Principles and Methods of
Adapted Physical Education and Recreation

Twelfth Edition

Kristi Roth, PhD, CAPE
Professor
University of Wisconsin—Stevens Point

Jean Pyfer, PED, CAPE
Professor Emeritus
Texas Woman's University

Lauriece Zittel, PhD, CAPE
Associate Professor
Northern Illinois University

David Auxter, EdD, CAPE
Senior Scientist
Research Institute for Independent Living

JONES & BARTLETT
LEARNING

World Headquarters
Jones & Bartlett Learning
5 Wall Street
Burlington, MA 01803
978-443-5000
info@jblearning.com
www.jblearning.com

Jones & Bartlett Learning books and products are available through most bookstores and online booksellers. To contact Jones & Bartlett Learning directly, call 800-832-0034, fax 978-443-8000, or visit our website, www.jblearning.com.

Substantial discounts on bulk quantities of Jones & Bartlett Learning publications are available to corporations, professional associations, and other qualified organizations. For details and specific discount information, contact the special sales department at Jones & Bartlett Learning via the above contact information or send an email to specialsales@jblearning.com.

08938-7

Production Credits

VP, Executive Publisher: David D. Cella
Publisher: Cathy L. Esperti
Acquisitions Editor: Sean Fabery
Vendor Manager: Sara Kelly
Director of Marketing: Andrea DeFronzo
VP, Manufacturing and Inventory Control: Therese Connell
Composition and Project Management: Cenveo® Publisher Services
Cover Design: Scott Moden
Rights & Media Specialist: Jamey O'Quinn
Media Development Editor: Troy Liston
Cover Images: Top center: ©Shutterstock/Studio 1One; Top right: ©Shutterstock/Jaren Jai Wicklund; Bottom: ©Getty Images/DisabilityImages
Printing and Binding: RR Donnelley
Cover Printing: RR Donnelley

Library of Congress Cataloging-in-Publication Data
Names: Roth, Kristi, author. | Zittel, Lauriece L., author. | Pyfer, Jean, author. | Auxter, David, author.
Title: Principles and methods of adapted physical education and recreation / Kristi Roth, Lauriece Zittel, Jean Pyfer, and David Auxter.
Description: Twelfth edition. | Burlington, MA : Jones & Bartlett Learning, [2017] | Includes bibliographical references and index.
Identifiers: LCCN 2016021005 | ISBN 9781284077810 (casebound : alk. paper)
Subjects: | MESH: Physical Education and Training—methods | Disabled Persons | Recreation
Classification: LCC GV445 | NLM QT 255 | DDC 790.1/96—dc23 LC record available at https://lccn.loc.gov/2016021005
****
6048

Printed in the United States of America
20 19 18 17 16   10 9 8 7 6 5 4 3 2 1

CONTENTS

This edition of *Principles and Methods of Adapted Physical Education and Recreation* aims to serve as a practical, evidence-based resource, just as previous editions have since its initial publication in 1969. This edition strives to continue to meet the needs of both undergraduate- and graduate-level students who are training to work with individuals with disabilities in an educational and recreational environment.

Having joined the author team with the 11th edition, Drs. Lauriece Zittel and Kristi Roth are now the book's lead developers, building on the exemplary work of Drs. Jean Pyfer and David Auxter in the previous editions. In addition to enjoying her retirement, Dr. Pyfer provided frequent feedback and guidance throughout the development process. There has been a strong effort to review each chapter and ensure that the content includes what is most practical for application in the education and recreation environment. As always, we have ensured the content is supported by current research.

We have carefully reviewed the feedback from external reviewers and vetted several chapters in development to ensure readability, applicability, and content quality. Several of our peers who are using the textbook in their courses indicated a need for the book to be more attractive to today's undergraduate student. To meet that need, we are excited to now publish with Jones & Bartlett Learning, which has helped create a visually attractive text with full-color photos and an easy-to-navigate layout. In tandem with this, all of the photos in the text have been updated.

Content Highlights

The textbook is divided into three parts: The Scope, Key Techniques, and Needs of Specific Populations. Each chapter in the text begins with Learning Objectives and concludes with Review Questions.

- Part I, "The Scope," includes a general overview of adapted physical education and recreation and the need and legal requirements for services and support. It includes updated information related to the Every Student Succeeds Act and recent relevant litigation.
- Part II, "Key Techniques," explores the process of qualification and delivery of services in the school environment, from determining educational needs through assessment to delivering services in the least restrictive environment. It includes an updated case study, evaluation report, and Individualized Education Plan (IEP) for physical education. This section has been strengthened by the inclusion of two new chapters: Chapter 8, "Teaching with Technology," and Chapter 9, "Transition Programming/ Community Recreation and Sport."
- Part III, "Needs of Specific Populations," delves into specific types of disabilities—including intellectual and developmental disabilities, autism spectrum disorders, specific learning disabilities, among others—and provides suggestions for intervention strategies. With this edition, these chapters now all utilize a consistent heading structure for ease of navigation.

New to This Edition

This edition has been thoroughly revised to reflect the latest standards and changes affecting the field of adapted physical education. Changes for this edition include the following:

- Part II, "Key Techniques," now includes two new chapters: Chapter 8, "Teaching with Technology," and Chapter 9, "Transition Programming/ Community Recreation and Sport." Chapter 8 explores the digital tools and resources available that can be used in teaching individuals with disabilities. Chapter 9, meanwhile, contains valuable content related to transitioning, community-recreation, and disability sport. This material was previously located throughout various chapters in the book and has been condensed into one chapter for ease of use and continuity. This content has also been updated to reflect current sport organizations and research in transition as applied to physical education for individuals with disabilities.

- All chapters have been updated to reflect the *Diagnostic and Statistical Manual of Mental Disorders, Fifth Edition* (DSM-5) current definitions and language.
- All chapters reflect the latest legislative changes, such as the Every Student Succeeds Act that was passed into law in 2015.
- Chapters 3, "Determining Educational Needs Through Assessment," and 4, "Developing the Individual Education Program," are based on a new case study. The sample assessment report reflects a new method for reporting test results and utilizes an updated test.
- Chapters in Part III, "Needs of Specific Populations," now incorporate a consistent heading structure for ease of content navigation. Each chapter begins with a definition of the type of disability being covered before walking through the incidence, causes, characteristics, and the physical education program. Case studies previously featured in these chapters are now found in the slides.
- Chapter 12, "Autism Spectrum Disorder," has been significantly revised to reflect changes in terminology, updated research, and the current evidence-based practices (EBPs) for individuals with autism spectrum disorder (ASD). Application of the 27 EBPs in the physical education setting is provided.

Instructor Resources

There has been a significant effort to provide support to instructors teaching with *Principles and Methods of Adapted Physical Education and Recreation*, and the instructor resources created for the 12th edition are more expansive and impactful than ever. Qualified instructors can access the following resources:

- Test Bank, containing more than 500 questions
- Slides in PowerPoint format, mapping to each chapter and incorporating a case study to frame class discussion

- Instructor's Manual, featuring active learning activities, an answer key for case studies found in the slides, and materials for a project-based final exam
- Screencast Lectures, providing real-life examples of chapter content and sharing valuable resources for further research

We hope you find the changes to this edition of *Principles and Methods of Adapted Physical Education and Recreation* beneficial, and we welcome your feedback to ensure that our revisions continue to meet your needs.

The authors would like to gratefully acknowledge the many contributions of individuals who provided their wisdom, effort, and support in the preparation of the 12th edition of this text. We rely not just on the scientific literature in disability research but also on the leadership of the many passionate adapted physical educators in the field. First and foremost, we would like to thank Dr. Jean Pyfer for her guidance as Dr. Laurie Zittel and Dr. Kristi Roth assumed the lead on this edition. Her wisdom is unending, her editorial feedback is swift and gentle, and her passion for ensuring our content useful, yet research-based, is appreciated. In the early stages of development for this edition, we also relied heavily on feedback provided by external reviewers. They, along with the many passionate professionals in the field of adapted physical education, helped guide and inform our content.

We would like to share that we strive to include the love and wisdom infused in this textbook by Dr. Carol Huettig. Although she is no longer physically present, her presence is felt on a daily basis and helps to guide our advocacy efforts for individuals with disabilities and the continued revision of this resource.

We also would like to thank the parents, children, and college students involved in our campus practica for their consent in using their inspirational photographs as we set about the daunting task of updating every photo in the book. We also would like to thank the various individuals and organizations who provided us with photos, including the United States Association of Blind Athletes and the Great Lakes Adaptive Sports Association.

Additional gratitude is shared with Jones & Bartlett Learning for their editorial assistance, guidance, and advocacy for the development of this edition.

Finally, we owe the deepest gratitude to our families for their unending support. This textbook reflects not only our passion for the field and for children with disabilities but also the love we receive from those who we call home.

MaryJo Archambault, MS, CTRS
Assistant Professor
Southern Connecticut State University
New Haven, Connecticut

Ann L. Boe, MS
Assistant Professor
Rockford University
Rockford, Illinois

Lauren Cavanaugh, PhD
Assistant Professor
Canisius College
Buffalo, New York

Rose M. Chew, PhD
Assistant Professor
Grambling State University
Grambling, Louisiana

Beatrice Darden-Melton, PhD
Assistant Professor
Norfolk State University
Norfolk, Virginia

Candice Howard-Shaughnessy, PhD
Associate Professor
Troy University
Troy, Alabama

Michelle Hsiu-Chen Liu, PhD
Assistant Professor
Averett University
Danville, Virginia

Gerard G. Lyons, EdD
Professor
Idaho State University
Pocatello, Idaho

PART I

The Scope

In Part I we provide an overview of adapted physical education—what the term means, its historical development, the benefits strong programs have to offer persons with disabilities, and the barriers we must overcome if we are to provide quality, outcome-based services in the future. The significant growth of adapted physical education has been supported through strong advocacy. We highlight national organizations as well as name the outstanding professionals who have led advocacy work to make adapted physical education a mandated educational service. Court decisions and federal legislation that have had an impact on physical education for individuals with disabilities is presented.

CHAPTER 1

Adapted Physical Education

OBJECTIVES

- Define adapted physical education.
- Explain physical education as a mandated, direct special education service.
- List several of the benefits of physical education for learners with disabilities.
- Briefly describe the many, varied roles of the adapted physical educator.
- Briefly explain the major advocacy events in the history of physical education for individuals with disabilities.

Adapted physical education is the art and science of developing, implementing, and monitoring a carefully designed physical education instructional program for a learner with a disability, based on a comprehensive assessment, to give the learner the skills necessary for a lifetime of rich leisure, recreation, and sport experiences to enhance physical fitness and wellness.

Adapted physical education (APE) and recreation are critical components for the well-being of children with disabilities. The Centers for Disease Control and Prevention, the federal agency responsible for promotion of the health of the nation, has stated that one of its highest

health priorities is participation in leisure physical activity. The contributions of adapted physical education to the U.S. public health goal are clear. The old notion of the "inoculation theory" that a dose of physical activity during the years of school will provide a health benefit for the rest of one's life has been discredited. Rather, to establish and maintain health, ongoing participation in physical activity is necessary. In addition to keeping children with a disability physically fit during the school years, adapted physical education must provide skills that involve physical activity that can be generalized into homes and communities for a lifetime.

Who Is Disabled?

There are persistently recurring myths and misconceptions among the public that disabilities are rare and refer only to highly observable physical impairments. The data on disability reveal a different picture:[11]

- There are approximately 56.7 million people with disabilities in the United States.
- The likelihood of having a severe disability is 1 in 4 for individuals 65 to 69 years of age.
- Persons 80 years of age and older are 8 times more likely to have a disability.
- The likelihood of having a severe disability is 1 in 20 for young adults 15 to 24 years of age.
- 9.4 million, noninstitutionalized adults experience difficulty with at least one activity of daily living.
- Approximately 30.6 million individuals experience difficulty walking or climbing stairs, or use assistive devices such as wheelchairs, canes, or crutches.

MYTH OF DISABILITY

There is a perception by many persons in the public that *disability* refers to persons who are in wheelchairs; however, in reality, the number of persons in wheelchairs is small. Most disabilities are invisible to the public because they are neuromuscular, cardiovascular, chronic respiratory, and/or mental disorders.

IMPACT OF DISABILITY

Nearly every extended family across three generations will most likely have a member with a disability. It is a costly social, public health, and moral issue. What determines a disability is the extent to which a person's physical and mental conditions limit his or her ability to meet the demands of his or her physical and/or social environments. Once a disability is identified, interventions should be implemented to lessen the impact of the disability. Adapted physical education strategies can help individuals improve functional capacity and avert further deterioration in physical and mental functioning.

DISABILITY CLARIFICATION

There are many federal definitions of disability. For instance, the Individuals with Disabilities Education Improvement Act's definition of disability refers to medical conditions associated with *adverse educational progress.* The Social Security definition of disability is associated with *ability to work,* not educational progress. Each of these definitions is limited. Because how one defines disability impacts the approach taken to address the disability, attempts have been made to clarify the causes and results of disabilities.

The Institute of Medicine (IOM) developed a model in collaboration with the Centers for Disease Control and Prevention and the National Council on Disability that builds on the World Health Organization (WHO) definition of disability.[5] The IOM model places disability within the context of health and social issues. It depicts the interactive effects of biological, environmental (physical and social), lifestyle, and behavioral risk factors that influence each stage of the disability process. Adapted physical educators and recreation specialists should use this model and become more active players at each stage of the disability process because they have the skills needed to intervene at several different stages in the process.

Depending on the circumstance, progressively greater loss of function may not need to occur, and the progression toward disability could be halted or reversed. Adapted physical education strategies can be applied at any of the stages that precede disability as well as in the disability stage itself. Intervention can focus on facilitating development, restoration of lost function, or prevention of complications (secondary disabling conditions) that can exacerbate existing conditions or lead to new ones.

The Process of Becoming Disabled

The disabling process involves disability risk factors, pathology, impairment, and functional limitation. Examples of stages of the disability process are depicted in **Table 1-1**. Quality of life or well-being can be affected at each stage of the disability process. An example of diminished health that could lead to a disability follows:

Disability risk factor: inadequate physical activity and nutrition
Symptoms: defects in insulin secretion and/or action (i.e., diabetes)
Physical impairment: affects vision and the lower extremities
Functional limitations: blindness or lower-limb amputations

A variety of personal and social environmental factors can influence the progression of disability and secondary disabling conditions. Some of these factors are health status, psychological state, socioeconomic status, educational

TABLE 1-1   Disabling Process Stages

Disability Risk Factors	Physical inactivity, poor nutrition, substance abuse, smoking, improper eating habits, risky behavior that places a person's health in danger, child abuse, risky sexual activity, domestic violence, lack of access to medical care, hypertension, arthritis, back pain, depression, postural disorders, and others
Symptoms	Joint pain, defects in insulin secretion and/or action, depression, low vision, hypertension, chronic cough, underachievement, and tiredness
Physical or Intellectual Impairment	Impaired organs of the body, such as the cardiovascular system, including the heart, musculoskeletal organs; mental health; vision; mental retardation; hearing; and the immune system
Functional Limitations	Inability to meet the demands of tasks in social and/or physical environments

attainment, and the presence of multiple conditions of disability. However, regardless of which of the factors is contributing to the condition, adapted physical educators and recreation specialists can moderate the situation by addressing the risk factors, utilizing evidence-based practices, employing assistive devices and technologies, and/or addressing the built environment.

Contributions by Adapted Physical Educators and Recreation Specialists

Risk factors are biological, environmental (social, physical), and lifestyle or behavioral characteristics that are causally associated with health-related conditions. Several specific examples are given in **Figure 1-1**. Identifying

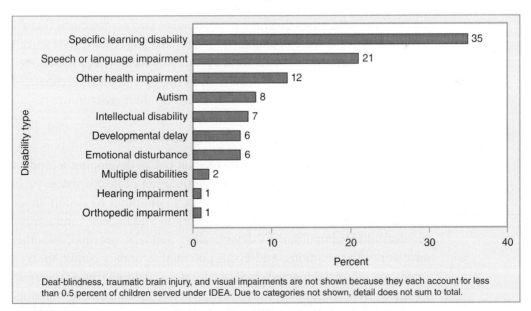

FIGURE 1-1   Percentage distribution of children ages 3–21 served under the Individuals with Disabilities Education Act (IDEA), Part B, by disability type: School year 2012–13.

U.S. Department of Education, Office of Special Education Programs, Individuals with Disabilities Education Act (IDEA) database, retrieved October 3, 2014, from https://inventory.data.gov/dataset/8715a3e8-bf48-4eef -9deb-fd9bb76a196e/resource/a68a23f3-3981-47db-ac75-98a167b65259. See Digest of Education Statistics 2014, table 204.30. http://nces.ed.gov/programs/coe/indicator_cgg.asp

such factors can be a first step toward streamlining a plan of action to combat the disabling process and develop appropriate interventions.

UTILIZING EVIDENCE-BASED PRACTICES AND ASSISTIVE DEVICES AND TECHNOLOGIES

Evidence-based practices and adaptations to help people with disabilities benefit from active lifestyles are essential. Knowing facts regarding types of disabling conditions, characteristics of the disabilities, teaching strategies, and specific suggestions of activities, modifications, and adaptations that will promote participation is necessary in order to effectively design developmentally appropriate and safe programming.

PHYSICAL ACTIVITY AND THE BUILT ENVIRONMENT

Modifying the "built environment" enables accommodation of persons with disabilities to reduce the discrepancy between their personal capabilities and the environment. Examples of well-known adaptations to the built environment for people with disabilities are ramps to buildings and swimming pools, buses that have provisions for easy access, curbs that are cut for wheelchair access, and entrances to buildings that enable wheelchair access. Great improvements to the built environment have occurred in the public in the past several years. These improvements have enhanced the ability of persons with disabilities to access their environments.

ADDRESSING POTENTIAL SECONDARY CONDITIONS

People with disabling conditions are often at risk of developing secondary conditions that can result in further deterioration of health status, functional capacity, and quality of life. Secondary conditions by definition are causally related to primary disabling conditions and include contractures, physical and cardiopulmonary deterioration, mental depression, and other adverse health conditions. Addressing potential secondary conditions is an important role of the adapted physical educator and the recreation therapist. Adapted physical educators and recreation personnel can, through development of skills and attitudes that generalize into recreational environments, impact the lifelong quality of life for persons who exit the educational setting for recreational/leisure living in the community.

ENRICHING THE LIVES OF OTHERS

The potential exists for the physical educator and the adapted physical educator to "do something," to make an incredible difference in the life of a learner with a disability and the learner's family.

Imagine the opportunities to "do something":

- Share with a mother and father the Boy Scout award ceremony in which their son, diagnosed with Asperger's syndrome, is presented his Swimming Merit Badge.
- Celebrate with a remarkable athlete named to the USA Wheelchair Basketball Team.
- Enjoy the "first walking steps" of a 20-month-old boy with Down syndrome who progressed because of a developmentally appropriate aquatics and motor development program.
- Spend time "in jail" to earn money for the Muscular Dystrophy Association.
- Share with a mother her delight that her son, diagnosed with autism, learned the skills necessary to go swimming with his younger brother at the community pool.
- Enjoy the success of an athlete who placed in the top 10 in the Boston Marathon, Wheelchair Division.
- Teach a child with a visual impairment to play Frisbee with a friend.
- Help a teenager with severe, multiple disabilities develop her own wheelchair aerobics routine to her favorite country-western music.
- Coach a Special Olympics team and be part of a worldwide program that currently serves millions of athletes worldwide.
- Help a student using a wheelchair learn to navigate an obstacle course and do a "wheelie."
- Teach a young boy with Duchenne muscular dystrophy skills to swim using an elementary backstroke, a skill he will be able to use throughout his life span.
- Coach a teenager with a hearing impairment who wrestles on his high school wrestling team.
- Teach a toddler or preschooler play skills necessary to engage in parallel play.
- Develop an inclusive, after-school leisure, recreation, sport, fitness, and wellness program.

- Race downhill alongside a young woman using a sit-ski.
- Design a behavior enhancement program for a young girl with a conduct disorder to help her monitor/improve her behavior in physical education.
- Develop a swimming program, emphasizing the freestyle and back crawl, for learners with dyslexia, to help them develop cross-lateral integration.
- Reassure the young mother of a 13-month-old boy with Down syndrome that his atlantoaxial instability simply requires wise choices of play and physical activity and need not significantly limit his opportunities.
- Lead an aqua aerobics session daily to meet the needs of older adults with osteoarthritis and osteoporosis.
- Develop sign language skills in order to communicate with your students who are deaf.
- Coach judo for the United States Association of Blind Athletes.
- Share skills, in the home, with a young mother of a significantly low-birthweight baby, so she can encourage and foster developmentally appropriate play.
- Help a young girl with spina bifida learn to ride a tricycle to encourage/foster her walking.
- Contact local leisure, recreation, and sport facilities and help them accommodate individuals with disabilities who would like to use the facilities.

Definition of Physical Education

Physical education for individuals with disabilities was specifically defined in PL. 108-446, the Individuals with Disabilities Education Improvement Act (IDEIA 2004). The term *physical education* means the development of

1. Physical and motor fitness
2. Fundamental motor skills and patterns
3. Skills in aquatics, dance, and individual and group games and sports (including intramural and lifetime sports)

The term includes special physical education, adapted physical education, movement education, and motor development. The three essential components of physical education for persons with disabilities are developing and implementing an individualized education program (IEP), assessing child performance, and teaching the defined curricula of physical education. When specially designed physical education is prescribed on the child's IEP, educators will provide physical education to ensure children and youth with disabilities have an equal opportunity to participate in those services and activities. Each child with a disability is to participate in physical education with children without disabilities to the maximum extent appropriate.[14]

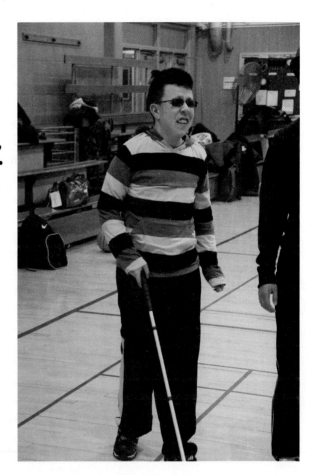

Definition of Adapted Physical Education

Adapted physical education is a direct special education service to be provided to all qualifying children. It is a carefully designed, modified physical education *instructional* program to accommodate a learner with a disability, based on a comprehensive assessment, to give the learner the skills necessary for a lifetime of rich leisure, recreation, and sport experiences to enhance physical fitness and wellness.

Benefits of Physical Education for Learners with Disabilities

Qualified and dedicated physical educators and adapted physical educators can "do something" because there are significant and long-term benefits of a quality physical education program for learners with disabilities. Programs can enrich well-being by providing the prerequisites to healthy leisure physical activity. More specifically, quality programs can promote:

- The development of equilibrium, sensory discrimination and integration, and sensorimotor function
- The development of locomotor and nonlocomotor skills
- The development of object-control skills
- The development of play, leisure, recreation, sport, and physical fitness skills
- The development of physical fitness for maintenance of activities of daily living and health/wellness
- The development of a repertoire of movement skills necessary for independent and functional living
- The development of physical and motor prerequisites to vocational skills required for independent living
- The prevention and management of chronic health conditions
- The prevention of secondary disabling conditions

The benefits of a quality physical education program for learners with disabilities cannot be minimized. The major obstacle, however, is that the benefits are not clearly understood by the local, state, and federal educational administrators who make program decisions and allocate budgets.

Roles of the Adapted Physical Educator

The adapted physical education teacher is the person responsible for developing an appropriate individualized physical education program for individuals with disabilities. The APE teacher is a physical educator with highly specialized training in the assessment and evaluation of motor competency and the implementation of programs in physical fitness, play, leisure, recreation, sport, and wellness. *The APE teacher is a direct service provider,* not a related service provider, because special physical education is a federally mandated component of special education services.[14] There has been confusion that APE is a related service due to circulation of misinformation and state education departments' misinterpretation of the federal law.

TABLE 1-2　Roles and Responsibilities the Adapted Physical Education Teacher May Assume

- Direct service provider (hands-on teaching)
- Assessment specialist, completing comprehensive motor assessments of individuals with disabilities and making specific program recommendations
- Consultant for physical education and special education professionals and paraprofessionals providing physical education instruction for individuals with disabilities
- IEP/multidisciplinary team committee member who helps develop and monitor the IEP
- In-service educator, providing training for those who will provide physical education instruction for individuals with disabilities
- Student and parent advocate
- Facilitator of a "circle of friends" for a learner with a disability
- Program coordinator who develops curricular materials and develops intra- and interagency collaborations to meet the needs of individuals with disabilities
- Transition facilitator who helps the IEP/multidisciplinary team develop an appropriate individual transition plan for those students preparing to leave school and move into the community
- Facilitator to coordinate efforts with existing health programs to ensure learners with disabilities have access to quality health care
- Coordinator to ensure individuals with disabilities have access to quality wellness and health promotion programs to reduce complications associated with secondary disabling conditions, such as hypertension, obesity, diabetes, and cardiovascular disorders
- Collaborator with community information outlets and local public policy makers
- Personal trainer/coach for individuals with disabilities exercising at home or participating in lifetime or competitive sports
- Disseminator of research/information regarding effective intervention in APE

Depending on the size of the school district, the numbers of students with disabilities who require adapted physical education, the caseload, and the unique skills of physical education and special education professionals, the APE teacher may assume any or all of the roles (see **Table 1-2**).

Prevalence

Child Find efforts to identify and serve children and youth with disabilities in the public schools have been successful. In the 2012–2013 academic year, more than 6.4 million learners with disabilities received special education services.[7] Information regarding the number of children with specific disabilities served by special education is included in Figure 1-1.

Each year, the U.S. Department of Education, Office of Special Education and Rehabilitative Services (OSERS), reports to Congress pertinent facts about the education of learners with disabilities. Recent data indicate:

- Children with disabilities in special education represent approximately 13% of the entire school-age population.
- Approximately twice as many males as females, receive special education services.
- Approximately 95% of school-age children who receive special education are enrolled in the regular schools.[7]

OSERS reports serving 750,131 preschool children with disabilities in 2012, or 6% of all preschoolers who lived in the United States. This represents a 50% increase in the number of children needing services since 1990–1991. The overwhelming number of preschoolers requiring special education intervention is related to, but not limited to, the following:

- Growing numbers of infants affected by drug and alcohol use in utero
- Inadequate prenatal care during pregnancy
- Drastically increased numbers of children being raised in poverty
- Inadequate nutrition
- Inadequate health care
- Housing and schools in toxic environments
- Increased numbers of children who are victims of abuse and neglect
- Parents with limited or no appropriate, nurturing parenting skills
- Medical technology that allows more premature and medically fragile infants to survive

Advocacy and Adapted Physical Education

The history of adapted physical education is rich and reflects significant growth. The National Consortium for Physical Education and Recreation for Individuals with Disabilities (NCPERID) was formed in 1973 to advocate, stimulate, and encourage significant service delivery, quality professional preparation, and meaningful research in physical education and recreation for individuals with disabilities. This commitment and advocacy for individuals with disabilities was evidenced when a group of adapted physical educators dedicated to providing appropriate programs for students with disabilities met in Washington, D.C. The purposes of their meeting were to define what constituted appropriate physical education for persons with disabilities and to develop a strategy for ensuring that physical education was identified in PL. 94-142, implemented in 1975. Some of the professionals who championed physical education as a mandated educational service, at that important meeting included Dr. David Auxter, Dr. Lane Goodwin, Dr. Jean Pyfer, and Dr. Julian Stein. They were successful in their lobbying efforts. That led to a national thrust to prepare physical educators with specialized training in providing programs for persons with disabilities.

In the spring of 1991, the NCPERID, in conjunction with the National Association of State Directors of Special Education (NASDSE) and Special Olympics International, conducted an "Action Seminar" on adapted physical education for state directors of special education and leaders of advocacy groups for individuals with disabilities. This conference had two goals:

- Identify the barriers that were preventing full provision of appropriate physical education services to individuals with disabilities.
- Establish an action agenda for addressing and resolving these problems.

To counter the trend of providing less than appropriate physical education experiences to students with disabilities, in 1994 the NCPERID published national standards for adapted physical education.[6] The purpose of the Adapted Physical Education National Standards (APENS) project was to ensure that physical education instruction for students with disabilities was provided by qualified physical education instructors.[1] To achieve this end, the project has developed national standards (refer to **Table 1-3**) for the profession and a national certification examination to measure knowledge of these standards. This major movement in the field of adapted physical education was led by visionary educator Dr. Luke Kelly. Under Dr. Kelly's careful supervision, the APENS standards and examination were developed maintaining a complete commitment to the process of ensuring validity and reliability.

TABLE 1-3   Adapted Physical Education National Standards (APENS) Categories

1. Human development
2. Motor behavior
3. Exercise science
4. Measurement and evaluation
5. History and philosophy
6. Unique attributes of learners
7. Curriculum theory and development
8. Assessment
9. Instructional design and planning
10. Teaching
11. Consultation and staff development
12. Student and program evaluation
13. Continuing education
14. Ethics
15. Communication

For more information regarding APENS standards, please go to the APENS website at www.apens.org.

This project was/is critically important to the field because, unlike other special education areas (learning disabilities, early childhood, etc.), most states did not/do not have defined certifications or endorsements for teachers of adapted physical education. In addition, the quality of physical education was compromised because the definition of who was "qualified" to provide physical education services to individuals with disabilities was left to the individual states and their respective certification requirements.

On May 10, 1997, the first national administration of the APENS certification exam was given at 46 sites around the country. A total of 219 teachers completed the exam, and 175 passed. To date there are more than 3,000 certified adapted physical educators (CAPEs), 3,127 who have passed and earned CAPE certification. Every state is currently represented; in many states there are more than 100 CAPEs (e.g., Texas).[4]

The consortium is now referred to as the National Consortium for Physical Education for Individuals with Disabilities (NCPEID) and has played a major role in shaping the direction of the adapted physical education profession. Its members, primarily adapted physical education and recreation professionals involved in teacher preparation, actively serve as advocates for favorable legislation and funding at the national, state, and local levels; disseminate information about new legislation; and stimulate and conduct research.[9]

Adapted Physical Education/Adapted Physical Activity Special Interest Group (APE/APA SIG) is affiliated with SHAPE America. Its mission is to promote quality movement experiences for individuals with disabilities through research, advocacy, publications, programs at conventions and workshops, position statements, standards of practice, and cooperation with other organizations committed to people with disabilities.[10]

In the spring of 1999, Dr. Jim Rimmer, director of the Center on Health Promotion Research for Persons with Disabilities, Department of Disability and Human Development, University of Illinois at Chicago, received a $7 million grant from the Centers for Disease Control and Prevention to establish the National Center on Physical Activity and Disability (NCPAD).[1] The NCPAD was developed through a cooperative venture of the University of Illinois at Chicago and the Secondary Conditions Branch of the Centers for Disease Control and Prevention. Currently the center is called the National Center on Health, Physical Activity and Disability (NCHPAD). Dr. Rimmer continues to direct the NCHPAD at the University of Alabama. The NCHPAD is

> a public health practice and resource center on health promotion for people with a disability. NCHPAD seeks to help people with a disability and other chronic health conditions achieve health benefits through increased participation in all types of physical and social activities, including fitness and aquatic activities, recreational and sports programs, adaptive equipment usage, and more.[8]

Professional publications dedicated to the discipline of adapted physical education have provided the field with rich information. The *Adapted Physical Activity Quarterly* (*APAQ*), the official journal of the International Federation of Adapted Physical Activity, was first published in 1983. *APAQ* is the journal in which professionals share their research regarding adapted physical activity. *Palaestra: Forum of Sport, Physical Education, and Recreation for Those with Disabilities,* edited by Dr. Marty Block is a quarterly publication released in cooperation with the United States Olympic Committee's Committee on Sports for the Disabled and the Adapted Physical Activity Council of the American Alliance for Health, Physical Education, Recreation and Dance (now SHAPE America), dealing with adapted physical activity for individuals with disabilities, their families, and professionals in the field. *Sports 'N Spokes,* for the past several decades, has been a magazine dedicated to the active wheeler. *Sports 'N Spokes* covers competitive wheelchair sports and recreational opportunities for individuals who use wheelchairs.

The need for quality adapted physical education and adapted physical activity programs is very clear. Unfortunately, many state education agency personnel, school board members, school district administrators, and parents have yet to understand the importance of physical education in the lives of all students, including those with disabilities. The value of physically active leisure for the health of Americans is well understood by some federal and state policy makers. Understanding the legal and moral value of providing physical education/activity to individuals of all abilities is critical.

Federal Legislation and the Civil Rights of Individuals with Disabilities

There is a long history of federal legislation that supports the education of learners with disabilities. Perhaps the most significant civil rights litigation tied to the education of learners with disabilities was *Brown v. Board of Education, Topeka, Kansas,* in 1954.[3] Though the litigants, parents, sued in protest over "tracking" their African American children into non-college-preparatory classes, the affirmation of the courts regarding the significance of education in the lives of ALL children was a landmark case. The court wrote:

> [Education] is required in the performance of our most basic responsibilities. . . . It is the very foundation of good citizenship. In these days, it is doubtful that any child may reasonably be expected to succeed in life if he [or she] is denied the opportunity of an education. Such an opportunity, where the state has undertaken to provide it, is a right that must be made available to all on equal terms.[3]

The rights of persons with disabilities became a central concern during the 1970s, when landmark court cases ruled that children with disabilities had a right to a free and appropriate education and training and persons in institutions had a right to rehabilitation. These court decisions paralleled and created the initiative for federal legislation such as the Rehabilitation Act of 1973[12] and the Education for All Handicapped Children Act of 1975 (PL. 94-142).[13] Before the enactment of the Education for All Handicapped Children Act of 1975, the special education needs of children with disabilities were not being fully met. More than one-half of children with disabilities did not receive appropriate educational services that would enable them to have full equality of opportunity. One million children with disabilities in the United States were excluded entirely from the public school system and did not go through the educational process with their peers.

At the beginning of the 1990s, the passage of the Americans with Disabilities Act (ADA) and in 2004 the Individuals with Disabilities Education Improvement Act (IDEIA) (the Reauthorization of IDEA) further addressed the rights of persons with disabilities. The ADA had a significant impact on the civil rights of individuals with disabilities in the public and private sectors.

The Rehabilitation Act of 1973, the Education for All Handicapped Children Act of 1975, the Americans with Disabilities Act of 1990, and the Individuals with Disabilities Education Improvement Act of 2004 are four pieces of legislation created to provide equal opportunity for individuals with disabilities. The similarities are

- Equity of services for individuals with disabilities when compared with those without disabilities
- Accessibility to environments and programs, so that there is equal opportunity to derive benefits from services in the public and private sectors
- Encouragement of integration of individuals with and without disabilities

Court decisions that have had an impact on the education of individuals with disabilities in the past several decades are historically sequenced and briefly summarized in **Table 1-4.**

TABLE 1-4   Federal Legislation That Has an Impact on Physical Education for Individuals with Disabilities

2015	Every Student Succeeds Act (ESSA) (P.L. 114-95)
	This act assures equal educational opportunity for all children.
2004	Individuals with Disabilities Education Improvement Act (IDEIA) (P.L. 108-446)
	This act aligns the educational services provided to students with disabilities with NCLB and reinforces inclusion and evidence-based education.
2003	Reauthorization of the Child Abuse and Protection Act (P.L. 108-83)
	The reauthorization of PL 93-247 retained the mandate that a person who suspects child abuse must report it or commit a felony.
2003	Reauthorization of the Amateur Sports Act
	The reauthorization reinforces the rightful place of "elite athletes" with disabilities in the community of "elite athletes" who participate in amateur athletics, particularly the Olympics and the Paralympics.
2003	Improved Nutrition and Physical Activity Act of 2003
	The act is designed to encourage collaboration of public schools with community resources; the intent is to include persons with disabilities. The act provides training for personnel to improve participation in physical activity, particularly to prevent arid ameliorate obesity.
2003	Workforce Reinvestment and Adult Education Act
	The act is designed to provide significant education opportunities for vocational training, including for individuals with disabilities. The recreation portion of the Rehabilitation Act of 1973 was reauthorized in this act.
2001	Physical Education for Progress Act
	The act is designed to improve physical education for ALL children, including children with disabilities in the public schools, by providing competitive grants.
2001	No Child Left Behind Act
	This act puts significant federal support behind the improvement of reading and mathematics scores and compromises other critical curricular areas, including physical education, health, history, art, computer science, and music.
1997	Reauthorization of IDEA (P.L. 105-17)
	The reauthorization emphasized education for learners with disabilities in the general education program and increased the emphasis on parental participation in the assessment and IEP process.

TABLE 1-4   Federal Legislation That Has an Impact on Physical Education for Individuals with Disabilities
(*Continued*)

1990	Americans with Disabilities Act (P.L. 101-336)
	The act expanded civil rights protections for individuals with disabilities in the public and private sectors.
1990	Individuals with Disabilities Education Act (IDEA)
	IDEA continued the emphasis on FAPE, IEP, LRE, and **physical education as a direct, educational service.**
1988	Assistive Technology Act (P.L. 103-218)
	This act made technology (basic and sophisticated) available to learners with disabilities so the learners could function within the public school system.
1975	Education for All Handicapped Children Act (P.L. 94-142)
	The act mandated (a) free, appropriate public education for all children with disabilities between the ages of 3 and 21 years; (b) individual education plan; (c) education in the least restrictive environment; and (d) **physical education as a direct, educational service.**
1973	The Rehabilitation Act (P.L. 93-112, Section 504)
	The act mandated that individuals with disabilities cannot be excluded from any program or activity receiving federal funds solely on the basis of the disability.

While the laws are designed to provide significant protection of individual education rights and to ensure access to programs and services, including leisure, recreation, sport, fitness, and wellness programs, there remain significant obstacles to the provision of quality services.

One of the significant problems that has emerged, in that the rights/assurances for individuals with disabilities are tied to the law, is that there is increasing litigation that "tests" the law. In particular, lawsuits against the public schools have proved incredibly costly in terms of both financial cost and human work hours. And, unfortunately, it has created a situation in which the parents with the most resources (money or power) can demand and receive for their children educational services that are not accessible to the children of the poor and disenfranchised, the children who inevitably need our services the most. (**Table 1-5** provides a few examples of the focus of these decisions.)

TABLE 1-5   Court Decisions (Litigation) That Have Had an Impact on the Education of Learners with Disabilities

2015	*Phyllene, W. v. Huntsville City (AL) Board of Education*
	A child was not evaluated for a suspected hearing impairment and therefore was not provided FAPE. The lack of medical information meant no meaningful IEP was developed.
2006	*Arlington Central School District Board of Education v. Pearl and Theodore Murphy*
	Parents are not entitled to recover fees for services rendered by experts in IDEA actions.[2]
2005	*Schaffer v. Weast*
	The burden of proof in a due process hearing regarding the IEP is on the parent if the state is silent on the matter. It limits parents' rights to acquire services they deem important from school districts.
2003	*Neosho School District v. Clark*
	School districts must develop and implement appropriate behavioral management plans (BMPs).
2002	*Girty v. School District of Valley Grove*
	The court required the school district to "prove" that a child with special needs cannot be accommodated in the general classroom with supplementary aids and services prior to placement in a special education program.

The Teacher's Reality

Teachers continue to play a critical role in the lives of children and youth. Good physical education teachers and adapted physical education teachers continue to be the "pied pipers" of the professionals who work with chil-

dren and youth. Children are drawn, of course, to teachers who love to do what children love to do—play and move. And those who truly love children and love to teach continue to be the backbone of this society. The profession becomes even more important as children have more and more needs that must be met.

Certainly, as physical educators and adapted physical educators, the very future of students with disabilities lies in the palms of our hands. And that future has not been placed in our hands gently; it has been thrust on us because of an incredible need for good teachers—physical education teachers who are committed to learners with disabilities—to step forward and make a difference. With imagination, we can transform our profession and focus our energies.

SUMMARY

Remarkable growth in physical education for individuals with disabilities has taken place. Certainly, the law has continued to provide the impetus for this growth. There have been major changes in the public schools in the past several decades. These changes had at once challenged and frustrated the physical educator with a commitment to serving children and youth with and without disabilities. Certainly, the physical educator in the twenty-first century must demonstrate increased skills in facilitating cooperative play and in developing critical thinking skills and must demonstrate cultural competence. Best practice in adapted physical education involves knowing who is disabled and providing evidence-based programs for all children with disabilities through generalizing skills acquired in physical education to long-term, lifestyle patterns in the home and community. There are increased opportunities for individuals with disabilities to lead full and healthy lives, enjoying leisure, recreation, fitness, sport, and wellness opportunities because of a quality physical education program.

REVIEW QUESTIONS

1. What is adapted physical education? How does it differ, if it does, from general physical education?
2. What are the similarities among the major pieces of legislation affecting physical education for individuals with disabilities?
3. What are the benefits of a quality physical education program for individuals with disabilities?
4. What is APENS? Briefly describe its impact on the field.
5. What is the NCHPAD? Describe its mission.

REFERENCES

1. Adapted Physical Education National Standards (APENS). www.apens.org
2. *Arlington Central School District Board of Education v. Pearl and Theodore Murphy*, No. 03-785-cv, July 28, 2006. (2nd Cir., 2005).
3. *Brown v. The Board of Education*, 347 US, 483 (1954).
4. Davis, T. personal communication, January 2015.
5. Institute of Medicine of the National Academies. (2006). *Disability in America: A new look*. Washington, DC. Retrieved from www.iom.edu
6. Kelly, L. E. (1994). *National standards for adapted physical education*. Washington, DC: U.S. Department of Education, Office of Special Education Programs.

7. National Center for Education Statistics. (2015). Institute of Education Sciences. www.nces.ed.gov
8. National Center on Health, Physical Activity and Disability. *Building Healthy Inclusive Communities*. www.nchpad.org
9. National Consortium for Physical Education for Individuals with Disabilities. www.ncpeid.org
10. SHAPE America, Adapted Physical Education/Adapted Physical Activity Special Interest Group (APE/APA SIG). www.shapeamerica.org
11. United States Census Bureau. (2012).
12. U.S. Department of Health, Education, and Welfare. (1990). Section 504 regulations for the Rehabilitation Act of 1973, Rehabilitation Act amendments of 1974, and Education of the Handicapped Act. 45 C.F.R. sec. 339–395.
13. U.S. 94th Congress. Pub. L. 94-142 (November 29, 1975).
14. US Department of Education, 36th annual report to congress on the implementation of the Individuals with Disabilities Education Act, 2014.

PART 2

Key Techniques

The types of services needed by learners are common; however, each individual has a unique profile that must be addressed in the most appropriate fashion. For learners to benefit fully from physical education, their specific needs must be identified, a program to address those needs must be designed, a teaching approach to facilitate each learner's needs should be provided in the most positive and least restrictive environment, and school systems must provide the necessary resources to ensure programmatic success. Teaching with technology in physical education is an essential part of working with individuals with disabilities to provide successful learning opportunities. Types of equipment and instruction with technology are provided in this part. Transition programming and community recreation and sport opportunities for individuals of various age groups and disabilities are presented to emphasize the importance of lifelong physical activity.

CHAPTER 2

Adapted Physical Education in the Public Schools

OBJECTIVES

- Briefly explain the adapted physical education program within the public schools. Give examples of a philosophy and definition.
- Briefly explain the mandates of three federal laws that have an impact on the education of learners with disabilities.
- Describe the personnel involved and function of the members of a quality motor development team.
- List inexpensive equipment that can be used in the physical education program for children with and without disabilities.
- Describe the six levels of involvement in a parent/school/community partnership and give examples of each.

Adapted Physical Education

Adapted physical education (APE) is usually, but not always, aligned administratively with special education, rather than the physical education department. This creates a huge problem for the adapted physical educator and, more important, for the child, because much of the time our children with disabilities receive their physical education instruction within the general physical education program. While general physical educators are responsible for the education of children with and without disabilities, the

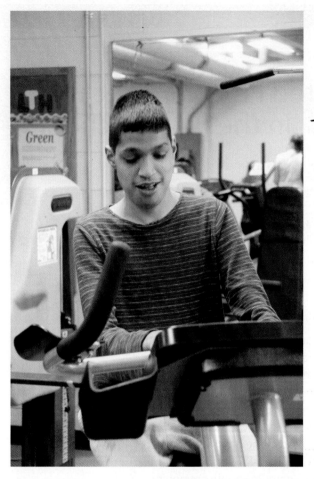

special education department controls the finances. Hence, decisions regarding personnel, such as hiring an APE specialist or making certain that paraprofessionals are attending physical education, are made by the special education department.

In a large school district or large special education cooperative, one member of the APE staff may be designated the lead teacher or department chair. This person will make decisions regarding the roles and assignments of the other APE staff members. This person is also directly accountable for the activities of the staff and reports to his or her immediate supervisor.

In small school districts, the principal determines what will occur in the school, and those decisions depend on the understanding that person has, as well as the resources that are available. If the principal is knowledgeable about the special education laws, an adapted physical educator may be sought to come to the district once or twice a month to test students and suggest modifications to the general physical educator. If the school district has access to a special service cooperative, the center may have an adapted physical educator on staff to provide testing, consulting, and workshops throughout the districts served by the center.

One of the major responsibilities of the adapted physical educator is to communicate regularly and effectively with his or her direct supervisor. Frequently, neither the director of special education nor the building principal understands the potential and importance of a quality APE program in the education of learners with disabilities. The adapted physical educator must be a vocal and tenacious advocate for the learner with a disability and for the field. The teacher should inform these persons about the requirements of the law and share legal updates and current articles describing state-of-the-art practices in APE.

The single most effective way to communicate the worth of the program is through demonstrated student results, based on measurable, observable outcomes and through student and parent testimony regarding the effectiveness of the program.

Timely information that clarifies the goals and objectives of the program and describes the "before and after" status of students receiving APE may help the administrator understand the value of the program. If possible, the administrator should be invited to attend a class or an activity that demonstrates quality programming to meet individual student needs and highlights the accomplishments of the students. It is vital that the adapted physical educator secure the support of district administrators and building principals if the program is to receive its share of district and school resources and if the adapted physical educator is to be considered a vital and integral part of the instructional team within the district.[8] The director of the APE program and the school's teachers are responsible for meeting federal, state, and local mandates regarding the provision of a quality physical education program for all children with disabilities who need a specially designed program in order to learn and grow. A district APE manual that outlines the components of a quality program should be on hand for administrators, parents, and teachers. The components of a quality APE program should include the following:

Philosophy
Definition of APE
Goals and objectives
Criteria for eligibility
Referral process
Assessment procedures
Individualized education program (IEP)
Instructional options/delivery models
Equipment
Accountability

PHILOSOPHY

A philosophy statement should outline the responsibility a school district has to follow the intent of federal legislation and provide quality physical education services to qualifying children with disabilities in preschool through transition. A very good example of such a statement appears in a guide written by the Maryland State Department of Education and nine individuals from the state's local school systems. The statement reads:[9]

> The philosophy of the Maryland State Department of Education is to provide all students, including those students with disabilities, an appropriate physical education program. All Maryland Public Schools must ensure that students with disabilities have access to a program that enables them to achieve the same goals in physical education as their non-disabled peers. If special services are required to assist students with disabilities to master these goals, services should be provided. Instructional methods, settings, materials, and time should be modified to create an appropriate educational environment comparable to that provided for students without disabilities.

DEFINITION OF ADAPTED PHYSICAL EDUCATION

APE is the art and science of developing, implementing, and monitoring a carefully designed physical education *instructional* program for a learner with a disability, based on a comprehensive assessment, to give the learner the skills necessary for a lifetime of rich leisure, recreation, and sport experiences to enhance physical fitness and wellness. See **Table 2-1** for the responsibilities of an adapted physical educator.

GOALS AND OBJECTIVES

The goals of the APE program should be consistent with those established by the state education agency for every learner who participates in physical education. This is critical, given the current emphasis on the inclusion of learners with disabilities in the general physical education program. The Maryland State Department of Education has developed its overall goal statement around five main points. The main objectives state that the physical education program should be:

- a planned instructional program with specific content
- part of the total curriculum to increase physical competence, health-related fitness, self-responsibility, and enjoyment

TABLE 2-1   Responsibilities of the Adapted Physical Educator

- Assessment and comprehensive evaluation within physical and motor development
- Development of the individual physical education plan (IPEP)
- Implementation of the IPEP
- Representation of APE at IEP or multidisciplinary team meetings
- Provision of direct instructional services to children with disabilities, when appropriate
- Consultation with general physical education and general special education personnel
- Consultation with community-based leisure, recreation, and sport facilities managers regarding program and facility accessibility
- Curriculum development and/or revision
- Communication with parents
- Management of budget
- Purchase and maintenance of equipment

- a program that can establish lifelong enjoyment of physical activity
- a program to enhance brain development to maximize academic performance
- a program that builds positive attitudes and habits[9]

CRITERIA FOR ELIGIBILITY

The specific criteria for eligibility for APE remain confusing and inconsistent from school district to school district and state to state. The local education agency must determine the eligibility criteria based on the interpretation of federal law by the state education agency. Eligibility criteria may be established based on the extent of the learner's gross motor delay, age-related performance, or score on a given standardized instrument. A few states have identified specific criteria for eligibility in APE.

The lack of criteria in other states makes it virtually impossible for itinerant APE consultants to serve learners with disabilities in the public schools consistently and fairly. Individuals hired to conduct comprehensive APE analyses are asked to determine if the student assessed "qualifies" for APE; without specific criteria, this decision is based solely on the experience and judgment of the individual consultant.[8]

REFERRAL PROCESS

Referral, assessment, and placement procedures are the very foundation of the APE program and are vital to ensure that each eligible student receives the appropriate intervention, an IEP. The instructional model for APE follows these steps:

1. Accumulation of information about the student
2. Screening and, with parental consent, a comprehensive assessment
3. Development of a program to meet the student's individual needs as part of the IEP/multidisciplinary team
4. Determination of the instructional modifications necessary to meet the learner's educational needs
5. Consideration of placement
6. Implementation of the program
7. Monitoring of progress

ASSESSMENT PROCEDURES

It is vital that an APE assessment be completed by a trained professional who has extensive experience in assessment in physical and motor development (see **Table 2-2**). Because it is unusual for a general physical educator to have specific training in the comprehensive assessment that identifies gross motor delays and their causes, many school districts hire APE specialists specifically for assessing and recommending an appropriate instructional program.

TABLE 2-2   Assessment Skills of the Adapted Physical Educator

The carefully trained adapted physical educator has unique skills to assess and evaluate gross motor performance within the following areas:

- Reflex and equilibrium development
- Sensory stimulation and discrimination skills
- Sensorimotor integration
- Locomotor and nonlocomotor competency
- Play, game, leisure, recreation, and sport-specific motor patterns
- Physical and motor fitness

INDIVIDUALIZED EDUCATION PROGRAM

The individualized education program (IEP) is the cornerstone of the educational process that ties together the parent and data from the comprehensive assessment and information from the child's classroom and physical education teacher, with a specific program to intervene to meet goals and objectives specially designed for the student. The IEP should contain specific physical education goals. If these goals are not written in the plan, it is often assumed that the student does not need to receive physical education services, especially if other motor services are written in the IEP. For example, if physical therapy goals are written in the IEP and physical education goals are not, it could be interpreted that the student's motor needs will be met by physical therapy alone. A related service such as physical therapy cannot replace a direct service such as physical education.

INSTRUCTIONAL OPTIONS/DELIVERY MODELS

A continuum of instructional options is the basis of a district's ability to provide physical education services within the least restrictive environment. APE is special education programming, not just a place or class period. For example, a qualifying student with a mild motor delay may receive physical education instruction in a general physical education setting with same-age peers. Peer tutors and/or a paraeducator may assist with accommodations and modifications. On the other hand, a student who is very involved motorically may receive instruction in a small-group setting or one-to-one with an APE specialist. See **Table 2-3** for a continuum of instructional options.

TABLE 2-3   Instructional Options

Required educational service by a CAPE or state-certified adapted physical educator.
Assessment and IEP development by a CAPE or state-certified adapted physical educator who serves as a regular consultant to the general physical educator, instruction by general physical educator.
Assessment and IEP development by a CAPE or state-certified adapted physical educator who serves as an occasional consultant to the general physical educator, instruction by general physical educator.
Assessment and IEP development by a general physical educator or special educator with occasional review by a CAPE or state-certified adapted physical educator, instruction by general physical educator.

The strategies used to ensure that a student receives the instructional services he or she deserves vary greatly, depending on a number of variables:

- The number of students served by the school district
- The location and geographical size of the school district
- The administrative hierarchy
- The administrative commitment to APE
- Parental interest in and commitment to APE
- The number of trained/certified adapted physical educators hired to teach within the district
- The caseload

A continuum of service-delivery models should be available to any student qualifying for APE services. The adapted physical educator and general physical educator, if appropriate, along with other IEP team members, should determine which delivery model will provide the student with the most success. Three of the most popular models are listed here:

1. *Direct services:* Designates direct physical education services provided by an APE specialist to students who qualify, as indicated by an assessment and evaluation of motor performance and other areas of need.
2. *Collaboration:* Designates services provided and/or implemented jointly with other school personnel to assist students in meeting individualized goals and objectives through all of the physical education options described. Services may be provided in a way intended to lead students progressively through various types of physical education options or in a way that combines elements of various options to meet the students' individual needs.
3. *Consultation:* Designates assistance given to parents, paraeducators, or general physical education teachers who conduct the general, modified, or specially designed physical education program options. Assistance may include suggestions for individualizing instruction by making modifications or adaptations, and identification of supplementary devices or assistive technology to facilitate skill development to meet a student's individual needs.

Increasingly, the well-trained adapted physical educator (e.g., national [CAPE] or state-certified professional) finds himself or herself thrust into the role of consultant, even though his or her preservice training focused on the provision of instructional services to learners with disabilities. See **Table 2-4** to consider the roles and responsibilities of the APE consultant. It also becomes increasingly important that the general physical educator be able to take advantage of the services of the APE consultant. Few teachers have received adequate training to prepare them for their collaborative roles. See **Table 2-5** for specific suggestions for the general physical educator to maximize time spent with the APE consultant.

EQUIPMENT

The physical educator or adapted physical educator is responsible for a great deal within the school community. The physical education teacher who

TABLE 2-4   Roles and Responsibilities of the Adapted Physical Education Consultant[3]

- Complete a comprehensive APE assessment.
- Make specific program recommendations.
- Work with the IEP/multidisciplinary team to develop an individual physical education program.
- Consider accommodations/modifications of the following instructional variables (refer to Chapter 6):
  - Curriculum
  - Assessment
  - Extent and nature of program participation
  - Instructional (personnel) support
  - Teaching style
  - Grading
  - Equipment
  - Management of behavior
- Work with the general physical educator:
  - Identify needs.
  - Develop a plan for addressing the needs.
  - Develop a system for accountability for both the consultant and the general physical educator/special educator.
  - Monitor progress.

TABLE 2-5   Strategies for the General Physical Educator to Maximize Use of the Adapted Physical Education Consultant[3]

- Make sure the APE consultant feels as if your gymnasium/school is his or her second home.
- Give the APE consultant a place to work (if possible, a phone) in your office or gymnasium.
- Put the APE consultant's scheduled visit on the bulletin board.
- Communicate with the APE consultant regularly via email or campus mail.
- If the APE consultant deserves a "thanks," do so regularly with cards, notes, or letters, with copies to the consultant's supervisor.
- Advise the APE consultant of upcoming IEP meetings (if the special education staff has advised you of the upcoming IEP meetings).
- Invite the APE consultant to PTA presentations, school-wide play days, holiday celebrations, and so on.
- Be sure to introduce the APE consultant to key building personnel.
- Be prepared for the consultant's visit with specific questions.
- When necessary, loan the APE consultant equipment needed for assessment/intervention.
- Regularly complete service logs or portfolio notes for the APE consultant.
- Videotape student performance or behavior, so that the consultant has all the information needed to intervene.

serves children with disabilities in the regular elementary physical education program may wish to supplement basic equipment needed for quality elementary physical education instruction with additional equipment. The following is a list of the basic equipment needed for such a program. This list also represents the basic requirements for an APE program in a more restricted environment:

a. Wide balance beams or balance boards (6, 8, 10, and 12 inches wide)
b. Oversize scooter boards
c. Shoe polish/washable paint for marking floors
d. Plastic hoops
e. Jump ropes
f. Polyspots of varying colors and shapes
g. Punch balls and beach balls
h. Balls (assorted sizes, types, textures)
i. Velcro paddles and Velcro balls for catching
j. Wands with ribbons attached
k. Beanbags (including large and heavy beanbags)
l. Huge group parachutes

m. Cage balls
n. Tug-of-war rope
o. Oversize tennis and badminton racquets
p. Oversize, soft, and short bats
q. Nerf-type soccer balls, footballs, and volleyballs
r. Junior-size balls
s. Height-adjustable equipment
t. Floor and incline mats
u. Carpeted barrels
v. Bells, drums, maracas, etc.

With some ingenuity, the teacher can provide an excellent APE program for students at the elementary school level with minimum equipment. Play equipment can be made inexpensively. Following are suggestions for inexpensive equipment for use in the physical education program:

a. Rope for skipping, making shapes, jumping over, and climbing under
b. Cardboard boxes to climb in and through, to catch with, and to use as targets (particularly empty refrigerator, television, and washer/dryer boxes)
c. Tape/chalk to make shapes on the floor for moving on, around, and in
d. Half-gallon or gallon plastic jugs for catching, throwing, and knocking over
e. Scrap lumber for balance beams
f. Yarn for yarn balls
g. Carpet squares to skate on, slide on, sit on, and use as targets
h. Old garden hoses to make hula hoops
i. Old ladders to walk on and through
j. Traffic cones for obstacle courses

Equipment for middle and secondary physical education for learners with disabilities is very similar to that used in general physical education. A few special pieces of equipment that may facilitate the performance of learners with disabilities in fitness, leisure, recreation, and sports activities include (a) beepers to attach to targets for the visually impaired/beeper balls; (b) oversize racquets, bats, golf clubs (large heads); (c) basketball standards with return nets; (d) junior size/lightweight balls; (e) portable bowling ramps and balls with retractable handles; (f) Goal balls; (g) fluorescent balls; (h) therapy balls; (i) adjustable net standards; and (j) guide ropes with moveable, plastic handles.

ACCOUNTABILITY

The adapted physical educator must be accountable for the delivery of appropriate education services. Taxpayer scrutiny regarding the use of funds in education has, particularly, highlighted the need for accountability. In some states, federal and state funding of the local special education program is based on the number of documented contact hours between the professional and the student. Contact hours are usually documented with a service log. Service logs are used to record daily involvement in the APE program. A sample of such a log is provided in **Table 2-6**. In addition to a daily log that accounts for time and student contact, the adapted physical educator, like other teachers in the district, may be responsible for submitting paperwork

TABLE 2-6   Sample Daily Service Log

Date	Service	Student(s) Served/School	Time
2/10	Direct service—teaching*	EC Class/Adams	8:00–9:00
	Direct service—teaching	S/Ph Class/Adams	9:00–10:00
	Travel to Cabell		10:00–10:15
	Motor/fitness assessment	J. Flores/Cabell	10:15–12:00
	Lunch/travel to White		12:00–12:45
	Consultation—PE teacher	K. Black/White	12:45–1:30
	Travel to office		1:30–1:45
	Written report	J. Flores/Cabell	1:45–3:15
	Prepare for IEP meeting		3:15–3:45
2/11	Direct service—teaching*	EC Class/Foster	8:00–8:45
	Direct service—teaching	HI Class/Foster	9:00–9:45
	Travel to Cabell		9:50–10:00
	IEP meeting	J. Flores/Cabell	10:30–12:00
	Travel/lunch		12:00–12:45
	Direct service—teaching	S/Ph Class/Grant	1:00–1:45
	Travel to community pool		1:45–2:00
	Direct service	MD students/district	2:15–3:30
	Swimming instruction		

*See attached lesson plans.

(i.e., lesson plans) to a building principal or to the lead teacher. APE teachers with large caseloads will find it impossible to manage the paperwork without the use of technology. Managing electronic IEP updates, tracking assessment data, lesson plan writing, and emailing daily instructional plans to paraeducators are just some of the uses. Having continual access to the files and being able to submit files to administrators provides accountability and organization.

Interaction with Other Special Education Personnel

Within the larger structure of the school district and local campus, the effective adapted physical educator works in close cooperation with other direct service providers and with related service personnel. The most crucial interactions are with the learner's general physical educator, special education teacher(s), and related service personnel. The relationship between the adapted physical educator and the physical therapist, occupational therapist, and recreation therapist, and in some districts the musical therapist, is particularly crucial, given the direct concern of each professional regarding the child's motor efficiency. Related service personnel play an important role in physical education programs for children with disabilities. In addition to providing services that will help the children benefit from the program, they may also enhance the program by:

- Communicating directly with medical personnel
- Identifying students with motor needs
- Making APE referrals
- Recommending specific exercises and activities
- Providing computer or assistive technology necessary for the student to learn auxiliary skills in physical education—for example, playing computer golf; indeed, there are virtual reality computer programs that allow students with limited movement potential to rock climb, whitewater raft, skydive, and participate in other physical activities

Professionals involved in the education of a learner with a disability must share their knowledge, expertise, and technical skill not only with the learner but also with each other. The use of a multidisciplinary team to provide services is an excellent way to ensure communication among service providers.[6] The most efficient way to ensure cooperation among the adapted physical educator and related service personnel is to formalize the relationship by forming a multidisciplinary motor development team. The members of the motor development team should include the adapted physical educator, the general physical educator, the physical therapist, the occupational therapist, and the recreation therapist. The speech therapist and/or vision specialist may also function as part of the motor development team depending upon the needs of the student. The multidisciplinary process is, however, complex and there may be some barriers to overcome and discuss as a team:[2]

- Philosophical differences
- Lack of time for collaborative meetings
- Lack of training regarding collaborative skills, including communication and listening skills; this appears to be a critical obstacle in the collaborative process[7]

Common functions of members of motor teams can include the following:

1. *To screen and evaluate students with functional and/or educational problems to determine needs for special services.* See **Table 2-7**, a motor team screening form developed in District 19, Oregon. This screening instrument gives direction to physical educators, special educators, and general educators who may need to refer children to the motor development team. Once the members of the motor development team receive the information, they decide which specialist should serve as the lead member of the evaluation process. That lead person initiates and organizes a subsequent full-scale gross motor evaluation, which reduces the amount of duplicated effort. For example, both the occupational therapist and the adapted physical educator routinely use the Bruininks-Oseretsky Test of Motor Proficiency-2. As a member of the motor development team, either the adapted physical educator or the occupational therapist may administer the test and share the results with other professionals on the team.

TABLE 2-7   District 19 Motor Team Screening Form

Name: _____ DOB: _____

Date of referral: _____ Grade: _____ Teacher: _____

School: _____

Specialist: _____ Physician: _____

Was student retained? _____ Yes _____ No

PE time: _____ Recess time: _____

Current disabling conditions: _____

_____

Does the student use adaptive equipment (braces, crutches, etc.)? _____

_____

Please check those items that have been observed:

Gross Motor

- Lacks age-appropriate strength and endurance
- Difficulty with run, jump, hop, or skip compared with others his or her age
- Stiff and awkward in his or her movements
- Clumsy, seems not to know how to move body, bumps into things, falls out of chair
- Demonstrates mixed dominance
- Reluctant to participate in playground activities
- Play pattern is inappropriate for age group (does not play, plays by self, plays beside but not with stereotypical) (Circle one.)
- Has postural deviations
- Complains of pain during physical activities
- Demonstrates unusual wear patterns on shoes and/or clothing

Fine Motor

- Poor desk posture (slumps, leans on arm, head too close to work) (Circle.)
- Difficulty drawing, coloring, copying, cutting
- Poor pencil grasp and/or drops pencil frequently
- Lines drawn are light, wobbly, too faint, or too dark
- Breaks pencil often
- Lack of well-established dominance after 6 years of age
- Student has difficulty using both hands together (stabilization of paper during cutting and paper activities)

(continues)

TABLE 2-7   District 19 Motor Team Screening Form (*Continued*)

Self-Care Skills

- Difficulty with fasteners (buttons, zippers, snaps, shoe tying, lacing) (Circle.)
- Wears clothes backwards or inside out, appears messy
- Difficulty putting clothes on or taking them off
- Difficulty with the eating process (opening packages, feeding self, spilling, using utensils) (Circle.)
- Oral-motor problems (drools, difficulty chewing, swallowing, difficulty drinking from straws) (Circle.)
- Needs assistance with toileting (wiping, flushing, replacing underwear/clothes) (Circle.)

Academic (Check those areas presenting problems.)

- Distractibility
- Following directions
- Hyperactivity
- Memory deficit
- Difficulty naming body parts
- Slow work
- Restlessness
- Organizing work
- Finishing tasks
- Attention deficit

Tactile Sensation

- Seems to withdraw from touch
- Craves touch
- Tends to wear coat when not needed: will not allow shirtsleeves pulled up
- Has trouble keeping hands to self, will poke or push other children
- Apt to touch everything he or she sees ("learns through fingers")
- Dislikes being hugged or cuddled
- Avoids certain textures of foods
- Dislikes arts-and-crafts activities involving different textures (clay, finger paints)
- Complains of numbness, tingling, and other abnormal sensations

Auditory Perception

- Appears overly sensitive to sounds
- Talks excessively
- Likes to make loud noises
- Has difficulty making self understood

TABLE 2-7   District 19 Motor Team Screening Form (*Continued*)

- Appears to have difficulty understanding teacher/paraprofessional/peers
- Tends to repeat directions to self

Visual Perception

- Difficulty discriminating colors and shapes doing puzzles
- Letter and/or number reversals after first grade
- Difficulty with eye-tracking (following objects with eyes, eyes and head move together)
- Difficulty copying designs, numbers, or letters
- Has and wears/doesn't wear glasses
- Difficulty transcribing from blackboard or book to paper
- Difficulty with eye-hand or eye-foot coordination (catching, striking, kicking)

Emotional

- Does not accept changes in routine easily
- Becomes easily frustrated
- Acts out behaviorally, difficulty getting along with others
- Tends to be impulsive, heedless, accident prone
- Easier to handle in large group, small group, or individually (Circle.)
- Marked mood variations, outbursts, or tantrums
- Marked out-of-seat behavior
- Noncompliant
- Unstable home situation
- Notable self-stimulatory behaviors

Additional Concerns:

_____

_____

Assigned to: _____

Date received: _____ Evaluation date: _____

2. *To develop an IEP as part of the total multidisciplinary team, to specifically address the child's motor needs.* Members of the motor team develop an IEP that addresses the needs of the child.
3. *To implement an intervention program that facilitates learning.* Once the IEP is approved by the entire IEP/multidisciplinary team, the members of the motor team implement the intervention program. Like the assessment, the intervention program is cooperative. Each member of the team addresses the child's motor needs. Instead of limiting focus to one component of motor development, all professionals

on the team share responsibility for implementing the program or designate one service provider to represent the team.

4. *To manage and supervise motor programs.* Each member of the motor team assumes a specific responsibility for the management and supervision of the program according to his or her expertise. If a team leader has been designated, each member of the motor team will communicate directly with that person regarding the student's progress.[4, 5]

5. *To document service delivery.* Careful documentation of services delivered is a vital part of the process. Each member of the team must be accountable not only to the child served but also to each other. This is often done by using a service provider log. (See **Table 2-8**, a sample of a motor team service provider log.) This type of log is vital for communication among professional members of the motor team. The log may also serve as crucial documentation of the services provided during the annual review of the child's progress.

6. *To cooperatively provide or create resources that help other professionals meet the motor needs of students with disabilities.* Members of the motor development team have specialized knowledge that should be shared with educators who are in daily contact with the learners. In some school districts or special service cooperatives, the members of the motor team have created motor development handbooks for use by teachers in early childhood classrooms, self-contained special education classrooms, or general physical education.

TABLE 2-8   Motor Team Service Provider Log

For this student, one of the program recommendations, based on a comprehensive motor assessment, was an exercise program to strengthen abdominal muscles and extensor, adductor, and abductor hip muscles.

Date	Service Provider	Child's Performance
11/12	C. Candler, OTR	Performed 15 abdominal curls while seated on a therapy ball, feet flat on floor
11/14	H. Unger, PT	Performed 10 long-sitting, hip abduction exercises, using a medium TheraBand for resistance
11/15	B. Huettig, CAPE	Swam 100 yards using a "lifeguard" front crawl with head out of the water
11/19	C. Candler, OTR	Performed 17 abdominal curls while seated on a therapy ball, feet flat on floor
11/20	B. Huettig, CAPE	Swam 125 yards using a "lifeguard" front crawl with head out of the water

7. *To conduct cooperative in-service motor development training for other school personnel, parents, and volunteers.* Professionals on the motor development team share functions yet retain professional integrity and expertise. Each has a unique contribution to students and professionals who provide direct or related instructional services to students with disabilities. The traditional emphasis by each professional who may function as a member of a motor team is illustrated in **Figure 2-1**. It is important to note that this model is not restrictive. The intent of the motor team is to share professional competency, judgment, and expertise.

This type of model for the delivery of services to children with motor deficits is particularly important in school districts and cooperatives

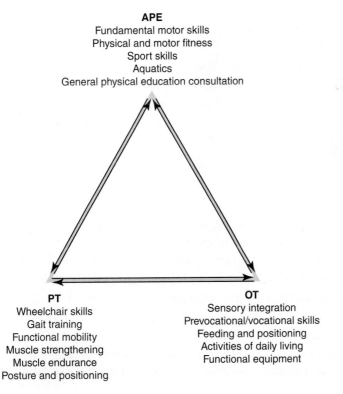

APE
Fundamental motor skills
Physical and motor fitness
Sport skills
Aquatics
General physical education consultation

PT
Wheelchair skills
Gait training
Functional mobility
Muscle strengthening
Muscle endurance
Posture and positioning

OT
Sensory integration
Prevocational/vocational skills
Feeding and positioning
Activities of daily living
Functional equipment

Figure 2-1   Motor Team

unable to locate sufficient numbers of certified, trained professional staff. For example, if a school district is unable to hire and retain a licensed physical therapist as part of the staff, it may be necessary for other professionals to implement the program designed by a contracted therapist. In school districts with limited APE teachers, it is vital that the general physical educator who provides direct service be provided information necessary to deliver appropriate educational services. Physical education services *must* be provided to students with disabilities enrolled in public education. Though federal law makes it infinitely clear that "lack of money" or "lack of personnel" is not an adequate reason for failure to provide the services, in reality the quality of those services will depend on the availability, training, and knowledge of the service providers.

Public Education

Federal education policy typically reflects congressional priorities and interests; those priorities and interests may or may not reflect the priorities of the people. More and more often, policies regarding the education of children with and without disabilities have been mandated by the federal courts and challenged within the state and federal judicial system. The U.S. Department of Education is challenged with the responsibility of interpreting federal legislation and helping the states implement such policies. Within the Department of Education are several subagencies responsible for setting the agenda and providing direction for each state. The Office of Special Education and

Rehabilitative Services (OSERS) has the primary responsibility for setting the agenda and providing direction regarding the delivery of educational services for students with disabilities.

THE STATE AND LOCAL EDUCATION AGENCY

A state education agency is responsible for implementing federal policy at the state level and interpreting federal legislation to meet the needs of learners in the state. The state education agency or department of public instruction within each state has specific guidelines and policies that must be followed by each local education agency. Historically, it has been important in the nation's educational system for the state education agency and the local education agency to be "empowered" to decide how to educate their children. While this guarantee of "rights" continues to be significant, it is important to note that there are states and local education agencies that do not honor or recognize the rights and the needs of children with disabilities and their families or hold them as priorities. When this is the case, it is the responsibility of the courts to interpret laws.

Typically, the state education agency is responsible for decisions regarding the instructional standards and the strategies that will be used to evaluate whether students served within the local education agency are meeting those standards. A local education agency or education cooperative, a cluster of small school districts without sufficient resources to provide education for their children independently, is responsible for implementing state policy and interpreting that policy to meet the needs of learners within the district or cooperative. It is the responsibility of the school to contribute to the fullest possible development of each student entrusted to its care. This is a basic tenet of our democratic structure. The notion of "home rule" is critical in the education of children within the United States. Since the founding of this country, citizens in individual communities have long held the belief that it is their responsibility and their right to educate their children. In most school districts, the responsibility for educating the district's children is placed in the hands of the members of a school board. In most communities, individuals who serve on this school board are elected officials, responsible to the voters for their performance. The school board is responsible for implementing state policy and interpreting that policy to meet the needs of learners within the particular school district.

The primary administrator within the school district is usually called the superintendent of schools or the chief executive officer. The responsibilities of the superintendent or chief executive officer include the assurance of a quality education for all children. This individual, particularly in a large district, often has associate superintendents who help with quality control and assist with decisions regarding student services, budget, personnel, and facilities and equipment. Within that structure, historically, an individual has been designated as the director of special education. That person is responsible for implementing school board policy as it relates to students who are in need of special education services in order to be successful learners and, ultimately, productive and capable citizens.

SITE-BASED MANAGEMENT

Site-based management is a strategy to increase school effectiveness by allowing the major players (e.g., the principal, teachers, parents, students, and community members) more control over policies and procedures that affect their school. The potential beauty of site-based management is that the very people responsible for the quality of learning are held directly accountable for that learning and are given greater decision-making authority in that process. However, the site-based management process is only as good as the building leader(s).

> *If the school has a visionary principal, virtually any management style will be effective in bringing about significant learning outcomes for children with and without disabilities.*

The physical educator and the adapted physical educator can and must ask to be a part of the school-based team. Far too often, excellent physical educators do their jobs quietly and without fanfare in the gymnasium without recognition. In this day of limited budgets and increased emphasis on the "academic subjects," the physical educator/adapted physical educator must be vocal, visible, and strident regarding the needs of children with and without disabilities. (See **Table 2-9**.)

TABLE 2-9 Unique Contributions of the Physical Educator in a Site-Based System

The adapted physical educator or general physical educator is uniquely trained to do the following:

- Develop school-based wellness programs for teachers, staff, students, and their parents
- Help develop a before- or after-school program to keep children in a safe and nurturing environment while parents work
- Assume leadership of a committee designed to develop positive relationships between community members and the school

SCHOOL–FAMILY PARTNERSHIPS

Epstein[1] has developed a model for the development of school/family/community partnerships to best serve the children within any given community. She has identified the following six types of involvement of families and community members within the schools:

Type 1: Parenting. Help all families establish home environments to support children as students.

Type 2: Communicating. Design effective forms of school-to-home communications about school programs and children's progress.

Type 3: Volunteering. Recruit and organize parent help and support.

Type 4: Learning at home. Provide information and ideas to families about how to help students at home with homework and other curriculum-related activities, decisions, and planning.

Type 5: Decision making. Include parents in school decisions, developing parent leaders and representatives.

Type 6: Collaborating with the community. Identify and integrate resources and services from the community to strengthen school programs, family practices, and student learning and development.

The following are suggestions for the adapted physical educator and general physical educator for increasing participation in each of the six types of involvement:

Type 1: Parenting

- Provide parents and members of the learner's extended family with information that will help them develop reasonable expectations regarding the motor development of their child with a developmental delay or disability.
- Provide parents and members of the learner's extended family with information regarding developmentally appropriate play (e.g., the child needs to learn to engage in cooperative play before he or she can engage in competitive experiences with success).
- Model appropriate play and motor intervention strategies for parents (e.g., toss a ball in a horizontal path when a student is learning to catch, so that the child is not overwhelmed by trying to track an object moving through horizontal and vertical planes).
- Share information with parents about strategies for making inexpensive equipment for the student to play with in the home (e.g., an old mattress or an old tire covered with a secured piece of carpeting makes a wonderful trampoline).
- Share information about community resources and opportunities for students with disabilities to participate in play; games; and leisure, recreation, and sport activities.
- Provide family support and information regarding securing health services for the student.
- Serve as an advocate for the parent and family.

Type 2: Communicating

- Use your computer to generate a physical education and/or APE newsletter or ask for a column or space in the school newspaper.
- Develop an APE website for the school and/or district to communicate with parents and community members.
- Send home brief notes to communicate with the student's family, such as the computer-generated certificate shown in **Figure 2-2**.
- Call a parent to praise the student's progress. Far too often, teachers communicate with parents only when there is a problem.
- Be an active participant in regularly scheduled parent–teacher conferences. Communicate to parents a willingness to meet at other times as well.
- Write positive comments on student report cards.

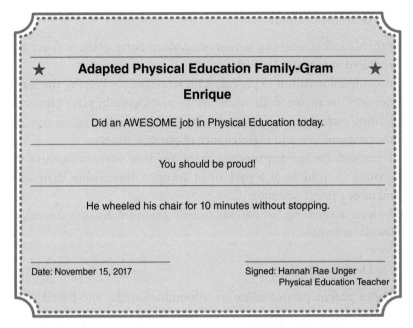

Adapted Physical Education Family-Gram

Enrique

Did an AWESOME job in Physical Education today.

You should be proud!

He wheeled his chair for 10 minutes without stopping.

Date: November 15, 2017

Signed: Hannah Rae Unger
Physical Education Teacher

Figure 2-2 A Customized Certificate is an Excellent Way to Communicate with a Atudent's Family

Type 3: Volunteering

Encourage parents to serve as the following:

- An assistant in classes
- A director or an assistant in before- and after-school recreation, intra- mural, or sports programs
- An assistant coach
- A director or an assistant on school play day
- The editor or publisher of the newsletter
- A parent-to-parent trainer
- A raffle organizer to raise money for equipment
- An assistant playground supervisor
- A clerical assistant to generate certificates, progress charts, etc.

Type 4: Learning at Home

- Provide information to parents regarding curriculum and activities required at each grade level.
- Provide information to parents with strategies for helping the learner develop the motor skills necessary to participate in play; games; and leisure, recreation, and sport activities; include information regarding the development and maintenance of physical fitness.
- Demonstrate age-appropriate activities that parents can use with groups of children at a park or in an open area within their apartment or project complex.
- Provide a calendar for parents to help them follow unit themes and special activities.

Type 5: Decision Making

- Invite parent participation as a member of the site-based school committee.
- Invite parent participation in a subcommittee of the parent-teacher association/organization (PTA/PTO) that addresses the physical education/APE program.
- In districts where there is a special education advisory committee, ensure that a parent with a commitment to physical education/APE is on that committee.

Type 6: Collaborating with the Community

- As the physical educator or adapted physical educator, ask to serve on boards or committees of community recreation and/or sports organizations.
- Develop a collaborative physical education or recreation program to meet the needs of learners within the community, using shared facilities, shared equipment, and, if possible, shared personnel.
- Recruit community personnel to help develop and build playgrounds for the schools. Particularly in large, urban districts, playgrounds are often nonexistent or antiquated.
- Invite the parents and other relatives of children into the school to teach games, sports, and dances of their country of origin (see **Table 2-10**).

TABLE 2-10   The School as Part of the Extended Family

Following are strategies for enhancing the family–school partnership:

- Find out what the parents really want from the school. What "outcomes" do they expect after their children receive educational services?
- Encourage many different types of parental involvement in the school, based on the comfort level of the parents.[1]
- Make communications with parents positive. Unfortunately, all too often, parents are contacted by the school only when their child is in trouble.
- Create parent-involvement opportunities that are sensitive to parents' work schedules, time constraints, needs for child care, etc.[1]
- Find and develop a small room, designated for the parents, that has child development information, computer/Internet access, access to a printer, etc.

SUMMARY

The provision of quality APE services for learners with disabilities requires a carefully designed referral, assessment, and instructional program. These programs reflect "quality services" when there is a cooperative effort between professionals and parents in order to meet the unique needs of the learner.

The physical education teacher and APE teacher must work together as advocates for a quality program for children with and without disabilities. Clearly, that communication is the most critical in the provision of services.

The quality APE program requires excellent communication among all involved. Adapted physical educators and general physical educators serving learners with disabilities may have a vital role as a member of a motor team made up of professionals with a particular commitment to developing skills to encourage lifelong physical activity.

REVIEW QUESTIONS

1. Explain the relationship between litigation and legislation that has an impact on the education of learners with disabilities.
2. Briefly explain how computer technology can be used to enhance physical education for learners with disabilities.
3. Explain the responsibilities of the motor development team in the provision of educational and related services for learners with disabilities.

REFERENCES

1. Epstein, J., et al. (2009). *School, family, and community partnerships: Your handbook for action* (3rd ed.). Thousand Oaks, CA: Corwin Press, Inc.
2. Horton, M., Wilson, S., & Gagnon, D. (2003). Collaboration: A key component for successful inclusion in general physical education. *Teaching Elementary Physical Education, 14,* 13–17.
3. Huettig, C., & Roth, K. (2002). Maximizing the use of APE consultants: What the general physical educator has the right to expect. *JOPERD, 73,* 32–35.
4. Kasser, S., & Lieberman, L. (2003). Maximizing learning opportunities through activity modification. *Teaching Elementary Physical Education, 14,* 19–22.
5. LaMaster, K., Gall, K., Kinchin, G., & Siedentop, D. (2003). Inclusion practices of effective elementary specialists. *Adapted Physical Activity Quarterly, 15,* 64–81.
6. Lieberman, L., & Houston-Wilson, C. (2009). *Strategies for inclusion: A handbook for physical educators.* Champaign, IL: Human Kinetics.
7. Lytle, R., Lavay, B., Robinson, N., & Huettig, C. (2003). Teaching collaboration and consultation skills to preservice and inservice APE teachers. *JOPERD, 74,* 13–16.
8. Lytle, R., Lavay, B., & Rizzo, T. (2010). What is a highly qualified adapted physical education teacher? *Journal of Physical Education, Recreation & Dance, 81,* 40–50. DOI: 10.1080/07303084.2010.10598433.
9. Maryland State Department of Education. (2009). *A guide for serving students with disabilities in physical education.* Baltimore, MD: Maryland State Board of Education.

CHAPTER 3

Determining Educational Needs through Assessment

OBJECTIVES

- Explain the purposes of assessment.
- List the different types of assessment.
- Identify four factors that must be considered when selecting an assessment instrument.
- Explain what is meant by administrative feasibility.
- Provide examples of techniques that can be used to organize test results.

It is becoming increasingly clear that traditional educational practices that have served our society well in the past must be modified to keep pace with changing societal demands, as well as the growing diversity of students being educated in our schools. It is apparent that, for our society to survive and grow, all students, regardless of gender, ethnicity, and functional capacity, must be adequately prepared to participate successfully in a multicultural society that is increasingly dependent on advanced technology.[4] School curricula must be designed to provide students with information, skills, and problem-solving capabilities that will enable them to function fully in the career and community of their choice. A critical component of an effective curriculum is a means for determining at what levels students are

functioning, the types of interventions needed to gain full benefits from their school experiences, their progress toward mastery of the school curriculum, and validation that what has been learned has application in the society. Appropriate assessment techniques can provide this information.

In this chapter a broad range of assessment information will be presented. The purposes of assessment, the types of instruments available to meet those purposes, ways to evaluate specific instruments to determine their appropriateness, and tips on administering tests have been included. Ways to arrange test results to facilitate interpretation will also be covered. Recommendations for instruments that can be used with students, who have specific types of disabilities, and ways to modify the testing situation to meet their needs, will be included in each of the chapters that address those populations.

Purposes of Assessment

Assessment is a problem-solving process that involves a variety of ways of gathering information. Testing is the administration of specific instruments that are used to gather assessment data.[7] Motor assessment instruments provide different types of information. It is important to match the selection of the instrument with the purpose of the assessment. Assessment instruments should provide the teacher information about what activities should be included in the curriculum. Too frequently, the teacher selects assessment instruments that reflect what is currently being taught. Assessment is an inseparable part of the student's ongoing educational program, and it is particularly critical for students with disabilities.

Assessment of students in educational settings has at least seven purposes.

1. To identify those who might be experiencing developmental delays
2. To diagnose the nature of the student's problem or delay
3. To provide information to use to develop the individualized education program (IEP) and determine appropriate placement
4. To develop instruction specific to the student's special needs
5. To evaluate student progress[7]
6. To determine support services needed[5]
7. To determine which skills need to be developed to enable the individual to access programs available in the community[5]

In addition to formal types of physical and motor assessments, quality adapted physical education (APE) programs usually include needs assessments to determine what supports and services are needed by each student to fully benefit from participation. Those types of assessments gather (1) student data, (2) support needs, and (3) services needed to generalize skills learned in the physical education program to the community.[5] Other types of information the APE teacher may want to gather are (1) student participation in extracurricular activities, (2) play and leisure-time preferences, (3) the extent to which the program is meeting the students' goals, and (4) student satisfaction with the program.

Matching Type of Assessment to Purpose

Both formal and informal tests serve important functions in the educational process. Formal tests are those that have been developed for a specific purpose and have been standardized. Informal tests are those that have been developed for a general purpose and have not been standardized. The purpose of the assessment should dictate the type of instrument selected and the standards the instrument must meet. The more critical the decisions that are made from the assessment, the more rigorous the requirements for the instrument the evaluator will use.

Informal techniques used for screening groups to determine whether any individuals are experiencing significant delays include checklists, activities used in the curriculum, and observation of students during their regular physical education class or during recess. Formal tests used to pinpoint specific areas of delays include physical fitness tests, gross motor development tests, and skill tests and/or motor proficiency tests that have been standardized. Whatever the method used, it is recommended that the information be recorded, so that documentation is available for the permanent record file. An example of an observational checklist that was developed for use in the Denton, Texas, Independent School District appears in **Table 3-1**. Using an informal test, once a teacher observes a student not performing to the level of his or her classmates, it is understood that more rigorous testing is necessary to determine the extent and type of delay. Parental approval is not required for informal testing; however, it is required for more in-depth testing.

Assessment information used for developing a student's IEP and for selecting appropriate activities can be gathered from a variety of sources, including parental reports, informal test procedures, and formal testing. Those areas found to be below expectations for the student's age become the present levels of performance that are required to be recorded on the IEP. Measurable annual goals written for the student are directly related to the present level of performance areas found to be lacking. Periodic reports to document the progress a child is making on the annual goals are shared with parents/guardians. The effectiveness of a physical education program can be continuously monitored by determining the extent to which the students are mastering goals that have been included on their IEPs.

For over 50 years, a standardized test that has been used to assess persons with intellectual disabilities is the Vineland Adaptive Behavior Scales. This test, which has just been revised, measures adaptive functioning and was influential in the defining and classification system of intellectual disability.[1] The Vineland is an interview for teachers, parents, and service providers that is designed to measure the level of adaptive functioning of persons from birth to 90 years of age in five domains: (1) communication, (2) daily living skills, (3) socialization, (4) motor skills, and (5) maladaptive behaviors. There is a teacher's edition for use with ages 3 years to 21 years, 11 months.

TABLE 3-1   Denton Independent School District Adapted Physical Education Pre-Referral/Referral Form

	Regular Educator	Educational Diagnostician	APE Teacher
	Initial ____ Date ____	**Initial** ____ Date ____	**Initial** ____ Date ____

Student _____ ID# _____ DOB _____

School _____ Type of Class (Unit) Teacher _____

Evaluation Requested by _____ Medical Concerns _____

Major concerns about student in Physical Education _____

_____

School Contact for APE Teacher _____

Method of Ambulation _____ Form of Communication _____

Below are some behaviors that indicate a student's ability to move efficiently and interact effectively with others. Please check (s) the appropriate response in the Regular Education (RE) column. If these tasks do not apply, list your concerns in the comment section on the back of this page.

	YES		SOMETIMES		NO	
PSYCHOMOTOR DEVELOPMENT	RE	APE	RE	APE	RE	APE
Demonstrates capability for voluntary movement						
Reacts to noise/activity/touch						
Rolls from front to back						
Sits assisted/unassisted						
Stands assisted/unassisted						
Walks in cross pattern						
Runs in cross pattern						
Ascends/descends stairs						
Jumps with mature pattern						
Hops (1 foot) with mature pattern						
Leaps with mature pattern						
Gallops with mature pattern						
Skips with mature pattern						
Slides with mature pattern						
Walks a straight line/heel-to-toe						
Stands on one foot for 5 seconds						
Catches an 8.5 inch ball with mature pattern						
Bounces and catches a playground ball to self						
Kicks a stationary ball with mature pattern						
Kicks a rolled ball with mature pattern						
Throws a ball with mature pattern						
Turns own jump rope using rhythmic form while jumping						

(continues)

TABLE 3-1   Denton Independent School District Adapted Physical Education Pre-Referral/Referral Form
(*Continued*)

PSYCHOMOTOR DEVELOPMENT	YES		SOMETIMES		NO	
	RE	APE	RE	APE	RE	APE
COGNITIVE DEVELOPMENT						
Can remember visual and/or auditory information						
Can understand cause and effect						
Exhibits appropriate on-task behavior						
Can follow directions						
AFFECTIVE DEVELOPMENT						
Indicates a dislike for physical activity						
Prefers to play solo						
Has a low frustration tolerance, cries easily						
Tends to be impulsive						
Is physically/verbally aggressive toward others/self						
Has a short attention span						
Distracts others						
Respects authority, rules, and others						
Student _____						

BODY MECHANICS/POSTURE: (Check all that apply)	YES		SOMETIMES		NO	
	RE	APE	RE	APE	RE	APE
☐ Posture – head/trunk/feet misalignment						
☐ Muscular/Skeletal/Neurological impairment						
☐ Underweight/Overweight						
MOBILITY SKILLS (NON-AMBULATORY: (Check all that the student demonstrates)						
☐ Transfers in and out of chair						
☐ Has acceptable range of motion						
☐ Can open doors						
☐ Can push up ramps						
☐ Can reverse direction						
☐ Can use brake						
☐ Can pivot in chair						
☐ Can perform a wheelie						
Teachers' Comments _____						

_____

_____

_____

_____

TABLE 3-1 Denton Independent School District Adapted Physical Education Pre-Referral/Referral Form (*Continued*)

Thank you for your time. Please return this completed form to the Special Education Diagnostician in your school.
....

To be filled out by the *Adapted Physical Educator*

Date of Classroom Visit(s): _____   _____   _____   _____   _____

Recommendations:

 ❑ The student is functioning within acceptable limits in regular Physical Education and does not need any further evaluation at this time.

 ❑ The student is able to be included in regular Physical Education class with appropriate modifications by either the regular Physical Educator or consultation services by the Adapted Physical Educator.

 ❑ The student appears to be experiencing difficulty in the area(s) indicated above and will need further screening/evaluation by the Adapted Physical Education Teacher for appropriate placement with some type of special services.

 ❑ The student can benefit from activities provided by the Classroom Teacher.

_____   _____   _____
              Signed   Date   Position

Courtesy Denton, Texas, Independent School District

Legal Mandates for Determining Present Level of Performance

The type of testing used for students with disabilities must conform to federal and state laws and district practices. Physical education for students with disabilities is broadly defined in the federal law. Those laws do not dictate the type of testing that should be done but do set the conditions surrounding the testing process. The 2004 Individuals with Disabilities Education Improvement Act (IDEIA) revisions generally restate longstanding policy set out in the prior regulations.[8] These requirements are located in **Table 3-2**.

In most school districts, the questions of whether testing is done and the type utilized are left to the discretion of individual teachers. Because appropriate testing is basic to designing a physical education program that will meet the needs of the student with a disability, it is critical to the effectiveness of a teacher.

The reauthorization of IDEIA (P.L. 108-446) revisions align IDEIA with Every Student Succeeds Act (ESSA, P.L. 114-95). In general, the IEP must be linked to each child's education in the general curriculum, and children with

TABLE 3-2 2004 IDEIA Evaluation Requirements

- Assessments may not discriminate on a cultural or racial basis.
- Assessments are provided and administered in the child's native language.
- A variety of assessment tools and strategies are used to gather functional and development information, including information provided by the parent, and information related to enabling the child to be involved in and progress in the general curriculum.
- The standardized tests used in the process must have been validated for the specific purpose for which they are used and must be administered by trained and knowledgeable personnel in accordance with the provided instructions.
- All variations from standard conditions must be described.
- Child is assessed in all areas related to the suspected disability, including, if appropriate, health, vision, and motor abilities.
- Assessment tools and strategies are used that provide relevant information that directly assists persons in determining the [physical] education needs of the child.
- Assessment tools, required in the general [physical] education program, must be administered to students with disabilities with modifications, if needed.

disabilities are to be assessed according to their state's content standards. The provisions for testing students in special education in the general curriculum apply only to the academic areas. There is no national test for physical education; however, there are content standards in physical education in some states.

The Every Student Succeeds Act (ESSA) reauthorizes the Elementary and Secondary Education Act of 1965 and replaces the No Child Left Behind Act (NCLB) of 2002. ESSA differs from NCLB in that states will now have more discretion in deciding how to intervene in low-performing schools. States will still test in math and reading in grades 3 and 5, and once in high school. Accountability plans will still need to be submitted to the Education Department but states can select their own long- and short-term goals as long as they address testing, English-language proficiency, graduation rates, and goals for closing achievement gaps. Although physical education is not specifically addressed in ESSA, schools could develop goals and incorporate physical education testing and standards into the prescribed curriculum. These state initiatives could be aimed at facilitating (1) children and youth with disabilities to participate in after-school programs that involve physical activity, (2) participation in school health programs, and (3) utilization of school personnel who demonstrate healthy lifestyles. All of these initiatives could be incorporated into the APE program.

Types of Assessment

Assessment data provides the teacher with information needed to develop a meaningful physical education program for each student as well as evaluate what learning takes place during the program (formative) and at the end of the program (summative).[6] What is meaningful depends a great deal on the knowledge and skill of the teacher as well as the time available to him or her. The teacher who wants to know if students can apply the skills taught in physical education to real-world settings will utilize authentic alternative assessments. Teachers who are committed to a predetermined curriculum will measure students' ability to demonstrate competence of the components of the curriculum (curriculum-based). The teacher who is preparing a transitional program for a student who is 14 years of age or older will conduct task analyses of activities available in the community (ecological inventory) and then will design a program to teach the missing skills to the student. The teacher who believes all activity should primarily contribute to physical fitness will measure fitness levels. The teacher of the young student will focus on the basic locomotor, object-control, and perceptual motor skills needed to be successful later with sport-specific activities. The teacher with advanced training in basic neurological building blocks will probe down through physical fitness tasks and sport, functional, and perceptual motor skills to determine if all the underlying sensorimotor components are functioning fully. The types of assessments and examples of tests available to address each of these kinds of assessments are presented in **Table 3-3**.

TABLE 3-3   Types of Assessments for School-Age Students

Authentic alternative assessment—Create a poster illustrating how to perform the key elements of a specific skill; create a video about sportsmanship and respect to post on YouTube[2]

Curriculum-based—Competency Testing for Adapted Physical Education (Louisiana); Motor Activities Training Program (National); Moving into the Future: National Standards for Physical Education (National); Skill Tests (Local)

Physical fitness—Brockport Physical Fitness Test: A Health-Related Assessment for Youngsters with Disabilities; Physical Best and Individuals with Disabilities

Functional skills—Mobility Opportunities via Education (MOVE); Test of Gross Motor Development (TGMD)

Sport skills—PE Metrics (SHAPE America); Special Olympic Sport Skill Guides (Special Olympics)

Perceptual/motor skills—Purdue Perceptual-Motor Survey

Sensorimotor skills—Southern California Sensory Integration Tests; DeGangi-Berk Test of Sensory Integration

The scoring method used for any given test depends on what the test is designed to measure. Tests are designed to measure a student's performance against established criteria, key elements in the task, or key elements in a series of tasks (refer to **Tables 3-4** and **3-5** and the content task analyses in **Tables 3-6, 3-7,** and **3-8**). Tests that measure performance against established criteria are either normative-referenced or criterion-referenced. *Norm-referenced* means an individual's performance can be compared with that of others of the same age and gender. Most physical fitness test items are norm-referenced. *Criterion-referenced* means the test is designed to provide information about an individual's mastery of a specific skill or behavior.

Some tests include both criterion-referenced and content-referenced scoring techniques. For example, the task of kicking a playground ball 30 feet from a running start could also require the evaluator to indicate whether the student demonstrated the following key elements of the task: backswing of the leg from the knee, contact with the foot, forward swing of the arm opposite the kicking leg, and follow-through by hopping on the nonkicking foot.

Checklists and ecological inventories are content-referenced because they are used to determine whether specific key elements of a task or a series of tasks are demonstrated. Checklists are frequently developed and used to delineate critical aspects of motor coordination and sport skills. The content task analysis of a softball throw is an example of such a checklist (see Table 3-6). Checklists are useful for screening one student or a whole class before beginning a unit of instruction. Through the use of the checklist, the teacher can determine which tasks need to be taught. Ecological inventories are developed to identify the behavioral contents (demands) of an environment. An example of an ecological inventory is shown in Table 3-7. That ecological inventory is a content analysis of a series of tasks that need to be mastered to participate in the activity of bowling in the community. Ecological inventories are particularly helpful when designing a transition program for students 16 years of age and older. A community-based ecological inventory

TABLE 3-4   Fitness Zone for Girls with Spinal Cord Injury

Age (yr.)	TAMT (pass/fail) NI	TAMT (pass/fail) HFZ[a]	Percent body fat[b] Very lean	Percent body fat[b] HFZ	Percent body fat[b] NI	Percent body fat[b] NI (health risk)	Triceps and calf skinfold[b,c] (mm) HFZ	Reverse curl (# completed) NI	Reverse curl (# completed) AFZ[a]	Seated push-up (# completed) NI	Seated push-up (# completed) AFZ[a]	Bench press (# completed) NI	Bench press (# completed) HFZ[a]	Dumbbell press (# completed) NI	Dumbbell press (# completed) HFZ[a]
10	F	P	≤11.5	11.6–24.3	24.4	≥33.0	11–32	0	≥1	≤4	≥5–20				
11	F	P	≤12.1	12.2–25.7	25.8	≥34.5	12–34	0	≥1	≤4	≥5–20				
12	F	P	≤12.6	12.7–26.7	26.8	≥35.5	13–36	0	≥1	≤4	≥5–20				
13	F	P	≤13.3	13.4–27.7	27.8	≥36.3	14–37	0	≥1	≤4	≥5–20	≤9	10–50	≤4	5–50
14	F	P	≤13.9	14.0–28.5	28.6	≥36.8	15–39	0	≥1	≤4	≥5–20	≤12	13–50	≤6	7–50
15	F	P	≤14.5	14.6–29.1	29.2	≥37.1	16–40	0	≥1	≤4	≥5–20	≤13	14–50	≤9	10–50
16	F	P	≤15.2	15.3–29.7	29.8	≥37.4	17–41	0	≥1	≤4	≥5–20	≤13	14–50	≤10	11–50
17	F	P	≤15.8	15.9–30.4	30.5	≥37.9	18–42	0	≥1	≤4	≥5–20	≤14	15–50	≤10	11–50

Age (yr.)	Grip strength (kg) NI	Grip strength (kg) HFZ[a]	Modified Apley (score) NI	Modified Apley (score) HFZ[a]	Modified Thomas (score) NI	Modified Thomas (score) HFZ[a]	Target stretch (score) NI	Target stretch (score) HFZ[a]
10	≤16	≥17	≤2	3	≤2	3	≤1	2
11	≤18	≥19	≤2	3	≤2	3	≤1	2
12	≤21	≥22	≤2	3	≤2	3	≤1	2
13	≤23	≥24	≤2	3	≤2	3	≤1	2
14	≤25	≥26	≤2	3	≤2	3	≤1	2
15	≤28	≥29	≤2	3	≤2	3	≤1	2
16	≤28	≥29	≤2	3	≤2	3	≤1	2
17	≤28	≥29	≤2	3	≤2	3	≤1	2

a. Based on data from Project Target (1998).

b. Reprinted, by permission, from The Cooper Institute, 2013, *Fitnessgram/Activitygram test administration manual*, updated 4th ed. (Champaign, IL: Human Kinetics), 62.

c. The Cooper Institute, 2013; *Fitnessgram/Activitygram test administration manual*, updated 4th ed. (Champaign, IL: Human Kinetics), 66, 102.

Winnick, & Short, Brockport Physical Fitness Test Manual, Human Kinetics

TABLE 3-5   Fitness Zone for Boys with Spinal Cord Injury

Age (yr.)	TAMT (pass/fail)		Percent body fat[b]				Triceps and calf skinfold[b,c] (mm)	Reverse curl (# completed)		Seated push-up (# completed)		Bench press (# completed)		Dumbbell press (# completed)	
	NI	HFZ[a]	Very lean	HFZ	NI	NI (health risk)	HFZ	NI	AFZ[a]	NI	AFZ[a]	NI	HFZ[a]	NI	HFZ[a]
10	F	P	≤8.8	8.9–22.4	22.5	≥33.2	11–29	0	≥1	≤4	≥5–20				
11	F	P	≤8.7	8.8–23.6	23.7	≥35.4	11–31	0	≥1	≤4	≥5–20				
12	F	P	≤8.3	8.4–23.6	23.7	≥35.9	10–31	0	≥1	≤4	≥5–20				
13	F	P	≤7.7	7.8–22.8	22.9	≥35.0	9–30	0	≥1	≤4	≥5–20	≤19	20–50	≤13	14–50
14	F	P	≤7.0	7.1–21.3	21.4	≥33.2	8–28	0	≥1	≤4	≥5–20	≤32	33–50	≤18	19–50
15	F	P	≤6.5	6.6–20.1	20.2	≥31.5	8–26	0	≥1	≤4	≥5–20	≤39	40–50	≤20	21–50
16	F	P	≤6.4	6.5–20.1	20.2	≥31.6	8–26	0	≥1	≤4	≥5–20	≤46	47–50	≤23	24–50
17	F	P	≤6.6	6.7–20.9	21.0	≥33.0	8–27	0	≥1	≤4	≥5–20	≤49	50	≤26	27–50

Age (yr.)	Grip strength (kg)		Modified Apley (score)		Modified Thomas (score)		Target stretch (score)	
	NI	HFZ[a]	NI	HFZ[a]	NI	HFZ[a]	NI	HFZ[a]
10	≤17	≥18	≤2	3	≤2	3	≤1	2
11	≤20	≥21	≤2	3	≤2	3	≤1	2
12	≤24	≥25	≤2	3	≤2	3	≤1	2
13	≤28	≥29	≤2	3	≤2	3	≤1	2
14	≤32	≥33	≤2	3	≤2	3	≤1	2
15	≤36	≥37	≤2	3	≤2	3	≤1	2
16	≤42	≥43	≤2	3	≤2	3	≤1	2
17	≤48	≥49	≤2	3	≤2	3	≤1	2

a. Based on data from Project Target (1998).

b. Reprinted, by permission, from The Cooper Institute, 2013, *Fitnessgram/Activitygram test administration manual*, updated 4th ed. (Champaign, IL: Human Kinetics), 61.

c. The Cooper Institute, 2013, *Fitnessgram/Activitygram test administration manual*, updated 4th ed. (Champaign. IL: Human Kinetics), 65, 101.

Winnick, & Short, Brockport Physical Fitness Test Manual, Human Kinetics

TABLE 3-6   Content Task Analysis of a Softball Throw

1. Demonstrate the correct grip 100% of the time.
   a. Select a softball.
   b. Hold the ball with the first and second fingers spread on top, thumb under the ball, and the third and fourth fingers on the side.
   c. Grasp the ball with the fingertips.
2. Demonstrate the proper step pattern for throwing the softball three out of five times.
   a. Identify the restraining line.
   b. Take a side step with the left foot.
   c. Follow with a shorter side step with the right foot.
3. Demonstrate the proper throwing technique and form three out of five times.
   a. Grip ball correctly.
   b. Bend rear knee.
   c. Rotate hips and pivot left foot, turning body to the right.
   d. Bring right arm back with the ball behind the right ear and bent right elbow leading (in front of) hand.
   e. Bend left elbow and point it at a 45-degree angle.
   f. Step straight ahead with the left foot.
   g. Keep the right hip back and low and the right arm bent with the ball behind the ear and the elbow leading.
   h. Start the throwing motion by pushing down hard with the right foot.
   i. Straighten the right knee and rotate the hips, shifting the weight to the left foot.
   j. Keep the upper body in line with the direction of throw and the eyes focused on the target.
   k. Whip the left arm to the rear, increasing the speed of the right arm.
   l. Extend the right arm fully forward, completing the release by snapping the wrist and releasing the ball at a 45-degree angle.
   m. Follow through by bringing the hand completely down and the right foot forward to the front restraining line.
4. Throw a softball on command three out of five times.
   a. Assume READY position between the front and back restraining lines with feet apart.
   b. Point the shoulder of the nonthrowing arm toward the restraining line.
   c. Focus eyes in the direction of the throw.
   d. Remain behind the front restraining line.
   e. Throw the softball on command.
   f. Execute smooth integration of skill sequence.

TABLE 3-7   Content Task Analysis of a Series of Tasks Needed to Bowl Independently

1. Can determine when bowling lanes are available.
   a. Finds the number of the bowling establishment in the phone book.
   b. Calls the bowling establishment to determine when open bowling is available.
2. Can get from home to the bowling establishment.
   a. Knows which bus to take to the bowling establishment.
   b. Walks to the nearest bus stop.
   c. Waits at the bus stop until the bus arrives.
   d. Checks the bus sign to make sure it is the correct bus.
   e. Gets on the bus.
   f. Checks with the bus driver to be sure the bus goes to the bowling establishment.
   g. Drops the fare into the box.
   h. Asks the driver to let him or her know where to get off.
   i. Moves to an empty seat and sits down.
   j. Listens for the driver's announcement of the correct stop.
   k. Pulls the cord to alert the driver that he or she wants to get off at the next stop.
   l. After the bus stops, departs from the bus.
   m. Checks to determine where the bus stop is for the return trip home.
3. Can reserve a lane, rent shoes, and select the appropriate ball.
   a. Goes to the counter and tells the clerk how many games he or she wants to bowl and asks for the correct-size bowling shoes.
   b. Pays for the games and shoes and receives the correct change.
   c. Takes a seat behind the lane that has been assigned and changes from street to bowling shoes.
   d. Searches for a ball that fits his or her hand span and is the correct weight.
   e. Selects a ball that fits and is not too heavy.
   f. Places the ball on the ball-return rack of the correct lane.
4. Can correctly deliver the ball.
   a. Picks up the ball with both hands.
   b. Cradles the ball in the nondominant arm while placing his or her fingers in the ball.
   c. Positions self in the center of the approach approximately 15 feet from the foul line.
   d. Holds the ball in both hands and aims.
   e. Walks to the line, coordinating the swing of the dominant arm and the walking pattern of the feet.
   f. Releases the ball from behind the foul line.

TABLE 3-7   Content Task Analysis of a Series of Tasks Needed to Bowl Independently (*Continued*)

    g. Follows through with the dominant arm.

    h. Watches the ball move down the lane and strike pins.

5. Can retrieve the ball and continue bowling.

    a. Walks back to the ball-return rack.

    b. Awaits the ball's return.

    c. Continues to aim and deliver the ball, being careful not to throw the ball while the pins are being reset.

6. Stops bowling when the electronic scoring device indicates that three games have been completed.

    a. Returns the ball to the storage rack.

    b. Changes back into street shoes.

    c. Returns the rented shoes to the counter.

    d. Exits the bowling establishment.

7. Can return home from the bowling establishment.

    a. Goes to the bus stop and awaits the bus.

    b. Checks the bus sign to verify it is the correct bus.

    c. Gets on the bus.

    d. Asks the bus driver if the bus goes to the street he or she is seeking.

    e. Drops the fare into the box.

    f. Asks the driver to let him or her know where to get off.

    g. Moves to an empty seat and sits down.

    h. Listens for the driver's announcement of the correct stop.

    i. Pulls the cord to alert the driver that he or she wants to get off at the next stop.

    j. Waits for the bus to stop before rising from the seat and departing the bus.

    k. Walks home.

Permission for the Special Olympics Sports Skills Instructional Program provided by Special Olympics, created by The Joseph P. Kennedy, Jr., Foundation. Authorizzed and accredited by Special Olympics, Inc., for the Benefit of Mentally Retarded Citizens.

TABLE 3-8   Content Task Analysis of a Locomotor Pattern—Run

1. Arms move in opposition to legs with elbows bent

2. Brief period where both feet are off the surface

3. Narrow foot placement landing on heel or toe (not flat-footed)

4. Nonsupport leg bent about 90 degrees so foot is close to the buttocks

From Test of Gross Motor Development-3. Courtesy of Dale Ulrich.

completed by a teacher will identify what activities are available in the community and the series of tasks a student needs to master to participate in those activities.

Evaluating Physical Fitness

There are at least four prevalent measures to assess the health of children and youth in special education that are related to participation in physical activity. These four tools are (1) the Body Mass Index, (2) physical examinations to assess readiness for participation in activity, (3) health risk instruments, and (4) health screenings.

The Body Mass Index (BMI) is a ratio of weight and height. It is calculated by dividing a person's weight in pounds by his or her height in inches squared and multiplying the answer by 703. (BMI = weight in pounds/height in inches [squared] × 703.) BMI in children is compared with children of the same gender and age. A child's BMI of less than the 5th percentile is considered underweight; a BMI of greater than the 95th percentile is considered overweight. In Arkansas, children are provided with calculators to assess if they have a healthy weight for their gender and age. The calculator automatically adjusts for differences in height, age, and gender.

Physical examinations are required for some children and youth who participate in sport activity. For instance, every athlete who participates in Special Olympics is to have a physical examination. Usually, a primary care physician examines the youngsters (1) to determine the type and degree of abilities and disabilities, (2) to review medications affecting strength and endurance, and (3) to act as a liaison with the athletes' parents and coaches.

Health risk assessments are a critical component of any wellness program. They take the form of a detailed health questionnaire that includes questions on lifestyle issues, such as exercise and weight. They provide information on health status and suggest areas for improvement. An overall risk score is provided.[3] Health screenings include measurements of height and weight, cholesterol levels, blood sugar levels, blood pressure, and/or BMI.[3]

Test Selection Criteria

As indicated earlier in this chapter, depending on the purpose for the assessment, both standardized tests and less formal instruments are useful when working with students with disabilities. Once the purpose of the assessment has been decided, an appropriate assessment instrument is selected. Factors that must be considered to select the right test are (1) the need for utilizing a standardized test; (2) the adequacy of test standardization; (3) administrative feasibility; and (4) the student's type of disability. Each of these factors will be discussed.

NEED FOR UTILIZING A STANDARDIZED TEST

IDEIA (2004) specifies that, in order to determine a child's eligibility for special services—in this case, special (adapted) physical education—a variety of assessment tools and strategies must be utilized. Although the requirement of utilizing standardized tests is not clearly stated, in IDEIA the intent is implicit. That is, whereby many types of information may be used *in addition to* standardized tests, standardized tests indicating that a student's performance significantly lags behind his or her peers are still required.[8] What is clear in the most recent amendments is that if an instrument is used for eligibility purposes, the adequacy of the person administering the test and the fact that the instrument is technically sound must be demonstrated. That is, the person administering the test must be adequately trained in administration and interpretation, and the test itself must be valid, reliable, and objective for the purposes it is being used.

STANDARDIZATION

To standardize a test means to give the test to a large group of persons under the same conditions to determine whether the test discriminates among ages and populations. When a test is going to be used for diagnostic purposes, adequacy of the standardized process must be verified. Questions that must be answered include the following: (1) Were the appropriate procedures used to select the population used to standardize the instrument? (2) Did the author(s) demonstrate an appropriate type and level of validity? (3) Did the author(s) establish an appropriate type and level of reliability? and (4) Did the author(s) verify the objectivity of the instrument?

Selecting the Standardization Sample

Ideally, the sample that is used for the standardization of an instrument should include the same percentage of individuals in the socioeconomic groups, geographic locations (South, East, North, Northeast, etc.), ages, genders, and races represented in the general population according to the latest population census. Hence, if the year 2010 U.S. census reports that 51% of the population is female and 49% is male, those percentages should be duplicated in the test sample. If, in the same census, it is reported that the U.S. population is 12% African American, 74% Anglo, 18% Hispanic, 4% Native American, 4% Asian, and 6%, then those percentages should be used to select the makeup of the sample to be tested. In addition, the test sample should include the ages of the persons with whom the test will be used selected at random from all areas of the country. Because few, if any, motor tests meet these stringent criteria, tests should be selected that come as close to the ideal as possible.

Establishing Validity

Test validity is a measure of how truthful an instrument is. A valid instrument measures what the authors claim it measures. There are three acceptable types of validity: (1) content-related, (2) criterion-related, and (3) construct.

Content-related validity is the degree to which the contents of the test represent an identified domain (perceptual motor, physical fitness), body of knowledge, or curriculum. Content-related validity pertaining to a domain or a body of knowledge is often determined by verifying that experts in the field agree about the components of the domain. To demonstrate content validity, first the author must provide a clear definition of what is being measured. Then, literature that supports the content is identified or the test is examined by a panel of judges selected according to a predetermined set of criteria (i.e., five or more publications in the field, recommended by three or more professionals as an authority in the field, etc.). The panel members independently review the items in the test to determine whether they are appropriate, complete, and representative. In the case of content-related validity pertaining to a curriculum, the test is usually constructed by a district-wide, statewide, or nationwide committee made up of professionals in the field. Those professionals select items to include in the tests that they believe are appropriate, complete, and representative of the physical education curriculum at each level (elementary, middle school, junior high, and senior high).

Appropriateness means that the most knowledgeable professionals would agree that items measure what it is claimed they measure. For example, if a test designer claims that the 50-yard dash measures cardiovascular function, few professionals would agree that the test content is appropriate.

Completeness is determined by whether there is a wide range of items or only a select few. To be complete, a test that is purported to measure physical fitness would be expected to sample cardiovascular endurance, upper-body strength, abdominal strength, leg power, lower back and hip flexibility, and percent body fat. If only one measure of strength and one measure of cardiovascular endurance were included, the test would be deemed incomplete.

For a test to be declared representative of a given domain, several levels of performance would be sampled. This is accomplished by including a range of items from simple to complex or allowing a set amount of time to complete as many of the same tasks as is possible. In physical fitness tests, the representative requirement is frequently met by allowing the student to perform to the best of his or her ability within a given period of time. That is, the number of sit-ups executed in 30 seconds is counted. Students with well-developed abdominal muscles will perform more sit-ups than those who are less well-developed. The content validity of a test is frequently as strong as the literature cited and/or the knowledge base of the professionals selected to evaluate and/or develop the test. The broader the literature base, and the more knowledgeable the professionals, the stronger the content validity.

Criterion-related validity indicates the test has been compared with another acceptable standard, such as a valid test that measures the same components. There are two types of criterion-related validity—concurrent and predictive. Concurrent criterion-related validity is achieved when the test scores on one test accurately reflect a person's score on another test at a point in time. For instance, if a student performs strongly on a 2-mile run, a strong performance on a bicycle ergometer test is expected. Predictive content-related validity means that the test scores can be used to predict accurately how well a student will perform in the future. Thus, if a student performs well on a motor ability test, the student should do well in a variety of sport activities.

Construct validity is the degree to which a test does what the author claims it will do. To establish this type of validity, an author sets out to develop a test that will discriminate between two or more populations. After identifying which populations the test should discriminate among, a series of studies is completed, measuring each of the identified groups with the test. For example, an author might claim that students with learning disabilities will do significantly more poorly on the test than will students with no learning problems. After the test is designed, it is administered to two groups of students who have been matched on age and gender. One group has verified learning disabilities; the other does not. Each group's scores are compared to determine whether they are significantly different. If the group with learning disabilities scores significantly lower than the group with no learning disabilities, construct validity is claimed.

Different statistical techniques are used to evaluate validity. In the case of content validity relating to a domain or a body of knowledge, percentage of agreement among the judges on the panel is reported. Acceptable content validity can be declared when the judges agree on the appropriateness of items included in the test at least 90% of the time. Content validity relating to a curriculum is generally achieved by majority vote of the professionals developing the test. Criterion validity is usually reported as a coefficient that is derived from correlating the sets of scores from the two tests being compared. Ideally, a correlation coefficient of between +0.80 and +1.00 is desirable. However, few motor tests reach this level of agreement. Construct validity is generally demonstrated by using a statistic that measures differences between the mean scores of each group. Thus, when construct validity is claimed at the 0.05 level of significance, it means that it is expected that the test will accurately classify an individual as belonging to one group rather than another 95 times out of 100.

Determining Reliability

Test reliability is a measure of an instrument's consistency. A reliable test can be depended on to produce the same scores at different times if no intervention, learning, or growth has occurred between test sessions. The two test reliability techniques used for most physical and motor tests are test-retest and alternate forms.

The test-retest technique is the most frequently used method for demonstrating reliability of physical and motor performance instruments. To establish test-retest reliability, the same test is administered to the same group of people twice in succession, and then the scores are correlated to determine the amount of agreement between them. The interval between administrations of the test should be carefully controlled. Never should a period of more than 2 weeks lapse between test administrations.

The alternate form reliability technique is also referred to as equivalent form reliability. When two tests are identified that are believed to measure the same trait or skill and have been standardized on the same population, they can be used to determine alternate form reliability. To estimate the degree to which both forms correlate, the tests are divided in half and administered to the same population. Half of the group are tested using Test A first and Test B second. The other half of the group will be tested with Test B first and then with Test A. The scores from Test A will be correlated with the scores from Test B to determine the amount of consistency (equivalency) between the tests.

Determining the extent to which sets of scores achieved during the testing sessions correlate is the most frequently used statistical method for estimating reliability. The stronger the correlation coefficient, the more reliable the test. A reliability coefficient between +0.90 and +1.00 is most desirable because it means that 90% of the two test scores were the same; however, the larger the sample tested, the smaller the size of reliability coefficient that is acceptable.

Determining Objectivity

Objectivity means freedom from bias and subjectivity. The clearer and more concise the instructions, the more objective the instrument. Test objectivity is determined by having two or more scorers independently evaluate the performance of a subject being tested. The scorers' results are then correlated to determine the amount of agreement. The greater the amount of agreement between the scores, the higher the correlation coefficient. An objectivity coefficient beyond +0.90 would be considered an acceptable level of objectivity because it would indicate that all scorers agreed on the scores given 90% or more of the time.

Administrative Feasibility

Administrative feasibility means how practical and realistic the test is. Several factors must be considered when attempting to determine whether a given test is administratively feasible to use for a given purpose.

Cost.   Resources available to purchase test manuals and equipment must be carefully considered. Costs of tests continue to increase; it is not uncommon for motor tests to range in cost from $250 to $1,000. To conserve resources, needed tests may be stored at a central source and made available for individuals to check out for brief periods of time.

Equipment. The amount and kind of equipment needed to administer tests vary widely. Frequently, it is possible to build, rather than purchase, equipment; however, some items, such as bicycle ergometers, may be out of the practitioner's price range. Standardized instruments will outline very specific guidelines for equipment use or include specific equipment with the purchase of the assessment kit. Many criterion-referenced, curriculum-based tests require equipment that is part of most physical education equipment inventories. School districts vary on their policy regarding homemade equipment because of liability issues.

Level of training to administer the test. Some tests require extensive training for accurate administration; indeed, some tests require evidence of professional training and certification of capability before the tests can be used. Other tests simply require practice and familiarity with the items. Professionals familiar with test administration, such as university professors who teach assessment courses, can be contacted to provide workshops for practitioners who are responsible for testing.

Level of training to interpret the test. Professional training in interpretation of test results is required for most tests. Educators should select tests they understand and can interpret accurately. Again, professionals can be retained to provide workshops in test interpretation.

Purpose of the test. How a test is to be used will determine which test to select. As indicated earlier, different types of tests are used for screening, diagnosing, and programming purposes. For a test to be useful, it must provide the needed information.

Length of time to administer. Limited time is available in school settings for test administration. However, too frequently a test selected because it can be administered in a short period of time yields little usable information. On the other hand, tests that require more than 45 minutes to 1 hour of administration time are unrealistic for school settings. Tests need to be selected that provide the needed information yet require a minimum of time to administer.

Personnel needs. Some tests can be used if adequate personnel are available to administer and score them. When paraprofessionals and/or volunteers are available, they must be carefully trained, particularly if they do not have a strong background in motor and physical development.

Standardization population. If the test information is going to be used to diagnose a student's movement challenges to determine whether special services are required, the test must be standardized on a population the same age as the student being tested. Practitioners sometimes avoid using the appropriate standardized test because they are aware that their student cannot adequately perform the items in the test. One of the purposes of a standardized test is to establish that the student is performing significantly below same-age peers.

TYPE OF DISABILITY

The type of disability a student has greatly impacts the assessment process. There are some tests available that have been developed for use with individuals with specific types of disabilities. These tests obviously should be used for diagnostic purposes to determine whether a student qualifies for special services. Other tests, both formal and informal with minor modifications, can be used to provide the information needed for developing the IEP and determining intervention programs. An overview of tests appropriate for use with individuals with disabilities is presented in **Table 3-9**. More information about tests that are appropriate for use with specific types of disabilities, as well as suggestions about how they might best be used, will be presented in the chapters in which distinctive populations are discussed.

Care must be exercised to select the assessment tool that is most appropriate and administratively feasible. Once appropriate assessment instruments have been selected, it is critical that the administration, interpretation,

TABLE 3-9   Selected Motor Tests Appropriate for Use with Individuals with Disabilities

Test	Source	Population	Components	Scoring Type
Adapted Physical Education Assessment Scale (APEAS II) *As of 2016 this test is being validated and not currently available.*	SHAPE America 1900 Association Drive Reston, VA 20191	Students who are unable to safely and successfully participate in general physical education, ages 4.5–17 years	Perceptual motor function, object control, locomotor skills, physical fitness, adaptive behaviors	Criterion-referenced
A recently updated standardized test that includes a DVD showing how to administer the items.				
Brockport Physical Fitness Test: A Health-Related Assessment for Youngsters with Disabilities (2nd ed.) (2014)	Human Kinetics Publishers Box 5076 Champaign, IL 61825	Visually impaired, intellectual disability, or orthopedic impairment, ages 10–17 years	Body composition, aerobic fitness, musculoskeletal functioning	Criterion-referenced
A health-related physical fitness test that includes modifications for different types of disabilities.				
Bruininks-Oseretsky Test of Motor Proficiency (BOT II) (2005)	http://pearsonclinical.com	Normal, mentally retarded, learning disabled, ages 4–21 years	Speed and agility, balance, bilateral coordination, strength, fine motor precision and integration, manual dexterity, upper-limb coordination	Normative-referenced
A standardized test composed of subtests that can be administered individually to determine underlying sensory input and ability level delays.				
Competency Testing for Adapted Physical Education (CTAPE) (2008)	Louisiana Department of Education Division of Educational Improvement and Assistance PO Box 94064 Baton Rouge, LA 70804	Ambulatory individuals, ages 6 years and older	Locomotor, manipulative, balance, sport, fitness, gymnastic, spatial relations	Content- and criterion-referenced
A task-analyzed curriculum-embedded program for all students with disabilities except for the most severely involved.				

TABLE 3-9   Selected Motor Tests Appropriate for Use with Individuals with Disabilities (*Continued*)

Test	Source	Population	Components	Scoring Type
I CAN K-3 (1998)	PRO-ED Publishing Co. 8700 Shoal Creek Blvd. Austin, TX 78757	Ambulatory individuals at the developmental ages 5–9 years	Locomotor, object control, orientation and personal-social participation	Criterion- and content-referenced
A task-analyzed curriculum-embedded program for moderate- to low-functioning individuals.				
Mobility Opportunities Via Education (MOVE) (1990)	Kern County Superintendent of Schools 1300 17th Street City Centre Bakersfield, CA 93301-6683	Nonambulatory, severely and profoundly involved of any age	A sequence of motor skills that leads to independent self-management	Content- and criterion-referenced
A task analyzed curriculum-embedded program to promote head, trunk, and limb control of severely involved individuals.				
Motor Activities Training Program: Special Olympics Sports Skill Program (2005)	Special Olympics International 1325 G Street, NW, Suite 500 Washington, DC 20005	Severe disabilities of any age	Mobility, dexterity, striking, kicking, aquatics, manual and electric wheelchair	Content-referenced
A task-analyzed program designed for persons with severe intellectual disabilities who are not yet able to compete in a rigorous sports program.				
Movement Assessment Battery for Children (Movement ABC-2) (2007)	http://pearsonclinical.com	Motor development delays, ages 3–12 years	Balance, fine motor, object-control, locomotor	Normative- and content-referenced
A standardized, updated version of the Stott-Henderson Test of Motor Impairment, designed to detect, quantify, and correct motor development delays.				

(continues)

TABLE 3-9   Selected Motor Tests Appropriate for Use with Individuals with Disabilities (*Continued*)

Test	Source	Population	Components	Scoring Type
National Standards & Grade Level Outcomes for K-12 Physical Education (2014)	SHAPE America 1900 Association Drive Reston, VA 20191	School-age individuals	Five national standards	Content-referenced
A national standards-based test assessing grade-level outcomes within the curriculum.				
Project M.O.B.I.L.I.T.E.E. Curriculum Embedded Assessment (1981)	http://www.twu .edu/downloads /inspire/Project _MOBILITEE-1.pdf	Moderately and low functioning, ambulatory and nonambulatory, any age	Cardiovascular, speed, agility, power, strength and endurance	Content- and criterion-referenced
A task-analyzed, curriculum-embedded program for ambulatory and nonambulatory individuals (available at no charge from address provided).				
Test of Gross Motor Development II (TGMD II; 2000)	PRO-ED Publishing Co. 8700 Shoal Creek Blvd. Austin, TX 78757	Motor development delays, ages 3–10 years	12 gross motor patterns, including locomotor and manipulative	Criterion- and normative-referenced
A test that can be used to identify critical components of locomotor and manipulative skills.				

and recommendations from the tests produce the type of information that can be used to design a physical education program that will contribute to the growth and independence of students, particularly those with disabling conditions. General guidelines for ensuring that the procedure results in appropriate educational programming are presented in the next section.

The Testing Process

Although selecting an appropriate test is a critical step in gathering meaningful assessment information, the most important phase of the process is to ensure that the information gathered is truly representative of the student's capability. The effective evaluator fully prepares for the testing session, conducts the testing with care, and analyzes the information gathered as soon after the session as possible.

PREPARATIONS FOR TESTING

In addition to administration of a motor test, a comprehensive evaluation will include review of the student's special education file, observation of the student, and conversations with appropriate personnel. The special education file review allows the evaluator to read the results of previous assessments, potential medical concerns, and applicable behavioral information. Observing the student in his or her current physical education placement, and if possible in the classroom and playground, allows the evaluator to select an appropriate motor test, gather information about how the student functions in that environment, and determine modifications that are currently being utilized. Finally, conversing with those who currently work or live with the student can assist with determining motivations and interests of the student, existing concerns, and student strengths. Potential individuals to talk with are related service providers, such as physical, occupational, and/or speech therapists, parents or guardians, classroom teachers, and the student.

File review, observations, and conversations will assist the evaluator in selection and administration of the test instrument. After an appropriate instrument has been selected, it is important to give careful thought to the testing process. Not only should the evaluator become thoroughly familiar and comfortable with the test, but others who are assisting should also. Having practice sessions in advance with peers and/or children who do not have disabilities or observing a videotape of the correct procedure to use followed by discussion of the critical aspects of each test item can be helpful. To avoid having to refer constantly to the test instructions during the actual testing session, evaluators may choose to prepare and use "crib" notes while testing. These notes can be used as reminders about what positions are required, time limitations, and unique cues that can be given during the testing session. With parental permission, evaluators may also choose to videotape the testing to allow review of skill performance after the assessment. Having the instrument in an electronic format with the ability to digitally document and score the performance on a mobile device can also be highly beneficial. When other personnel are going to assist with the testing session, they should be trained to the point where it is evident that they are clear about how the test items are to be administered and scored. Once everyone is confident about the test procedures, decisions must be made about how, where, and when the test will be administered.

ADMINISTERING THE TEST

Tests can be administered individually or in groups and whenever possible in a natural rather than a contrived setting. Diagnostic tests are most frequently administered individually; however, screening and programming tests can be given to groups during the physical education period. When groups are tested, the gymnasium can be divided into stations, with each station designated for a particular test item, or the skills from the test can be built into the lesson activities for the day.

Regardless of the procedure being used, it is important that a well-lighted, comfortably cooled, uncluttered area be selected. The more removed from noisy events and traffic zones, the better. Equipment that is required for the testing session should be placed near the location where it will be needed and arranged so that it is accessible but not distracting to the students. The best time to administer tests is midmorning or midafternoon. Whenever possible, avoid administering tests early or late in the day, just before or after lunch, after a student has been ill or prior to or just after an exciting event. If the student being tested takes medication, it may also be helpful to determine their medication schedule and select a time when the medication is midcycle. Regardless of the time of day the tests are administered, the evaluators' attitude toward the students is a critical factor in obtaining optimum performance efforts.

The test situation should be a positive experience for the students. Students who feel encouraged and valued will be motivated to try harder than will students who feel threatened and demoralized by the testing situation. Evaluators should show interest in each child and offer words of encouragement. However, it is important to not tell the student he or she has performed a skill well, when the execution is not mature. This can result in the reoccurrence of incorrect execution. Correction and feedback can be provided after the practice trial, but not during the trials that are scored. Unusual behaviors and ways of executing movements demonstrated during the session should be noted on the score sheet. Avoid rushing the students, verbally comparing their performance with those of others, and providing clues not permitted by the test. Some practical considerations to keep in mind are the following:

1. The test should be administered by an individual who can communicate in the child's preferred language and/or form of communication. If an adult is not available, use a bilingual peer to interpret the instructions.
2. How a child performs a task often can be more informative than whether the child is successful with the movement. Watch for extraneous arm, trunk, or leg movements and unusual head positioning as the child performs. Record these observations.
3. Keep the testing conditions as comfortable as possible. Students often perform better when the surroundings are free from distractions and the evaluator is relaxed and unhurried. Spend a few minutes talking with the children to establish rapport, and convey your interest in them.
4. Keep the number of observers appropriate for the student's comfort level. The student may be hesitant to perform in front of peers or parents. When they are insecure about their ability to perform, they will try too hard or fail to give their best effort if people are watching them.
5. If executing an informal assessment, repeat trials when you think the child might be able to perform adequately if given more time or is less tense. If a student is having difficulty with a given task, go on to easier tasks until he or she regains some confidence. Then go back to a task that was failed earlier and try again.
6. Observe the student on different days if possible. Children are just like adults—they have their good days and their bad days. If the testing can be spread over two or three days, the child will have the opportunity to show different performance levels.
7. Limit testing time to reasonable periods. Many students will perform best for a period of 30 to 60 minutes. If the time is too brief, the child does not have time to get warmed up and into the procedure. If you go beyond an hour of testing time, fatigue and distractibility often interfere with performance.

A sensitive evaluator keeps the student's best interest in mind at all times. Focusing on the test rather than the student distorts test results and gives an inaccurate picture of the student's true capabilities. On completion of the

testing session, observations and scores must be recorded, organized, and interpreted.

ORGANIZING AND INTERPRETING THE TEST RESULTS

Once you have the test results in hand, it is important to analyze them as soon as possible. The shorter the time lapse between administering and interpreting the results, the easier it is to remember how the student performed individual tasks in the test. To facilitate reporting and interpreting the data, the test results should be organized. Test performance can be charted, grouped according to strengths and challenges, or reported according to subset or subtest scores. Regardless of how the test results are organized, development of a report summarizing all results of the evaluation can be highly beneficial for the IEP team as they determine the student's educational needs and make recommendations for IEP goal development and placement. A sample report appears in **Table 3-10.** The student tested was Noah. Previous testing revealed Noah exhibits a developmental delay and subsequent need for special education services, so a criterion-referenced test, the Louisiana Competency Test of Adapted Physical Education, was administered to determine appropriate IEP goals.

Test data provide a record of how the student performed in comparison with established normative standards. However, little information from which to establish goals and to develop an intervention program is available through testing alone. For instance, by viewing the charted test results, it appears that Noah's upper-body coordination is not a problem area because he was able to strike a ball with a bat, dribble a basketball, and complete a bounce pass. However, Noah struggles to execute skills requiring upper- and lower-body strength as well as balance.

Highlighting Noah's strengths and challenges without providing subtest scores provides more information than simply charting the test results. Grouping test information according to strengths and challenges provides

TABLE 3-10   Adapted Physical Education Evaluation

ADAPTED PHYSICAL EDUCATION REPORT

Initial Evaluation

Student: Noah Lott   **DOB:** 3/15/2002

School: Riverside Middle School   **Evaluator:** Kristi Roth

Date of Report: 1/16/2016   **Date of Evaluation:** 9/20/2015–12/13/2015

General Information:

Noah consistently participates in physical education with a positive attitude. He genuinely enjoys physical education and loves to play and compete. He was assessed using the Louisiana Competency Test for Adapted Physical Education (CTAPE) Level V, in the gym at his school, Riverside Middle School. Noah, the evaluator, a physical therapist, and an occupational therapist were present during the evaluation. Level V of the CTAPE is an assessment tool for students aged 13 years to 14 years and 11 months that is used to determine the student's current level of motor ability in various locomotor, sport, gymnastics, and fitness skills. Upon completion of the assessment, the student receives a percentage score indicating his or his level of motor deficit: average (70%–100%), mild motor deficit (45%–69%), moderate motor deficit (20%–44%), or severe motor deficit (0%–19%). Noah, who has Down syndrome, was assessed due to concerns in his ability to demonstrate success in the inclusive competitive sports units, even with modifications. He consistently behaved and cooperated throughout the entire assessment process. Selected test items are identified below.

CTAPE Test Level V (Ages 13 years–14 years and 11 months)

Overall Percentage Score: 30% (Moderate Motor Deficit)

Skill	Measurement & Total Score	Observed Every Time	Observed at Least Once	Not Observed	Comments
Striking (Bat)	5 trials (Made contact 3 times) Score: 25/48 Mean: 24	• Proper grip • Bat off shoulder	• Square stance • Elbows away from body • Wrists cocked • Full swing (+180°) • Follow through	• Weight shift	• Very little lower-body movement and weight shift. Feet remained planted. • Little weight shift perhaps due to weak balance?
Football Pass 30 feet	0 out of 5 trials Score: 0/5 Mean: 3			• Reaching of distance requirement.	• Ball seemed too large. Should have used a smaller football. • Throw went about 10–15 feet.

(continues)

TABLE 3-10   Adapted Physical Education Evaluation (*Continued*)

Skill	Measurement & Total Score	Observed Every Time	Observed at Least Once	Not Observed	Comments
Dribble a Basketball	3 trials Score: 7/12 Mean: 6	• Fingertip contact • Ball at waist or below	• Without stopping or losing control	• Change hands at each object	• Dribbled with both hands on occasion.
Bounce Pass	3 trials (Ball reached receiver at chest height 2 times) Score: 13/18 Mean: 9	• Ball held chest high • Fingers spread • Elbows bent • Forcefully extending elbows	• Weight shifted toward receiver • Hit a target spot on the floor 2/3 distance from the passer		
Jump Turn	3 trials Score: 2/6 Mean: 4	• Begin in standing position		• Turn 360° • Land without losing balance	• Lost balance and nearly fell over upon landing.
Walk-outs	1 trial Score: 2/8 Mean: 5	• Begin on hands/feet		• Hands walk forward to push-up position • Hands walk backward to starting place • Did not perform 5 consecutive walk-outs	• Did not perform properly. Begin in correct position, and slowly moved to the ground.
Standing Long Jump	3 trials Score: 2/24 Mean: 14		• Prep crouch • Forceful arm swing at lift-off	• Backward arm swing • Balanced two feet, bent knee landing • Did not jump a distance of 48 inches	• Performed a leap instead of a jump, taking off on right foot and landing on left.

TABLE 3-10   Adapted Physical Education Evaluation (*Continued*)

Skill	Measurement & Total Score	Observed Every Time	Observed at Least Once	Not Observed	Comments
Vertical Jump	1 trial Score: 1/20 Mean: 14		• Prep crouch	• Did not jump a distance of 6 inches • Balanced on two feet, bent knee landing • Did not jump 10 times consecutively	• Took off on right foot only. • Perhaps unsure of what a true "jump" looks like.
Jumping Jacks	1 trial Score: 4/16 Mean: 11	• Begin standing arms at side (feet together)	• Jump to side stride/arms overhead • Jump back to starting	• Not rhythmically • Did not perform 10 consecutive jumping jacks	
Jog / Walk ½ Mile	1 trial Time: 9:45 Mean: 6:00				• Sprinted for about 50 feet, and then would walk for about 50 feet. This was a repetitive pattern.

Observations:

During observations in his physical education classes at Riverside Middle School, Noah consistently participated and put forth effort. The vast majority of the time, he would follow directions without needing the directions repeated. Noah would willingly help clean up equipment upon request of the teacher. Prior to the beginning of class, he was observed talking to his friends, and giving them hugs on occasion. Noah was social with all of his peers. Noah is fully included in physical education and Noah always appeared to be safe. He experiences success with most modifications; however, during game play he struggles to stay involved. He was observed in archery, football, resistance training, basketball, and dance units. Often times when working with a partner, not including the dance unit, Noah would be paired with another student with a disability who was at a similar skill level. During the archery unit, Noah required minimal assistance to pull the bow back to generate enough power to shoot the arrow to the target. During the football unit, he and another student passed, and punted the football back and forth from a distance of approximately 15 feet. When the distance was moved back to 30 feet, Noah struggled to throw and punt the ball the entire distance. During the flag football game Noah needed reminders about the direction of play and was often out of position despite verbal prompting from his peers. He was observed getting frustrated and standing on the side with his arms crossed. During the resistance training unit, Noah performed all exercises required with verbal direction from a teacher or student helper.

(continues)

TABLE 3-10   Adapted Physical Education Evaluation (*Continued*)

During basketball, Noah was able to make a basket from the free throw line. He also participated in a 3-on-3 game with general physical education students with minimal verbal guidance from a teacher or student helper, however during a full-court game Noah again stood to the side and removed himself from play. Noah functionally participated with the rest of his classmates during the dance unit, and did not require more redirections than any of his peers. When running, he would often challenge student helpers to a race. Noah was consistently motivated by competition and interaction with his peers.

Conversations:

A conversation with Noah's APE teacher revealed that Noah is a consistently motivated student. His teacher noted that Noah enjoys games and competitions in physical education. Also, Noah's special education teacher shared that Noah desires to fit in with his peers. Noah loves pop music and can be motivated in class and at home through music. Noah's physical educator has noted that Noah could work on balance, strength, and coordination skills. It was noted that Noah requires extensive verbal and physical prompting to properly execute a jump. He has performed a proper jump before, but often needs assistance. Another conversation with one of Noah's special education paraprofessionals revealed that Noah seems to sincerely enjoy physical education. The paraprofessional also noted Noah is a very caring individual at school, especially to his younger brother who is in sixth grade. Lastly, when speaking to Noah, he mentioned he really enjoys basketball and loves PE, but not when he gets tired.

Conclusions:

1. Noah enjoys basketball and is able to dribble, pass, and shoot a basketball successfully without assistance.

2. Noah functionally participates in the majority of physical education activities while being safe and successful.

3. Noah's scores on skills involving lower-body strength and coordination indicate below average ability in these areas, which can impact his success in activities involving jumping, balancing, and/or kicking.

4. Noah's inability to throw a football an average distance and maintain control of a basketball while dribbling indicate reduced upper-body strength and coordination.

5. Noah enjoys and is motivated by social interaction with his peers.

6. Noah requires access to verbal and physical prompting from a teacher or student helper to ensure he experiences success in physical education.

Recommendations:

1. Continued placement in inclusive physical education will be best for Noah's psychomotor, cognitive, and affective development due to the appropriate physical challenges, assessments, and social interaction it entails.

2. More advanced basketball skills such as three-point shooting, running while dribbling with one hand, and passing while moving may be good areas for IEP goals. Other IEP goal considerations include upper- and lower-body strength exercises, jumping, catching, and/or balancing exercises.

3. The presence of a paraprofessional or student helper would benefit Noah in physical education to provide him with verbal or physical prompting when needed.

4. Doing simple resistance exercises such as push-ups, sit-ups, lunges, or resistance band exercises would increase his strength and lead to greater success in physical education. These could be done while listening to music.

ready reference to areas of concern while acknowledging the student's stronger points. However, the evaluator must be trusted to determine accurately what constitutes a strength and a challenge. With this form of reporting, it is possible to determine what Noah can and cannot do, but his performance cannot be compared with that of others his age. Comprehensive reporting will include informal observations and conversations, which not only assist with determination of Noah's needs, but will also be beneficial for Noah's future physical educators.

When the test results are going to be used to determine whether a student's performance is significantly delayed to require special services, comparison with age-expected results is necessary and required by law. Usually, any total or subtest score that falls beyond one standard deviation below the mean or below the 25th percentile or 1 year below the performance expected for the age of the child is considered a deficit area. But do not rely on those scores alone. Poor performance on individual tasks is a clue to deficit areas. If a child does well on sit-ups but poorly on push-ups, we cannot conclude that strength is adequate. Rather, we note that improvement of shoulder girdle strength is a very definite unique need.

When the information is going to be used to develop an IEP, determine goals, and/or design educational programs, descriptive rather than comparative information is needed. Additionally, information about how a movement was performed will provide clues to determine what the underlying difficulty is and where to focus the intervention program.

SUMMARY

Assessment has become an integral part of the educational process. Students are evaluated for the purpose of (1) identifying those who have developmental delays, (2) diagnosing the nature of the student's problem or delay, (3) providing information to use to develop the student's IEP, (4) developing instruction specific to the student's needs, and (5) evaluating student progress. Evaluation instruments can be classified as informal or formal. Informal evaluation involves observing movements in a variety of settings, gathering information from parents, and/or using a checklist or clinical test. Formal evaluation involves using a standardized test instrument. Tests can be used to measure mastery of a general or specific curriculum, mastery of a functional or sport skill, level of physical fitness, perceptual motor development, or sensorimotor status. Performance is measured using a criterion or content reference. Criterion-referenced tests measure performance against a standard, whereas content-referenced tests are used to determine whether all components of a task or a series of tasks are demonstrated.

Which instrument is selected depends on established policy, whether standardization is required, administrative feasibility, and the student's type of disability. A variety of tests are available that are very useful for fitness and motor programming for students with disabilities. Evaluators should be trained in test administration and interpretation. Information gathered from assessment must be organized, interpreted, and reported in ways that facilitate communication and program development.

REVIEW QUESTIONS

1. What is the difference between a formal and an informal test?
2. What are the purposes of assessment?
3. When must a standardized test be used?
4. What is curriculum-based assessment?
5. What is administrative feasibility?
6. Describe, compare, and contrast techniques for organizing test data.

REFERENCES

1. Community-University Partnership for the Study of Children, Youth, and Families (2011). *Review of the Vineland Adaptive Behavior Scales-Second Edition (Vineland-II).* Edmonton, Alberta, Canada.
2. Fencl, M. (2014). Fun and creative unit assessment ideas for all students in physical education. *Journal of Physical Education, Recreation, & Dance, 85,* 16–21, DOI: 10.1080/07303084.2014.855589.
3. Ferrera, M., & Grudzien, L. (2006). Impact of ADA and IDEA on wellness program design. *J Deferred Compensation, 11*(2), 48–57.
4. Henson, K. (2015). *Curriculum planning: Integrating multiculturalism, constructivism, and education reform.* Long Grove, IL: Waveland Press, Inc.
5. Jansson, L., Sonnander, K., & Wiesel, F. (2005). Needs assessed by psychiatric health care and social services in a defined cohort of clients with disabilities. *Euro Arch of Psych, 255,* 57–64.
6. Lund, J., & Kirk, M. (2010). *Performance-based assessment for middle and high school physical education.* Champaign, IL: Human Kinetics.
7. Salavia, J., Ysseldyke, J., & Witmer, S. (2013). *Assessment: In special and inclusive education.* Belmont, CA: Wadsworth.
8. United States Department of Education, Office of Special Education Programs. (2006). IDEA Regulations: Changes in initial evaluation and reevaluation.

CHAPTER 4

Developing the Individualized Education Program

OBJECTIVES

- Briefly explain educational accountability.
- List the specific components of the individualized education program (IEP).
- Write a measurable annual goal for an IEP. The goal should be appropriate for a physical education program.
- List the individuals who should attend the IEP/multidisciplinary team meeting. Describe their function within the IEP/multidisciplinary team meeting.
- Explain some strategies a professional can use to encourage parents to take an active role in the IEP meeting.
- Briefly describe the heightened role of the parents in the IEP process.

Every student in the United States is entitled to a free, public education. This is true of every student with a disability, as well. However, each student with a disability has unique abilities and unique needs. The very nature of a disability simply enhances that uniqueness—and requires that the student be taught more carefully.

The 108th Congress of the United States determined that many students with disabilities were not eligible for special education services in the

Individuals with Disabilities Education Improvement Act (IDEIA). Specifically, in order to be eligible for special education, a student must have a "clinical definition" of disability, determined by multidisciplinary testing, and must exhibit "adverse educational performance."[25] This has broad-based and significant implications for students with mild disabilities. Literally, students with mild intellectual disabilities, mild learning disabilities, or mild emotional disturbances may now be deprived of their access to an education modified to meet their unique needs. For a student with a disability to qualify for physical education, that service must be specified on the IEP.

To ensure that every student with a disability receives an appropriate education, the Education of the Handicapped Act of 1975 (P.L. 94-142) mandated that an IEP be developed for each student with a disability. The IEP should be the cornerstone of the student's education. It should be a living, working document that the teacher and parents use as the basis for the instructional process.

> *The IEP is not a piece of paper; it is a process in which parents, educators, and the student work together to ensure that the student is able to achieve his or her designated goals.*[26]

The IEP requires that educators and administrators be accountable for the education of the student with a disability. The IEP process, through which a student's education is planned and delivered, requires a specific education program to be developed for each student with a disability. The federal mandates regarding the development of the IEP and the content of the IEP necessitate accountability. (See **Table 4-1.**)

Educators and administrators must be able to document the student's needs, based on a comprehensive assessment and evaluation, and to outline, specifically, the methods, techniques, and procedures that will be used to educate the student, while keeping in mind the student's specific and unique needs. Many educators are, however, deeply concerned that the intent of

TABLE 4-1   Contents of the Individualized Education Program

The IEP must include the following:

- A statement of the student's present level of performance
- How the student's disability affects involvement and performance in the general physical education class
- How the disability affects the student's involvement and progress in the general curriculum
- A statement of goals
- A statement of how progress toward the annual goals will be measured
- Indications of how the student can be involved and progress in the general curriculum
- A statement describing how each of the student's other needs that result from the student's disability will be met
- A statement describing special education and related services
- A statement describing supplementary aids and services
- A statement of program accommodations or modifications or supports for school personnel that will advance the student toward attaining educational goals
- A statement of services needed for the student to participate in extracurricular and other nonacademic activities
- A statement describing how the student is to be educated so he or she can participate with other students with and without disabilities
- An explanation of the extent, if any, to which the student will participate with students without disabilities in the general class
- A statement describing how the student's parents will be regularly informed, at least as often as parents of students without disabilities, of their student's progress
- A statement that provides information of the extent to which progress is sufficient to enable the student to achieve his or her goals by the end of the year
- Beginning at age 14 years, a statement of transition service needs that focuses on the student's course of study
- Beginning at age 16 years, a statement of needed transition services of interagency responsibilities or any needed linkages
- A plan for positive behavioral management if the student is disruptive

the law regarding the IEP has virtually been ignored. The IEP has too often become paperwork completed for the sake of doing paperwork. *All too often, the IEP is neither individualized nor special.* Espin et al. wrote,

> Although most special educators would agree that an individual focus is what makes special education special and that the IEP is the key to tailoring individual programs, questions have been raised recently regarding the extent to which individual programming remains central to special education. Most specifically, concerns have been raised regarding the extent to which the same degree of individual tailoring occurs in inclusive settings—general

education classrooms where students with disabilities are educated with their peers—as in noninclusive settings—where students receive special education outside the general education classroom.[9]

The emphasis on education within the general education program may have had a significant negative impact on the individualization long associated with quality special education programs. Teachers serving students with disabilities in "inclusive settings" are less likely than teachers in resource or self-contained classrooms to develop IEPs that meet the intent and specifications of the law.[9]

Professional Personnel Who May be Involved in the Individualized Education Program and/or the Individual-Transition Plan

The variety of personnel who provide both direct and related services and who may be involved in the initial evaluation and in the student's subsequent individually designed education program are described in this section. Direct services are those to be provided as part of the student's special education. These include (1) instruction conducted in the classroom, in the home, in hospitals and institutions, and in other settings, and (2) instruction in physical education. The personnel involved in the provision of these services are described in the following paragraphs.

DIRECT SERVICE PROVIDERS

Special Educators

Special educators are professional personnel who have received specific training in the techniques and methodology of educating students with disabilities. In the past, special educators were trained primarily to provide instruction to students with one particular disability. For example, special educators received training and subsequent certification in "mental retardation" (now referred to as intellectual disability), "emotional disturbance," or "deaf education." Today, most professional preparation programs provide training that leads to a general special education certification. This training and certification may better prepare educators to serve students who have more than one disability.

The level and type of instruction provided to students with disabilities depend on the student's present level of performance and expectations for future performance. For example, special educators working with students who have profound intellectual disorders and who are medically fragile require sensory stimulation experiences and health care (e.g., catheterization, tube feeding, medication) to meet their unique sensory and developmental needs. Special educators working with students who are on the autism spectrum and developmentally delayed need to provide a very structured prevocational, self-care program. Special educators teaching students with a history of abuse and subsequent emotional disorders may use a pre-academic or academic curriculum within the framework of a structured, positive behavior management program. The special educator, a classroom teacher, has primary responsibility for the student with disabilities.

Generally, as the student's primary teacher, the student's special educator is responsible for the implementation and monitoring of the IEP. The special educator should work closely with other professionals, including the physical educator and the adapted physical educator, to ensure that the student acquires developmentally appropriate motor skills. The physical educator should regularly communicate with the special educator/classroom teacher.

Hospital/Homebound Instructors

Hospital/homebound instructors are trained professionals who provide special education instruction to students who are hospitalized or who, because of severe medical disabilities, cannot be educated within the typical school setting. The education is the same, only the setting is different. Increasingly, parents of students with disabilities are opting to provide home-based instruction. Educators will need to provide services in the home.

Instructors in Institutions and Other Settings

For a variety of reasons, some students, particularly those with profound developmental delays and multiple disabilities, and increasingly those with severe emotional and behavioral disorders, receive their education within an institutional setting. Within recent years, court mandates have significantly improved the quality of both instruction and care within these facilities.

Adapted Physical Educators

The art, the science, and the profession of adapted physical education (APE) are described throughout this text. The role of the adapted physical educator, as part of the IEP/multidisciplinary team, is summarized in this section.

Adapted physical educators are physical educators with specialized training. Specifically, these professionals have training in the assessment and evaluation of fundamental motor skills, motor and physical fitness, individual and team sports, aquatics, and dance. They are responsible for the development of the student's individual physical education program (IPEP), the implementation of the student's IPEP, and the processes of teaching and managing the behavior of students with disabilities in a venue that emphasizes play, leisure, recreation, sport, and physical fitness skills.

Due, specifically, to the original work of Dr. Luke Kelly, University of Virginia, a certification in APE is now available to trained professionals who meet "rigorous" standards of professional preparation and who complete/pass a comprehensive examination. Fulfilling the criteria mandated by the Adapted Physical Education National Standards (APENS) allows the adapted physical educator to use the title "certified adapted physical educator," or "CAPE."[10] Many states, however (California, Louisiana, and Minnesota, for example), have extensive certifications, which indicate a significant professional commitment and comprehensive training, as well.

Physical education is mandated by law as a direct education service, not a related service. Adapted physical educators with specific training and knowledge in the neurodevelopmental process may intervene at a variety of levels, depending on the extent of their training and commitment (see **Table 4-2**).

> *The initial passage of P.L. 94-142, 1975, mandated that physical education is to be a vital part of each student's special education program. In fact, physical education was the only curricular area designated specifically as a required, direct service. The intent of the law was that specially trained adapted physical educators would provide quality, direct, hands-on, daily physical education instruction to students with disabilities. A lack of financial and personnel resources, as well as a lack of commitment to physical education, in general, has made this scenario a dream, rather than a reality.*

General Physical Educators

The intent of those who carefully crafted the wording of P.L. 94-142 was for physical educators with special training and certification to meet the unique motor needs of students with disabilities as part of their comprehensive education.[17] Increasingly, general physical educators are being asked to provide direct physical education instruction to learners with disabilities. General physical education professionals are, typically, professionals with a state

TABLE 4-2   Adapted Physical Education Levels of Intervention

Adapted physical educators with specific training and knowledge in the neurodevelopmental process may intervene at a variety of levels:

- Reflex integration
- Equilibrium development
- Sensory stimulation and sensory discrimination
- Sensorimotor development
- Body image and body cathexis
- Motor planning
- Locomotor and nonlocomotor skills
- Object-control skills
- Patterns for leisure, recreation, and sport skills
- Skills and knowledge related to physical fitness

certification or license in physical education. In many states, the educator has an all-level certification that indicates the individual has the necessary education and skills to provide physical education instruction for learners from kindergarten through high school.

The general physical educator, typically, has specific training in the following:

- Motor development
- Motor learning
- Pedagogy, particularly as it relates to human movement
- Anatomy and physiology
- Exercise physiology
- Biomechanical analysis of movement
- Curriculum models (i.e., adventure education, fitness education, sport education)

More and more learners with disabilities are receiving their physical education instruction from general physical education teachers within the general curriculum. This is effective only if the general physical educator has access to the personnel (APE consultant), paraeducators, and resources necessary to provide quality instruction.

Vision Specialists

Historically, a student with a severe visual impairment received educational services within a segregated environment. Typically, educational services were delivered in a separate residential school facility or within a self-contained room in a given school building. In that setting, the student's primary teacher was a vision specialist, a teacher specially trained to meet the educational needs of the student with a severe visual disability.

The increased emphasis on inclusion of learners with disabilities in the general curriculum has changed that scenario. Specifically, the learner with a visual impairment, whenever possible, is educated in his or her home school with support from vision specialists and orientation and mobility specialists. Students who are totally blind, legally blind, or partially sighted and those who have multiple disabilities (whose visual loss is only one of their impairments) may be educated with support within the regular education classroom in school districts embracing the concept of inclusion.

Vision specialists have the skills necessary to complete a visual evaluation and educational assessment to determine the extent of visual disability and the types of intervention that will make possible a successful educational experience. The vision specialist/teacher focuses on modification of instruction, which may include specific visual, tactile, and auditory learning techniques. Other modifications also may be required for the student to learn in the designated education setting. The specialist may suggest augmentative aids, such as a computer with auditory input/output capability, or a text enlarger, to meet the unique needs of the student.

Orientation and Mobility Specialists

Orientation and mobility was added to the Amendments to IDEA of 1997 as a direct educational service. Orientation and mobility means services provided to students who are blind or visually impaired to enable them to use skills systematically to orient them within their environments in their schools, homes, and communities.[25]

Orientation and mobility services help students improve spatial and environmental concepts and use information received by the senses, such as sound and vibrations. Travel training is often an integral part of the individual transition plan, the special education program that is designed to prepare students for post-school activities. The orientation and mobility specialist works with the student and his or her general or special educators to help the student develop the skills necessary, for example, to use a cane or to successfully ascend and descend school bus stairs. The orientation and mobility specialist focuses on helping the learner develop the skills necessary to access his or her environment.

RELATED SERVICE PROVIDERS

The law also specifies and defines related services. As indicated earlier in the chapter, these are services that must be provided to the student with disabilities so that the student can benefit from instruction. There are several related services that may assist the student to benefit from special education. The list of related services is not exhaustive and may include other corrective or supportive services, such as music or dance therapy, if they help the learner benefit from special education. The related service providers are described in the following paragraphs.

Audiologists

Audiologists are trained to complete a comprehensive evaluation of a student's hearing capabilities. This includes an evaluation of the student's response to the qualities of sound—intensity, pitch, frequency, and timbre. Based on the results of the evaluation, the audiologist makes recommendations to school personnel. The audiologist may suggest, for example, simple modifications in the educational environment of the student with a mild hearing impairment to facilitate learning; specifically, the student may be placed close to the teacher for instructional purposes. The audiologist may recommend that a hearing aid be provided for the student with a more severe hearing disability and may work closely with trained special educators who will help the student develop total communication skills, including sign language, speech reading, and oral language.

In addition, the audiologist may create and administer programs for prevention of hearing loss, as well as counsel parents and teachers regarding hearing loss. The audiologist may also determine students' needs when selecting and fitting an appropriate hearing aid and evaluating the effectiveness of amplification.[25]

Counseling Services

Counseling services are provided by qualified social workers or other qualified personnel, such as psychologists and guidance counselors.[25] Counseling services are becoming increasingly important in the total education process for all students, particularly students with disabilities. The school-based counselor may serve students with disabilities by implementing programs designed to enhance self-esteem, to teach students to identify and avoid sexual abuse, to share techniques for values identification and clarification, or to teach techniques and methods for dealing with grief.

Students with disabilities living within dysfunctional families may need more comprehensive intervention. These students may need individual counseling services in order to benefit from educational services. Because the family unit must be addressed if counseling is to be of value and have long-lasting effects, the most effective programs involve each member of the family in the counseling process.

Medical Diagnostic Service Personnel

Medical diagnostic services must be provided for a student who needs these services in order to benefit from his or her education. Many school districts have working partnerships with a hospital or rehabilitation facility, so that students who require medical diagnostic services can be referred to medical diagnostic service personnel at that hospital or center. It is important to note, however, that the law does not mandate medical services, just medical diagnostic services.

To be eligible for special education services, a student with an orthopedic impairment or another health impairment must be diagnosed as having a disability; this diagnosis must be made by a licensed physician. For a student to be identified as "emotionally disturbed," a licensed psychologist or psychiatrist must confirm the diagnosis.

Occupational Therapists

Occupational therapists improve, develop, or restore functions impaired or lost through illness, injury, or deprivation, so that individuals can function independently.[25] Occupational therapy must be made available to a student with a disability who requires this service in order to allow the student to be successful in the educational environment.[5] The American Occupational Therapy Association has adopted occupational therapy domains[2] that are the focus of occupational therapists in all settings. See **Table 4-3** for aspects of the domain of occupational therapy.

Occupational therapists working within the educational setting have had to define their role and focus in relation to special education. As a result, the school-based therapist has had to develop a strategy to function within the educational model rather than the medical model. This is, primarily, due to the lack of funding promised by the Congress when P.L. 94-142 was passed. The American Occupational Therapy Association has described the occupational therapist serving in the schools in the following way:

> Occupational therapists and occupational therapy assistants are part of the education team within a school district. The profession of occupational therapy is concerned with a person's ability to participate in desired daily life activities or "occupations." In the schools, occupational therapy practitioners use their unique expertise to help students to prepare for and perform important learning and school-related activities and to fulfill their role as students. In this setting, occupational therapists (and occupational therapy assistants, under the supervision of the occupational therapist) support academic and

TABLE 4-3 Occupational Therapy Domains as Defined by the American Occupational Therapy Association[2]

Occupations	Client Factors	Performance Skills	Performance Patterns	Contexts and Environments
Activities of living (ADLs)*	Values, beliefs, and sprituality	Motor skills	Habits	Cultural
Instrumental activities of daily living (IADLs)	Body functions	Process skills	Routines	Personal
	Body structures	Social interaction skills	Rituals	Physical
Rest and sleep			Roles	Social
Education				Temporal
Work				Virtual
Play				
Leisure				
Social participation				

*Also referred to as *basic activities of daily living (BADLs) or personal activities of daily living (PADLs)*.

American Occupational Therapy Association (2014). Framework: Domain and practice. 3rd ed. *The American Journal of Occupational Therapy*, 68, 1–48.

nonacademic outcomes, including social skills, math, reading and writing (i.e., literacy), behavior management, recess, participation in sports, self-help skills, prevocational/vocational participation, and more, for students and students with disabilities, 3 to 21 years of age. Practitioners are particularly skilled in facilitating student access to curricular and extracurricular activities through supports, designing and planning, and other methods. Additionally, they play a critical role in training parents, other staff members, and caregivers regarding educating students with diverse learning needs.[3]

The school-based occupational therapist contributes to the student's school success in a number of ways. The therapist may help students using wheelchairs to move independently within the school by teaching them to carry a lunch tray on their lap, manage a ramp to and from the playground, and move through crowded halls without running into classmates. The therapist may assist a student with a learning disability by providing sensorimotor training to ready the student to receive instruction. The occupational therapist usually has significant education and training in the skills necessary to promote sensory integration.

The occupational therapist will often work in cooperation with the physical educator, particularly to ensure student success in managing travel around the gymnasium or playground, in developing strategies to maximize the development of appropriate social skills and play behavior, and in contributing to the individualized physical education plan.

Paraeducators

Paraeducators are education support professionals (ESP) who are hired to provide direct or indirect services in schools. They perform many of the routine duties that used to be required of teachers. Three-fourths of these individuals work with special education students. Their roles include instructional and noninstructional assistants; teacher or program assistants; preschool caregivers; building, bus, and playground monitors; crossing guards; and nonmanagerial supervisors.

Parent Counselors and Trainers

Parents of students with disabilities are very important participants in the education of their students. This echoes the mandates of the federal law that the parent is the student's first and primary teacher. Helping parents gain the skills that will enable them to help their students meet the goals and objectives of the IEP or the individual family service plan (IFSP) is critical.[25] The services provided by parent counselors and trainers are vital to those facing the reality of raising a student with a disability. This counseling and training are even more crucial for a single parent raising a disabled student. The grief, financial struggles, loneliness, and fears are often overwhelming.

Parent counseling and training also focus on helping the parent(s) develop appropriate expectations regarding the student's growth and development. The parent must be helped to develop realistic, yet hopeful, goals for the student.

Physical Therapists

The physical therapist is trained to provide services that address range of motion, maintenance, and development of muscle tone, gait therapy, and mobility assistance with and without physical aids or equipment. The physical therapist can be a vital and integral part of the motor development team. The therapist brings to the student with disabilities a vast wealth of information regarding human motion.

One of the major problems facing the public schools that are attempting to meet the mandates of the federal law is that it is increasingly difficult to hire a physical therapist to work within the schools. The services of physical therapists are sought by hospitals, rehabilitation facilities, and nursing homes. Generally, the public schools cannot compete financially to hire and retain physical therapists.

Psychologists

Psychological services for students with disabilities, and if necessary for their parent(s), have been designated as a related service. Their responsibilities include:

- Administer psychological and educational tests
- Interpret assessment results
- Interpret information about the student's behavior and condition related to learning

- Consult with other staff members in planning school programs to meet the special needs of students
- Conduct behavioral evaluations
- Plan and manage a program of psychological services
- Provide psychological counseling for parents and students
- Assist with developing positive behavior-intervention strategies

Many school districts provide these services by hiring a psychologist or psychiatrist as a consultant or on a per-student basis. Larger school districts may hire school-based psychologists as part of the assessment and intervention team.

These professionals are involved in the assessment of students with disabilities referred because of conduct, behavioral, or emotional disorders; aggressive behavior toward other students or their parent(s); severe depression; suicidal tendencies or attempted suicides; or reports of sexual or physical abuse or serious neglect.

Recreation Therapists

Therapeutic recreation specialists usually play their significant role in hospital and rehabilitation programs. Few school districts have the resources to hire and retain these personnel. The school-based recreation therapist has the following responsibilities: "(a) assessment of the interests, resources, level of participation, social capability, and physical limitations of a person with a disability, (b) education for leisure activities, (c) increasing the independence of a person with a disability, and (d) providing recreation activities that are nonstructured and more suited to the wants and needs of the person with a disability."[20]

The school-based recreation therapist provides instruction so that individuals with disabilities will be able to make wise choices in the use of leisure time. The intent is to provide instruction so students will be able to participate in community-based leisure activities. Because of the commitment of recreation therapists to community-based, lifetime activity development, these professionals may play a vital role in the development of the student's individual transition plan (ITP). The student's IEP in middle school and high school must include specific goals and objectives related to community-based leisure and recreation activities.

Rehabilitation Counselors

Rehabilitation counselors provide services in individual or group sessions that focus specifically on career development, employment preparation, and achievement of independence and integration in the workplace and community. These services include vocational rehabilitation services funded under the Vocational Rehabilitation Act of 1973 as amended.[25]

The rehabilitation counselor focuses on helping the learner with a disability gain the confidence and learn the skills necessary to function as typically as possible. Most rehabilitation counseling and rehabilitation services address the needs of the learner with adventitious injuries or disabilities; these are injuries or disabilities that occur after the student has already experienced typical development.

Rehabilitation counseling addresses grief; specifically, the individual with a new injury or disability must grieve the loss of function or ability before he or she can get on with life. This counseling also addresses strategies for the re-establishment of self-esteem. Techniques are taught so that the student can adapt or compensate for the injury or disability and live a full life. Play, games, leisure, recreation, and sports have been found to be effective tools in the rehabilitation process. Indeed, most major rehabilitation facilities encourage participation in these activities to facilitate recovery and development.

Assistive Technology Service Personnel

Technology is part of our society and all individuals should have access to technology that is available for communication, interaction, and access to information. Some individuals with specific disabilities will require certain types of technology to access information. The Assistive Technology Act of 2004 (P.L. 108-364) is a reauthorization of the 1998 act, brought about to change the purpose. The previous technology-related acts were in place to help states build systems to be certain that individuals with disabilities had access to the assistive technology (AT) they needed. The Assistive Technology Act of 2004 defined AT in the following way: "any item, piece of equipment, or product system, whether acquired commercially, modified, or customized, that is used to increase, maintain, or improve functional capabilities of individuals with disabilities."[16]

AT devices can be "low-tech," "medium-tech," or "high-tech," as the examples below show:

- power and manual wheelchairs, scooters, canes, walkers, and standing devices
- augmentative communication devices (speech-generating devices), voice amplifiers, and speech-recognition devices
- durable medical equipment and medical supplies, such as patient lifts and incontinence supplies
- orthotics and prosthetics, such as hearing aids and electric larynxes
- accessibility adaptations to the home, workplace, schools, group homes, nursing facilities, ICF/MRs, and other places (e.g., ramps, stair glides, lifts, grab bars, flashing smoke detectors, lever doorknobs, and environmental controls)
- special equipment to help people work, study, and engage in recreation, such as enlarged computer keyboards, reachers, amplified telephones, magnifiers, voice-recognition software, and adaptive sports equipment
- accessibility modifications in the community, such as audio systems on public transportation, talking ATMs, and voting machines for the blind[6]

Educational personnel who provide AT services perform any service that directly assists an individual with a disability in the selection, acquisition, or use of an AT device, including:

a. the evaluation of the needs of an individual with a disability, including a functional evaluation of the individual in the individual's customary environment;

b. purchasing, leasing, or otherwise providing for the acquisition of AT devices by individuals with disabilities;

c. selecting, designing, fitting, customizing, adapting, applying, maintaining, repairing, or replacing of AT devices;

d. coordinating and using other therapies, interventions, or services with AT devices, such as those associated with existing education and rehabilitation plans and programs;

e. training or technical assistance for an individual with disabilities, or, where appropriate, the family of an individual with disabilities;

f. training or technical assistance for professionals (including individuals providing education and rehabilitation services), employers, or other individuals who provide services to, employ, or are otherwise substantially involved in the major life functions of individuals with disabilities; and

g. a service consisting of expanding the availability of access to technology, including electronic and information technology, to individuals with disabilities.[16]

The Quality Indicators for Assistive Technology (QIAT) Consortium has developed a self-evaluation matrix and recommends the following be considered for IEP teams when implementing AT for students:

- The education agency has guidelines for documenting AT needs in the IEP and requires their consistent application.
- All services that the IEP team determines are needed to support the selection, acquisition, and uses of AT devices are designated in the IEP.
- The IEP illustrates that AT is a tool to support achievement of the goals and progress in the general curriculum by establishing a clear relationship between student needs, AT devices and services, and the student's goals and objectives.
- IEP content regarding AT use is written in language that describes how AT contributes to achievement of measureable and observable outcomes.
- AT is included in the IEP in a manner that provides a clear and complete description of the devices and services to be provided and used to address student needs and achieve expected results.[18]

As the availability of technology to the general public has escalated dramatically, so have the nature and types of technology available to students with disabilities. For example, Microsoft Windows has a feature called "Sticky Keys," which makes it easier to push a designated computer key. Xybernaut and IBM have developed computer systems with touch screens, voice recognition, and icons that are touch-activated.[22] A remarkable technology available for students with disabilities is universal design. A student using this technology is able to have text materials highlighted; the text changed to a different, more readable font; or the particular material presented at a lower reading level. The use of personal data assistants (PDAs) may be very useful for learners with mild disabilities to help them coordinate their learning.[22]

School Health Service Personnel

School health services must be provided to students with disabilities. In most school districts, the school health service personnel are nurses. These health services include monitoring immunization records and monitoring and/or completing health procedures, such as catheterization or tracheostomy tube suction. School health services for students with disabilities become more complex as more students who are medically fragile pursue their right to a free, appropriate public education as mandated by IDEA and Section 504 of the Rehabilitation Act.

Social Workers

Some of the specific tasks done by social workers include:

- preparing social or developmental histories of students with disabilities,
- conducting group or individual counseling with parents and students,
- working in partnership with parents regarding aspects of the student's living situation that affect the student's adjustment to school, and
- assisting in developing positive behavior-intervention strategies.

The licensed social worker intervenes within the family, seen as part of the total community, and helps the student with disabilities and his or her family deal with issues that directly relate to the disability—discrimination, fear, guilt, substance abuse, student abuse, medical expenses, and the intrusion of well-meaning professionals into their lives. The social worker is trained to assist the family in coping with the vast and often-complex system designed to provide support for families in trouble. The social worker can, for example, help a parent apply for Aid for Dependent Students or, if necessary, unemployment compensation.

In some large school districts, community social service agencies have opened offices within the schools to improve access to needed social services. This strategy has proved valuable in providing assistance to non-English-speaking students and their families.

Speech Therapists

Speech and language therapy has as its goal the improvement of communication behaviors of students whose speech and/or language deficits affect educational performance. The areas assessed by a speech and language therapist would include:[21]

- semantics (language content or meaning)
- syntax (language structure or grammar)
- pragmatics (language use or function)
- phonology (the sound system of language)

Service delivery in speech and language programs was historically based on a medical model in which the speech therapist provided therapy to students with speech and language deficits in a clinical, isolated setting. That is, the clinician would provide speech and language programming in a setting removed from the student's regular education or special education classroom. That practice is changing.

Current, innovative practice in speech and language programs is based on the notion that speech and language are a basic and integral part of the student's total life experience. Speech and language therapy should be embedded within the total academic and nonacademic curriculum.

To allow classroom-based therapy to occur, the speech therapist functions collaboratively with the student's regular educator and/or special educator. A smart, motivated therapist is eager to collaborate with the adapted physical educator and general physical educator because the distinct advantages identified in classroom-based language instruction pertain to the physical education "classroom" or APE "classroom," as well. In fact, the nature of physical education makes it an exciting, language-rich opportunity. Students involved in dance, play, and games are functioning within their most natural environment; this environment demands communication in a variety of forms—gestures, signs, expressive facial behaviors, and expressive/receptive speech.

In addition, the therapist collaborates with the physical educator or adapted physical educator because of the obvious relationship between gross and fine motor development and the development of speech and language. Indeed, movement is speech; speech is movement.

Transportation Specialists

In *Alamo Heights v. State Board of Education* (1986), the court mandated that transportation, like other related services, must be included on the student's IEP.[1] The Office of Civil Rights has decreed that a student with a disability should not have to ride the school bus longer than other students. The Office of Civil Rights has also indicated it is a violation of civil rights if a student with a disability has a shorter instructional day than other students because of the school bus schedule. In addition, the student with a disability should have the same access to extracurricular, before-school, or after-school programs as any other student.[24] If the student needs an aide (transportation specialist) on the bus during transportation to and from school, litigation indicates it should be included on the IEP as well.

Transition Service Personnel

One of the major transition services offered by transition service personnel is vocational education. A quality vocational education program includes a comprehensive assessment of vocational potential and capabilities. The student with a disability is given the opportunity to demonstrate his or her unique skills and talents, so that appropriate job training can be provided. As the student enters middle school and high school, the focus of the education provided is vocational, if appropriate. Special education instruction focuses on the skills necessary to function within a workplace. Actual work-related opportunities are provided in "work production" or "work simulation" classes. Some progressive school districts have job placement opportunities for students with disabilities in the last years of their special education career. In fact, some provide "job coaches" to work "shoulder to shoulder" with a student with a disability at the actual job site to assist the student with the technical aspects, as well as the social nuances, of the job. For example, if the student is being trained as a maid for a major hotel chain, the job coach accompanies the student to the hotel, both wearing the same uniform as every other employee, and helps the student learn the day-to-day routine and processes involved in being a successful employee.

Each of the professionals described previously brings a special expertise to the student with a disability. Seldom does one student require the services of all these specialized professionals. However, the intent of the law is that these personnel must be made available, if necessary, for the student to benefit from the educational process.

Seldom are all these professionals on-staff personnel within a given district. Small school districts may rely on a special education center to provide such services. These centers are called by different names in different states. When this type of special education center is not available, school districts hire their own specialized personnel on a contractual basis or refer students to private practitioners and/or hospitals or rehabilitation centers for assessment/evaluation services and/or programming.

Description of Each Component of the IEP

PRESENT LEVEL OF EDUCATIONAL ACHIEVEMENT

The IEP must include a statement of the present level of educational achievement, including the "academic" and "functional performance" of the student. It is important that the statement of the student's present level of educational achievement be based on current, relevant information about the student. Information should be obtained from a variety of sources:

1. Information from the student's parents. There is an increased emphasis on parental involvement in every phase of the student's education. Increasingly, the emphasis in the public schools is on involvement of the parent and/or extended family in the decisions made with/for a student with a disability.
2. The most recent evaluation of the student
3. District-wide assessment results
4. Input from the student's general physical educator and/or APE teacher

The statement describing the present level of educational achievement, including academic and functional performance, must include how the student's disability affects his or her involvement and progress in the general educational curricula or, in the case of infants, toddlers, and preschoolers age 3 to 5 years, their participation in appropriate activities. Appropriate activities are age-relevant developmental abilities or milestones that typically reflect the development of children of the same age.

One of the purposes of assessment is to determine the student's present level of educational achievement and need for specially designed education and physical education. These assessments are needed to ensure the student's involvement and progress in the general education and physical education curriculum and any needed adaptation or modifications to the general curriculum.

The comprehensive determination of a student's present level of educational achievement developed by the IEP team should include the following:

1. Intellectual assessment
2. Educational assessment
3. Developmental needs
4. Sociological information
5. Emotional/behavioral assessment
6. Physical examination or health update
7. Speech and language assessment
8. Language dominance assessment
9. Motor and play assessment
10. Community-based leisure/recreation/sport and fitness assessment
11. Vocational or prevocational assessment
12. Related services assessment(s)
13. Functional assessments. It appears to be critical that the adapted physical educator and the physical educator remember the focus of the curriculum—play, movement, leisure, recreation, sports, and fitness—and not be forced into a position to deliver services to enhance "functional" skills associated with those of daily living.

The statement describing the learner's present level of achievement in physical education must always be based on the results of more than one assessment instrument in order to ensure reliability and validity. A comprehensive statement of the student's present level of performance in physical education may include a description of:

1. Motor output that may cause one to suspect a sensory-input system dysfunction
    a. Inappropriate reflex behavior
    b. Equilibrium dysfunction
    c. Sensory integration deficit
    d. Motor-planning deficit

2. The learner's locomotor and nonlocomotor competency
3. The learner's physical and motor fitness level
4. The learner's ability to participate in a variety of play, games, leisure, recreation, and sport and fitness activities
5. The learner's ability to participate in a variety of rhythms, dance, and aquatic activities
6. The learner's ability to use community-based resources to enable participation in play, games, leisure, recreation, sports, and fitness activities

The comprehensive assessment that determines the present level of performance is critical to the development of the IEP. A valid and extensive understanding of the student's present abilities and skills is the basis for the development of the student's annual goals.

GOALS

Measurable annual goals are critical to the strategic planning process used to develop and implement the IEP for each student with a disability.

Once the IEP/multidisciplinary team has determined measurable annual goals, the team can develop specific strategies that will be most effective in achieving those goals. The annual goals should address the student's needs that result directly from the student's disability if the disability interferes with the student's ability to make progress in the general curriculum.

Edelen-Smith[8] has suggested that only if the service provider (teacher or related service personnel) and parents believe a goal on an IEP is valid and meaningful will that individual make a concerted effort to help the student achieve that goal. Edelen-Smith suggests eight elements that are vital if the goals are to be perceived as being valid by professionals, parents, and the student (see **Table 4-4**). The annual goals must include four concepts:

- An action (what?)
- Conditions under which the action should occur (how?)
- A criterion for mastery of a specific task (at what level?)
- A performance better than the student's present level of educational performance

Action Concept

The action portion of the annual goal indicates what the learner will do when performing the task. It is important that the action be stated in verb form,

TABLE 4-4 Edelen-Smith's Criteria for Establishing Valid Goals

1. *Conceivable:* If all parties can conceive of the *outcome* that will result if these particular goals are met, the goals will have particular value for the student.

2. *Believable:* The student, parent, and professionals must believe the goal can be met. To be believable, the goal must also be consistent with family, cultural, and societal value systems.

3. *Achievable:* The comprehensive assessment, if done well, will provide data that make it possible to suggest goals that will be challenging but achievable.

4. *Controllable:* The student must feel as if he or she has had input in decisions regarding personal goals; if the student has had no control, the student will feel un-empowered.

5. *Measurable:* The goal must be written so it can be measured.

6. *Desirable:* The goal must be something the student wants to achieve and the parent(s) and teacher(s) want him or her to achieve.

7. *Stated with no alternative:* In order for a student, parent, or teacher to take a goal seriously, it must be perceived as a significant target, not one that will be adjusted without demonstrated effort.

8. *Growth facilitating:* The goals must seek desirable behaviors instead of seeking to eliminate undesirable behaviors.

Data from Edelen-Smith, P. (1995). Eight elements to guide goal determination. *Intervent School Clin*, 30 (5): 297–301.

such as "throw," "strike," "kick," "do a sit-up," "serve a volleyball," "walk a mile," or "complete a 30-minute aerobic dance workout."

Conditions

The conditions under which the action should occur describe how the learner is to perform at the task. It is important to be exact. Changing the conditions makes a task easy or more difficult, inefficient or efficient, simple or more complex. Examples of conditions are:

- "With eyes closed and nonsupporting leg bent to 90 degrees, the student will … "
- "From a prone position, the learner will …"
- "Keeping the back straight and arms at the side of the body, the student will …"
- "Floating on her back, the swimmer will …"

If the conditions are not specified, it is impossible to determine the student's true capability and what activities are needed to make progress. If the conditions are not precise, it is unclear how the student is to perform the task, and once again the value of the goal is lost.

Well-written goals include what, how, and at what level the behaviors are to be performed. Inappropriate goals fail for several reasons:

- "Run as fast as you can."
Conditions: The condition, distance, or environmental arrangements are not specified.
Criterion: Neither an objective, a measurable distance, nor a specified time has been included in the goal. "As fast as you can" is subjective. The students may believe they are running as fast as they can, but the teacher may have a different opinion.
- "Walk on a balance beam without falling off."
Conditions: The width of the balance beam and the position of the arms make the task more or less difficult. Neither of these is specified.
Criterion: The distance to be traveled or distance over time is not specified.
- "Swim to the end of the pool."
Conditions: The stroke is not specified.
Criterion: Swimming pools are different lengths. It is unclear the exact distance the student is to swim.

Criterion of Mastery

The criterion for mastery of a task in the annual goal is the standard at which the task should be performed. Being able to perform the task to criterion level indicates mastery of the task and, hence, student progress. Reaching a criterion serves notice that one prerequisite in a series has been mastered and that the student is ready to begin working toward the next step. Measures for task mastery can take several forms (see **Table 4-5**):

- Number of repetitions (10 repetitions)
- Number of repetitions over time (20 repetitions in 15 seconds)
- Distance traveled (8 feet on a balance beam without stepping off)
- Distance traveled over time (200 yards in 25 seconds)
- Number of successive trials without a miss (4 times in a row)
- Specified number of successful responses in a block of trials (3 out of 5)

TABLE 4-5   Measurable Goals, Including Action, Condition, and Criteria

The student will run 1 mile in 10 minutes 30 seconds.

Action:	Run
Condition:	1 mile
Criteria:	10 minutes 30 seconds

The student will walk on a balance beam, 4 inches wide, heel to toe, with eyes closed and hands on hips, for 8 feet.

Action:	Walk
Condition:	A balance beam 4 inches wide
Criteria:	Heel to toe, eyes closed, and hands on hips for 8 feet

The student will swim the breaststroke 50 meters in 1 minute 30 seconds.

Action:	Swim
Condition:	Breaststroke 50 meters
Criteria:	1 minute 30 seconds

The learner will roll his or her wheelchair through a 5-cone, figure-8 obstacle course in less than 2 minutes.

Action:	Roll wheelchair
Condition:	Through a 5-cone obstacle course
Criteria:	Less than 2 minutes

- Number of degrees of movement (flexibility in degrees of movement from starting to ending positions)
- Mastery of all the stated conditions of the task

Although not required in all situations by IDEA, it is critical that the adapted physical educator provide short-term objectives or benchmarks for the general physical educator or the paraprofessional who is responsible for providing physical education services to the student. These are vital if effective instruction is to occur. These benchmarks make it possible for the general physical educator and the paraprofessional to ensure that progress toward the goal is occurring. A sample Present Level of Educational Performance, Goals, and Benchmarks, as documented on an I-4 form, for Noah Lott can be found in **Table 4-6**.

SPECIFIC EDUCATIONAL SERVICES

The dates of the initiation, the duration, the frequency, and the location of all services and supports must be made clear. In the broadest sense, the "specific

TABLE 4-6   Individualized Physical Education Program

INDIVIDUALIZED EDUCATION PROGRAM: PRESENT LEVEL OF ACADEMIC ACHIEVEMENT AND FUNCTIONAL PERFORMANCE

Form I-4

Name of Student: <u>Noah Lott</u>   DOB: <u>03/15/2002</u>   Duration of IEP: <u>1/20/2016–1/19/2017</u>

Describe the student's strengths and the concerns of the parents about the student's education.

Noah has many strengths in physical education. Among his greatest strengths is his willingness to participate and give maximal effort. With little to no hesitation, Noah participates in almost every physical education activity. He is very cooperative as well, and consistently tries hard. He really enjoys socially interacting with his peers. This includes talking with friends before class, getting along with everyone during class, and taking part in competitions. Some of his psychomotor skills involve shooting a basketball, dribbling a basketball, throwing, catching, and striking. These strengths come as no surprise as Noah enjoys and is very talented at basketball. There were no recorded concerns of his parents because they were not contacted.

Describe the student's present level of academic achievement and functional performance including how the student's disability affects his or her involvement and progress in the general education curriculum. For preschool children, describe how the disability affects involvement in age-appropriate activities. *(Note: Present level of performance must include information that corresponds with each annual goal.)*

Noah consistently demonstrates mature, cooperative behavior in physical education. He sincerely seems to enjoy physical education for the social interaction, and skill development opportunities. Noah was recently evaluated with the Louisiana Competency Test for Adapted Physical Education Level V. The test identifies the student's present level of motor deficit based on their test item scores compared to the mean scores. Noah scored 30%, as 7 of the 10 test items he scored were below the mean. This indicated he has a moderate motor deficit. Although Noah put forth great effort and happily participated during the test, it was revealed he has several skill areas that need to be addressed. During the jump turn test item, where he was given 3 trials to execute proper full-jump turns, Noah scored a 2 out of a possible 6 points. He did in fact begin in the proper position, which earned him 2 points, but failed to turn a full 360° and did not land on balance. A need for balance improvement was an underlying observation throughout the assessment. During the standing long jump test, Noah was given three trials to jump as far as possible using correct form. He scored 2 out of a possible 18 points on this skill. He was given points for being observed at least once using a preparatory crouch and forcefully swinging his arms at lift-off, but failed to jump the required 48 inches while ending with a balanced two-feet, bent-knee landing. This test item, along with the vertical jump test, indicates a need for improved balance and lower-body strength. Noah scored a 1 out of 20 on the vertical jump test. Once again, he scored 1 point for being observed using a preparatory crouch at least once, but did not jump a distance of the required 6 inches while using a balanced two-feet, bent-knee landing 10 consecutive times. Noah's performance on the walk-out test indicated insufficient upper- and lower-body strength as well. Noah scored a 2 out of 8 on the walk-out test. The goal was to complete 5 consecutive walk-outs but Noah did not appear to have the strength to maintain the proper push-up position and work his way back up to a bridge position. An interesting test item was the football pass test, where Noah was given 5 trials to pass the football within the reach of a receiver 30 feet away. He did not score any points on this test, as he was not able to throw the football 30 feet.

(continues)

TABLE 4-6   Individualized Physical Education Program (*Continued*)

This indicated that Noah should also attempt to improve his upper-body strength, which will help him experience more success in activities involving throwing and shooting. In certain activities, Noah may need additional demonstrations and/or verbal or physical prompting in order to stay focused on the task at hand; however, rarely does his lack of focus affect his fellow classmates. After a simple reminder or prompt, Noah will often refocus and continue participating. As Noah exhibits a developmental delay in some of his gross motor and fitness skills, he requires individualized assistance and IEP goals to ensure his safety and success in general physical education.

Will the student be involved full-time in the general education curriculum or, for preschoolers, in age-appropriate activities?   X Yes   ☐ No

(If no, describe the extent to which the student will not be involved full-time in the general curriculum or, for preschoolers, in age-appropriate activities.)

Noah will participate in general physical education.

Measurable annual academic or functional goal to enable the student to be involved in and progress in the general education curriculum, and to meet other educational needs that result from the student's disability. *(Note: present levels of academic achievement and functional performance must include information that corresponds with each annual goal.)*

Upon review: ☐ Goal met   ☐ Goal not met

1) Noah will perform a vertical jump 10 inches off the ground, without losing balance upon landing 5 out of 7 trials.

2) Noah will shoot a basketball at a hoop from 20 feet away and hit the rim or backboard 5 out of 7 trials.

3) Noah will perform 3 consecutive walk-outs using mature form, 2 out of 3 trials.

Procedures for measuring the student's progress toward meeting the annual goal:

- **Rubrics**
- **Checklists**
- **Digital Videos**
- **Digital Pictures**

Will the student participate in an alternate assessment aligned with alternate achievement standards for students with disabilities in any subject area?   X Yes   ☐ No

(If yes, include benchmarks or short-term objectives for the student.)

1) Noah will perform a vertical jump 10 inches off the ground, without losing balance upon landing 5 out of 7 trials.

    a. Noah will perform a vertical jump 6 inches off the ground 5 out of 7 trials.

    b. Noah will perform 6 dumbbell squats of at least 40 total pounds without stopping 2 out of 3 trials.

TABLE 4-6   Individualized Physical Education Program (*Continued*)

> 2) Noah will shoot a basketball at a hoop from 20 feet away and hit the rim or backboard 5 out of 7 trials.
>   a. Noah will shoot a basketball at a hoop from 15 feet away and hit the rim or backboard 5 out of 7 trials.
>   b. Noah will throw a 10-pound medicine ball a distance of 5 feet, using both hands 5 out of 7 trials.
> 3) Noah will perform 3 consecutive walk-outs using mature form, 2 out of 3 trials.
>   a. Noah will perform 1 walk-out using mature form 3 out of 5 trials.
>   b. Noah will perform 5 push-ups without stopping 2 out of 3 trials.
>
> **When will reports about the student's progress toward meeting the annual goal be provided to parents?**
>
> Reports on Noah's progress in physical education will be provided to his parents every 9 weeks. Also, Noah will have a visual portfolio with digital pictures and video clips of his progress. This will be accessible by all members of the IEP team, including Noah's parents.

educational services to be rendered" means what professional services (e.g., APE, remedial reading, speech and language therapy) will be made available to the student. Every professional service and educational activity should be chosen/designed to help the student attain the annual goals.

The services to be provided must be clearly stated on the IEP, so that the extent of the commitment of school district resources, personnel, equipment, and facilities will be clear to parents and other IEP team members.[25] The specification of the extent of services should include:

- Dates of initiation of services
- Duration of services
- Number of minutes a particular service will be delivered to the student per day, week, or month. For example: Speech and language therapy, 30 minutes, 2 days per week. A range may specify the services—for example, the student will participate in general physical education three times a week for 30–45 minutes.
- Location at which the services will be provided—for example, the APE services may be provided at the local fitness center, so that the student has the opportunity to learn the skills necessary to enjoy, use, and benefit from the services available in the community.

RELATED SERVICES

Related services are intended to help the student with disabilities benefit from special education. APE is special education, and subsequently not a related service. Related services can be used to help students with disabilities benefit from APE services. The goals of related service personnel may be a vital part of the student's IEP and should be consistent with those established for special education services, such as APE. These services should focus on offsetting or reducing the problems resulting from the student's disability that interfere with learning and physical education performance in school. Examples of related services, which commonly help students with disabilities benefit from physical education, are physical therapy, occupational therapy, and speech-language therapy.

Depending on the unique needs of the student, other developmental, corrective, or supportive services may be required to help a student with a disability benefit from special education. Such services include nutrition services and service coordination between school-based physical education services and community-based agencies for health promotion purposes.[25]

EXTENT TO WHICH THE STUDENT WILL NOT PARTICIPATE IN REGULAR EDUCATION

IDEA requires national assessment in states' ability to improve participation of children with disabilities in the general education curriculum. The IEP/multidisciplinary team's determination of how each student's disability affects the student's involvement and progress in the general curriculum should be included in the student's IEP.

If the IEP team believes that the least restrictive environment (LRE) for a student with a disability is not the general physical education setting, it is vital for aids and services, accommodations, and modifications to be attempted before consideration of an alternative placement. If the LRE is an alternative physical education placement, such as small-group physical education, then access to the general curriculum should still be provided. The general physical education curriculum should be mirrored in that alternate setting.

MODIFICATIONS/ACCOMMODATIONS NEEDED FOR THE STUDENT TO PARTICIPATE IN STATEWIDE AND DISTRICT-WIDE ACHIEVEMENT TESTS

Consistent with congressional mandates regarding access to the general curriculum is an increased emphasis on the participation of students with disabilities in state- and district-mandated achievement tests. This can apply in physical education if the school district has mandated fitness testing. If the IEP/multidisciplinary team believes that the student cannot participate in this fitness assessment, it is the responsibility of the team to explain why the test is inappropriate and to offer an alternative. Equal access would involve provision of necessary modifications to allow for testing or utilization of fitness testing designed for individuals with disabilities, such as the Brockport Physical Fitness Test.

STATEMENT OF NEEDED TRANSITION SERVICES

The individual transition plan (ITP) facilitates the student's movement from school to post-school activities. Effective transition programs provide students with the skills necessary to live successfully after graduation from high school.

Beginning at the age of 16 years, or earlier if the IEP team or the state the student lives in determines it to be necessary, the IEP/multidisciplinary team, in determining appropriate measurable annual goals and services for a student, must determine the planned instructional and educational experiences that will prepare the student for transition from secondary education to post-secondary life.[25] Also at this time, a statement that describes the process by which a student with a disability will make the transition into community-based living must be included on the IEP. All students with disabilities should have appropriate physical education to prepare them for independent living and community participation, which includes quality leisure, recreation, sports, and physical fitness experiences, and vocation, which often requires a healthy level of fitness.

POSITIVE BEHAVIOR MANAGEMENT

According to IDEIA, all students with a disability who violate a code of student conduct may be removed from their current placement and placed in an appropriate interim alternative educational setting, placed in another setting, or suspended for not more than 10 consecutive school days. If the student has a disability, within those 10 days the student's IEP team must review all relevant information in the student's file to determine if the conduct in question was a result of the student's disability or was a direct result of the local education agency's (LEA) failure to implement the IEP. If the disability or the LEA is found to be at fault, immediate steps must be taken to remedy the situation.

If the conduct was a result of the student's disability, the IEP team must conduct a functional behavioral assessment and implement a behavioral intervention plan (BIP) for the student. If a plan was already in place, that plan is reviewed and modified to better address the behavior.

School personnel also have the right to move a student with a disability to an alternative educational setting for not more than 45 days if the student knowingly possesses or uses illegal drugs; sells or solicits the sale of a controlled substance; carries a weapon to or possesses a weapon at school, on school premises, or to a school function; or has inflicted serious bodily injury upon another person, while at school or a school event.[25]

Positive behavior management strategies have proven to be successful in preventing and controlling disruptive behavior in the schools. Appropriate positive behavior management strategies should be included in the contents of the IEP when the student's behavior interferes with his or her learning or disrupts the learning of others.[25] Special educators (including adapted physical educators), related service personnel, general educators, school administrators, school counselors, and parents need to work in concert to develop and implement a positive behavior management plan. The focus, as in any good behavior management plan, needs to be on prevention of disruptive or inappropriate behavior.

There are a number of very creative ways to help establish the behavior management plan, as part of the IEP process. Behavior management plans are also called behavior intervention plans (BIPs). A BIP should include a specific description of the behavior impacting learning, the data collected regarding the behavior, such as the antecedent and frequency and intensity of occurrence, the prevention strategy, behavioral goal, and supports that will be provided to remediate the behavior. The three common approaches used to remediate behavior are the behavioral approach (contracts, reward systems), biophysical approach (medication, relaxation), and humanistic approach (character development, personal responsibility).[12] Tournaki and Criscitello have suggested that another way to enhance the behavior of students who struggle to behave appropriately is to use reverse-role tutoring; students with disabilities become tutors for students without disabilities.[23]

In that role, the students with disabilities demonstrate improved behavior in the classroom. Another strategy that has proven successful is the use of dialogue journals that allow the student and the teacher to share feelings and emotions without direct, personal communication.[19] It appears that students are more likely to share their feelings within a context that does not require face-to-face communication. These strategies, and others, should be included in the student's IEP. School-wide implementation of a positive behavior management plan that is consistent throughout the school building is the most effective strategy for success when using behavior management techniques.

PROJECTED DATES FOR INITIATION AND TERMINATION OF SERVICES

The projected dates for beginning and terminating educational and related services must be included on the IEP. This is just one more technique intended to ensure accountability. All IEPs must include a date when services should begin and an anticipated date when goals will be reached.

APPROPRIATE OBJECTIVE CRITERIA AND EVALUATION PROCEDURES

Each IEP must include a description of the techniques/strategies used to determine the student's present level of performance and to determine whether the student accomplishes each of the goals on the IEP. These must include how the student's progress toward meeting the goals will be measured and when periodic reports on the progress will be provided.

ADDITIONAL COMPONENTS OF MOST SCHOOL-BASED IEP DOCUMENTS

It is important for the physical educator to be aware that there are many other pieces of information included in most school-based documents. Because the IEP document has often become the basis of litigation by parents and/or advocacy groups and is highly scrutinized by review teams from the state department of public instruction and/or federal grant agencies, the actual document has become increasingly complex. It is not unusual for this document to be between 25 and 50 pages long. This additional information, often kept as records within the principal's office, but often included on the IEP, includes:

1. Information about the student:
   a. Name
   b. Identification number
   c. Birth date
   d. Native language/mode of communication
2. Information about the parent or guardian:
   a. Address
   b. Phone numbers (work, home, emergency)
   c. Contact person/phone for parent without access
   d. Native language/mode of communication
3. Determination of eligibility statement (i.e., does the student have a disability as determined by federal mandates?)
4. Determination of placement or placement options along the service delivery continuum
5. Assurance of placement close to home and/or home school and a specific explanation if the student must receive services in a different setting
6. Waiver/nonwaiver status for state education agency-mandated examinations and specific techniques that will be used to ensure the student every opportunity to participate in state and local education agency assessments and, if that is not possible, modifications of assessments that will be provided
7. Specific modifications in instructional strategies to ensure learning throughout placement continuum
8. Goals for extended-year service (summer school) if it is feared that regression may occur without such service
9. Modified standards for participation in extracurricular activities, if necessary
10. Assurances that
    a. Placement in special education is not a function of national origin, minority status, or linguistic differences
    b. Placement in special education is not directly attributable to a different culture or lifestyle or to lack of educational opportunity
    c. Education will be provided in the student's least restrictive environment

Participants in the IEP/Multidisciplinary Team Meeting

The following individuals must attend the IEP meeting:

1. The parents or legal guardian of the student
2. Not less than one regular education teacher of the student (if the student is or may be participating in the regular education environment). This may be the general physical educator if the student is to participate in the general physical education program.
3. Not less than one special education teacher of the student or, where appropriate, not less than one special education provider of the student
4. A representative of the school administration. This person must have the authority to allocate school district resources. In most school districts, the principal or the principal's designee fills this role in the meeting.
5. An individual who can interpret the instructional implication of evaluation results and who also might be one of the other listed members
6. At the discretion of the parent or the school district, other individuals who have knowledge or special expertise regarding the student, including related services personnel as appropriate
7. Whenever appropriate, the student with a disability[25]

When a student is in transition, whether from preschool to elementary school, elementary school to middle school, middle school to high school, or high school into the community, it is absolutely critical that there are representatives from the student's present and eventual placements if the transition process is to be "seamless" and appropriate. Without participation of the professionals at both schools or placements, precious time will be lost in the education of learners with disabilities.

In addition, the following personnel should be part of this IEP meeting:

1. Any direct or related service personnel who have assessed the student (APE specialist, occupational therapist, speech-language pathologist, etc.). The IDEIA regulations do not expressly mandate that the IEP/multidisciplinary team include related services personnel. However, it is critical that those individuals attend the meeting if a particular related service is to be discussed at the meeting.
2. The school nurse, particularly if the student has a chronic and/or serious medical condition (e.g., asthma, AIDS, cancer) and/or requires

special medical procedures (e.g., tube feeding, catheterization) in order to function in the school environment

3. An interpreter, as required

4. Representatives of the community agencies that will be responsible for implementing individual transition plans (after the student reaches age 16 years)

Difficult and occasionally adversarial relationships between parents and school districts have created situations in which a parent may bring an advocate or a lawyer to an IEP meeting. If a student or parent advocate is present, the meeting should continue as scheduled; the advocate is representing the best interests of the student and/or parent and usually represents a nonprofit agency devoted to ensuring rights for students and adults with disabilities. The advocate may be helpful to the parent and other members of the IEP team as strategies for developing and implementing the best possible IEP are discussed. If the parent brings a lawyer without providing appropriate prior notice to the school district, so that the district's counsel can also attend, the meeting must be terminated and rescheduled, so that both sides (the student and/or parent and the school district) are represented by counsel.

The intent of the IEP meeting is that every individual who cares about the student and who has data regarding the student's performance should meet with every other individual with important information about the student and share this information, so that, in the end, the student receives the best possible education. Unfortunately, in the real world this is not always possible. For example, an APE specialist may be serving as a consultant for more than 300 students. There may be only one physical therapist serving an entire district. As a result, not all the people who are serving the student can attend every meeting. APE teachers who find themselves in this situation should be certain that the person making the physical education report understands the evaluation results and why it is important to follow the physical education recommendations. They also should contact key members of the IEP team, including the student and parents and share with them details regarding the student's progress prior to the meeting and inform them of their pending absence. Maintenance of a visual portfolio, including pictures and video clips of the student's progress, is the best method of relaying clear student growth.

The IEP Meeting Agenda

A productive IEP meeting should proceed as follows:

1. The principal or meeting leader welcomes all participants and thanks them for attending. This sets the tone for a cooperative effort.
2. Individuals attending the meeting either are introduced by the meeting leader or introduce themselves.
3. Meeting participants review the agenda for the meeting. Although an agenda is not required by federal mandates, it has proven very useful in keeping meeting participants on task. In addition, it helps create the proper mindset in the participants; *the IEP meeting is a business meeting* and should be treated as such.
4. At this point, the committee members should also agree on an individual who will take minutes of the meeting. These minutes are invaluable in the IEP process and in the maintenance of records. In IEP meetings that last 3 to 4 hours, it is almost impossible to remember what was said and by whom, and while the IEP document should reflect committee consensus, it often does not address important concerns regarding the student's education. In addition, in the event that a professional serving the student was unable to attend, the minutes will bring that person "up to speed" about the committee's decisions. These minutes should become a valuable part of the student's comprehensive educational record and an attachment to the IEP.
5. The principal or meeting leader should begin the meeting by expressing a personal interest in the student and comment on at least one of the student's strengths.
6. The principal or meeting leader should explain the reason for the meeting. This may include:
   a. Admission to special education: initial assessment/evaluation
   b. Review of assessment and/or the program
      1. Three-year comprehensive re-evaluation
      2. Annual review
      3. Parent's request to reconsider any component of the existing IEP for any reason
      4. Disciplinary review
   c. Dismissal from special education

7. Each participant then addresses the student's present level of educational performance. It is vital that the parents be encouraged to begin that discussion and to provide their insight into their student's progress. This is consistent with mandates that the parents be much more involved in the total education of their student. Asking the parents to start the discussion validates the parents and increases the likelihood that they will be active participants in the meeting. Then, each professional reports on the student's present level of performance within that person's area of expertise. This includes a concise report that includes the names of the tests administered, the results of the testing (including strengths and deficits demonstrated by the student), and the goals that should be set for the student. Whenever possible, the physical educator should relate findings to results found by other professionals (e.g., poor balance often can be tied to fine motor delays, visual problems can be tied to reading difficulties, poor self-concept can be associated with motivational problems in the classroom). If the meeting has been called at the parent's request or is a result of an ongoing disciplinary problem, the involved participants should indicate specific behaviors that have necessitated the meeting.

8. An open discussion among the people present at the meeting is the next step. During this discussion, the needs of the student and strategies for meeting these needs are explored. At this point, the true multidisciplinary nature of the meeting should surface. Each person must be willing to recognize the value of the services that other persons, particularly the parents, have to offer, as well as the value of his or her own expertise. The knowledgeable adapted physical educator or general physical educator will understand and appreciate services that can be provided by other professionals; however, he or she must also recognize that many activities in physical education can accomplish the physical and motor goals of the student in an interesting, novel fashion unique to the discipline.[13]

9. The committee must then determine appropriate annual goals. Agreement must be reached among the participants about which of the student's needs are most pressing and which goals should take precedence over others. Most states have determined specific expectations for their students at given age levels and within specific content areas. Whenever possible, the annual goals developed for the student with a disability

should be similar to those expected by state department of education policies; the regulations regarding the use of benchmarks make this possible.

10. After determining appropriate annual goals, the committee must consider the educational services that will be required for the student to meet goals and accomplish objectives. When contributing to these decisions, the physical educator should focus on the present level of educational performance evidenced by the student in the physical and motor areas. If, through testing, the student is found to have significant deficits, such as reflex abnormalities, vestibular delays, or range-of-motion limitations, and the physical educator does not believe the student can be included in the general physical education program, referral to a related therapy may be the best recommendation. Such a recommendation does not mean the student should not or cannot participate in some type of physical education class. It simply means that the related therapies should focus on the immediate low-level deficits while the student continues to participate in a physical education program that is designed to reinforce the intervention programs provided by the other services. *None of the related service therapies should replace physical education; however, they should be used to help the student take a more active role in the physical education class.*

11. The committee must then consider the extent to which the student will be educated in the regular education program. Given increased emphasis on education in the general education curriculum/program, this is often one of the most difficult and potentially confrontational parts of the IEP meeting. Once again, the physical educator must remember that his or her services are valuable, regardless of the student's demonstrated functioning levels. Under no circumstances should the physical educator agree that the student should automatically be included in a regular physical education class or that motor services can better be implemented by an occupational or a physical therapist. Unfortunately, some parents and school personnel continue to perceive physical education as supervised "free play." Their perception that physical education is a nonacademic experience causes them to devalue physical education.

12. Transition must be considered in three situations:
    a. If the student has just turned 3 years of age and is entering a public school preschool program

    b. If the student is turning 6 years of age and will be leaving preschool for a school program

    c. If the student is approaching his or her 16th birthday and decisions need to be made to prepare the student for community transition when leaving school

Note: Enlightened educators understand the need for consideration of transition during every phase of the student's life when major changes are to be encountered, including, in addition to those listed previously, a student's transition from elementary school to middle school and the student's transition from middle school to high school. Whenever possible, a significant meeting regarding transition should also occur when the student's family is moving into another school zone, school district, or state. Technology can make such communication easy and inexpensive.

13. The committee must agree on dates for initiation and review of services.

14. The members of the committee must discuss and agree on the criteria for evaluating the student's progress toward IEP goals.

15. The minutes of the meeting should be read, carefully, so that any participants can ask for clarification.

16. The meeting leader should briefly summarize the meeting and ask if any member of the committee has any additional questions or comments. All participants should sign the IEP document.

If the parents do not concur with the recommendations made by school personnel and refuse to sign the IEP, the IEP/multidisciplinary team must be reconvened—in most cases, within 10 school days—to address the issues. If the parents ultimately continue to disagree, the parents then have the right to secure counsel.

Each state is responsible for ensuring the following:

- Mediation is a voluntary process and is not used to deny a parent the right to due process.
- A qualified, impartial mediator who is well trained conducts the mediation process.
- A list of trained and qualified mediators is available to the school and parents.
- The schools are prepared to assume the cost of the mediation.

An alternative to mediation is due process. Due process involves a hearing, presentation of evidence, sworn testimony, and cross-examination. Lawyers and/or nonlawyer advocates may be involved in this process. The hearing officer will make a judgment, which can be appealed at the state and/or federal level. During due process the student is entitled to remain in his or her current placement with the current level of services until the matter is resolved.

Encouraging and Maximizing Parent Participation in the IEP Process

Parents must be a significant part of the IEP process. In fact in *Doug C. v. Hawaii,* the U.S. Court of Appeals indicated that the scheduling of IEP meetings should ensure the parent's availability has priority, not the other members on the team.[7] The concerns of parents and the information they provide, with their unique perspective, must be considered in developing and reviewing IEPs. There are specific mandated parent/guardian rights that must be made clear to the parent(s) or guardian(s) before a student is evaluated and either admitted to or dismissed from a special education program.

Most school districts distribute a parent rights manual developed by their state education agency when the student is first referred by the parent or guardian, members of the extended family, classroom teachers, physical education teachers, social workers, daycare personnel, medical personnel, student protective services personnel, and/or workers in homeless shelters. Usually, a case manager or transition specialist gives the parent rights manual to the parent.

Parents and guardians need to be advised of their rights in their native language or mode of communication. While most state education agencies have parent rights manuals developed in at least two languages

(English and Spanish), translators must be used to explain parent rights to those parents who use another language. It should be noted, though, that this process has become overwhelming, particularly for many large, urban school districts. It is not unusual for students and parents within a given school zone to speak hundreds of different languages/dialects and represent that many different cultures.

In addition, the law is clear in its intent—it is not enough to simply hand parents a booklet explaining rights that they may or may not be able to read, much less understand; it is crucial that they really do understand, and a professional must use parent-friendly language to make these rights clear.

In the comprehensive assessment process, the parent or guardian has the right to:

- Receive written notice (in native language) before the school assesses the student
- Receive information about the abilities, skills, and knowledge that are to be assessed
- Give or refuse consent for that assessment
- Inspect and review all assessment records before the IEP meeting
- Expect that the assessment information will be considered at the IEP meeting
- Expect that tests and other assessment materials will be administered in the form of communication that will yield accurate results
- Expect that no single procedure will be used as the sole basis for admission, placement, or IEP decisions
- Seek one external assessment, an independent educational evaluation, within reason, at the school district's expense, if the parent or guardian disagrees with the results of the evaluation
- Request mediation or a due process hearing if agreement on assessment procedures or results cannot be reached

In regard to the IEP meeting, the parent or guardian also has the right to:

- Receive written notice of the IEP meeting before the meeting that explains the purpose, time, and location of the meeting and who will attend

- Receive written notice of what the school proposes for the student as a result of the meeting
- Have the IEP meeting scheduled at a time that is convenient for the parent or guardian and the school. It is considered best practice for the school administrator to make every effort to schedule at a time when both parents, or a parent and grandparent, can attend the meeting together. (If the parent or guardian is unable to attend, the school must contact the parent or guardian via a visiting teacher or personal conference.)
- Have an interpreter present if the parent or guardian is deaf and/or uses a language other than English
- Bring others to the meeting for support or advocacy
- Be an active and important participant in the IEP meeting and discuss any service the parent or guardian thinks the student needs
- Have the meeting reconvened at a later date if the parent or guardian disagrees with the recommendations of the committee
- Seek judicial intervention (due process) if the parent or guardian and school continue to disagree regarding the student's assessment, placement, or services
- Obtain an independent evaluation at public expense and to know where it may be obtained. For example, if the parent disagrees with the assessment report provided by the district's adapted physical educator, the parent may request an independent assessment.
- A written notice at a reasonable time before the school proposes and changes identification, evaluation, or educational placement
- An impartial hearing officer from the state education agency
- Be accompanied and advised by counsel and/or individuals with special knowledge or training with respect to students with disabilities
- Appeal if aggrieved by the findings and decisions made in the hearing

In order for the IEP to be a living, breathing document that ensures educational progress and specifies the focus of the education program, it must be reviewed consistently. The law requires that this be done at least annually, or more frequently, if necessary.

Parents must also be informed about the educational progress of their children, at least as often as are parents of children without disabilities, particularly as the information relates to progress in the general curriculum.

This is particularly important for the general physical educator, who is usually expected to provide a report card or progress report every 6 weeks for all the students he or she teaches. If the parents of children without disabilities get a physical education progress report every 6 weeks, the parents of children with disabilities must also receive a progress report every 6 weeks.

Attendance at IEP meetings may be difficult for some parents; however, it is important to empathize with the parents and work with them to ensure they are active participants in the meeting. Consider some of the reasons parents of a student may not attend or participate in the IEP meeting (see **Table 4-7**). Understanding these reasons helps identify strategies for increasing the likelihood the parents will participate. Parents of a learner with a disability may miss the IEP meeting, or fail to participate actively, if present, for a number of reasons.

TABLE 4-7   Obstacles to Parental Attendance at or Participation in the IEP Meeting

- The parent may be in one of several stages of the grief cycle, which makes it difficult, if not impossible, to address his or her student's specific education needs.
- The parent is overwhelmed by the educational system and chooses to avoid interacting with professionals.
- The parent, despite repeated attempts at notification, is unaware of the meeting. Difficulty notifying parents is typical in non-English-speaking families. It is also typical if parents are illiterate. Difficulty with notification is a particular issue with homeless families; as a rule, they are so transient it is difficult to maintain contact over the period of time required to complete the evaluation and/or paperwork.
- The parent is unable to attend the IEP meeting at the time it is scheduled. A constantly changing work schedule may be one reason for this problem. This is particularly true of migrant farm workers and other members of a temporary workforce.
- The parent cannot find transportation to the meeting site.
- The parent is unable to find a babysitter and is hesitant to take other, younger students to the meeting.
- The parent's cultural background is such that he or she feels obligated to accept the decisions of the professionals involved; as such, the parent feels as if he or she has no input of value.
- The parent may have serious personal problems, developmental disabilities, or emotional disturbances, drug-related or otherwise, that preclude participation, without careful assistance, in the IEP process.

To enhance parent participation in the IEP meeting, the climate of the meeting must be parent-friendly. Following are some specific strategies for ensuring this.

DUTIES OF THE PROFESSIONALS

- Emphasize the positive. All parents want to hear good reports about their child; it is difficult for any parent to be bombarded by what their child cannot do.
- Use parent-friendly language. Explain assessment results and discuss goals and objectives without professional jargon or acronyms. The parents will be better able to make good judgments if they understand what is said.
- Use a parent's exact words, describing the IEP goal. There is nothing more enabling for parents than having their thoughts and words embraced. The other bonus is that the parents will be much more likely to encourage their child to accomplish a goal they have understood and articulated.
- If possible, use audiovisual technology to share information with parents about their child. If it is true that a picture is worth a thousand words, a videotape of the child performing a movement activity may be worth a million words.
- Relate to common experiences whenever possible to enhance communication. The physical educator is in a particularly good position to develop rapport with the parent because most parents can identify with movement, play, leisure, and recreation experiences more readily than with a specific academic curriculum.
- Talk directly to the parent and not to the other professionals at the meeting. This is particularly important if there is an interpreter. Look at the parent and not at the interpreter.
- Listen to the parents. Body language and facial expressions must reflect openness to their thoughts and feelings.

Encouraging and Maximizing Student Participation in the IEP Process

If at all possible, the student should be involved in the IEP meeting. In actuality, only students with the most severe and profound disabilities would have difficulty participating in some way. After all, it is the student's performance that is being reviewed and the student's plan that is being discussed and developed. Student involvement in the IEP development process has resulted in an increase in academic achievement.[4] However, in a study analyzing IEP meetings that involved students, it was found that students participated in the meeting 3% of the time, even though many of the special educators in the meeting estimated the student participated "a lot."[15] The largest barrier to student participation in the IEP meeting is a lack of training in self-representation. Strategies for training students for participation in the IEP meeting include verbal rehearsal, role-playing, instructional videos, and verbal, visual, and physical prompts.[15] Self-directed IEP meetings, in which the student is trained in how to direct his or her own IEP meeting, can significantly increase student active engagement, expression of interests and transition desires, identification of skills and limits, and memory of IEP goals.[11, 14]

Many of the strategies for making the parent feel like a vital part of the IEP process can also make the student feel like a vital part of the IEP process. For example, professionals must make eye contact with the student while talking, instead of looking at other professionals in the room. In addition, the following are strategies for getting students' input concerning their goals and objectives. Before the IEP meeting:

1. Ask the middle or high school student to meet with his or her teachers and therapists to discuss and write goals/objectives that the student believes will be challenging but attainable. If writing is difficult, the student can record his or her goals and objectives on a tape recorder. Then the student will be prepared with input for the IEP meeting.
2. Ask the elementary school student to express his or her desires regarding goals or objectives in the following ways:
   a. Tell what he or she would like to learn to do.
   b. Draw a hero and describe the qualities he or she likes in that hero.
   c. Describe the things a friend does that he or she would like to be able to do. Use a tape recorder or allow the student to make a magazine collage representing his or her particular skills, abilities, and interests.
   d. Tell a story about his or her favorite character and describe the things the character does that he or she would like to do.
   e. Make a list of the things he or she does best.
   f. Describe the things he or she wants to do when he or she grows up.

Finally, and perhaps most important, professionals cannot hesitate to include goals and objectives in the student's language on the IEP. It will help the student and his or her parents/guardians feel intricately involved in the process. If the student does not attend the IEP meeting, the school must take other steps to ensure that the student's preferences and interests are carefully considered.

SUMMARY

The process of designing individualized education programs (IEPs) in physical education for the student with a disability is a basic component of effective programming. The role of the parents in this process has been heightened. In addition, there has been an increased emphasis on the provision of services in the general curriculum and program.

The type of physical education program developed for each student will depend on the student's identified needs. After the student has been assessed to determine specific levels of present performance and needs, the IEP/multidisciplinary team determines goals. Not later than age 16 years, an individual transition plan (ITP) must be developed that ensures the student's ability to function in a community when leaving the school setting.

REVIEW QUESTIONS

1. Explain the importance of and difference between the IEP and ITP.
2. Explain the role of the adapted physical educator and physical educator in the development and implementation of the IEP and ITP.
3. How can the physical educator or adapted physical educator engage a parent or a student in an IEP/multidisciplinary team meeting?
4. Describe a physical education program that promotes transition for students with disabilities.

REFERENCES

1. *Alamo Heights v. State Board of Education*, 790 F 2d 1153 (5th Cir 1986).
2. American Occupational Therapy Association. (2014). Framework: Domain and practice. 3rd ed. *The American Journal of Occupational Therapy*, 68, 1–48.
3. American Occupational Therapy Association. (2010). Occupational therapy in school settings. Retrieved from www.aota.org
4. Barnard, B., & Lechtenberger, D. (2010). Student IEP participation and academic achievement across time. *Remedial and Special Education*, 31, 343–349.

5. Clark, G. (2001). Children often overlooked for occupational therapy services in educational settings. *School System Special Interest Section Quarterly, American Occupational Therapy Association, 8,* 1–3.

6. Disability Rights Network of Pennsylvania. (2008). *Assistive technology for persons with disabilities: An overview.* Retrieved December 15, 2009, from http://drnpa.org/File/publications/assistive-technology-for-persons-with -disabilities—an-overview.pdf

7. *Doug C. v. Hawaii.* US Court of Appeals. 13 June 2013. Print.

8. Edelen-Smith, P. (1995). Eight elements to guide goal determination for IEPs. *Intervent School Clin, 30,* 297–301.

9. Espin, C., et al. (1998). Individualized education programs in resource and inclusive settings: How "individualized" are they? *J Special Ed, 33,* 164–174.

10. National Consortium for Physical Education and Recreation for Individuals with Disabilities, Kelly, L. (Editor). (2006). *Adapted physical education national standards.* Champaign, IL: Human Kinetics.

11. Johnson, D. R., & Sharpe, N. M. (2000). Issues influencing the future of transition programs and services in the United States, *National Transition Network, Institute on Community Integration, University of Minnesota,* 31–48.

12. Lavay, B., French, R., & Henderson, H. (2007). A practical plan for managing the behavior of students with disabilities in general physical education. *Journal of Physical Education, Recreation & Dance, 78*(2), 42–48.

13. Lytle, R., Lavay, B., Robinson, N., & Huettig, C. (2003). Teaching collaboration and consultation skills to preservice adapted physical education teachers. *JOPERD, 74,* 41–43.

14. Martin, J., Van Dycke, J., Christensen, W., & Greene, B. (2006). Increasing student participation in IEP meetings: Establishing the self-directed IEP as an evidenced-based practice. *Exceptional Children, 72*(3), 299–316.

15. Martin, J. E., Van Dycke, J. L., Greene, B. A., Gardner, J. E., Christensen, W. R., Woods, L. L., & Lovett, D. L. (2006). Direct observation of teacher-directed IEP meetings: Establishing the need for student IEP meeting instruction. *Exceptional Children, 72*(2), 187–200.

16. Public Law 108–364. (2004). Assistive Technology Act of 2004. (H.R. 4278), 108th Congress of the United States.

17. Pyfer, J. personal communication, Fall 2015.

18. Quality Indicators for Assistive Technology Consortium. (2012). Quality indicators for assistive technology services with QIAT self-evaluation matrices. Retrieved from http://www.qiat.org

19. Regan, K. (2003). Using dialogue journals in the classroom. *Teaching Except Child, 36,* 36–41.

20. Shapiro, D., & Sayers, L.K. (2003). Who does what on the interdisciplinary team regarding physical education for children with disabilities? *Teaching Except Child, 35,* 32–38.

21. Shipley, K., & McAfee, J. (2016). *Assessment in speech-language pathology: A resource manual.* Boston, MA: Cengage Learning.
22. Technology—The great equalizer. (2003). *Today* (Council for Exceptional Children), *10*, 1, 5.
23. Tournaki, N., & Criscitello, E. (2003). Using peer tutoring as a successful part of behavior management. *Teaching Except Child, 36*, 22–29.
24. U.S. Department of Education, Office of Civil Rights. (2012). *Disability rights: Enforcement highlights.* Washington, D.C.
25. U.S. Department of Education: 34 CFR Parts 300 and 301: Assistance to states for the Education for Children with Disabilities and Preschool Grants for Children with Disabilities. *Federal Register.* August 14, 2006.
26. Walsh, J. (1998). *How to propose an IEP, run an ARD, develop a BIP, and comply with procedural safeguards.* Austin, TX: Walsh, Anderson, Brown, Schulze & Aldridge, P.C.

CHAPTER 5

Teaching to Meet Learners' Needs

- Recognize the differences between the top-down and the bottom-up teaching approaches.
- Discriminate between functional and sport skills.
- Give an example of a content analysis.
- Identify three functional adaptations a physical educator could make to accommodate students with disabilities.
- Explain programmed physical education instruction.

There is no question about the importance of motor development. In addition to its being a critical component of movement efficiency, it is also widely believed to underlie perceptual, cognitive, and affective function.[3] How infants' bodies grow and change has been widely studied in this country since 1920. From that time through the 1940s, child development specialists carefully observed and documented hundreds of motor milestones normally developing children demonstrate during their first few years of life. Those observations became the basis for the majority of motor development screening instruments available to us today. Such instruments are frequently used to determine whether an infant is progressing neurologically at the expected rate because motor milestones are among the first visible indicators of central nervous system maturation.[10]

However, even though motor development screening instruments can be used to identify where a child is performing in comparison with normal expectations, such instruments do not provide information indicating what is interfering with delayed development. That information must be predicted from formal sensory input, sensory integration or psychological tests developed specifically for those purposes, or informal clues provided by the child.

Developmental psychologists, movement scientists, neuroscientists, and others are joining forces to try to build on the work of the early developmentalists to better understand the processes by which infants and children gain mastery over their bodies. Careful studies are being conducted to determine what aspects of nature and nurture are critical for maximal motor development. Advanced technology is being used to identify and monitor factors that impact favorably on a child's motor competence.

Physical educators who teach individuals with disabilities agree that their primary goal is to facilitate the development of purposeful skills for each student. There are, however, a variety of approaches to programming from which physical educators can select. They range from general physical education activities believed to benefit all children, regardless of degree of function, to developmentally sequenced activities that serve as building blocks of motor development, to activities that enhance very specific skills.

Which approach a physical educator selects depends on the amount of time available, the age and readiness level of the students, the capabilities of the teacher, and the number of individuals available to assist the teacher. In this chapter, the levels of function that contribute to sport and functional skills, ways to facilitate development at each of those levels, and adaptations that can be made to accommodate individuals with differing abilities will be addressed.

Levels of Motor Function

The ultimate goal of physical education for individuals with disabilities is to equip them with motor skills that contribute to independent living. To plan these programs systematically, it is desirable to distinguish clearly the levels of function that contribute to the acquisition of the many specific sport skills.

Each of these levels makes a unique contribution to independent functioning: (1) basic neurological building blocks, (2) integration processes, (3) functional skills, and (4) sport and recreational skills (see **Table 5-1**). The physical educator, who understands the interrelatedness of these levels

TABLE 5-1   Motor Development Model

Motor Output		
Sport Skills		
Dribbling, shooting, rebounding, spiking, volleying, serving, trapping, pitching, tumbling, punting, diving, skiing, batting		
Functional Skills		
Locomotor	**Object Control**	
Rolling, crawling, walking, running, hopping, jumping, sliding, galloping,	Kicking, catching, throwing, striking, bouncing	
Integration Processes		
Perceptual Motor	**Physical Fitness**	**Motor Fitness**
Balance	Strength	Agility
Laterality	Flexibility	Power
Spatial awareness	Muscular endurance	Speed
Ocular-motor control	Cardiovascular endurance	Coordination
Cross-lateral integration		
Body image		
Basic Neurological Building Blocks		
Primitive reflexes		
Postural/equilibrium reflexes		
Vestibular, kinesthetic, refractive and orthoptic vision, tactile		

and can select intervention activities to facilitate functioning at any given level, depending on a student's needs, will realize success.

The functioning of the basic neurological building blocks depends on the integrity and operation of the sensory input systems. These systems include primitive and equilibrium reflexes, vestibular, kinesthetic, refractive and orthoptic vision, and tactile. Before information can reach the central nervous system for processing, these systems must be intact and functional. The physical educator who automatically assumes these systems are functioning and that adequate stimulation is reaching the central nervous system disregards an important component of purposeful movement.

The second level of functioning is the integration processes. Like the basic neurological building blocks, these prerequisites enhance the acquisition of skill. If the basic neurological building blocks are functioning, integration processes develop concurrently with quality movement experiences. The integration processes include the perceptual-motor, physical fitness, and motor fitness categories. Examples of perceptual-motor abilities are balance, cross-lateral integration, laterality, directionality, body image, and spatial awareness. Physical fitness prerequisites are muscular strength, flexibility, muscular endurance, and cardiovascular endurance. Motor fitness consists of power, agility, speed, and motor coordination.

The uppermost levels of motor development are functional and sport and recreation skills. Skills are motor behaviors that are specific to either functional living or a sport or recreational activity. Examples of functional skills are the basic locomotor skills, such as walking, running, hopping, and skipping, and the object-control skills, such as throwing, bouncing, and kicking. Sport and recreational skills include shooting a basketball, serving a tennis ball, skiing, and trapping a soccer ball. Functional skills, such as walking and running, usually emerge as the central nervous system prerequisite components mature. Proficiency at specific individual and team sport skills is usually developed through repetitious practice of the skill itself.

Incidental Versus Planned Learning

Most individuals learn from everyday interaction with the environment. This is particularly true if the environment is varied and the learner possesses all the prerequisites needed to convert environmental stimulation into motor patterns. This is known as *incidental learning*. The more ready an individual is (i.e., the more developed the neurological, cognitive, and motor functions are), the more that can be gained from interaction with the environment. Conversely, the fewer the number of developed prerequisites, the less a person gains from environmental exchanges.

An individual with a disability is often denied opportunities to interact with varied environments. This is a hindrance because, for the central nervous system to develop normally, a wide variety of stimulation is necessary.[12] Thus, attempts to protect these children from interaction with the environment often delay their development. Because of these delays, learners with disabilities do not always gain as much from incidental learning, as do other learners.

Teachers of children with disabilities must be particularly sensitive to the needs of their students. Until a teacher determines the needs of students, appropriate intervention strategies cannot be selected. The physical education teacher must ensure that each student's motor learning improves. The general approach of providing a wide variety of activities to all students gives no assurance that motor learning will result. It is true that the children may have fun and could gain some physical fitness from their activities; however, the students will not make the same gains as would be possible if activities were selected specifically to meet the needs of the learners. There are many activities available that are enjoyable for all children in a class that meet the needs of individual learners. The effective teacher will select those activities that benefit all of the children in his or her class.

Facilitating Skill Development

Children and youth with disabilities frequently demonstrate physical and motor development lags. As a result, they often have difficulty learning chronologically age-appropriate skills. When developmental deficits become apparent, decisions about how to address the deficits have to be made. Questions that need to be answered include whether it is necessary to modify the teaching strategy used or will modifications/adaptations best accommodate the student's needs. In the following sections, two teaching techniques and several functional adaptations that are effective for accommodating the student with special needs will be presented.

TEACH SPECIFIC SKILLS: TOP-DOWN

Teaching the skill directly is known as using the task-specific approach. Advocates of this approach stress what skills an individual will need for productive independence as an adult in the community where he or she lives. In the case of the physical educator, the targeted behaviors focus on the functional and recreational sports skills that an individual would have an opportunity to participate in as an adult in the community. The top-down approach places emphasis on the end of the skill sequence, the final motor countdown as an adult, rather than what is to be taught next. When using the top-down approach, it is necessary to monitor carefully the progress of learners with disabilities as they move from elementary to middle schools to high schools and then into adult life. To ensure that functional skills are being taught, it is necessary to gather information about the lesser restrictive environments the individual will function in as an adult. This approach emphasizes teaching skills and behaviors that are absolutely necessary for a person to function in a community environment.

To determine which skills an individual has in relation to skills that will be needed for ultimate functioning in the community requires the completion of an ecological inventory (community-based assessment). An ecological inventory provides critical information about current and future school and community environments. Selecting age-appropriate skills tends to maximize the normalization process during the life of a person with a disability. When using ecological assessment data, a major departure from traditional procedures is the need to take students into the community to do part of the instruction. This enables the student to practice the skills in a natural setting.

When using a task analysis approach to assess students' repertoires, the educator can determine which motor skills are present and which are yet to be learned. Once the deficient skills are determined, they are prioritized and analyzed to determine which portions have not yet been mastered, and the specific missing components are taught using a direct teaching method.

In general, there are two types of task analysis, content analysis of discrete tasks and content analysis of continuous skills. Examples of each appear in **Table 5-2**. An example of a content analysis of a discrete task is given in **Table 5-3**, and an example of a content analysis of continuous skills is presented in **Table 5-4**. Once a task analysis is completed and the missing

TABLE 5-2   Task Analyses and Educational Performance

Type of Analysis	Type of Task	Examples
Content analysis of discrete tasks	Discrete tasks broken down into parts that make up the entire task	Dressing, lay-up shot in basketball
Content analysis of continuous skills	Continuous task broken down into components that contribute to the skill	Running, jumping, throwing

TABLE 5-3   Content Analysis of the Discrete Task of Executing a Lay-Up Shot in Basketball

1. Bounces a basketball with one hand
2. Bounces a basketball at waist height with one hand
3. Runs while bouncing a basketball at waist height
4. Takes a short step and jumps vertically off the foot opposite the shooting hand
5. Times the jump to occur just before the body reaches the area under the basket
6. Releases the ball at the top of the jump
7. Directs the ball to a point on the backboard that will permit the ball to rebound from the backboard into the basket
8. Controls the body when coming down from the jump

TABLE 5-4   Content Analysis of the Continuous Task of Running

Characteristics of Proficient Hopping
• Balance effectively on the support foot
• Support leg extends fully at take-off and flexes at landing
• The thigh of the nonsupport leg pumps back and forth with the hop
• Arms pump in opposition to the swing leg's pendular motion
• Forward lean of the body

Courtesy of Gallahue, D. L., Ozmun, J. C., & Goodway, J. D. (2012). *Understanding Motor Development.* New York, NY: McGraw-Hill.

components are identified, a person using a task-specific top-down teaching approach would either teach each of the components found to be lacking or teach the entire movement from beginning to end.

Task analyses can be very formal or quite informal. Tests that are content-referenced are truly sets of analyzed tasks because they provide the components of each task in the test. However, frequently the physical educator relies on observation of performance to determine what parts of the task are inefficient. For example, if the physical educator observes that the student is performing all parts of the basketball lay-up task correctly except timing the jump to occur just before the body reaches the area under the basket and directing the ball to the correct point on the backboard, those are the two components that are selected and taught directly.

To correct the jump timing problem, it might be necessary to mark an area on the floor where the jump should be executed for a right-hand lay-up. The student practices approaching the mark and landing on it consistently with the left foot. When that movement becomes habitual, the student practices the approach and adds a jump off the left foot when reaching the mark on the floor. Then, to direct the student's attention to the correct place to rebound the ball, an area could be marked on the backboard. The student then practices the correct approach, jump, and striking the outlined area on the backboard with the ball in one continuous motion. Minor adjustments may need to be added to modify the amount of force the student uses when releasing the ball.

Once a skill is learned, it should be practiced under a variety of conditions to ensure the learner's ability to use the skill in different situations and environments. Conditions that can be modified include time (fast/slow, even/uneven), space (straight/circular/zig-zag, high/low, alone/with others, inside/outside), force (light/heavy, soft/hard), and flow (synchronized/unsynchronized, run/walk/hop, twist/turn).

The task-specific top-down approach is probably the most realistic and expedient type to use with individuals with severe disabilities and higher-functioning individuals in middle school and beyond, but it may be inappropriate for younger children with disabilities. The essential question to ask when trying to decide whether to use this approach is, "How much time is available?" Facilitating basic neurological building blocks and integration processes prior to teaching specific skills takes time, perhaps years. When the individual with a disability is older and severely involved and there is a limited amount of time available to develop functional skills needed to live in a natural environment, the task-specific approach is the most efficient intervention strategy.

ELIMINATE DEFICIENCIES: BOTTOM-UP

Motor development is a progressive process. For each of us to learn to move efficiently, we must first be able to take environmental information into the central nervous system. Then it must be processed or integrated, so that it can be used to direct movement patterns and skills. Only after the information is received and processed can the brain direct the muscles to work. If anything goes wrong before the information reaches the muscles, movement is inefficient or nonexistent. Advocates of the developmental approach agree that the ultimate goal of education is to produce productive adults who can function independently in their communities. To achieve this goal, the developmentalist would intervene in a child's life as early as possible to determine whether age-appropriate basic building blocks, integration processes, and skills were functional. If any age-appropriate developmental blocks were found to be deficient when the child was tested, then the developmentalist would select activities to promote development of the deficient areas. Thus, if a child were found to have a severe orthoptic (eye alignment) problem that would interfere with eye-hand coordination development, the child would be referred to a visual behavioral specialist for correction of the problem. If a child demonstrated failure to develop equilibrium reactions and/or adequate vestibular (inner ear) function, which are critical for balance development, activities to promote development in those areas would be prescribed.

The developmental approach can be considered a bottom-up teaching strategy because the evaluator tries to determine the lowest level of motor function and correct that problem before addressing specific skills (review Table 5-1). Once the developmentalist determines which basic neurological building blocks and integration components appear to be poorly developed, activities that promote the functioning of each area found to be lacking are selected. The rationale is to ensure that the supporting building blocks and integration processes are fully functioning, so that skill development will be facilitated.

In the following section, each of the basic neurological building blocks and perceptual motor integration processes will be described. Examples

are provided to demonstrate what it may look like if the systems are not fully developed, and individual activities that promote development will be suggested.

BASIC NEUROLOGICAL BUILDING BLOCKS

The primitive reflexes and the vestibular, visual, kinesthetic, tactile, and auditory systems, as well as the equilibrium reflexes, are considered basic input systems because sensations arising from these systems' receptors provide the basic "stuff" from which integration processes and motor skills are built. These systems normally develop during the first 5 years of life. After they are functioning, perceptual-motor, physical fitness, motor fitness, and motor skill development occurs. Should any one or a combination of these systems fail to develop fully, all motor development is delayed and/or interfered with in some way.[1] For this reason, it is imperative to identify and remediate basic input system delays as early in life as possible. The point at which it becomes too late to attempt to facilitate development of any of these systems is not really known. However, if such delays are still present at age 12 years, the educator's time might better be spent teaching the child to accommodate to the delay. See **Table 5-5** for an informal screening test that can be used to identify sensory input delays.

Reflexes

Reflexes are innate responses that all typically developing children are born with (see **Table 5-6**). Reflexes that affect movement are of interest to the physical educator because students whose reflex maturation is delayed have inefficient movement patterns. In general, there is a series of reflexes that should appear and disappear during the first year of life. These early (primitive) reflexes are layered over by (integrated into) voluntary movement patterns. As a child begins to move voluntarily, a different set of reflexes appears. These later automatic patterns are equilibrium or postural reflexes. They help maintain upright posture and should remain with us throughout life.

TABLE 5-5   Sensory Input Systems Screening Test

Reflex Test Items—Check Pass or Fail	Pass	Fail
1. Tonic labyrinthine supine—(TLS) While lying on back, can bend knees to chest, wrap arms around knees, and touch head to knees. Child should be able to hold position for 10 seconds.		
2. Tonic labyrinthine prone—(TLP) While lying facedown on mat with arms at side, child can lift head and upper body and hold off mat for 5 seconds.		
3. Positive support reaction—(PSR) Child is able to jump into air and, on landing, flex ankles, knees, and hips while maintaining balance for 5 seconds.		
4. Equilibrium reactions When placed on a tilt board, child will move hands out to side and maintain balance for 3 seconds when the board is suddenly tipped 15 degrees to one side and then to the other side (check each side independently). Check child in each of these positions: a. Seated, start with hands in lap—move right. b. Seated, start with hands in lap—move left. c. On two knees, start with hands on hips—move right. d. On two knees, start with hands on hips—move left. Place child on all fours on tilt board and tip board 15 degrees to one side and then to the other. Child can maintain "all fours" position while holding head in a neutral position. e. When tipped to right. f. When tipped to left.		

Vestibular Test Items—Check Pass or Fail

1. Seat child in a desk chair that can be rotated 360 degrees. Have child rest hands in lap or on arms of chair. Child should tip head down slightly (30 degrees). Turn chair 10 complete turns in 20 seconds (1 complete rotation every 2 seconds). Stop chair and watch child's eyes. Child's eyes should flick back and forth for 7 to 13 seconds. After a 2-minute rest, repeat turning procedure in opposite direction. Check eye movement again.

   a. Turn to right.

   b. Turn to left.

(continues)

TABLE 5-5   Sensory Input Systems Screening Test *(Continued)*

Reflex Test Items—Check Pass or Fail	Pass	Fail

Fixation (Ocular Control)—Check Pass or Fail

1. Child should sit in a chair facing a seated evaluator. Child can fixate with both eyes on an object held 18 inches in front of the nose at eye level for 10 seconds.

2. Child should sit in a chair facing a seated evaluator. Cover child's left eye with your hand or a card. Child can fixate with the right eye on an object held 18 inches in front of the nose at eye level for 10 seconds.

3. Child should sit in a chair facing a seated evaluator. Cover child's right eye with your hand or a card. Child can fixate with the left eye on an object held 18 inches in front of the nose at eye level for 10 seconds.

NOTE: Any tendency to turn the head to one side or to blink excessively, or for the eyes to water, could be an indication that the child needs to be referred to a visual developmental specialist for a refractive and orthoptic visual exam.

Ocular Alignment (Depth Perception)—Check Pass or Fail

NOTE: On all of the following items start with the child looking at the object with both eyes. Then cover 1 eye and begin your observation.

1. Child is seated in a chair facing a seated evaluator. Child can fixate on an object held 18 inches in front of the nose at eye level without moving the right eye as left eye is covered for 3 seconds. (Note whether the right eye moves and in what direction.)

2. Child is seated in a chair facing a seated evaluator. Child can fixate on an object held 18 inches in front of the nose at eye level without moving the left eye as the right eye is covered for 3 seconds. (Note whether the left eye moves and in what direction.)

Convergence-Divergence Ocular Control—Check Pass or Fail

1. Child is seated in a chair facing a seated evaluator. Child can visually follow with both eyes an object moved slowly from 18 inches directly in front of the nose (eye level), to 4 inches from the eyes (midpoint), and back to 18 inches. (Note whether the eyes move equally without jerking.)

Visual Tracking—Check Pass or Fail

1. Child is seated in a chair facing a seated evaluator. Child can visually pursue with both eyes without moving the head an object held 18 inches from the eyes as the object is moved in the following patterns:

   a. A square (12-inch sides)

   b. A circle (8- to 10-inch diameter)

   c. An *X* (10-inch lines)

   d. A horizontal line (12 inches)

TABLE 5-5 *Sensory Input Systems Screening Test* (*Continued*)

Reflex Test Items—Check Pass or Fail	Pass	Fail

2. Child is seated in a chair, with the left eye covered, facing a seated evaluator. Child can visually pursue with the right eye without moving the head an object held 18 inches from the eyes as the object is moved in the following patterns:
   a. A square (12-inch sides)
   b. A circle (8- to 10-inch diameter)
   c. An **X** (10-inch lines)
   d. A horizontal line (12 inches)
3. Child is seated in a chair, with the right eye covered, facing a seated evaluator. Child can visually pursue with the left eye without moving the head an object held 18 inches from the eyes as the object is moved in the following patterns:
   a. A square (12-inch sides)
   b. A circle (8- to 10-inch diameter)
   c. An **X** (10-inch lines)
   d. A horizontal line (12 inches)

NOTE: During all tracking tasks, note any tendency for the eyes to (1) jump when the object moves across the midline of the body, (2) jump ahead of the object, (3) jerk while pursuing the object, (4) water, or (5) blink excessively. The watering and/or excessive blinking could be an indicator of visual stress, and such cases should be referred to a visual developmental specialist for a refractive and orthoptic visual exam.

Kinesthesis—Check Pass or Fail

1. Can touch finger to nose 3 times in alternating succession with index fingers while eyes are closed. (Failure if the child misses the tip of the nose by more than 1 inch.)

Courtesy Jean L. Pyfer, Texas Woman's University, Denton, TX, and Robert Strauss, Trinity University, San Antonio, TX.

A child is considered developmentally delayed in reflex development if any of the following conditions exist:

1. The primitive reflexes do not appear during the first year of life.
2. The primitive reflexes appear at the normal time but do not disappear by the end of the first year.
3. The postural reflexes do not appear by the end of the first year of life.
4. Postural reflexes do not persist throughout life.

TABLE 5-6   Primitive and Postural Reflex Development

	Month												
Primitive Reflexes	0	1	2	3	4	5	6	7	8	9	10	11	12
Moro	X	X	X	X	X	X	X						
Startle								X	X	X	X		
Search	X	X	X	X	X	X	X	X	X	X	X	X	
Sucking	X	X	X	X									
Palmar-mental	X	X	X										
Palmar-mandi bular	X	X	X	X									
Palmar grasping	X	X	X	X	X								
Babinski	X	X	X	X									
Plantar grasp					X	X	X	X	X	X	X	X	X
Tonic neck	X	X	X	X	X	X	X						
Postural Reflex													
Labyrinthine righting			X	X	X	X	X						
Optical righting							X	X	X	X	X	X	X
Pull-up				X	X	X	X	X	X	X	X	X	X
Parachute and propping					X	X	X	X	X	X	X	X	X
Neck righting	X	X	X	X									
Body righting							X	X	X	X	X	X	X
Crawling	X	X	X	X									
Stepping	X	X	X	X	X								
Swimming	X	X	X	X	X								

From: Gallahue, D., Ozmun, J., & Goodway, J. (2012). *Understanding motor development* (6th ed). New York, NY: McGraw Hill.

Primitive Reflex

When the symmetrical tonic neck reflex is present, the upper limbs tend to flex and the lower limbs extend when the neck is flexed. If the neck is extended, the upper limbs extend and the lower limbs flex. If this reflex does not become fully integrated within the first year of life, the child will demonstrate the following:

1. Instead of using a cross pattern creep, the child may bunny hop both knees up to the hands.
2. If, while creeping, the child lowers the head, the arms will tend to collapse.
3. If, while creeping, the child lifts the head to look around, movement of the limbs ceases.

Activities that require the child to keep the arms extended while the head is flexed, and the arms flexed while the head is extended, will promote integration of this reflex. Examples of such activities include the following:

1. While balancing on hands and knees, look down between the legs; then look up at the ceiling. Keep the arms extended and the legs flexed.
2. With extended arms, push against a cage ball while looking down at the floor.
3. Practice doing standing push-ups against a wall while looking at the ceiling.
4. Do pull-ups (look up when pulling up, and look down when letting oneself down).

Postural/Equilibrium Reflexes

Equilibrium reactions help us maintain an upright position when the center of gravity is suddenly moved beyond the base of support. If the equilibrium/postural reactions are not fully developed, children fall down often, fall off chairs, and avoid vigorous running games.

Labyrinthine and optical righting reactions cause the head to move to an upright position when the body is suddenly tipped. Once the head rights itself, the body follows. Thus, these reflexes help us maintain an upright posture during a quick change of position. Without these reflexes, the child will fall down often during running and dodging games and even tend to avoid vigorous running games.

The labyrinthine reflexes are under control of the inner ear, whereas the optical righting reactions are primarily controlled by the eyes. Labyrinthine reflexes are facilitated when the head is moved in opposition to gravity. Any activity requiring the child to move the head in opposition to the pull of gravity will promote development of this reflex. Poorly developed optical righting reactions most frequently accompany orthoptic visual problems (poor depth perception). Once the depth perception problem is corrected, the optical righting reactions begin to appear.

The body righting reflex enables segmental rotation of the trunk and hips when the head is turned. As a result of this segmental turning, children can maintain good postural alignment and maintenance of body positions. Without it, for example, when doing a log roll, the child will tend to turn the knees, then the hips, and then the shoulders. To promote development of the body righting reflex, the child should practice turning the head first, then the shoulders, followed by the hips. The child should start slowly and then increase the speed from both a standing position and a back-lying position.

Almost all of these types of equilibrium reactions are the result of the stimulation of muscle spindles and/or the Golgi tendon apparatus. Both muscle spindle and Golgi tendon apparatus reactions result from sudden stretch (or contraction) of the muscles and tendons. To promote these postural/equilibrium reactions, the child should participate in activities such as the following, which place sudden stretch (or contracture) on the muscles and tendons:

1. Bouncing on an air mat while lying down, balancing on all fours, or balancing on the knees
2. Tug of war
3. Scooter activities with a partner pulling or pushing the child who is seated on the scooter

Vestibular System

The vestibular receiving mechanism is located in the semicircular canals of the inner ear. As the body moves, sensory impulses from the vestibular system are sent to the cerebellum and to the brainstem. From these two areas, information about the position of the head is sent to the extraocular muscles of the eye, to the somatosensory strip in the cerebral cortex, to the stomach, to the cerebellum, and down the spinal cord. Accurate information from this mechanism is needed to help position the eyes and to maintain static and dynamic balance. When maturation of the system is delayed, students may demonstrate the following problems:

1. Inability to balance on one foot (with the eyes closed)
2. Inability to walk a balance beam without watching the feet
3. Inability to walk heel-to-toe
4. Inefficient walking and running patterns
5. Delays in ability to hop and to skip

Concentrated activities to remediate balance problems that result from poor vestibular function should be administered by someone trained in observing the responses of such a child. However, some activities can be done in fun, nonthreatening ways in a physical education class or on a playground with the supervision of parents or teachers.

Anyone who uses vestibular stimulation activities with children should observe closely for signs of sweating, paleness, flushing of the face, nausea, and loss of consciousness. These are all indications that the activities should be stopped immediately. Spinning activities should not be used with children prone to having seizures.

The following vestibular stimulation activities should be nonthreatening to most children:

1. Log roll on a mat, changing directions frequently.
2. While prone on a scooter, spin by crossing hand-over-hand; stop and change direction.
3. Lie on a blanket and roll self up and then unroll.
4. Play on spinning playground equipment.

Kinesthetic System

The kinesthetic receptors are specialized proprioceptors located in the joints, muscles, and tendons throughout the body. Information from the kinesthetic receptors informs the central nervous system about the position of the limbs in space. As these joint receptors fire, sensory impulses are sent to the brain and are recorded as spatial maps. As the kinesthetic system becomes more developed, judgment about the rate, amount, and amplitude of motion needed to perform a task improves. Refined movement is not possible without kinesthetic awareness. Possible signs of developmental delays of the kinesthetic system are

1. Inability to move a body part on command without assistance
2. No awareness of the position of body parts in space
3. Messy handwriting
4. Poor skill in sports that require a "touch," such as golf ball putting, basketball shooting, and bowling

Activities to promote kinesthetic function include any activities that increase tension on the joints, muscles, and tendons. Some activities that have proven useful in promoting kinesthetic function are:

1. Games involving pushing (or kicking) a large cage ball
2. Lying prone on a scooter, holding onto a rope, and being pulled by a partner
3. Using the hands and feet to propel oneself while seated on a gym scooter
4. Doing any type of activity while wearing wrist and/or ankle weights

Visual System

Both refractive and orthoptic vision are important for efficient motor performance. Refractive vision is the process by which the light rays are bent as they enter the eyes. When light rays are bent precisely, vision is sharpest and clearest. Individuals who have poor refractive vision are said to be nearsighted (myopic) or farsighted (hyperopic) or have astigmatism. The following are demonstrated by children with refractive visual problems:

1. Tendency to squint
2. Tendency to rub the eyes frequently
3. Redness of the eyes

Orthoptic vision refers to the ability to use the extraocular muscles of the eyes in unison. When the extraocular muscles are balanced, images entering each eye strike each retina at precisely the same point, so that the images transmitted to the visual center of the brain match. The closer the match of the images from the eye, the better the depth perception. The greater the discrepancy between the two images that reach the visual center, the poorer the depth perception. Children with poor orthoptic vision (poor depth perception) demonstrate the following:

1. Turning the head when catching a ball
2. Inability to catch a ball or a tendency to scoop the ball into the arms
3. Tendency to kick a ball off center or miss it entirely
4. Persisting to ascend and descend stairs one at a time
5. Avoidance of climbing apparatus

The physical educator is not trained to test for or correct refractive and orthoptic visual problems. However, a screening test can be administered by a vision specialist and used to determine whether the possibility of a serious orthoptic (depth perception) problem exists. Individuals who fail the ocular alignment portion of a screening test should be professionally evaluated by a behavioral visual specialist (optometrist or ophthalmologist who has specialized training in orthoptics). Either an optometrist or an ophthalmologist should evaluate students suspected of having refractive vision problems.

Tactile System

The tactile receptors are located throughout the body and respond to stimulation of body surfaces. Some of the receptors lie close to the surface of the body; others are located more deeply. A well-functioning tactile system is needed for an individual to know where the body ends and space begins and to be able to discriminate tactually among pressure, texture, and size. Children who are tactile-defensive are believed to have difficulty processing sensory input from tactile receptors. Behaviors demonstrated by the child who is tactile-defensive may include:

1. Low tolerance for touch (unless the person doing the touching is in the visual field of the student)
2. Avoidance of activities requiring prolonged touch, such as wrestling or hugging

3. Avoidance of toweling down after a shower or bath unless it is done in a vigorous fashion
4. Tendency to curl fingers and toes when creeping

Activities believed to stimulate the tactile system and promote sensory input processing should begin with coarse textures and progress (over time) toward finer texture stimulation. A sequence of such activities follows:

1. Present the child with a variety of textured articles (nets, pot scrubbers, bath brushes). Have the child select an article and rub it on his or her face, arms, and legs. (A child who is tactile-defensive will usually select the coarsest textures to use for this activity.)
2. Using an old badminton net, play "capture me" while crawling around on a mat. The teacher should toss the net over the child as the child tries to crawl from one end of the mat to the other. When the child has been captured, rub the net over exposed parts of the body as the child struggles to escape. Repeat the activity with the child chasing and capturing the teacher.
3. Construct an obstacle course with several stations where the child must go through hanging textures (strips of inner tube, sections of rope) and/or squeeze through tight places.
4. Using a movement exploration teaching approach, have the students find various textures in the gym to rub a point or patch against (e.g., rough, smooth, wavy).

PERCEPTUAL MOTOR PROCESSES

Integration processes, including perceptual motor, emerge after sensory input systems begin to stabilize, usually during the fifth through the seventh years of life. Development of these processes requires not only intact information from the sensory input systems but also the capacity to integrate those signals in the brain. Weakened, distorted, or absent signals from the sensory input systems will detract from the development of integration processes as well as all other motor performance. This is not to say that specific motor skills cannot be taught in the absence of intact sensory information. Specific motor skills can be taught, but only as splinter skills. A splinter skill is a particular perceptual or motor act that is performed in isolation and does not generalize to other areas of performance. If hard neurological damage or age of the learner prevents development of the sensory input systems, it becomes necessary to teach splinter skills. In such cases, the top-down approach (task analysis) is recommended. If, however, it is believed that sensory input systems are fully functioning and cortical integration is possible, practice in the following activities should promote development of a wide variety of perceptual-motor abilities.

Balance

Balance is the ability to maintain equilibrium in a held (static) position or moving (dynamic) position. Balance ability is critical to almost every motor function. Some literature suggests that, until balance becomes an automatic, involuntary act, the central nervous system must focus on maintaining balance to the detriment of all other motor and cognitive functions.[1] Balance, once believed to be a result of combining some sensory input system signals, is now seen as a skill that is learned from using many systems, including all available sensory systems, many muscles, and passive biomechanical elements, as well as many different parts of the brain.[5] Clues to poor balance development include:

1. Inability to maintain held balance positions (e.g., stand on one foot, stand heel-to-toe) with eyes open
2. Inability to walk heel-to-toe on a line or on a balance beam
3. Tripping or falling easily
4. Wide gait while walking or running

Activities that can be used to promote static balance include:

1. Freeze tag—play tag; the child who is caught is "frozen" until a classmate "unfreezes" by tagging the child; "it" tries to freeze everyone.
2. Statues—each child spins around and then tries to make himself or herself into a "statue" without falling first.
3. Tripod—child balances by placing forehead and both hands on the floor; knees balance on elbows to form tripod balance.
4. Child balances bean bags on different parts of the body while performing balancing positions.

Activities that can be used to promote dynamic balance include:

1. Hopscotch
2. Various types of locomotor movements following patterns on the floor
3. Races using different types of locomotor movements
4. Walking forward heel-to-toe between double lines, on a single line, and then on a balance beam; make this more demanding by having the child balance a bean bag on different body parts (e.g., head, shoulder, elbow, wrist) while walking the balance beam.

Laterality

Laterality is an awareness of the difference between the two sides of the body. Children who have not developed laterality often demonstrate balance problems on one or both sides. Delays in the development of laterality may be indicated by the following types of behavior:

1. Avoiding the use of one side of the body
2. Sliding sideways in one direction better than the other
3. Using one extremity more often than the other
4. Lacking a fully established hand preference

Laterality is believed to develop from intact kinesthetic and vestibular sensory inputs. If these two input systems are believed to be functioning adequately, then a child will benefit from activities that require differentiation between the two sides of the body. Examples include the following:

1. Wear ankle and/or wrist weights on the weak (unused) side of the body while climbing on apparatus; moving through obstacle courses; and kicking, bouncing, throwing, or catching a ball.
2. Walk a balance beam while carrying objects that weigh different amounts in each hand (e.g., carry a small bucket in each hand, with different numbers of bean bags in each bucket).
3. Push a cage ball with one hand only.
4. Use only one hand in tug of war.

Spatial Awareness

Spatial awareness is the ability to perceive the position of objects in space, particularly as they relate to the position of the body (see **Figure 5-1**).

Development of spatial awareness is believed to depend on vestibular, kinesthetic, and visual development. Problems may be indicated by:

1. Inability to move under objects without hitting them or ducking way below the object
2. Consistently swinging a bat too high or low when attempting to hit a pitched ball
3. Inability to maintain an appropriate body position in relation to moving objects
4. Inability to position the hands accurately to catch a ball

If it has been determined that none of the prerequisite input systems are delayed, spatial awareness can be facilitated by practice in the following activities:

1. Set up an obstacle course with stations that require the child to crawl over, under, and through various obstacles.
2. Place a 10-foot taped line on the floor. Give the child a bean bag and ask him or her to place the bean bag halfway down the line. If the child makes an error, ask him or her to walk from one end of the line to the other, counting the number of steps. Then have the child divide the number of steps in half, walk that far, and place the bean bag down at that point. The child should then stand to the side of the line and look from one end of the line to the bean bag. Continue practicing until the

Figure 5-1   A Child Must Have Spatial Relationship Abilities to Fit the Body through the Circular Tunnel

child is successful at estimating where, on several different lengths of line, the midpoint is.

3. Repeat Activity #2 with the child wearing ankle weights.
4. Place several chairs around the room with varying distances between them. Ask the child to point to the two chairs that are closest together, farthest apart, or a given distance from one another (e.g., 3 feet, 10 feet, 6 feet). If the child makes an error on any task, have him or her walk the distance between the chairs and/or measure the distance with a measuring tape.

Ocular-Motor Control

Ocular-motor control includes the ability to fixate on and visually track moving objects, as well as the ability to match visual input with appropriate motor response (see **Figure 5-2**). Observed deficiencies might include:

1. Failure to locate visually an object in space
2. Failure to track visually a softball when attempting to hit it
3. Failure to track visually a fly ball or ground ball
4. Failure to keep a place when reading
5. Difficulty using scissors or tying shoelaces
6. Poor foot–eye coordination
7. Messy handwriting

Ocular control can be improved with practice if a child does not have serious orthoptic (depth perception) problems. If an individual does have depth perception problems, participation in ocular control activities can worsen the visual difficulties. Once it is ascertained that no depth perception problems exist, the activities in the next sections can be used to promote ocular control of the eyes.

Fixation

1. Child sits and rocks back-and-forth while keeping his or her eyes on a piece of tape on the wall directly in front of him or her.
2. Child lies on back with eyes fixated on a point on the ceiling. Child then stands up (or does a series of stunts) while continuing to fixate on the spot.

Figure 5-2   Activities That Contribute to the Development of Visual Systems

3. Child is in a standing position, fixating on a designated point on the wall. Child then jumps and turns 180 degrees and fixates on a designated point on the opposite wall.

4. Child is in a standing position, fixating on a designated point on the wall. Child then jumps and turns completely around (360 degrees) and again fixates on the original point.

Convergence/Divergence

1. Draw two *X*s on the chalkboard (at shoulder height of the child) approximately 36 inches apart. Have the child stand centered about 2 inches in front of the board and move his or her eyes back and forth between the two *X*s.

2. Have the child sit at a table and look from an object on the table to an object on the wall directly ahead; continue back-and-forth 10 times. The table should be about 15 inches from the wall.

3. The child sits with arms extended and thumbs up, looking back-and-forth from one thumb to the other.

4. The child sits with one arm extended and the other flexed, so that the hand is about 6 inches from the nose with thumbs up. Have the child look back-and-forth from one thumb to the other 10 times.

Visual Tracking

1. The child lies on his or her back. Have the child visually track lines, pipes, or lights on the ceiling, without moving the head.

2. The child lies on his or her back. Attach a small ball to a string and swing the ball horizontally above the child's head. The child should track the swinging ball with his or her eyes and then point to it as it swings. (The ball should be suspended approximately 16 inches above the child's head.)

3. The child throws a ball up in the air and follows the path of the ball with his or her eyes until it hits the floor. Repeat several times and encourage the child not to move his or her head while tracking the ball.

4. The child sits or lies on his or her back, then hits a suspended ball with the hand and visually tracks the movement of the ball.

Cross-Lateral Integration

Cross-lateral integration is the ability to coordinate the use of both sides of the body. It normally follows the development of balance and laterality. A child who has not developed cross-lateral integration by age 8 years is said to have a midline problem because there is difficulty using the hands efficiently at and across the center of the body. Teachers will note the following problems demonstrated by a child with a midline problem:

1. Difficulty using both hands to catch a ball
2. Tendency of eyes to jump when trying to track visually an object that is moving from one side of the body to the other
3. Inability to master a front crawl stroke with breathing while trying to swim
4. Inability to hop rhythmically from one foot to the other
5. Tendency to move the paper to one side of the body when doing paper-and-pencil tasks

Activities that will promote cross-lateral integration are as follows:

1. The child crawls down a rope or line on the floor, crossing hands back-and-forth over the line (rope) going forward, then crossing feet back-and-forth while crawling backward.
2. The child picks up objects (from right side of body) with the right hand and places them in a container on the left side of the body. This should be repeated using the left hand, picking up one object at a time.
3. The child practices swimming the front crawl with breathing.

Body Image

Body image is a broad concept that includes how people picture their body, attitude toward their body, and knowledge of personal bodily capabilities and limitations. Body image develops from all sensory input system information as well as from experiences with the body. Indications of a poorly developed body image are:

1. Lack of knowledge of where body parts are located
2. Distorted drawings of self
3. Lack of knowledge about what specific body parts are for
4. Poor motor planning

Activities that can be used to facilitate a child's body image include

1. Give verbal commands to the child (e.g., touch your knees, touch your ankles, touch your ears, touch your shoulders).
2. Have the child stand with eyes closed. The teacher touches various body parts, and the child identifies them. Then have the child touch the same part that the teacher touches and name the part.
3. Trace an outline of the child's body on a large piece of paper or with chalk on the floor. Then have the child get up and fill in the details (e.g., facial features, clothes, shoes). Have the child name all the body parts. Leave out a part and see if the child notices.
4. Draw an incomplete picture of a person on the chalkboard and have the child fill in the missing parts.

Studies have shown that children who experience an early rich and varied environment demonstrate increased cognitive and scholastic performance at age 11 years.[9] Frequently, children with disabilities have not had that opportunity. For this reason, the physical educator is in an ideal position to provide a rich movement experience to promote these youngsters' development.

When attempting to determine whether to use a bottom-up approach in the APE program, the teacher must again ask, "How much time is available?" The younger the child, and the more time available to the teacher, the more appropriate it is to use this strategy. Examples of how each of these two teaching methods is applied to achieve the same principles are given in **Tables 5-7** to **5-11**.

TABLE 5-7   Teaching Approaches and Their Relation to Growth and Development Principles

Principle	Implication	Bottom-Up Teaching Approach	Top-Down Teaching Approach
Each individual is unique.	Every child has a different motor profile.	Test for sensory input deficits and intervene to eliminate those before testing and programming for higher-level abilities and skills.	Test for specific functional motor skill deficits. If some are found, probe down into specific abilities that contribute to those skills. If deficits are found, probe down into sensory input areas.
	Every child learns at his or her own rate.	Select activities that appeal to the child and use those until the deficits are eliminated.	Program activities at the highest level of dysfunction. If the child does not learn quickly, probe down into contributing components for deficits.
Children advance from one stage of development to a higher, more complex stage of development.	Activities are selected appropriate to the level of development.	Select activities that are appropriate for the stage of development the child demonstrates.	Select activities specific to the skill deficits the child demonstrates. Begin an intervention program at the developmental level the child demonstrates.

(continues)

TABLE 5-7 Teaching Approaches and Their Relation to Growth and Development Principles (*Continued*)

Principle	Implication	Bottom-Up Teaching Approach	Top-Down Teaching Approach
	Progression to the next stage of development depends on physiological maturation and learning.	When a child appears to have mastered one stage of development, select activities appropriate for the next level of development.	When a child masters lower levels of a specific skill, select activities to promote learning of a more complex aspect of that skill.
Children learn when they are ready.	As neurological maturation takes place, we are capable of learning more. There are critical periods of learning.	Test from the bottom up and begin instruction with the lowest neurological deficit found. It is assumed the child will learn fastest if instruction is begun at the developmental stage at which the child is functioning.	Analyze a specific task from the top down until the present level of educational performance is found. The level of instruction determined by empirical testing verifies that the child is ready to learn.
Development proceeds from simple to complex.	Development begins with simple movements that eventually combine with other movements to form patterns.	Eliminate reflex and sensory input delays before teaching higher-level abilities and skills.	Functional skill deficits are identified. The pattern of the skill is analyzed to determine contributing components. Behavioral programs are constructed and implemented to develop pattern deficits.
	Development progresses from large to small movements (from gross to fine patterns).	Promote reflex and vestibular development to stabilize balance. Once balance becomes automatic, control of the limbs will follow.	Program to synthesize patterns that contribute to a specific skill.

TABLE 5-8 Teaching Approaches and Their Relation to the Generalization Process*

Principle	Implication	Bottom-Up Teaching Approach	Top-Down Teaching Approach
Generalization procedures	Activities to promote generalization are selected in particular ways.	Activity is selected to develop sensory input systems, reflexes, and abilities that are believed to be prerequisite to many skills that could be used in a variety of environments.	Functional age-appropriate activities are selected to promote appropriate skills in a variety of natural environments.
Generalization process	There is a degree to which the learning environment matches the natural environment.	At the basic levels (reflexes, sensory inputs, and abilities), the environment is controlled only to ensure that the basics are learned. No attention is paid to the type of environment the eventual skills will be used in.	Skills are practiced in environments that correspond closely to the environment in which the skill will be used (e.g., practice shooting baskets in the gym).
Retention	The more meaningful the skill, the longer it is remembered.	It is believed that, once basic reflexes, sensory input systems, and abilities emerge, they remain stable (unless the child is traumatized in some way).	Activities are reviewed immediately after a lesson and then periodically to ensure retention.
Overlearning	Overlearning occurs when a skill or an activity is practiced after it has been learned.	Overlearning occurs as the basic levels are interwoven into higher skill levels.	Ability levels prerequisite to skills should be substantially greater than minimum entry requirements needed to fulfill the needs of the task.

*A task is not considered learned until it can be demonstrated in a variety of environments.

TABLE 5-9   Teaching Approaches and Their Relation to the Attention of the Learner

Principle	Implication	Bottom-Up Teaching Approach	Top-Down Teaching Approach
Get the attention of the learner.	Help the child attend to relevant rather than irrelevant cues.	Permit the child to participate in a free activity of his or her choice each day if the child enters the room and immediately focuses on the beginning task.	Keep bats, balls, and other play equipment out of sight until time of use.
	Give a signal (sometimes called a "ready signal") that indicates a task is to begin.	Structure each day's lesson the same way, so that the child knows that, when a given activity ends, the next activity will begin.	Teach the child precise signals that indicate a task should begin.
Provide the appropriate stimulation.	Stimulate the child to focus on the desired learning task.	Make the activities enjoyable, so that the child will want to continue the task.	Use precise, detailed instruction that is designed around eliciting attention through the use of the following hierarchy: Visual or verbal input only Combined visual and verbal input Combined visual, verbal, and kinesthetic instruction

PHYSICAL FITNESS

Physical fitness is composed of strength, flexibility, muscular endurance, and cardiovascular endurance. *Strength* refers to muscular strength, which is the ability to contract a muscle against resistance. *Flexibility* is the range of motion possible at any given joint. *Muscular endurance* is the ability to continue to contract a muscle against resistance. *Cardiovascular endurance* is the ability of the heart and vessels to process and transport oxygen from the lungs to muscle cells for use. It has been demonstrated that good

TABLE 5-10 Teaching Approaches and Their Relation to Managing the Instructional Environment

Principle	Implication	Bottom-Up Teaching Approach	Top-Down Teaching Approach
Impose limits for use of equipment, facilities, and student conduct.	Children should learn to adhere to rules that are necessary in a social context.	Students are not permitted access to equipment and areas unless they have been given permission by the teacher.	The equipment and facilities a student has access to are specified in the behavioral program.
Control the social interaction among children.	Inappropriate social behavior among children may disrupt class instruction.	The teacher must consider the performance level and emotional stability of each child when grouping children for activities.	Tasks and environments are structured to reduce adverse interaction with peers.
Do not strive for control in all situations.	Children with disabilities must develop social skills that will promote social interaction in the natural environment. For this to occur, students must have an opportunity to adjust to situations independent from supervision or with minimum supervision.	Select activities that will meet the long-range goals of the students and promote social interaction. Pair children so that their interaction contributes to both students' objectives— for example, a child who needs kinesthetic stimulation might be given the task of pulling a child who needs to ride a scooter for tonic labyrinthine prone inhibition.	The students are permitted to interact with others as long as progress toward short-term objectives is occurring.

nutrition and a high level of physical fitness contribute to one's health and enjoyment of life. Because an active lifestyle is critical for persons with disabilities, an exemplary APE program continually promotes physical fitness.

Developing and maintaining an appropriate level of physical fitness is critical for persons with disabilities because, frequently, the disabling condition itself interferes with the ability to move efficiently. The problem is compounded when physical fitness levels are not adequate, because appropriate

TABLE 5-11   Teaching Approaches and Their Relation to the Nature of the Activity and Quality of the Experience

Principle	Implication	Bottom-Up Teaching Approach	Top-Down Teaching Approach
Learning occurs best when goals and objectives are clear.	Clear goals provide incentives for children to learn.	The desired outcome is clear to the teacher (e.g., 5 seconds of postrotatory nystagmus). The child may be advised of another goal (e.g., stay on the spinning scooter until it stops).	The goal and ongoing measurement of the attainment of the objectives that lead to the goal are shared by the teacher and the child.
Actively involve the student in the learning process.	The more learning time and the less idle time, the more learning will occur.	The child stays active because activities that are enjoyable to the child are selected.	When and if the child learns to self-instruct and self-evaluate or do so with the help of peer tutors, the student will be active throughout the period.
Discourage stereotyped play activities that develop rigid behaviors.	Permitting children to participate in the same activity day after day deters learning.	The teacher must initiate new activities as soon as lack of progress is evidenced.	The ongoing collection of data makes lack of progress immediately apparent to the teacher and the child and serves notice that the activity should be changed.
Program more for success than failure.	Every satisfying experience decreases anxiety and increases confidence.	The teacher selects activities the child enjoys and from which the child gains a feeling of accomplishment.	The increment of the step sizes in the behavioral program is constantly modified to match the ability of the learner.

levels of muscular strength, joint flexibility, muscular endurance, and cardiovascular endurance are requisite for movement efficiency. A sedentary lifestyle that results from inadequate levels of fitness can lead to chronic disorders that diminish health and limit mobility, ability to work, and other major life functions.

Several factors may contribute to poor physical fitness, including health status, developmental delays, lack of recreational opportunity, lack of confidence by the child or the caregiver, and poorly designed physical education programs. Developmental delays that can impact physical fitness levels include abnormal reflex development, delayed vestibular function, poor vision, delayed cross-lateral integration, inadequate spatial awareness, poor body image, and any other factor that limits the ability to move efficiently.

MOTOR FITNESS

Agility, power, speed, and coordination are the four components of motor fitness. Agility, the ability to change position in space quickly and accurately, is dependent on the visual, kinesthetic, and vestibular systems. Should any of these systems be delayed, agility is compromised.

Power, or explosive strength, requires the ability to rapidly contract and coordinate muscles to perform to maximum effort.[5] Power is frequently evaluated by using a standing long jump. Thus, strength is a primary contributor to power. When the standing long jump is used to measure power, the physical educator is reminded that strength of the hip adductor and abductor muscles, as well as the quadriceps, greatly impacts that movement. The stronger the hip stabilizers and flexors, the greater the distance jumped. In addition to muscular strength, good kinesthetic and vestibular information is critical to jumping performance.

Speed is the ability to move quickly in a short period of time. Speed is dependent on reaction time and movement time. Thus, the time it takes to hear and respond to a signal, as well as how quickly a person moves after initiating the movement, is critical to speed. Speed is frequently measured using a 50-yard dash. Obviously, a person will be able to demonstrate greater speed if the vestibular, kinesthetic, and auditory systems are fully functioning; the primitive reflexes are integrated; and the postural/equilibrium reflexes are well developed. Speed is also dependent on the number of fast-twitch muscle fibers that can be recruited during the movement. Fast-twitch muscle fibers are believed to be genetically determined.

Coordination is "the ability to integrate separate motor systems with varying sensory modalities into efficient patterns of movement."[5] To demonstrate coordination, individuals are required to perform a series of moves accurately and quickly. Gross motor coordination involves the whole body; thus, balance, agility, and rhythm must be synchronized to enable a smooth, efficient movement pattern. Hand–eye and foot–eye coordination require the ability to use visual information, muscular control, and kinesthetic information while maintaining balance. Should any one of the visual, kinesthetic, or vestibular systems or the primitive or equilibrium reflexes be compromised, the efficiency of the movement is impacted.

The Motor Development Model (review Table 5-1) is integral to any physical education curriculum and can be customized for the individual needs of students with disabilities. The most expeditious way to manage an average-size class in a public school, using the individualized approach, is by using a variety of stations arranged around the gymnasium, with a different activity performed at each station. Each activity is graduated from simpler moves to more demanding requirements. The needs of individual children are determined ahead of time, and each child performs only the level of the activity that is appropriate for that student. Video and static visual displays as well as rubrics can be used to help students self-evaluate and complete independent and guided practice, which can facilitate development of skills at their own rates.

Evidence-Based Practice and Response to Intervention

An approach receiving increased attention in educational circles is evidence-based practice. *Evidence-based practice* refers to utilizing instructional procedures and curricula that have been validated as effective by scientific research and/or the best available evidence. This evidence can come in several forms and does not all have the same strength. A hierarchy of evidence has been proposed to assist in identifying types and strength of evidence to support evidence-based practice (**Table 5-12**).[6]

Several scientifically based instructional strategies for physical education are explicit instruction, direct instruction, task analysis, and peer tutoring.[11] In addition to the need to use scientifically based instruction, it

TABLE 5-12   The Hierarchy of Evidence

1. Systematic reviews of randomized control studies
2. Randomized control studies
3. Longitudinal cohort studies
4. Quasi-experimental or cross-sectional studies
5. Longitudinal case studies
6. Cross-sectional single-subject or case studies
7. Consensus of public experiences
8. Expert opinions
9. Anecdotal information

is important that physical education follows an evidence-based curriculum. The essence of an evidence-based curriculum is objective measurement of a child's progress in response to intervention (RTI). RTI is a framework for support for students who may be struggling in the general education environment. RTI is centered around three tiers of intervention in which each tier provides increasing levels of support if the student continues to exhibit need.[2] RTI can function both independently and within the special education process. Regardless, the core purpose of RTI is to ensure implementation of continuous measurement of progress, provision of supports, and utilization of evidence-based practice.

Many adapted physical educators use evidence-based practice and response to intervention through the inherent IEP process. By initial and ongoing assessment of student needs, establishment of goals and objectives, and modification of instruction and provision of supports based on student progress, instructors are responding to the intervention provided.

Modifications or Adaptations

Modifications or adaptations change the demands of the task, rules, the environment, the equipment, or the instruction to permit students with disabilities to participate. Making modifications in accordance with a child's needs may enable immediate participation in age-appropriate activities selected to enhance specific skills. Following is a list of modifications for children with physical, sensory, or motor deficits. In these examples, modifications are necessary for the student with a disability to participate in chronologically age-appropriate physical education activities.

- Children who are blind can receive auditory or tactual clues to help them locate objects or position their bodies in the activity area.
- Individuals who are blind read through touch and can be instructed in appropriate movement patterns through manual kinesthetic guidance (i.e., the instructor manually moves the student through the correct pattern) or verbal instructions.
- Children who are deaf can learn to read lips or learn signing, so that they understand the instructions for an activity.
- Children with physical disabilities may use walkers, wheelchairs, or crutches during their physical education classes.
- A child with asthma may be permitted to play goalie in a soccer game intermittently, which requires smaller cardiovascular demands than the running positions.
- Rules may be changed to accommodate the variety of ability levels demonstrated by children in the class.
- A buddy, peer tutor, or paraprofessional may be assigned to help the student with special needs execute the required moves or stay on task.

- Small-sided games may be utilized to reduce distractions, the playing field, and demands.
- Modified equipment, such as auditory balls, larger or brightly colored objects, lighter objects, or tethered objects can be used.

For a larger list of modifications, please see the Project INSPIRE website at www.twu.edu/inspire.

Generalization to Community Environments

Time spent teaching skills in physical education training settings is wasted if the individual with disabilities cannot demonstrate competency in sport and recreation settings other than the school's and in the presence of persons other than the original teachers. To ensure that generalization to community environments and activities occurs, simulated training conditions need to be developed. Although there are few studies in physical education that have examined the generalization of motor skill and sport performance from instructional to community environments, it is known that when accommodations and opportunities are provided for persons with disabilities to interact in the community with persons without disabilities, the programs are successful. The American Youth Soccer Organization's VIP (very important person) program is an outstanding example of a creative way to include players with disabilities in regular leagues. The rules used by VIP teams are modified somewhat and the fields they play on are smaller. Peer buddies may be included initially; however, as the persons with disabilities gain in skills and knowledge of the game, use of peer buddies is gradually lessened.[7]

On the other hand, the literature on simulated settings versus training in the applied settings on nonphysical education tasks is mixed. It is critical that instruction not cease until the individual uses the new skills spontaneously and correctly in the community.

Commercial Programs

Several physical and motor programs are available commercially. Everyone Can![7] is based on the achievement-based curriculum model and provides assessments, instructional activities, games, and resources for teachers seeking to meet diverse needs in their classroom. Mobility Opportunities Via Education (MOVE)[8] is a curriculum to facilitate mobility skills for students with severe disabilities.

Parental Involvement

Parents should always be informed of their children's educational performance levels and the progress toward meeting the goals and objectives of the school curricula. IDEIA requires that the parents be apprised of the educational status of their children and informed of their child's progress in the general curriculum and in meeting their IEP goals, at least as often as their peers without disabilities. When the instructional strategies, assessment, and programming described in this chapter are followed by the teacher and the information is shared with the parents, there will be no question about the child's educational process. Consistent parental involvement aids in the consistent implementation of the activities, interventions, and modifications and promotes successful transition.

SUMMARY

Physical educators have traditionally included exercises, games, sports, rhythmic activities, and gymnastics in their curricula. Often these activities are selected according to teacher bias. More recently, teachers have been sensitized to the need to provide appropriate learning environments for students who demonstrate a wide range of abilities. These teachers are exercising greater care in selecting meaningful activities to include in their programs. Even when following a set curriculum, more attention is being paid to selecting activities that will meet a variety of learners' demonstrated needs.

The goal of a physical education program for students with disabilities is the development of motor behaviors that assist ultimate functional responses in community environments. Maximizing performance of the many specific skills of the physical education curriculum is the unique role of the adapted physical educator. The physical educator must determine which skills are needed and select appropriate instructional strategies to ensure that learning occurs. Regardless of the teaching approach used, functional adaptations may need to be made to enable the student to fully participate safely and successfully in the physical education curriculum.

REVIEW QUESTIONS

1. Identify three perceptual-motor abilities.
2. What are the differences between bottom-up (developmental) and top-down (task-specific) approaches?
3. Name two sensory input systems, two categories of integration processes, and two specific skills.
4. What is incidental learning? Why are some children with disabilities unable to learn as much through incidental learning as children without disabilities?
5. What is evidence-based practice?
6. Why is it important to use RTI?

REFERENCES

1. Abbruzzese, G., & Berardelli, A. (2003). Sensorimotor integration in movement disorders. *Mov Disord*, *18*(3), 231–240.
2. Dauenhauer, B. D. (2012). Applying response to intervention in physical education. *Strategies*, *25*(5), 21–25.
3. Dunn, J. M., & Frederick, H. (1985). *Physical education for the severely handicapped: A systematic approach to a data based gymnasium.* Austin, TX: PRO-ED.
4. Gallahue, D., Ozmun, J., & Goodway, J. (2012). *Understanding motor development: Infants, children, adolescents, adults.* New York, NY: McGraw-Hill.
5. Haywood, K. M. & Getchell, N. (2014). *Lifespan motor development* (6th ed.). Champaign, IL: Human Kinetics.
6. Jin, J., & Yun, J. (2010). Evidence-based practice in adapted physical education. *Journal of Physical Education, Recreation & Dance (JOPERD)*, *81*(4), 50–54.
7. Kelly, L., Wessel, J., Dummer, G., & Sampson, T. (2010). *Everyone can!: Skill development and assessment in elementary physical education.* Champaign, IL: Human Kinetics.
8. Kern County Superintendent of Schools. (1990). *Mobility opportunities via education.* Bakersfield, CA.
9. Lavay, B., & Semark, C. (2001). Everyone plays—Including special needs children in youth sport programs. *Palaestra*, *17*(4), 40–43.
10. Raine, A., Reynolds, C., Venables, P. H., Mednick, S. A. (2002). Stimulation seeking and intelligence: A perspective longitudinal study. *J Pers Soc Psychol*, *82* 663–674.
11. Stephens, T. L., Silliman-French, L., Kinnison, L., & French, R. (2010). Implementation of a response-to-intervention system in general physical education. *Journal of Physical Education, Recreation & Dance*, *81*(9), 47–53.
12. Wright-Ott, C. A., Escobar, R. J., & Leslie, S. Encouraging exploration. *Rehab Manage*, June 2002. Retrieved from www.rehabpub.com

CHAPTER 6

Delivering Services in the Least Restrictive Environment

- Define least restrictive environment.
- Compare and contrast the least restrictive environment and inclusion.
- Suggest strategies for preparing the school and community for the least restrictive environment.
- Describe the nine instructional variables that can be modified to accommodate a learner with a disability in the least restrictive environment.
- Evaluate an existing physical education program to determine its appropriateness for students with disabilities.

The Least Restrictive Environment and Inclusive Education

There are strong and passionate voices that support the inclusion of students with disabilities in the general education program and equally strong and passionate voices that believe the concept of least restrictive environment (LRE), if appropriately implemented, better addresses the unique needs of learners with disabilities. Inclusion is a philosophy in which "all individuals can participate in physical activities that enable them to be motorically, cognitively, and affectively successful within a community that embraces diversity."[37] The intent of the IDEIA (2004) was, and continues to be, that

there must be a *continuum of services* and service delivery models, so that the unique needs of every learner with disabilities can be met. The LRE is a *civil right* that was guaranteed to all children in *Brown v. Board of Education* in 1954. See **Table 6-1** for the courts' interpretation of LRE.

The ARC, for people with intellectual and developmental disabilities, has a strong position on the inclusion of individuals with intellectual

TABLE 6-1   Least Restrictive Environment Determination, as Mandated by the Courts[44]

School district determinations regarding the LRE should be based on the following:

- Has the school taken necessary steps to maintain the child in the general classroom?

  What supplementary aids and services were used?

  What interventions were attempted?

  How many interventions were attempted?

- Benefits of placement in general education (with supplementary aids and services) vs. special education
  - Academic benefits
  - Nonacademic benefits (e.g., social, communication, peer-model)
- Effects on the education of other students
  - Is the education of other students adversely affected (e.g., if the student is disruptive)?
  - Does the student require a great deal of attention from the teacher, compromising the education of the other children?
- If the student is being educated in a setting other than the general classroom, is he or she interacting with peers without disabilities to the maximum extent appropriate? In what academic settings is the student integrated with peers without disabilities? In what nonacademic settings is the child integrated with peers without disabilities?
- Is the entire continuum of alternative services available?

disabilities that has significant implications for the adapted physical educator and the general physical educator:

Children should:
   Live in a family home;
   Have access to the supports that they need;
   Grow up enjoying nurturing adult relationships both inside and outside a family home;
   Enjoy typical childhood relationships and friendships;
   Learn in their neighborhood school in a general education classroom that contains children of the same age without disabilities;
   Participate in the same activities as children without disabilities;
   Play and participate with all children in community recreation; and
   Participate fully in the religious observances, practices, events, and ceremonies of the family's choice.
Adults should have the opportunity to:
   Have relationships of their own choosing with individuals in the community, in addition to paid staff and/or immediate family;
   Live in a home where and with whom they choose;
   Have access to the supports they need;
   Engage in meaningful work in an inclusive setting;
   Enjoy the same recreation and other leisure activities that are available to the general public; and
   Participate fully in the religious observances, practices, events, and ceremonies of the individual's choice.[36]

   TASH, the vocal and primary advocate for students with severe disabilities, strongly supports inclusive education:

THEREFORE BE IT RESOLVED, THAT TASH, an international advocacy association of people with disabilities, their family members, other advocates and people who work in the disability field, affirms that all students with disabilities shall be provided a quality, inclusive education that assures full and meaningful access to the general education curriculum. To achieve such an education, support services must be provided as needed, programs and curricula must be modified as needed, and students must receive such supports, supplementary aids and services as are necessary in an inclusive setting. The expectation shall be that every school community shall provide a quality, inclusive education for all students with disabilities that is predicated on a shared vision of high expectations for all students and a commitment to a set of learning goals or standards that are strong, clear, understood, and put into practice.[35]

The position statement of the American Association for Active Lifestyles and Fitness, now SHAPE America, states that each child, with and without a disability, has the right to be a physically educated person. AAPAR's powerful position statement, "Physical Education for Infants, Children, and Youth with Disabilities," (2004), begins as follows:

> Physical activity provides meaningful movement experiences and health-related fitness for all individuals in order that they may have the opportunity to acquire the motor skills, strategies, and physical stamina necessary for a lifetime of rich leisure, recreation and sport experiences to enhance physical fitness and wellness. A quality physical education program provides the foundation for a healthy, happy, and physically active lifestyle. Infants, children, and youth with disabilities have the right to receive the full range of benefits from physical education just as their able-bodied peers. Benefits include the development of motor skills and physical fitness, as well as the opportunity to participate in play, active leisure, aquatics, recreation, outdoor adventure, and sport experiences.[1]

The emphasis of the Office of Special Education and Rehabilitation Services (OSERS) has also been on the education of learners with disabilities within the general education program. According to the Individuals with Disabilities Education Improvement Act 2004 (IDEIA 2004),

> Access to the general education curriculum means that students with disabilities are actively engaged in learning the content and skills that define the general education curriculum. It isn't enough to simply be *placed* in the general education classroom—students must be actively engaged in learning the content and skills that define that curriculum.[5]

Access to the general education curriculum has evolved because of the significant efforts of parents, professionals, and advocates devoted to the right to educational equity of children with disabilities. Federal law continues to indicate that children with disabilities should be educated in the least restrictive environment (LRE). That is, children with disabilities have the right to be educated with typically developing children whenever appropriate. But that means that a continuum of service delivery options should be available for the individualized education program (IEP) team to consider. In 2012, 61.5% of students ages 6 to 21 years served under IDEIA (2004) were educated in the general education classroom 80% or more of the day.[40]

According to Kasser and Lytle (2005):[14]

> Inclusion is a philosophy that asserts all individuals, regardless of ability, should participate within the same environment with necessary support and individualized attention. Inclusion is more than simply placing individuals together—it's a belief that all individuals belong and are valued. (p. 5)

Inclusive education has been defined as education in which the following are true:

- All students are welcomed into the general education classes in their home/neighborhood school.
- Students are educated in groups that represent the greater society (i.e., approximately 10% of the students in any class/school have identified disabilities).
- A zero-rejection philosophy is in place, so that no student, regardless of the nature or severity of the disability, is excluded from access to the general education class.
- Students with varying abilities share an educational experience, with specific modifications and accommodations to meet individual needs.
- Special education support is available within the context of the general education program.[18]

Because of the growing national movement toward acceptance of the philosophy of inclusion and the implementation of educational practice to promote inclusion, this text includes a variety of strategies for meeting the needs of students with disabilities in an inclusive setting. Our decision to provide this information is not intended to imply an endorsement of the notion that all students' needs can best be met in the general physical education setting. We are deeply committed to the notion that the LRE mandates better protect the individual rights and ensure a quality physical education experience. General guidelines, including types of activities that will meet the needs of all students in various school levels, are included in this chapter, and more specific strategies are addressed in each of the chapters dealing with specific disabilities.

Certainly, the LRE mandate has had a huge impact on general physical educators, librarians, art teachers, and computer teachers in schools because, typically, children who may not be able to be included with children without disabilities in the so-called academic programs are included in physical education, library, art, computer, and recess times. The courts continue to assert the rights of learners with disabilities to be educated in inclusive environments.

LRE AND DEVELOPMENTALLY APPROPRIATE PRACTICE IN PHYSICAL EDUCATION

The IEP or multidisciplinary team is responsible for determining the appropriate education for a student. There should be a continuum of placement and instructional opportunities for learners with disabilities. If children with disabilities are to be included in the general physical education program, the physical educator must be using developmentally appropriate practices. That is, the physical educator engages the learners in the class in activities that are age- and interest-appropriate for the learners. For example, learners with disabilities can most effectively be included in the general physical education curriculum for first and second graders if the emphasis in the program is the acquisition and refinement of basic locomotor and nonlocomotor patterns, movement exploration, cooperative play activities, and elementary rhythms and dance. If inappropriate practices are being used—for example, team sports and competitive games—children with disabilities, like all young learners who are not "superstars," are doomed to failure and frustration.

The same is true of general physical education at the high school level. If the general physical educator concentrates on instruction in leisure and recreation skills for use as adults in post-school years and emphasizes the development of physical fitness, for example, most learners with disabilities can be successful in the general physical education environment.

Preparing for the Least Restrictive Environment—A Proactive Approach

All too often, inclusive education was something that "happened" within a given school community. Any change, particularly a dramatic change, in an educational environment must be preceded by careful and systematic preparation to ready all involved in the process. A model blue-ribbon school, Marvel Springs School, established an entire school culture in its efforts to be inclusive. According to Stockall and Gartin,

> A learning community was established that embraced children with disabilities and students at risk and created a school world that embodied specific cultural rules. First, no child was excluded from opportunities to socially interact with others. Second, school faculty modeled ways to mark signs of ability in all children and actively searched for positive markers of success. Finally, they established a context of caring and cooperation among all students. These subcultural rules guided teachers' actions and decisions about their teaching practices. The consciously attended to and marked signs of social interaction supported these beliefs.[34]

For inclusive practice to be effective within a given community and school, significant forethought and preparation must occur and include consensus building, values modification, and comprehensive in-service education. In this section, suggestions are made for ensuring that the LRE is created by preparing the community, administrators, parents, children, teachers, and paraprofessionals.

PREPARING THE COMMUNITY

An increased emphasis on school–community partnerships necessitates a broad-based public relations campaign to help focus community interest on issues tied to the quality of life of individuals with disabilities. Within a given community, visible, capable, and effective individuals with and without disabilities need to be part of a public relations campaign to educate and motivate its citizens to embrace appropriate inclusion in the schools. It is particularly critical that the school board—elected representatives of the public—has adopted a philosophy that emphasizes appropriate inclusion.[13] The school board—representatives of the taxpayers who continue to be overwhelmed with the financial responsibility of educating their children—must be able to communicate carefully and effectively to all its citizens the benefits of appropriate inclusive practice. This is particularly important if learners with disabilities are to have the opportunity to make a meaningful transition into the community.

THE BUILDING PRINCIPAL: THE KEY TO EFFECTIVE INSTRUCTIONAL PROGRAMS

Without a primary building administrator who is deeply committed to the philosophy and ideal of quality instruction for ALL learners, school-wide education programs for children with disabilities, particularly inclusion programs, can be poorly applied and practiced. See **Table 6-2** for a summary of the practices of principals who encourage and support inclusive practices. Unfortunately, all too often children with disabilities are included in general physical education, art, music, library, and computer classes without careful regard to the unique needs and abilities of the child or the unique needs and abilities of the teacher. The IEP/multidisciplinary

TABLE 6-2   The Building Principal: The Key to Successful Inclusion in Physical Education

An administrator who values and supports the education of diverse learners is absolutely critical to successfully implementing inclusive practices. The administrator will do one or more of the following to ensure that quality physical education is received by all:

1. Decrease the class size by hiring additional professional personnel or arranging alternate scheduling patterns.
2. Decrease the student–teacher ratio by assigning trained paraprofessionals to assist the teacher and ensuring they do their job.
3. Decrease the student–teacher ratio by assigning school volunteers to assist the physical educator in the gymnasium.
4. Use creative alternative scheduling patterns for service delivery. Perhaps it is more prudent to have students attend a quality physical education class three times a week if the class size is limited to 30 students than to have them attend a large, ineffective baby-sitting service daily if class size is in excess of 80 students.
5. Arrange for university/community college interns to provide vital extra hands.

In addition to limiting the student–teacher ratio in physical education, the administrator must also provide support for the physical educator by addressing other concerns:

1. The physical educator must be encouraged to attend classes and in-service presentations that address the education of children with disabilities in the general physical education program.
2. The physical educator must be given release time to participate actively as part of the motor development team or the multidisciplinary team in the assessment/evaluation of the child's gross motor skills and in the creation and implementation of the child's individual motor education plan (IMEP) or individual physical education plan (IPEP).

team may suggest that a child with a disability be integrated in the general education curriculum—based solely on the social needs of the child—in order to meet parental demands for placement with typical children without jeopardizing student performance in the so-called academic components of the curriculum.

Administrative support for the appropriate inclusion of children with disabilities in general education, including general physical education, is vital if a nurturing educational environment is to be created. If the principal believes some children with disabilities may be integrated effectively into the general physical education program, and that meets the child's social, physical, or motor needs, then the administrator must support the physical educator in a number of ways.

The federally mandated participation of students with disabilities in state and district assessments may redirect school administrators to focus their efforts on the performance of students in special education. Unfortunately, many school administrators believe physical education and adapted physical education (APE) are simply peripheral or so-called special activities and focus their energies on test scores in the "general" education program.

PREPARING PARENTS

Perhaps the most important phase of a successful inclusion program is the education and preparation of parents of children with and without disabilities. Certainly, a broad-based public relations campaign within the community is a good start, but carefully designed parent education programs are vital. On their website, the National Consortium of Physical Education for Individuals with Disabilities (NCPEID) provides links and resources for parent education.[28] Parents of children with disabilities are often the primary advocates of inclusive programming for their children. However, some parents of children with disabilities are fearful of the general education program. Parents fear their child may be teased or hurt, laughed at, and ridiculed by children without disabilities. The best way to deal with these types of fears is to ask the physical educator to talk to the parents about strategies to work toward an LRE and invite parents to visit the general physical education program before the IEP/multidisciplinary team considers the possibility of the child's attending the class. If the parents have the opportunity to see a caring, nurturing teacher and a well-organized, child-centered physical education program, their fears will likely be reduced.

Preparing the parents of children without disabilities for inclusion may be the most difficult part of the development of inclusive programming. Most parents of children without disabilities are supportive of inclusive efforts if, and only if, they believe their children's education will not be compromised. Parents of children without disabilities are concerned that:

- The teacher's time and energy will be exhausted dealing with a learner with disabilities.
- School resources and tax dollars will be allocated disproportionately for learners with disabilities.
- Their child's learning will be disrupted by a child with inappropriate learning behaviors—aggressive, acting out, and refusal behaviors, in particular.
- Their child will begin to mimic inappropriate behaviors demonstrated by children with disabilities.
- Their child's safety will be compromised by a child with physically aggressive behavior.
- Their child's emotional well-being will be compromised by a child who is verbally aggressive or who uses inappropriate language.
- Their child's health will be compromised by a child who vomits, drools, spits, is not toilet trained, or has a communicable disease (e.g., AIDS, syphilis).

The single most important strategy for preparing parents of children without disabilities for inclusive programming is gradual and thoughtful inclusion of children with mild disabilities, at first. It appears that this is particularly effective if very young children with disabilities are included with their peers. If parents of children without disabilities can see that their children's education is not compromised, and, in fact, if they learn some important social skills about dealing with others, they will be more likely to support inclusive educational practices.

If infants, toddlers, and preschoolers grow up learning together, as young adults there will be no question of "who belongs." In fact, if a school district is deeply committed to effective, inclusionary practice with a minimum of heartbreak, the district would begin inclusive education in their preschool program; then children would grow up together into elementary school, then junior high school and, later, high school.

In fact, if inclusive practice is done well, there are innumerable benefits for all children. According to Rogers,

- The presence of an included classmate should provide opportunities for growth for the entire class.
- Classmates can develop a sense of responsibility and the enhanced self-esteem that results from such responsibility.
- Classmates' understanding of the range of human experience can be enhanced.
- Children can benefit from their classmates with disabilities as role models. As a result of advancements in medical science that allow most people to live even longer lives, most of those children without disabilities will survive to become persons with disabilities themselves one day.
- Classmates are enriched by the opportunity to have friends with disabilities who successfully manage their affairs and enjoy full lives.[32]

To ensure that this is a positive experience for all children, helping children without disabilities to understand what it is like to have a disability is an excellent first step.[23] Children respond well to empathy experiences in which they have the opportunity to feel what it is like to have a disability. These empathy experiences help a child, in a concrete way, learn and accept.

In the physical education classroom, empathy experiences designed to help learners without disabilities understand the person with a disability might include the following:

1. Navigate an obstacle course in a wheelchair.
2. Wear mittens when trying to play catch with a friend.
3. Play in the gymnasium and on the playground using only gestures or sign language for communication.

4. Wear a headset to cut out hearing and attempt to play in a game.
5. Wear eye patches.
6. Kick a ball while supporting self on crutches.
7. With a yardstick splint on the dominant arm, catch, throw, and dribble with the nondominant hand and arm.
8. Participate in a pool exercise/game using blindfolds.

One of the most significant means of preparing an environment for a learner to be successfully included is to identify and encourage a circle of friends to be in place before the inclusion experience is attempted.[30] This helps provide a vital, caring, and humane transition into general education services. (See **Table 6-3**, which addresses peer friendships.) A child with a disability is given the opportunity to make friends in a controlled, reverse mainstream setting before attempting to move into the general education/physical

TABLE 6-3   Improving Friendships between Children with and without Disabilities

The teacher must

- Model friend-first behavior.
- Provide opportunities at the beginning of the school year and intermittently throughout the year for children to get to know one another.[33]
- Use books, videos, and songs/dances that encourage friendship.[33]
- Teach specific skills for being "friends." Increasingly, students go to school without the interpersonal skills necessary to create and maintain friendships.
- Ensure opportunity to practice the specific skills for being "friends." The skills are specific and "learned" and need to be practiced.[45]
- Reinforce and reward "friendly" behaviors.
- Teach children specific skills for handling a peer's rejection.
- Provide structure, to encourage appropriate social interactions.[19]
- Be knowledgeable of any social skill goals written into the IEP.
- Identify and assign roles in a "cooperative learning" experience to foster friendship. For example, one child in the group could be specifically charged with being a "cheerleader" for the other group members.
- Help children create a "circle of friends" before moving into a new educational environment. For example, if a child is going to begin participating in general physical education, *before* the child starts, he or she should already have a "circle of friends" in place, ready to welcome the child into the learning environment.

education setting. For example, if a 6-year-old girl with Down syndrome is hoping to participate in the general education/physical education program, several 6-year-old girls are asked to meet and play with the child in her classroom, preferably during a time in which interaction might occur (e.g., center time). Then, after the child has made friends, she is included in the general education/physical education program, more comfortable because of her friends.

Preparing older students, middle and high school age, for inclusion needs to be approached altogether differently. These students are more likely to be accepting of an individual with a disability if they are able to understand the disability on an intellectual level.[8] Honest communication of information regarding the nature of a disability will reduce fear. They are also more likely to interact with a classmate with a disability if given a leadership role (e.g., as a peer tutor or personal assistant). Only the truly mature adolescent is able to deal with peer pressure issues to only "hang with the in crowd." Selective assignment and recruitment of tutors and personal assistants must be used.

PREPARING PROFESSIONALS, INCLUDING THE GENERAL PHYSICAL EDUCATOR

Clearly, undergraduate and graduate professional education programs need to be restructured to focus on real-world applications. An increased emphasis on the skills necessary to provide services to students with very diverse characteristics/needs is critical. The general educator must be prepared to meet the diverse needs of children representing a wide variety of cultures, races, languages, socioeconomic classes, abilities, and disabilities.[38] An increased emphasis needs to be placed on the professional skills necessary to work in collaboration with other professionals.

Parent panels have been used effectively in the preparation of professionals who will be serving children with disabilities. The parent panel would consist of meetings between parents and the instructional staff to discuss information about disabilities and effective intervention strategies.[19]

For a child with even a mild disability to be educated in the general physical education class, careful preparation must be made. Three variables must be considered before deciding to place a child in the general education/physical education program:

1. The professional preparation of the educator to teach a child with disabilities
2. The attitude of the educator toward learners with disabilities
3. The nature of the educator's previous experience working with learners with disabilities

The first variable to be considered in the decision to include children with disabilities in general education/physical education programs is the professional preparation of the teacher. An introductory-level APE class at the undergraduate level that addresses the attitudes and feelings of preprofessionals is the basis of such preparation.[15] It is particularly critical that the preparation include hands-on experiences with children with disabilities in the physical education setting.[17] It appears that the nature of the practicum is critical in the quality of the experience as well. The controlled practicum, on a university campus, is characterized by the following:

- The faculty member is actively involved in ongoing supervision.
- Students are served in small teacher–student ratios.
- Students with disabilities are carefully selected for participation.

If the physical educator did not acquire knowledge of ways to accommodate a learner with disabilities in the general curriculum during undergraduate or graduate professional preparation, the educator must be provided access to this information through in-service preparation before a child with disabilities is included in the general program. Subsequent, ongoing in-service training is vital in order to keep professional staff on the cutting edge in the provision of services to learners with disabilities in a general physical education setting.

The second variable that must be considered before placing a child with a disability in the general classroom is the teacher's attitude toward teaching those with disabilities. If the teacher has a negative attitude about including a learner with a disability in the class, the learner will know it instantly and be devastated by it; the learner with a disability simply cannot be placed in a classroom or gymnasium in which he or she is not valued. Teachers may have negative attitudes toward students with disabilities for a variety of reasons, but attitudes are learned behaviors that, when necessary, can be changed with training.[15] Providing physical educators the knowledge and skills necessary to work effectively with students with disabilities in the general classroom may increase positive attitudes toward them. Teachers may have negative attitudes toward students with disabilities because they do not know how to teach them.

Block and Obrusnikova suggest that the general physical educator is an important part of creating a positive and successful inclusive setting. They suggest the following:[3]

- have a positive attitude
- take responsibility for teaching all children in the class
- model appropriate behavior
- include the student with a disability in as many activities as possible
- individualize the curriculum and instruction
- reinforce positive interactions, and
- be knowledgeable about the student

PREPARING THE PARAEDUCATOR

The role of the paraeducator in the public schools is a very important one. A paraeducator must now have specific training/education prior to being hired to assist in the school community. Training and education in the areas of reading, mathematics, science, and social studies is most helpful. The more training our paraeducators have, the better the outcomes for our children.

The paraeducator is often the key to the success of a learner with a disability in the general physical education program.[20] Paraeducator personnel are often willing, but grossly underpaid, members of the teaching staff. Increasingly, however, paraeducators who work within special education are involved in significant instructional behaviors. These include tutoring, gathering and maintaining data, implementing behavior management plans, preparing instructional materials, and collaborating with teachers. These staff members can be the single most important force in the school life of a child with a disability. If a paraprofessional is given

TABLE 6-4   Paraeducator Roles

A dedicated and well-trained paraeducator may serve in the following roles:

- Ensuring access to the general physical education setting
- Providing physical and emotional support for the learner with a disability
- Serving as an advocate for the learner
- Implementing the IEP
- Supplementing instruction by providing individualized learning experiences
- Being the child's "best friend"
- Communicating with the other professionals serving the child[7]
- Communicating with the child's parents/caregivers
- Documenting intervention and the child's progress[7]

specific training, he or she can better meet the needs of the child. With success in intervention, the paraprofessional will be enabled and reinforced to continue (see **Table 6-4**).

In-service training needs to be concrete and specific to the needs of the individual children the paraprofessional is expected to serve. The single most important part of the training is the management of the learner's behavior. If the paraprofessional can help the learner behave appropriately, the general educator/general physical educator will be more likely to embrace the learner in the gymnasium and on the playground.

Variables Affecting Instruction in Physical Education in the Least Restrictive Environment

It is critical that instruction, not placement, be the deciding factor in the process of educating a learner with a disability. Unfortunately, all too often learners with disabilities are "placed" in a particular educational setting and left there to learn or fail. The most critical factor in the instruction of learners with disabilities is a comprehensive assessment. The assessment drives and is the basis for the development of the IEP. Then, and only then, should decisions be made regarding instruction and placement in the LRE.

In complete disregard of the LRE mandates of the federal law, a huge majority of our children are receiving their physical education services in the general physical education program. Generalizations regarding what is least or most restrictive are inappropriate when considering individual instruction for learners with disabilities. The determination of least or most restrictive must be carefully considered by the IEP/multidisciplinary team. Careful consideration must be given to the variables that affect instruction in physical education in the LRE. Each of the following variables can be considered on a continuum (see **Figure 6-1**).

• Accessibility
• Curriculum
• Program participation
• Support personnel
• Teaching style
• Management of behavior
• Grading
• Assessment
• Equipment

Figure 6-1   Least Restrictive Environment Considerations

ACCESSIBILITY AND THE LRE

Accessibility is a critical issue in the determination of the LRE. Facilities for physical education at the elementary, middle, and high school level vary extensively from district to district and from state to state. Most schools have an indoor gymnasium/play area and an outdoor playground area available for class use. Some school districts have no gymnasium and rely entirely on outdoor facilities. Some inner-city schools, however, have no viable (safe, weapon-free, gang-free) playground area, and often the gymnasium is too small to allow appropriate activities.

It is, of course, necessary to evaluate the facilities with regard to the appropriateness for all learners. In addition, it is vital that the physical educator critically evaluate the facility with the unique needs of learners with disabilities in mind. The physical educator must ask the following questions regarding the learning environment:

- Is the indoor gymnasium/play area architecturally accessible for a student who uses a wheelchair, a walker, or crutches?
- Can the student with a physical or neurological disability make an easy transition from the indoor gymnasium/play area to the outdoor playground area?
- If the gymnasium/play area is not architecturally accessible, what accommodations can be made to ensure that a student is not limited by a disability?
- If the student is unable to make an easy transition from the indoor to the outdoor play area—because of stairs, for example—what

accommodations can be made to ensure that the child is not limited access to the program by the disability?
- Can the play areas be modified to provide a safe, secure, and nurturing learning environment for all learners?
- Are there accessible washrooms close to the indoor gymnasium/play area and the outside playground area?
- Can all learners, including those with disabilities, be safely evacuated from the indoor gymnasium/play area in the event of a fire?

It is important for the teacher to understand that Section 504 of the Rehabilitation Act of 1973 and subsequent legislation—specifically, the Americans with Disabilities Act of 1990—mandate that all new public facilities be built to ensure access for individuals with disabilities. In the event, however, that the teacher is serving in an old building, the law mandates that a "reasonable accommodation" must be made to ensure that the student has access to programs offered to others. For example, if the primary pathway from the gymnasium to the playground is down a set of stairs, a student using a wheelchair may be unable to get to the playground by that route. A reasonable accommodation is for the physical education teacher to have the entire class take an accessible route—one with a ramp, for example—so that the learner using the wheelchair feels part of the group. The gymnasium and playground areas can be modified to make them more user-friendly for learners with disabilities:

- A constant sound source could be placed in the gymnasium or on the playground to allow the student with a visual impairment to orient himself or herself in both settings.[2]
- A "safety strip" made of a material different from that of the major play area could surround the gymnasium or playground area to warn the visually impaired or blind student of walls or fences.
- The playground area must be completely surrounded by fences if a learner with a conduct disorder, a student with autism, or a "wanderer" or "runner" is to be allowed to play and/or recreate outside. Actually, given the present climate in the society, it is critical that all school property is surrounded by a fence with gates that can be locked or supervised to control access to the school.

- The gymnasium should be well-lighted to ensure use by a student with a visual disability.
- The gymnasium should have good acoustics to ensure that a learner with a hearing impairment can hear the teacher's instructions. Materials to absorb sound and prevent it from bouncing around the environment are critical for the learner with Asperger's syndrome or autism.
- The teacher should have access to a microphone to speak at levels that can be heard by a student with a hearing impairment.
- Major equipment should always be stored in the same place in the gymnasium to provide consistency for learners with visual impairments or autism.

CURRICULAR VARIABLES AFFECTING INSTRUCTION IN THE LRE

The adoption of a given curriculum for use by some or all students within a given district is a critical variable affecting instruction in the creation of an inclusive learning environment. Increasing emphasis is being placed on the use of universally designed materials, so teachers need to teach only one flexible curriculum in order to meet the needs of all of their students. In order to implement universal design in the physical education curriculum, the teacher should consider (1) the attributes of the learner, (2) the objectives of the class, and (3) the modification variables.[23]

The curriculum must be considered when determining instruction in the LRE:

- *NASPE National Standards for Physical Education as the basis of the school curriculum.* The National Association for Sport and Physical Education has determined the standards of performance in physical education. If possible, learners with disabilities should participate in this curriculum.
- *State education agency "essential elements" in physical education as the basis of the school curriculum.* Most states have developed their own standards or "essential knowledge and skills" for all curricular areas, including physical education. These essential elements may not be as global as those outlined by NASPE.
- *Local education agency physical education curriculum.* Many local districts have developed their own curriculum. Curricula developed at the

local level tend to reflect the interests and attitudes of local school and community personnel.

- *Modified physical education curriculum.* Considering the needs and interests of all learners in the physical curriculum will guide necessary modifications. A universally designed curriculum is an efficient approach to ensure that the curriculum is accessible and least restrictive.

In determining the LRE, there are many alternatives that may be considered by the IEP committee (see **Figure 6-2**):

- *Full, independent participation in general physical education.* In actuality, the general physical educator has coped with the notion of inclusion for years. It has been relatively standard, albeit inappropriate, practice to give students the opportunity for "socialization" in art, music, and physical education to pacify parents interested in having their child educated with typically developing peers.
- *Full, independent participation in general physical education with younger students.* Occasionally, it may be appropriate to integrate children with disabilities into physical education classes with younger children. This strategy, viable only at the elementary school level, may be appropriate with children with delayed social and play skills. Under no circumstances, however, should a child with a disability be integrated into a physical education class serving children more than two years younger. To place a first grader with a mild conduct disorder into a physical education class with kindergartners may be a humane and creative way of allowing the child to develop the social and play skills he or she lacks. However, it would be inappropriate to place a fourth grader in a kindergarten class.

↑

Full, independent participation in general PE
Full, independent participation in general PE with younger children
Independent participation in general PE in some units
Independent participation in some phases of the general PE class
Participation in general PE with specific APE instruction
Separate, but equal, APE with typical peers (reverse mainstreaming)
Separate, but equal, APE with peers with disabilities
APE in home, hospital, or institution

Figure 6-2   Program Participation Variables Affecting Instruction in the LRE

The child is not "included" in that learning environment; the child is set apart for ridicule by the very nature or differences in size and interests.

- *Full, independent participation in some units in general physical education.* On occasion, a decision about instruction in the LRE must be made on a unit-by-unit basis. For example, a learner with a behavior disorder may be able to participate independently in individual activities, such as bowling, bocci, or inline skating, but would be overwhelmed by a large-group game or sport activity.

- *Full, independent participation in some phases of the daily lesson in general physical education.* A learner on the autism spectrum, for example, may be able to participate in the structured warm-up/fitness phase of the physical education class but would be unable to handle a group game or sport.

- *Participation in general physical education with specific APE instruction.* A student with Duchenne muscular dystrophy, for example, may be able to participate in the "relaxation" phase of the daily lesson. However, when the rest of the class is involved in a group game or competitive sport activity, the student should receive specific instruction in leisure and recreation activities, such as fishing or bocci.

- *APE in the school building with typically developing peers.* In the event that a student requires a program participation limitation—separate, but equal, APE—a reverse mainstreaming model may be adopted. In that model, with parental permission, students without disabilities may be invited to participate in a physical education program specifically designed for students with disabilities.

- *Separate, but equal, APE in the school building with peers with disabilities.* Students with severe disabilities and/or delays may need to receive their physical education within a separate APE class. This may, in fact, be the LRE for a student with severe behavior disorders, Rett syndrome, or severe/profound intellectual disability.

- *APE in the home, hospital, or institutional setting.* Students with profound disabilities and/or chronic, terminal illness may need to receive physical education, as well as the rest of their educational services, in an institutional setting, the hospital, or their home. Students with an illness or injury that requires hospitalization or causes them to be homebound for more than 4 weeks (this timeline may vary from state to state) require educational services, including physical education, in the hospital or home.

ASSESSMENT VARIABLES AFFECTING INSTRUCTION IN THE LRE

In order to determine the physical and motor needs of children with disabilities, a valid and reliable assessment must be completed. Accurate assessment data will guide decisions regarding LRE placement as well as IEP goals and objectives, and allow the physical educator to monitor progress.[21, 22]

Legislation requires that children with disabilities have equal opportunities to participate in programming, including assessments. In the event that a child is not able to fully participate in a given school-wide assessment, then an alternative assessment must be offered.[39]

The challenge of including students with disabilities in state- and district-wide assessments is great. Generally, students receiving special education services may participate in the education process in three ways: (1) in standard tests administered to all other students; (2) through the use of approved accommodations; and (3) through an alternative assessment designed to measure the progress of students who cannot participate, meaningfully, in the standard assessment process.[9]

SUPPORT PERSONNEL VARIABLES AFFECTING INSTRUCTION IN THE LRE

The IEP/multidisciplinary team must carefully consider the learner's need for instructional support from a teacher, paraprofessional, volunteer, or peer buddy (see **Table 6-5**). In addition, the IEP/multidisciplinary team must

TABLE 6-5   Support Personnel Variables Affecting Instruction in the LRE

Student requires no support.
General PE teacher has APE consultant.
Same-age peer buddy
Older peer buddy
Older student as teacher assistant
Adult volunteer as teacher assistant
Physical education paraprofessional provides support.
Special education paraprofessional provides support.
APE teacher provides support in general physical education program.
APE specialist as teacher

assess the child's need for support from a highly trained adapted physical educator as a consultant or as a direct service provider.

- *No support required.* The LRE in terms of support is that in which the general physical education teacher requires no support in order to provide services. An IEP, however, is required if a student is to receive services in APE.
- *General physical educator with APE consultant support.* The general physical educator provides instruction and relies on an APE consultant for assessment/evaluation, IEP development, and program recommendations.
- *Same-age peer buddy.* Often, the only accommodation that must be made to allow a learner with a disability to function effectively within the general physical education class is to ask another child to be a special buddy. The buddy is asked to include the learner in play, games, or activities. Often, this is the only "ice-breaker" necessary to allow the student to thrive in the general program. Trained peer tutors appear to be effective in improving the motor performance of learners with disabilities in the inclusive physical education setting.[12] (See **Table 6-6**.)

TABLE 6-6   Peer Tutor Instructions

Job description: peer buddy

Peer buddy: Molly Pyter

Student: Cole Huettig

Physical education teacher: Dave Auxter

Physical education: Monday, Wednesday, and Friday. 8:00 to 8:45

Every time your class goes to PE,

1. Walk behind Cole in line. Take his hand if he starts to get out of line. Tell him, "Cole, walk with me, please." If he says, "No," drop his hand.
2. Sit next to Cole in the gymnasium.
3. Follow Mr. Auxter's direction so that Cole can watch you and learn from you.
4. If Cole is not doing what the class is doing, tell Cole, "Watch me."
5. During free play, ask Cole, "Will you play with me?" If he says, "No," leave and go play with other friends.
6. If Cole does play with you, tell him, "I like playing with you, Cole."
7. If Cole hits, spits, or tries to wrestle with you, leave him and tell Mr. Auxter.

TABLE 6-7   Classwide Peer Tutoring Model[41]

The beauty of the classwide peer tutoring model is that children with and without disabilities alike can serve interchangeably as peer tutors, depending on the activity. The following are steps to teach the classwide peer tutoring model:

1. Develop specific task sheets with criteria for successful performance for discrete skills.
2. Provide a model—teacher demonstration, demonstration by skilled student, or videotape.
3. Allow the students an opportunity to practice the skill.
4. Distribute the specific task sheets and criteria.
5. Provide a demonstration of the peer tutoring process.
6. Review the process.

Peers are powerful facilitators of learning.[41] Once instruction becomes specific, it is not difficult for students to learn what it is they are to do and then communicate information to their peers. The peer instruction or modeling can be done by students with and without disabilities. Buddies must know what is to be done and have the ability to communicate with the learner.

The buddies should receive the same type of preservice and in-service training as does the professional, although the learning needs to be adapted, so that it is developmentally appropriate. A classwide peer tutoring model is presented in **Table 6-7**.

Empathy experiences are particularly valuable in the training of peer buddies. Also, just like paraprofessionals, the buddy should have a specific job description (review **Table 6-8**). In close cooperation with the student's classroom teacher, this experience can be valuable for the peer buddy, as well as for the child with a disability.

- *Older peer buddy*. A student who is unable to function within the general physical education class with a same-age buddy may thrive if given the opportunity to work with an older buddy. This buddy should be carefully trained to help meet the special needs of the student without interfering with instruction and without setting the child apart from the others. This older, more mature student should receive training in the nature of the disability, in techniques for communicating effectively with the learner, and in methods of helping the learner (to move his or her wheelchair, for example, or, if blind, to orient himself or herself in the gymnasium). Older students may serve as excellent models and, if

TABLE 6-8   Strategies for Developing Student Support Programs in General Physical Education

1. Discuss student support programs (peer buddy and older student assistant) in APE with the local campus administrator. At the request of the campus administrator, usually the principal, present program guidelines to the site-based management school committee.

2. Discuss the student support plan with the classroom teachers whose students will be affected. Suggest that the program be used as a reinforcer for good work in the classroom. For example, those students who have turned in homework assignments each day of a given week would be given the opportunity to serve as "peer buddies" or "student assistants" in the following week.

3. Secure permission of parents of students without disabilities in order for them to participate in the program. Outline potential benefits of participation in the program for students involved:

    a. Opportunity to learn responsibility

    b. Opportunity to assume a leadership role

    c. Chance to interact with children with different needs and abilities

4. Schedule a preservice orientation meeting for all teachers, students, and their parents. Include

    a. A description of the program

    b. Roles/responsibilities of all involved

    c. Characteristics of children with disabilities (use empathy experiences)

5. Provide in-service training for all teachers and students involved in the program. Invite parents to attend as well.

6. Develop a specific schedule for each classroom teacher whose children will be involved in the program.

7. Plan ongoing in-service education during each class period. Spend a few moments before each class reminding the student support personnel of their roles and responsibilities.

8. Informally evaluate the performance of the student support personnel; provide positive feedback whenever possible.

9. Honor the student support personnel at the end of the year in the student award assembly. *The greater the student perception of program importance, the greater the participation and personal investment.*

carefully chosen, may serve as a magnet to draw other students toward the student with a disability (see Table 6-8).

- *Older student as teacher's assistant.* Teacher's assistants in physical education can be indispensable in individualized learning environments. They can assume several responsibilities that contribute to class management and record progress in physical education, such as setting up and storing equipment before and after class, collecting data on themselves and others, and assisting with the instruction of younger students. These students are often honor students who are released from school or are scheduled with younger and slower-learning children. These students need to be thoroughly familiar with the programming if their assistance is to be valuable.

- *Adult volunteer as teacher's assistant.* The adult volunteer must be carefully trained to meet the needs of the student with a disability in the general physical education classroom. This may be a more effective instructional environment (the least restrictive one) for a learner with a behavior disorder that another child could not manage but a trained adult could manage.

As funds become increasingly scarce, administrators and teachers are becoming more and more dependent on the use of volunteer resources to continue or improve programs. The effective recruitment and retention of volunteers is enhanced by effective communication. However, it is important for the general physical education teacher or APE teacher to understand the nature of the volunteer to effectively use the volunteer to meet program goals (see **Table 6-9**).

Parents may take an active role as adult volunteers within the physical education program. As with other volunteers, it is critical that parents receive training for their task. Downing and Rebollo wrote, "Parental roles

TABLE 6-9   Strategies for Increasing Volunteer Support in the Gymnasium

1. Develop a poster recruiting campaign that features the fact that it is "fun" and a great "change of pace" to work with children with disabilities in a play, leisure, recreation, or sport setting.

2. Actively recruit volunteers on the basis of their athletic skills; it is easier to recruit someone who has the perception of being needed because of particular skills.

3. Form a "dad's club" that allows fathers to contribute to their child's education in a format in which they may be comfortable.

4. Indicate the potential for learning new skills, particularly those that might be marketable. This is particularly valuable in recruiting individuals who are unemployed or seeking alternative employment opportunities.

5. Share program goals and objectives with the volunteer. Share specific goals and objectives for specific children the volunteer serves.

6. Write a specific job description for the volunteer. This is the key to successful volunteer recruitment and retention. The volunteer needs to understand his or her role within the program.

7. Ensure that the volunteer is recognized for his or her efforts. Help the children in the program express their thanks. This is perhaps the most valuable form of recognition for most volunteers. Develop a systematic strategy for recognizing the volunteer. This includes "volunteer highlights" in the APE newsletter, thank-you notes, plaques, and/or recognition dinners.

as support personnel and/or adjunct educators of their children can only be as effective as their preparation to serve in these capacities."[17]

Schools and school districts have begun the process of actively recruiting volunteers to work with children within the schools. Schools may be "adopted" by a corporation or a civic organization. Corporate employees or members of a civic group may each serve the school in a unique way as a part of the "adopt a school" program.

The use of volunteers in the schools can greatly enhance the opportunities that can be given to children with disabilities. The physical educator can provide a chance for children to thrive and grow through the encouragement and help of program volunteers.

Physical Education Paraeducator to Provide Support

The student's least restrictive physical education environment may be the general physical education class with the support and assistance of a physical education paraeducator. This paraeducator literally serves as a second physical education teacher, who focuses interest and efforts on the children with special needs. Many paraeducators contribute greatly to the successful inclusion of a child with a disability in the general education setting. (See **Table 6-10**.) In some instances, the general physical education teacher should insist that, if one or more learners with disabilities are to be included in the physical education class, a paraprofessional must be available (see **Table 6-11**).

In many school districts, paraprofessionals or teacher's aides are assigned to assist a teacher in a given program without regard to their training or background in physical education. As such, it is possible that the physical education teacher will need to ensure that the paraprofessional attend

TABLE 6-10   Perceptions of Paraprofessionals Regarding Their Role in Inclusion Programs[26]

- Paraprofessionals assumed an advocate role for "their" students being included.
- Paraprofessionals sought to make the experience positive for the general education teacher with whom they worked.
- They feel responsible for controlling all student behaviors to avoid disruption in the classroom.
- They believed they were a critical liaison among parents, the general education teacher, and other school personnel involved with the child (school nurse, etc.).
- They believed themselves to be "experts" regarding the student to whom they were assigned.

TABLE 6-11   Example of Specific Responsibilities for a Special Education Paraprofessional

Class 1, 8:00–8:45

7:55

Go to Room 109 to accompany Michelle to the gym. Insist she push her own chair.

8:00–8:15

Roam throughout the gymnasium while children are doing warm-up exercises, encouraging all the children to do well. If necessary, remind Michelle to do her modified warm-ups, which are posted on the wall.

8:15–8:40

Monitor Michelle's interactions with others in the class. Record and describe any inappropriate interactions on her behavior chart in the teacher's office. Refer to the description of appropriate and/or inappropriate behaviors on her chart.

8:40–8:45

Accompany Michelle to her room.

preservice and in-service programs regarding physical education and, if students with disabilities are to be served, regarding physical education for children with disabilities.

At the very least, the paraprofessional must have the opportunity to share the same types of learning experiences recommended for teachers. One of the most significant aspects of the supervision of a paraprofessional is the description of the paraprofessional's role and responsibilities. Most school districts have a generic job description for the paraprofessional. This description is, however, often vague regarding the specific role and responsibilities of the paraprofessional. In addition, the job description for the paraprofessional is usually prepared for the individual who will assist a classroom teacher. The duties and responsibilities of the paraprofessional working in the gymnasium are different from the duties and responsibilities of the paraprofessional in the classroom.[6] As such, the general physical education teacher or APE teacher must work closely with the building principal to design a specific job description, particularly if the paraprofessional is to help teach children with disabilities.

A specific job description significantly alleviates potential problems. If respective roles and responsibilities are clear to both the physical education teacher and the paraprofessional, they can work together as a professional team, serving children in the best possible way. In addition, the wise physical educator should take every opportunity to reinforce the efforts of the paraprofessional. For, example, the physical educator should write a letter to the principal praising the efforts of the paraprofessional. A copy should be shared with the paraprofessional. Or the physical educator should routinely orchestrate a class "thank-you" for the paraprofessional with cards, cake, and punch.

Special Education Paraprofessional to Provide Support

The presence of a special education paraprofessional in the gymnasium is more restrictive than if the student works with a physical education paraprofessional because of the stigma attached to having a "special ed" teacher accompany the learner to class. Every bit of information that applied to the physical education paraprofessional applies to the special education paraprofessional as well (review Table 6-11).

Adapted Physical Educator to Provide Student Support

For a student to function within the general physical education program, it may be necessary for an APE specialist to intervene with the student in the gymnasium. Unfortunately, few school districts have adapted physical educators who actually provide direct instructional service to students. In some school districts, an APE specialist may be able to provide hands-on services once a week or once a month. A good model lesson may be helpful for the general physical educator and the paraprofessional, however.

Adapted Physical Educator as Teacher

Many school districts have not made a strong commitment to quality APE programming. In some schools, for example, the caseload of the adapted physical educator may be more than 200 students; there is no way that quality service can be delivered in that situation. A separate, but equal, service for students with disabilities, who may be unable to benefit from general physical education, has become a luxury, not a reality.

The adapted physical educator may provide direct service in some institutions or with a very specific type of student—those with traumatic brain injuries, for example—but, in general, staff priorities cause this form of direct service to students with disabilities and their parents to be rare.

TEACHING STYLE AS A VARIABLE AFFECTING INSTRUCTION IN THE LRE

The teaching style of the general physical educator must be considered carefully if a learner with a disability is to be taught in the general physical education class. It is clear that most teachers have a set teaching style and in some cases are unwilling or unable to change that style. For example, there may be two physical educators in the same large high school. The IEP committee may need to evaluate the teaching style of both teachers to determine in which class the learner is likely to succeed. Certainly, a willingness to work with a student with a disability and a commitment to educating all are necessary and desirable traits in a teacher selected to work with a learner with a disability.

The selection of an instructional approach appears to be based heavily on the teacher's experience. Professional preparation training programs continue to produce teachers who are most likely to teach the way they have been taught. This cycle, unfortunately, continues to place teachers who remain teacher-directed and teacher-focused and who believe themselves to be the "givers of knowledge" in direct contact with students who would be more successful if given the opportunity to direct their own learning, to discover, and to take responsibility for their own learning. Following are different types of instructional strategies.

- *Learner's individually designed program.* The essence of this teaching style is that the focus is on each student and his or her needs. A teacher who is already focusing on individual students can easily accommodate and serve a student who just happens to have a disability. The learner is empowered to design and develop a series of tasks and activities that meet his or her needs, and the teacher serves essentially as a consultant— the teacher helps the student by asking important questions, reinforcing appropriate tasks and activities, and redirecting the student's efforts if the tasks or activities are not developmentally appropriate.
- *Guided discovery.* In this teaching style, the teacher asks questions, chooses and develops activities, and plans events to lead a student to a predetermined answer or solution.[4] The most common guided discovery

teaching style in physical education is movement exploration. For example, a student who uses a wheelchair may be guided through the following activities at the same time as his or her ambulatory peers:

1. Can you move in a large circle on the floor?
2. Can you move in a large circle on the floor in a different way?
3. What can you do to make the circle smaller?
4. What can you do to make the circle even smaller?

- This type of approach empowers all movers and respects the individual's unique responses to movement problems and challenges. This teaching style is one in which learners with disabilities can be easily included.
- *Self-check*. In this teaching style, the teacher shares with the learner the skills needed to perform a task or an activity individually.[4] The teacher has established criteria for successful accomplishment of a given task, so that the individual learner can evaluate his or her own success. If the teacher is serving a student with a disability, the teacher can help the student establish challenging, yet attainable, standards for success. Once again, the emphasis on meeting the needs of individual students facilitates the inclusion of students with disabilities.
- *Reciprocal style*. This teaching style is characterized by the establishment of learning partnerships.[4] While the teacher determines the activity or task and establishes the criteria for success, students work in partnership to provide each other feedback regarding performance. This teaching style easily accommodates learners with disabilities, even those who require the support of a same-age or older peer buddy to be successful. If every student has a learning buddy, it is easy for the learner with a disability to have a buddy as well.
- *Command style*. This teaching style has often been called the traditional teaching approach.[4] The teacher explains an activity, demonstrates it, and expects each learner to replicate it. The teacher-controlled atmosphere allows little individual variation in performance. Though this sounds restrictive, this teaching style may be exactly what a learner with a conduct disorder or autism needs in order to learn. The structure may prove very helpful.

The needs of learners demand that teachers of children, with and without disabilities, examine strategies to meet those needs. Most certainly, teachers have to focus on active rather than passive learning. Children, like adults, learn by doing, not by watching and certainly not by listening. And it is critical that teachers honor and respect the various ways that children learn. [27]

MANAGEMENT OF BEHAVIOR AS A VARIABLE AFFECTING INSTRUCTION IN THE LRE

The behavior of students with and without disabilities in a general education setting is often the major factor that determines the students' success or failure within that setting. A proactive, positive behavior management program is the key to the successful inclusion of students with disabilities in the general education program.[16] Increasingly, inappropriate behavior is a critical problem in the public schools. Children with and without disabilities are exhibiting inappropriate behavior. There are a myriad of reasons, but the result is that it is difficult for the teacher to teach and difficult for the learner to learn.

Identical Behavioral Expectations

Inappropriate behavior in the physical education classroom is the reason most often given that physical education teachers do not want a learner with a disability in the gymnasium. If a learner with a disability is to be readily accepted in the general physical education program, by the teacher and students alike, the learner must be able to meet the behavioral expectations and standards set for every other learner. Too often, a learner with a disability is excluded from the physical education environment, not because of a motor delay but because of the learner's inability to follow class rules (see **Table 6-12**).

Slightly Modified Behavioral Expectations

General physical educators are often willing to include a learner with a disability in the general physical education program if it requires making only minor changes in behavioral expectations. For example, if a student with an attention deficit disorder is unable to sit on a given spot while listening to directions, the teacher may accommodate the student by allowing the student to stay within a larger space (e.g., a free-throw circle).

TABLE 6-12   Skills Needed for Success in the General Program

One of the keys to the inclusion of children with disabilities in the general physical education program is teaching *all* the children the skills they need to be successful within the program.

These specific behaviors include:

- Following directions
- Asking and answering questions
- Beginning and completing tasks
- Getting, using, and returning equipment
- Sitting, standing, and walking in line

Individually Designed Reinforcement System

As an example of this behavior management system, a deeply committed physical educator teaching a high school student with Down syndrome was willing to abide by the recommendations of the IEP committee and completed a behavior checklist each week to be sent home to the student's parents. When the student willingly participated in class activities more than 50% of the time, she earned a coupon, which she could use to rent a video on the weekend.

Individually Designed Behavior Management Plan

The most restrictive environment is one in which the student with a disability has an individual behavior management plan (BMP) that is different from the plans of his or her classmates. An individual BMP is almost impossible to implement in a physical education class without the support of an additional trained adult in the gymnasium. Under no circumstances should a student, even an older student, be put in the position of implementing a BMP for another student. The ethical and legal implications of a student being given the responsibility of managing the behavior of another student are frightening.

According to IDEIA 2004, schools have a responsibility to provide appropriate behavioral supports, individualized where necessary, to children who require them. Supports may include a functional behavioral assessment (FBA) and related behavior intervention plan. Conducting individualized FBAs and intervention plans is the job of the administration and teachers. Professional development will be necessary to be certain assessments and plans are completed accurately.[31]

GRADING AS A VARIABLE AFFECTING INSTRUCTION IN THE LRE

If the school district has made a commitment to parents of children without disabilities to provide report cards every 6 weeks (six report cards per academic year), parents of children with disabilities have a right to have a report card explaining their students' progress every 6 weeks.

Grading is one of the most difficult issues facing the general physical educator (any educator, for that matter). All too often, children with disabilities are "placed" in the general physical education program, and the IEP/multidisciplinary team has made no recommendations regarding modifications/accommodations in grading.

Same Expectations in Grading and Reporting Grade

In terms of instruction, the LRE in the physical education program is one in which learners with disabilities are able to meet the same expectations in all phases of the grading process. That includes the motor, physical fitness, knowledge, and behavioral components of grading. The teacher is able to use the same state or local assessments for the learner with a disability as he or she uses for other children and is able to report the results on the same instrument.

Modifications of Expectations in Grading and Reporting Grade

Occasionally, a learner with a disability participates successfully in the general physical education program with basic modifications in expectations for grading and in the way that grade is reported to parents. For example, a student with severe dyslexia may need to have written tests administered verbally. A high school student with a mild intellectual disability may be required to answer only every third question on a written test. Or a student with spina bifida who uses a wheelchair may be asked to "roll" instead of "run" in the cardiovascular-respiratory endurance phase of the physical fitness test. The modifications made must be reported on the standard school report card.

Individual Plan for Grading and Reporting Grade

A grade in any subject should promote educational goals and should reflect educational aims and objectives. For programs to be most effective, established objectives must indicate the desired goals of instruction, so that they become the criteria on which grades are based. If the criteria are valid, successful measurement will result in valid evaluation. The grade, if one desires to translate behavioral performance, could reflect how well these criteria have been met.

The complexity of grading in physical education classes is magnified when an attempt is made to evaluate the performance of students with disabilities. The one common denominator among all students is the mastery of individual performance objectives. If students are graded on the basis of how well they meet their IEP objectives, a student with poor posture, a student with a cardiac disorder, a student who is obese, and a student who has just had surgery can all be properly evaluated for their grades in the class. In the case of a student with a disability, the student's IEP may be used as the tool for reporting progress (grade) to parents.

EQUIPMENT AS A VARIABLE AFFECTING INSTRUCTION IN THE LRE

Making instructional modifications for students with disabilities in physical education may be as simple as finding a different type of equipment for the student to use while learning.

- *Same equipment.* Every learner within the class shares and uses the same equipment.
- *Similar but different equipment.* It is possible to improve instructional modifications simply by changing the type of equipment available for student use. For example, a student with juvenile rheumatoid arthritis may not be able to participate in a volleyball game with a real volleyball but may be successful in a "volleyball" game that uses a beach ball, instead. A child with a visual impairment may experience difficulty tracking a typical playground ball but would be able to participate in a game of catch if the ball were a bright, fluorescent color.
- *Specially designed equipment.* It is possible to enhance opportunities for inclusion by providing the learner with a disability with specially designed equipment to meet his or her needs. For example, a student with cerebral palsy may be able to bowl by using an "automatic grip release" or a ramp. A student with a below-the-knee amputation may be able to participate in a downhill skiing unit with an "outrigger" ski pole.

Instruction within the LRE is a dynamic and evolving process. Unlike a determination of "placement," in which a student receives services without regard for acquisition of motor behaviors, social behaviors, or self-abusive behavior, carefully designed instruction requires the physical educator to evaluate constantly the student's needs within each continuum.

Working Document for the IEP Committee: Least Restrictive Environment in Physical Education

The Irving, Texas, Independent School District designed a special education program design matrix for the IEP/multidisciplinary committee in its consideration of the LRE within the general education program. The strength of this document is that it provides the members of the IEP committee with a working document that emphasizes a student's strengths and considers the realities of the general education experience. The committee members then try to match the student's strengths with the educational opportunity that will be provided.

This type of proactive effort in determining the LRE for learners with disabilities may be modified for use in physical education as well. Examples of matrixes for a unit and a daily plan are presented in **Figures 6-3**, **6-4**, and **6-5**.

Program Design Matrix

To facilitate positive and constructive admission, review, and dismissal meetings (ARDs) for all students, this program design matrix was developed at Irving Independent School District. It was during a difficult ARD that this matrix was scratched out for all participants to see a "picture" of the student. Because it focused on the strengths of the student, the ARD was able to maintain a proactive focus that generated an individual education program (IEP) for the student's needs. The successful and positive ARD supported the need for this matrix.

The following is a guide to implement the matrix.

1. The matrix is given to the teacher before the ARD to fill in the schedule of a regular school day. Copies are to be made to hand to all those attending the ARD.
2. After review of student's testing, progress, etc., you could begin the use of the matrix, explaining that this will help develop the IEP and programming for the student.
3. Next, identify strengths of the student. Everyone should participate and feel comfortable with the identified strengths before doing a cross-check with the classroom schedule.
4. As you do a cross-check, mark an X in the appropriate box and column to signify the student's specific strength(s) that could allow the student to be able to be successful in the classroom. It does not mean that the child could not get support if needed.
5. Empty boxes could indicate areas of concern that the ARD committee needs to address or that a box is not applicable. Circling an activity identified as an area of need will alert the committee to be sure to develop strategies to meet the student's needs in that area. Through ARD discussion, areas that could provide support through modification, consultation, pullout, collaboration, etc., could be identified. It is not to be assumed that support services are to be provided at the specific time scheduled for an activity identified as an area of need. The time assigned will allow the ARD committee to see how much time during the day is needed to program for special education support. The bottom boxes allow times to be totaled, which will help transfer information onto the time sheet.
6. Support suggestions can include equipment, peer tutor, buddy classmate, modifications to the lesson or activity, support personnel, etc.

A

Figure 6-3   Student: Janet Wells; Date October 31, 2015

Courtesy Irving (Texas) Independent School District.

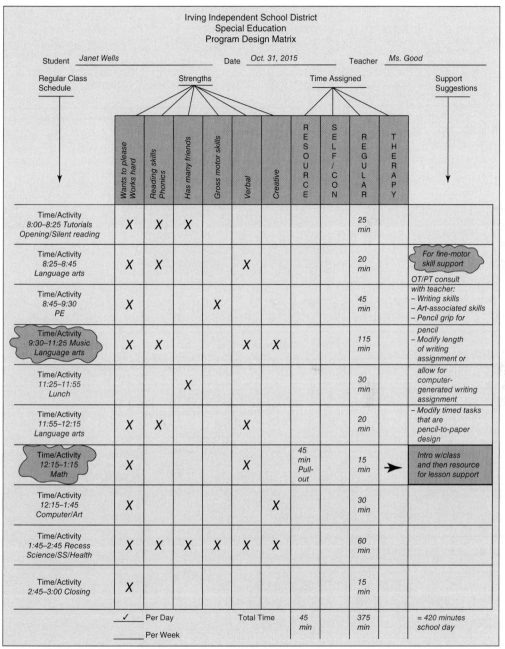

Figure 6-3   Student: Janet Wells; Date October 31, 2015 (*Continued*)

Least Restrictive Environment Design Matrix (Unit)
High School Physical Education
First Semester

Student _Julia Hernandez_   Date _3/3/2016_

Adapted Physical Education Teacher _Brett Favre_

Physical Education Teacher _Mr. Garcia_

Activity/Unit	Student Strengths					Support Suggestions
	Good runner	Excellent flexibility	Works well independently	Responds well to music	Follows directions	
September, Weeks 1 & 2 Fitness Evaluations	✓	✓			✓	
September, Weeks 3 & 4, October, Weeks 1 & 2 Individual Fitness	✓	✓			✓	
October, Weeks 3 & 4 Archery			✓		✓	
November, Weeks 1 & 2 Flag Football						_Remove for separate, but equal program with low pupil-staff ratio_
November, Weeks 3 & 4 Soccer						
December, Weeks 1 & 2 Volleyball						
December, Week 3 Creative Dance			✓	✓		

Figure 6-4   Student: Julia Hernandez; Date March 3, 2016

Least Restrictive Environment Design Matrix
First Grade Physical Education
Daily Lesson Plan

Student   _Dione Haley_   Date _9/7/2016_

Adapted Physical Education Teacher _Mr. Peters_

Physical Education Teacher _Cassandra Williams_

Activity/ Unit	Student Strengths				Support Suggestions
	Basic locomotor skills	Balance	Rhythmic ability	Responds well to 1–1 instruction	
9:40–9:45 Roll				✔	Pair with a buddy for roll/directions
9:45–9:55 Warm-Ups to Music			✔		
9:55–10:10 Movement Exploration	✔				
10:10–10:20 Large-Group Activity				✔	Pair with a buddy for parallel activity
10:20–10:25 Relaxation				✔	Pair with a buddy for relaxation activity

Figure 6-5   APE Teacher Mr. Peters; PE teacher Cassandra Williams

Figure 6-4 is an illustration of how the student's strengths are matched by unit(s) in which the student is likely to experience success. Focusing on the student's strengths is of particular value in the IEP/multidisciplinary team meeting. Parents are often much more receptive to the ideas of the committee members if the emphasis is on what the student can do, rather than what the student cannot do. In Figure 6-5, the student's strengths are matched with each phase of the daily lesson plan in the first-grade physical education program.

If an IEP/multidisciplinary team is truly focused on providing the best possible instruction for a student, within the federally mandated least restrictive learning environment, accommodations can and must be made to ensure success. Careful consideration of the student's abilities, the schedule and plan of the general physical educator, and the availability of support can all influence decisions involved in the construction of an appropriate learning environment.

SPECIFIC STRATEGIES FOR CREATING AN LRE FOR LEARNERS WITH DISABILITIES

In the following sections, specific instructional strategies for instructing learners with disabilities in the general physical education program are considered at the elementary, middle, and high school levels.

Elementary Physical Education

Williams[43] addressed the fact that many activities typically used in elementary physical education programs are inappropriate; not only for children with disabilities but for any child. He identified the "Physical Education Hall of Shame" to help physical educators take a close look at decisions regarding games that are inappropriate for any learner (see **Table 6-13**).

The intent of this ageless Hall of Shame is to encourage educators to focus on developmentally appropriate activities to avoid the following:

- Embarrassing a child in front of his or her peers
  - One student performing while the others watch[42, 43]
  - One line, one ball, one chance to participate[42, 43]
- Eliminating students from participation to allow only one "winner"
- Low participation time and low activity time
- Placing learners at serious risk for injury and harm

TABLE 6-13 Activities Included in the Physical Education Hall of Shame[42]

- Dodgeball
- Duck, duck, goose
- Giants, elves, and wizard
- Kickball
- Musical chairs
- Relay races
- Steal the bacon
- Line soccer
- Red rover
- Simon says
- SPUD
- Tag

- "Rolling out the ball"[42]
- Inappropriately sized equipment, such as 10-foot-high basketball hoops in elementary schools
- Using exercise as punishment
- Allowing students to choose teams[42, 43]

Young children who are still in the process of developing their basic sensory systems and their perceptual-motor integration processes are best served by using the bottom-up developmental model. As often as possible, activities that address specific areas of development should be incorporated into the activity of children demonstrating delays. When programs are delivered in a general physical education program, it is possible to address the specific needs of the children with delays and still benefit other students within the class.[10]

The Middle and High School Physical Education Program

One of the most successful techniques for designing physical education classes that appeal to and accommodate a wide range of ability levels is described in the book *Changing Kids' Games*, by Morris and Stiehl. These authors suggest that an excellent way to pique students' interest and involvement in a physical education class is to engage them in a process that puts them in control of many aspects of the games included in the curriculum. They propose using a games' analysis technique in classes to enable students and teachers to identify and modify any aspect of a game or sport. Using a visual chart, a teacher can lead the students through a process of systematically identifying the components that are included in the six categories that constitute a game.

The six categories included in every game are purposes, players, movements, objects, organization, and limits. Each category includes several components that have the potential to be changed, depending on the wishes of the group. The categories and their components are as follows:

1. *Purposes.* The purposes of a game include developing motor skills, enhancing self-worth, improving fitness, having enjoyment, gaining satisfaction, and developing cognitive skills. When deemed necessary, the components may be subdivided to identify specifics, such as which motor skills, aspects of fitness, and cognitive skills are included in the game.

2. *Players.* Analysis of the players category yields characteristics such as the number of players required, whether individual performance or group cooperation is needed, and the makeup of the groups. To create greater opportunities for students to be involved in a game, the number of team members could be increased, all teams could be made coeducational, efficient and inefficient movers could be placed on the same team, and students with disabilities and/or different cognitive levels could be included.

3. *Movements.* The components of the movements category include types (body awareness, locomotor versus nonlocomotor, reception versus propulsion, and physical attributes); locations, including personal space (levels, directions, and pathways) and general space; quality (force, flow, and speed); relationships (objects, players, and group); quantity (number, unit of time, distance, and location); and sequences (task order within an episode). Students should be given the opportunity to alter the types of movement demands, so that everyone has a chance to participate fully. Individual games could be changed to partner or small-group efforts, and a variety of pathways from which players could choose could be built into the game. Players could be given the opportunity to play for a predetermined score rather than for time or vice versa.

4. *Objects.* The discussion of objects will center around the types and uses of the objects, the quantity needed, and their location. A game that

requires everyone to use the same implements does not require much imagination. Why not give everyone the opportunity to use a batting tee, or to swing at a slow pitch rather than a fast pitch, or to catch with the mitt of choice rather than the one the rules call for?

5. *Organization.* Organizational patterns include patterns in the game (lines, circles, or scattered), number of players in the pattern, and locations of the players (close to one another or far apart, etc.). Differences among students can become less discouraging if the students are given opportunities to change things, so that they can be successful. Permitting the volleyball server to stand as close to the net as he or she chooses, designating specific players who have a difficult time keeping up to execute all of the throw-ins in soccer, working with peer partners who can help interpret written personal fitness program instructions, or allowing a hit after two bounces of the tennis ball can turn a dreaded class into a positive, uplifting experience.

6. *Limits.* Limits in games have to do with what is expected of players (the kind of participation and the movements that are necessary) and the environmental conditions (boundaries, time limits, scoring, and rules). Wider boundaries, modified rules, shoulder instead of forward rolls, spotting instead of executing a cartwheel, smaller goals to defend, and more than one chance to execute a correct serve can include students who might never have had the opportunity to participate in a game with their classmates.

Students can be wonderfully creative when they are given an opportunity to analyze the components in a familiar game and are invited to invent ways to alter it by changing one or more components. In the beginning, the teacher may have to provide some examples—such as, if the game requires the use of one ball, what changes to the game would be necessary if two or more balls were used? How could the rules be changed if three rather than two teams were included in the game?

COLLABORATION TO CREATE AN LRE

The collaborative process, one in which two or more professionals share responsibilities and, subsequently, thoughts and ideas, is often difficult for educators. It is particularly distressing to some professionals when the need for collaboration is thrust on them by programs or administrators. The most successful collaborations are those that spring from grassroots, teacher-based efforts and that emerge naturally as professionals learn to trust each other and themselves. Shared responsibility necessitates significant communication and specific delineation of responsibilities.[14] General, ongoing team meetings are necessary if this type of communication is to work. In addition, there must be a way for team members involved in the collaboration to communicate with others generally. Many teachers have found shared lunch periods and common planning periods to be good times to discuss common problems and to create solutions.

Maguire[25] noted that there are four types of skills necessary for collaboration between educators in the school setting:

1. Exchanging information and skills
2. Group problem solving
3. Reaching decisions by consensus
4. Resolving conflicts

Exchanging Information and Skills

All professionals involved in collaboration must be able to share information and skills in a nonthreatening, nurturing way. As is true of all collaborative efforts, a teacher who is confident of his or her ability is delighted to share and receive information and skills from others. While this type of information sharing can be accomplished in formal, in-service training experiences, often the most effective information sharing occurs in small doses as professionals work together on an ongoing basis. This type of mutual learning occurs when teachers learn from watching another's behavior (modeling), observe another teacher's portfolio assessment, and share assessment/evaluation data.

Group Problem Solving

Historically, teachers have had their own autonomous classroom or gymnasium. Decisions made within their rooms have been made independently. Collaborative teaching necessitates that teachers learn to make group decisions and solve problems together. The skills required for group problem solving include:

- Identifying the problem
- Stating the problem

- Listing solutions
- Comparing solutions
- Deciding on the solution to the particular problem
- Reaching decisions by consensus

Reaching Decisions by Consensus

Although it is a more time-consuming process than making decisions by a vote, the collaborative process necessitates that all team members feel comfortable with group decisions. To reach consensus requires open and honest communication and, by necessity, a willingness to give and take for the sake of the program. For example, if a local campus received a small grant allocation and needed to determine how best to use the money to serve its students, the teachers (and, in the best educational environment, the students) would meet to discuss and prioritize needs. Together, all involved would come to a decision that all could accept.

Resolving Conflicts

As is true of any human community, conflicts may arise among members of that community. Teachers involved in a collaborative effort may find that there are times when disagreements occur and conflicts arise. One of the most important aspects of a collaborative effort is the willingness of those involved to address disagreements and conflicts openly and honestly. Left to fester, disagreements and conflicts will grow out of proportion. This type of open discussion requires professionals who are secure in their own skills and competencies. In the event that professionals cannot solve a dispute by themselves, a negotiator may be required to help find resolution.

The Consultant's Contribution to an LRE

The significant impetus toward including learners with disabilities in general physical education has drastically and dramatically changed the nature of APE in schools and, at the same time, the nature of services provided by the adapted physical educator. Many adapted physical educators have been thrust into the role of consultant. For many physical educators specially trained to provide services to children and adults with disabilities, the process of changing roles from direct service provider to that of consultant has been difficult.[24] The general physical educator can indeed provide an excellent program for students with disabilities if their APE consultant provides the following services:

- Assessment and evaluation of motor performance
- Evaluation of the learning environment
- Collaborative development of the IEP
- Monitoring of student progress toward annual goals and benchmarks
- Collaboration in the development of a portfolio assessment
- Help in solving student-related problems, particularly related to behavior
- Grading of modifications
- Curriculum modifications
- Activity modifications
- Demonstrations of teaching behavior
- Work with parents to foster their participation in program development
- Communication skills
- Provision of specialized equipment

With this type of comprehensive support, a student with disabilities may be able to learn and thrive in the general physical education setting, and the general physical educator will be willing to serve children with special needs.

In the event that the student is unable to participate successfully without additional personnel support, the APE consultant may play a crucial role in the creation of a setting that is inclusive. The APE consultant can:

1. Create a personnel support program
2. Identify student needs
3. Determine the least intrusive personnel continuum that will meet the student's needs (e.g., a peer buddy is much less intrusive than a full-time paraprofessional)
4. Develop a training program
5. Write specific job descriptions for support personnel

It is vital that important communication be established with the principal, teachers, and parents of students with and without disabilities if a successful student support program is to be implemented. (Specific strategies to follow when initiating student support programs in physical education were presented in Table 6-8.) In addition, communications with building personnel are a vital part of this process.

Perhaps the most important thing a quality APE consultant can do is honor the role of the general physical educator. The general physical educator has specific, usually state-based, mandates regarding the curriculum, the essential knowledge and skills that are expected by the state education agency. The APE consultant, while focused on the child with a disability, must make sure that the recommendations made to the general physical educator are consistent with the curriculum and class format.[11]

Creating concise job descriptions may be the single most important part of the process of serving as a consultant to the general physical educator. Specifically, a job description allows the APE consultant to ensure some quality control and takes a huge load off the shoulders of the general physical educator. The job description should include specific task requirements, dates/time involved, the extent of responsibility, the hierarchy of authority, and allowance for "storms." (Sample job descriptions used in a large, urban school district APE consultancy are presented in **Tables 6-14** and **6-15**.)

TABLE 6-14 Job Description for an Adult Volunteer in an Elementary Physical Education Program

Volunteer: Beth Ann Huettig

Students: Alex, Talitha, Lashundra, and Jesus

Physical education teacher: Jean Pyfer

Physical education: Tuesday and Thursday, 10:10 to 10:50 A.M.

- Provide instructional support for Alex, Talitha, Lashundra, and Jesus
- Please use the following strategies for encouraging appropriate behavior:
  1. Praise the child if "on task."
  2. Praise another child, in close proximity, who is "on task."
  3. Remind the child verbally regarding the task—for example, "Alex, we are all doing warm-ups now," or "Alex, I'd like you to join the other children and do your sit-ups."
  4. Physically assist the child with the task. For example, sit down next to Talitha and help her hold on to the parachute handle.
- If the child demonstrates "off-task" or disruptive behaviors after using the four steps, request the teacher's assistance.
- Beth, remember you are responsible solely to me. If one of the children is abusive or aggressive, please let me intervene.

TABLE 6-15   Job Description for a Paraprofessional for Middle School Physical Education

To: Mr. Chen, special education assistant, self-contained classroom, Carthage Middle School

From: Jean Pyfer, APE consultant

Responsibilities for: Alejandro Moreno

Physical education: 11:00 to 11:50 A.M. every day

- Allow Alejandro to wheel himself to the gymnasium every day. Please leave 5 minutes before passing time, so that Alejandro will not be late.
- Please watch quietly as Alejandro does his modified warm-ups with the class. Please note that his exercises are posted in the coach's office on the back of his door. He knows his exercises, but he may "pretend" he doesn't to avoid them.
- As the class begins the group activity, please use another student (one who hasn't dressed for activity) to work on skills with Alejandro. For example, if the class is playing basketball, demonstrate to the student how to bounce pass to Alejandro. Carefully monitor the activity to ensure that his peer is not too rough.
- When the class begins laps at the end of class (outside or inside), Alejandro should start his as well. At the beginning of the year he was able to roll 2 times around the gymnasium in 10 minutes. Build, please, throughout the year by adding 1 lap per month. I would like him to be able to roll 6 times around the gymnasium in 10 minutes. Reward good effort with the football cards I gave you.
- You are responsible for Alejandro's safety and well-being in the gymnasium. If you have difficulty with his behavior, call me and we will develop a specific behavior management plan. If he has a "bad" day (swearing, refusing, etc.), report it to his classroom teacher.

Each job description is written in very different terms, using different language, depending on the sophistication of the service provider. It is vital that the information in the job description also be shared verbally for the support person who is unable to read. A translator may be required to communicate the components of the job description to a student, volunteer, or paraprofessional who uses a language not used by the consultant.

The job description can be used informally, as a simple method of communicating with support personnel. If it is determined that the job is not being done well—that is, the student with disabilities is not being served well—several options exist, including:

1. Evaluate job performance in relation to the job description and provide supervisory support. Revise the job description if necessary.
2. Find another peer buddy, older student assistant, or volunteer.
3. Use the job description as a type of contract, and ask school personnel to sign the contract in the presence of the building principal.

A letter written to motivate, as well as educate, a general physical education teacher is a great tool. This type of letter is extremely effective for building cooperative teams with school personnel because it is personal and it compliments the physical education teacher. This is particularly important in school settings in which the teachers do not feel empowered (most schools, unfortunately). An APE consultant willing to take the time to thank and honor a general physical educator for service to students with disabilities will have created a strong support network. A letter, at once thanking the teacher and reminding him or her of the needs of his or her students, also provides a summary and review of communication that is important documentation of one's program and efforts. Copying the letter to the physical educators' principal and any other administrative "higher-ups" is reinforcing to the teacher and reminds the administrators of the importance of APE.

Remembering to take the time to thank school personnel who serve students well is important. A simple handwritten or computer-generated thank-you note is a marvelous tool for reinforcing good efforts and developing a team of individuals willing to serve students with disabilities. Perhaps most effective is a note, voice tape, or work of art created by the student (with the help of the classroom teacher or art teacher) to thank his or her peer buddy, older student assistant, volunteer, or paraprofessional. This type of thank you is also very important for the general physical educator. A sample of a note sent to a paraeducator who served children very well is presented in **Table 6-16**. Sending a copy to building principals, district

TABLE 6-16   "Thank-You" Memo Sent to a Paraprofessional

MEMO

To: Sharon Black

From: Carol Huettig, APE consultant

Subject: Deundrae Bowie, Dunbar Learning Center

Date: December 1, 2015

I can't thank you enough for your efforts on Deundrae's behalf. He is so lucky to have you as a mentor and friend. Your willingness to provide him with special help has truly enhanced the quality of his life. His dribbling skills have really improved, as has his ability to maneuver his wheelchair.

I thank you, once again, for your professionalism, dedication, and concern for your students.

cc: Mr. Moore, principal, Dunbar Learning Center; Dr. Pittman, area coordinator physical education coordinators, and area special education coordinators enhances its impact.

One of the most difficult aspects of being an APE consultant is having a great deal of responsibility and very little, if any, authority. The consultant must be accountable for his or her actions and for the supervision provided to school personnel. Job descriptions, letters that outline responsibilities and summarize conversations, correspondence regarding support personnel programs, and copies of thank-you notes help document efforts. As important, the APE consultant must do the following:

1. Keep a copy of original assessment data, as well as the written report shared with the IEP committee.
2. Attend as many EEP meetings as possible. There is simply no substitute for face-to-face communication with parents, general educators, building personnel, and related service personnel.
3. Keep a copy of the IEP and carefully document visits to campus sites to monitor achievement of goals/objectives.
4. Maintain careful logs that document:
   a. Direct student contact, including the date, length of time spent with the student, and the purpose on that date (e.g., assessment, team teaching, or modeling teaching behavior)
   b. Time spent in consultancy, including the date, length of time spent in collaboration, personnel with whom he or she consulted, and the purpose on that date (e.g., modifying grading, modifying activities, or developing a behavior management program)
   c. The nature and extent of parent communication
   d. The nature and extent of any communication with the student's physician and/or related service personnel
5. Be visible on the local school campus. In addition to signing in at the office, make a point of speaking to the building principal, the office secretary, the child's general and/or special educator, and the physical educator.
6. Send a note home to the student's parent if the student has made progress or has accomplished a goal/objective and leave copies with the child's general and/or special educator and the physical educator.
7. Keep transportation logs to verify campus visits.

One of the unique difficulties associated with the consultancy is demonstrating, in a systematic way, the efficacy of the program and the effect it has on the lives of students with disabilities. As more and more school districts and school systems demand accountability of their staff members, the responsibilities of the consultant become more clear—the consultant must keep and maintain a paper trail to document service delivery.

SUMMARY

APE has changed dramatically since inclusion was widely embraced as an educational philosophy and LRE a necessary practice. General physical educators are becoming increasingly responsible for providing instruction to students with disabilities. There are instructional strategies and procedures that can be used to ensure that appropriate services are provided.

Physical educators deeply committed to providing quality APE services have to cope with, adjust to, and create new collaborative and consultative procedures for providing services in inclusive settings. Careful preparation, communication, and documentation are needed for the process to work.

REVIEW QUESTIONS

1. What are the nine instructional variables that can be addressed to accommodate learners with disabilities in the least restrictive environment?
2. How can the least restrictive environment design matrixes included in this chapter be used to evaluate appropriate physical education services for a student with disabilities?

REFERENCES

1. AAHPERD. (2004). www.aahperd.org
2. American Foundation for the Blind. (2003). www.afb.org/education /jtlipaper.html
3. Block, M., & Obrusnikova, I. (2007). Facilitating social acceptance and inclusion. In Block, M. *A teacher's guide to including students with disabilities in general physical education* (3rd ed.). Baltimore, MD: Paul Brookes Publishing.
4. Buck, M., Lund, J., Harris, J., & Cook, C. (2007). *Instructional strategies for secondary school PE* (6th ed.). Boston, MA: McGraw-Hill.
5. Cortiella, C. (2006). *NCLB and IDEA: What parents of students with disabilities need to know*. Minneapolis, MN: The Advocacy Institute, University of Minnesota, National Center on Educational Outcomes.

6. Davis, R. W., Kotecki, J. E., Harvey, M. W., & Oliver, A. (2007). Responsibilities and training needs of paraeducators in physical education. *APAQ, 24*, 70–83.

7. Doyle, M. B. (2008). *The paraprofessional's guide to the inclusive classroom: Working as a team.* Baltimore, MD: Paul Brookes Publishing.

8. Duckworth, S. V., & Kostell, P. H. (1999). The parent panel: Supporting children with special needs. *J Assoc Childhood Education International, 75*(4), 199–203.

9. Erickson, R., et al. (November/December 1998). Inclusive assessments and accountability systems: Tools of the trade in educational reform. *Teaching Except Child*, 4–9.

10. Huettig, C., Simbeck, C., & Cravens, S. (May 2003). Addressing fears associated with teaching all our children. *Teach Elem Physical Education, 14*(3), 7–12.

11. Huettig, C., & Roth, K. Maximizing the use of APE consultants: What the general physical educator has the right to expect. *JOPERD 73*(l), 32–35.

12. Hughes, C., Fowler, S. E., Copeland, S. R., Agran, M., Wehmeyer, M. L., & Church-Pupke, P. P. (2004). Supporting high school students to engage in recreational activities with peers. *Behavior Modification, 28*, 3–27.

13. Idol, L. (1997). Key questions related to building collaborative and inclusive schools. *J Learn Dis 30*(4), 384–394.

14. Kasser, S., & Lytle, R. (2005). *Inclusive physical activity: A lifetime of opportunity.* Champaign, IL: Human Kinetics.

15. Kozub, F., & Lienert, C. (2003). Attitudes toward teaching children with disabilities: Review of literature and research paradigm. *Adapted Physical Activity Quarterly, 20*, 323–346.

16. Lavay, B., French, R., & Henderson, H. (2006). *Positive behavior management in physical activity settings.* Champaign, IL: Human Kinetics.

17. Lavay, B., Lytle, R., Robinson, N., & Huettig, C. (2003). Teaching collaboration and consultation skills to preservice and inservice APE teachers. *JOPERD, 74*(5), 13–16.

18. Learning Disabilities Association of America. (2007). www.ldnatl.org/positions /inclusion/html.

19. Lee, S-H., Yoo, S-Y., & Bak, S-H. (2003). Characteristics of friendships between children with and without mild disabilities. *Education and Training in Developmental Disabilities, 38*, 157–166.

20. Lieberman, L. J. (2007). *Paraeducators in physical education: A training guide to roles and responsibilities.* Champaign, IL: Human Kinetics.

21. Lieberman, L., & Houston-Wilson, C. (2009). *Strategies for inclusion: A handbook for physical educators* (2nd ed.). Champaign, IL: Human Kinetics.

22. Lieberman, L., & Houston-Wilson, C. (2011). Strategies for increasing the status and value of adapted physical education in schools. *Journal of Physical Education, Recreation, and Dance, 82*, 25–28.

23. Lieberman, L., Lytle, R., & Clarcq, J. (2008). Getting it right from the start: Employing the universal design for learning approach to your curriculum. *Journal of Physical Education, Recreation and Dance, 79,* 32–39.

24. Lytle, R. K., & Hutchinson, G. E. (2004). Adapted physical educators: The multiple roles of consultants. *APAQ, 21,* 34–49.

25. Maguire, P. (1994). Developing successful collaborative relationships. *JOPERD, 65*(l), 32–36.

26. Marks, S. U., Scharder, C., & Levine, M. (1999). Paraeducator experiences in inclusive settings: Helping, hovering or holding their own? *Except Child, 65*(3), 315–328.

27. Mosston, M., & Ashworth. (2008). Teaching physical education (1st online ed.). Retrieved from http://www.spectrumofteachingstyles.org/ebook

28. National Consortium for Physical Education and Individuals with Disabilities. (2013). Links and resources for parents. www.ncpeid.org

29. No Child Left Behind Act. (January 8, 2002). www.edu.gov/nclb/landing.html

30. O.A.S.I.S.: Circle of Friends. (2003). www.udel.edu/bkirby/asperger/socialcircle.html

31. Ravensberg, J. D., & Tobin, T. J. (2006). *IDEA 2004 final regulations: The reauthorized functional behavioral assessment.* Educational and Community Supports, College of Education, University of Oregon.

32. Rogers, J. (May 2–3, 1993). The inclusion revolution. *Research Bulletin.* Phi Delta Kappa, Center for Evaluation, Development and Research.

33. Searcy, S. (1996). Friendship interventions for the integration of children and youth with learning and behavior problems. *Preventing School Failure, 40*(3), 131–134.

34. Stockall, N., & Gartin, B. (2002). The nature of inclusion in a blue ribbon school: A revelatory case. *Exceptionality, 10*(3), 171–188.

35. TASH. (2003). http://tash.org/inclusion/res02inclusiveed.htm

36. The Arc. (2009). Position statement on inclusion. www.thearc.org

37. Texas Woman's University Project Inspire. (2007). www.twu.edu/INSPIRE.2003

38. Trent, S., Kea, C., & Oh, K. (2008). Preparing pre-service educators for cultural diversity: How far have we come? *Exceptional Children, 74,* 328–350.

39. Tripp, A., & Zhu, W. (2005). Assessment of students with disabilities in physical education: Legal perspectives and practices. *Journal of Physical Education, Recreation, and Dance, 76,* 41–47.

40. United States Department of Education, Office of Special Education and Rehabilitative Services. (2014). *Thirty-sixth annual report to Congress on the implementation of the individuals with disabilities education act.* Washington, DC.

41. Ward, P., & Ayvazo, S. (2006). Classwide peer tutoring in physical education: Assessing its effects with kindergartners with autism. *APAQ, 23,* 233–244.

42. Williams, N. (1994). The physical education hall of shame, part 2. *JOPERD*, *65*(2), 17–20.

43. Williams, N. (1996). The physical education hall of shame, part 3. *JOPERD*, *67*(8), 45–48.

44. Yell, M. L. (1995). Least restrictive environment, inclusion and students with disabilities: A legal analysis. *J Spec Ed*, *28*(4), 389–404.

45. Yu, S. Y., Ostrosky, M., & Fowler, S. (2011). Children's friendship development: A comparative study. *Early Childhood Research and Practice*, *13*. http://ecrp.uiuc.edu/v13n1/yu.html

CHAPTER 7

Enhancing Student Behavior

OBJECTIVES

- Give the four fundamental assumptions about behavior management.
- Describe techniques that can be used to identify behaviors that need to be learned or changed.
- Name and describe five techniques that can be used to facilitate performance of a skill or behavior.
- Differentiate between behavior management techniques for reducing disruptive behaviors in a group setting versus with individuals.
- Give three examples of techniques to facilitate generalization.
- Identify the characteristics of effective classroom management rules.
- Name five critical mistakes a teacher cannot afford to make.
- Identify the circumstances that permit school personnel to suspend or expel a student with a disability.

Classroom management is a major concern in the schools in the United States and teachers feel they have very little training in the area.[25] Teachers who feel unprepared to address behavior challenges may experience more difficulty with behavior management plans and be less willing to implement individualized programming.[2, 14] Behavior problems, lack of discipline, student safety, and violence in schools are concerns.[31] More and more children are going to school from homes where socially acceptable behavior is not taught. Children who are raised in homes where cultural, religious, and

ethnic expectations differ vastly from the expectations of the schools cannot expect to thrive in school settings. Children from homes where patterns of abuse, verbal and physical, are the norm cannot be expected to demonstrate kindness and consideration for others, let alone wait quietly in line and take turns. Their everyday world has taught them to look out for themselves first and to mistrust adults. How do teachers manage the behavior of children who are being raised in environments that, instead of meeting their basic needs, constantly threaten their safety and well-being?

In the past, teachers who became overwhelmed with a student's behavior would refer the "problem" to special education or to the school psychologist to be fixed. However, more recently, educators are coming to understand that the problem may not rest solely with the child. It is becoming clear that the structure of the learning environment, the types of behaviors that are taught directly, and the kinds of interactions that are allowed to routinely occur in that environment are critical factors that impact the behavior of students.

Leading educators and recent legislation address the need to maximize positive learning environments while minimizing problematic behavior. Rather than using negative behavior management techniques that have been used in the past, positive behavioral support plans are being promoted.[26] Negative intervention strategies, such as verbal reprimands, time-outs, corporal punishment, and denial of privileges, may solve immediate problems, but are rarely effective in eliminating undesirable behaviors.[16] School administrators, teachers, and staff have important roles in creating and maintaining a learning environment and providing the support necessary to enable all students to learn and benefit from their educational experience. The person in most direct contact with the student, the teacher, has the primary responsibility for ensuring positive student outcomes.

Effective teachers are emotionally stable, flexible, and empathetic toward students, as well as proactive rather than reactive. The most effective teachers plan in advance, give clear instructions, demonstrate consistency, teach to learners' strengths, model behavioral expectations, follow through on consequences, affirm positive behavior, and teach students developmentally appropriate behaviors and socialization skills.[11] These teacher behaviors result in improved student performance levels and lead to a reduction of undesirable behaviors.

In this chapter, we will discuss effective discipline practices, ways to identify problematic performance and behavior, and techniques for maximizing student performance.

Assertive, Effective Discipline

ESTABLISHING THE RULES

As a teacher you have the right to teach, you have the right to ask for help, and you have the right to be safe. Students have the right to learn, the right to ask for help, and the right to be safe. Teachers who establish clear and positive rules for the learning environment honor these basic premises.[5] These teachers are consistent, establish clear and concise rules and expectations, and have clear and concise consequences tied to the behavior. Their classroom management rules are positive, specify proper student behavior in observable terms, and have specific, observable consequences.[3] The management rules should be developed at the beginning of the school term and involve the students. The number of rules should be limited to five to seven and be written in terms the students can understand. Consequences for breaking the rules should also involve the students and be clearly stated. The rules should be displayed in a prominent place and the students should frequently be reminded about them.

It is important that the teacher remember that a child has a right to choose to misbehave. When those occasions arise, the student must be reminded that his or her behavior was his or her choice, and then the consequence must always be offered as a choice. A proven way to ensure that students follow the rules is to catch students being good and then praise them for following the rules. Other proven strategies are staying close to the student, providing signals when the rules are not followed, giving verbal redirection, and remaining unemotional but firm when intervening.

Several mistakes a teacher must avoid are listed in **Table 7-1**. These mistakes must be avoided because they communicate very negative messages to students. It is imperative that teachers honor students' individuality and treat all students equally. Inconsistency sends a definite message that some students are "better" than others. Demonstrating anger informs the student

TABLE 7-1 Critical Mistakes a Teacher Cannot Afford to Make

- Be inconsistent in expectations, demeanor, and behavior
- Treat children differently
- Be volatile
- Criticize a child in front of others
- Ask a child to do a particular task
- Compare students using posted charts and grades
- Be sarcastic
- Make vague, negative statements about the student
- Use corporal punishment
- Use consequences that are disproportionate to the act
- Use consequences that are unrelated to the act
- Select consequences that you can't administer evenly, calmly, and without anger
- Ignore inappropriate behavior when you are too exhausted to deal with the student and the behavior
- Delay consequences to meet your schedule
- Threaten
- Threaten without being able to follow through
- Use exercise as punishment
- Punish the whole class for the misbehavior of one child

that acting out is an acceptable behavior. Criticizing students in front of others is demeaning and demoralizing. Asking a child to do something like "Jon, will you sit down?" gives the student the opportunity to refuse. Once that happens, the teacher has few positive options left. Comparing students publicly through the use of posted charts and grades enables other students to observe who has performed more poorly than others (a public put-down). Sarcasm should not be used because students frequently do not understand sarcasm, and it is a clear sign the teacher is unable to positively control the situation. Vague, negative statements such as "I can't believe you just did that," "What a stupid thing to do," and "What did you just say?" do nothing to convey to the student what is expected. Using corporal punishment teaches the student that physically abusing another is acceptable behavior. Selecting consequences that are disproportionate, unrelated to the act, and can't be administered evenly, calmly, and without anger communicates to students very mixed and negative messages that can be interpreted in a variety of ways. When you ignore behavior that is dangerous to the student or others, you inadvertently inform the student that the behavior is acceptable. For consequences to be effective, they must be immediate. Threats such as "Just you wait, young man," "So help me, you're going to regret doing that," "Don't make me come over there," and "That's it, you're dead meat" convey nothing to the student except you do not know how or you choose not to deal with the problem immediately. Using exercise as punishment teaches the student exercising is negative rather than positive. Punishing the whole class for one child's misdeeds may lead to disapproval and possible retaliation by the child's peers. The teacher who understands and avoids making these critical mistakes is a teacher who has successfully created a positive learning environment in which all students feel valued, know they can expect answers to their questions, and feel safe to learn.

In addition to creating a positive learning environment, the teacher who serves children with various physical, mental, and emotional disabilities frequently needs several methods for identifying problematic performance and behavior as well as strategies to systematically structure the learning environment to enhance those students' opportunities to learn. Students with disabilities who have ongoing behavior problems must have a formal behavior management plan that has been developed in conjunction with the parents.[24] Methods for identifying problematic behaviors and strategies for structuring the environment are described in the following section.

Identifying Problematic Performance and Behavior

NEED TO ASSESS AND MONITOR PERFORMANCE AND BEHAVIOR

According to Cowart,[8] an experienced adapted physical education (APE) teacher, "Good teaching practices include instructional strategies matched to each student's learning style, curriculum appropriate for that student, and applying good reinforcement practices." The two most common techniques for assessing and monitoring a student's progress are through actual testing and observation. The initial assessments and observations are used to determine present levels of performance, so that the student's individualized educational program (IEP) can be developed. Once that program is implemented, ongoing observation is necessary to determine whether the student is benefiting from the intervention strategies selected. In addition to monitoring physical and motor performance, the student's behavior must also be noted because, if a student misbehaves, instruction slows until the teacher is able to address that problem. When, for whatever reason, it is observed that learning is not occurring, the teacher must determine why. That is to say, the problem must be identified and addressed.

DEFINE THE PROBLEM

The teacher is alerted to the existence of a problem when any of the following occurs: (1) no progress is being made toward the instructional objectives, (2) tasks are not being completed in a timely manner, (3) the teacher is having to spend an inordinate amount of time with one student, (4) a student is disrupting other students, or (5) a student is behaving in an unacceptable fashion. At this point, the teacher must evaluate the situation to determine exactly what the problem is and why it is occurring.[7]

After determining what problem is occurring, it is critical that the problem be clearly stated in observable terms that convey what is occurring, when, where, how often, and the strength (intensity). Examples are "When Thomas attempts to perform a basketball lay-up shot, he misses the basket because he always overruns the point at which he should be releasing the ball" and "At the end of her first week in class, when Marquitta arrived at the jump rope station, she picked up one end of a rope and began swinging it rapidly around her head endangering other students at that station." Each of these examples is a description of what is occurring, when, where, how often, and at what intensity. Once the problem has been identified, the possible cause for the behavior must be determined.

DETERMINE WHY THE PROBLEM IS OCCURRING

When trying to determine why a problem is occurring, the teacher asks himself or herself several questions that address instruction, the curriculum, and reinforcement.[8] Instructional questions would center on whether the student understands the task, whether the student needs additional assistance, and/or whether the demonstration of the task was sufficient for the student to replicate the skill. In the case of Thomas, the instructional question might be "Does Thomas require some specific cues to understand when to jump and how to release the ball?" In Marquitta's case, the question might be "Are the types of jump rope activities that we expect to be performed at that station understood by Marquitta?"

An example of a curricular question is "Has Thomas been taught the lead-up skills necessary to be successful with his lay-up shots?" To address Marquitta's behavior, we might ask ourselves whether she has recently transferred from a school where jumping rope was not included in the physical education program.

Reinforcement questions should address whether the student is trying to obtain something, avoid something, or both obtain and avoid something; to access sensory stimulation; and/or to communicate.[7] In Thomas's case, the question might be, "Is Thomas deliberately dribbling past the basket to avoid trying to make a successful shot, so that he will get more individual attention from me?" In the case of Marquitta swinging the rope around her head, we might wonder if she is attempting to avoid a jumping task or whether she is trying to communicate something to other students.

ADDRESS THE PROBLEM

The answers to the questions will determine the next steps the teacher will take to impact the performance of the student. Sometimes quickly thinking through your observations of the student experiencing the problem will help with the solution. However, there are times when more information must be gathered before the nature of the problem is understood, and yet immediate action must be taken. As we think about Thomas's problem, we are reminded that he doesn't usually misbehave to get extra attention, so we can assume that there is something about the way the skill is performed that needs to be corrected. A task analysis of the skill components will help pinpoint the error as occurring because Thomas is not timing his jump correctly or he does not understand where the ball must contact the backboard to rebound into the basket. But when a student's behavior is disruptive to the class, immediate intervention is required and solutions thought out later.

Because Marquitta's behavior is endangering others, the teacher needs to immediately tell Marquitta to stop and possibly redirect her to another task, such as being one of two turners of the long jump rope. If she chooses not to cooperate, she is given other options that are included in the class rules. By intervening, the teacher has solved the immediate problem;

however, to prevent similar problems in the future, the reason Marquitta chose to misbehave in the first place must still be determined. Frequently, talking privately with the student who is disruptive will provide insight into the problem. In Marquitta's case, she may tell you that one or more of the students in her group made fun of the way she dressed or talked and she just got "mad" and decided to hurt them back. In this case, the effective teacher will (1) find a way to help Marquitta understand that striking out at others in anger is never productive in the long run, (2) restructure the class to separate her temporarily from those who were teasing her, and (3) praise Marquitta's good behavior (or dress or bilingual ability) in the presence of the class.

Usually, experienced teachers who have worked with hundreds of students are able to intuit the right intervention strategy more readily than inexperienced new teachers. But the primary goals for all teachers are to maximize student performance and minimize distractions.

Self-management is another technique that should be encouraged when a student is ready to regulate his or her own behavior to address the problem and establish ownership and independence. Teaching self-management of behavior to students with disabilities is important. The technique requires that the control over behavior be shifted from the teacher or parent to the student.[32] Self-management leads students toward a more self-determined lifestyle and provides them with control of their own behaviors in and out of school. The effectiveness of a variety of self-management procedures has been demonstrated in classroom settings. It has been shown that students can regulate their behavior by selecting appropriate goals; by self-instructing; and by self-monitoring, reinforcing, and evaluating responses.[17] Self-management procedures consist of one or more of the following strategies:

- *Goal setting.* Teaching students to select numerical targets to achieve leads to higher performance than not selecting goals or selecting vague goals.[15]
- *Self-instruction.* Teaching individuals to direct their own task performance is critical for independent functioning.[32]
- *Self-evaluation.* Teaching individuals to observe, record, evaluate their performance according to a standard, and reward their own successes promotes ongoing growth and independence.

Maximizing Student Performance

As Cowart[8] reminds us, "Good teaching practices include instructional strategies matched to each student's learning style, curriculum appropriate for that student, and applying good reinforcement practices." In this section, these three practices will be discussed.

Solid instructional practices include clarity of instruction, appropriate intervention, and provision for feedback.[8] The most effective teachers keep their instructions to a minimum. Clear and concise directions are a must in the physical education setting. The less time spent with the teacher talking and the more time spent with the students practicing, the better. When it is noted that several students are experiencing difficulty, the activity should be halted and additional instruction given. When additional assistance is needed by a few students to enable them to perform effectively, physical assistance can be provided and/or verbal and/or sign clues can be used until the task is mastered.

Effective physical education curricula include activities and skills that are age appropriate and consistent with students' needs, material and equipment appropriate for the students' capabilities, and a learning environment that supports what is being taught.[8] Sometimes students misbehave because the activities are too difficult, too easy, or too boring, or they require too much standing around. Novice learners, whether because of age or inability to understand, cannot be expected to be successful if the racquets, the standards, and other activity equipment cannot be easily managed by them. Frequently students with physical disabilities can participate in most activities if the activity or the equipment is modified to meet their unique needs. Learning environments that are uncluttered, clearly marked, and accessible to all learners are inviting places that make participation enjoyable.

APPLYING GOOD REINFORCEMENT PRACTICES

As stated earlier, positive reinforcement practices are good reinforcement practices. When students feel safe, valued, and successful, their performance improves and their misbehavior decreases. The discussion that follows focuses on positive reinforcers because they yield the most lasting results. Positive reinforcers include teacher or peer praise, stickers, a paper certificate, positive notes to parents, sports equipment, medals, first in line and squad leader privileges, selection of activities a student enjoys doing, and success on a task. Positive reinforcement is constructive because it helps individuals feel good about themselves.

Selection of Reinforcers

Reinforcers may be intrinsic (internal) or extrinsic (external). Intrinsic reinforcement comes from within the learner. Often, knowledge of success on a task or the satisfaction of participating is sufficient reinforcement. Extrinsic reinforcement comes from outside the learner. Examples of extrinsic reinforcement are praise and other rewards from a person who acknowledges the learner's achievement. One objective of a reinforcement program is to move the learner from dependence on extrinsic reinforcers to a search for intrinsic reinforcers. Once learners no longer have to rely on teachers for feedback, they can direct their own learning. It is important that both the learner and the teachers agree on what the reinforcer will be and how the system of reinforcement will work.

Reinforcement Procedures

Contingency management is a way of controlling the use of reinforcers. A contingency agreement is an agreement between the student and the teacher that indicates what the student must do to earn a specific reward. A token economy is a form of contingency management in which tokens (external reinforcers) are earned for desirable behavior. This type of system can be used with a single student, selected groups of students, or classes of students. Five main elements of a token economy include:[21]

1. The identification of specific target behaviors
2. The identification of tokens for conditioned reinforcement
3. The development of a menu of backup reinforcement options to award appropriate behavior
4. The creation of an explicit protocol for exchanging conditioned reinforcers for backup reinforcers
5. The development of procedures for fading the use of the token economy system

Token economy systems that have proved successful in the physical education program include those that allow students to cash in their tokens to buy the following:

- A given number of minutes of supervised free play
- The right to lead class warm-up exercises
- The right to choose a class activity for 5 to 10 minutes on a given day
- The privilege of being the "assistant" teacher for a given class
- The privilege of 5 to 10 minutes of uninterrupted one-on-one play time with the physical education teacher
- The right to eat lunch with the physical education teacher
- A poster of a sports star

Recreation and Sport Equipment   Relatively inexpensive recreation and sport equipment can be purchased to support the token economy system. Children love having the privilege to earn jump ropes, balls, juggling scarves, and hacky-sacks. Parent–teacher associations often are willing to organize fund-raising to help provide the physical education teacher with this type of equipment. There are corporations that have fund-raiser/promotional campaigns (e.g., Box Tops) that may help the physical education teacher secure this type of equipment without buying it out of an already small budget or an equally small personal salary.

Frequency of Reinforcement

The frequency of distributing reinforcers should be carefully controlled, so that the student continues to strive toward desirable goals. The frequency that reinforcers are given is called the reinforcement schedule. Schedules of reinforcement should move from continuous (a reinforcer every time the desirable behavior occurs) to a fixed ratio (e.g., one reinforcer for every three instances of desirable behavior). Interval reinforcement schedules provide reinforcement after an established period of time. The schedule should be changed eventually to a variable-interval ratio (e.g., one reinforcer for every three instances of desirable behavior followed by one reinforcer for every five instances of desirable behavior, or one reinforcer every minute followed by one reinforcer every three minutes). The variable-interval ratio is the most effective because, when students are unable to predict when they will be reinforced, they tend to persist at a task.

Peer Tutoring

Peer tutoring has been shown to increase instructional effectiveness for persons with disabilities. Peer tutoring involves using same-age peers or older peers to interact with children with disabilities to keep them on task.[6] Both the child with a disability and the peers benefit from the interaction. The benefits to students with and without disabilities include: (1) increased academic learning time,[18] (2) increased moderate to vigorous physical activity,[1] (3) enhanced motor performance,[29] (4) age-appropriate role models, and (5) development of social behaviors and communication skills. Peer tutors gain from the experience by (1) increasing acceptance of individual differences, (2) developing a deeper sense of social justice and advocacy for others, (3) increasing self-esteem, and (4) developing a better understanding of how to communicate with and provide assistance to people with disabilities. Peer tutoring programs are most effective when a training program has been incorporated.[18] Starting out with one or two classes and moving to more classes with more peers will allow the program to grow slowly but effectively.[20]

MINIMIZING DISTRACTIONS

Much of the previous discussion concerns the uses of reinforcement to increase efforts toward learning tasks. Very often, reinforcement procedures are used to decrease undesirable behaviors. The undesirable behaviors must be eliminated or substantially reduced, so that the student can focus attention and effort on positive learning habits.

Because of self-concept and attention deficits, children with disabilities may disrupt classrooms and make it difficult for themselves and others to learn meaningful motor skills. When behavior management strategies are applied to classroom management, they must be systematic, consistent, and concerned with both preventing disruptive behavior and promoting positive behavior. There are two levels of classroom management: one for the group and another for individuals within the group.

Managing Group Behavior

There are some techniques for managing behavior that are particularly effective for groups. These include positive teacher attitudes, prevention, establishment and enforcement of class rules, teacher intervention, flexibility in planning, appeals to values, control of the environment, and student leadership opportunities.

Positive teacher attitudes have a powerful impact on the learning of social behavior and physical skills. Some behaviors a teacher can demonstrate that will motivate a class to perform to their maximum include:

1. Be positive. Students work harder to gain rewards than they do to avoid punishment.
2. Teach enthusiastically. Use a comfortable verbal pace, varied inflection, and an encouraging tone of voice.
   a. Set realistic expectations. Students will strive toward goals they believe they can accomplish.
   b. Inform students about their progress. Students need to know they are on track and improving.
   c. Reinforce every legitimate effort. Students are more motivated to persist when their efforts are noticed and reinforced.

The single most effective method for managing behavior is prevention. The most significant technique for controlling behavior is to "catch 'em being good." This proactive teaching response, in which the teacher consistently and enthusiastically embraces "good" behavior, allows the teacher and the students to focus on good behavior. It is crucial that, when addressing the behavior of a child or children, the focus is on behavior. When praising a child for good behavior, it is necessary that other children understand that it is the behavior that is being praised, so that those not being praised do not get the unintentioned message that they are somehow "bad." Examples of appropriate responses include the following:

- "Juan, thank you for being such a good listener."
- "I really like the way Thelma is following directions."
- "Carlos, I'm really proud of you for putting your ball away."
- "Way to be, Jason! I like the fact that you shared your toy with Julianna."

The good teaching technique of "catch 'em being good" is one of the basic elements of preventive planning, which consists of establishing class rules and enforcing them in the least intrusive ways possible. Rules for class conduct should communicate to students the behavior expected by the teacher. Effective class rules should (1) be few in number, (2) be a statement of behavior desired from the student, (3) be simple and clearly stated in a positive way, and (4) explain guidelines that the teacher can enforce. For example, a well-stated rule is "When lined up at the door waiting to pass to the next class, keep your hands to yourself." Clearly stated expectations lead to appropriate classroom behavior. They provide learners with rules of conduct and identify behavior that will be rewarded. It is suggested that a list of rules be placed where students can observe it each day. The consequences for breaking rules should also be made clear to the students. These must be posted in the native languages of the children served. For example, if a school serves a large number of Hispanic students, rules and consequences should be posted in both English and Spanish. When serving young children or nonreaders, rules and consequences must be reviewed before each class period; in some situations, rules and consequences may need to be repeated periodically throughout the class.

Rules cannot take care of every situation; often, there is disruptive behavior not covered by the rules. The difficult decision each teacher must make is whether to intervene and stop the disruptive behavior. Teachers have a responsibility to interfere with behaviors that:

- Present a physical danger to self or others
- Are psychologically harmful to the child and others
- Lead to excessive excitement, loss of control, or chaos
- Prohibit continuation of the program
- Lead to destruction of property
- Encourage the spread of negativism in the group
- Lead to conflict with others outside the group
- Compromise the teacher's ability to deliver effective instruction

If the teacher does decide it is necessary to intervene to control disruptive behavior, several techniques are effective. Some specific techniques to manage disruptive students in a physical education setting are as follows:

- **Planned ignoring.** Much of children's behavior is designed to antagonize the teacher. If this behavior is not contagious, it may be wise to ignore it and not gratify the child.

- **Signal interference.** The teacher can use nonverbal controls, such as hand clapping, eye contact, frowns, and body posture, to indicate to the child disapproval and control.
- **Proximity control.** The teacher can stand next to a child who is having difficulty. This is to let the child know of the teacher's concern regarding the behavior.
- **Interest boosting.** If a child's interest is waning, involve the child actively in class activities of the moment and let him or her demonstrate the skill that is being performed or discussed.
- **Reduction of tension through humor.** Humor is often able to penetrate a tense situation, with the result that everyone becomes more comfortable.
- **Hurdle lesson.** Sometimes a child is frustrated by the immediate task. Instead of asking for help, the child may involve his or her peers in disruptive activity. In this event, select and structure a task in which the child can be successful.
- **Restructure of classroom program.** If the teacher finds the class irritable, bored, or excited, a change in program might be needed.
- **Support from routine.** Some children need more structure than others. Without these guideposts, they feel insecure. Structure programs for those who need it by clearly defining the rules, boundaries, and acceptable limits of behavior, as well as adhering to the same general routine each day.
- **Direct appeal to value areas.** Appeal to certain values that children have internalized, such as a relationship between the teacher and the child, behavioral consequences, awareness of peer reaction, and appeal to the teacher's power of authority.
- **Removal of seductive objects.** It is difficult for the teacher to compete against balls, bats, objects that can be manipulated, and equipment that may be in the vicinity of instruction. Either the objects have to be removed or the teacher has to accept the disorganized state of the group.[27, 28]

HANDLING THE DISRUPTIVE BEHAVIOR

The behavior problems of students with disabilities frequently contribute to their placement in special physical education programs. When students with disabilities are placed in the physical education class, teachers are often concerned that their problem behaviors will interfere with the operation of the classroom.

Behaviors that interfere with classroom instruction, impede social interaction with the teacher and peers, or endanger others are considered classroom conduct problems. Examples of inappropriate classroom behaviors are talking out, fighting, arguing, swearing, using equipment or facilities inappropriately, being noncompliant, and avoiding interactions with others. Breaking of the rules of the game, poor sportsmanship, and immature and withdrawn behaviors also fall under this category. Behaviors that interfere with the special student's motor skill development are considered skill problems. Typical skill problems result from poor attending behavior and failure to attempt tasks with a best effort.

Problem behaviors are exhibited in one of three ways: (1) there is a low rate of appropriate behaviors, (2) there is a high rate of inappropriate behaviors, or (3) the appropriate behavior is not part of the student's repertoire. Knowing the characteristics of the behavior is important, because different management strategies are linked to each.

1. *Low rate of appropriate behaviors.* Students with low rates of appropriate behaviors do exhibit appropriate behaviors, but not as frequently as expected or required. For example, a student may be able to stay on task only 50% of the time. Also, students may behave appropriately in one setting but not in another. For instance, the special student may work well on individual tasks but find it difficult to function in group games. To alleviate these problems, the teacher sets up a systematic program to generalize on-task behaviors from one situation to another. An example of facilitating the generalization of on-task behavior toward functioning in a group setting is to gradually move a student from an individual task to a task that is paralleled by another student, to a task where two students assist each other in being successful (such as taking turns spotting one another during free weight lifting).

2. *High rate of inappropriate behaviors.* Inappropriate behaviors that occur frequently or for long periods are troublesome to teachers. Examples are students who do not conform to class rules 30 to 40 times a week, those who talk during 50% to 60% of class instruction, those who use profanity 5 to 10 times in one class period, and those who are off task 70% to 75% of the class period. To overcome these high rates of inappropriate

behavior, the physical education teacher attempts to decrease the frequency or duration of the undesired behavior by increasing appropriate behaviors that are incompatible. For instance, to decrease the incidence of hitting a peer while in class, the teacher can increase the rate of performing tasks or decrease the time between tasks.

3. *Appropriate behavior not part of the student's repertoire.* Students may not yet have learned appropriate behaviors for social interaction or classroom functioning. For instance, they may not know sportsmanship conduct in class games. Teachers must provide instruction to help students acquire new behaviors. Behavior problems do not occur in isolation. Events or actions of others can initiate or reinforce inappropriate behaviors. To understand and manage classroom problems, the teacher should examine the student in relation to the target behavior. For example, classmates who laugh at clowning or wisecracks tend to reinforce that type of disruptive behavior; as a result, the disruptive student continues to exhibit the undesirable behavior. Students show inappropriate behavior when they have not learned correct responses or have found that acting inappropriately is more rewarding than acting appropriately. These behavior problems do respond to instruction.

Several methods for decreasing inappropriate behavior are available. Walker and Shea[30] have proposed the following continuum of behavior modification interventions:

1. *Reinforcement of behavior other than the target behavior.* A reinforcer is given at the end of a specified period of time, provided that a prespecified misbehavior has not occurred during the specified time interval.
2. *Reinforcement of an appropriate target behavior.* A reinforcer is given following the performance of a prespecified appropriate target behavior.
3. *Reinforcement of incompatible behaviors.* A reinforcer is given following the performance of a prespecified behavior that is physically and functionally incompatible with the target behavior.
4. *Extinction.* The reinforcer that has been sustaining or increasing an undesirable behavior is withheld.
5. *Stimulus change.* The existing environmental conditions are drastically altered to ensure that the target behavior is temporarily suppressed.

6. *Reprimand.* This is a form of punishment that involves verbally addressing a student for inappropriately exhibiting a target behavior. The reprimand should:
   - Be specific to the inappropriate behavior
   - Address the behavior, not the child
   - Be firm and administered immediately
   - Be accompanied by loss of privileges
   - Include a statement of appropriate behavior
   - Be done in a calm voice privately followed by observation of the child's reaction, so that the effect of the reprimand can be evaluated

7. *Nonexclusionary time-out*
   a. Restriction to a place in a separate area of the gymnasium but able to observe activities
   b. Removal of materials (work, play)

8. *Physical restraint.* Physical restraint may be used only if it is included on the child's behavior management plan. If the child loses control or becomes violent, physical restraint may be used by a person trained in the proper technique. Following the incident the parents must immediately be contacted.

9. *Negative practice or satiation.* The target behavior is eliminated by the continued and increased reinforcement of that behavior.

10. *Overcorrection.* This punishment procedure requires the individual who misbehaves to improve the environmental effects of the misbehavior and/or repeatedly perform the appropriate form of the target behavior in the environment in which the misbehavior was exhibited.

11. *Exclusionary time-out*
    a. Temporary distraction. When a student's behavior has reached the point at which he or she will not respond to verbal controls, the student may have to be asked to leave the room (to get a drink, wash up, or deliver a message—not as punishment, but to distract the student).
    b. Quiet room/think station. Some schools provide quiet spaces for students to use when it becomes necessary to remove oneself from a group setting to ponder about the misbehavior. The student should be continuously monitored, and the length of time should be limited to 2 to 10 minutes.
    c. In-school suspension

12. *Response cost lottery.* Students are given a predetermined number of slips of paper. Each time the student violates a class rule, he or she must relinquish one slip of paper. The names of the students are written on the slips of paper the students still have at the end of a given time period and are placed in a hat for a lottery drawing. The winner of the drawing receives a prize.

CONSISTENT MANAGEMENT TECHNIQUES

There is consensus that successful schools use systems of firm, consistent management. Research confirms that clearly structured, secure environments permit students to master the objectives of the program.

The preconditions for the application of learning principles are that there must be a precisely defined short-term instructional objective, and there must be incentives for the learner to master the objective. If either of these preconditions is not satisfied, the effect of the program is minimized. Effective learning is the result of mutual understanding between the student and the teacher. The student must understand what is expected and the consequences of not performing to expectations. Homme[12] provides nine rules to follow when using behavior management techniques:

1. Praise the correct objective.
2. Praise the correct objective immediately after it occurs.
3. Praise the correct objective after it occurs and not before.
4. Objectives should be in small steps, so that there can be frequent praise.
5. Praise improvement.
6. Be fair in setting up consequences for achieving objectives.
7. Be honest and provide the agreed-on consequences.
8. Be positive, so that the child can achieve success.
9. Be systematic.

Praise the Correct Objective

To implement this principle effectively, persons involved with instruction (teachers, school administrators, parents, and related service personnel) must know precisely the objective or behavior that the learner is to carry out. That behavior must be praised only if it is achieved. The application of this principle must be consistent among all persons who work with the child.

There are two ways that this learning principle can be violated by a teacher, parent, or school administrator. First, he or she may provide praise even though the objective has not been achieved; second, he or she may neglect to provide praise even though the objective has been achieved. In the first case, the learner is being reinforced for doing less than his or her best and consequently will have a lessened desire to put forth maximum effort on subsequent trials. In the second case, if the teacher does not deliver the agreed-on consequence (explicit or implicit), the student's desire to perform the instructional task again will be reduced.

Praise Immediately after Completion of the Task

Learners need to receive feedback immediately after task performance. Immediacy of feedback on task performance is particularly important with children functioning on a lower developmental level. If there is a delay between task performance and feedback, the child may be confused as to what the praise is for. For example, if a child walks a balance beam correctly but confirmation of task mastery is provided late (for instance, as the child steps off the beam), the behavior of stepping off the beam may be strengthened to a greater degree than the desired objective of walking the beam.

Praise at the Appropriate Time

If a child is praised for performing an objective before it is completed, there is a good chance that he or she will expend less effort to meet the objective.

Make Sure Objectives Are in Small Steps

If the step size is small, there will be a greater rate of success. As has been indicated, disruptive behavior may be triggered by lack of success. This principle may therefore be applied in attempts to control disruptive behavior in the classroom. Thus, if a child often exhibits many different types of disruptive behavior, objectives can be postulated to reduce the occurrence of these disruptive behaviors in small steps. For children with disabilities, learning by small steps permits much needed success.

Praise Improvement

The acquisition of skill toward an objective should be praised. Providing appropriate consequences for improvement may in some instances violate the principle of praising the correct objective. However, on tasks that cannot be broken into small steps, it is necessary to praise improvement. To do so, the instructor must know precisely the student's present level of educational performance. When the performance reflects an improvement on that level, the student must be reinforced with praise. Improvement means that the learner is functioning on a higher level than before. Therefore, it is unwise to praise or provide positive consequences to students who perform at less than their best effort, because to do so may encourage them to contradict their potential.

Be Fair in Setting Up Consequences

When there are specific objectives to be achieved to develop skills or appropriate classroom behavior, specific consequences can be arranged to support the development of these objectives. However, if such arrangements are to be made between the learner and the teacher, there must be equity between the task and the incentives. If the learner does not have sufficient incentive to perform the tasks or to behave appropriately, he or she is unlikely to do so. This learning principle operates at very early ages.

In one clinical experience, a target objective was set up for an 18-month-old boy with Down syndrome to learn to walk. The task involved walking from one chair to another, which was placed 8 feet away. If the child walked the full distance, he was allowed to play for 15 seconds with the toys that were placed on top of the chairs. When this period elapsed, he would return to the task of walking a prescribed distance of 8 feet 1 inch, a short distance farther than the previous time. After a time, the child refused to participate in the activity. The child's mother suggested that he be permitted to play with the toys for 30 seconds rather than 15 seconds. This procedure was used, and the child again engaged in the instructional task. It was inferred that the child would participate in tasks if the opportunity to play was commensurate with the effort put forth to master the objective. This is an example of equity between incentive and performance.

Be Honest

Agreements between teachers and learners must be honored by both. If there is an implicit or explicit arrangement between the teacher and the learner and the teacher does not follow through with the arrangement when the

learner has upheld his or her end of the bargain, then the learning conditions will be seriously weakened. It is not uncommon for teachers to inadvertently forget the arrangements that have been made. Therefore, it is important for teachers to have records of arrangements between themselves and learners. Forgetting the preconditions between learner and teacher may have a negative impact on the pupil's learning at a subsequent time.

If the teacher requests that a learner perform a specific task, the teacher must not provide the desirable consequences unless the learner achieves the proper objective. Honest delivery of the agreed-on consequences is similar to praise for the correct behavior. However, praise for the correct behavior usually connotes a specific short-term task, whereas an agreed-on consequence may involve a contractual arrangement between two parties. Principals and teachers who set policies may achieve positive results with the application of this principle.

Be Positive

The objective should be phrased positively, so that the learner can achieve the stated objective (e.g., "Walk to the end of the balance beam"). An example of a negative statement is "Don't fall off of the balance beam." In the negative instance, the child is avoiding failure, and there can be little value in mastering the desired behavior.

Be Systematic

To make the greatest positive impact on children with disabilities, it is necessary to apply all the learning principles all the time. Inconsistency confuses the learner with regard to the material to be learned and the type of behavior to maintain during class. The consistent use of behavior management strategies enhances a child's ability to learn desirable behaviors. This learning principle is the most difficult one for teachers of children with emotional disturbances to master.

CONTINGENCY CONTRACTING

Contingency contracting is a method used to individualize instruction to respond to the interests, needs, and abilities of children. This type of behavior contracting is a written agreement between the student and the teacher.[10] When the students satisfactorily complete the conditions of their contracts, they receive something they have identified. Contingency contracts can be used to teach a new behavior, maintain existing behaviors, and decrease inappropriate behaviors. The values of contingency contracts are that (1) the technique can be used with fairly large groups of students, (2) they allow for delay of reinforcement during busy periods, (3) they allow one reinforcer for reinforcing many behaviors, and (4) reinforcers can be given without interruption of teaching the class.

Support in School to Manage Behavior

The IDEIA (2004) amendments clearly indicate to what extent students with disabilities may be disciplined. The amendments emphasize the fact that, if a student's undesirable behavior is related to the child's disability, positive behavioral interventions, strategies, and supports that address that behavior should be included in the student's IEP. However, the student with a disability may be suspended or expelled from the school setting for any infringement of the school's rules of conduct to the same extent as students without disabilities. When a child with a disability has been disciplined by removal from school for more than 10 days, the school must convene an IEP meeting and develop a functional behavioral assessment plan. After developing the plan and the assessment, the school must convene an IEP meeting to determine appropriate behavioral interventions to use with the student. When necessary, an interim alternative setting will be selected to enable the student to continue to participate in the general curriculum.

If a formal behavioral intervention plan (BIP) is necessary to support a student who is struggling in a learning environment, the plan should be clearly documented in the IEP. A proactive approach being used in schools is called positive behavioral support (PBS). This approach is a framework used to structure interventions for managing behaviors. The intervention incorporates a tiered system for differentiating instruction and monitoring the progress of students.[4] The approach should be data-driven and the intervention structured around that data to systematically teach appropriate behaviors.[13] A teaching/learning environment that uses PBS should remain flexible and adapt to the changing needs of the student. In a physical education setting that may mean supporting a student with a peer tutor or incorporating social stories into the class.[4]

Discipline

Teachers report behavior problems as one of their greatest school-related concerns and challenges.[9] Spending classroom time managing students' behavior has a negative impact not only on the teacher but also on student performance.[19] Children exhibiting problem behaviors experience a type of school day that is vastly different from that of their typical peers.[23]

Severe problem behavior, such as aggression and self-injury, may compromise the quality of life for persons with disabilities and others.[22] Disruptive classroom behavior is a major factor in teacher stress and discontent and significantly affects a teacher's capacity to maintain a productive learning environment. Student interactions with teachers as a result of problem behavior command twice the amount of attention than do those of nondisruptive students.[23]

The teacher who uses the assertive effective discipline techniques presented in this chapter can significantly reduce behavior problems and in so doing, contribute to a positive learning environment.

SUMMARY

Learning is facilitated and changes in behavior occur when a systematic process is used. New skills and behaviors can be learned and inappropriate behaviors can be diminished when appropriate procedures are followed. First, the behavior to be learned or changed must be identified. Second, intervention strategies and appropriate reinforcers must be selected. Finally, reinforcement must be consistently applied and change in behavior validated. The maintenance of a learned skill or behavior can be verified through re-evaluation in the educational or community setting. The true measure of learning is the extent to which the skill or behavior generalizes across several environments and contributes to independent functioning. Students with disabilities who are expelled or suspended from school must be provided a functional assessment and an intervention program that will be implemented in an alternative setting.

REVIEW QUESTIONS

1. What techniques can be applied to maximize student achievement in motor skill development?
2. What are some positive teacher techniques that can be used to adapt instruction to the needs of the learner?
3. Name and describe some behavioral techniques for facilitating the development of positive behavior.

4. What are some techniques that can be used to manage disruptive classroom behavior?
5. List some types of reinforcers.
6. What are some of the teacher characteristics that can maximize the development of motor and social skills for individuals with disabilities?
7. Under what circumstance can a student with a disability be expelled or suspended from school?

REFERENCES

1. Ayvazo, S., & Ward, P. (2009). Effects of classwide peer tutoring on the performance of sixth grade students during a volleyball unit. *The Physical Educator*, *66*(1), 12–22.
2. Baker, P. H. (2005). Managing student behavior: How ready are teachers to meet the challenge? *American Secondary Education*, *33*(3), 51–64.
3. Bicard, D. F. (2000). Using classroom rules to construct behavior. *Middle School J*, *31*(5), 37–45.
4. Buchanan, A., Hinton, V., & Rudisill, M. (2013). Using positive behavior support in physical education. *Journal of Physical Education, Recreation & Dance*, *84*(5), 44–50. DOI: 10.1080/07303084.2013.779534.
5. Canter, L., & Canter, M. (2002). *Assertive discipline: Positive behavior management in today's classroom* (3rd ed.). Los Angeles: Lee Canter and Associates.
6. Cervantes, C., Lieberman, L., Magnesio, B., & Wood, J. (2013). Peer tutoring: Meeting the demands of inclusion in physical education today. *Journal of Physical Education, Recreation & Dance*, *84*(3), 43–48. DOI: 10.1080/07303084.2013.767712.
7. Collier, D., & Reid, G. (2003). Preventing and coping with difficult behaviors. *Palaestra*, *19*(3), 36–45.
8. Cowart, J. (2000). Managing student misbehavior in adapted physical education by good teaching practices. *Palaestra 16*(l), 40–45.
9. Darling-Hammond, L. (2003). Keeping good teachers: Why it matters, what leaders can do. *Educ Leadership*, *60*(8), 6–13.
10. Downing, J. A. (2002). Individualized behavior contracts. *Intervention in School and Clinic*, *37*, 168–172.
11. Hester, P., Gable, R. A., & Manning, M. (2003). A positive learning environment approach to middle school. *Childhood Education*, *79*(3), 130–136.
12. Homme, L. (1977). *How to use contingency contracting in the classroom*. Champaign, IL: Research Press.
13. Horner, R. H. (2000). Positive behavior supports. *Focus on Autism and Other Developmental Disabilities*, *15*(2), 97–105.
14. Jordan, A., Schwartz, E., & McGhie-Richmond, D. (2009). Preparing teachers for inclusive classrooms. *Teaching and Teacher Education*, *25*, 535–542.
15. Karvonen, M., Test, D. W., Wood, W. M., Browder, D., & Algozzine, B. (2004). Putting self determination into practice. *Exceptional Children*, *71*, 23–41.

16. Kennedy, C. H. (2002). Toward a socially valid understanding of problem behavior. *Education and Treatment of Children, 25*(1), 142–153.
17. King-Sears, M. (2006). Self-management for students with disabilities: The importance of teacher follow-up. *International Journal of Special Education, 21*, 94–108.
18. Klavina, A., & Block, M. (2008). The effect of peer tutoring on interaction behaviors in inclusive physical education. *Adapted Physical Activity Quarterly, 25*, 132–158.
19. Lambert, M. C., Cartledge, G., Heward, W. L., & Lo, Y. Y. (2006). Effects of response cards on disruptive behavior and academic responding during math lesson by fourth-grade urban students. *J of Positive Beh Interv, 8*(2), 88–99.
20. Lieberman, L. J., & Houston–Wilson, C. (2009). *Strategies for inclusion: A handbook for physical educators* (2nd ed.). Champaign, IL: Human Kinetics.
21. Maggin, D. M., et al. (2011). A systematic evaluation of token economies as a classroom management tool for students with challenging behaviors. *Journal of School Psychology, 5*, 529-554. DOI: 10.1016/j.jsp.2011.05.001.
22. McLaughlin, D. M., Carr, E. G. (2005). Quality of rapport as a setting event for problem behavior. *J of Positive Behav Interv, 7*(2), 68–91.
23. Morgan, P. L. (2006). Increasing task engagement using preference or choice making. *Remed Spec Educ, 27*(3), 176–187.
24. *Neosho School District v. Clark.* 315 F.3d 1022, 1028–1029 (8th Cir. 2003).
25. Pavri, S. (2004). General and special education teacher's preparation needs in providing social support: A needs assessment. *Teacher Education and Special Education, 27*, 433–443. DOI: org/10.1177/088840640402700410.
26. Reinke, W., Herman, K., & Stormont, M. (2013). Classroom-level positive behavior supports in schools implementing SW-PBIS: Identifying areas for enhancement. *Journal of Positive Behavior Interventions, 15*(1), 39–50. DOI: 10.1177/1098300712459079.
27. Simonsen, B., Fairbanks, S., Briesch, S., & Myers, D. (2008). *Evidence-based practices in classroom management: Considerations for research to practice education and treatment of children, 31*, 351–380. Published by West Virginia University Press. DOI: 10.1353/etc.0.0007.
28. TeacherVision. Working with emotionally and behaviorally challenged students. In partnership with the Council for Exceptional Children.
29. Temple, V., & Stanish, H. (2011). The feasibility of using peer-guided model to enhance participation in community-based physical activity for youth with intellectual disability. *Journal of Intellectual Disabilities, 15*(3), 209–217.
30. Walker, J. E., & Shea, T. M. (1999). *Behavior management: A practical approach for educators.* Columbus, OH: Charles E. Merrill.
31. Warger, Eavy & Associates. (1999). *Prevention strategies that work.* Reston, VA: Warger, Eavy & Associates.
32. Wood, S. J., Murdock, J. Y, & Cronin, M. E. (2002). Self-monitoring and at-risk middle school students. *Behavior Modification, 26*, 605–626.

CHAPTER 8

Teaching with Technology

OBJECTIVES

- Identify a variety of technologies for use in adapted physical education.
- Describe guidelines for technology selection.
- List resources for identifying and evaluating technology tools.
- Examine the benefits of technology in adapted physical education.

The rapid evolution of technology has significantly impacted the opportunities for accommodations, data collection, and instructional strategies in adapted physical education. Apps, Web 2.0 and cloud-based services, software, and devices can be used to improve services for students with disabilities. The Advanced Standards for Physical Education developed by the former National Association for Sport and Physical Education (NASPE), now SHAPE America, identify the benefits of using instructional technology for a variety of purposes, including differentiation or meeting the needs of varied level learners.[7] Instructional technologies, such as video feedback of skill performance, can improve the skill execution of the student being recorded.[15] Research in the use of current technology in adapted physical education is just beginning. An unpublished study found varied outcomes in two students with autism who used the app Proloquo2Go in physical education. In an analysis of activity time before and after using

Courtesy of Kristi Roth

the app on an iPod touch, one participant's activity time went from 26% (pre) to 34% (post), and the other participant went from 27% (pre) to 49% (post). The participants' physical education teachers also responded positively to the use of the app. However, they noted that the use of the device was inconsistent between both participants and often depended on the participants' moods.

Special education instruction is meant to be individualized due to the wide array of abilities of individuals with disabilities. As a result, the effectiveness of the technology selected will vary and may not meet the needs of all students. Careful discussion must occur among all members of the individualized education program (IEP) team when considering the use of potentially expensive technology for individual students. Factors to consider include the current level of functioning of the student, any barriers the student might be struggling with, whether there is an appropriate solution within the technology, and what data supports the idea that the student may benefit from using the technology.[8] Cognitive level of functioning, behavior, and interests can all affect the success of using technology with individuals with disabilities. It is important that technologies are selected only if they help achieve a learning outcome or goal better than if the technologies were not in use. Careful selection of tools and strategies will ensure the time, effort, and expense of technology are beneficial. It is important for physical educators to answer a series of questions prior to the use of technology as an instructional or administrative tool. These are identified in **Table 8-1**.

Prior to using any technology, particularly those that involve visual or written documentation of student progress that is stored or shared through the Internet, the technologies and, if applicable, their Terms of Service and Privacy Statements should be carefully reviewed and approved by the technology administration for the school district. Following is a description of technologies that can assist students with disabilities and their physical

TABLE 8-1 Technology Selection Considerations

1. What is the cost?
2. Is the tool easy to use for both you and your students?
3. Does the tool ensure student information is secure?
4. Is there evidence of effectiveness?
5. Does the tool work on multiple platforms or devices?
6. Does the tool allow you to solve a problem?
7. Can the tool work within your school infrastructure? Does it require connectivity to function? Can this be accessed from multiple devices?
8. Does the tool detract from or enhance the lesson?

educators with assessment, instruction, equipment provisions, communication, administrative tasks, and behavior management.

Assessment

In adapted physical education, cumulative (summative) and ongoing (formative) assessment is necessary to meet federal regulations and develop and maintain effective individualized education programs.[5] This assessment can also assist with instructional and programmatic evaluation. A number of technologies are available to facilitate summative and formative assessment.

For initial qualification of special education services, as well as for re-evaluations, administration of a formal test is required. Historically, test administrators kept the test score sheet on a clipboard during test administration and documented scores and notes with a pencil during test administration. For physical educators, juggling a clipboard, papers, and pencil in addition to the equipment required for testing and demonstration while providing student assistance, can prove difficult. By transferring the test into an electronic format, the evaluator is able to score the test on a mobile device that can fit in his or her pocket and record video and voice comments on the same device for later reference. A licensed copy of the Test of Gross Motor Development-2 (TGMD-2) or Adapted Physical Education Assessment Scale-II (APEAS-II) can be converted to a spreadsheet and

Courtesy of Kristi Roth

uploaded to an app such as Numbers for electronic scoring on a mobile device that fits in a pocket. Another option is to convert the assessments into a Google Form, which allows for instant transfer to a spreadsheet. Tutorial recordings available online show how to use Google Forms to develop an electronic version of a licensed TGMD-2. Observation notes can be written on a mobile device with a stylus or finger using apps such as Notability or Penultimate. They also can be dictated and converted into text using the built-in voice-recognition tools found in apps such as Notes and Google Docs.

Google Forms can also be used for peer assessment or self-assessment in physical education. Rubrics and checklists, which include videos and pictures of skill demonstrations, can be linked to mobile devices and utilized for assessment or review. Adult volunteers or paraprofessionals can also use these tools to aid in assessment.

Once IEP goals are established, it is necessary to document progress toward meeting those goals. Electronic documentation allows educators to share results instantly and have visual evidence of student progress. Any camera can record student skill performance; however, when paired with a secure cloud-based service, this documentation can be shared instantly with IEP team members. An example would be if the school district has a Google Apps for Education (GAFE) service. Folders for students can be created in the educator's GAFE Drive and when photos and videos are taken of student performance, they can be uploaded to their folders. IEP team members can be given permission to view this visual documentation at their convenience. Visual evidence of student growth can be a highly effective advocacy tool for physical educators.

It is also beneficial to maintain daily documentation of when IEP goals are addressed in physical education. This can be easily tracked through a Google Form, which can be accessed through any mobile device. Developing a Form with student first names only, and key terms from their IEP goals, allows physical educators to quickly input student progress on their goals. Video tutorials showing how to develop a Google Form for IEP goal tracking can be found online. There are also several apps that run on mobile devices that can be helpful when documenting progress. Easy Portfolio and Three Ring are two apps that allow for development of digital portfolios for students. Both apps accommodate photos, videos, and written documentation; provide reports; and allow for a parent account so progress can be monitored by all IEP team members if desired.

Instruction

Assessment forms the basis for instruction. Determining student individual needs allows for personalized learning. Many technologies are available for instructional integration. YouTube offers a wide range of videos that can be projected and followed along with the class. This allows the physical educator to work individually with students while they follow the video. When using YouTube videos in class, teachers can utilize SafeShare.tv to show the video without suggested videos or advertisements. Ensure YouTube's Terms of Service are reviewed to guarantee compliance with Fair Use in the classroom. There are many Just Dance videos available for students to dance along with; Cosmic Kids Yoga has engaging yoga lessons for children; and Zumba Fitness has a channel that includes Zumba Kids videos. In addition, many chair-exercise routines are available, as well as several workout videos featuring individuals who ambulate with wheelchairs exercising alongside their peers without disabilities.

There are also many apps available that integrate well with the typical physical education curriculum. Many of these apps have been reviewed by Jarrod Robinson at http://thepegeek.com. An abbreviated list of apps effective for students, particularly those with disabilities, is located in **Table 8-2**.

There is also a public Google document titled iPad Apps for Autism,[1] which provides a comprehensive summary of many apps useful to students with disabilities. In a study by Ptomey et al. (2015), students with intellectual disabilities successfully lost weight with a monitored healthy diet and physical activity tracked by an app on a mobile device (Lose It!) and a wireless activity monitor (Fitbit). Participants reported that the app was easy to use and 42% of participants independently entered information into the app regarding food and activity.[11] Apps can be utilized in small group or one-to-one settings or projected to an entire class. Projection of apps and

TABLE 8-2 Apps for Adapted Physical Educators

App Name	Use
SpecialRef	Reference dictionary with special-education terms
ASL Dictionary	ASL words with corresponding videos
Autism Apps	List of apps being used for students with autism and other special needs
Behavior Tracker Pro	Track behaviors using recorded videos, data, and graphs
IEP Checklist	Tool to use during IEP meetings to record information verbally and written
Team Picker	Divides your class into teams, separated by gender and/or friend status
Stories2Learn	Create personal social stories for students
ClassDojo	Behavior tracking and IEP goal tracking
PE Apps	List of PE apps broken down into a variety of categories
First Then Visual Schedule	Visual schedule
ShowMe	Take or upload picture. Draw on it. Record voice.
Interval Run	Verbal cues for when to walk and when to run
Team Shake	Put class into teams. Can sort by ability level, gender, etc.
Letter Quiz	Put body into the letter you see
AlphaBaby Free	Put body into the shape you see
C-Fit Dance	Elementary dance lessons
Simply Yoga	Yoga workouts
Daily Ab Workout	Ab workouts
Daily Arm Workout	Arm workouts
Daily Butt Workout	Butt workouts
FitnessClass	TONS of fitness videos, some free
Scoreboard Lite	Keep score
PE Games	PE games in a variety of categories
Tandalay PLAY	PE games
BaM Video Delay	Video clip playback in four screens or manual slow motion
C-Fit Yoga	Yoga routines for classrooms
Easy Assessment	Enter student names and rubrics or scores on assessments
Remind	(Web and app) Text class without getting cell numbers

videos from a mobile device in a gymnasium can be accomplished by a variety of methods. If the teacher is using an Apple device (such as an iPad or iPhone), an AppleTV can be connected to a projector and the Apple device will stream wirelessly, allowing the teacher to roam the area with the device in his or her hands and pause when needed. Other options for displaying a mobile device are AirServer and Reflector. These programs can be purchased for a minimal fee and downloaded onto a laptop. The laptop can then be connected to the projector and the content from the mobile device will stream wirelessly through the laptop. If direct connection to the projector is preferred, a VGA or HDMI adapter can be purchased to allow connection from the mobile device to the projector. It should be noted that video streaming can be impacted by Internet speed and broadband availability. Testing of the streaming should be attempted prior to display during class. Some videos may need to be downloaded and saved onto a device prior to class to eliminate streaming issues.

Utilizing one of the many videoconferencing tools online is another dynamic way to engage students in the physical education classroom. Skype, Google Hangouts, and FaceTime are three tools that are easily accessible and allow educators to take virtual field trips, complete mystery hangouts, or connect with athletes who participate in international games or with Paralympians. Classes can even have dance competitions with schools in other parts of the country. For physical educators who are teaching students who struggle with communication, practicing speech and eye contact through video can be highly beneficial. Google+ provides communities for educators to connect via video. There is a database of educators from all over the world who wish to connect with other educators, which can be found at www.eduhangout .org. Another method to connect with educators around the world is through Twitter. Searches for #physed and #adaptedpe provide many Tweets of modified equipment, games, and strategies applicable to the field.

Video can also be used locally to improve instruction. Many students need repetition of instruction and demonstration of skills. Recording skill demonstrations with short verbal cues allows students to watch instructional videos repeatedly to aid in mastery. If teaching in stations, teachers can set up a video display of the skill to perform at each station. They also can link to external sources that demonstrate skill performance. The Physical Educator website (www.thephysicaleducator.com) has several printable posters, QR codes, and video clips of sport skills,

reducing the need for physical educators to create their own. Students can use recording apps such as Ubersense, Coach's Eye, and Dartfish to play back their execution, watch the execution in slow motion, and even compare their execution to a highly skilled performance.

Another instructional technology tool for physical education is exergaming. Exergaming is the activity of playing video games that involve exercise or physical activity. Video games can assist in mirroring the general physical education curriculum in a small group or one-on-one instructional setting. Exergaming has been shown to increase the physical activity levels of students in physical education.[3, 13] Several augmented reality (AR) sport games, such as ARBasketball and ARSoccer, allow students with limited movement to shoot baskets or kick balls. EyeToy is another tool that puts the student into the screen through a small camera and allows him or her to play soccer, karate, dance, table tennis, volleyball, football, and track and field with limited movement. The Wii can simulate many of those same activities and can be ideal for students with more upper-body mobility. If the student has difficulty holding onto a Wii remote, a soccer shin guard can hold it in place on his or her arm. Some exergames are available through the Internet. VI Fit is a program that can be loaded onto a computer and utilized with a Wii remote to provide vibrotactile and audio cues to allow students with visual impairments to engage in bowling, tennis, or pet-n-punch exergaming.[16]

Equipment

Modified equipment, such as the shin guard mentioned previously, is key to successful support for many students with disabilities. There are several pieces of technology-related equipment that can accommodate the needs of diverse learners. Students who ambulate in a wheelchair can participate in a Dance Dance Revolution game through the use of the Hand Dance Pro. Students with very limited movement can participate in bowling by using a bowling ramp and the Poss-I-Bowl, which is a device that releases the ball down the ramp when a big red switch is pressed. There are also many auditory devices available to assist students with attention and/or visual impairments. Basket-balls, soccer balls, softballs, and foam and playground balls can be ordered with bells or beeping modules in them. When purchased separately, beep-ing modules can assist with tracking or the location of targets and goals. Fitness equipment with enhanced technology includes the talking pedometer that announces pedometer data to the student, talking ropeless jump ropes, and a wheelchair roller that functions as a treadmill for individuals who ambulate in wheelchairs. Researchers at the University of Nevada, Reno, are developing a drone that guides runners with visual impairments around a track.[6] Three-dimensional printers are being used to build modified equip-ment for use in physical education.[9] The Rehabilitation Engineering Research Center on Recreational Technologies (www.rectech.org) is a US Department of Education grant funded center that develops recreation technology for individuals with disabilities. Included in their equipment is a Wii Fit Board for individuals who ambulate in wheelchairs, adaptive game controllers, and a Wii Mat, which takes the place of a Wii controller and has sensitivity adjustments and accommodations to play with hands or feet.

Communication

It is important to engage students with disabilities in identification of modification preferences to build self-advocacy skills and independence. This is not always easy as students with disabilities sometimes have com-munication methods that are not always easy to understand. They also can struggle with receptive and expressive language, be confused by social cues, overwhelmed by sensory information, and puzzled by verbal inter-action. Communication through technology provides the structure and direct visual contact needed by many individuals with disabilities. The growth of technology has provided a large number of options for aided augmentative and alternative communication (AAC). Often students with disabilities work with their speech-language pathologist to determine the most appropriate AAC device for their needs. Some students use simple communication devices such as button communicators (e.g., BIGmack, in which pre-recorded statements are vocalized when a button is touched), or communication books that contain pictures for students to select for communication. More advanced communication devices and programs are also available. DynaVox makes a variety of devices that are often secured to a wheelchair or placed on a table top. The devices contain pictures, letters, sentences, and even offer word prediction, for a student to select either by touching or by eye pointing. The selected images or words are voiced by the device. There is also software and apps that can be run on computers and mobile devices, and do not require a DynaVox. The use of iPads, tablets, smartphones, and iPods overcomes some of the common barriers associated with assistive technology, in that they are easy to use and are socially accepted.[8] Proloquo2Go, iCommunicate, iComm, and TouchChat are just a few of the AAC apps available. Mobile devices are becoming more accessible to all users with apps such as BrailleTouch, which allows users to type using braille. Most mobile devices are constructed with accessibility features such as VoiceOver. Dot is a braille smartwatch, which has an anticipated market launch in 2016.[2] It is important for the physical educator to remain an active participant of the IEP team and to work closely with the speech-language pathologist to ensure proper and effective use of communication devices in physical education. The primary device used by the student should be used consistently throughout his or her entire education, home, and work environment. Physical education can sometimes require accommodations to ensure students still have the ability to communicate even though they may be engaged in gross motor skills.

In the physical education setting, there is always a risk that the device could be thrown, kicked, or dropped. A durable case for whichever device is being used (e.g., smartphone, iPad, iPod, Android tablet) can be very important. For example, a mobile device can be well cushioned in a portable speaker system, such as the iMainGo 2, and iPads or other tablets can be fastened to a wall with a mount, such as a PadTab.[12]

Administration

Scheduling IEP meetings can be a cumbersome process. Often physical educators are not notified of IEP meetings, or unable to attend due to scheduling conflicts. Doodle.com can be an effective scheduling tool for IEP teams. This tool allows the case manager to create a schedule poll for the group and group members can select their availability, and see each other's availability. There are options for calendar integration and comments. Because student personally identifiable information is confidential, when using tools such as Doodle it is safe to utilize the student's first name only.

Some adapted physical educators travel for their jobs. Documentation of services provided at each school is necessary for accountability and advocacy. Utilization of mobile devices for voice-to-text dictation of services can save time for itinerant adapted physical educators. These notes can be easily saved and emailed to administration or IEP team members. Additional dictation can include modification or behavior-management tips for general physical educators after an observation. Remind.com is a tool that allows teachers to set up text message reminders for a class without the need to exchange cell phone numbers. This tool can be used to remind physical educators or case managers of a pending consultation by an adapted physical educator or upcoming IEP meetings. With parental and student consent, Remind can be used as a social reinforcer for engaging in daily physical activity. Individuals are more likely to exercise if reminded of their intent to exercise through text messaging.[10] Adapted physical educators can schedule text message reminders to be sent throughout the year using this tool. This can also be used to remind families of community-based activities available throughout the year.

Behavior Management and Classroom Structure

Mobile devices can assist with managing and documenting behavior. This is easier to implement with small groups, in one-on-one instructional settings, or with the assistance of a paraprofessional. The Autism Tracker and Behavior Tracker Pro apps can be used in the classroom, community, or at home to document positive and negative behaviors and daily routines. They also provide graphs that help to easily identify possible antecedents of behaviors, empowering educators when designing the optimal educational setting for students with autism. This data collection is often managed by a special educator or case manager. Once the information is gathered and a plan is developed to aid the student in his or her behavior, this plan should be implemented in the school and home environments. There are several apps that can assist with managing student behavior.

Positive behaviors can be reinforced with the iReward app, which allows students to earn stars when they reach specific goals. Students who function well with a token reward system can earn a token for every successful activity performed. Upon earning a set number of tokens, the student can go to a "play zone"—a mat set up on its side in the corner of the gym—and have time to play a game on the iPad. The time can be monitored by a timer app, such as Autism Timer, and the time can be regularly reduced to fade the reinforcer. This timer app provides a visual of the time changing, which can help students understand how much time they have left in the play zone. Additional apps for behavior management are identified in **Table 8-3**.

Many students with disabilities exhibit improved behavior if provided with clear structure during physical education. Visual schedules are one of the evidence-based practices for students with autism.[14] The physical educator can utilize a variety of tools for visual schedule development and previewing of the day's activities. Developing a QR code that is linked to a Google Doc with the day's activities identified through text, pictures, and/or videos, allows students to scan the code with their own mobile devices. If this code is placed in their homeroom or classroom, students can scan the code at their convenience and allow for required processing time. The teacher can change the content on the Google Doc each class to depict the current day's activities.

Visual schedules can also be developed through apps. The First Then Visual Schedule will allow physical educators to customize a schedule of class routines and daily lessons. Options within many visual schedule apps allow for students to check off tasks once they are complete, providing closure to assist with transition to a new task, uploading of videos and photos to

TABLE 8-3   Behavior-Management Apps

App Name	Features
ClassDojo	Behavior tracking and recognition, student and parent monitoring, reporting
Time Timer	Visual timer
iReward	Reward system and token board
Calm Counter	Timer to help people calm down. Social story on anger and calming down
iPrompts	Visual schedules, timers

individualize the content for the user, and even voice recording for instructions to students. This also can be utilized effectively when students are working in stations and required to complete tasks independently.

Mobile devices can also provide structure to students whose learning style requires social stories. For students who struggle when entering a loud gym containing many objects and visual distracters, a mat can be set on its side to serve as an "entry tunnel," which reduces the visual stimulation. The student can read through a social story on the iPad, using the apps Stories2Learn, Pictello, or iCommunicate, while simultaneously adjusting to the auditory stimuli. When the student is ready, he or she can enter the gym area. This gradual introduction to the environment, along with a visual representation of the lesson for the day, often gives students with autism the structure they need to succeed.

Some students with disabilities respond better to words than to pictures for social stories. These can simply be the written steps of the daily activities or tasks. A typed story or story written on a small whiteboard can accommodate this need; however, these are often hard to save and access if needed for reuse. The ShowMe app allows physical educators to write out the steps to a skill, motor pattern, or an activity with a stylus, and the student can check off each step upon completion. For example, steps for tee-ball would include: hold the bat, look at the ball on the tee, step, swing, put the bat down gently, run to the orange cone, and touch the base with your foot (often students with disabilities struggle to understand the term *base*, so it is helpful to have a visual cue here). The steps can be reviewed by the students while waiting for their turn to bat. Once the steps are entered into the app on the iPad, they will be available for future use.

Tablet technology can also be used as an extrinsic or intrinsic motivator for students with disabilities.[4] If the IEP team determines that tablets are a desired reward for the student, then the student can earn time using the tablet by completion of tasks throughout his or her day, including in physical education.

© Helga Smith/Shutterstock

Students may also enjoy recording themselves performing skills or tracking their progress in fitness activities, such as the number of push-ups completed in one minute, and seeing their performance improve over time.

Many of the technologies described in this chapter involve the use of mobile devices and/or Web 2.0 tools. Teachers wanting to integrate such devices into physical education are encouraged to request the school community, businesses, and even cell phone providers to donate old phones, iPods, and other mobile devices to the physical education program. The only requirement for many of the strategies described previously is the device and, for some tools, internet access. Most old devices can be used for this purpose and economically provide a one-to-one educational setting.

SUMMARY

The rapid growth of technology can be overwhelming for some, however, there are many benefits to learning effective use of such tools for teaching students with disabilities in physical education. Software, apps, cloud-based services, and equipment should be carefully considered to ensure the benefits of the tool outweigh the potential challenges. Consultation with district technology personnel is necessary to ensure appropriate security measures are followed when using instructional technologies. Technology selection should be discussed with the IEP team and is most effective if implemented consistently throughout the home and school environment.

Technology can be used by the adapted physical educator and student to facilitate assessment, instruction, equipment provisions, communication, administrative tasks, and behavior management. Mobile devices, such as tablets and smartphones should have protective covering and mounting and storage options when used in the gym environment. Offering the school as a donation center for old devices can help school districts with the acquisition of technology.

REVIEW QUESTIONS

1. Describe five considerations when selecting technology for student use in physical education.
2. Identify three steps to ensure student security when using apps and cloud- or web-based services.
3. Give some examples of how technology can be used to enhance instruction.
4. Give three examples of how technology can be used to assist the adapted physical educator with assessment.

5. Identify two pieces of modified equipment that are considered assistive technology and describe how they can be used in the physical education curriculum.
6. Describe strategies for using technology as an extrinsic motivator.

REFERENCES

1. Docs.google.com. (2016). *iPads & autism apps recommendations*. Retrieved from https://docs.google.com/spreadsheets/d/1q-R9HD0PCzcSWjh-CBM03AldQ3f3O1BIOqwWH-bmMNc/pub?hl=en&single=true&gid=0&output=html
2. Fingerson.strikingly.com. (2016). *Dot(Fingers On)*. Retrieved from http://fingerson.strikingly.com/
3. Fogel, V. A., Miltenberger, R. G., Graves, R., & Koehler, S. (2010). Evaluating the effects of exergaming on physical activity among inactive children in a physical education classroom. *Journal of Applied Behavior Analysis, 43*, 591–600.
4. French, R., Henderson, H., Lavay, B., & Silliman-French, L. (2014). Use of intrinsic and extrinsic motivation in adapted physical education. *Palaestra, 28*(3), 32.
5. Individuals with Disabilities Education Act, 20 U.S.C. § 1400 (2004).
6. Couch, C. (2015). Fitness technology that helps the blind get moving. *MIT Technology Review*. Retrieved from http://www.technologyreview.com/news/542426/fitness-technology-that-helps-the-blind-get-moving/
7. National Association for Sport and Physical Education. (2009). National standards and guidelines for physical education teacher education. (Third edition / revised by Initial Physical Education Teacher Education Standards Task Force, National Association for Sport and Physical Education, Advanced Physical Education Teacher Education Standards Task Force, National Association for Sport and Physical Education, eds.).
8. Newton, D. A., & Dell, A. G. (2011). Assistive technology. *Journal of Special Education Technology, 26*, 347–349.
9. Open BioMedical Initiative. (2015). *Help this teacher 3D print assistive fitness equipment for disabled children*. Retrieved from http://www.openbiomedical.org/help-this-teacher-3d-print-assistive-fitness-equipment-for-disabled-children/
10. Prestwich, A., Perugini, M., & Hurling, R. (2009). Can the effects of implementation intentions on exercise be enhanced using text messages? *Psychology & Health, 24*(6), 677–687.
11. Ptomey, L., Sullivan, D., Lee, J., Goetz, J., Gibson, C., & Donnelly, J. (2015). The use of technology for delivering a weight loss program for adolescents with intellectual and developmental disabilities. *Journal of the Academy of Nutrition and Dietetics, 115*(1), 112–118.
12. Roth, K. (2013). Adapt with apps. *Journal of Physical Education, Recreation & Dance, 84*(2), 4–6.

13. Shayne, R. K., Fogel, V. A., Miltenberger, R. G., & Koehler, S. (2012). The effects of exergaming on physical activity in a third-grade physical education class. *Journal of Applied Behavior Analysis, 45*(1), 211–215.

14. Simpson, R. L. (2005). Evidence-based practices and students with autism spectrum disorders. *Focus on Autism and Other Developmental Disabilities, 20*(3), 140–149.

15. Uhl, B., & Dillon, S. (2009). Dartfish video analysis in secondary physical education: A pilot study. Poster session at the American Alliance for Health, Physical Education, Recreation, and Dance annual convention. Tampa, FL.

16. Vifit.org. (2016). *Tactile/audio exergames for players who are blind.* Retrieved from http://vifit.org/

CHAPTER 9

Transition Programming/Community Recreation and Sport

- Define transition services in the public school.
- Examine community opportunities for students of all abilities.
- Define recreation and sport opportunities for individuals with developmental disabilities.
- Define recreation and sport opportunities for individuals with sensory and physical disabilities.
- Examine Deaflympics, Special Olympics, and Paralympics.

Transition

The Individuals with Disabilities Education Improvement Act (IDEIA, 2004) mandates that a transition plan be in place for any qualifying student no later than the age of 16 years, but can begin as early as the age of 14 years. The focus of this transition period will be on activities such as vocational education, independent living, and adult and continuing education.[10] Community participation is not part of the mandate and therefore if active participation in recreation, sport, and/or physical activity programming is to take place, the adapted physical educator or general physical educator has to be proactive in setting up goals with the multidisciplinary team.[21] Active participation in community recreation, sport, and

physical activity programming after leaving the school-based setting is only effective if a student has had the opportunity to learn, while in school, the skills needed to function with success in the community. The role of the adapted physical educator and general physical educator (GPE) becomes important, as they should have the knowledge and community network to link parents and family members of students with disabilities to community recreation and sport venues. The role in interaction with parents and family members of learners with disabilities is critical in the "outcomes" of adapted physical education (APE). If adapted physical educators have not been an integral and critical part of the transition process, individuals with disabilities, as adults, tend not to be active participants in community recreation and sport experiences.

The primary goal of participating in recreation, sport, and/or physical activity programming is no different for individuals with or without disabilities. Developing functional skills and a healthy lifestyle to be able to work and live independently is the goal.[22] The ability to work all day with the mental and physical stamina to be successful requires good levels of physical and motor fitness. Having endurance, strength, flexibility, balance, agility, and general coordination is necessary for maintaining a full day of work and independence.[13]

A framework used in special education for transition planning called the taxonomy of transition programming[25] outlines five primary areas of focus for professionals working with students with disabilities and their families. **Table 9-1** outlines how Roth and Columna[21] applied this taxonomy to physical education transition planning.

A school district should have a solid *program structure* in place for students and families going through transition. For physical education, this structure and approach to transition should be part of an APE manual and clearly outline the steps necessary to move a student and family from assessment, and programming, to post-school opportunities upon graduation.

TABLE 9-1   Taxonomy of Transition Programming in Physical Education

1. Program structure
   - Transition plan
   - Transition handbook
   - Schedule flexibility
   - Peer development
2. Student-focused planning
   - Authentic assessment
   - Interest surveys
   - IEP/ITP goals
3. Student development
   - Social skills
   - Task analysis
   - Skill attainment
   - Transfer of skills
4. Interagency collaboration
   - YMCA
   - I Can Do It, You Can Do It
   - Best Buddies
   - Special Olympics
5. Family involvement
   - Family training
   - Open house
   - Parent workshops

Taken from: Roth, K., & Columna, L. (2011). Collaborative strategies during transition for students with disabilities. *Journal of Physical Education, Recreation & Dance, 82*, 50–55. DOI: 10.1080/07303084.2011.10598.

A top-down approach is the most effective way to ensure *student-focused planning* is in place. Discussing with the student what recreation, sport, and/or physical activity interests he or she has upon graduation will guide the assessment and planning. Options and experiences within the school setting and community setting should be outlined for students so they have a clear picture of what is available to them as they move through their transition years. Involving the parents and other family members in this discussion is critical as they will be the ones who assist with post-school goals. Although the APE or GPE specialists may not be the primary instructors of the program, they are the ones who have the expertise to assess and write activity goals for the professional providing the instruction. Writing the individualized transition plan (ITP), much like an individualized education program (IEP), will guide programming and evaluation for the student.

Once the recreation, sport, and/or physical activity programming interests and opportunities are identified, and skills assessed, the APE or GPE specialist can focus on *student development* and write the ITP. With the overall goal being functional independence in an activity setting, assessing the cognitive and affective skills of the student will be essential too.[21] For example, if a student with an intellectual disability has a strong interest in playing tennis on a unified Special Olympics team in the near future, he or she will need the social skills as well as the sport skills to be a successful teammate. Collaboration with other members of the multidisciplinary team will help provide this holistic picture of skills in all domains.

With the ultimate goal being a healthy lifestyle, one role of the APE or GPE specialist in developing transition goals for students with a disability is making sure they learn the skills necessary to access recreation, sport, and physical activity programming and how to move through a facility and/or program independently.[22] *Interagency collaborations* should begin early in a transition program. Representatives from community organizations can assist with transition goal planning.[21] For example, a representative from the community YMCA could help identify what specific skills a student would need to independently access the YMCA's fitness facility or pool. Starting right in the school-based setting is a good way to begin to learn most of the necessary steps to being independently in a community setting. Often because of vocational education planning and training, the 14- to 16-year-old student who has a transition plan is on a different school-day schedule than his or her same-age peers. They may be receiving much of their instruction in a school-based life-skills classroom and part of their day in the community for vocational training. Therefore the student on a transition plan may not have access to APE or GPE class times to take fitness classes or learn how to use exercise equipment. In this case the APE or GPE specialist would work with the classroom instructor or paraprofessional to carry out the specific goals. This collaboration would mean scheduling time to train the classroom instructor or paraeducator. For example, if a transition goal was to spend 3 days per week on cardiovascular endurance training and 2 days a week on strength training, the APE or GPE specialist would need time to train the professionals instructing and overseeing the program on the equipment and safety precautions of being in the exercise/weight room.

Family involvement throughout the transition years is essential. Communicating with parents and family members about how to maintain involvement in recreation, sport, and/or physical activity programming will help them to identify and schedule such programming for their adult children upon graduation. Empowering parents will help ensure that involvement in community activity continues.[21]

SETTINGS FOR TRANSITION GOALS

The APE or GPE specialist involved with transition programming should be familiar with community-based settings where a transition plan could be implemented. Working with a local fitness center, YMCA, or recreation center is not only age-appropriate, it is also an opportunity for the student to practice the skills necessary to access the facility or program independently. Additionally, stepping into the community develops relationships and networks that will assist students and their families post-school. Having personnel who run the facility get to know the students, understand their skills, and be aware of what assistance they could require may minimize barriers associated with people with disabilities accessing facilities for activity.[19]

Depending on a school's location, another option is to connect a school district with a local college or university for transition programming. An APE or GPE specialist could collaborate with program directors or faculty members on campus to utilize a student recreation center or physical activity facility. Volunteer students on campus could be trained to assist with goal implementation. A great example of such collaboration is one run by Dr. Robert Arnhold at Slippery Rock University (SRU). The SRU Transition Achievement Program (TAP) consists of a transition program for high school students with intellectual and other developmental disabilities. It also consists of a postsecondary education program for high school completers with intellectual disabilities. The transition services are delivered in the areas of job training, educational, health, and life-skills training. School districts collaborate with the university and transition goals are met on campus.[20]

Community Sport and Recreation

The opportunity for students with disabilities to be physically active in community settings outside of school should be encouraged and promoted. Participating in community sport and recreation promotes inclusion, can increase physical functioning, and enhance self-esteem and overall well-being.[14] Knowing that collegiate level inclusive sport opportunities exist, high school student athletes should be seeking sport club opportunities in the community just like their peers without disabilities. The Eastern College Athletic Conference is an example of adaptive sport opportunity at the college level. They offer NCAA-sanctioned, varsity level competition in sports like wheelchair basketball, sled hockey, sitting volleyball, and several others. High school athletes with physical disabilities and visual impairments can now look forward to continuing their athletic ambitions at the college level along with their able bodied peers.

APE or GPE specialists should be aware of what sport and recreation opportunities exist in or near their community and based upon the interests of students and their families, connect them with coaches and community recreation leaders. Encouraging this connection in the community will further increase the chances that students will stay connected to community opportunities for sport, recreation, and/or physical activity programming post-school years.

Summer programming is also often available in many communities. Camp Abilities is a one-week summer sporting opportunity for students who are blind, have a visual impairment, or those who are deaf-blind. The camp can be found in over 15 states and several countries internationally. The camp provides children and teens with several recreation and sport opportunities.

Community programming associated with the Paralympic movement may be found at a local YMCA, park district, BlazeSports club, or Paralympic sports club. These sport programs provide training and skills for students with physical and visual disabilities wishing to train competitively with goals of competing in the Paralympics as well as for those who just enjoy sport and want to remain active.[9] Locating a program can begin by searching the United States Paralympic website. Paralympic sport clubs (PSCs) are one example of a network of community-based organizations across the United States sponsoring camps, clinics, and competitions at the local level.[26] Originating in 2007, the PSC network operates with the following objectives:[27]

- Developing community-based sport clubs that recruit and involve youth and adults with physical and visual impairments in sports and physical activity
- Developing a comprehensive, community-based PSC network as a foundation for the Paralympic athlete pipeline
- Providing community-based sport program opportunities for injured service members and veterans to continue sport participation upon their integration back into their home communities
- Creating a national, unified, community-based PSC network that provides a grassroots branding campaign to educate Americans on the opportunities and benefits inherent in sport and physical activity as practiced by people with physical and visual impairments

The Great Lakes Adaptive Sports Association (GLASA) in northern Illinois provides a good example of a community-based program supporting children and adults with physical and visual disabilities through

TABLE 9-2   Great Lakes Adaptive Sports Association Sport and Recreation Programs

Boccia	Track and field
Cycling	Horseback riding
Swimming	Judo
Wheelchair football	Yoga
Wheelchair basketball—Prep and JV	CrossFit training at CrossFit Kilter
Golf	Goalball
Tennis	Power soccer
Powerlifting and strength conditioning	Road racing
Kayaking	Sled hockey
Sailing	
Waterskiing	

sport.[7] GLASA is a recognized PSC and serves athletes in northern Illinois and southern Wisconsin. **Table 9-2** lists the sports offered to participants. GLASA operates under the following mission: to promote and support the optimal development and well-being of youth, adults, and military veterans who have a physical or visual disability through the provision of inclusive recreation, fitness, and competitive sport activities.[7]

GLASA coordinates with local, regional, and national partners to provide programming. Examples of collaborators include local park districts (e.g., Chicago Park District), sporting organizations (e.g., USA Hockey, U.S. Paralympics), disability-specific associations (e.g., Spinal Cord Injury Association of Illinois, Spina Bifida Association of Illinois), and hospitals and rehabilitation facilities (e.g., Lurie Children's Hospital, The Rehabilitation Institute of Chicago).

The APE or GPE specialist can help students and their families get connected to PSC programs by searching the PSC website and viewing sport options by impairment group for summer and winter sports.

BlazeSports America is a legacy of the 1996 Atlanta Paralympics and another example of an organization promoting sport for children and adults with disabilities. BlazeSports America's mission is to: *change the lives of children and youth, adults and veterans with physical disabilities through adaptive sport and recreation.* The organization's goals are:

- to provide sport, recreation, and physical activity opportunities for people with physical disability in sport comparable to those provided nondisabled, nationally and internationally
- to foster character development, productive lives, healthy lifestyles and self-sufficiency for people with physical disability through sport
- to use cutting-edge training, distance-learning opportunities, and fresh ideas as a vehicle to build capacity of local service providers
- to build positive perceptions of people with physical disability
- to promote peace building, human rights, and equity through sport[2]

Another popular, community-based sport program is the Challenger Division of Little League.[12] Challenger players are those with physical and/or intellectual disabilities. Children can begin as young as 4 years of age and continue for as long as they are enrolled in high school. The game can be played as tee-ball, coach pitch, player pitch, or a combination of all three. The Challenger Division may also incorporate "buddies." Buddies assist players, if necessary, with batting, running bases, and fielding and typically are peers that play on a baseball or softball team. This inclusive aspect of the Challenger Division is positive for children with and without disabilities.

Most communities have a parks and recreation association to care for, develop, and oversee community parks and recreation gathering places and programming. In smaller, rural locations more than one community or municipality may work together to support their parks and recreation associations. Within a parks and recreation association, families should be able to seek programming for students and adults with disabilities. These programs are typically referred to as special recreation programs within a larger park district. For example, the Chicago Park District provides special recreation programming under a specific unit. The special recreation unit of the Chicago Park District provides adaptive sports, Paralympic sports, Special Olympics, and recreation programming for individuals who are deaf/hard of hearing and/or blind/visually impaired.[3]

Some park districts and municipalities combine their resources and create their own special recreation cooperatives. The state of Illinois has what is called the Special Recreation Association Network of Illinois (SRANI). It is a very structured, organized listing of all special recreation programs. As of 2013 there were 33 special education cooperatives serving 206 Illinois communities.[24] An APE or GPE specialist or family member can visit the SRANI website to find the cooperative or program closest to their community. For example, the Fox Valley Special Recreation Association is a cooperative including seven different community parks and recreation associations.[6]

Deaflympics, Special Olympics, Paralympics

In the world of disability and sport, there are three different Olympic games. Some school-age students, especially those who get involved in recreation, sport, and/or physical activity programming, may find themselves wanting to, and being encouraged to, compete as young adults and adults in disability sport. The Deaflympics, Special Olympics, and Paralympics all have a unique history, regularly scheduled international summer and winter competition, diverse sport offerings, and a specific classification system. Each requires rigorous training to compete.

DEAFLYMPICS

Sport for individuals who are deaf dates back to the late 1800s with organized sport clubs. The first competition, named the Silent Games, was held in Paris in 1924. At that first competition, nine countries were represented. After those initial games, the International Committee of Silent Sports (CISS) was formed to oversee the Silent Games. In 1979 the name was changed to the International Committee of Sports for the Deaf (ICSD).[4] The ICSD is recognized by the International Olympic Committee (IOC) as an International Federation with Olympic standing.[11, 1] The Deaflympics is run in 4-year intervals with summer and winter competitions.[4] See **Table 9-3** for the summer and winter sport offerings. For several years the CISS (now the ICSD) committee struggled with classifying a deaf athlete. In

TABLE 9-3　Deaflympic Summer and Winter Sport Offerings

Summer Games		Winter Games
Athletics	Swimming	
Badminton	Table tennis	Alpine skiing
Basketball	Taekwondo	Cross-country skiing
Beach volleyball	Tennis	Curling
Bowling	Volleyball	Ice hockey
Cycling road	Wrestling freestyle	Snowboard
Football	Wrestling Greco-Roman	
Handball		
Judo		
Karate		
Mountain bike		
Orienteering		
Shooting		

1979 the committee made the decision that an athlete with a minimum of a 55-decibel hearing loss in the better ear would qualify for competition.[4] Hearing aids are not permitted, only sign language. This allows for no spoken language between athletes and eliminates hearing directions from coaches. Twenty-two summer games have been held since 1924 and 17 winter games have run, the first games held in 1949. The 2017 games will be held in Samsun, Turkey.[4]

SPECIAL OLYMPICS

Sport can be viewed as a significant life experience for all athletes, those with and without an intellectual disability.[8] The Special Olympics hosts an international audience with 4.5 million athletes, ages 8 years old and up, from more than 170 countries.[23] Eunice Kennedy Shriver is the founder of Special Olympics and dedicated her life to changing the worldview of the potential and abilities of individuals with intellectual disabilities through sport. Jamaal Charles, running back for the Kansas City Chiefs, got his first sporting opportunity, at the age of 10, through Special Olympics. He found his talent and ability in a supportive and nurturing environment. The concept of the "games" started as a sport day camp for individuals with intellectual disabilities in the early 1960s. The first official International Special Olympic Games took place in the summer of 1968 at Soldier Field in Chicago. Attending those first games were approximately 1,000 athletes from 26 states in the United States, Canada, and France.[11] The most recent reported census numbers, in the year 2015, showed that participation in Special Olympic events and competitions totaled more than 94,000.[23] The mission of Special Olympics is to:

> … provide year-round sports training and athletic competition in a variety of Olympic-type sports for children and adults with intellectual disabilities, giving them continuing opportunities to develop physical fitness, demonstrate courage, experience joy, and participate in sharing of gifts, skills, and friendship with their families, the Special Olympic athletes, and the community.[23]

Special Olympics runs summer and winter games and competitions locally, regionally, nationally, and internationally. Athletes of degrees of intellectual disability are grouped by ability for competition. See **Table 9-4** for all Special Olympic sport offerings.

Several global programs and initiatives within Special Olympics have been developed to involve athletes, coaches, and families from around the world. Unified Sports is one of those initiatives. It is an offering through Special Olympics that brings together athletes with and without intellectual disabilities to form teams.[15] With the goal of social inclusion to promote friendships and understanding, athletes of similar age and ability are brought together to train and compete.[23]

TABLE 9-4   Special Olympic Summer and Winter Sport Offerings

Alpine skiing	Cycling	Handball	Snowboarding
Aquatics	Equestrian	Judo	Snowshoeing
Athletics	Figure skating	Kayaking	Softball
Badminton	Floorball	Netball	Speed skating
Basketball	Floor hockey	Open-water swimming	Table tennis
Bocce	Football	Powerlifting	Tennis
Bowling	Golf	Roller skating	Triathlon
Cricket	Gymnastics, artistic	Sailing	Volleyball
Cross-country skiing	Gymnastics, rhythmic		

The Young Athletes program is another Special Olympics initiative developed in 2004 to offer motor skill development for children 2.5 through 8 years of age. The programming focuses on those fundamental skills that are the building blocks for future sport involvement. Play activities are organized for children to improve physical and psychological development.[15]

The Motor Activity Training Program (MATP) was developed for individuals who are more severely impacted by their disability and unable to participate in other sports and programs offered by Special Olympics. The MATP is often used as part of a physical education program and includes warm-ups, physical fitness, motor fitness, and motor skill development.[15] See **Table 9-5** for other global initiatives offered through Special Olympics.

TABLE 9-5　Global Initiatives within Special Olympics[15]

1. Coaching excellence and coaching model
2. Partnerships with international (regional) sports federations
3. Sports Resources Teams (SRT)
4. Extended quota for high-level athletes
5. Athletes Leadership Program (ALP)
6. Young Athletes program
7. Youth volunteer initiatives
8. Unified Sports program
9. Motor Activity Training program
10. Healthy Athletes program

PARALYMPICS

The Paralympic games are held each year the Olympic games are held and in the same venue. In fact, *para* means "equal to."[16] Historically, the first games for individuals with disabilities were organized by Sir Ludwig Guttmann to give veterans of World War II competitive sport opportunities. In 1948 he organized the Stoke Mandeville Games in England for wheelchair athletes.[5] The games were officially named the Paralympics when they were held in Seoul, South Korea, in 1988. That year the games were referred to as the "modern games." Today, an Olympic bid has to be summited jointly by

TABLE 9-6   Paralympic Summer and Winter Sport Offerings

Alpine skiing	Football 5-a-side	Snowboarding
Archery	Football 7-a-side	Swimming
Athletics	Goalball	Table tennis
Badminton	Ice sledge hockey	Taekwondo
Biathlon	Judo	Triathlon
Boccia	Powerlifting	Wheelchair basketball
Canoe	Rowing	Wheelchair curling
Cross-country skiing	Sailing	Wheelchair dance sport
Cycling	Shooting	Wheelchair fencing
Equestrian	Sitting volleyball	Wheelchair rugby
		Wheelchair tennis

the Olympic and Paralympic Committees. The summer and winter games are held every 4 years.[16] See **Table 9-6** for a list of all summer and winter Paralympic sports. A total of 14 summer Paralympic games have been held and 11 winter games have been held since the first games in Rome, Italy, in 1960. **Table 9-7** lists the host cities the International Paralympic Committee has chosen for the summer and winter games through 2022.

Athletes competing in each Paralympic sport must be classified, by a classification panel, into one of the following impairment types:

Impaired muscle power
Impaired passive range of movement
Limb deficiency
Leg length difference
Short stature

TABLE 9-7   Paralympic Host Cities through 2022

Summer 2016→Rio de Janeiro
Winter 2018→Pyeongchang
Summer 2020→Tokyo
Winter 2022→Beijing

Hyertonia

Ataxia

Athetosis

Vision impairment

Intellectual impairment[18]

The classification system is in place to ensure that an athlete's impairment is minimized. Athletes are grouped into sport classes after determining the degree of activity limitation imposed by their impairment. Then it is determined how athletes are grouped together.[17]

SUMMARY

The Individuals with Disabilities Education Improvement Act (IDEIA, 2004) mandates that no later than 16 years of age a qualifying student will need to have an individualized transition plan in place. The goal of this plan will be to get the student and his or her family familiar with community-based programming so that upon graduation the student is familiar with options and ways to access recreation, sport, and/or physical activity programming. The taxonomy of transition programming in physical education takes a top-down approach. That is to say, the programming should be student-focused and based upon the student's interests and skills. Community settings may include fitness centers, YMCAs, recreation centers, park districts, and so on. Programs that run Paralympic sport clubs, BlazeSports, and/or special recreation programming provide students with options for being involved in recreation, sport, and/or physical activity programming. For students with disabilities who are interested in team and individual sport and want to train as athletes, the Deaflympics, Special Olympics, and Paralympics could be options. Maintaining a healthy, active lifestyle is the overall goal.

REVIEW QUESTIONS

1. According to IDEIA, at what age should the transition plan begin?
2. What is an ITP?
3. Why is it critical to have family involvement during the transition years?
4. Give some examples of community settings where an ITP can be carried out.
5. Compare and contrast the Deaflympics, Special Olympics, and Paralympics.

REFERENCES

1. Ammons, D., & Eickman, J. (2011). Deaflympics and the Paralympics: Eradicating misconceptions. *Sport in Society: Cultures, Commerce, Media, Politics, 14*, 1149–1164. DOI: 10.1080/17430437.2011.614772.

2. BlazeSports America. (2016). www.blazesports.org/

3. Chicago Park District Special Recreation. www.chicagoparkdistrict.org

4. Deaflympics. (2016). http://www.deaflympics.com/sports.asp

5. DePauw, K. (2012). A historical perspective of the Paralympic games. *Journal of Physical Education, Recreation and Dance, 83*, 21–22, 31.

6. Fox Valley Special Recreation Association. www.fvsra.org

7. Great Lakes Adaptive Sport Association. www.glasa.org

8. Harada, C., & Siperstein, G. (2009). The sport experience of athletes with intellectual disabilities: A national survey of Special Olympics athletes and their families. *Adapted Physical Activity Quarterly, 26*, 68–85.

9. Hunter, D. (2012). Community programs, sport clubs, and clinics for adapted sport. *JOPERD, 83*, 25–26.

10. Individuals with Disabilities Education Improvement Act. (2004). Pub. L. 108-446, 118 Stat. 2647 et seq.

11. Legg, D., Emes, C., Steward, D., & Steadward, R. (2004). Historical overview of the Paralympics, Special Olympics, and Deaflympics. *Palaestra, 20*, 30–35, 56.

12. Little League Baseball and Softball. (2016).

13. Lorenzi, D.G., & Arnhold, R.W. (2015). Getting involved in transition planning. *Journal of Physical Education, Recreation & Dance, 86*, 3–4. DOI: 10.1080/07303084.2015.1076638.

14. Murphy, N., Carbone, P., & Council on Children with Disabilities. (2008). Promoting the participation of children with disabilities in sports, recreation, and physical activities. *Pediatrics, 121*, 1057–1061. DOI: 10.1542/peds.2008-0566.

15. Myśliwiec, A., & Damentko, M. (2015). Global initiative of the Special Olympics movement for people with intellectual disabilities. *Journal of Human Kinetics, 45*, 253–259. DOI: 10.1515/hukin-2015-0026.

16. Paciorek, M. (2011). *Adapted sport.* In Winnick, J. (Editor): *Adapted physical education and sport* (5th ed.). Champaign, IL: Human Kinetics.

17. Paralympic Games. (2016). International Paralympic Committee. http://www.paralympic.org/paralympic-games/summer

18. Paralympic Games. (2016). http://www.paralympic.org/classification

19. Rimmer, J., Riley, B., Wang, E., Rauworth, A., & Jurkowski, J. (2004). Physical activity participation among people with disabilities: Barriers and facilitators. *American Journal of Preventative Medicine, 26*, 419–425. DOI: 10.1016/j.amepre.2004.02.002.

20. Arnhold, R. personal communication, January 12, 2016.

21. Roth, K., & Columna, L. (2011). Collaborative strategies during transition for students with disabilities. *Journal of Physical Education, Recreation & Dance, 82,* 50–55. DOI: 10.1080/07303084.2011.10598629.
22. Samalot-Rivera, A., López-Alemán, A., & Volmar, V. (2015). Increasing transition opportunities for youth with disabilities: Steps to follow in program selection. *Journal of Physical Education, Recreation & Dance, 86,* 57–59. DOI: 10.1080/07303084.2015.1009808.
23. Special Olympics. (2016). www.specialolympics.org
24. Special Recreation Association Network of Illinois. (2013). http://www.specialrecreation.org/find-my-service
25. Test, D. W., Fowler, C. H., Richter, S. M., White, J., Mazzotti, V., Walker, A. R., et al. (2009). Evidence-based practices in secondary transition. *Career Development for Exception Individuals, 32,* 115–128.
26. United States Olympic Committee. (2016). *Paralympics.* Retrieved from http://findaclub.usparalympics.org
27. United States Olympic Committee. (2015). *Paralympic sport club annual report 2014.* U.S. Paralympics Division.

PART 3

Needs of Specific Populations

In this part, specific types of disabilities and suggestions for intervention strategies are described. While we recognize that each person has unique qualities and needs, for ease of communication we have grouped similar age groups and conditions together. Each condition is defined, characteristics are given, means of testing are suggested, and specific programming and teaching techniques are detailed. The conditions addressed in each chapter have been organized to be consistent with the 2004 amendments to the Individuals with Disabilities Education Improvement Act. Categories of conditions/diagnoses discussed in this part include intellectual disability, autism spectrum disorder, specific learning disabilities, emotional disturbance, physically disabling conditions, communication disorders, visual impairments, and other health impairment.

CHAPTER 10

Infants, Toddlers, and Preschoolers

OBJECTIVES

- Explain the difference between IDEIA mandates for early childhood intervention (for children birth to 3 years of age) and preschool programs (for children 3 to 5 years of age).
- List and describe Howard Gardner's forms of intelligence and explain the implications for assessment and intervention.
- Describe the infant–family interaction process.
- Explain effective modeling techniques for parents who are trying to improve motor and play skills in their infant or toddler.
- Describe developmentally appropriate practice in assessment and intervention in preschool learning environments, including preschool movement programs.
- Discuss strategies for identifying a child's anger and helping the child deal with the anger.
- Design an active learning center for indoor and outdoor play.
- Describe strategies to develop an anti-bias active learning center.

Early and developmentally appropriate intervention during the crucial years in which central nervous system development is "plastic," marked, and pronounced has a profound impact on cognitive, language, social-emotional, and motor performance. Attention to these factors is important for all children; however, it is critical for children who are born with disabilities or

developmental delays or who are at risk for failure.

In this chapter we examine the most recent theories of intellectual development, as well as the gross motor, cognitive, receptive and expressive language, symbolic play, drawing, fine motor, constructive play, self-help, and emotional characteristics of the typically developing child from birth through 5 years of age. Techniques for identifying the developmental level of young children and intervention strategies to facilitate their developmental processes are explained. In addition, federal mandates that address required services for at-risk infants, toddlers, and preschoolers are discussed. The central role of the parents and other family members, including the extended family, in this process is emphasized. The characteristics and importance of developmentally appropriate learning environments designed to facilitate the primary learning tool of the young child—play—are highlighted.

The Potential of Quality Early Intervention

There is a window of opportunity in which quality, family-based early intervention can make a significant difference in the lives of an infant, a toddler, or a preschooler and, subsequently, his or her family and the greater community.[53] During the early years of a child's life, there are incredible opportunities to enhance central nervous system function. A quality early childhood intervention (ECI) program can have lasting positive results: higher scores on intelligence tests, higher scores on reading and mathematics tests, and an increase in the probability that the individual will study at the college level and be employed. This type of program can reduce the likelihood that the individual will require special education, will become pregnant as a teenager, and will be incarcerated or served by the juvenile justice system.[34, 54]

The Eight Types of Intelligence—The Philosophical Foundation of Effective and Appropriate Early Intervention

A socially valid physical education program for preschoolers at risk, with developmental delays or disabilities, is based on the premise that professionals, parents, and other family members acknowledge, recognize, accept, and embrace the notion that there are eight types of intelligence.

Howard Gardner, in his classic works *Frames of Mind: The Theory of Multiple Intelligences* [18] and *Intelligence Reframed: Multiple Intelligences for the 21st Century,* suggests that, if educators are to conceptualize cognition, it must be considered in a far broader realm than that typically used to identify or quantify an individual's ability to think and learn. Specifically, Gardner suggests that the instruments used typically to assess and evaluate intelligence tend to ignore many types of human intelligence in lieu of measuring those that are easiest to measure—namely, linguistic and mathematical abilities. Although the first eight intelligences have been used for decades, more recently another type of intelligence, existential intelligence, has been discussed. This type of intelligence would describe children who ask deep questions and demonstrate curiosity about the meaning of life, death, and how we got here.[51] Here we will focus on the long-standing eight intelligences as they apply more to young children.

Gardner's theory of multiple intelligences has been widely embraced by enlightened educational communities. His theory continues to be ignored by those satisfied with the status quo.

Gardner defines intelligence as the ability to solve problems or create products valued within one or more cultural settings. His emphasis on multicultural settings is of particular value in consideration of the philosophy. His work continues to gain recognition as educators seek to explore and define strategies to evaluate the intelligence of children representing a wide variety of cultures and as they seek educational intervention strategies that meet their diverse needs.

Widely used norm-referenced linguistic and mathematically based "intelligence tests" have widespread cultural, racial, socioeconomic, and gender biases. Historically, these tests have been used to include children in learning environments and experiences, as well as to exclude them. The tracking of African American and poor children, which provided the impetus for *Brown v. Board of Education* (Kansas), 1954, is a practice that, unfortunately, still exists. If Gardner's theory of multiple intelligences were widely embraced and practiced, educational assessment would more appropriately and equitably evaluate the performance and potential performance of all children. Educational intervention would be more appropriate and equitable, and more children would love school and want to stay in school to learn.

Movement and play programs would be embraced as a vital and integral part of the total education process. Movement and play would be recognized for their significant potential in the lives of young children.

Educators, lawmakers, voters, school board members, and state education agency personnel must acknowledge that there are at least eight types of intelligence. In order to thrive and grow, our society needs individuals with each of these types of intelligence. The educational system must nurture each child and honor the child's intelligence. Each of Gardner's theorized intelligences is considered in the following sections with examples of the behaviors of infants, toddlers, and preschoolers that reflect these intelligences.[51]

LINGUISTIC INTELLIGENCE

Linguistic intelligence is expressed in and through the use of oral language (receptive and expressive) and written language (reading and writing). It represents a sensitivity to and interest in the use of words, the sound and rhythm of words, and the functions of language—to express wants and needs, to convince, to share, and to explain. The young child demonstrates this intelligence by cooing and babbling, scribbling and drawing, asking questions, repeating nonsense rhymes, telling stories, listening to stories, identifying simple words or signs, and rote counting.

LOGICAL-MATHEMATICAL INTELLIGENCE

Logical-mathematical intelligence is an individual's ability to group and sequence objects, to order and reorder them, to describe their quality and quantity, and to see and understand patterns. The young child demonstrates this intelligence by separating dinosaurs from zoo animals; stacking rings, diminishing in size, on a base; collecting sticks and separating the long ones from the short ones; sequencing blocks in patterns, such as three blue, two red, and three blue; and arranging balls from the largest to the smallest.

MUSICAL INTELLIGENCE

Musical intelligence is an individual's ability to recognize sounds and distinguish one from another, identify and see patterns in music, be sensitive to rhythm and time variables, know and appreciate timbre and tone, and express feelings and emotions through music. The young child demonstrates this intelligence by seeking one "favorite" musical instrument; moving the body to a beat; using pots and pans as drums; turning off the CD player if he or she does not like the music; asking to sing a favorite song, over and over; clapping or toe tapping to a particular rhythm or beat; singing or humming; and "rapping" a favorite song.

SPATIAL INTELLIGENCE

Spatial intelligence includes the ability to identify shapes and differentiate between objects in terms of size, to see commonalities in shape or size, to perceive the visual world accurately, to perform simple transformations of visual images, and to recreate a graphic image of a visual representation, such as a map or graph. The young child demonstrates this intelligence by putting puzzles together, building a block structure, building a "Lego" bridge, drawing self, sorting objects by shape and size, copying a given figure, drawing a particular shape in a variety of positions,[23] identifying a child who is larger or smaller than self, and identifying a child who is taller or shorter than self.

BODILY-KINESTHETIC INTELLIGENCE

Bodily-kinesthetic intelligence is characterized by the ability to use the body in highly differentiated and skilled ways, for expressive and goal-directed purposes. The young child demonstrates this intelligence by crawling, creeping, and walking in, around, and between objects; using gestures to express needs and wants; using facial expressions to convey emotions; reaching to get a favorite toy; rolling over; hurling a ball; catching a rolled ball; jumping over a set of blocks, arranged in an ever-taller sequence; kicking a ball; using the body to pretend to be "mad," "sad," or "glad"; and carrying a toy from the toy box to the play area.

INTERPERSONAL INTELLIGENCE

Interpersonal intelligence is one in which an individual can identify and empathize with the feelings and emotions of others. The young child demonstrates this intelligence by crying if another child cries, telling a parent or another caregiver if a friend is hurt or sad, comforting a friend who is upset, noticing that the parent or caregiver is having a "bad day," and engaging in cooperative play.

INTRAPERSONAL INTELLIGENCE

Intrapersonal intelligence is one in which the individual is able to identify his or her own feelings, emotions, and motives and is basically inner-directed (i.e., internally driven). The young child demonstrates this intelligence by seeking solitary play experiences; judging his or her own art project; keeping a journal of pictures, drawings, or symbols that reflect feelings; expressing emotion in housekeeping play experiences; and preferring an independent plan-do-review process to a group process.

NATURALIST INTELLIGENCE

In later works, Gardner identified the eighth form of intelligence. At first, he suggested that it might be a "spiritual" intelligence.[22] In more recent works he has called it "naturalist" intelligence. In fact, it appears that this intelligence is probably a combination of "spirituality" and a profound sense of "nature." The young child demonstrates this intelligence by collecting and sorting leaves or taking loving care of a class rabbit.

Developmentally Appropriate Assessment of Infants, Toddlers, and Preschoolers

While some educators have embraced the move toward assessment that acknowledges multiple forms of intelligence, there is a desperate need for assessment processes that are developmentally appropriate and sensitive to the unique needs of infants, toddlers, and preschoolers. This is critical because screening and identification of delay drives eligibility. Eligibility drives decisions regarding goals and objectives on the individualized education program (IEP) or individual family service plan (IFSP). Goals and objectives drive placement and programming decisions.

Developmentally appropriate assessment of movement and play for infants, toddlers, and preschoolers should incorporate play-based, transdisciplinary practices and the development of a movement/play portfolio assessment process to follow the child from infancy through adulthood.

Mandates specific to screening and identification are included in P.L. 99–457.[46] This legislation calls for:

1. A multidisciplinary approach to screen and identify children from birth through 5 years of age
2. Identifying infants and young children with known disabilities and developmental delays and, at states' discretion, identifying children from birth through 2 years of age who are at risk for developmental delays
3. Planning comprehensive services for young children with special needs, including a model of periodic re-evaluation, and
4. Involving the family in all levels of screening, identification, and intervention.

The expansion of services mandated by P.L. 99–457 has enabled the physical educator to become more fully involved in identifying and remediating delays evidenced by a wider range of young children. This provides a significant opportunity to have a positive impact on the lives of growing numbers of children at risk in those critical early periods of life to help ready them for school.

Recommendations for Screening and Assessment of Infants, Toddlers, and Preschoolers

The following recommendations for assessing young children with disabilities are supported by the Division for Early Childhood (DEC) of the Council for Exceptional Children (CEC) to ensure a child- and family-centered, team-based approach:[14]

1. The process is a shared experience between the professionals involved and family members.
2. All information and data generated about the young child are solely to benefit the child's growth.

3. All steps in the process should be individualized to the specific needs of the child and his or her family in order to answer any and all questions posed.
4. The process should "... integrate the child's everyday routines, interests, materials, caregivers, and play partners ..." (p. 10)
5. Develop a shared partnership between professionals and families for communication regarding the design of learning environments.

Selected motor assessment instruments that are appropriate for use with infants, toddlers, and preschoolers are included in **Table 10-1**.

Transdisciplinary, play-based assessment (TPBA) is an example of a developmentally appropriate strategy for assessing infants, toddlers, and preschoolers. The TPBA method allows a team to observe a young child in his or her most natural play environment. While a play facilitator interacts with a child, the team records information about the child, collecting information in four domains: cognitive, social-emotional, communication and language, and sensorimotor.[27] **Table 10-2** provides a list of motor development delay indicators.

The assessment process must be transdisciplinary; that is, it should be done by a team of individuals with a commitment to infants, toddlers, and preschoolers representing various disciplines. The child's parents are the most important members of the team—the parents are the best source of information about the child. In order for the assessment process to yield meaningful information, the infant, toddler, and/or preschooler and his or her family members must be honored and respected. Neither the child nor the family members should be put in an uncomfortable situation.

Professionals with unique abilities and skills in one or more of the domains are a vital part of the team as well. These professionals include, but are not limited to, (1) an educational psychologist, (2) a speech and language therapist, (3) an occupational therapist, (4) a physical therapist, (5) an adapted physical educator with specific training and experience working with young children, (6) a play therapist, and (7) a music therapist. A transdisciplinary approach to assessment with infants, toddlers, and preschoolers allows the team members to gain vital information about the child's development and to share that information with other professionals.

The adapted physical educator may add a unique perspective to the transdisciplinary team because of specific competencies. Cowden and

TABLE 10-1   Selected Motor Assessment Instruments for Infants, Toddlers, and Preschoolers

Test/Description	Source	Age	Motor Components	Reference
Alberta Infant Motor Scale (AIMS) (1994)				
A tool for assessing the early postures of the developing infant	Piper & Darrah: Motor Assessment of the Developing Infant W.B. Saunders Company 6277 Sea Harbor Drive Orlando, FL 32821	Birth–19 mos	Prone, supine, sit, stand postures	Content-referenced
Bayley Scales of Infant Development III (2005)				
This revised scale is sensitive to differences between children who are at risk for developmental delay and those who are not.	Harcourt Assessment 3052 Smidmore Street Marrickville, NSW 2204	1–42 mos	Posture, locomotor, fine motor	Norm-referenced
Brigance Diagnostic Inventory III (2013)				
A widely used, teacher-friendly scale that also includes speech and language, general knowledge and comprehension, social and emotional development, literacy manuscript writing, and math and science, daily living skills assessment techniques	Curriculum Assoc., Inc. 5 Esquire Road North Billerica, MA 10862	Birth–7 yrs	Preambulatory, fine motor, gross motor	Norm-referenced Criterion-referenced

(continues)

TABLE 10-1   Selected Motor Assessment Instruments for Infants, Toddlers, and Preschoolers (*Continued*)

Test/Description	Source	Age	Motor Components	Reference
Callier-Azusa Scale (1978)				
A developmental scale designed to aid in the assessment of deaf-blind children and children who have profound disabilities. It also includes daily living skills, cognition, communication and language, and social-developmental milestones.	The University of Texas at Dallas The Callier Center for Communication Disorders 1966 Inwood Road Dallas, TX 75235	Birth–7 yrs	Postural control, locomotion, fine motor, visual-motor and visual, auditory, and tactile development	Content-referenced
Developmental Assessment of Young Children, 2nd Ed. (2012)				
Includes scoring for adaptive behavior, cognitive, communication and social-emotional domains	Pearson 19500 Bulverde Road San Antonio, TX 78259	Birth–5 yrs	Physical development	Norm-referenced
Developmental Indicators for the Assessment of Learning (DIAL-4) (2011)				
A screening tool for assessing large groups of children. Includes concepts, language, self-help, and social development	Pearson 19500 Bulverde Road San Antonio, TX 78259	2.6–5.11 yrs	Motor skills	Norm-referenced

TABLE 10-1   Selected Motor Assessment Instruments for Infants, Toddlers, and Preschoolers (*Continued*)

Test/Description	Source	Age	Motor Components	Reference
Denver Development Screening Test II (DDST II) (1990)				
This easy-to-use screening tool also includes screening for speech-language, cognitive, and social-emotional skills (self-help).	Denver Developmental Materials, Inc. PO Box 371075 Denver, CO 80237-5075	Birth–6 yrs	Gross motor skills, fine motor, adaptive skills	Content-referenced
Hawaii Early Learning Profile (HELP) (1995)				
A curriculum-embedded developmental checklist that also includes cognitive, language, social, and self-help skills	VORT Corp. PO Box 601321 Palo Alto, CA 94306	Birth–6 yrs	Gross motor, fine motor, self-help	Content-referenced
Miller Assessment for Preschoolers (1988 Rev.)				
An instrument that also includes evaluation of a child's speech and language and cognitive abilities and provides guidance in determining whether a child's behavior during testing ranges from severely dysfunctional to normal	The Psychological Corp. 555 Academic Court San Antonio, TX 78204-2498	2.9–5.9 yrs	Sense of position and movement, touch, basic movement patterns, gross motor, fine motor	Content-referenced

(continues)

TABLE 10-1   Selected Motor Assessment Instruments for Infants, Toddlers, and Preschoolers (*Continued*)

Test/Description	Source	Age	Motor Components	Reference
Movement Assessment of Infants (1980)				
An instrument that enables the evaluator to determine whether a child is developing normally during the first year of life	Movement Assessment of Infants PO Box 4631 Rolling Bay, WA 98061	Birth–12 mos	Muscle tone, primitive reflexes, equilibrium reflexes, volitional movement	Content-referenced
Peabody Developmental Motor Scales-2 (2000)				
A curriculum-embedded assessment tool that is widely used by preschool teachers	Pearson 19500 Bulverde Road San Antonio, TX 78259	Birth–6 yrs	Fine motor, gross motor	Norm-referenced
Test of Gross Motor Development-2 (2000)				
A commonly used motor assessment for elementary children.	PRO-ED 8700 Shoal Creek Boulevard Austin, TX 78757	3–10 years	Locomotor skills, object-control skills	Criterion-referenced, Norm-referenced

TABLE 10-2   Motor Development Delay Indicators: Age 3 Years and Older*

I. Muscle tone status (check all that apply):

   a. Low tone (proprioceptive problems):

      Difficulty holding up head   _____

      Slumped posture   _____

      Tendency to put legs in a W position when sitting   _____

   b. High tone (overflow/tension):

      Stiff body movements   _____

      Fisting of one or both hands   _____

      Grimacing of mouth or face when concentrating   _____

TABLE 10-2   Motor Development Delay Indicators: Age 3 Years and Older* (*Continued*)

II. Strength and endurance—demonstrates any of the following:

    Tires during play before other children

    Has breathing difficulties sometimes

    Gets out of breath before other children

III. Equilibrium/extensor muscle control (check all that apply):

    a. Does not raise and control head when:

Lying facedown	_____
Balancing on hands and knees	_____
Sitting	_____
b. Does not roll from front to back	_____
c. Does not prop on forearms	_____

    d. Does not reach for a toy when:

Lying facedown	_____
Balancing on hands and knees	_____
Sitting	_____
e. Cannot remain standing without support	_____

IV. Equilibrium/flexor muscle control (check all that apply):

    a. Has difficulty with the following moves from a back-lying position:

Rolling from back to front	_____
Sitting up	_____
Standing up	_____
Reaching for toy	_____

V. Equilibrium when moving (check all that apply):

Does not use sequential movement when rolling (head, shoulders, hips, followed by legs)	_____
Stands/walks/runs on balls of feet	_____
Uses a wide base of support during walk/run	_____
Loses balance when suddenly changing directions	_____
Does not put arms and hands out to break fall	_____
Avoids walking on narrow supports (balance beam, curb)	_____

(continues)

TABLE 10-2   Motor Development Delay Indicators: Age 3 Years and Older* (*Continued*)

VI. Visual status (indicators of depth perception problems)—
demonstrates any of the following:

Both feet are not off ground momentarily when running	_____
Does not jump down from bottom step	_____
Watches feet when moving on different surfaces	_____
Marks time when ascending and descending stairs	_____
Avoids climbing apparatus	_____
Turns head when catching ball	_____
Cannot bounce and catch playground ball with both hands	_____
Misses ball when kicking	_____

(NOTE: Children demonstrating three or more of the preceding
eight behaviors should be referred to a visual developmental
specialist for an orthoptic visual examination.)

VII. Coordination (check all that apply):

a. Does not bring the hands together at midline when:

Lying down	_____
Sitting up	_____

b. Does not demonstrate the following:

Uses arms in opposition to legs when crawling	_____
Uses arms in opposition to legs when walking	_____
Uses arms in opposition to legs when running	_____
Arms are bent at waist height when running	_____
Use of both arms to assist during jump	_____
Slides leading with one side of body	_____
Gallops	_____

c. Does not demonstrate the following when kicking:

Swings kicking leg behind body when preparing to kick	_____
Follows through with kicking leg after contact	_____

TABLE 10-2   Motor Development Delay Indicators: Age 3 Years and Older* (*Continued*)

VIII. Additional information

    a. What are the primary means of moving during play?

    ———————————————————————————

    b. What motor skills does the child avoid?

    ———————————————————————————

    c. Can the child imitate a movement pattern that is
       demonstrated?   —————————

    d. Can the child demonstrate a sequence of movements
       when requested to do so?

    ———————————————————————————

    e. Check the stages of play the child demonstrates:

       Solitary (onlooker or ignores others)   —————————

       Parallel (plays alongside or with similar toys)   —————————

       Associative (follow the leader)   —————————

       Cooperative (social interaction)   —————————

IX. Comments/observations/concerns:

———————————————————————————

Torrey[10] suggest the "adapted motor developmentalist" should have the following competencies:

- Knowledge of normal and abnormal motor development
- Curriculum- and judgment-based assessment techniques
- Appropriate response-contingent toys and materials for sensory stimulation and physical and motor development
- Strategies for relaxation, socialization, and play

The more traditional assessment/evaluation model is inappropriate for infants, toddlers, and preschoolers for a number of reasons:

- Infants, toddlers, and preschoolers are not comfortable with strangers. It is frightening to meet a stranger, much less be asked to leave a parent or "more comfortable" adult to go with a stranger into a room to "play."

- Young children are uncomfortable outside of their natural setting—their home, their neighborhood, their child-care setting—and will not behave naturally when asked to perform outside of their natural setting.
- A young child may be asked to play with an evaluator, but the child does not control the situation—the unfamiliar adult does. The child is asked to play without favorite toys and, to facilitate evaluation, the child may find a toy he or she enjoys playing with and then be asked to return the toy to move on to another task.
- Assessment protocols often discriminate against a child with a disability. For example, most "intelligence tests" rely heavily on language and prelogical/mathematical skills; the child's performance may be significantly negatively affected.
- Many developmental assessment scales assume that there is a typical developmental sequence; many children with disabilities do not acquire developmental milestones in a typical way.
- Many of the tasks that infants, toddlers, and preschoolers are asked to perform have little or no meaning for the child or the child's parents. Unfortunately, this has been part of the clinical "mystique," which has presumed that the professionals have the answers and the parents are dependent on the professionals for information.

The assessment of movement and play behaviors in infants, toddlers, and preschoolers requires a special sensitivity to the fact that major developmental changes occur during the crucial years from birth to age 5 years. Whenever possible, the assessment and evaluation of an infant, a toddler, or a preschooler should be completed in the child's most natural environment—the child's home, child-care setting, or neighborhood play area. In addition to being sensitive to the child's natural environment, the assessment must be culturally, linguistically, socio-economically, and gender sensitive.

The Portfolio Assessment Process

Sensitivity to the fact that assessment is not, and should never be, a 6-month, annual, or 3-year comprehensive event but, rather, a day-to-day, ongoing process has led educators to the portfolio assessment. Just as caring parents have historically saved documentation of their child's progress—pictures, drawings, height/weight information, "new" words, and so on—caring educators must begin to save, carefully, documentation of the progress of the children they teach.

Danielson has identified three types of portfolios:[11]

1. Display, or showcase, portfolio. The display portfolio captures, usually with photos, the many activities in which children engage in a classroom. It is a picture of what goes on in the classroom but does not document a child's performance or development. A display portfolio shows only a child's best work and, subsequently, does not accurately reflect actual consistent performance.

2. Working portfolio. One way to get more accurate documentation of how a child is growing and developing is in a working portfolio. It shows the process of learning new concepts and applying new understanding to tasks. The teacher and child have evidence of strengths and challenges that align with learning objectives. The information is useful in guiding and designing instructional goals.

3. Assessment portfolio. An assessment portfolio is a collection of student work that represents what the student has learned. The most effective portfolios also contain the student's reflection about what he/she has gained from the assignment. Danielson and Abrutyn wrote, "Documentation for assessment purposes must be more than photos and work samples. Teacher commentary becomes an essential source of information for evaluating the work. . . . Identifying what makes a quality piece of work or an informative work sample for portfolio collection is critical."[11]

If the parent and teacher are sensitive to the fact that their roles should not be intrusive but, rather, supportive—not as the director of learning but as the facilitator of learning, the portfolio is a natural and obvious conclusion. If the educator is actively watching and learning—from the children—the teacher will become adept at documenting each child's progress.

The adapted physical educator has a great deal to contribute to the child's total portfolio. In fact, this specialist may contribute information and data to the portfolio for all types of intelligence. Sharing these types of data with the early childhood educator helps validate the active play and learning process and encourages teachers and parents to perceive the adapted physical educator as a professional who can and does make a significant contribution. The following are examples of movement and play data that can be collected to reflect each of the eight types of intelligence.

LINGUISTIC INTELLIGENCE

- A toddler says, "ball," when he or she wants the teacher to roll the ball to the child; the teacher records the utterance on the child's daily log.
- The child sings a simple "rap" song while jumping; the teacher videotapes the child.

LOGICAL-MATHEMATICAL INTELLIGENCE

- A child builds a tower with giant soft blocks, and the teacher takes a picture of the structure.
- A group of children line up to form a "train," and the teacher videotapes the group performing to the song "Chug-a-Long Choo Choo."

MUSICAL INTELLIGENCE

- Several children dance to Hap Palmer's "What a Miracle"; the teacher videotapes the child being assessed.
- A child walks to the beat of a drum; the teacher notes the progress.

SPATIAL INTELLIGENCE

- A toddler can trap a 13-, 10-, 8-, or 6-inch ball rolled to the child sitting in a V-sit position; the parent notes the ability and shares the information with other team members.
- An infant crawls toward and reaches a toy; the preschool movement/play specialist records that on the ongoing motor development assessment instrument.

BODILY-KINESTHETIC INTELLIGENCE

- A 2-year-old toddler hurls a ball; the teacher records the progress on the child's portfolio.

- A 5-year-old with Down syndrome climbs up and down a set of five stairs, holding the railing; the teacher records the milestone.

INTERPERSONAL INTELLIGENCE

- A child engages in parallel play in a sandbox; the teacher videotapes the play.
- A child identifies the children he or she likes to play with and those he or she does not like to play with; the teacher records this on a sociogram.

INTRAPERSONAL INTELLIGENCE

- A child describes the way he or she feels when playing a simple game with a friend; the teacher catches this on audiotape.

NATURALIST INTELLIGENCE

- A child names a flower on a nature walk; the teacher notes it.
- A child describes how he or she feels chasing his or her shadow; it is recorded on audiotape.

Contemporary communication, technology, and computer capabilities make it possible for parents and teachers to save vast amounts of information about the development of young children. Baby boomers have sepia photographs of their grandparents as children. The children of the 2000s have audio and visual memories stored in "clouds."

The technology exists to begin for every infant a portfolio that can follow the child throughout his or her development. The beauty lies in the capability to store information that could increase the likelihood that infants, toddlers, and preschoolers grow and learn in the best possible way. When an infant makes the transition into a toddler program, when that toddler makes the transition into a preschool program, and when that preschooler makes the transition into kindergarten, his or her teachers will have a comprehensive record of the child's progress.

The most significant questions related to the assessment process with infants, toddlers, and preschoolers include, but are not limited to, the following:

1. Does the assessment process yield important information that relates to eligibility, placement, and programming?
2. Does the assessment process do no harm? Is the infant, toddler, or preschooler safe both emotionally and physically?
3. Does the assessment discriminate against children on the basis of culture, socioeconomic base, ability, or gender? It must not.
4. Does the process provide information that the parents and other practitioners can use?

Assessment can be intrusive. A transdisciplinary, play-based approach to assessment completed in the child's natural ecosystem reduces the potential for the assessment to frighten the child or parent. Assessment can also be discriminatory. Recognizing eight types of intelligence and monitoring progress using a portfolio assessment minimize that possibility as well.

Ages and Stages—Understanding Typical and Atypical Development

It is vital that the adapted physical educator be aware of the development of the whole child. It is also necessary for the educator to embrace the notion that there is no such thing as a "typical" child. Each child is a unique being who develops in a unique way.

The description of the approximate ages at which a child usually acquires a new skill is charted in **Table 10-3**. Certainly, the educator must know what is typical in order to work with a child with delays or disabilities. But it must be understood that each child develops uniquely. For example, it is not uncommon for an abused or neglected child to demonstrate typical gross and fine motor development yet show marked delays in social-emotional, cognitive, receptive, and expressive language development. It is not uncommon for a child struggling to learn English as a second language to demonstrate typical gross and fine motor development but show delays in play behavior and receptive and expressive language development.

TABLE 10-3 Ages and Stages of Typical Child Development

Months	Typical Gross Motor Development	Typical Play Development	Typical Fine Motor/ Constructive Play	Typical Cognitive Development
0–3	Optical righting (2 mos)—child uses vision to align head when body is tilted; labyrinthine righting prone (2 mos)—when body is tilted, head orients to normal position	Gets excited when a toy is presented; shakes rattle if placed in hand	Puts fist in mouth; brings hands to chest and plays with hands and fingers; refines movements that satisfy needs (e.g., thumb sucking)	Follows object with eyes; continues actions to produce interesting reactions (e.g., kicks, coos, babbles)
3–6	Labyrinthine righting supine (6 mos)—when body is tilted, head orients to normal position; body righting (6 mos)—when body is tilted, body orients to normal position	Smiles, laughs in response to parent's speech, smile, or touch; enjoys simple songs, tickling, vocal games	Early grasping patterns emerge, plays with hands and feet; rubs, strikes, and shakes things to make noise; develops reaching patterns; uses both hands together; reaches for and grasps objects	Uncovers partially hidden object; imitates simple familiar actions
6–12	Supine and prone equilibrium reactions (6 mos), crawling (6–7 mos); hands and knees equilibrium reactions (8 mos); creeping (7–9 mos); sitting equilibrium reaction (10–12 mos); cruises holding on to furniture	Likes to bang things together; begins to imitate social games; prefers play with a parent to play with a toy; bites/chews toys; explores environment with adult help	Imitates simple actions (e.g., clapping, lying down); thumb begins to help with grasp; loves to shake and bang toys; begins to move intentionally; real pincer emerges at 12 months; begins to release objects	Uncovers hidden object; imitates somewhat different actions; puts familiar actions together in new combinations; moves to get toy

(continues)

TABLE 10-3   Ages and Stages of Typical Child Development (*Continued*)

Months	Typical Gross Motor Development	Typical Play Development	Typical Fine Motor/ Constructive Play	Typical Cognitive Development
12–18	Standing equilibrium (15 mos); walks up stairs, marking time; stands alone; walks alone with wide base of support; starts and stops walking; pushes a playground ball back and forth with a partner; makes a whole-body response to music; pulls or pushes a toy while walking	Enjoys piling objects and knocking them down; engages in solitary play; swings on a swing; plays alone contentedly if near an adult; likes action toys but plays with a variety of toys; uses realistic toys on self (e.g., pretends to brush hair with brush)	Stacks hand-sized blocks; combines objects; puts on/takes off pan and jar lids; takes objects out of a container; begins to scribble; holds crayon in hand with thumb up	Modifies familiar actions to solve new problems; imitates completely new actions; activates toy after adult demonstration
0-3	Begins to find ways to calm and soothe self (e.g., sucking); draws attention to self when distressed; learns adults will answer (if, indeed, an adult answers); likes face-to-face contact; responds to voices	Notices faces of others; coos in response to pleasant voice; may stop crying when someone enters room	Cries and makes vowel-like sounds; uses "different" kinds of cries; makes pleasure sounds	Depends on parent for everything
3-6	Cries differently in response to adults; shows excitement when adult approaches to lift, feed, or play; regards adult momentarily in response to speech or movement; smiles when parent smiles; laughs and giggles; smiles at mirror image	Turns eyes and head toward sound; responds to sound of own name	Varies tone to express feelings; makes new sounds; stops making sounds when adult talks; begins vocal play; squeals; babbles, coos; "talks" to toy or pet	Depends on parent for everything

TABLE 10-3   Ages and Stages of Typical Child Development *(Continued)*

Months	Typical Gross Motor Development	Typical Play Development	Typical Fine Motor/ Constructive Play	Typical Cognitive Development
6-12	Asserts self; demonstrates curiosity; tests relationship with caregiver; exhibits anxiousness over separation; shows awareness of difference between parent and "stranger"; gives hugs and kisses; likes to play simple adult–child games; exhibits sensitivity to other children (e.g., cries if another child cries); demonstrates emotions—joy, fear, anger	Shows interest in sounds of objects; understands and recognizes own name; understands "no" and "stop"; imitates simple sounds; gives objects on request	Makes same sounds over and over; uses gestures; imitates adults' sounds; enjoys simple games, such as "peek-a-boo"; appears to sing along with familiar music; asks for toys/food by pointing and making sounds; says "da-da" and "ma-ma"	Pulls off own socks; feeds self finger foods; holds bottle independently to drink
12-18	Demonstrates initiative; imitates; "me do it" attitude; explores (if feels safe; exploration inhibited if child feels insecure); begins to comply with simple requests; resists change; demonstrates affection with parent; follows simple one-step directions; initiates interactions with other children	Recognizes names of people and some objects; points to some objects; responds to a simple command; points to one to three body parts when asked; acknowledges others' speech by eye contact, speech, or repetition of word said	Jabbers; understands simple turn-taking rules in simple play; tries to communicate with "real words"; uses one to three spoken words; calls at least one person by name	Spoon-feeds and drinks from cup with many spills; sits on toilet, supervised, for 1 minute

(continues)

TABLE 10-3 Ages and Stages of Typical Child Development *(Continued)*

Months	Typical Gross Motor Development	Typical Play Development	Typical Fine Motor/ Constructive Play	Typical Cognitive Development
18–24	Walks down stairs, marked time, 1 hand held; walks backward; hurls a tennis ball while standing	Engages in parallel play; likes play that mimics parent's behavior; adds sounds to action (e.g., talks to a teddy bear); play themes reflect very familiar things (e.g., sleeping, eating); engages in play beyond self (e.g., child holds doll and rocks it)	Builds tower of four blocks; turns a key or crank to make a toy work; fits simple shapes into form boards; pours/dumps objects out of a container; scribbles vigorously; begins to place scribbles in specific place on paper	Points to pictures of animals or objects; chooses pictures to look at; points to mouth, eyes, nose; looks for familiar person who has left room; uses stick to get out-of-reach toy
24–30	Runs; jumps over a small object; stands on tiptoes momentarily	Likes rough and tumble play; pretends with similar objects (e.g., a stick becomes a sword); uses a doll to act out a scene; imitates adult activity in play (e.g., pretends to cook or iron)	Stacks five or six objects by size; nests cups by size; puts together simple puzzles; dresses/ undresses dolls; strings objects; turns doorknob; scribbles begin to take on forms and become shapes; imitates circular, vertical, and horizontal strokes; rolls, pounds, and squeezes clay	Points to and names pictures; likes "read-to-me" books; loves stories that include him or her; points to arms legs, hands, fingers; matches primary colors
30–36	Walks to and kicks a stationary playground ball; climbs on/off child-sized play equipment	Shares toys with encouragement; plays with other children for up to 30 minutes; pretend play reflects child's experience; pretends with dissimilar objects (e.g., a block becomes a car)	Draws a face; makes pancakes with clay; moves fingers independently; snips on line using scissors	Understands "front"/"back" and "in"/"out"; matches objects that have the same function (e.g., comb, brush)

TABLE 10-3   Ages and Stages of Typical Child Development *(Continued)*

Months	Typical Gross Motor Development	Typical Play Development	Typical Fine Motor/ Constructive Play	Typical Cognitive Development
36–48	Stands on one foot for 5 seconds: walks up stairs, alternating feet; runs contralaterally; hops on "best" foot three times; catches a bounced playground ball; throws a ball homolaterally; does a simple forward roll	Plays with an imaginary friend; prefers playing with other children to playing alone; pretends without any prop (e.g., pretends to comb hair with nothing in the hand); pretends after seeing, but not experiencing, an event; assumes "roles" in play and engages others in theme; acts out simple stories	Builds 3-D enclosures (e.g., zoos); makes specific marks (e.g., circles, crosses); draws a simple face; drawings represent child's perceptions (adult should not try to name/label); makes balls and snakes out of clay; cuts circles with scissors	Fills in words and phrases in favorite books when an adult reads; corrects adult if adult makes an error in reading (or tries to skip part of the story); points to thumbs, knees, chin; matches brown, black, gray, white; names red and blue when pointed to; matches simple shapes; understands "over"/"under"; classifies animals, toys, and modes of transportation
18-24	Expresses emotions by acting them out; likes cuddling; follows simple rules most of the time; begins to balance dependence and independence; "no" becomes a favorite word; remains unable to share	Recognizes common objects and pictures; follows many simple directions; responds to "yes" or "no" questions related to needs/wants; listens as pictures are named; points to five body parts when asked; understands approximately 300 words	Uses simple two-word phrases (e.g., "Bye-bye, Daddy" or "Cookie, more"); uses simple words to request toys, reject foods, or answer simple questions; favorite word may be "no"; names familiar objects; has an expressive vocabulary of at least 25 words; refers to self by name	Chews food; begins using fork

(continues)

TABLE 10-3 Ages and Stages of Typical Child Development *(Continued)*

Months	Typical Gross Motor Development	Typical Play Development	Typical Fine Motor/ Constructive Play	Typical Cognitive Development
24-30	Separates easily from mother in familiar situations; exhibits shyness with strangers; has tantrums when frustrated; imitates others' actions; may be bossy and possessive; identifies self with children of same age and sex	Understands simple questions; understands pronouns ("I," "me," "mine"); follows a related two-part direction; answers "what" questions; understands approximately 500 words	Begins to put together 3- and 4-word phrases; says first and last name; uses "I" and "me"; asks simple questions; uses "my" and "me" to indicate possession	Uses spoon, spills little; takes off coat, puts on coat with help; washes and dries hands with help; gets drink from fountain; helps when being dressed; tells adult regarding need to use toilet in time to get to toilet
30-36	Comforts others; relates best to one familiar adult at a time; begins to play with others with adult supervision; is conscious of and curious about sex differences	Listens to simple stories; follows a two-part direction; responds to simple "yes" or "no" questions related to visual information; points to pictures of common objects by use (e.g., "Show me what you eat with"); understands approximately 900 words	Begins to tell stories; plays with words/ sounds; has 300-word vocabulary; asks "why" and "where" questions; adds "ing" to words	Stabs food with fork and brings to mouth; puts on socks and shirt
36-48	Begins to say "please" and "thank you"; shows affection for younger siblings; enjoys accomplishments and seeks affirmation; begins to form friendships	Answers "who," "why," and "where" questions; responds to two unrelated commands; understands approximately 1,500 words	Begins to use tenses, helping verbs; uses simple adjectives— "big," "little"; uses language imaginatively when playing; uses three- or four-word sentences; repeats simple songs; asks lots of questions; uses speech to get/keep attention of others; has 900- to 1,000-word vocabulary; repeats simple rhymes	Eats independently, with little help; brushes hair; spreads with knife; buttons/unbuttons large buttons; washes hands independently; uses tissue, with verbal reminder; uses toilet independently, with assistance to clean and dress self; puts on/ takes off shoes and socks (Velcro closures); hangs up coat (child-sized cubbies)

TABLE 10-3   Ages and Stages of Typical Child Development (*Continued*)

Months	Typical Gross Motor Development	Typical Play Development	Typical Fine Motor/ Constructive Play	Typical Cognitive Development
48–60	Walks down stairs, alternating feet; walks to an even beat in music; jumps forward 10 times consecutively; hops on nonpreferred foot; catches using hands only; gallops with one foot leading; slides in one direction; throws contralaterally; swings on a swing and self-propels	Plays a table game with supervision; acts out more complex stories; creates stories that reflect that which child has not experienced; plays cooperatively with two or three children for 15 minutes	Prints first name; repeats patterns in structure (e.g., 3 red blocks, 3 blue, 3 red); draws self with primary and secondary parts; creases paper with fingers; begins to distribute shapes/ objects evenly on paper; begins to draw bodies with faces; completes eight-piece puzzle; threads small beads on string	Follows along in a book being read; tries to read book from memory; names green, yellow, orange, purple; names circle and square when pointed to; understands "forward"/"backward," "above"/"below"; classifies food/people
60–72	Gallops with either foot leading; may skip; bounces and catches tennis ball	Plays several table games; engages in complex sociodramatic play	Combines drawings of things the child knows (e.g., people, houses, trees); draws pictures that tell stories; folds paper diagonally and creases it; colors within the lines; pastes and glues appropriately	Retells story from a picture book; reads some words by sight; names triangle, diamond, rectangle when pointed to; understands "right"/"left"; classifies fruits and vegetables; matches letters
48-60	Begins to describe feelings about self; acknowledges needs of others and may offer assistance; starts to initiate sharing; tends to exaggerate; shows good imagination	Understands approximately 2,500 words; knows words associated with direction (e.g., "above," "bottom")	Uses adjectives; uses past tense; can retell a story; defines simple words; can describe differences in objects; can describe similarities in objects; uses five- to six-word sentences	Cuts easy food with knife; does laces; buttons smaller buttons; uses toilet independently; uses zipper

(continues)

TABLE 10-3   Ages and Stages of Typical Child Development *(Continued)*

Months	Typical Gross Motor Development	Typical Play Development	Typical Fine Motor/ Constructive Play	Typical Cognitive Development
60-72	Asks for help from adults; cares for younger children; waits for turn for adult attention; has "best friend"; seeks autonomy	Participates in conversation without dominating it; understands words related to time and sequence; understands approximately 10,000 words; understands opposites	Participates in give-take conversation; uses words related to sequence; uses "tomorrow" and "yesterday"	Dresses self completely; makes simple sandwiches; brushes teeth alone; likes to make simple purchases; can assist in setting table, making beds; has complete independence in bathing

An understanding of typical development allows the educator to better meet the needs of the child in early intervention and preschool programs for children with disabilities.

ACTIVE START: RECOMMENDATIONS REGARDING ACTIVITY FOR INFANTS, TODDLERS, AND PRESCHOOLERS

Childhood obesity is now prevalent in infants, toddlers, and preschoolers; thus, it is critical that professionals and parents committed to the health and well-being of young children address childhood obesity in their homes and classrooms. SHAPE America has released recommendations regarding activity for infants, toddlers, and preschoolers in the hope that their health would be maximized and obesity prevented. Titled "Active Start: A Statement of Physical Activity Guidelines for Children Birth to Five Years,"[45] the resource provides five guidelines each for infants, toddlers, and preschoolers, respectively. An example of a few of the guidelines are:

- Infants should be in settings that encourage physical movement and do not restrict movement for prolonged periods of time. Infants should move in/through basic activities, such as rolling, crawling, and creeping.
- Toddlers should get at least 30 minutes of activity every day. The activities should include early movement skills, such as running, jumping, and throwing.

- Preschoolers should get at least 60 minutes of activity every day.
- Toddlers and preschoolers should not be sedentary for more than 1 hour at a time, except, of course, when sleeping.

The adapted physical educator is critical in the process of helping parents develop activity programs for their infant, toddler, or preschooler with a disability in the child's natural setting. Critical to this process is ensuring that children are engaged in developmentally appropriate PLAY, not participating in exercise regimens.

Early Intervention Programs—Birth to 3 Years

INFANTS, TODDLERS, AND THEIR FAMILIES

The strategies for intervention with infants and toddlers are significantly different from those used in traditional educational programs. Consistent with the direction of the Office of Special Education Programs (OSEP), legislation has emphasized the importance of the family unit in providing early services to young children. The family takes a central role in providing for young children, particularly those children with high probability for lagging in their developmental process. Central to early intervention is a respect for the family unit—in whatever form that takes.

The 36th Annual Report to Congress indicates that between 2003 and 2012 there was a 21.6% increase in the number of infants and toddlers being served under IDEIA part C. In 2012, 87.3% of infants and toddlers received early intervention services in the home and only 7.6% in community-based settings.[47]

The shift toward embracing the family in the early intervention process represents a philosophical and pedagogical shift from past practices. The growing societal awareness of the importance of early intervention for positively impacting the quality of children's lives and the current national emphasis on parental involvement in programs for at-risk children can dramatically modify the educational experiences of all children.

Strategies for fostering the participation of parents in early intervention programs are summarized in **Table 10-4**.

TABLE 10-4 Fostering Parents' Participation in Early Intervention Programs[43, 39]

- The emphasis should be on families, not children alone.
- Program practices should be directly tied to the characteristics and circumstances of the families served.
- The emphasis should be on expanding the parents' strengths.
- Frequent, personal, and enabling conversation appears to be the key to parent–faculty relations.
- Parents must be honored in and for their lives and roles separate from that of "parent."

INFANT–PARENT RELATIONSHIPS IN FAMILIES WITH AN INFANT WITH A DISABILITY

The myriad of actions and representations of the infant and parents, especially when complicated by actions and representations of members of the extended family, are difficult enough in the growth and development of an infant or a child who develops typically. The process is much more complex when the infant or child has a developmental delay or disability.

There are early indicators that an infant may be at risk for delay and/or disability. Typically, these infants present one of two profiles: the "model" baby or the "irritable" baby. The model baby is lethargic, prefers to be left alone, and places few demands on parents. These behaviors, which cause these babies to be perceived to be "good" babies, may be due to neurological or neuromuscular pathology. A typically developing infant seeks contact with the parents, particularly the mother, engages in social interaction (at 7 weeks the infant seeks to make eye contact), and makes his or her needs known.

The irritable baby cries excessively, sleeps fitfully, is difficult to console (does not respond to rocking or caress), and has difficulty nursing or eating. Mothers of infants later diagnosed as having attention deficit disorder or attention deficit hyperactivity disorder have suggested that the fetus is irritable within the uterus and that the kicking and other fetal movements are not like those of other children. Again, these behaviors may have a neurological or neuromuscular basis.

Other behaviors associated with atypical infant development (potential indicators of developmental delay or disability) are the following:

- Lack of response to sound (parent's cooing or singing)
- Lack of response to parent's presence (face or smile)
- Limited imitation of parent's expressions, gestures, or vocalizations

- Difficulty with gaze behavior (avoiding eye contact or staring)
- Limited response to parent's play attempts
- Unnatural attachment to objects

Comprehensive and early medical evaluation of infants makes it possible for a child with a potential for developmental delay or disability to be identified early in many cases. In fact, many potential delays or disabilities can be identified when the fetus is in utero.

Early identification of an at-risk fetus or infant provides the parents with early warning and may give them the opportunity to begin the grief process. However, this grief process is as complex and multidimensional as the actions and representations of the infant, parents, and members of the extended family. Typically, the grief process is similar to that described by Kübler-Ross in her classic works regarding death and dying. The grief of parents and others when confronting the delay or disability of an infant is often much more profound than that of an individual dealing with the death of someone who has lived a long and purposeful life.

The contrast between the expectations and dreams for the infant and the reality is often vast. The parent who dreams of his or her child's being the first female president of the United States grieves unbelievably when the parent learns that that is most probably not an option for her daughter with Down syndrome. The father who dreams of his son as a professional hockey player grieves terribly when he learns his son has Duchenne muscular dystrophy and that, unless there is a cure soon, playing professional hockey is probably not an option.

The stages of grief that a parent may experience in response to an infant with a delay or disability are detailed in **Table 10-5**. Also presented is a range of appropriate responses from the professional educator. The parent moves through these phases of grief in a fluctuating way—simple events may cause the parent to experience all these feelings all over again. For example, if the infant is still unable to walk at age 3 years, the parent may begin the grieving process all over again. If the child requires placement in a preschool program for children with disabilities at age 3 years, the parent may need to envision the dream all over again. If the child cannot make a transition into kindergarten on entering school, the parent may face denial and anger

TABLE 10-5   Stages of Parental Grief and the Educator's Role in Response to Infants with Developmental Delays or Disabilities

Stage	Parent's Behavior	Role of the Educational Professional
Denial	The parent does not acknowledge that the infant has a delay or may have a disability. In the initial stages of grief, this is a self-protective mechanism that keeps the parent from being totally destroyed by this information.	During this time, the professional working with the parent may help in the following ways: • Share information about the infant and the infant's progress; far too often, the parent is exposed only to what the infant cannot do rather than what the infant can do. • Deal with the present rather than projecting the future. • Express a willingness to listen. Use open-ended questions to allow the parent to discuss feelings and thoughts. • Share information in simple, direct writing, so that the parent can review the information in private and on the parent's terms.
Negotiation	During this stage, parents may try to negotiate, or "make a deal" with, their God or a force in the universe. The parents may promise to "do good works" in order to have their infant cured.	The professional working with the infant and the parent should continue to work with the parent as if in denial.
Guilt/Grief	During this stage, the parent may experience tremendous guilt and grief. This is particularly true if the cause of the delay or disability is genetic or a result of parental alcohol or other drug abuse. This is often a time in which parents blame each other for the child's disability. This is difficult if there is no blame to be had; it is devastating if one of the parents' behaviors did, indeed, have a cause–effect relationship in the disability.	The professional working with the infant and the parents should: • Encourage parents to express guilt and "get it in the open." • Encourage parents to examine their belief system. • Help parents meet other parents who have experienced the same thing—contact existing support groups or help parents make contact with parents of other infants. • Share realistic expectations regarding their infant's development. • Reinforce any parental attempt to play or interact with the infant.

TABLE 10-5   Stages of Parental Grief and the Educator's Role in Response to Infants with Developmental Delays or Disabilities (*Continued*)

Stage	Parent's Behavior	Role of the Educational Professional
Depression	The parent may become overwhelmed with the contrast between the expectation and the reality. Stern described a mother's reaction to having a severely disabled infant as a narcissistic wound.[15] The depression, ultimately, allows parents to abandon their dream and may help the parent move to self-acceptance.	The professional dealing with the parent who is depressed must do so with great care, because the parent is very fragile at this time. The professional must keep an open line of communication that is nonjudgmental and caring.
Anger	Though this may be the most difficult stage for the professional to deal with, when the parent finally gets angry, the parent is on the way to healing (a process that may take a lifetime).	During this time, the professional must: • Acknowledge that anger directed toward him or her may be displaced (or the parent may simply be angry with the motor specialist). • Encourage the parent to express anger. • Encourage the parent's effort to play with the child and help the parent develop skills to avoid directing the anger toward the child.

all over again. The professional working with the parent must consistently focus on honest, open communication and redirect the parent to focus on the child's abilities rather than disabilities.

EARLY INTERVENTION IN NATURAL, FAMILY-CENTERED SETTINGS

Best practices in early intervention (EI) acknowledge that infants and toddlers between birth and 3 years of age must be educated in their most natural environments with a family-centered approach. Although many infants and toddlers do receive services in their own home, some do spend time outside the home in regulated and unregulated child-care centers.[47] Children receiving care outside of the home may do so because of the following:

- Parents/families unable to provide care within the home
- Parents/families unwilling to provide care within the home

- Parents/families living in poverty and the subsequent need for both parents (if there are two parents) to work
- Requirements for job training and work for parents receiving social support services
- Single parents, particularly young women, trying to support their children

The Division of Early Childhood (DEC) of the Council for Exceptional Children has developed well-documented and carefully validated[29] recommendations regarding best practices in EI and early childhood special education.[13] The recommendations were developed to help teachers and families improve learning outcomes for young children. The focus on intervention in natural settings is in direct response to programs that in the past served typically developing infants and toddlers as well as infants and toddlers with developmental delays or disabilities, in training/school centers or provided programs in hospital-based or university-based clinical settings. McWilliams[30] conceptualized *early intervention in natural environments* (EINE) as a five-component model:

1. Understanding the family ecology,
2. Functional intervention planning,
3. Integrated services,
4. Effective home visits, and
5. Collaborative consultation to child care.

More recently the model has been referred to as routines-based early intervention (RBEI).[31] The approach is family-centered, within natural environments, to improve the lives of young children and their families.

Intervention within a child's natural setting has many advantages. The first, and most important, is that an infant or a toddler will be most at ease in the familiar environment. The specialist will have the opportunity to see the child moving in his or her most natural play environment and will be able to develop a movement/play program designed to work within that context. The second advantage is that the specialist will have an opportunity—in the home, in the child-care setting, in the neighborhood recreation center, and on the community playground—to provide meaningful intervention with the parent in a context familiar to the parent or other caregiver. Strategies can be developed to help the parent develop skills for facilitating the child's development in the environment most familiar to both the parent and the child. The likelihood that the parent will become an active participant in the child's learning is enhanced.

There are, however, some disadvantages and problems associated with the provision of services in the natural setting. These disadvantages and problems, which are increased in inner-city and other poverty-stricken areas, including Native American reservations and camps for transient migrant workers, include the following:

- The safety of the professional may be compromised within a community, particularly in the late afternoons and evenings. Unfortunately, there are some homes and neighborhoods in which the lives of professionals (even when traveling in pairs) are in jeopardy.
- The health of the professional may be compromised in homes in which basic health care standards are not met (lack of cleanliness or appropriate immunizations).
- The provision of services in a clinical setting provides professionals the opportunity, if only for a brief time, to meet an infant's or a toddler's basic health and safety needs. For example, infants and toddlers are often bathed and fed nutritious meals while attending the clinic. That type of opportunity is not readily available in some homes and neighborhoods.
- The professional feels as if he or she has no base and only limited connection with other early childhood professionals.

According the *DEC Recommended Practices*,[13] the promotion of active participation by families is a priority. Three themes are emphasized:

1. *Family-centered practices:* Practices that treat families with dignity and respect; are individualized, flexible, and responsive to each family's unique circumstances; provide family members complete and unbiased information to make informed decisions; and involve family members in acting on choices to strengthen child, parent, and family functioning.
2. *Family capacity-building practices:* Practices that include the participatory opportunities and experiences afforded to families to strengthen existing parenting knowledge and skills and promote the development

of new parenting abilities that enhance parenting self-efficacy beliefs and practices.

3. *Family and professional collaboration:* Practices that build relationships between families and professionals who work together to achieve mutually agreed-upon outcomes and goals that promote family competencies and support the development of the child.

The "family-centered approach" has become the foundation of EI. Families are seen as having enormous strengths and making the critical difference that enables a child to reach his or her potential. In the family-centered approach, families are allowed to choose their role at each stage and professionals are there not to direct but to support the family and provide services.[25] Given the large number of children being raised in poverty who are in need of EI services, it is important to note that "parents as teachers" programs have been found to have some success, particularly with very poor families.[49] It has also been established that quality intervention to prepare parents as "teachers" can be effective, particularly if the program is well-defined, if parents are reinforced for effective behavior and educational intervention, and if the training was generalized into the home environment.[19]

To consider movement and play intervention with an infant or a young child, it is vital that the adapted physical educator be sensitive to the unique needs of the child within the family unit and to the needs of the parent(s) in response to the child. The interactions of the child and parent may be seriously compromised if the infant has a disability or if the parent is ill prepared for the role.

Being sensitive to the families of infants, toddlers, and preschoolers with disabilities is much more complex, given the vast diversity in the families served in early childhood intervention programs and their ethnic, cultural, linguistic, and economic characteristics. And, certainly, although there are a myriad of educational materials available to the professional serving learners with disabilities and their families, the most difficult process is selecting and using materials that are appropriate for each child and his or her family.[35] Suggestions for providing culturally competent services are outlined in **Table 10-6**.

In order to support the family of an infant or toddler with a disability, developmental delay, or one who is at risk for a developmental delay, an individualized family service plan (IFSP) is written. It is expected that the

TABLE 10-6 Cultural Competence[41]

- The family, in whatever form, must be the focus of treatment and services.
- Many Americans with diverse racial/ethnic backgrounds are bicultural or multicultural. As a result, they may have a unique set of needs.
- Families make choices based on their cultural backgrounds. Service providers must respect and build on their own cultural knowledge as well as the families' strengths.
- Cross-cultural relationships between providers and consumers may include major differences in worldviews. These differences must be acknowledged and addressed.
- Cultural knowledge and sensitivity must be incorporated into program policy making, administration, and services.
- Natural helping networks, such as neighborhood organizations, community leaders, and natural healers, can be a vital source of support to consumers. These support systems should be respected and, when appropriate, included in the treatment plan.
- In culturally competent systems of care, the community, as well as the family determines direction and goals.
- Programs must tailor services to their consumers—the family.
- When programs include staff who share the cultural background of their consumers the programs tend to be more effective.

family-centered IFSP process—including assessment, IFSP development, and service delivery—relate to the family's ability to choose services that reflect and support the child in the family's natural settings. Natural settings include:

- Home
- Family and for-profit or nonprofit agency child-care settings
- Church and synagogue programs and activities
- Community playgrounds
- Park and recreation department programs and activities
- Library "reading times"

The assessment and the IFSP must provide information regarding the infant or toddler's eligibility and the level of functioning in the following areas:

- Cognitive development
- Physical development, including vision and hearing, gross and fine motor skills, and nutrition status

- Communication development
- Social-emotional development
- Adaptive development or self-help-skills[46]

In addition, the assessment must include the child's unique strengths and needs and his or her ability to function in settings that are natural or normal for the child's peers who do not have disabilities, including home and community settings in which children without disabilities participate.[38]

Mandates ensure that each family has a plan of services that meets the unique needs of the child and family and reflects and supports the collaborative partnership between parents and professionals. The program must provide service coordination and an IFSP for all eligible children. The IFSP must:

- Be written within 45 days of referral
- Be jointly developed through a face-to-face meeting of a team of professionals that includes the parents
- Be based on information from a comprehensive evaluation and assessment performed by an interdisciplinary team
- Be developed to include the services to be provided, the child's ability to function in natural environments, and the family's ability to meet the child's needs
- Coordinate services with all other providers, including child-care providers
- Address the need for assistive technology assessment, services, and devices
- Include a statement that describes the child's health and medical history
- Include a statement that describes the present level of development
- Contain major outcomes and strategies for achieving outcomes
- Include frequency, intensity, location, and method (FILM) of delivering services
- Contain a summary of opportunities for inclusion in family and community life and life with peers
- Address starting dates and expected length of services
- Include medical and other services required and the method of payment
- Include a transition plan, beginning at 2 years of age, into preschool programs[46, 47]

MOVEMENT AND PLAY IN THE INDIVIDUAL FAMILY SERVICE PLAN

The single most important factor in the development of the IFSP is that the goals and objectives must reflect the family's preferences, hopes, dreams, and realities. The trend toward intervention within the natural context can be effective only if the goals and objectives (and the specific strategy for accomplishing these objectives) are functional, can be generalized, can be integrated within the natural setting, are measurable, and reflect a hierarchical relationship between long-range goals and short-term objectives. It is critical to put real-life skills into the IFSP.[37] This is true of movement and play, as well. The following are examples of real-life goals and objectives:

- *Functionality*. Will the movement or play skill increase the child's ability to interact with people and objects in the environment? For example, facilitating the development of sitting equilibrium increases the likelihood that a child will be able to sit and play with a toy. An appropriate annual goal may be "The child is able to retain sitting equilibrium while being bounced on a mattress with hands held."
- *Generality*. Can the movement or play skill be used in several different settings? For example, if a child is able to grasp and release small objects, the child can (1) at home—help pick up toys and put them in a bucket, (2) at child care—build with large Duplo blocks, and (3) on the playground—collect and stack twigs. An appropriate annual goal may be, "The child is able to grasp and release a variety of small objects."
- *Integrated into natural setting*. Can the movement or play skill be used within the child's daily environment? For example, if a child is able to participate in parallel play, he or she can (1) at home—sit and look at a book while the parent looks at a newspaper, (2) at child care—share a water table with another child, and (3) on the playground—share a sandbox and engage in filling and pouring like another child. An appropriate annual goal may be, "The child is able to engage in parallel play with adults and peers."
- *Measurable*. Can the movement or play skill be measured? A goal or an objective is of no use if the educator or parent cannot determine if the objective has been met. For example, "The child will be able to run better" is not an appropriate goal or objective. An appropriate annual

goal may be "The child will be able to run, using arms in opposition to the legs."

- *Hierarchical annual goals and objectives.* Can the movement/play goals and objectives be expressed in hierarchical fashion? The only appropriate annual goals and objectives are those in which the objectives can build on one another, leading to an annual goal.[37]

ROLE OF THE ADAPTED PHYSICAL EDUCATION SPECIALIST WITH INFANTS AND TODDLERS IN NATURAL SETTINGS

The role of the adapted physical educator is the same in each of the natural settings. The first responsibility is the completion of a comprehensive, developmentally appropriate, ecological assessment and the initiation of the portfolio assessment process. The APE specialist is, then, responsible for working closely with the parents or other caregivers to help them understand the importance of play in the lives of their child. Most young children learn to play naturally and without specific professional intervention. However, young children with disabilities may need specific intervention. This is particularly true of young children with severe disabilities. Huettig, Bridges, and Woodson wrote,

> While play appears to evolve naturally in typically developing children, children with severe and profound disabilities must often be taught to play. Acquiring play skills is a complex process for children with severe and profound disabilities. . . . These children often have many hours of idle, nonproductive time if they are not able to develop play skills.[23]

It is critical that parents be involved in the process of helping their infants and toddlers, particularly those with severe and profound disabilities, to learn to play. Infants and toddlers are more responsive to adults who are playful than to those who are not and will develop stronger bonds with parents who play than with those who do not.[33]

The most effective strategy for introducing developmentally appropriate play to parents is to engage parents, with their children, in activities that are reinforcing to both. The following activities are reinforcing to both the parent and the child and will encourage the development of the child's central nervous system.

STRATEGIES AND TECHNIQUES FOR ENHANCING SENSORY STIMULATION

Vestibular Stimulation

1. Hold and rock the infant or toddler in your arms or rock in a rocking chair.
2. Bounce the infant or toddler on your lap with the child lying on his or her stomach, sitting, and standing.
3. Gently pat the bed or couch cushion next to the infant or toddler while the child lies prone.
4. Dance, holding the infant or toddler in your arms.
5. Carry the child in a baby backpack.

Tactile/Proprioceptive Stimulation

1. Do infant massage. Hold (or lie down next to) the infant or toddler and gently stroke the child with the fingertips and fingers. Apply slightly more pressure as the massaging hand moves down the long bones in the arms and legs and down the spine.
2. Play with the child's fingers and toes.
3. Introduce Koosh balls and squishy animals for the child to hold and feel.
4. Grasp the child's feet and gently pump up and down while chanting or singing a simple song: "Molly is kicking, kicking, kicking, Molly is kicking all day long" (sung to "London Bridge").
5. Lift and move the child's arms and legs; stretch and bend.
6. Use different types of materials to rub gently on the child's body—flannel, silk, cotton, fake fur, terry cloth, feathers, sponge, and so on.
7. Wiggle the child's fingers and toes in water, sand, cereal, whipped cream, and so on.
8. Help the child do finger play in a scoop of pudding on the child's high-chair tray.
9. Play simple games, such as "This Little Piggy," while touching and pulling gently on the baby's toes and fingers.
10. Let the child pound on chunks of refrigerated cookie dough.
11. Put pillows on the floor for the child to crawl and creep on or over.
12. Let the toddler push and pull objects, such as laundry baskets.

Auditory Stimulation

1. Talk, coo, and sing to the baby.
2. Read. If the parent cannot read, help the parent select audiotapes or CDs of simple books or, better still, urge the parent to participate in a parent/child literacy program.
3. Tell the child simple stories that include the child. Use the child's name often in the story.
4. Expose the infant or toddler to different types of music—classical, jazz, rock, and country-western.
5. Allow the infant or toddler to stimulate his or her own auditory system using rattles.
6. Attach a large jingle bell to the child's arm or foot using a ponytail holder; help the child kick the foot.

Visual Stimulation

1. Expose the newborn to black/white contrasts.
2. As the infant matures, expose the baby to vibrant, primary colors.
3. Imitate the baby's gestures and expressions.
4. Encourage the child to look at self in a mirror.
5. Jiggle a brightly colored toy or noisemaker in front of the child's face. When the child's eyes locate the object, jiggle it again.

Olfactory Stimulation

1. Hold the child very close to your body, allowing the child to pick up the body's unique odor.
2. Expose the child to the varying odors of perfumes and spices.

STRATEGIES AND TECHNIQUES FOR ENHANCING THE DEVELOPMENT OF EQUILIBRIUM BEHAVIORS

Supine Equilibrium

1. With the infant or toddler supine, jiggle a bright toy or noisemaker above the child's face (no closer than 12 inches to the child's face).
2. With the child supine on your lap, with the head supported by a hand under the head, gently bounce the infant or toddler on your lap.

3. Put a brightly decorated sock on the baby's foot to encourage the child to reach for his or her toes.
4. Lie on your back with the child supine on your chest. Supporting the child's head and body, roll from side to side.

Prone Equilibrium

1. With the infant or toddler in the prone position, place a bright toy or noisemaker in front of the child's head to encourage the child to lift the head.
2. With the infant or toddler in the prone position, walk your fingertips up the child's back, with fingers on each side of the spine.
3. Use textures to stimulate the muscles in the baby's back and neck. Try using a paintbrush, washcloth, and sponge.
4. Lie on your back with the child prone on your chest. Supporting the child's head and body, roll from side to side.
5. Put a rolled-up towel under the child's shoulders, allowing the hands and arms to move freely in front of the child. Blow bubbles for the child to track or use a music box or rhythm instrument to encourage the child to hold the prone position, bearing weight on the forearms.

Sitting Equilibrium

1. Hold the child on your lap, supporting the child's head on your chest, and gently rock from side to side.
2. Hold the child on your lap, supporting the child's head on your chest, and gently bounce the child up and down.
3. Prop the child up in a sitting position using pillows. Put toys or musical wind-ups above eye level to encourage the child to hold the head up.
4. Place the baby in a highchair, an infant seat, or a walker. Hold a toy in front of the child and encourage the child to reach for it.
5. Prop the baby in a corner in a sitting position with pillows for support. Encourage the child to reach for a toy and play with it while sitting.
6. When the child can sit independently, place a number of toys within the child's reach and a number just beyond easy reach, so that the child has to adjust equilibrium to get the toys.
7. Play games such as "Pat-a-Cake."

8. With the child seated on a mattress or pillow, gently pull or push the child to force the child to regain equilibrium.
9. Let the older child sit on a rocking horse or the like.
10. With the child in a sitting position, put a bucket in front of the child and objects to be placed in the bucket at the sides and near the back of the child.
11. Put a wheeled toy in front of the child and let the child roll it back and forth, causing the child to need to readjust equilibrium.

Standing Equilibrium

1. With the child supine, put the palms of your hands against the bottom of the child's feet and push gently.
2. After the child has head-righting capabilities, hold the child in a standing position with the child's feet on your lap. Bounce the child and gently move the child from side to side, keeping the feet in contact with the lap.
3. Play "Soooooo Big"—lift the child above your head while keeping the child in a vertical position.
4. While supporting the child in standing position, "dance" back and forth, and forward and back, keeping the child's feet in contact with the floor.
5. Let the child stand on your shoes as you dance around the room.

STRATEGIES AND TECHNIQUES FOR DEVELOPING SIMPLE LOCOMOTOR COMPETENCY

Rolling

1. Gently lift the infant's right hip from the supine toward the side-lying position; alternate and lift the left hip from the supine toward the side-lying position. Let the return happen naturally.
2. If the infant is supine, place a favorite toy on either side of the child's head to encourage the child to roll the head to look for the toy.
3. Place the child on a blanket or towel on the stomach or back. Gently raise one side of the blanket to assist the child in rolling to the side. (Do not use this activity if the infant arches his or her back during the roll.)
4. Jiggle a favorite toy or noisemaker in front of the child's eyes (never closer than 12 inches) while the child lies supine; when the child focuses on the toy, slowly move it to a position at the side of the child's head on the crib mattress.

5. Place the child on a small incline, so that the child has a small hill to roll down.

6. With the child supine, gently bend one leg and bring it across the midline of the body. Go slowly, so that the child's body follows the movement.

Pull to Sitting

Sit with your back against a support and with your knees bent to make an incline for the child to lie on. The baby lies with the head near the knees and the hips cradled by your chest, so that the child faces you. Carefully, and with head support, round the baby's shoulders toward you and lift the baby into a sitting position. As the baby develops strength and sitting equilibrium, gradually reduce the amount of support.

Crawling

1. Sitting on the floor with your legs stretched out, place the child over your leg and shift the child so that the child's hands are in contact with the floor, and gently roll the child toward his or her hands, so that the child gradually takes more weight on the hands.

2. Repeat 1, but this time shift the weight so that the child gradually takes more weight on his or her knees.

3. Place the child on a carpet or mat and remove shoes and socks. Place a favorite toy in front of the child to encourage the child to move toward the toy. If needed, help the child move by placing a palm against the child's foot, so that the child has something to push off from.

Creeping

1. Place a bolster or rolled-up towel in front of the child and encourage the child to creep over it to get to a favorite toy.

2. Make a simple obstacle course with sofa cushions, pillows, rolled-up towels, and rolled-up newspapers and encourage the child to move through the obstacle course toward a favorite toy.

Pull to Standing

1. Place a favorite toy on the edge of the seat of a sturdy, cushioned chair or sofa; when the child expresses interest in the toy, move it back just a little from the edge.

2. When the child is in a sitting or kneeling position, periodically throughout the day grasp the child's hands and pull gently to standing.

Cruising

1. Put a small, child-sized chair with metal feet on a tile or wooden floor. Help the child pull to stand near the chair and "cruise," holding weight on the chair.
2. Put several well-cushioned chairs close together and increase interest in cruising by placing toys on the chair seats.

STRATEGIES AND TECHNIQUES FOR FACILITATING/SCAFFOLDING SYMBOLIC PLAY BEHAVIOR

1. Imitate the infant or toddler's facial expressions and gestures.
2. Demonstrate simple strategies for the child to communicate the following and model parent response:
   a. Behavioral regulation
      1. Requesting objects
      2. Requesting actions
      3. Protesting
   b. Social interaction
      1. Greeting
      2. Calling
      3. Requesting social routine
      4. Requesting permission
      5. Showing off
   c. Joint attention[26]
      1. Commenting
      2. Requesting information
      3. Providing information

STRATEGIES AND TECHNIQUES FOR SCAFFOLDING LEARNING

Pretend play, or symbolic play, is an important part of the child's growth process. The adapted physical educator may help the parent develop the scaffolding skills necessary to gently nudge the child toward more sophisticated symbolic play as he or she moves through the sequence of development of symbolic play skills.[50, 16]

Following is the "typical" sequence in which young children develop "pretend play" skills. Understanding this sequence can make it possible for the teacher and parent to more readily facilitate "pretend play" behavior.

Pre-Pretense or Accidental Pretense   The child puts a comb in his or her hair or a telephone to his or her ear. The adult can help scaffold learning by responding, "Emily, you're combing your hair," or the adult can pretend to put a telephone to his or her own ear and say, "Hello, Hannah. This is . . ."

Self-Pretend   The child pretends to do familiar things. The most typical are eating and sleeping. The adult can help scaffold learning by saying, "Is it good? Can I have some, too?" or the adult can cover the child and say out loud, "Ssshhhh, Molly is sleeping."

Other-Pretend   The child pretends to do things that he or she has seen significant others do. For example, the child may pretend to feed a baby or drive a car. The adult can help scaffold learning by saying, "Lashundra, what a good mommy you are being, feeding your baby." Or the adult may sit down next to the child and make "vvvvvvroooom" sounds. The adult may facilitate other-pretend play by providing appropriate props after a trip—for example, to the grocery store: garbage bags, boxes of food, an old wallet.

Imaginary Objects and Beings   The child not only uses a variety of real or child-sized replicas of real objects in play but also uses imaginary objects to engage in pretend behavior. For example, the child might ride an imaginary horse or pretend a block is an ice cream cone. The adult may provide support for play by joining in—riding an imaginary horse while twirling a rope or giving the child another "scoop" of ice cream. This type of play is best facilitated when the child has access to props—blocks, for example—that can be anything.

Animated Play   The child uses toy people and toy animals, for example, and assigns them words or actions. The toy dog may run across the yard while "woofing." The adult can facilitate play by running and rolling over.

DEMONSTRATING HOW SIMPLE MATERIALS FOUND (IN THE HOME OR OTHER SETTINGS) CAN BE USED TO FACILITATE PLAY AND THE DEVELOPMENT OF GROSS MOTOR AND FINE MOTOR SKILLS

1. Use mattresses as "trampolines."
2. Provide pillows as "mountains" for climbing over and rolling down.
3. Provide wooden spoons, strainers, funnels, and old pans to make music or "cook."

4. With the child lying on a quilt, pick up an edge of the quilt to help the child roll from the stomach, to the back.
5. Put a favorite toy just out of reach of the child to encourage crawling, creeping, cruising, or walking to the toy.

DEMONSTRATING THE USE OF SIMPLE TOYS

1. Securely attach objects (large hair curlers, clean jar lids, plastic rings) to a dowel and tie it across the crib.
2. Put dry oatmeal, cereal or macaroni in film canisters.
3. Make building blocks out of 2 × 4s (saw and sand the blocks).
4. Recycle empty cereal boxes as building blocks.
5. Use cardboard rolls from paper towels and toilet paper for building and rolling.
6. Make available things to crumple and crinkle—waxed paper, aluminum foil, tissue, used wrapping paper, newspaper, and so on.
7. Clean a 1-liter soda bottle and fill it with water. To enhance the effect, add food coloring. Close the lid tightly and seal with duct tape. To help the child with discrimination of weight, put varying amounts of water in a number of bottles.

HELPING THE PARENT (OR OTHER CAREGIVER) SELECT TOYS THAT FACILITATE COMMUNICATION BETWEEN THE CAREGIVER AND THE CHILD

1. Toys that draw attention to the parent's actions
   a. Push toys that make noise
   b. Musical instruments
   c. Rattles
2. Toys that draw attention to the parent's face
   a. Bubbles
   b. Pinwheels
   c. Scarves
3. Toys that facilitate reciprocal interaction
   a. Puppets
   b. Push toys (cars, trains, trucks)
   c. Balls

HELPING THE PARENT SELECT TOYS THAT EMPOWER THE CHILD

1. Toys that allow the child to see cause–effect (bang pan with spoon and make noise)
2. Toys the child can push and pull
3. Toys with which the child can follow the action (ball is dropped into the top and rolls down the series of chutes)

Preschool Programs—Ages 3 to 5 Years

A comprehensive, family-focused early childhood intervention program based in natural settings has the potential to prepare a 3-year-old child for participation in "regular day care" or for continued home/community involvement. If a child deemed at risk for developmental delays exhibits a disability at 3 years of age, the child will usually make the transition into a preschool program for children with disabilities within a community agency or public school program.[13]

The 36th Annual Report to Congress reported the following "settings" in which preschoolers with disabilities received educational services during fall 2012:[47]

Regular early childhood setting—37.2%
Early childhood special education—23.6%
Separate school, residential facility and home—4.9%
Other—6.5%

The components necessary for children to achieve their potential are:

- Health
- Nutrition
- Family and community stability
- Cultural competence
- Self-esteem
- Quality of early learning experience

If a preschooler has each of these six components in his or her life, the child will be more likely to have a quality life. The importance of a quality preschool learning experience has been well documented in the research literature. The most noteworthy of the studies is the Perry Preschool Project,[3,2,6] which is a comprehensive, longitudinal study of 123 African American children from families with low incomes—children who were believed to be at risk for school failure. The results were astonishing and demonstrated lasting benefits of quality preschool education. This is consistent with the findings of the Abecedarian Project (ABC) of the effectiveness of birth-to-5 intervention. When compared with the control group, the individuals in the experimental group demonstrated the following:

- Improved cognitive performance during early childhood
- Improved scholastic performance during school years
- Decreased delinquency and crime
- Decreased use of welfare assistance
- Decreased incidence of teenage pregnancy
- Increased graduation rates
- Increased frequency of enrollment in postsecondary education and vocational training programs
- Increased employment

The long-term health effects on the birth-to-5 intervention group are positive and show much stronger effects than the school-age group. It cannot be ignored that when discussing health status and obesity prevention, the early childhood years for quality programming are essential.[6]

Unfortunately, preschoolers are being bombarded by a host of forces over which they have little or no control. In order for preschool education to be effective, teachers must address the children's anger and fears. Certainly this is most effective if done in concert with the family. The typical causes of anger in toddlers and preschoolers are addressed in **Table 10-7**.

TABLE 10-7   Typical Causes of Anger in Preschoolers[28]

- Conflict over possessions or space. Children get angry if another child takes a toy with which they are playing or moves into a space, such as a spot at the sand table, that they had "claimed."
- Physical assault. Children get angry if jostled, pushed, or hit.
- Verbal aggression. Children, like other individuals, get angry if teased, taunted, or ridiculed.
- Lack of recognition or acceptance. Children get angry particularly, if not allowed to participate, if they want to play and peers say "no."
- Compliance issues. Children may get angry when asked to do something they believe interferes with their plans, such as washing their hands, putting away toys, or stopping to go to the bathroom.

TABLE 10-8 Helping Toddlers and Preschoolers Develop Skills to Deal with Anger[28]

- Create a safe environment for expression of emotion.
- Model responsible anger management and discuss it with the children.
- Help children develop self-regulatory anger management skills.
- Help children give a name to their anger. Teachers typically encourage children to "use your words...."
- Encourage children to talk about situations that cause anger.
- Read books and talk about books that help children talk about anger.
- Use "thinking puppets" to discuss anger within the curriculum.

Strategies the teacher can use to help young children deal with their anger constructively are outlined in **Table 10-8**.

It is also critical that preschool educators help young children deal with the realities of violence in their lives. Strategies a teacher can use to help a preschooler deal with violence in his or her life are listed in **Table 10-9**.

The preschool educator is also faced with the reality of teaching many children whose language he or she does not share. It is not uncommon for a teacher in a preschool program for children with disabilities to be working with children who represent four or five different linguistic backgrounds. In a typical prekindergarten or kindergarten class in an urban, core area, the children may speak as their first languages as many as 15 languages. When combined with other factors affecting so many children—poverty, abuse, parents with limited parenting skills—the language issue becomes overwhelming. When it is difficult to communicate with a child, it is difficult to teach and to provide support, love, and care. The developmental sequence

TABLE 10-9 Helping Young Children Deal with Violence[36]

Early childhood educators can help young children deal with violence by:
- Helping children identify violence, find a name for it, and talk about its consequences
- Talking *with* children about real-world violence
- Recognizing and responding to children's traumatic reactions to violence
- Training young children in basic violence-related safety and self-protection
- Eliminating "disciplinary" violence against children
- Supporting families trying to help children cope with violence
- Providing a safe haven for young children and their families

TABLE 10-10 Developmental Sequence of Second-Language Acquisition in Young Children[21]

Preproduction
Child has minimal comprehension, does not verbalize but rather nods "yes" and "no" and/or draws or points.
Early Production
Child has little comprehension, produces one- or two-word responses, uses key words and familiar phrases and past-tense verbs.
Speech Emergence
Child has good comprehension, can produce simple sentences, makes grammar and pronunciation errors, and frequently misunderstands jokes.
Intermediate Fluency
Child has excellent comprehension and makes few grammatical errors.
Advanced Fluency
Child has a near-native level of speech.

of second language acquisition is illustrated in **Table 10-10**. Strategies for teachers of preschoolers who use English as a second language are outlined in **Table 10-11**.

The incredible diversity of children creates a situation in which it is difficult for a teacher, school district, or state education agency to determine an

TABLE 10-11 Basic Strategies for the Teacher of Second Language Learners

- Rely heavily on nonverbal communication.
- Rely heavily on demonstrations.
- Use visual images—pictures, graphics, photographs—to help communicate.
- Combine gestures with the important words in a sentence.
- Use a buddy system to pair an outgoing English-speaking child with a second-language learner.[64]
- Establish and keep a predictable routine in the class.
- Use graphics to help the students anticipate activities.
- Use music and simple dances in which the sequence of movements is very predictable.
- Use favorite music, dances, and movements often.

effective assessment and curricula to meet their needs. Increasingly, however, preschool programs are using curriculum-based measures to serve children. These include curriculum-embedded, curriculum-compatible, and normative curriculum-compatible programs.[40]

A quality preschool learning environment is one in which expectations for children's performance are high and the learning environment encourages active exploration. A quality learning environment for 3- to 5-year-old children is play-based.[27] A child's natural drive to play is encouraged, fostered, and respected. Play is a vehicle through which a child's motor, language, social-emotional, and cognitive skills are scaffolded in and through interaction with another child or a gentle, caring adult. Play by any name—symbolic play, fantasy play, make-believe, pretend play, dramatic play, imaginative play—is the foundation or focus of the development of cognition, social-emotional skills, and language.

Vygotsky emphasized the role of representational play, or fantasy play, as a leading factor in child development:

> Play creates a zone of proximal development in the child. In play, the child always behaves beyond his average age, above his daily behavior; in play it is as though he were a head taller than himself. As in the focus of a magnifying glass, play contains all developmental tendencies in a condensed form and is itself a major source of development.[48]

In most child-care and preschool settings, this play-based, quality educational environment is one that is center-based. That is, there are unique, separate, and distinct areas within the classroom that are specifically designed and equipped for active exploration. Heroman, Dodge, Berke, Bickart, Colker, Jones, Copley, and Dighe[20] recommend interest areas for the preschool classroom in order to guide children's development and learning. Example interest areas may be:

Blocks
Dramatic play
Toys and games
Discovery
Art
Sand and water
Library

Music and movement
Cooking
Computers
Outdoors

An interest area gives children the opportunity to explore and interact with a wide variety of materials that engage a whole spectrum of senses, encourages sensory integration, and allows the children to be involved in an extended process of pretend and real play. For example, a dramatic play area may include the following:

- Child-sized furniture, including a stove, refrigerator, sink, comfortable chair, sofa, kitchen table and chairs, doll bed, and stroller
- Play props, including pots and pans, cooking and eating utensils, a coffee pot, glasses and cups, a broom, and a mop
- Baby dolls reflecting diversity—cultures, genders, and abilities
- Doll clothes
- Dress-up clothes, including hats, scarves, and costume jewelry
- A full-length mirror
- Cash registers with toy money

A puppet theatre and puppets reflecting a variety of people, animals, and so on may also encourage pretend and real play. An area that can be used to simulate a post office, grocery store, or restaurant and the necessary props to stimulate play may also encourage pretend play.

Given this type of play support, the young child who is just developing pretend play skills will be nudged toward more sophisticated play. Eventually, the child will not need actual objects to stimulate play but will be able to substitute any object for another in play.

QUALITY MOVEMENT, PLAY, AND WELLNESS EXPERIENCES IN PRESCHOOL PROGRAMS

Garcia and colleagues wrote,

Common sense suggests that happy and successful experiences early in life predispose people to enjoy physical activity. If that is true, school administrators, early childhood educators, motor development specialists, and physical educators have a tremendous opportunity to influence the health of the next generation by providing movement program opportunities to young children.[17]

Certainly, the need for quality movement, play, and wellness experiences exists for ALL children, but there is a critical need for quality programs for children with disabilities. Huettig and O'Connor wrote,

> Creating an environment in which preschoolers with disabilities become "well" and develop early skills tied to a lifelong understanding and practice of wellness requires the educator/caregiver and parent to address physical fitness, nutrition, emotional health, and the other dimension of wellness on a daily basis. Most important, we must remember and recognize the fact that play is the vehicle and the process in and through which a child can embrace wellness.[24]

The key to developing a quality movement, play, and wellness program for young children is dependent on developmentally appropriate practice. Sanders wrote,

> Developmentally appropriate practices in movement programs recognize children's changing capacities to move and promote such changes. A developmentally appropriate movement program accommodates a variety of individual characteristics in children, such as developmental status, previous movement experiences, fitness and skill levels, body size, and age.[44]

Researchers at the University of North Carolina (Chapel Hill)[32] created the Nutrition and Physical Activity Self-Assessment for Child Care (NAP SACC) to assess policies in child-care centers around nutrition and physical activity. This initiative is an effort to promote healthy weight in young children attending child care. The components of NAP SACC are:

- Children provided with at least 120 minutes of active playtime each day.
- Teacher-led physical activity provided to children two times per day.
- Outdoor active playtime provided two times per day.
- Outdoor play space includes open, grassy areas and a track/path for wheeled toys.
- Indoor play space available for all activities, including running.
- Wide variety of fixed play equipment provided to accommodate the needs of all children.
- Large variety of portable play equipment available for children to use at the same time.

- Outdoor portable play equipment freely available to all children.
- Television or videos rarely or never shown.
- Children are not seated for periods longer than 30 minutes.
- Visible support for physical activity provided in classrooms and common areas through use of posters, pictures, and displayed books.
- Prominent display of sedentary equipment (e.g., televisions, videos, and electronic games) should be limited.
- Staff should join children in active play.
- Staff should encourage children to be active.
- Active playtime should never be withheld as punishment, and additional active playtime should be given as a reward.
- Physical activity education is provided to children by using a standardized curriculum at least one time per week.
- Physical activity education opportunities should be offered to parents two times per year.
- Physical activity training (not including playground safety) should be provided for staff two times per year.
- Written policies on physical activity should be followed.

Unfortunately, developmentally inappropriate practices have emerged in movement programs for young children. A young child cannot be expected to do the following:

- Sit and wait "forever" for a turn
- Sit and listen "forever" to directions given by an adult
- Participate in an activity predetermined by an adult and be given no choice regarding participation
- Participate in large-group activities when the child is not yet able to play with another, one-to-one
- Share equipment before the child is ready to share equipment
- Use modified equipment—mini-basketballs, shortened baskets, large plastic bats—with a stereotypical *adult* expectation regarding the use of the equipment
- Perform skills for which he or she is not ready, because the teacher or parent does not understand developmental sequence (e.g., a 5-year-old trying to bat an arched, pitched ball)
- Play cooperatively or compete with other children when the child is developmentally at onlooker, solitary play, or parallel play stage

Given the critical issue of childhood obesity, it is important for the physical educator to understand the need of children, with and without disabilities, to MOVE in order to develop and maintain health and wellness. Not only is physical activity basic to the child, but physical activity provides an opportunity for preschoolers to equalize calorie intake and expenditure. NASPE (2001) physical activity guidelines for preschoolers include the following:[45]

- **Guideline 1**: Preschoolers should accumulate at least 60 minutes of structured physical activity each day.
- **Guideline 2**: Preschoolers should engage in at least 60 minutes—and up to several hours—of unstructured physical activity each day, and should not be sedentary for more than 60 minutes at a time, except when sleeping.
- **Guideline 3**: Preschoolers should be encouraged to develop competence in fundamental motor skills that will serve as the building blocks for future motor skillfulness and physical activity.
- **Guideline 4**: Preschoolers should have access to indoor and outdoor areas that meet or exceed recommended safety standards for performing large-muscle activities.
- **Guideline 5**: Caregivers and parents in charge of preschoolers' health and well-being are responsible for understanding the importance of physical activity and for promoting movement skills by providing opportunities for structured and unstructured physical activity.

Developmentally appropriate movement, play, and wellness programs for preschoolers with and without disabilities should provide young children access to neurodevelopmentally appropriate activities that enhance the development of equilibrium; sensory discrimination; sensorimotor function (body image and motor planning); basic locomotor and nonlocomotor competency; cross-lateral integration; object-control skills; and fitness.

The Indoor Active Learning Center

The active learning center for preschoolers with and without disabilities should provide children with the opportunity to move, self-test, explore, interact, and play. Ideally, the APE specialist should create the active learning center *with* the children. The educator should be sensitive to the needs of the children and create and re-create the environment on the basis of the materials and equipment to which the children are drawn. The following materials and equipment enhance the learning environment and encourage active exploration and active experiences in movement and play:

- Mats of different types and densities, including "crash-type" mats
- Large, foam-filled forms of different shapes (pyramids, cubes, donut holes, etc.) for kids to roll on, jump on, and climb in, around, over, and through
- Large, empty boxes for children to climb in, around, over, and through
- Giant tumble balls (17-, 23-, and 30-inch)
- Hippity hops
- Large balls for catching (10- to 13-inch)
- A wide variety of small balls and bean bags to throw
- Tricycles and child-sized safety helmets
- Scooters and child-sized safety helmets
- Wagons and wheelbarrows
- A variety of scooter boards, with and without handles (Sportime has some excellent "huge" scooter boards that two children can share.)
- Sheets and blankets to make forts and tunnels
- Steps for climbing and a slide for sliding
- An incline ramp
- Nets and ropes for climbing
- Big trucks, cars, and so on.
- Hula hoops
- Parachutes (6-, 12-, and 20-foot)
- Tug-of-war rope and shorter ropes for pulling and jumping over
- Cones
- Paper and markers to identify a play area (e.g., Pooh's house)

In the indoor learning center, the children have the opportunity to use their vivid imaginations, while moving:

1. The children may pretend to be people cutting and stacking firewood and shoveling snow.
2. The children may pretend to be ice skaters, skating on pieces of waxed paper on the wood or tile floor.
3. The children can use large building blocks to make snow forts and have a "snowball" fight using yarn balls or rolled-up white socks.
4. The children can ride tricycles and pretend to be snowmobilers.
5. The teacher can fold a large rope between panels of a mat. Several children can ride on the "sleigh" while the teacher and other children are the horses. To make it even more fun, the children can jingle "sleigh bells" and sing "Jingle Bells."
6. The teacher can push children lying prone on scooter boards, and the children can pretend to be sledding.

Movement is an end in itself. Children need to move, and they must be given every opportunity to do so. It may be easier, however, for the APE specialist to convince other preschool educators to involve children in gross motor activity if the teachers believe the activity will reinforce learning that occurs in other centers or supports a given "theme." The opportunities for learning that are inherent in the active learning center are endless and meet the needs of young children to use their bodies and to participate in play, all the while reinforcing other learning.

As mentioned earlier, the equipment, materials, and other props simply help the adapted physical educator establish the learning environment. The learning opportunities are endless. They are endless, however, only if each child has adequate play opportunities. There is nothing as sad as seeing a group of young children in a huge, open play space with only two or three balls to share.

Careful preparation of the play environment will maximize learning opportunities and minimize the potential for arguments. The key to the preparation of any learning environment for young children is the creation of at least 2.5 play units (play materials, equipment, and spaces) per child. Sharing is one of the things that preschoolers really struggle with—to force them to do something for which they are developmentally unprepared is to create conflict between children. Fewer play units increases the likelihood that children will argue about materials, equipment, and space.

Wilson[52] describes the different types of play units:

- Simple play unit: a play area that occupies one child and is not conducive to cooperative interaction
- Complex play unit: a play area that occupies up to four children, such as a sand table with pouring utensils for each child or a puppet stage with puppets for each child
- Super play unit: a play area that occupies up to eight children, such as a dramatic play area with eight costumes or a block area with at least 25 interlocking or 50 unit blocks per child

With young children, the leap from independent, solitary play in a simple play unit to play in a complex play unit may be overwhelming. A "partner" play unit is developmentally appropriate as children learn to deal first with one other child and then with small groups of children. Teachers must create opportunities for play with only one other child as well. A play unit analysis for indoor active play centers is presented in **Table 10-12**.

The Outdoor Active Learning Center

The outdoor play experience for young children with developmental delays or disabilities should be an extension of learning that occurs within the home, daycare center, recreation center, neighborhood playground, and active learning center. As in every other setting, the outdoor play of young children needs to be respected and valued, and it may serve as a scaffold for the development of:

- More complex and sophisticated play
- Gross and fine motor skills
- Interpersonal skills
- Communication and language

The outdoor active learning center must also provide adequate play units if the environment is to enhance learning. An example of an outdoor active play center play unit analysis is found in **Table 10-13**.

TABLE 10-12   Active Learning Center, Indoors: Play Unit Analysis

Following is a sample evaluation of an indoor active learning center that a preschool APE specialist would complete before involving young children in its use. Required: 2.5 play units per child

Materials, Equipment, Spaces	Number of Play Units
Simple Play Units (1 Point Each)	
5 tricycles	5
3 wheelbarrows	3
2 small slides (height = 6 feet)	2
2 small balance beams (6 inches wide, 6 feet long)	2
6 scooter boards (2 feet × 3 feet)	6
3 wooden trucks	3
3 plastic fire trucks	3
2 "jumpin jiminy"	2/26 play units
Partner Play Units (2 Points Each)	
3 small pull wagons (1 child pulls, 1 rides)	6
2 two-seat rockers	4
6 huge (refrigerator/stove), empty boxes	12/38 play units
Complex Play Units (4 Points Each)	
1 CD player with songs for dancing	4/42 play units
Super Units (8 Points Each)	
1 large parachute with handles for 16	16/58
Play area is adequate to support quality play of 27 children.	38 play units

The opportunity to play and learn outdoors is as vital to a child as the air he or she breathes. Children, as resilient people, will find a way to play—in almost any outdoor setting. Being able to use "outside voices" and to do the things that come naturally to many children—running, jumping, climbing, swinging, hanging—creates the opportunity for a joyful learning experience. However, as Rivkin reminds us,

> Although no person or government planned it, habitats for children, especially in industrialized countries, have been greatly altered—often destroyed.... Children's access to outdoor play has evaporated like water in sunshine.[42]

TABLE 10-13   Active Play Center, Outdoors: Play Unit Analysis

Following is a sample evaluation of an outdoor play area that a preschool APE specialist would complete before involving young children in its use. Required: 2.5 play units per child

Materials, Equipment, Spaces	Number of Play Units
Simple Play Units (1 Point Each)	
5 tricycles	5
3 wheelbarrows	3
2 small slides (height = 6 feet)	2
2 small balance beams (6 inches wide, 6 feet long)	2
6 scooter boards (2 feet × 3 feet)	6
3 wooden trucks	3
3 plastic fire trucks	3
2 "jumpin jimmy"	2/26 play units
Partner Play Units (2 Points Each)	
3 small pull wagons (1 child pulls, 1 rides)	6
2 two-seat rockers	4/10 play units
Complex Play Units (4 Points Each)	
1 water table (with a spoonful of dishwashing detergent)	4/4 play units
2 buckets	
2 measuring cups	
2 watering cans	
4 bubble makers	
Super Units (8 points each)	
1 large sandbox	8
5 buckets	
5 shovels	
4 rakes	
4 pancake turners	
2 sieves	
1 small parachute with handles for 8	8
1 large play structure	8/24 play units
Play area is adequate to support quality play of 25 children.	64 play units

Unfortunately, this alteration and destruction of play environments for children—the ruination of their habitats—have significantly compromised the quality of young children's lives. In many urban environments, children simply cannot "go out to play" for fear of drive-by shootings or kidnapping, contact with drug paraphernalia, and contact with toxic substances. In fact, many children have the opportunity to play outdoors only under the supervision of teachers and assistants in a daycare or preschool program. An integral part of a total early childhood education program, the outdoor play experience should be a part of the daily schedule.[8] Children must have the opportunity to play outside every day. The only exception, of course, is during inclement or dangerous weather, including weather "warnings," storms with lightning, severe heat or severe cold, and, particularly for children with asthma and other respiratory problems, ozone and other pollution alerts.

Most preschool educators would agree that the ideal outdoor play setting is one in which the child has the opportunity to interact with and learn from nature. This gives the child with a "naturalistic" intelligence the opportunity to learn and grow and use that intelligence.[51] It not only is vital for the child's physical and social development but may inherently be vital for the development of his or her soul. The ideal preschool outdoor play area is nature-based (**Figure 10-1**) and includes the following:

- Flowers, bushes, and trees native to the area
- Natural play surfaces: grass (short and tall grasses), dirt, sand, hills, and valleys
- Apparatus for climbing, swinging, and hanging: trees, rocks, vines
- Apparatus for balancing, self-testing: tree stumps, fallen logs
- Play areas for digging and pouring: dirt/mud, sand, stream/pond
- Play materials for building and stacking: rocks, twigs
- Play materials for sorting and classifying: flowers and weeds, leaves, seeds (acorns)

In the event that the outdoor play area is not in a natural setting, there are still ways for the creative adapted physical educator to help design an outdoor play area that meets the

Figure 10-1   Natural Outdoor Play Area

fundamental needs of young children (see **Figure 10-2**). The "asphalt" play area could include the following:

- Flowers, bushes, and trees native to the area (flower boxes, potted trees, potted bushes)
- Play surfaces: wood chips, sand, dirt, pea gravel, incline ramps
- Apparatus for climbing, swinging, hanging, and sliding: net climbers, tire climbers, swings, slides, steps/ladders, horizontal poles, vertical poles
- Apparatus for balancing, self-testing: railroad ties, 4 × 4s
- Play areas for digging and pouring: sandbox, dirt/mud, sand table, sand, water table, plastic swimming pool, sprinkler, garden plots

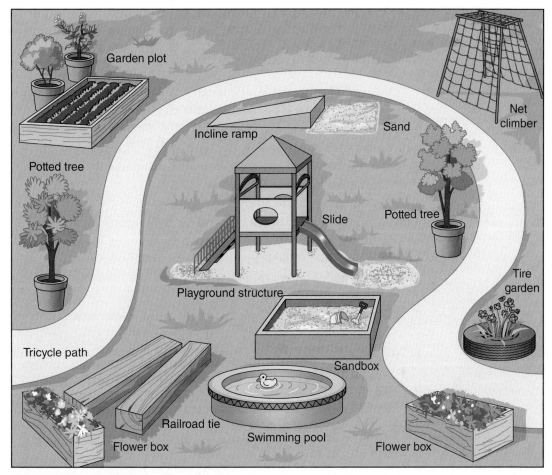

Figure 10-2 "Asphalt" Outdoor Play Area

- Play materials for building and stacking: plastic blocks, rocks, wooden blocks, twigs

In some inner-city areas, it is virtually impossible to maintain a developmentally appropriate outdoor play area because of theft and vandalism. Large play structures that can be cemented into the ground may be the only option to provide any play spaces for children. Educators have to be concerned about parts of those play structures that can be disconnected to be sold to gain recycling dollars. There are some creative play structures that provide access for all children that are difficult to disassemble and difficult to hurt.

BASIC STANDARDS FOR THE PRESCHOOL OUTDOOR PLAY AREA

The following must be considered to determine the safety and developmental appropriateness of the outdoor play area:

1. Is the outdoor play area large enough to allow children to move freely (75 to 100 square feet per child)? If the play area is not that large, can scheduling patterns be devised to limit the number of children using the outdoor play area at any given time?
2. Can the teachers and assistants see all the children in the outdoor play area without obstruction?
3. Is the area accessible to all children?
4. Is the area adjacent to bathrooms and water fountains? Are those accessible to all children?
5. Is there a phone available in the event of an emergency?
6. Does the outdoor play area provide areas that are sunny and areas that are shaded?
7. Is the area fenced in to provide protection? Is there an area that serves as a buffer between the street and the play area?
8. Are there child-sized places to rest and relax (e.g., child-sized picnic tables or benches)?
9. Is the area free of debris, litter, and broken glass?
10. Are playground structures no taller than twice the height of the tallest preschooler using the play area?
11. Does any of the equipment have rust, cracks, or splinters?
12. Are there any hazards, such as sharp edges or places where a child can be pinched?

Preschool-age children with more severe disabilities may need more assistance during play. **Table 10-14** is a checklist that can be used to evaluate the extent to which a child with a severe disability is active in an indoor and/or outdoor setting.

Responsibilities of the Adapted Physical Education Specialist

If preschoolers with disabilities are receiving services from an APE teacher, it is usually as a consultant rather than as a direct service provider. The general physical educator may work with preschoolers who are 3, 4, or 5 years

TABLE 10-14   Preschool Movement/Play Checklist for Children with Severe Disabilities

Student:_____ Age:_____ Date:_____	**Yes/No**

1. Is the child in a position to participate in all phases of the movement/play activity? If the child uses a wheelchair or crutches, is the activity taking place on a surface that is accessible?
2. Does the child participate in the same movement/play activities as the other children? If not, are the modifications kept to a minimum?
3. Does the child engage in movement/play activities at the same time as the other children?
4. Is the child actively involved, or does the child spend a great deal of time watching others play/move?
5. Does the child receive physical assistance from the adult only when absolutely necessary?
6. Is the adult careful not to interrupt the play of the child?
7. Does the child receive only the most non-obtrusive prompts from the adults to help the child participate in the activity?
8. Do other children seek out child for play (e.g., ask the child to play)?
9. Does the child seek out other children for play?
10. Does the child have gestures, signs, or pictures to help him or her communicate if the child is unable to communicate verbally?
11. Do teachers interact with the child the same way as they do with the other children—the same type of praise, stickers, hugs, etc.?
12. Does the child have the same opportunities as other children for responsible roles in the active learning center (e.g., selecting music, distributing equipment)?

old but in many school districts the early childhood educator is responsible for addressing the child's gross motor and play needs. The responsibilities of the adapted physical educator who works directly with preschoolers and/or consults with other teachers should include the following:

1. Address the gross motor and play goals/objectives on the IEPs of each of the children with disabilities.
2. Collect data for each child's portfolio assessment, those children with and without disabilities.
3. Create a learning environment in which all the children, those with and without disabilities, have the opportunity to work on gross motor and play skills; the key to a successful, developmentally appropriate motor/play learning environment is the work done before the children are present to prepare the learning environment.
4. Coordinate and plan the learning experience to support the theme or focus of the child-care or preschool program.

5. Model appropriate motor and play behavior for all students.
6. Encourage and support age-appropriate interaction among all students.
7. Provide support for the children with disabilities who are having difficulty with a gross motor or play skill, not by separating the children for individual instruction but by encouraging a small group of children to work together.
8. Model and provide consultative support for the early childhood educators and assistants and other preschool regular and special educators and their paraprofessionals.
9. Communicate with parents through notes and newsletters (see **Tables 10-15** and **10-16**).

An example of including all children in a learning center that reflects a preschool theme is provided in **Figure 10-3**. In this example, the theme for the week was "transportation," and the adapted physical educator created an active learning center to support that theme. The active learning center, indoor or outdoor, for preschoolers with and without disabilities designed to support a transportation theme would include the following:

- A marked roadway for automobiles, buses, and trucks with tricycles, scooter boards, and wagons, including stop signs and so on
- An incline ramp with crash mat to simulate an airplane takeoff
- Different-sized boxes for the children to decorate as race cars, police cars, fire trucks, and so on
- A roadway created with a series of mats to provide varied surfaces for the cars to move on
- An obstacle course for the automobiles, buses, and trucks to move on, over, between, and through

Once the active learning center is designed to expand on the theme, the role of the adapted physical educator is that of *facilitator*.[55] Following are examples of techniques that can be used to address IEP goals/objectives and still serve all the children in the program:

- If a 4-year-old with Down syndrome is having difficulty with jumping skills and performing a vertical jump[9] using a definite flexion-extension

TABLE 10-15   Parent Note

PARENT NOTE
It is very important that you know…
You can be very proud of _____. Your child did some great things this week:
Played in a small group
Caught a bounced 6-inch playground ball
You could help at home by
Complimenting play at home that doesn't include fighting
Playing catch with your child
Thank you for sharing your great kid with me.
Emily Unger, Preschool Motor Specialist

TABLE 10-16   Preschool Newsletter

Newsletter September 2, 2016	
Dear Parents,	
We are learning a great deal together… and want you to know how well we are doing!	
We are learning to	*Things to do at home*
Walk on a 6-inch balance beam	Hold your child's hand while the child practices walking on a curb.
Throw a small ball, overhand, at a target	As you finish looking at the paper, wad up each piece of paper and ask the child to throw it as hard as possible.
Jump	Rake leaves with your child and jump into them.
Act out stories	Tell your child a story and act it out together.
Identify body parts	Ask your child to draw a picture of you and ask the child to explain it to you.
	Go on a nature walk and collect leaves, seeds, etc.

pattern with hips, knees, and ankles is one of her short-term objectives, the teacher may position himself or herself near the "airplane takeoff area" and offer to spot for all the children as they run and jump into the crash pad. All children gravitate to a teacher who is actively supporting and encouraging children. In this way, the teacher can work on the child's IEP goals without singling the child out from the others.

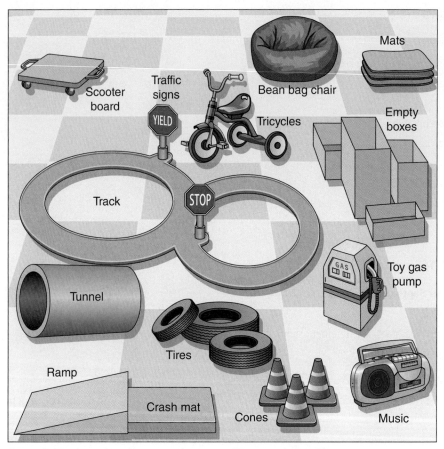

Figure 10-3   Active Learning Center to Support a Transportation Theme

- If a 3-year-old child with low muscle tone is having difficulty lifting his head and shoulders when in a prone position, the teacher may sit on the floor and play "supergirl" or "superboy" by letting children get on scooter boards on their stomachs and then pushing them, so that they race until they run out of gas.
- If a 5-year-old with spina bifida is using a manual wheelchair to ambulate and one of her annual goals is "Elaine will be able to stop and start her

wheelchair to avoid bumping into other children in the hallway," the teacher can help her decorate her wheelchair as a police car and then work with all the children on starting/stopping activities in the figure-eight raceway.

ACTIVE LEARNING CENTER TO SUPPORT A TRANSPORTATION THEME

- If a 4-year-old child with ADHD (who has difficulty playing with other children) has an annual goal that reads "Jeremiah will be able to participate in a small-group cooperative play activity," the teacher may invite three or four children to play "Freeze," an active parallel play experience.

ATYPICAL PLAY BEHAVIOR

The adapted physical educator needs to be sensitive to the play behavior of young children because atypical play behavior may be an indicator of developmental delays or reflect problems in the child's personality and social functioning.[1]

The preschool movement/play specialist, always a careful observer of young children at play, must be sensitive to the following types of idiosyncrasies in play:

1. Significant preoccupation with a single play theme may be an indicator of a behavior disorder or an autistic-like behavior. Most young children seek repetition as a means of gaining and keeping control of their environment. Any parent who has been urged to read a story "one more time" or any teacher who has grown weary of a particular song or dance understands this phenomenon.
2. Unchanging repetition of a play theme may indicate the following:
   a. An emotional disturbance or a cognitive delay
   b. A need for control of part of the child's life, as is typical of children living with abuse and neglect or parental drug abuse
3. Unusual or morbid play themes (drive-by shooting, funeral) may indicate that a child has had the experience and is trying to put it into perspective.
4. Imitation of sexual acts and practices may indicate that the child is being or has been sexually abused or molested.
5. Lack of awareness of other children may indicate:
   a. A developmental delay (in children age 3 years or older)
   b. An emotional disorder
   c. Autism or pervasive developmental disorder

6. Fragmentary play—an inability to sustain play—
   a. In children older than 3 years may indicate a developmental delay or attention deficit disorder
   b. May indicate that a child is unable to cope with a significant, acute, or chronic trauma
7. Difficulty separating self from a play role (e.g., the child is a Power Ranger, not Sally playing "Power Ranger") may be typical of a child who has been treated aggressively.
8. Difficulty joining groups at play without disrupting others may be typical of a child with a developmental delay.
9. A tendency to lash out and spoil the play (knock down the block structure) of other children may indicate the child has a disability that makes it difficult to participate, so the child acts out in frustration.

MANAGEMENT OF BEHAVIOR IN THE PRESCHOOL LEARNING ENVIRONMENT

If educators design a learning environment that is more child-directed versus teacher-directed, behavior management is simplified.[55] The following environmental variables encourage developmentally appropriate, play-based learning to minimize problems:

- A small student–teacher ratio (young children demand and require the attention and care of adults; a ratio of no more than 8:1 is vital)
- Age-appropriate, child-driven activity
- A routine that the child can count on during the day, every day
- Child choices regarding activity
- A daily schedule sensitive to a child's basic needs—nutritious snack and lunch time, quiet or nap time
- A daily schedule that provides an opportunity for solitary, partner, small-group, and large-group activities
- A daily schedule that allows for a mix of indoor and outdoor play
- A quiet place to which a child can retreat at any time during the day
- An adequate number of play units (there must be a sufficient number of materials, so that children are not expected to share)

If these basic variables are controlled, most children's behavior will be managed as well. To encourage consistency, just as in any other setting, rules must be clear, concise, brief, and understandable.

The most basic strategy for establishing a positive learning environment in which a preschooler will be successful is to be proactive and to "catch 'em being good" whenever possible.

CULTURAL DIVERSITY IN THE ACTIVE LEARNING CENTERS

The APE specialist needs to be particularly sensitive to the diverse cultures, languages, socioeconomic backgrounds, genders, and abilities/disabilities of the children served. Even very young children begin to develop stereotypical notions regarding performance and potential. The wisest responses from educators are to openly address issues related to culture, socioeconomic forces, gender, gender preference, age, and ability/disability and, specifically, to be willing to address the many questions that young children will raise.[12]

To create a learning environment that encourages anti-bias within the active learning center, the adapted physical educator may do the following:

1. Display posters and photographs of people that reflect a broad variety of cultures, socioeconomic status, gender, age, and ability/disability.
   a. Posters and photographs should empower all children.
   b. Posters and photographs should correctly reflect daily life with an emphasis on movement, sport, recreation, and leisure activities.
2. Use various types of music common to the cultures of the children in the program.
   a. Use a broad assortment of music that features males and females as lead performer.
   b. Choose a broad assortment of music that features young and old performers.
   c. Use music that reflects diversity: "You Are Super the Way You Are" (*Joining Hands with Other Lands*), "Mi Casa, My House" (*Joining Hands with Other Lands*), "Somos El Barco" (*Head First and Belly Down*), "Sister Rosa" (The Neville Brothers), "Native American Names" (*Joining Hands with Other Lands*), "La Bamba" (*Dancin' Magic*), "Shake It to the One You Love the Best" (*Shake It to the One You Love the Best*, Cheryl Mattox).
   d. Use music that honors young children as they are: "Ugly Duckling" (*We All Live Together*, Volume IV, Greg and Steve), "What a Miracle" (*Walter the Waltzing Worm*, Hap Palmer), "Free to Be You and Me" (*Free to Be You and Me*, Marlo Thomas), "Self Esteem" (B.E.S.T. Friends).

3. Use music that includes culturally distinctive instruments.
4. Provide a variety of cultural musical instruments:
   a. Kenyan double stick drum
   b. Zulu marimba
   c. Indian sarangi
   d. Mexican guiro
   e. West African balaphon
   f. Japanese den den
   g. Native American dance bells
   h. Chilean rainstick

5. Teach dances that reflect a variety of cultures and experiences.
   a. Ask parents and grandparents of the children to teach the songs and dances of their childhood.
   b. Provide materials of color that have cultural connotations to enhance celebrations and studies of different cultures (e.g., red and gold to celebrate Chinese festivals; red, white, and green to represent the Mexican flag for Cinco de Mayo celebrations).
6. Introduce simple games that reflect a variety of cultures and experiences. Ask parents and grandparents of the children to teach simple games.
7. Use language that is gender-free when referring to the activities and play of children. If the child, for example, is zooming around the room "pretending to be," be certain the words you use reflect no bias. The child is a "firefighter," a "police officer," or a "postal worker."
8. Read and act out stories of children involved in diverse play, sport, leisure, and recreation experiences.

SUMMARY

The APE specialist has a unique role to play in the child development process. The professional must be a consultant, or a teacher of teachers—including the parent.

A developmentally appropriate learning environment for infants, toddlers, and preschoolers is one in which adults are sensitive to the unique needs of the children and are responsive to those needs. The learning environment allows active exploration with others and with materials. A developmentally appropriate learning environment for movement reflects the same needs.

A heightened respect for the family unit, in whatever form, has dominated "best practices" in early childhood intervention and preschool education. In addition, the emphasis has been placed on providing intervention within the most "natural" setting—the home, church, child-care center, community center, or neighborhood park.

REVIEW QUESTIONS

1. Compare and contrast the behavior of a typically developing infant, toddler, or preschooler with that of an infant, a toddler, or a preschooler who has a delay or disability.
2. Explain the differences between the individual family service plan and the individualized education program.
3. List each of Howard Gardner's eight forms of intelligence discussed in this chapter and give examples of behaviors tied to each.
4. Describe techniques that parents or teachers could use to improve an infant's or a toddler's motor and play skills.
5. Describe developmentally appropriate assessment practices for preschool-age children.
6. Describe developmentally appropriate intervention programs for preschool-age children.
7. Describe a developmentally appropriate preschool learning environment.
8. Explain strategies the physical educator could use to encourage "anti-bias" in the curriculum.

REFERENCES

1. Allen, E., & Cowdery, G. (2015). *The exceptional child: Inclusion in early childhood education* (8th ed.). Belmont, CA: Cengage Learning.
2. Barnett, W. S. (2011). Effectiveness of early educational intervention. *Science, 333*(6045), 975–978. DOI: 10.1126/science.1204534.

3. Berrueta-Clement, J., et al. (1985). Changed lives: The effects of the Perry Preschool Program on youths through age 19. *Monographs of the High/Scope Educational Research Foundation, No 8.* Ypsilanti, MI: High/Scope Press.
4. Blue-Banning, M., Summers, J., Frankland, H., Nelson, L., & Beegle, G. (2004). Dimensions of family and professional partnerships: Constructive guidelines for collaboration. *Exceptional Children, 70*(2), 167–184.
5. Bricker, D. (2000). Inclusion: How the scene has changed. *Topics Early Child Spec Educ, 20*(1), 14–20. Retrieved online, EBSCO host.
6. Campbell, F., Conti, G., Heckman, J., Moon, S., Pinto, R., Pungello, E., & Pan, Y. (2014). Early childhood investments substantially boost adult health. *Science, 343*(6178), 1478–1485. DOI: 10.1126/science.1248429.
7. Center for Parent Information and Resources. (2014). *Providing early intervention services in natural environments.* Retrieved from www.parentcenterhub.org
8. Charles, C., & Louv, R. (2009). *Children's nature deficit: What we know—and don't know.* Children and Nature Network. Retrieved from www.childrenandnature.org
9. Cheatum, B. A., & Hammond, A. A. (1999). *Physical activities for improving learning and behavior: A guide to sensory motor development.* Champaign, IL: Human Kinetics.
10. Cowden, J., & Torrey, C. (1995). A ROADMAP for assessing infants, toddlers, and preschoolers: The role of the adapted motor developmentalist. *APAQ, 12,* 1–11.
11. Danielson, C. L., & Abrutyn, L. (1997). *An introduction to using portfolios in the classroom.* Alexandria, VA: Association for Supervision and Curriculum Development.
12. Derman-Sparks, L., & Edwards, J. (2009). *Anti-bias education for young children and ourselves.* Reston, VA: National Association for the Education of Young Children.
13. Division of Early Childhood. (2014). *DEC recommended practices in early intervention/early childhood special education.* Retrieved from www.dec-sped.org
14. Division of Early Childhood (DEC). (2007). *Promoting positive outcomes for children with disabilities: Recommendations for curriculum, assessment, and program evaluation.* Missoula, MT.
15. Dunn, L., & Kontos, S. (1997, July). What have we learned about developmentally appropriate practice? *Young Children,* 4–13.
16. Florez, I. (2011, July). Developing young children's self-regulation through everyday experiences. *Young Children,* 46–51.
17. Garcia, C., Garcia, L., Floyd, J., & Lawson, J. (2002). Improving public health through early childhood movement programs. *JOPERD 73*(l), 27–31.
18. Gardner, H. (1983). *Frames of mind: The theory of multiple intelligences.* New York: Basic Books.

19. Hancock, T., Kaiser, A., & Delaney, E. (2002). Teaching parents of preschoolers at high risk. *Topics in Early Childhood Special Education, 22*(4), 191–213.

20. Heroman, C. (2010). *The creative curriculum for preschool* (5th ed.). Teaching Strategies, LLC.

21. Hill, J., & Bjork, C. (2013). *Classroom instruction that works with English language learners* (2nd ed.). Alexandria, VA: Association for Supervision and Curriculum Development.

22. Gardner, H. & Shores, E. F. (1995, Summer). Howard Gardner on the eighth intelligence: Seeing the natural world—An interview. *Dimens Early Child,* 5–6.

23. Huettig, C., Bridges, D., & Woodson, A. (2002). Play for children with severe and profound disabilities. *Palaestra, 18*(1), 30–37.

24. Huettig, C., & O'Connor, J. (1999, January/February). Wellness programming for preschoolers with disabilities. *Teach Except Child,* 12–17.

25. Iversen, M., Shimmel, J., Ciacera, S., & Prabhakar, M. (2003). Creating a family-centered approach to early intervention services: Perceptions of parents and professionals. *Pediatric Physical Therapy.* DOI: 10.1097/01 .PEP.0000051694.10495.79.

26. Kasari, C., Freeman, S., & Paparella, T. (2006). Joint attention and symbolic play in young children with autism: A randomized controlled intervention study. *Journal of Child Psychology and Psychiatry, 47*(6), 611–620. DOI: 10.111/j.1469-7610.2005.1567.x.

27. Linder, T., Anthony, T., Bundy, A., Charlifue-Smith, R., Hafer, C., Hancock, F., & Rooke, C. (2008). *Transdisciplinary play-based assessment* (2nd ed.). Baltimore, MD: Paul Brookes Publishing.

28. Marion, M. (2008). Helping young children manage the strong emotion of anger. *Early Childhood News.* Retrieved from www.earlychildhoodnews.com

29. McLean, M., Snyder, P., Smith, B., & Sandall, S. (2002). The DEC recommended practices in early intervention/early childhood special education: Social validation. *J Early Intervention, 25*(2), 120–128.

30. McWilliam, R. (2013). *Early intervention in natural environments (EINE): A five-component model.* Division of Child Development, Department of Pediatrics, Vanderbilt University Medical Center, 2013 presentation. www.kdec.org

31. McWilliam, R. (2010). *Routines-based early intervention: Support young children and their families.* Baltimore, MD: Paul Brookes Publishing.

32. McWilliams, C., Ball, S. C., Hales, D., Vaughn, A., & Ward, D. S. (2009). Best-practice guidelines for physical activity at childcare. *Pediatrics, 124,* 1650–1659.

33. Milteer, R., Ginsburg, R., & Council on Communications and Media Committee on Psychosocial Aspects of Child and Family Health. (2012). Clinical report: The importance of play in promoting healthy development and maintaining strong parental bond: A focus on children in poverty. *Pediatrics, 129*(1), e204–e213. DOI: 10.1542/peds.2011-2953.

34. National Association for the Education of Young Children. www.naeyc.org

35. National Association for the Education of Young Children. (2012). Supporting cultural competence. *Trend Briefs*, (4), Reston, VA.

36. National Institute of Mental Health. (2013). Helping children and adolescents cope with violence and disasters. *National Institutes of Health,* NIH Publication No. 13-3518.

37. Notari-Syverson, A., Shuster, S. (1995, Winter). Putting real-life skills into IEP/IFSPs for infants and young children. *TEACHING Except Child,* 29–32.

38. Parlakian, R. (2012). Inclusion in infant/toddler child development settings: More than just including. *Young Children, 67*(4), 66–71.

39. Popp, T., & You, H. K. (2014). Family involvement in early intervention service planning: Links to parental satisfaction and self-efficacy. *Journal of Early Childhood Research.* DOI: 10.1177/1476718X14552945.

40. Pretti-Frontczak, K., Kowalski, K., & Brown, R. (2002). Preschool teachers' use of assessments and curricula: A statewide examination. *Excep Child, 69*(2), 109–123.

41. Quality Benchmark of Cultural Competence Project. (2009). www.naeyc.org

42. Rivkin, M. (1995). *The great outdoors: Restoring children's right to play outside.* Washington, DC: National Association for the Education of Young Children.

43. Rouse, L. (2012). Family-centered practice: Empowerment, self-efficacy, and challenges for practitioners in early childhood education and care. *Contemporary Issues in Early Childhood, 13*(1). DOI: 10.2304/ciec.2012.13.1.17.

44. Sanders, S. *Active for life: Developmentally appropriate movement programs for young children.* Washington, DC: National Association for the Education of Young Children, in cooperation with Human Kinetics, Champaign, IL.

45. SHAPE America. (2009). *Active Start: A statement of physical activity guidelines for children from birth to age 5* (2nd ed.). Reston, VA.

46. U.S. Congress. (1986). Pub. L. 99-457, *Amendments to the Education of the Handicapped Act.*

47. United States Department of Education, Office of Special Education and Rehabilitative Services. (2014). *Thirty-sixth annual report to Congress on the implementation of the Individuals with Disabilities Education Act.* Washington, DC.

48. Vygotsky, L. (1978). The role of play in development. In Cole, R., et al., editors: *Mind in society.* Cambridge, MA: Harvard University Press.

49. Wagner, M., Spiker, D., & Inman, M. (2002). The effectiveness of the parents as teachers program with low-income parents and children. *Topics in Early Childhood Special Education, 22*(2), 67–82.

50. White, R. (2012). The power of play: A research summary on play and learning. *Institute on Child Development.* University of Minnesota for Minnesota Children's Museum.

51. Wilson, L. (2014). The second principle. Retrieved from www.thesecondprinciple.com

52. Wilson, R. (2012). *Nature and young children: Encouraging creative play in natural environments* (2nd ed.). New York: A David Fulton Book.

53. Zero-to-Three. (2014). *Early care and education*. Retrieved from www .zerotothree.org
54. Zero-to-Three. (2014). *Putting infants and toddlers on the path to school readiness: An agenda for the administration and 113th congress*. Retrieved from www.zerotothree.org
55. Zittel, L. L. (2011). Early childhood adapted physical education. In Winnick, J. (editor), *Adapted physical education and sport* (5th ed.). Champaign, IL: Human Kinetics.

CHAPTER 11

Intellectual and Developmental Disabilities

OBJECTIVES

- Define intellectual disability as it appears in the Individuals with Disabilities Education Act.
- Explain how the American Psychiatric Association definition of intellectual disability differs from the American Association on Intellectual and Developmental Disabilities definition of intellectual disability.
- Identify three common causes of intellectual disability.
- Identify typical physical developmental delays that individuals with intellectual disability may exhibit.
- Describe how physical education needs might differ for persons with mild intellectual disability and persons with severe intellectual disability.
- Describe modifications the physical educator should make when programming exercise for students with intellectual disability.

Intellectual disability is not a fixed, unalterable condition that condemns an individual to a static, deprived lifetime of failure to achieve. Rather, cognitive, psychomotor, and affective behaviors are dynamic processes that, if properly stimulated, can be developed further than ever before imagined. Early concepts of intellectual disability viewed the condition as an inherited disorder that was essentially incurable. This notion resulted in hopelessness on the part of professionals and social and physical separation of

Photo by Kristi Roth

persons who had an intellectual disability. After years of research and innovative programming, it is now recognized that intelligence and the ability to function independently depend on the readiness and experience of the child, the degree and quality of environmental stimulation, and the types of support systems provided.

In the late 1960s and early 1970s, institutions that served persons with intellectual disabilities began designing and implementing educational programs intended to help those persons develop independent living skills to enable them to function in community settings. As institutionalized individuals rose to the challenge of these educational programs, a movement began to promote their placement in communities. During the 1970s, thousands of persons with intellectual disabilities were removed from institutions and allowed to take their rightful place as contributing members of communities. As institutions began to develop viable educational programs, public schools took up their responsibility toward young children with intellectual disabilities who lived in the communities. School systems hired professionals trained in appropriate teaching techniques to provide educational opportunities for these children. As a result of efforts by both institutions and public school systems, a large majority of individuals with intellectual and developmental disabilities are living, going to school, and working in the community. Today these individuals have more opportunities for optimum social, functional, and occupational success than ever before. The social awareness and commitment required to maximize the physical and social community opportunities for individuals with intellectual disabilities continues to grow.

Definition

Two professional associations have developed diagnostic criteria for an intellectual disability. Both the American Psychiatric Association (APA) and the American Association on Intellectual and Developmental Disabilities (AAIDD) have similar definitions of intellectual disability. They both indicate that intellectual disability is characterized by significant limitations both in intellectual functioning and in adaptive functioning and origination before the age of 18 years.[2, 5] The only difference between the two definitions is the categories within adaptive functioning. The APA describes adaptive functioning as the areas of communication, social skills, personal independence at home or in community settings, and school or work functioning.[5] The AAIDD categorizes adaptive functioning in conceptual, social, and practical skills.[2]

Although the definitions are similar, the APA and the AAIDD vary in the severity codes used to further determine the severity of the intellectual disability. Historically, the APA utilized IQ scores and the AAIDD utilized adaptive functioning to determine severity of the intellectual disability. However, in the Diagnostic and Statistical Manual of Mental Disorders-5 (DSM-5),[5] the APA now also bases the severity code on adaptive functioning.

The severity codes identified within the DSM-5 are identified below:

- **Mild:** Individuals who can achieve some academic success, are mostly self-sufficient with supports, and can live independently within their community. This encompasses about 85% of people with intellectual disabilities.
- **Moderate:** Individuals who need support for social interaction and decisions, have adequate communication skills, and can perform most independence skills with extended support. Employment can be attained with limited conceptual requirements for performance. About 10% of individuals with intellectual disability are categorized as moderate.
- **Severe:** Individuals in this category require daily assistance with self-help skills. They also require safety supervision and often need supported housing. Communication skills are very basic. This comprises about 4% of those diagnosed with intellectual disabilities.
- **Profound:** These individuals are dependent upon others for all aspects of daily care. They often also have physical and/or sensory limitations. Twenty-four-hour care and support are needed. Individuals with profound intellectual disability comprise about 2% of the population diagnosed with intellectual disability.

AAIDD also recommends categorization of individuals with intellectual disability. However, instead of classifying based on severity,

TABLE 11-1   Levels of Support Required by Individuals with Intellectual Disabilities

Intermittent	Supports are on an as-needed basis. Supports may be high- or low-intensity when needed. Supports often only needed during times of stress, transition, or uncertainty.
Limited	Mild supports may be needed to navigate everyday situations (e.g., employment training, activities of daily living).
Extensive	Regular and ongoing supports are required; however, some self-care tasks can be completed independently.
Pervasive	Supports are constant. High-intensity, provision across environments. They are potentially life-sustaining in nature.

the AAIDD classifies based on level of support. This is determined through standardized assessment. As of this publication, the AAIDD is developing the Diagnostic Adaptive Behavior Scale (DABS). Additionally, the AAIDD publishes the Supports Intensity Scale (SIS) for determination of support requirements.[2] The level of support required will differ according to the needs of each individual. Four levels of support are presented in **Table 11-1**.

It is important to note within an educational context, that the term used for identification of an individual with an intellectual disability is inconsistent. Cognitive disability and intellectual disability are terms used within different school districts and states. In a legal context, Rosa's Law (P.L. 111-256) amended all federal laws to replace the term "mental retardation" with the term "intellectual disability."[59] However, the Individuals with Disabilities Education Act of 2004 (IDEA) still identifies intellectual disability as mental retardation in its resources found online. IDEA 2004 defines mental retardation as:

> Significantly sub-average general intellectual functioning existing concurrently with deficits in adaptive behavior and manifested during the developmental period that adversely affects a child's educational performance.[58]

Incidence

Approximately 1.5% to 2.5% of the total population of the United States have an intellectual disability.[55] The individuals with less severe forms of intellectual disability (those needing intermittent and limited support) are often associated with lower socioeconomic groups. Those individuals with the more severe forms that require extensive or pervasive support are in all levels of socioeconomic groups.[7] In 2012, 7.3% of students ages 6 years through 21 years were classified as having an intellectual disability and were served under IDEA, Part B. This was a 0.3 percentage point decrease from reports in 2003.[57] In 2012, the percentage of students with intellectual disabilities who spent 80% or more of the day inside the regular class was 13.1%.[60] Of those with intellectual disabilities, 48.7% were educated inside the regular class less than 40% of the day. About 87% of these persons are only a little slower than average when learning new skills and information. The other 13% score below 50 on IQ tests and need more intensive support throughout their lives.[57]

Causes

In two-thirds of children with an intellectual disability, the cause is unknown. Intellectual disabilities can occur in one of the following timeframes:

- Prenatal (e.g., chromosomal and genetic, congenital infections, and drug and toxin exposure)
- Perinatal factors (e.g., CNS bleeding, high forceps delivery, prematurity, low birth weight, multiple births, preeclampsia, or perinatal asphyxia)[2]
- Postnatal factors (e.g., severe malnutrition; environmental deprivation; accidents leading to head injury; lead or mercury poisoning; viral infection such as meningitis, measles, or whooping cough; or inadequate early intervention and/or special education services)[56]

Advances in research and vaccines have significantly improved the prevention of intellectual disabilities. Examples include the Hib, measles, Photo by Kristi Roth and rubella vaccines, as well as improved screening and treatment for phenylketonuria (PKU) and Rh disease. The three most common causes of intellectual disabilities are fetal alcohol syndrome, Down syndrome, and fragile X syndrome.

FETAL ALCOHOL SYNDROME

Fetal alcohol syndrome (FAS) is the leading known cause of an intellectual disability. Estimates of the number of individuals born with FAS range from 2.2 per 1,000 to 1 per 100 live births.[38] It is caused by maternal alcohol use during pregnancy, and it usually results in lifelong consequences, including intellectual disabilities, learning disabilities, and serious behavioral problems.[38] The most severe form of FAS results from the mother's heavy drinking during pregnancy; lesser degrees of alcohol abuse result in milder forms of FAS.

Both anatomical and cognitive modifications can accompany the condition. More than 80% of all children with FAS have pre- and postnatal growth deficiencies, microcephaly, and characteristic facial features (saddle-shaped nose and gap between the front teeth). Students with this syndrome have difficulty receiving and processing information. Common characteristics include hyperactivity, impulsivity, attention and memory deficits, inability to complete tasks, disruptiveness, poor social skills, need for constant supervision, and disregard for rules and authority.[39]

Although there is no cure for FAS, treatment can improve the development and outcomes of the child. Early intervention services are the most impactful of these treatments. Many individuals with FAS rely on medication to assist with the behavioral symptoms that may inhibit learning or independence. It is important that the physical educator is aware of what medication their students with FAS may be prescribed and understands the potential side effects of those medications.

DOWN SYNDROME

Down syndrome is the most common chromosomal disorder leading to intellectual disabilities. In about 95% of the cases, there is an extra chromosome #21. The incidence rates are about 1 in 700.[42] The following are some physical characteristics of individuals with Down syndrome:

- Small skull
- Slanting, almond-shaped eyes

- Ears slightly smaller than average
- Flat-bridged nose
- Protruding tongue
- Palmar crease
- Short stature
- Short fingers
- Short limbs
- Short neck
- Overweight
- Substantial delays in reflex integration
- Varied levels of intellectual disability
- Looseness of joints
- Lack of muscle tone during infancy

There has been considerable research interest in the specific physical and motor characteristics of individuals with Down syndrome. When compared with the general population, people with Down syndrome may differ in the following ways:[45]

- They demonstrate less power and strength.
- They function lower than average on cardiovascular measures.
- They have deficient leg strength associated with lower cardiovascular measures.
- They begin the aging process earlier than expected.
- They have less capability for decision making that relates to motor control.
- They have difficulty in planning goal-directed movements.[25]
- They have a greater incidence of obesity.
- They may have atlantoaxial instability.
- They may have hearing loss.
- They may have vision problems.
- They may have heart abnormalities.
- They may have problems with hormones and glands.

The atlantoaxial segments of the cervical spine of some children with Down syndrome tend to develop localized anomalies that are in danger of atlantoaxial dislocation. Atlantoaxial instability (AAI) is a greater than normal mobility of the two upper cervical vertebrae—C1 and C2—at the top of the neck. This results in an unstable joint. The condition exposes the victims to possible serious injury if they forcibly flex the neck, because the vertebrae may shift and thereby squeeze or sever the spinal cord. A dislocation involves an actual displacement of the bone from the normal position in the joint. AAI can be gradual and progressive. Awareness of the significance of AAI can aid in the prevention of injuries of the upper cervical spine level.[30]

Symptomatic AAI is extremely rare in individuals with Down syndrome. The two types of symptoms of atlantoaxial dislocation are observable physical symptoms and neurological signs.[1, 13] Some of the physical symptoms are as follows:

- Fatigue
- Difficulty in walking, abnormal gait
- Neck pain, limited neck mobility, torticollis (head tilt)
- Weakness of any of the extremities
- Uncoordination and clumsiness[34]

The following are some of the neurological signs associated with atlantoaxial dislocation:

- Spasticity
- Sensory deficits
- Hyperreflexiveness[30]

The incidence of AAI is in question. The range of incidents is reported to be from 10% to 30% of the Down syndrome population. However, the American Academy of Pediatrics' (AAP) Committee on Sports Medicine reports 15%.[3] Previous guidelines from the American Academy of Pediatrics, Special Olympics formulated policies for the participation of athletes with Down syndrome who may have AAI. As a precaution, Special Olympics has developed a policy requiring that all athletes with Down syndrome receive neck X-rays before they participate in its nationwide competitive program. In 2011, the AAP revised its recommendation for standard X-rays for children with Down syndrome who are asymptomatic for AAI. Due to the rarity and inconsistency of positive X-ray results, the AAP recommends cervical X-rays only if a child is symptomatic for AAI.[4] The Special Olympics does not intend to change its policies requiring X-rays prior to participation.

TABLE 11-2   Guidelines to Follow When Individuals with Down Syndrome Participate in Physical Education and/or Special Olympics

1. Check the medical files to determine which individuals have the atlantoaxial instability condition.
2. If there is no record of neck X-ray results, with the principal's permission, contact the parents and explain the importance of screening.
3. Discuss the medical options and the situation with the student's parents or guardians.
4. Have the parents sign a consent form allowing the child to participate in the physical education program.
5. If there is no record of neck X-ray results, restrict participation in gymnastics, diving, the butterfly stroke in swimming, the diving start in swimming, the high jump, soccer, and any warm-up exercises that place pressure on the neck muscles.
6. Design a physical education program with activities that are not contraindicated for those with atlantoaxial instability.
7. Watch for the development of the symptoms indicating a possible dislocation.
8. Adhere to the physician's recommendations.

Professionals in physical education need to be aware of the potential injury-inducing activities and situations for persons with AAI. The adapted physical educator should be aware of each student's medical status, including the condition of the atlantoaxial joint, as well as the symptoms of AAI. District policy should be established with consultation from area physicians and parents, providing guidance for physical education and athletics in the requirement of cervical X-rays prior to participation. Results of medical examinations should be kept in the student's permanent health file at the school. Recommended guidelines for physical education and athletic programs are presented in **Table 11-2**.

FRAGILE X SYNDROME

Fragile X syndrome (FXS) is the most common inherited cause of intellectual disabilities.[31] Prevalence rates are estimated to be 1 in 4,000 males and 1 in 6,000 females, with males being more severely affected than females.[31]

Cause

FXS is a result of a single gene disorder. The gene on the X chromosome that causes FXS is called the Fragile X Mental Retardation 1 (FXMR1) gene.[10,52] This gene makes a protein that is needed for normal brain development.[16] Fragile X syndrome usually expresses itself less fully in females because they have two X chromosomes, one normal and one abnormal. Because males have only one X chromosome, the condition manifests itself more fully. In addition, two distinct categories of variation as the fragile X locus have been identified. A mosaic premutation results in milder deleterious features than the fuller, nonmosaic mutation. The fuller mutation is the one associated with the developmental delays that affect development.[31]

Characteristics

Approximately 95% of the males with the full mutation have an intellectual disability (moderate to severe range), whereas only about 60% of the females with the full mutation have an intellectual disability;[8] however, those who are not labeled as having an intellectual disability usually demonstrate learning disabilities.

There are several differences in the physical features between the genders, with males being more affected than females. When full expression of the condition prevails, there are several distinct physical features in males, but they are often not apparent until after puberty. These features include a large head size, long face, prominent forehead and chin, and protruding ears.[27] These traits become more prominent with age, with the face narrowing and lengthening. Other distinguishing characteristics in males are large testicles, strabismus, mitral valve prolapse, hypotonia, and joint laxity.[22, 44] Males demonstrate autistic-like behaviors, such as hand flapping, perseveration, word repetition, body rocking, hand biting, and poor eye contact.[47] Many of these children are hyperactive, have attention deficits, and engage in aggressive outbursts.[37] Autism spectrum disorder is present in 30% of people with the full mutation.[24] Females have an increased prominence of the ears but few of the physical characteristics that males demonstrate. They tend to be shy, depressed, anxious, hypertensive, and somewhat hyperactive as children and socially impaired as adults.[31]

Most young boys with the full mutation of FXS demonstrate a moderate intellectual disability and exhibit a significant reduction in adaptive behavior as assessed by the Vineland Adaptive Behavior Scales over time, and show a significant decline in IQ.[26, 62] Interestingly, many of these males maintain good verbal expressive skills and are socially engaging; however, they tend to avoid direct eye contact during conversation, they have a short attention span, they are hyperactive, and they demonstrate motor delays.[22]

Approximately 33% of females with FXS have a mild intellectual disability; those who do not, usually have learning disabilities, particularly in mathematics.[35] Most females with FXS, regardless of degree of severity, demonstrate deficits in short-term memory for nonverbal information, deficits in mental flexibility, and visual-motor performance deficits.[31]

Both genders frequently have sensorimotor integration deficits, which result in delayed balance (probably related to recurring middle ear infections), poor coordination, motor planning deficits, and tactile defensiveness.[22]

The physical limitations of males require careful motor programming. Hypotonia and joint laxity could predispose students to a tendency to hyperextend joints during contact sports; strabismus could create depth perception difficulties that limit success in games and sports requiring object control; and a prolapsed mitral valve might limit cardiovascular endurance.[46]

Characteristics of Individuals with Intellectual Disabilities

Regardless of the specific cause of the intellectual disability, the characteristics of these individuals can be quite diverse in cognitive, social, and physical functions. They may have more difficulty learning at home, in school, and in the community; thus, they need more support systems to enable them to enjoy a satisfying life. Some athletes with intellectual disabilities are extremely adept at sports. On the other hand, some persons with intellectual disabilities struggle with inclusive sports and need modification of the activities to be successful. Other persons with severe intellectual disabilities may not be ambulatory or have the physical capability needed to independently participate in play of any sort.

Because of the diversity within the group, it is difficult to generalize a set of characteristics to the total population. However, the cognitive and physical characteristics of this population provide basic guidelines and alert the physical educator to the potential nature of the physical education programs they need.

COGNITIVE CHARACTERISTICS

In addition to the considerable variability in intelligence as measured by standardized tests, individuals demonstrate variance in processing information, comprehension, and memory. The cognitive limitations associated with intellectual disabilities include difficulty in organizing thoughts, persistence in using incorrect methods even when they have repeatedly resulted in failure to learn through imitation, and difficulty in evaluating self. However, there are aspects of intelligence that may be superior to many with so-called "normal intelligence." For instance, some persons with an intellectual disability have phenomenal memories.

As a group, persons with intellectual disabilities are not as adept in perceptual attributes that relate to motor skills as are comparable nondisabled individuals. They may be clumsy and awkward and lack balance, which affects their ability to perform motor tasks efficiently, which may inhibit the learning of motor skills. Motor delays are very common among persons who have a severe intellectual disability. Delays in developing postural reflexes impact the development of basic tasks such as grasping objects, holding the head up, sitting, standing, and walking. In addition, these delays, to varying degrees, negatively affect their motor and physical capabilities.

The lack of or delayed success in motor abilities early in development can impact perceived competence, which relates directly to motivation, self-esteem, and social development.[65] Even youngsters with mild intellectual disabilities often inaccurately perceive their competence to perform motor skills. And regardless of involvement in activity, perceived competence does not necessarily increase. Some studies have demonstrated that, although female adolescents with an intellectual disability improve their athletic performance when involved in integrated sports, their perceived athletic competence suffers.[40] Other studies have shown that poor physical education experiences in high school have a negative impact on the activity levels of adults with intellectual disabilities.[18]

The severity of the intellectual disability can be a factor that impacts experiences in physical education. Persons with severe intellectual disabilities often have adverse performance in social, cognitive, language, and motor development. They also often have difficulty interacting with others. This may stem from abnormal behavior, including self-abusive acts as well as behavior that is injurious to others. Furthermore, stereotyped behaviors, such as rocking back and forth, waving the hands in front of the eyes, and making strange noises, may also adversely affect social interaction with others. In addition, those who have a severe intellectual disability may have problems with self-help skills, such as dressing, feeding, and basic motor functioning. These can all impact participation in physical education. However, adaptations and support can enable individuals with severe or low-incidence disabilities to access the general physical education curriculum and these supports should be provided to them.

Three necessary areas for successful participation in physical education are attention, memory, and decision making. Attention, regardless of how it is defined, is generally considered to be a critical aspect of information processing. As a result, attention plays a prominent role in a wide range of cognitive and behavioral activities. Two important aspects of learning motor skills are the attention that one gives to the instructional task and the ability to remember and respond to movement cues. Individuals with intellectual disabilities may have a more difficult time performing tasks when some interference occurs. Thus, once they are on task, they are less likely to be distracted by extraneous cues and information. Persons with intellectual disabilities can improve their movement accuracy if they are helped to understand and remember essential movement information. Common strategies for remembering this information include the use of short verbal cues, tactile prompting, repetition, acquisition of the skill within the environment and constraints it will be used, and observation of video clips of the skill performance.

Decision-making capability varies widely among persons with intellectual disabilities. Some persons with an intellectual disability may be able to make decisions that enable independent functioning in the community, while some may be totally dependent on others for cognitive decisions. When applied to physical activity, individuals with cognitive disabilities are less able to spontaneously predict the changing conditions of a motor task when compared with persons without disabilities. They are slower than others to estimate the amount of time needed to plan activities[21] and to intercept moving objects.

Additional research has shown that persons with an intellectual disability can be made aware of exertion levels during physical exercise[6] and can successfully engage in self-management practices.[9] However, the severity of the disability can impact this success. Many persons who have a severe intellectual disability have impaired cognitive and language development, which requires adaptations and repetition in instruction. They also may lack the ability to generalize skills learned in one setting to another setting, requiring additional supports in transitioning.

PHYSICAL CHARACTERISTICS

There is an increasing frequency of chronic health conditions among persons with intellectual disabilities. They have a higher incidence of heart disease and thyroid disorder.[32] Children and adolescents with intellectual disabilities are more likely to be overweight and have a higher incidence of obesity than their non-disabled peers.

Health promotion that involves physical activities directed at persons with intellectual disabilities can significantly improve this group's health status. To enable individuals with an intellectual disability to improve their health status and ability to function well in their job settings, physical educators must make a significant effort to include and promote strength and cardiovascular and endurance activities in each student's curriculum and work carefully with the individualized education program (IEP) team as they develop the student's individual transition plan.

Many individuals who have an intellectual disability have postural abnormalities, including malalignment of the trunk or the legs. One of the most obvious postural deficiencies is that of the protruding abdomen, which may be associated with obesity and/or lack of abdominal strength. In addition, because of depth perception problems and/or delayed vestibular and equilibrium reflex development, there may be a tendency to hold the head flexed, externally rotate the legs, and use a wide base of support when walking and running. Persistent postural abnormalities can cause reduced balance and musculoskeletal difficulties, placing individuals with intellectual disabilities at higher risk of falls and chronic pain due to malalignment. It is believed that effective programs of physical activity can significantly impact physical and psychomotor deficiencies. Clinical intervention programs that begin early in life can promote reflex integration, vestibular function, and kinesthetic impulses that affect muscle tonacity. Development of these input systems is critical to gaining locomotor and object-control patterns and skills. Ulrich et al.[56] demonstrated facilitation of stable walking patterns through the use of treadmill programming. Lahtinen, Rintala, and Malin reported individuals with intellectual disabilities exhibited a significant decrease in the ability to perform static balance tasks from adolescence (25%) to adulthood (10%).[28] Subsequently, engagement of students with intellectual disabilities in activities addressing balance and core strength can improve functional outcomes.

Children and youth with intellectual disabilities have lower aerobic fitness and muscular strength than their typically developing peers.[19, 12] The performance gap is greater in the area of muscular fitness than it is for aerobic fitness.[23] Additionally, the developmental trajectories in physical fitness are similar for children with and without disabilities, meaning the gap between the two groups remains consistent throughout childhood in the areas of physical fitness. The gap, however, is narrower for children with milder disabilities.[23] One study reported that between the ages of 8–10 years old, children with intellectual disabilities exhibited an increase in running speed; an increase in aerobic endurance and explosive strength was observed between the ages of 10–11 years; and an increase in handgrip strength (indicating muscular strength) was observed between the ages of 11–12 years. These increases could be caused by a variety of factors, including maturation and/or sport participation; regardless, these could be indicators of critical periods for development in these areas for children with intellectual disabilities.

There is strong evidence that physical fitness, including cardiovascular endurance, can be developed through training.[20] Davis, Zhang, and Hodson assessed elementary school youth with intellectual disabilities on their BMI, PACER run, modified curl-up, medicine ball throw, and sit-and-reach tests. The participants then engaged in an 8-week activity program 5 days per week, for 30 minutes per day. The participants exhibited a statistically significant improvement in the areas of cardiovascular endurance, muscular strength and endurance, and flexibility. Moderate decreases in BMI were also observed.[14] Similar results have been found in a 12-week program to improve muscular strength in high school students with mild intellectual disabilities.[50] These studies verify that, when individuals with intellectual disabilities are given appropriate practice opportunities and guidance, they demonstrate improved levels of fitness and motor performance.

Individuals with intellectual disabilities who have not been given opportunities to exercise and build work capacity will often demonstrate low levels of function, as well as low muscle mass and strength. When provided instruction in physical fitness and given opportunities to practice, they demonstrate improvement, but at a slower rate than their peers who do not have an intellectual disability. Fernhall[17] indicates that individuals with intellectual disabilities may take between 16 and 35 weeks to show improved VO_2 max; however, functional capacity gains frequently occur sooner.

Although those with intellectual disabilities may be less capable in strength, flexibility, agility, coordination, and balance, investigations using subjects who have intellectual disabilities indicate that it is possible to strengthen all muscle groups as well as cognitive functioning when using appropriate training regimes.[11] Pastula et al. found that moderate-intensity exercise can significantly improve the processing speed, as tested by the Woodcock-Johnson III, of young adults with intellectual disabilities.[43] Additionally, regular participation in physical fitness activities improves reaction time in individuals with intellectual disabilities.[64]

Individuals who have an intellectual disability have developmental lags in intellectual quotients and usually have parallel lags in motor development. **Table 11-3** shows the mental and chronological ages of individuals who have an intellectual disability with a conversion of motor behaviors one would expect from individuals with delayed mental ages.

TABLE 11-3   Conversion of Behavior in Physical Education Activity Adjusted for Mental Age of Persons with Moderate Intellectual Disabilities

Chronological Age	Activities for Normal Children by Chronological Age	Activities for Those with Mild Intellectual Disabilities Adjusted for Mental Age	Mental Age
4 to 8 years	Generalization of running, jumping as subroutines into play activity; low organized games (i.e., follow the leader, tag).	Learning to run; balance on one foot; manipulate objects; engage in activity that requires simple directions.	2 to 4 years
8 to 12 years	Can play lead-up games to sport skills that involve throwing and catching. Can play games of competition where there is team organization. Can learn rules and play by them.	May be able to generalize running and locomotor skills into play activity. May be able to play games of low organization and follow simple direction. May socially interact in play; may play by self or may play in parallel.	4 to 6 years

TABLE 11-3   Conversion of Behavior in Physical Education Activity Adjusted for Mental Age of Persons with Moderate Intellectual Disabilities (*Continued*)

Chronological Age	Activities for Normal Children by Chronological Age	Activities for Those with Mild Intellectual Disabilities Adjusted for Mental Age	Mental Age
12 to 17 years	Can play games of high organization. Can further develop skills that involve racquet sports and balls and require high levels of skill. Can participate in team games and employ strategies in competitive activity.	Can participate in modified sport activity. Is better in individual sports (e.g., swimming, bowling, and track), where there is a minimum of social responsibility. Can throw and catch balls, but it is difficult to participate in meaningful competitive activity.	6 to 8 years
Over 17 years	Can participate independently in recreational activities in their chosen community.	Can participate in community recreational sport and physical activity in special programs and with assistance from others.	Over 10 years

The Physical Education Program

Knowledge of the characteristics of persons who have intellectual disabilities provides information about the types of programs that need to be implemented to serve them. However, designing entire physical education programs around these characteristics for the purpose of teaching groups of these persons may not meet the needs of the individuals within the group. Clearly, the assessed needs of each individual must be taken into consideration when ensuring all students' needs are met in the physical education program. Well-designed physical education programs can promote physical and motor gains. The use of necessary supports in the physical education environment, including paraprofessional, modifications, and possibly alternative placements such as one-on-one or small-group physical education, can help individuals with cognitive disabilities overcome or accommodate for many of the cognitive factors that impact motor skill development and active living.

TESTING

As in all cases of students with disabilities, motor skill level; physical fitness; ability to understand rules, strategies, and instructions; and ability to emotionally manage the general physical education environment should be carefully assessed before decisions are made as to what type of physical education program is needed. If testing shows a student to be deficient in any of these areas, determination should be made whether supplementary aids and services can be provided to allow for successful inclusion. If those supports are unsuccessful, an aligned physical education program should be provided in an alternative placement. Program adjustments may be required to ensure maximum benefit for students with intellectual disabilities.

Development of the IEP requires that present functioning levels be determined. Preference should be given to measuring physical fitness, locomotor skills, object-control skills, and balance. Lavay et al.[29] reviewed three physical fitness tests to determine their validity for use with individuals with an intellectual disability and concluded that all three tests were appropriate. The items included in the tests were sit and reach for flexibility; strength measures, including grip strength, sit-ups, isometric push-ups, and bench press (for age 13 years and older); and run, jog, march, walk, exercise bicycle, or propel oneself in a wheelchair or on a scooter board for 12 minutes while maintaining a heart rate between 140 and 180 beats per minute for cardiovascular endurance. Winnick and Short's Brockport Physical Fitness health-related test for youth is an excellent test, for use with youngsters between the ages of 10 and 17 years.[61] Other acceptable ways to evaluate the functioning levels of this population are task analysis and observation of the students as they perform a hierarchical sequence of activities.

Fernhall et al.[16] caution about the importance of determining whether any potential congenital cardiovascular problems exist prior to beginning testing, particularly for individuals with Down syndrome. One of the most difficult problems of testing individuals with intellectual disabilities is determining whether poor comprehension or poor motor development is the reason for their inability to perform a specific task. Because it is difficult to determine whether a student who has an intellectual disability understands directions given during test situations, the suggestions presented in **Table 11-4** may help the evaluator elicit the best performance possible.

TABLE 11-4   Techniques for Improving Response to Requests to Perform Test Items

1. If after the student has been told what to do the response is incorrect, demonstrate the position or movement.
2. If demonstration does not elicit the correct performance, manually place the student in or through the desired position or pattern.
3. Use positive reinforcement (praise, tokens, free play) to encourage the student.

CURRICULUM DESIGN

Physical education programs should be based on the nature and needs of the learner. As with students without disabilities, every effort must be made to provide each student who has an intellectual disability with an appropriate physical education program that will promote motor growth and development. Whenever possible, students who have an intellectual disability should be included with their peers into general physical education classes. Following a standards-based curriculum,[36] with modifications and supports, and utilization of the principles of Universal Design for Learning, many students with intellectual disabilities can be successful in this setting. If they cannot participate safely and/or successfully in regular classes, alternative placements should be considered and appropriately identified as the least restrictive environment on the student's Individual Education Program. Regardless of placement, equal access to the general curriculum should be ensured. Subsequently, if students are educated in an alternative placement, the general curriculum should still be followed with modifications and supports implemented. Regardless of the student's placement, if a comprehensive evaluation reveals the student requires adapted physical education services, annual individual goals related to physical education should be developed and continually addressed.

As with the general physical education curriculum, students should receive sensory integration activities, particularly vestibular, kinesthetic, and tactile stimulation, as early in life as possible. These types of activities are often standard in a pre-K to 2nd grade physical education curriculum. If the standard physical education curriculum is not the LRE for a student with a disability, mirroring the general curriculum, with expectations similar to that of his or her peers, is imperative. The skills addressed will include those addressed for same-age peers, with modifications as necessary. This includes locomotor skills, jumping, balancing, and object control skills. Sport and fitness skills should be addressed once the fundamental skills are mastered. If the student who has an intellectual disability has a propensity toward excessive body fat, this problem will be detected when the FITNESS-GRAM or a similar fitness test is given early in the school year to all students, through review of existing IEP data, or through assessment for qualification of adapted physical education services. Every student identified as having excessive body fat should be provided with appropriate strength-building, aerobic activities, and, possibly, nutritional counseling to reduce body fat stores. Activities such as weight training could contribute muscle tone and greater joint stability, as well as enhanced self-esteem.

Older students should be taught to perform culturally relevant community-based recreational skills that can be used throughout their lives to promote and maintain a healthy lifestyle.[66] After leaving school, individuals must be able to find recreation using the skills and activities they learned in school. Opportunities for such recreation should be available to persons of all ages and capability levels. Those who have not had opportunities to participate and to learn motor skills should be provided with instruction in skills and ways of using leisure time for physical activity. Programs in which students with intellectual disabilities learned leisure skills and applied them in the community-based setting during school, more frequently produced "graduates" who continue participation in community-operated and commercial health and fitness programs.[48]

In addition to instruction in a community-based setting during school, active recreational opportunities for children who have intellectual disabilities should be provided after school, during school vacations, and after formal educational training. There should be adequate provision in the recreation program for vigorous activity, such as sports, dancing, active games, swimming, and hiking. Intramural and community sports leagues should be provided to reinforce skills developed in the instructional program. In addition, winter snow games should be made available. Camping and outdoor education programs are other ways of affording expression of skills and interests.

TEACHING STRATEGIES

A physical educator can make a tremendous difference in every student's life, including those with intellectual disabilities. Because of the individual variation among persons with this condition, it is difficult to make generalizations that may be helpful when providing instruction of activities. However, as a guide, some strategies for teaching physical education to individuals with intellectual disabilities appear in **Table 11-5**.

The teaching methodology selected to use with the individual who has an intellectual disability depends on his or her level of functioning. All children who have an intellectual disability should engage in a bottom-up developmental program early in life because they need to develop their

TABLE 11-5   Strategies for Teaching Physical Education to Persons with Intellectual Disabilities

1. **Use methods that are compatible with individualized instruction.**

    Use strong visual, tactile, and auditory stimuli for the children who are more severely involved, because these often bring the best results.

    Have many activities available, because the attention span is short.

    "Overteach" concepts and constantly reinforce attempts.

    Keep verbal directions to a minimum. They are often ineffective when teaching children who are more severely disabled.

    Use demonstration as an effective instructional tool. It is particularly effective to use a peer demonstrator.

    Use **manual guidance** as a method of instruction. The proprioceptors are great teachers of movement. The less ability the child has to communicate verbally, the more manual guidance should be considered as a tool for instruction.

    Help students develop sound self-management procedures, so that they can learn to plan and complete tasks independently, evaluate their own performance, compare their performance with a standard, and make adjustments.

    Provide opportunities for choice of activities to foster self-motivation and decision making.

2. **Involve students actively in activities they can do successfully.**

    Structure the environment in which the activity takes place so that it challenges the students yet frees them from the fear of physical harm and gives them some degree of success.

    Analyze tasks involved in activities to be sure you are clear about all the components of the skill you are about to teach.

    Work for active participation on the part of all the students. Active involvement contributes more to neurological development than does passive movement.

    Modify the activity so that each child can participate up to his or her ability level.

    Place the student in a less demanding position if they struggle with the position they are in.

3. **Facilitate participation in group activities.**

    Use markers to indicate where students are to participate.

    Use peer partners during group exercises.

    Use a token or point system to reward compliant behavior.

4. **Interact appropriately with students.**

    Be patient with smaller and slower gains of students who are more severely involved. Often, gains that seem small when compared with those of their peers are tremendous for these students.

    Do not underestimate the ability of students who have an intellectual disability to perform skilled movements. There is a tendency to set goals too low for these children.

    Convey to all students that they are persons of worth by reinforcing their strengths and minimizing their weaknesses.

(continues)

TABLE 11-5   Strategies for Teaching Physical Education to Persons with Intellectual Disabilities (*Continued*)

5. **Teach for generalization to community environments.**

Remember that children with lower levels of cognition must be taught to play. This means that physical education programs are responsible for creating the play environment, developing the basic motor skills that are the tools of play, identifying at what play level (self-directed, onlooker, solitary, parallel, associative, or cooperative) the child is functioning, and promoting development from that point.

Use effective maintenance and generalization programs to ensure that the skills attained in physical education are used in community settings. If possible, teach the skills within the community-based setting that will be used for leisure, recreation, or sports participation.

Create a safe play environment but do not necessarily provide security to the extent that the students are unduly dependent on you for physical safety.

sensorimotor and perceptual motor systems, as well as learn the basic elements of fundamental movement skills. A bottom-up approach is critical for persons who are severely or profoundly involved because of the extent to which they are motorically delayed. The bottom-up approach to instruction involves ensuring the sensory and fundamental "building blocks" are mastered prior to instruction in more complex skills. For example, ensure a potential vestibular system disorder is addressed prior to teaching an advanced balancing skill, such as a cartwheel.

However, older individuals with an intellectual disability learn specific skills best with a defined instructional procedure that uses a top-down teaching approach. That procedure includes (1) assessing the present level of the student in defined target skills; (2) arranging the skills in an appropriate sequence, so that objectives can be identified; (3) providing clear cues during the instructional process; (4) providing precise feedback immediately after the task is completed; (5) including strategies to promote generalization of skills to meaningful community environments; and (6) measuring and evaluating the performance gains to enable appropriate subsequent instructional decisions. An example of teaching with the top-down approach would be to have students play a soccer game and provide cues for dribbling and kicking during the game.

Reducing error in the initial phase of learning fundamental movement skills is more likely to result in mastery of form and accuracy of the skill.[9] Subsequently, providing necessary modifications to skills upon introduction of those skills is important. For example, allowing students to throw at a large target, while standing close, and backing up and reducing the size of the target as skill performance dictates, will result in more positive outcomes than making adjustments to the distance and size of the target when the student does not exhibit proficiency.

The teacher should use pictures and concrete examples whenever possible. The greater the teacher's success at presenting the "whole picture," the easier it will be for the student to learn.

Behavior modification coupled with task analysis is usually recommended when teaching students who have intellectual disabilities. This system involves selecting a signal or a request to cause the desired behavior. After selecting the skill to be taught, divide it into its component parts. Teach the parts using backward or forward chaining. If the task is a continuous one (such as running or jumping), shaping, rather than task analysis, is more appropriate. Once the physical skill has been performed, reinforce the student.

Numerous studies have demonstrated that individuals who have intellectual disabilities benefit from physical fitness training coupled with reinforcement.[49, 54, 63] Stopka et al.[53] report significant results for secondary students with intellectual disabilities when using a twice-weekly program consisting of 5 to 10 minutes of warm-up and stretching, 20 to 25 minutes of resistance training or weight training, and 20 to 30 minutes of sports and recreational skills and games. When determining repetitions, they recommend weight be increased for 17- to 22-year-olds when 8 to 12 repetitions can be easily performed and for 13- to 17-year-olds when 15 to 20 repetitions can be easily performed.

Fernhall[16] recommends that the following modifications be made when working with individuals with an intellectual disability:

1. Exercise intensity should be between 60% and 80% of maximal functional capacity.
2. Exercise should be supervised.
3. Provide a longer training duration to achieve the desired effects.
4. Motivational techniques, such as token rewards, may be necessary to maintain adherence to the program.
5. Strength training using machines rather than free weights should be incorporated whenever possible because this may have important ramifications for vocational productivity and independence.

Appropriate motivation, high teacher expectations, and carefully designed learning sequences appear to be the keys to promoting learning among individuals who have an intellectual disability.

MODIFICATIONS

Integrated sports involve players with and without disabilities participating together. Modifications are made to the sport, which do not significantly compromise the nature of the game. An example of modified basketball rules include: (1) a player with disabilities can travel and double dribble; (2) players without disabilities cannot dribble, shoot the ball, or pass to a teammate without a disability; and (3) only players with disabilities can shoot. To increase scoring, another modification to the game could be to award one point when the ball hits the rim. This modification provides more reinforcement to the conditions of play.

To provide additional individual support to players who need it, players without disabilities can be paired with a player with a disability and a "player-coach." This player-coach then provides direct instruction as to when and to whom the ball should be passed, when to dribble, and when to shoot. These specific behaviors can be reinforced through verbal encouragement or prompting. Thus, play and technical instruction are combined. When using this procedure, the stimulus cues and reinforcement by player-coaches are withdrawn as the player with a disability improves social and physical skills and can perform tasks without the cues.

As with all modifications, the level of support and modifications selected will depend on the needs of the players with the disabilities. All players should be challenged in order to progress in the activity, so as competency increases, supports and modifications should be removed.

Photo by Kristi Roth

Modifications for Students with Severe Intellectual Disabilities

Technological advances have facilitated communication and functional participation of individuals with severe intellectual disabilities. MOVE International is an example of a program that uses activities and supports for improving the movement capability of persons with severely limited mobility.[33] Physical education, which develops the motor capabilities of this group, is an integral part of their education.

Many children who have a severe disability demonstrate delayed motor development milestones early in life and learn more slowly than children who do not have a disability. Early childhood intervention programs may help offset the marked motor delays that more involved children demonstrate when they reach school age.

As students in this classification grow, the general physical education setting is not always the LRE. They often receive services in a small-group, one-on-one, or reverse-inclusion setting. When designing the curriculum for this setting, two main considerations are the student's individual needs and the general physical education curriculum. Additionally, special considerations must be made for students with severe disabilities. Many of these students spend a great deal of the instructional day, or day at home, in wheelchairs, in recliners, or on pillows or bolsters. When designing the APE program, the physical educator should work closely with both physical and occupational therapists, who often test students who are severely involved to determine their range of motion and level of reflex development. Consultation with the therapists and creative modification of traditional physical education activities will benefit students who are severely delayed. IDEA 2004 requires students with disabilities to have equal access to the general curriculum. Subsequently, the curriculum followed in the general physical education setting should be mirrored if the student is receiving services in an alternative placement. For example, if the general physical education class is in a softball unit, a student with a low-incidence disability can catch a ball with a Velcro mitt and strike a ball by knocking it off a cup set on his or her wheelchair tray. Examples of aligned activities for students with severe disabilities can be found at the following link: https://goo.gl/ZK3bJT

Many students with profound delays respond particularly well to music. Music can be calming and encourage relaxation. Utilization of music as a cue to start and stop activity addresses the multisensory and structural needs of many students with severe disabilities. Additionally, music can be a positive reinforcer to maintain engagement in aerobic and gross motor activities.[41]

Special Olympics International has developed training materials for use with individuals with severe disabilities.[51] Activities in the Special Olympics Motor Activities Training Program (MATP) are broken down into the following components: dexterity, reaching, grasping, releasing, posture, head control in prone and supine positions, sitting in a chair, rolling, crawling, use of an electric wheelchair, and sensory, visual-motor, auditory-motor, and tactile awareness. Each of these activities is sequenced to maximize the potential for learning. The motor development curriculum promotes improvement in coordination and control of the body when performing a variety of motor activities. It is designed to develop age-appropriate sport and recreation skills as well as physical fitness, sensory awareness, and the sense of being part of a group. Included in the curriculum is a motor activities assessment instrument that should be used to evaluate mobility, dexterity, striking, kicking, and aquatic activity, as well as manual and electric wheelchair mobility skills. Also included are Special Olympics activities specifically adapted for athletes with severe disabilities. These include aquatics, track and field, basketball, bowling, gymnastics, softball, volleyball, and weight lifting. Each sport is task-analyzed for inclusion of the motor activities in the guide. Criteria and standards are identified to inform the teacher as to when the skill or task has been mastered. Furthermore, data sheets on which to record the types of instruction used (physical assistance, physical prompts, demonstration, verbal cues, and visual cues) are included. Spaces are also provided for recording the type of reinforcement used (e.g., edible, social, token), as well as the schedule of reinforcement (continuous, fixed, or intermittent).

AQUATICS

The aquatic environment can afford a student with profound impairment a singular opportunity for freedom. There are remarkable floatation devices that can help the student maintain a relatively upright position in the water and allow any cause–effect reaction.

Most aquatic educators do not recommend the widespread use of floatation devices when teaching students with disabilities to swim. However, it is unlikely that students with severe disabilities will learn to swim independently and safely without assistance. The floatation devices simply increase freedom from restraint. Large floatation mats may be helpful for students with severe contractures. Massage in a warm-water environment may be very helpful in maintaining circulation and preventing further contractures.

Because many students with profound intellectual disabilities have significant difficulty maintaining thermal equilibrium, care must be taken to watch for signs of overheating—flushed face and rapid respiration—or significant cooling—blue lips, shivering, chattering teeth, goose pimples, and so on. The student must be removed from the pool if these signs exist.

Photo by Paul Haas

Students with an educational/medical diagnosis of profound intellectual disability may retain significant primitive reflexes that interfere with movement in the water in the same way the reflexes interfere with movement on dry land. The aquatic environment is great for these learners, however, because the viscosity of the water reduces gravity's impact on movement.

Attention must also be given to apparatus attached to the body, as well as the toileting habits of the students. Stomas used for providing oxygen or other nutrients to the body or for removing body water must be covered securely with waterproof tape. Tips for instruction of learners with intellectual disabilities can be found in **Table 11-6**.

For more information refer to Project INSPIRE Aquatics Pages: http://twu.edu /INSPIRE.

Photo by Kristi Roth

TABLE 11-6   Aquatics for Learners with Intellectual Disabilities

- In an aquatic environment, a small teacher–student ratio is necessary. Students with mild intellectual disability can be served safely in/through small-group instruction (one teacher to four to seven children). Students with profound intellectual disability require careful, well-trained, one-to-one instruction.

- A whole-part-whole approach to instruction appears to be most effective particularly when dealing with stroke skills. The use of David Armbruster's (famous coach of the University of Iowa swimming team and extraordinary swimming teacher) technique in which the student is introduced to all swimming strokes via the human stroke or dog paddle is particularly viable. Once the student can human stroke (dog paddle) on his or her stomach, each side, and back, the foundation is laid for the development of each of the basic swimming strokes. Then refinement of stroke mechanics and technique can be introduced.

- When possible, use the least invasive/directive strategy to provide instruction. Keep verbal instruction simple. Use one-word and two-word directions. If possible, keep verbal instructions simple but age-appropriate. For example, don't ask a teenager to lie on his or her "tummy"; it is much more appropriate to ask the student to lie on his or her stomach. Pair the verbal instruction with a simple physical demonstration to clarify instruction.

- It is vital that the demonstration be done in the same place as the activity should be performed. For example, it is very confusing for a student with an intellectual disability to watch an instructor demonstrate the arm pattern for the back crawl with the instructor standing. Preferably, the instructor demonstrates in the water in the proper position; if that is not possible, the instructor should lie on the pool deck to demonstrate.

- If necessary, pair strong tactile and proprioceptive cues using patterning with a simple verbal (or sign) associative cue. For example, hold the student's hand and move it through a pulling motion, pairing that with the word (or sign) "pull." The student with intellectual disability will find it easier to manage his or her own behavior if given the opportunity to choose a particular activity or activity sequence. For example, the teacher can give the student the opportunity to decide if he or she wants to practice flutter kicking first or practice back float first.

- Using "if-then" strategies may be particularly effective in dealing with stubborn students—for example, "If and only if you bob five times will you be allowed to play with the beach ball."

- Repetition is key to learning in the student with an intellectual disability and developmental delays. The instructor can ensure this will happen without boredom by modifying the activity to involve other students and different types of equipment. For example, the student can practice the flutter kick while doing the following:
  - Being towed by the teacher
  - Kicking at a beach ball
  - Wearing fins
  - Going "fast" and "slow"
  - Going as part of a song. "If you're happy and you know it 'kick your feet.'"

For more information refer to Project INSPIRE Aquatics Pages: http://twu.edu/INSPIRE.

SUMMARY

Intellectual disabilities are characterized by significant limitations both in intellectual functioning and in adaptive behavior as expressed in conceptual, social, and practical adaptive skills. Intellectual disability begins before age 18 years but may not always be of lifelong duration. The prevalence of intellectual disabilities in the population is approximately 3%.

Physical educators can expect to have students with intellectual disabilities in the classes they teach. Those students' motor skills and physical fitness levels may be equal to or lower than those of students who do not have intellectual disabilities, yet their ability to achieve skills for active living is equal to that of their peers. Carefully selected teaching strategies and program adaptations will yield positive motor development results. Students should be tested to determine their specific motor strengths and weaknesses, as is true for most performance abilities. Physical education programs should be designed around these test results as well as meet the objectives of the general curriculum.

Physical education programs should provide assistance for transition of the recreational skills acquired in physical education classes to independent, integrated recreational activity in the community. Participation in recreation, home programs, and Special Olympics should be encouraged. Special Olympics has taken the lead in developing programs to include individuals who have intellectual disabilities in integrated sports activity.

REVIEW QUESTIONS

1. How does the IDEA definition of mental retardation differ from the American Association on Intellectual and Developmental Disabilities' definition of intellectual disability?
2. What specific medical considerations must the physical educator be aware of when teaching students with fetal alcohol syndrome, fragile X, or Down syndrome?
3. What types of physical education program modifications need to be made for individuals with Down syndrome who have atlantoaxial instability?
4. What types of modifications are recommended for use when programming fitness exercises for persons with intellectual disabilities?
5. What are five specific teaching strategies that can be used with persons with an intellectual disability?
6. What Special Olympics programs are available for persons with intellectual disabilities?

REFERENCES

1. Alvarez, N., Kao, A., Schneck, M. J., & Talavera, F. (2011). Medscape reference. Retrieved from http://emedi cine.medscape.com/article/1180354-overview

2. American Association on Intellectual and Developmental Disabilities. (2010). *Definition, classification, and systems of support* (11th ed.). Washington, DC.

3. American Academy of Pediatrics Committee on Sports Medicine. (1995). Atlantoaxial instability in children with Down syndrome. *Pediatrics, 96*, 151–154.

4. American Academy of Pediatrics. (2011). Health supervision for children with Down syndrome. *Pediatrics, 128*(2), 393–406.

5. American Psychiatric Association. (2013). *Diagnostic and statistical manual of mental disorders* (5th ed.). Washington, DC.

6. Arnold, R., Ng, N., & Pechar, G. (1992). Relationship of rated perceived exertion to heart rate and workload in mentally retarded young adults. *APAQ, 9*, 47–53.

7. Beers, M. H., & Berkow, R. (Eds.). (2006). *The Merck manual of diagnosis and therapy*. Whitehouse Station, NJ: Merck Research Laboratories.

8. Bailey, D. B., Raspa, M., Olmsted, M., & Holiday, D. B. (2008). Co-occurring conditions associated with FMR1 gene variations: Findings from a national parent survey. *American Journal of Medical Genetics Part A, 146*(16), 2060–2069.

9. Capio, C. M., Poolton, J. M., Sit, C. H. P., Holmstrom, M., & Masters, R. S. W. (2013). Reducing errors benefits the field-based learning of a fundamental movement skill in children. *Scandinavian Journal of Medicine & Science in Sports, 23*(2), 181–188.

10. Centers for Disease Control and Prevention. (2006, September). Fragile X syndrome. http://www.cdc.gov/ncbddd/single_gene/fragileX.htm

11. Chanias, A. K., Reid, G., & Hoover, M. L. (1998). Exercise effects on health-related physical fitness of individuals with an intellectual disability: A meta-analysis. *APAQ, 15*, 119–140.

12. Croce, R. V., Pitetti, K. H., Horvat, M., & Miller, J. (1996). Peak torque, average power, and hamstrings/quadriceps ratios in nondisabled adults and adults with mental retardation. *Arch Phys Med Rehabil, 77*, 369–372.

13. Davidson, R. G. (1988). Atlantoaxial instability in individuals with Down syndrome: A fresh look at the evidence. *Pediatrics, 81*, 857–865.

14. Davis, K., Zhang, G., & Hodson, P. (2011). Promoting health-related fitness for elementary students with intellectual disabilities through a specifically designed activity program. *Journal of Policy and Practice in Intellectual Disabilities, 8*(2), 77–84.

15. Ellis, D. N., Cress, P. J., & Spellman, C. R. (1992). Using self-management to promote independent exercise in adolescents with moderate mental retardation in a school setting. *Educ and Train of Ment Retard, 27*, 51–59.

16. Fernhall, B. Mental retardation. In Durstine, J. L. (Ed.). (1997). *Exercise management for persons with chronic diseases and disabilities*. Champaign, IL: Human Kinetics.

17. Fernhall, B., Pittetti, K. H., Vukovich, D. S., Hensen, T., Winnick, J. P., & Short, F. X. (1998). Validation of cardiovascular fitness field tests in children with mental retardation. *Amer J of Ment Retard, 102*, 602–612.

18. Frey, G. C., Buchanan, A. M., & Rosser Sandt, D. D. (2005). "I'd rather watch TV": An examination of physical activity in adults with mental retardation. *Mental Retard, 43*(4), 241–254.

19. Gillespie, M. (2003). Cardiovascular fitness of young Canadian children with and without mental retardation. *Education and Training in Developmental Disabilities, 38*, 296–301.

20. Golubovic, S., Maksimovic, J., Golubovic, B., & Glumbic, N. (2012). Effects of exercise on physical fitness in children with intellectual disability. *Research in Developmental Disabilities, 33*, 608–614.

21. Grskovic, J. A., Zentail, S. S., & Stormont-Spurgin, M. (1995). Time estimation and planning abilities: Students with and without mild disabilities. *Behavior Disorders, 20*, 197–203.

22. Hagerman, R. (2003). *The ARC's Q&A on Fragile X.* Retrieved from http://thearc .org/faqs/fragqa.html

23. Hartman, E., Smith, J., Westendorp, M., & Visscher, C. (2015). Development of physical fitness in children with intellectual disabilities. *Journal of Intellectual Disability Research, 59*(5), 439–449.

24. Hersh, J. H., & Saul, R. A. (2011). Health supervision for children with fragile X syndrome. *Pediatrics, 127*(5), 994–1006.

25. Hodges, N. J., Cunningham, S. J., Lyons, J., Kerr, T. L., & Digby, E. (1995). Visual feedback processing and goal directed movement in adults with Down syndrome. *APAQ, 12*, 52–59.

26. Klaiman, C., Quintin, E. M., Jo, B., Lightbody, A. A., Hazlett, H. C., Piven, J., & Reiss, A. L. (2014). Longitudinal profiles of adaptive behavior in fragile X syndrome. *Pediatrics, 134*(2), 315–324.

27. Lachiewicz, A. M., Dawson, D. V., & Spiridigliozzi, G. A. (2000). Physical characteristics of young boys with fragile X syndrome: Reasons for difficulties in making a diagnosis in young males. *American Journal of Medical Genetics, 92*(4), 229–236.

28. Lahtinen, U., Rintala, P., & Malin, A. (2007). Physical performance of individuals with intellectual disability: A 30-year follow-up. *Adapted Physical Activity Quarterly, 24*(2), 125.

29. Lavay, B., McCubbin, J., & Eichstaedt, C. (1995). Field-based physical fitness tests for individuals with mental retardation. In Vermeer, A., & Davis, W. E. (Eds.). *Physical and motor development in mental retardation.* Basel: Karger.

30. Leshin, L. (2003). *Atlantoaxial instability: Controversy and commentary.* Retrieved from www.ds-health.com/aai.htm

31. Merck Manuals Consumer Version. (2015). *Intellectual Disability—Children's Health Issues.* Retrieved December 30, 2015, from http://www.merckmanuals .com/home/children's-health-issues/learning-and-developmental-disorders /intellectual-disability

32. Morin, D., Mérineau-Côté, J., Ouellette-Kuntz, H., Tassé, M. J., & Kerr, M. (2012). A comparison of the prevalence of chronic disease among people with and without intellectual disability. *American Journal on Intellectual and Developmental Disabilities, 117*(6), 455–463.

33. M.O.V.E., MOVE International. Bakersfield, CA. www.MOVE-International.org.

34. Msall, M. E., Reese, M. E., DiGaudio, K., Griswold, K., Granger, C. V., & Cooke, R. E. (1990). Symptomatic atlantoaxial instability associated with medical and rehabilitative procedures in children with Down syndrome. *Pediatrics, 85,* 447–449.

35. Murphy, M. M. (2009). A review of mathematical learning disabilities in children with fragile X syndrome. *Developmental Disabilities Research Reviews, 15*(1), 21–27.

36. National Center on Universal Design for Learning. www.udlcenter.org

37. National Institute for Childhood Disorders. (2007). *What Are the Signs and Symptoms of Fragile X?* Retrieved from www.nichd.nih.gov/publications/pubs /fragileX/sub9.cfm

38. National Organization on Fetal Alcohol Syndrome. (2007). *What Policy Makers Should Know.* Retrieved from www.nofas.com/resources/factsheets/FASD

39. National Organization on Fetal Alcohol Syndrome. (2007). *What School Systems Should Know About Affected Students.* Retrieved from www.nofas .com/resources/factsheets/FASD

40. Ninot, G., & Delignéres, D. (2005). Effects of integrated and segregated sport participation on the physical self for persons with intellectual disabilities. *J of Intellectual Disability Research, 49*(9), 682–689.

41. Owlia, G. (1991). *Influence of reinforcers on motorized bicycle on-task time of profoundly mentally retarded adolescents.* Unpublished doctoral dissertation, Texas Woman's University, Denton.

42. Parker, S. E., Mai, C. T., Canfield, M. A., Rickard, R., Wang, Y., Meyer, R. E., & Correa, A. (2010). Updated national birth prevalence estimates for selected birth defects in the United States, 2004–2006. *Birth Defects Research Part A: Clinical and Molecular Teratology, 88*(12), 1008–1016.

43. Pastula, R. M., Stopka, C. B., Delisle, A. T., & Hass, C. J. (2012). Effect of moderate-intensity exercise training on the cognitive function of young adults with intellectual disabilities. *The Journal of Strength & Conditioning Research, 26*(12), 3441–3448.

44. Patel, B. D. (1994). The fragile X syndrome. *British J of Clinical Practice, 48*(1), 42–44.

45. Pitetti, K., Baynard, T., & Agiovlasitis, S. (2013). Children and adolescents with Down syndrome, physical fitness and physical activity. *Journal of Sport and Health Science, 2*(1), 47–57.

46. Pitetti, K. H., Rimmer, J. H., & Fernhall, B. (1993). Physical fitness and adults with mental retardation: An overview of current research and future directions. *Sports Medicine, 16,* 23–56.

47. Roberts, J. E., Hatton, D. D., Bailey, D. B. (2001). Development and behavior of male toddlers with fragile X syndrome. *J of Early Intervention*, *24*(3), 207–223.

48. Roth, K. (2007). Transition in physical recreation and students with cognitive disabilities: Graduate and parent perspectives. *Education and Training in Developmental Disabilities*, *42*(1), 94–106.

49. Silliman, L. M., & French, R. (1993). Use of selected reinforcers to improve the ball kicking of youths with profound mental retardation. *Adapted Physical Activity Quarterly*, *10*(1), 52–69.

50. Smail, K. M., & Horvat, M. (2006). Relationship of muscular strength on work performance in high school students with mental retardation. *Education & Training in Developmental Disabilities*, *41*(4), 410–419.

51. Special Olympics. (2007). www.specialolympics.org

52. Steinbach, P. (1993). Molecular analysis of mutations in the gene FMR-1 segregating in fragile X families. *Hum Genet*, *92*, 491–498.

53. Stopka, C., Pomeranz, J., Siders, R., Dykes, M. K., & Goodman, A. (1999). Transitional skills for wellness. *Teach Ex Child*, *7*, 6–11.

54. Taylor, J., French, R., Kinnison, L., & O'Brien, T. (1998). Primary and secondary reinforcers in performance of a 1.0 mile walk/jog by adolescents with moderate mental retardation. *Perc Motor Skills*, *87*, 1265–1266.

55. The ARC of the United States. (2007). www.thearc.org

56. Ulrich, B. D., Ulrich, D. A., Collier, D. H., & Cole, E. L. (1995). Developmental shifts in the ability of infants with Down syndrome to produce treadmill steps. *Phys Ther*, *75*, 17–23.

57. U.S. Department of Education. (2006). *IDEA Trend Data*. Retrieved from www.ideadata.org

58. U.S. 108th Congress. (2004). Pub. L. 108-446, Improved Educational Results for Children with Disabilities Act, Congressional Record 150: sec. 11653–11660, Washington, DC.

59. U.S. 111th Congress. (2010). Pub. L. 111-256, Rosa's Law, Washington, DC.

60. U.S. Department of Education. National Center for Education Statistics. https://nces.ed.gov/fastfacts/display.asp?id=64

61. Winnick, J. P., & Short, F. X. (2014). *The Brockport Physical Fitness Test* (2nd ed.). Champaign, IL: Human Kinetics.

62. Wright-Talamante, C., Cheema, A., Riddle, J. E., Luckey, D. W., Taylor, A. K., & Hagerman, R. J. (1996). A controlled study of longitudinal IQ changes in females and males with fragile X syndrome. *American Journal of Medical Genetics*, *64*(2), 350–355.

63. Yang, J. J., Porretta, D. L. (1999). Sport/leisure skill learning by adolescents with mild mental retardation: A four-step strategy. *APAQ*, *16*, 300–315.

64. Yildirim, N. Ü., Erbahçeci, F., Ergun, N., Pitetti, K. H., & Beets, M. W. (2010). The effect of physical fitness training on reaction time in youth with intellectual disabilities. *Perceptual and Motor Skills*, *111*(1), 178–186.

65. Yun, J., & Ulrich, D. A. (1997). Perceived and actual physical competence in children with mild mental retardation. *Amer J on Ment Retard, 102,* 147–160.
66. Zetts, R. A., Horvat, M. A., & Langone, J. (1995, June). Effects of a community-based progressive resistance training program on the work productivity of adolescents with moderate to severe intellectual disabilities. *Educ Train Ment Retard Dev Disab,* 166–178.

CHAPTER 12

Autism Spectrum Disorder

OBJECTIVES

- Briefly describe autism spectrum disorder.
- Give examples of "best practices" in teaching physical education to students with autism spectrum disorder.
- Give examples of physical education activities appropriate for learners with autism spectrum disorder.
- Explain simple strategies to encourage appropriate behavior in learners with autism spectrum disorder.
- Explain the team-based approach in assessment of and individualized education program development for individuals with autism spectrum disorder.
- Briefly explain instructional and behavioral methodologies used for individuals with autism spectrum disorder.
- Describe the most commonly used evidenced-based practices to use with students with autism spectrum disorder in physical education.

Photo by Kristi Roth

Definition

Individuals with autism spectrum disorder (ASD) present an exciting, wonderful, and ever-challenging opportunity for physical educators. Their unique approach to life, their reaction to sensory stimulation within the environment, and their fascinating human interaction and communication/language skills provide the opportunity for adapted and general physical educators to test and teach skills that promote success in lifetime physical activity.

The primary classification system used to identify autism spectrum disorder is the DSM-5 system developed by the American Psychiatric Association.[1] The DSM-5 significantly altered the classification system for individuals with ASD. The DSM-IV individuals with ASD could have been identified as having one of four separate disorders related to autism. These included autistic disorder, Asperger's disorder, childhood disintegrative disorder, or pervasive developmental disorder not otherwise specified (PDD-NOS). The range of diagnostic criteria that sometimes overlapped with each other caused inconsistency in diagnoses. Individuals who were previously diagnosed with one of these four types of autism spectrum disorder will retain those diagnoses; however, initial diagnoses as identified by the DSM-5 will fall under the umbrella term of autism spectrum disorder.[1]

ASD is characterized by persistent deficits in social communication and interaction in a variety of settings, and restricted, repetitive patterns of behavior, interests, or activities. These symptoms must be present in the early developmental period, significantly impair the individual, and not be due to an intellectual disability. Current estimates are that 35% of individuals with ASD score above the IQ cutoff for intellectual disability (70, depending on the test).[12] In addition to meeting one of the previously described characteristics, individuals with ASD will also be identified by their level of severity. See **Table 12-1** for the DSM-5 diagnostic criteria and description of the levels of severity for ASD.

TABLE 12-1   Diagnostic Criteria for Individuals with Autism Spectrum Disorder

For a formal diagnosis of autism, the DSM-5 system identifies the following diagnostic criteria:

A. Persistent deficits in social communication and social interaction across multiple contexts, as manifested by the following:

1. Deficits in social-emotional reciprocity, ranging, for example, from abnormal social approach and failure of normal back-and-forth conversation; to reduced sharing of interests, emotions, or affect; to failure to initiate or respond to social interactions.

2. Deficits in nonverbal communicative behaviors used for social interaction, ranging, for example, from poorly integrated verbal and nonverbal communication; to abnormalities in eye contact and body language or deficits in understanding and use of gestures; to a total lack of facial expressions and nonverbal communication.

3. Deficits in developing, maintaining, and understanding relationships, ranging, for example, from difficulties adjusting behavior to suit various social contexts; to difficulties in sharing imaginative play or in making friends; to absence of interest in peers.

B. Restricted, repetitive patterns of behavior, interests, or activities, as manifested by at least two of the following, currently or by history (examples are illustrative, not exhaustive; see text):

1. Stereotyped or repetitive motor movements, use of objects, or speech (e.g., simple motor stereotypies, lining up toys or flipping objects, echolalia, idiosyncratic phrases).

2. Insistence on sameness, inflexible adherence to routines, or ritualized patterns of verbal or nonverbal behavior (e.g., extreme distress at small changes, difficulties with transitions, rigid thinking patterns, greeting rituals, need to take same route or eat same food every day).

3. Highly restricted, fixated interests that are abnormal in intensity or focus (e.g., strong attachment to or preoccupation with unusual objects, excessively circumscribed or perseverative interest).

4. Hyper- or hyporeactivity to sensory input or unusual interests in sensory aspects of the environment (e.g., apparent indifference to pain/temperature, adverse response to specific sounds or textures, excessive smelling or touching of objects, visual fascination with lights or movement).

C. Symptoms must be present in the early developmental period (but may not become fully manifest until social demands exceed limited capacities, or may be masked by learned strategies in later life).

D. Symptoms cause clinically significant impairment in social, occupational, or other important areas of current functioning.

E. These disturbances are not better explained by intellectual disability (intellectual developmental disorder) or global developmental delay. Intellectual disability and autism spectrum disorder frequently co-occur; to make comorbid diagnoses of autism spectrum disorder and intellectual disability, social communication should be below that expected for general developmental level.

(continues)

TABLE 12-1 Diagnostic Criteria for Individuals with Autism Spectrum Disorder (*Continued*)

Severity Level	Social Communication	Restricted, Repetitive Behaviors
Level 3 "Requiring very substantial support"	Severe deficits in verbal and nonverbal social communication skills cause severe impairments in functioning, very limited initiation of social interactions, and minimal response to social overtures from others. For example, a person with few words of intelligible speech who rarely initiates interaction and, when he or she does, makes unusual approaches to meet needs only and responds to only very direct social approaches.	Inflexibility of behavior, extreme difficulty coping with change, or other restricted/repetitive behaviors markedly interfere with functioning in all spheres. Great distress/difficulty changing focus or action.
Level 2 "Requiring substantial support"	Marked deficits in verbal and nonverbal social communication skills; social impairments apparent even with supports in place; limited initiation of social interactions; and reduced or abnormal responses to social overtures from others. For example, a person who speaks simple sentences, whose interaction is limited to narrow special interests, and who has markedly odd nonverbal communication.	Inflexibility of behavior, difficulty coping with change, or other restricted/repetitive behaviors appear frequently enough to be obvious to the casual observer and interfere with functioning in a variety of contexts. Distress and/or difficulty changing focus or action.
Level 1 "Requiring support"	Without supports in place, deficits in social communication cause noticeable impairments. Difficulty initiating social interactions, and clear examples of atypical or unsuccessful response to social overtures of others. May appear to have decreased interest in social interactions. For example, a person who is able to speak in full sentences and engages in communication but whose to-and-fro conversation with others fails, and whose attempts to make friends are odd and typically unsuccessful.	Inflexibility of behavior causes significant interference with functioning in one or more contexts. Difficulty switching between activities. Problems of organization and planning hamper independence.

Modified from DSM-5.[1]

Incidence

ASD is the fastest growing developmental disability in this country. It occurs in all racial, ethnic, and socioeconomic groups. It is approximately five times more common among boys than girls. In 1990 it was estimated that the prevalence of pervasive developmental disorder was 2 per 10,000 children. In 2010 the Centers for Disease Control and Prevention estimated that 1 in 68 children born in the United States was diagnosed with ASD.[9] It is unclear how much of this increase is due to a broader definition of ASD and better efforts in diagnosis or a true increase in incidence of the disorder. The United States Department of Education, National Center for Education Statistics, reported that more than 498,000 children, from ages 3 to 21 years, received educational services in the broad category of "autism" during the 2012–2013 school year.[53]

Causes

The causes of ASD have been widely studied. Despite extensive research and hypotheses, the exact cause of ASD has not been identified. There are several conclusions on which scientists agree. Genetics are a contributing risk factor for the development of ASD. Children who have a sibling with ASD are at a higher risk of also having ASD. Children born to older adults are at a higher risk for having ASD. ASD has been linked to certain genetic or chromosomal conditions such as fragile X syndrome, and to prescription drugs taken during pregnancy such as valproic acid.[9] There has been widespread speculation in the popular press that ASD is caused by the mumps, measles, and rubella vaccine given to young children. However, there is no significant research to support that theory and major research indicates there is no relationship.[29]

The neurological basis of ASD may include chromosomal defects; disorders of neuron cell migration; congenital brain malformation, including megalencephaly (large brain); electrophysiological abnormalities; and defects in neurotransmitter and receptor structure.[3, 8, 50, 56] The amygdala may be central in autistic behavior because of its specific roles in the control of emotional and social function, affect, and the understanding of the intentions of others.[47]

There are also concerns that toxins in the environmental ecosystem may be related to an increase in the incidence of ASD.[13] The toxins may also have a negative impact on the genetic endowment of individuals. Although the exact cause(s) of autism has not been identified, there is evidence that the combination of genetic and environmental factors creates the greatest risk.

Characteristics

Every individual with ASD is unique. However, it is helpful for the physical educator to understand "typical" characteristics of ASD.

Research has identified other cognitive, motor/physical, language, behavioral, and psychosocial characteristics as well. Many children with ASD have difficulty completing academic tasks within the school setting, although this may have no relationship to their intelligence. Learners with ASD may simply find it difficult to function within the school environment.

Learners with ASD may exhibit gross and fine motor delays.[18, 37] In a comparison of children ages 7–10 years, with and without autism, children with autism exhibited significant deficits in two fundamental skills on the Movement Assessment Battery for Children (MABC-2), catching a ball and static balance.[55] Both of these skills form the basis for many skills in physical education. Students with ASD exhibit reduced motivation for physical activity, lower levels of cardiovascular endurance, and a limited number of physical activities that prove appealing. Individuals with ASD also exhibit poor or delayed motor skills, particularly in the areas of balance, hand–eye coordination, and perceptual motor skills.[16] Learners with autism may also display unusual gross and fine motor behaviors. Rapin noted,

> Motor stereotypes are often striking and, besides hand flapping, may include pacing, spinning, running in circles, twirling a string, tearing paper, drumming, and flipping light switches.[38]

Most learners with ASD struggle with expressive and receptive language. To communicate an intention, the learner with ASD may use atypical means, such as having temper tantrums, grabbing a teacher's hand to take the teacher where the learner wants the teacher to be, and performing self- and other-aggression.[43] To communicate verbally, the learner may use the following language patterns:

- Echolalia, echoing the language of another
- Neologisms, made-up words or sounds

- Singing or sing-songing of particular words or phrases or humming
- Poorly articulated and agrammatical speech
- Jargon
- "Overlearned scripts," repeating words

In addition, children with ASD typically have difficulty with behavior, and most experience difficulties in psychosocial experiences, including difficulty engaging in cooperative activities, difficulty attending to others, difficulty with appropriate engagement gaze, difficulty attributing emotions to others, and failure to develop age-appropriate play behaviors.[29, 30, 54] Many students with ASD have difficulty in social situations. They may have difficulty responding to typical social stimuli, such as having their names called; difficulty with spontaneous verbal or nonverbal greeting or "good-bye"; and difficulty establishing eye contact.[11, 20, 21] However, they appear to be sensitive to another human in distress.[6]

© wallybird/Shutterstock

During unstructured, unplanned free play, children with autism, when compared with children without autism matched on mental age, play with fewer toys, are less focused on play, seldom initiate interaction or communication with their play partners, and appear to prefer solitary play.[4, 15, 22, 26, 46] They play better, however, in more structured play experiences.

Dr. Temple Grandin, a high-functioning individual with autism, wrote that she and others with autism tend to identify with *Star Trek* heroes Data and Mr. Spock. She said, "I couldn't figure out what I was doing wrong. I had an odd lack of awareness that I was different. I thought the other kids were different. I could never figure out why I didn't fit in."[44]

There are particular characteristics of individuals with ASD that have a dramatic impact on their ability to learn:

- Learners with autism may be unable to impose meaning on their experiences. Their personal reality is apparently unrelated to actual experiences and events.

- They may be distractible and have difficulty focusing on what is important in the educational environment.
- They may focus on minute details and fail to grasp the "bigger picture."
- They may have difficulty with abstract concepts and symbols.
- They may find it easy to understand and remember individual facts or concepts but have difficulty combining or integrating ideas.
- They may have difficulty organizing acts or thoughts in a logical sequence.
- They may learn a fact or concept in one situation but be unable to generalize to another, similar situation.
- They are often very persistent in seeking out and getting what they want—whether it is a particular smell, object, or toy.
- They may be anxious. This is often a combination of biological and psychological factors.
- They may process sensory stimuli in atypical ways.[8]

Howard Gardner, in his classic work *Frames of Mind,* suggested that individuals with autism demonstrate a variety of intelligences, including logical-mathematical and musical, but have particular difficulty with intelligences associated with social-emotional skills, the interpersonal and intrapersonal types of intelligence.[17] In the broadest sense, if educators and other professionals were to embrace the notion that there are different types of intelligence and, thus, different ways to assess and teach EVERY learner, the needs of ALL LEARNERS could be met.

The Physical Education Program

TESTING FOR AUTISM SPECTRUM DISORDER

A powerful case can be made for the use of transdisciplinary and portfolio assessment strategies for the learner with ASD. A comprehensive eco-behavioral portfolio assessment, completed by parents together with professionals representing a variety of fields and interests, is crucial if the educational progress of the learner with ASD is to be measured. This is vital if the student's IEP is to be appropriate and will maximize progress. This type of assessment is particularly important for the learner with ASD because most traditional assessment strategies require performance-on-request behavior that is typically impossible for learners with ASD.

Ongoing observational data regarding the learner in a variety of settings are vital to the entire process: in the home; in natural settings; in a variety of school settings, including the classroom, and particularly the playground; in small- and large-group activities; in structured and free play; in academic /prevocational work programs; and in community-based leisure, recreation, and sport venues. As many students with ASD have sensory system dysfunction, inclusion of a comprehensive sensory assessment can be highly valuable when determining individual needs.[41] An occupational therapist is a key member of the motor assessment team, particularly when it involves assessing student sensory system functioning. The student's motor competency is a critical part of the evaluation process.[39] A portfolio assessment appears to be the most viable strategy for gaining valid and appropriate information. However, some adapted physical educators have used the Test of Gross Motor Development-II and the Louisiana Competency Test of Adapted Physical Education effectively with learners with "high-functioning" autism.[5] When assessing students with ASD, several strategies will promote validity and improve student engagement. These include the use of visual supports, such as video, pictures, and visual schedules; administration of the test in an environment which is most conducive for the student, such as an indoor space with limited distractions; the inclusion of peer tutors or a paraprofessional whom the student responds well to; the use of modified equipment if the student is unable to perform a skill with the equipment specified in the test; the use of reinforcers for completion of skill attempts; and the use of short, verbal cues and demonstrations rather than long verbal descriptions of skills to be performed.[7]

CURRICULUM DESIGN

Based on the information gained in and through the portfolio assessment process, the IEP must be developed to meet the unique needs of the learner, as mandated by federal law. Only then should consideration be given to the appropriate placement in which the IEP goals and objectives can be met.

The Reauthorization of IDEA, 1999, and recent litigation support the intent of Congress to allow individuals with disabilities to participate, whenever possible, within the general program, using the general curriculum. The decision about the physical education placement of the learner with ASD remains, however, one that must be made by the multidisciplinary IEP team or committee. The general physical education program may be very restrictive for learners on the ASD continuum. Decisions about placement must be made carefully and include choices of curriculum, assessment, program participation, support personnel, equipment, grading, teaching style, behavior management, and gymnasium environment.

High-functioning learners with ASD are capable of successful placement within the general physical education setting if the general physical education teacher is well organized, teaches developmentally appropriate activities, uses age-appropriate behavior management strategies, focuses on cooperative rather than competitive activities, and uses the teaching strategies outlined later in the chapter. Certainly, the learner with ASD who is not a behavior problem in the classroom is most likely to be successful because the teacher will be more receptive and, by example, will help other children be receptive.[42] For many learners with ASD, however, the general physical education class is restrictive because the nature of the physical education experience often includes large numbers of learners moving, with a great deal of noise and poor acoustics, in a relatively unstructured environment.[32] The curriculum and pace of learning for students with ASD present additional challenges. Children with ASD exhibit difficulty regulating force and timing when performing motor skills.[49] Subsequently, sport and activities that require rapid decision making, decreased reaction time, and varied play area distances can present many challenges for students with ASD.

Many variables need to be considered before deciding to place a learner with ASD in the general physical education setting. Learners with ASD who require more support often need to receive physical education instruction within a reverse-inclusion, small-group, or one-on-one setting. In order to give these learners the opportunity to interact with typically developing peers, the reverse-inclusion class, where other learners without disabilities are included in the small-group physical education experience, can be ideal. Learners without disabilities in a reverse-inclusion class require training on the nature and needs of their peers with ASD.

The types of activities that learners with ASD can experience success in the physical education program depends on the severity of the disorder and the age of the learner. However, *daily* vigorous aerobic exercise is critical because it reduces self-stimulatory and off-task behavior, increases time on academic and vocational tasks, and, as important, improves gross motor performance.[14, 17, 23, 25] Physical education programs for individuals with ASD, at all levels of development, should include exercise that promotes the development of cardiovascular-respiratory endurance.

The learner with ASD is usually more successful in closed, individual activities.[36] For example, the middle or junior high school learner with ASD may be very successful in activities such as bicycling, bowling, darts, Frisbee golf, croquet, horseshoes, swimming, and walking/jogging/running on a treadmill or track. Relaxation training is also a significant component of the physical education curriculum.

Courtesy of Kristi Roth

Children with ASD who are particularly sensitive to others but who struggle with their social behaviors, may find themselves teased and secluded from others. Difficulty dealing with their social-emotional issues makes it even more important for learners this age to participate in vigorous aerobic activities at least 1 hour per day. The vigorous activity allows the learners to better control impulses and other behavior. Learners with ASD tend to have the most success in walking, jogging, running, stationary cycling, stationary rowing, basic aerobic dancing, swimming, and inline skating.[40]

TEACHING STRATEGIES

Physical educators experience teaching challenges in one or more of the following areas when teaching students with ASD: inattentive and hyperactive behaviors, social impairment, emotional regulation difficulties, difficulties understanding and performing tasks, narrow focus and inflexible adherence to routines and structure, isolation by classmates, negative effects on classmates' learning, and need for support.[32]

For learners who fall under the broad umbrella of ASD, teaching strategies in physical education are, essentially, consistent with good teaching. In this section, teaching strategies found effective for individuals with ASD will be considered for the general physical education class and/or a more separate learning environment, if required, to ensure success. In addition to general teaching strategies that physical educators have found useful, evidence-based practices should be utilized to the maximum extent when teaching students with ASD. Evidence-based practices (EBPs) are interventions that have been proven effective through scientific research. As of this publication, there have been 27 focused EBPs for individuals with ASD.[57] They can be found in **Table 12-2**. A brief description of how selected EBPs can be implemented by physical educators is below.

TABLE 12-2   Evidence-Based Practices for Individuals with Autism Spectrum Disorder

Antecedent-based intervention (ABI)
Cognitive behavioral intervention (CBI)
Differential reinforcement of alternative, incompatible, or other behavior (DRA/I/O)
Discrete trial teaching (DTT)
Exercise (ECE)
Extinction (EXT)
Functional behavior assessment (FBA)
Functional communication training (FCT)
Modeling (MD)
Naturalistic intervention (NI)
Parent-implemented intervention (PII)
Peer-mediated instruction and intervention (PMII)
Picture exchange communication system (PECS)
Pivotal response training (PRT)
Prompting (PP)
Reinforcement (R+)
Response interruption/redirection (RIR)
Scripting (SC)
Self-management (SM)
Social narratives (SN)
Social skills training (SST)
Structured play group (SPG)
Task analysis (TA)
Technology-aided instruction and intervention (TAII)
Time delay (TD)
Video modeling (VM)
Visual support (VS)

National Professional Development Center on Autism Spectrum Disorder.

Exercise

Aerobic exercise has been directly linked to improvements in behavior, impulse control, attention span, sensory integrative function, and motor skills in students with ASD.[25, 33, 34, 48] Alternating aerobic activity with motor skills can improve attention and performance. For example, allowing a student with ASD to hit a tennis ball against a wall with a partner for 10 minutes, followed by 3 minutes of jogging or riding a stationary bike, can help a student with ASD focus and perform better upon returning to the wall.

Modeling

Physical educators should rely heavily on modeling for students with ASD. Demonstration of skills by the teacher, paraprofessional, or peers provides students with ASD the visual cues necessary for expected performance. Verbal reinforcement is often not necessary, as this increases the processing required for interpretation of the skill expectations. Video modeling, where the student watches a recorded demonstration of the skill, is also effective in helping students with ASD improve performance.[28, 31]

Peer-Mediated Instruction and Intervention

When typically developing peers interact with and/or help students with ASD, in-class performance and attention are often improved.[35] When implementing a peer-tutor program, it is important to train the peer tutors on strategies for engaging their peer with ASD.

Picture Exchange Communication System

When using the pictures exchange communication system (PECS), the student is taught to exchange a picture of a desired item or experience for the actual item or experience. An example in physical education would be to have small, laminated pictures of the student's preferred activities, such as basketball or treadmill, and when the student would like to participate in these activities, he or she gives the picture of it to the teacher. This encourages communication. This system can be expanded to using the Premack Principle, where the student must complete a required activity prior to receiving time to participate in the desired activity. For example, if the student requests time to play basketball, he or she "first" can be required to complete 10 exercise ball crunches and "then" he or she receives 2 minutes of free play with a basketball.

Prompting

Touch and verbal prompting can result in increased engagement in desired activities. When prompting students with ASD, it is important to know if they exhibit tactile defensive behavior, meaning they are sensitive to touch and may require gentle touch with a verbal warning. It is important to initially demonstrate the desired activity with or without a short verbal prompt (depending on the verbal processing skills of the student). If the student does not display a response, a touch prompt might prove helpful. If the student still does not respond, manual physical assistance for the full range of motion can provide the student with the guidance required to understand expectations. When using this more restrictive form of prompting, teachers should always have a goal of reducing the prompts as the student makes progress toward demonstrating an appropriate response.

Reinforcement

Providing students with a reinforcement or reward for expected performance can be significantly beneficial in helping students understand the desired skill. Students are motivated by different reinforcers so it is important to get to know the student to determine what reinforcers will be effective. Using reinforcers that are regularly used in the classroom and home environment is recommended. An example of using reinforcers would be if the student enjoys having coins in his or her pocket, if he or she bats a ball and runs from home plate to first base, he or she earns one coin. The student receives a coin for each additional base. Providing reinforcers intermittently and increasing the number of tasks to complete prior to receiving a reinforcer can increase independent performance in class.[51]

Scripting

Writing a script of the situation or skill and having the student with autism read through that script prior to the event or class can help the student understand the expectations of the activity, improve performance, and decrease anxiety.[30] These scripts should be read or listened to repeatedly prior to the event. Scripting can be used to teach engagement in peer activities. For example, a script can be developed to teach a child how to ask for a ball from a peer.

The script would include the statement "When I want the ball, I say to Alex, 'Pass,' and put my hands out. Alex will then throw me the ball and I will catch it."

Social Narratives

Social stories are brief, individual short stories that describe a social situation and provide specific behavioral cues. The stories provide a brief who, what, when, where, and why of a social situation. The stories help ensure a child's understanding of social information for various settings and provide instruction for initiating, responding to, and maintaining appropriate social interactions.[45] An example of a social story can be found in **Figure 12-1**.

Technology-Aided Instruction and Intervention

Technology has provided opportunities for highly effective communication and structure for students with autism. There are many apps that can run on

My name is _____. I am going to PE for the first time today. It is OK that I am a little scared. There will be a lot of children. There will be a lot of noise.

The teacher's name is Miss Chavez. She has colored circles on the floor where we will sit when we get to the gym. I am going to be able to sit by my buddy _____. That will be good because I like _____.

Miss Chavez starts class with music. That's good because I like to move to music. Then we will run around the gym. That's cool because I am a good runner. Then we will play a game. I can watch my buddy _____ so I know what I should do.

When we finish our game we all sit down on our circles again. Then, we fine up to leave to go back to class.

I'll say good-bye to Miss Chavez when I leave the gym.

Following is a sample social story for an adolescent struggling with peers' teasing in the gymnasium.

Today when I go to the gymnasium, I'll remember it is OK for me to be angry if kids in the gym tease me. But, if I get angry, I'll use the "STOP, THINK, DO" strategy before I do anything. If I can, I'll turn around and walk away.

I'll stay with my friend ____. We'll go to the stationary cycling fitness station where we can ride side by side.

Today, I'll ride 5 miles in 35 minutes. Then, I only have 405 more miles to get to Juneau, Alaska.

Figure 12-1 *Physical Education Social Story*

a small mobile device that is in the pocket or clipped to the student. Visual schedules, social stories, video modeling, and speaking apps are those most commonly used in physical education. Several apps facilitate communication and provide structure for students with ASD.[24] Autism Speaks maintains a database of apps for students with autism.[2]

Video Modeling

In video modeling, children watch a videotape of a model engaging in a target behavior; subsequently, the children implement it. Children with autism find watching themselves on videotape highly motivating.[28] Video modeling provides an interesting opportunity for teaching learners with autism age-appropriate social interaction and play behaviors.[31] Video modeling gives learners with autism the opportunity to prepare, so that their behaviors are more appropriate in a social setting. Recording a demonstration of the skill or description and demonstration of the rules to a game or activity can meet the visual learning requirements of many students with ASD. These can be "previewed" in the classroom or at home prior to physical education, allowing the student to come to physical education prepared.

Visual Supports

There are many types of visual supports that can be integrated into physical education. These can include photographs, drawings, objects, written words, or lists. First-then boards and visual schedules are the two most common visual supports used in physical education. Examples of these can be found in **Figure 12-2**.

In addition to evidence-based practice, additional strategies can meet the individualized needs of students with ASD in physical education. Specific teaching strategies based on individual characteristics of students with ASD are identified in **Table 12-3**. One of the most effective strategies for teaching

Courtesy of Kristi Roth

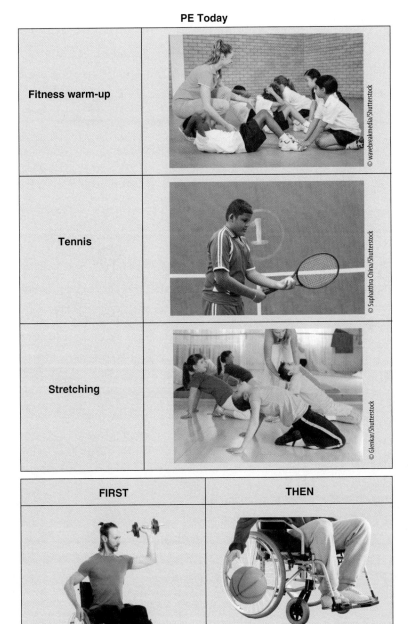

Figure 12-2 Physical Education Visual Schedule

TABLE 12-3   Specific Strategies for Teaching Learners with Autism Spectrum Disorder

Academic Difficulties

- Capitalize on the learner's typically excellent memory skills.
- Use graphics, pictures, and/or demonstrations.

Insistence on Sameness

- Provide a predictable environment.
- Maintain a consistent routine and minimize transitions.

Impairment in Social Interaction

- Place the learner in situations in which his or her reading, vocabulary, and memory skills can be viewed as an asset by peers.
- Create a bully-free learning environment for the sake of all.
- Pair students with a peer tutor to help the student learn appropriate social skills and to reduce their tendency to be reclusive.

Limited Range of Interests

- If possible, designate a time during the day in which the learner can discuss his or her preoccupation or interest.
- Initially individualize learning opportunities and experiences to build on the specific interest of the learner.

Poor Concentration

- Use frequent teacher interaction, feedback, and redirection.
- Time work sessions; start with short and build to longer sessions.
- Establish a signal to alert the student to "refocus."

Poor Motor Planning

- Teach skills in small chunks.
- Remove time constraints when learning new skills.[52]
- Teach skills in a predictable environment.

Poor Motor Coordination

- Use visual and verbal cues, such as dots to step on for opposition.
- Demonstrate skills next to or in front of the student mirroring the skills.[52]
- Involve the learner in a health-fitness curriculum, rather than a competitive sports program.

Poor Imitation Skills

- Ensure skills are goal-oriented and the purpose of the action is explained.
- Provide a sensory reward for performance of a skill.

Sensory Sensitivities

- Minimize background noise and fluorescent lighting.
- Watch carefully for signs that the student is becoming overwhelmed by stimuli—self-abusive behaviors, crying, flushing, or hyperventilation.

Modified from Williams, http://www.sasked.gov.sk.ca/curr_nst/speced/asper.html

children with ASD is to engage them in activities that reinforce their significant interest area to encourage and motivate them to move. For example, at the elementary school level, a child with a fascination with dinosaurs could throw "dinosaur" beanbags at dinosaur targets. At the middle school level, a learner with a fascination with trains could calculate the time it would take a train to travel from one part of the country to another and compare that to the time it would take him or her to ride a stationary bicycle that distance. At the high school level, a student with a fascination with transportation could run on a treadmill while watching Grand Prix races or stationary bicycle while watching the Tour de France. General teaching strategies for students with ASD are described in **Table 12-4**.

TABLE 12-4   General Teaching Strategies for Physical Education

Adopt a "gentle teaching" philosophy.

- Ensure that the learner has every possible opportunity to succeed in the physical education learning environment. Start slowly, with simple skills, and build on them gradually.

Establish and maintain a consistent class routine.

- Each learner should have a separate and carefully marked "home base." The learner with ASD may be most comfortable if the home base is on the periphery of the gymnasium or other learning environment, rather than in the center.
- The physical educator should ensure that each class has the same routine.
- If warm-ups are to be done to music, the physical education teacher should use the same songs over and over; a new song may be introduced after others have been mastered.
- If a given motor skill is to be practiced, the same class organization and equipment should be used. If the class is working on catching, for example, the teacher should use the same size and color ball.
- When using terms to describe a given activity or motion, the teacher should use the same term every time. For example, if each learner is assigned a plastic dot to serve as his or her home base, the teacher should refer to the plastic dot by calling it "dot" and not "circle."

Use joint activity routines.

- Use natural, teachable moments to help the learner acquire skills. For example, when the student enters or exits the gymnasium, he or she should be expected to greet the teacher, verbally or using a gesture.

Use a visual schedule.

- Place a horizontal visual schedule in a central place on the gymnasium wall to allow the learner with ASD to predict the next event.

(continues)

TABLE 12-4 General Teaching Strategies for Physical Education (*Continued*)

Use picture exchanges.

- If the learner with ASD has difficulty understanding the simple visual symbol schedule, the physical educator can use a picture exchange system to help the student more effectively predict the sequence of events. The individual learner with ASD may have his or her own visual schedule, with each component on an individual card. As each event is about to begin, the learner pulls the card from his or her schedule and puts it in a pile, face down, until the entire class is completed.

Provide opportunities for social interaction.

- Carefully trained and sensitive peer buddies may encourage appropriate social interaction.
- Create and maintain a bully-free learning environment.

Allow choice making to encourage participation.

- Give the learner two options from which he or she can choose. This is enabling and gives the learner some critical control over his or her environment. For example, while holding each ball in his or her hands, the teacher asks, "Ricardo would you like to throw the red or the yellow ball?" and waits for the learner to grasp one ball, or "Dominique, do you want to start at the 'push-up' station or the 'sit-up' station?"

Spend quality floor time with the learner.

- Get down on the floor with young learners with ASD to interact at their eye level.
- Ensure that the activities are developmentally appropriate. A learner with ASD is much more likely to be successful, for example, in a first-grade general physical education class if the teacher is concentrating on the foundations of locomotor and nonlocomotor patterns, object-control skills, and basic rhythmic activities than if the teacher is inappropriately focusing on team sports.

Address the interests of the learner with ASD.

- Part of the lesson should focus specifically on the strengths of the individuals with ASD. If the elementary school learner with ASD has a particular interest in animals, for example, the student should be given the opportunity to describe an animal before members of the class act like the animal. If the high school learner with Asperger's syndrome, for example, has a particular interest in aerodynamics, the learner with ASD should have an opportunity to explain the principles of aerodynamics before his or her classmates throw a Frisbee.

Acknowledge and honor the learner's difficulty attending to task.

- Provide frequent feedback.
- Use simple redirection strategies to return the learner's attention to task. For example, the physical educator could remind the student, "John, which station is next on your list?" or "Lisa, how many push-ups have you already done?"

TABLE 12-4   General Teaching Strategies for Physical Education (*Continued*)

Be consistent with behavior management systems.

- Adopt the behavior management system used by the learner's classroom teacher and the learner's parents.
- Develop a behavior contract for learners with Asperger's syndrome and "high-functioning" autism. This also needs to be consistent with that used in other parts of the curriculum.
- Redirect inappropriate behaviors. Because the learner with ASD often does not understand cause–effect relationships, it is ineffective to scold the learner for misbehavior or to say, "No." It is much more effective to redirect existing behavior. For example, if the learner is kicking furniture, replace the furniture with a ball.
- Simplify the task if the learner is misbehaving while attempting a task. Often, a learner with ASD "acts out" as a result of frustration. Simplifying the task at hand may allow the learner to succeed at the task while reducing inappropriate behaviors.
- If the learner is acting out or is out of control, moving the learner to a less stimulating area may allow the learner to regain control of his or her behavior. An ideal place in the gymnasium is a beanbag chair or soft chair just inside the teacher's office.

Allow for self-regulation.

- Teach students a visual signal, such as holding up three fingers, that they can give the physical educator when they are getting overwhelmed and need a break.
- Provide a quiet corner, such as a corner with mats up on their side blocking the general space, to allow students to take a break by swinging in a hammock, coloring, or listening to music.[19]
- Provide the student with a backpack with books in it to pick up and wear when they need proprioceptive input for calming and focusing.

SUMMARY

Autism spectrum disorder is the large umbrella term for the condition in which individuals experience communication difficulties, abnormal behaviors, and poor social skills. Physical education programs require set routines and careful transitions between each part of the instructional day. The key component in a quality physical education program for learners with ASD is daily, vigorous aerobic activity.

REVIEW QUESTIONS

1. Describe potential characteristics that may contribute to the diagnosis of ASD.
2. Briefly describe why there should be a primary emphasis on cardiovascular-respiratory /aerobic activity with individuals with ASD.

3. Explain evidence-based practices and describe several that have been proven effective when teaching students with ASD.

4. Describe common challenges students with ASD experience in physical education and identify strategies to accommodate those challenges.

5. Explain some strategies the general physical education teacher could use to help learners with ASD experience success in the program.

REFERENCES

1. American Psychiatric Association. (2013). *DSM-5 Autism Spectrum Disorder.* Retrieved from http://www.dsm5.org/Documents/Autism%20Spectrum%20 Disorder%20Fact%20Sheet.pdf

2. Autism Speaks. (2015). *Autism Apps.* Retrieved from https://www .autismspeaks.org/autism-apps

3. Bailey, A., et al. (1998). A clinicopathological study of autism. *Brain, 121,* 889–905.

4. Bashe, P. R., & Kirby, B. (2001). *The oasis guide to Asperger syndrome.* New York: Crown.

5. Berkeley, S., Zittel, L., Pitney, L., & Nichols, S. (2001). Locomotor and object control skills of children diagnosed with autism. *APAQ, 18*(4), 405–416.

6. Blair, R. J. (1999). Psychophysiological responsiveness to the distress of others in children with autism. *Personality Ind Diff, 26,* 477–485.

7. Breslin, C., & Liu, T. (2015). Do you know what I'm saying? Strategies to assess motor skills for children with autism spectrum disorder. *Journal of Physical Education, Recreation and Dance, 86*(1), 10–15.

8. Culture of Autism. (2003). *From theoretical understanding to educational practice.* Retrieved from http://www.mplc.co.uk/eduweb/sites/autism/culture .html#cult

9. Centers for Disease Control and Prevention. (2015). *Facts about ASD.* Retrieved from http://www.cdc.gov/ncbddd/autism/facts.html

10. Colombo-Dougovito, A. (2015). Successful evidence-based practices for autism spectrum disorder and their use for the development of motor skills in physical education. *Palaestra, 29*(2), 34.

11. Dawson, G., et al. (1998). Children with autism fail to orient to naturally occurring social stimuli. *J Autism Dev Disord, 28,* 479–485.

12. Dykens, E. M., & Lense, M. (2011). Intellectual disabilities and autism spectrum disorder: A cautionary note. In Amaral, D., Dawson, G., & Geschwind, D. (Eds.), *Autism spectrum disorders* (261–269). New York: Oxford University Press.

13. Edelson, S. B., & Cantor, D. S. (1999). Autism: Xenobiotic influences. *J Advance Med, 12*(l), 35–46.

14. Elliott, R., et al. (1994). Vigorous, aerobic exercise versus general motor training activities: Effects on maladaptive and stereotypic behaviors of

adults with both autism and mental retardation. *J Autism Dev Disord, 24,* 565–575.

15. Fisher, E. (1999). Recent research on the etiologies of autism. *Infants Young Child, 11*(3), 1–8.

16. Fournier, K. A., Hass, C. J., Naik, S. K., Lodha, N., & Cauraugh, J. H. (2010). Motor coordination in autism spectrum disorders: A synthesis and meta-analysis. *Journal of Autism and Developmental Disorders, 40,* 1227–1240.

17. Gardner, H. (2011). *Frames of mind: The theory of multiple intelligences.* New York: Basic Books.

18. Green, D., Charman, T., Pickles, A., Chandler, S., Loucas, T., Simonoff, E., & Baird, G. (2009). Impairment in movement skills of children with autistic spectrum disorders. *Developmental Medicine and Child Neurology, 51,* 311–316.

19. Groft, M., & Block, M. (2003). Children with Asperger syndrome: Implications for general physical education and youth sports. *JOPERD, 74*(3), 38–43.

20. Hobson, R. P., & Lee, A. (1998). Hello and goodbye: A study of social engagement in autism. *J Autism Dev Disord, 28*(2), 117–127.

21. Hobson, R. P., & Lee, A. (1999). Imitation and identification in autism. *J Child Psychol Psychiat, 40*(4), 649–659.

22. Kasari, C. (1993). Focused and social attention of autistic children in interactions with familiar and unfamiliar adults: A comparison of autistic, mentally retarded, and normal children. *Develop Psychopath, 5,* 403–414.

23. Kern, L., et al. (1982). The effects of physical exercise on self-stimulation and appropriate responding in autistic children. *J Autism Dev Disord, 12,* 399–419.

24. Krause, J., & Taliaferro, A. (2015). Supporting students with autism spectrum disorders in physical education: There's an app for that! *Palaestra, 29*(2), 45.

25. Levinson, L., & Reid, G. (1993). The effects of exercise intensity on the stereotypic behaviors of individuals with autism. *APAQ, 10,* 255–268.

26. Libby, S. (1998). Spontaneous play in children with autism: A reappraisal. *J Autism Dev Disord, 28,* 487–497.

27. Madsen, K. M., et al. (2002). A population-based study of measles, mumps, and rubella vaccination and autism. *New Eng J Med, 347*(19), 1477–1482.

28. Maione, L., & Mirenda, P. (2006). Effects of video modeling and video feedback on peer-directed social language skills of a child with autism. *J of Positive Behav Interv, 8*(2), 106–118.

29. Meyer, I., & Minshew, N. (2002). An update on neurocognitive profiles in Asperger syndrome and high functioning autism. *Focus Aut Dev Dis, 17*(3), 152–160.

30. Morrison, R., Sainato, D., Benchaaban, D., & Endo, S. (2002). Increasing play skills of children with autism using activity schedules and correspondence training. *J Early Intervention, 25*(l), 48–72.

31. Nikopoulos, C., & Keenan, M. (2003). Promoting social initiation in children with autism using video modeling. *Behav Intervent, 18,* 87–108.

32. Obrusnikova, I., & Dillon, S. R. (2011). Challenging situations when teaching children with autism spectrum disorders in general physical education. *Adapted Physical Activity Quarterly, 28*(2), 113–131.

33. Oriel, K. N., George, C. L., Peckus, R., & Semon, A. (2011). The effects of aerobic exercise on academic engagement in young children with autism spectrum disorder. *Pediatric Physical Therapy, 23*, 197–193. DOI: 10.1097 /PEP.0b013e318218f149.

34. Pan, C. Y. (2008). School time physical activity of students with and without autism spectrum disorders during PE and recess. *Adapted Physical Activity Quarterly, 25*, 308–321.

35. Pan, C., Tsai, C., & Hsieh, K. (2011). Physical activity correlates for children with autism spectrum disorders in middle school physical education. *Research Quarterly for Exercise and Sport, 82*(3), 491–498.

36. Pan, C. Y. (2014). Motor proficiency and physical fitness in adolescent males with and without autism spectrum disorders. *Autism, 18*, 156–165.

37. Provost, B., Lopez, B. R., & Heimerl, S. (2007). A comparison of motor delays in young children: Autism spectrum disorder, developmental delay, and developmental concerns. *Journal of Autism and Developmental Disorders, 37*, 321–328.

38. Rapin, I. (1997). Autism. *New Eng J Med, 337*(2), 97–104.

39. Reid, G., & Collier, D. (2002). Motor behavior and the autism spectrum disorders. *Palaestra, 18*(4), 20–27.

40. Reid, G., & O'Connor, J. (2003). The autism spectrum disorders: Activity selection, assessment, and program organization. *Palaestra, 19*(l), 20–27.

41. Rinner, L. (2001–2002). Sensory assessment for children and youth with autism spectrum disorders. *Assessment for Effective Intervention, 27*(1&2), 37–46.

42. Robertson, K., Chamberlain, B., & Kasari, C. (2003). General education teachers' relationships with included students with autism. *J Autism Devel Disorders, 33*(2), 123–130.

43. Rollins, P. R. (1999). Early pragmatic accomplishments and vocabulary development in preschool children with autism. *Am J Speech-Language Path, 8*, 181–190.

44. Sacks, O. (1993, December 27). A neurologist's notebook: An anthropologist on Mars. *New Yorker* 106–125.

45. Sansosti, F. J., Powell-Smith, K. A., & Kincaid, D. (2006). Using social stories to improve the social behavior of children with Asperger syndrome. *J of Positive Behav Interv, 8*(1), 43–56.

46. Schoen, S., & Bullard, M. (2002). Action research during recess: A time for children with autism to play and learn. *Teach Except Child, 35*(1), 36–39.

47. Schultz, R., & Klin, A. (2002). Genetics of childhood disorders: XLIII. Autism, Part 2: Neural foundations. *J Am Acad Child Adolesc Psychiatry, 41*(10), 1259–1262.

48. Srinivasan, S. M., Pescatello, L. S., & Bhat, A. N. (2014). Current perspectives on physical activity and exercise recommendations for children and adolescents with autism spectrum disorders. *Physical Therapy, 94*(6), 1–46.

49. Staples, K. L., & Reid, G. (2010). Fundamental movement skills and autism spectrum disorders. *Journal of Autism and Developmental Disorders, 40*, 209–217.

50. Szatmari, P. (1998). Genetics of autism: Overview and new directions. *J Autism Dev Disord, 28*(5), 351–368.

51. Todd, T. (2012). Teaching motor skills to individuals with autism spectrum disorders. *Journal of Physical Education, Recreation & Dance, 83*(8), 32–48. DOI: 10.1080/07303084.2012.10598827.

52. Todd, T., & Reid, G. (2006). Increasing physical activity in individuals with autism. *Focus On Autism & Other Developmental Disabilities, 21*(3), 167–176.

53. U.S. Department of Education. National Center for Education Statistics. https://nces.ed.gov/fastfacts/display.asp?id=64

54. Volkmar, F., Paul, R., Klin, A., & Cohen, D. (2005). *Handbook of autism and pervasive developmental disorders: Diagnosis, development, neurobiology, and behavior. Autism and the autism spectrum disorder.* Hoboken: John Wiley & Sons.

55. Whyatt, C. P., & Craig, C. M. (2012). Motor skills in children aged 7–10 years, diagnosed with autism spectrum disorder. *Journal of Autism and Developmental Disorders, 42*(9), 1799–1809.

56. Williams, K. (1995). Understanding the student with Asperger syndrome: Guidelines for teachers. *Focus on Autistic Behavior, 10*(2). Modified with permission from Barb Kirby, Web Master, O.A.S.I.S. web page, http://www.udel.edu/bkirby/asperger/karen_williams_guidelines.html.

57. Wong, C., Odom, S. L., Hume, K., Cox, A. W., Fettig, A., Kucharczyk, S., & Schultz, T. R. (2014). *Evidence-based practices for children, youth, and young adults with autism spectrum disorder.* Chapel Hill: The University of North Carolina, Frank Porter Graham Child Development Institute, Autism Evidence-Based Practice Review Group.

CHAPTER 13

Specific Learning Disabilities

- Define specific learning disability.
- Identify the types of behavior problems youngsters with a learning disability frequently demonstrate.
- List six motor/physical developmental delays youngsters with a learning disability might demonstrate.
- List at least three teaching strategies a physical educator could use to promote learning for students with specific learning disabilities.
- Identify three techniques that might be effective in keeping a student with a specific learning disability on task during a physical education class.

Probably no disability has proven to be more controversial or has undergone more name changes than what we now call *specific learning disability*. Confusion about the condition is reflected in the number of terms associated with disability. Over the past 30 years, individuals with these disabilities have been classified as perceptually handicapped, brain injured, brain damaged, minimal brain dysfunctionate, dyslexic, and developmentally aphasic.

Every term was selected in an attempt to convey the fact that persons with a specific learning disability have normal intelligence but fail to demonstrate the same academic competencies that most individuals do whose IQs fall within the normal range.

Definition of Specific Learning Disability

Specific learning disability is defined in the Individuals with Disabilities Education Improvement Act (IDEIA) of 2004 and the Diagnostic and Statistical Manual of Mental Disorders (DSM-5).[6] It is a disorder in one or more of the basic psychological processes involved in understanding or using language, spoken or written, which may manifest itself in the imperfect ability to listen, think, speak, write, spell, or perform mathematical calculations. Such disorders include perceptual disabilities, brain injury, minimal brain dysfunction, dyslexia, and developmental aphasia. The term does not include children who have learning problems that are primarily the result of visual, hearing, or motor disabilities; intellectual disability; emotional disturbance; cultural factors; environmental or economic disadvantage; or limited English proficiency.[18] Children with a learning disability have normal intelligence but demonstrate difficulties in one or more specific areas of learning.[40]

IDEIA (2004) regulations require that each state adopt criteria for determining whether a child has a learning disability. States are not required to use the IQ-discrepancy model (i.e., difference between a student's cognitive and achievement test scores),[32] but they must use a process for identifying a student based on the child's response to scientific, research-based interventions and may use other alternative research-based procedures. The significant point being that the methods the states use must be validated by research.[10] To be certain that a suspected specific learning disability is not caused by a lack of appropriate instruction, schools must provide evidence that the child in question was provided appropriate instruction in a regular education setting, by qualified teachers. Additionally, data-based evidence of assessments of achievement must be provided to parents.[38]

The most common types of learning disabilities include problems with math (dyscalculia), reading and spelling (dyslexia), handwriting (dysgraphia), and motor tasks (dyspraxia). Deficits and disorders associated with learning disabilities are often in the areas of information processing and include auditory and visual processing deficits, understanding and/or using verbal and nonverbal abilities (developmental aphasia, dysnomia, expressive language), executive functioning deficits, and attention deficit/hyperactivity disorder.[30] Many children and adolescents who have been identified as having a learning disability also have concurrent emotional and behavior problems.[22, 34] And, as would be expected of individuals who despite their best efforts continue to fail, self-esteem is reduced.

Incidence of Specific Learning Disability

Children with learning disabilities are the largest population of students receiving special education services. According to IDEIA (2004), in 2012, 40% of students with disabilities, ages 6–21 years, were diagnosed with specific learning disability.[39] Speech and language impairments (18.2%) are the next most common disability category.[14] Sixty-six percent of the children identified as having specific learning disability are boys[30]; however, there is growing speculation that both genders are equally affected. Referral bias and test bias are two reasons for boys being identified more frequently. Boys who are frustrated in school tend to be more disruptive than girls and therefore referred for special education services more often. Also, many of the tests used to diagnose learning disabilities were designed and standardized on boys. It is plausible that boys and girls reflect their learning disability differently.[35] In 2012, children with specific learning disability comprised 3.4% of the total population of children ages 6–21 years. This is a slight decrease from 4.3% of the total population in 2003.

Causes of Specific Learning Disability

Children who were once believed to be prone to daydreaming, inattentive, mischievous, or just plain "dumb" in school do, indeed, have an organic basis for their behaviors. A learning disability is often referred to as a "hidden disability" because no physical signs are present.[28] However, a learning disability is a neurobiological disorder. Because of differences in brain structure and/or function, individuals learn differently and process information in a way that is different.[35] The exact causes of a learning disability are unknown but risk factors such as heredity,[19] low birth weight, and poor nutrition may contribute.[40]

Technologically sophisticated equipment has been used to document neurological differences in the brains of persons with specific learning disability as compared with individuals without learning disabilities.[35, 4] However, the specific impact of neurological differences, the subcategories of the disability, and the causes have not been identified. The best we can do at this point in time is to describe the behaviors demonstrated by this varied group of learners and share whatever has been found to work successfully with them.

For more than 45 years theorists postulated that sensory-perceptual-motor functioning delays underlay specific learning disability. Technology developed in the past decade has enabled researchers to demonstrate neurological differences in individuals with learning disability; however, the extent to which these deficits are tied to academic performance is still unknown. During the 1960s, when the perceptual-motor theories of Getman, Kephart,[25] and Frostig and Maslow[20] were emerging, great hope was placed in using physical activity to "cure" learning disabilities. The perceptual-motor pioneers proposed that the basic "stuff" from which cognitive information is constructed included perceptual and motor components. Educational researchers speculated that, if they could identify that perceptual-motor delays exist and intervene with a movement program to overcome the delays, cognitive function would be facilitated. Special educators with little or no background in motor development seized on these theories as the possible answer to the academic learning problems manifested by individuals with learning disabilities. Kephart's and Frostig and Maslow's programs of activities were tried on groups of students with learning disabilities. Almost without exception, the wholesale application of these theories proved disappointing to the academic community. In most cases, the students with learning disabilities improved in perceptual-motor function but demonstrated no immediate change in reading or mathematical ability. As a result, many special educators abandoned the notion that there could be a causative relationship between motor and cognitive functioning.

As the perceptual-motor theories faded in popularity, other neuropsychological theories emerged that advanced the belief that cognitive function could be facilitated by controlling types and qualities of sensory and motor experiences. These theories differed from earlier ones in that they advanced the notion that, prior to efficient perceptual-motor and cognitive functioning, sensory input stimuli must be organized, so that it can be used by the central nervous system.

Prominent advocates of a definitive relationship among the sensory, motor, and cognitive domains were Ayres,[2, 3] deQuiros and Schrager,[12] and Dennison.[11] Ayres, a well-known researcher in the area of sensory integration therapy, advocated that "learning and behavior are the visible aspects of sensory integration"[2] and that sensory integration results from sensory stimulation and motor activity. DeQuiros and Schrager believed that primary learning disabilities have their bases in vestibular, perceptual modalities, and cerebral dysfunctions. They advocated the use of sensory-perceptual-motor activities to assuage vestibular and perceptual problems. Dennison built on Sperry and Ornstein's model of brain function and developmental optometry's theories and developed a program of specific movements to use to enable individuals to access different parts of the brain. He called his approach Educational Kinesiology.[5]

Research evidence suggests that sensory-integration may have a positive outcome in sensorimotor skills and motor planning. Additionally, in a systematic review of research evidence looking at sensory integration intervention approaches, positive outcomes were found in socialization, attention, behavioral regulation, reading, and reading related skills. Studies that have reported academic gains from sensory integration therapy programs suffer from sampling, group assignment, treatment, and analysis inadequacies.[29]

Interest in the relationship between motor skill performance, aerobic exercise, and academic skills continues.[17] It will take well-designed research studies to tease out the existence of the specific types of sensory and motor components that exist concomitantly with cognitive challenges.[21] Once the underlying delays are identified, intervention programs will need to be developed and used with children who have learning disabilities. After that, longitudinal studies that follow individuals who have been exposed to contemporary sensory-perceptual-motor intervention programs will need to be carried out. To understand the problem and potential solutions, dialogues among educators, neurologists, visual and hearing specialists, and researchers will need to be initiated and fostered. The questions to be answered must be approached with open minds, honest and critical analysis, and persistence.

Characteristics of Specific Learning Disability

All children differ in their psychomotor, cognitive, and behavioral characteristics. Likewise, children with learning disabilities differ from one another, and there is considerable overlap in abilities between children with learning disabilities and other children. However, there are some similar group characteristics that differentiate individuals with specific learning disabilities from individuals who lack disabilities. Understanding each child's challenges and considering how those challenges will impact his or her communication, self-help, play, and independence is critical.

Children can differ in motor performance for many reasons, including (1) neurophysiological differences, (2) sensory input processing differences, (3) problems processing information, (4) language differences, (5) memory deficits, and (6) short attention span. (See **Table 13-1.**)

NEUROPHYSIOLOGICAL DIFFERENCES

Functional magnetic resonance imaging (fMRI) is a safe and noninvasive method used to produce images of the brain.[13, 7, 9]

Most of the research on learning disability has been done by cognitive theorists. However, in the past 20 years there has been increased emphasis on neurophysiological functioning of the brain as it relates to learning disability. Studies of the brains of individuals with specific learning disabilities

TABLE 13-1   Characteristics That Affect Motor Performance

Neurophysiological differences
Sensory input processing differences
Problems processing information
Language differences
Memory deficits
Short attention span

have been done using electroencephalography (EEG), auditory brain stem–evoked response (ABER), regional cerebral blood flow (rCBF), and magnetic resonance imaging (MRI). More recently, functional magnetic resonance imaging (fMRI) has been used to examine brain functioning. Unlike a mere image of the brain that is produced with MRI, the fMRI produces a movie of the brain.[9] The fMRI is a safe and noninvasive method to help researchers monitor brain activity. The purpose of this research is to determine whether any significant differences exist between the brain structure and function of individuals with and without learning disabilities. Some differences have been reported.

Kim, Relkin, Lee, and Hirsch[26] used fMRI to better understand acquisition of native versus second language learning in adults and children. Researchers have also reported significant differences in regions of blood flow,[9] parietal dysfunction affecting acquisition of math processing tasks,[33] and disrupted neural activity during reading tasks.[36] Neurophysiological tools such as these show great promise for the early identification of children with specific learning disabilities. Once unique brain structure and function profiles are identified and correlated directly to specific learning difficulties, it will be possible to develop educational intervention strategies specific to each child's needs.

SENSORY INPUT PROCESSING DIFFERENCES

An analysis of neurological building blocks important to skilled motor performances indicates that exteroceptors (e.g., eyes, ears, and tactile receptors) and proprioceptors (e.g., vestibular and kinesthetic receptors) are important avenues for receiving information from the environment. Deficits in receiving and processing information from these senses may result in deficits in the performance of physical activities.[1]

There is strong evidence that persons with learning disabilities may be impaired in their ability to balance.[23] Good balance depends on accurate information from the vestibular system as well as normal reflex and visual depth perception development. When vestibular information is not received or processed efficiently, impaired balance results. In addition, persisting primitive reflexes and a delay in the development of postural (equilibrium) reflexes also inhibit a person's ability to achieve and maintain balance. Visual depth perception deficiencies interfere with the ability to use visual cues in the environment to assist in balancing. Impaired balance interferes with postural and locomotor efficiency as well as foot–eye and hand–eye coordination.

Children with learning disabilities also may possess deficits in kinesthetic perception (an awareness and control of body parts in space). Recent literature that points out the low muscle tone demonstrated early on by children with learning disabilities supports deficits in kinesthetic perception. When the kinesthetic receptors are not fully functioning, information about precise position and rate of movement of body parts in space does not reach the central nervous system. Kinesthesis is an essential prerequisite for sophisticated, refined sport skills that require precise movements, such as putting a golf ball, shooting a basketball, setting a volleyball, and performing any other movements that require qualitative forces for success. Most physical education activities require kinesthetic perception. Thus, kinesthesis is considered an important prerequisite for movement control, which generalizes to many other physical and sport activities.

Many children who have learning disabilities are uncoordinated and lack control of motor responses. Individuals with poorly developed balance and kinesthetic systems tend to have problems in changing direction or body position. As a result, these individuals commonly have difficulty learning to perform efficient specific sport and motor skills.

There is evidence to suggest that children with learning disabilities may also have developmental coordination disorder (DCD) as a coexisting condition.[24, 27, 8] Jongmans, Smits-Engelsman, and Schoemaker[24] found that children with this comorbidity had perceptual-motor deficits while Tsai, Wu, and Huang[37] reported difficulties with static balance. Iversen et al.[23] suggested that children identified with dyslexia be screened for possible motor difficulties.

PROBLEMS PROCESSING INFORMATION

There is evidence that many persons with learning disabilities differ from their unaffected peers as a result of their inability to process information efficiently.[14, 30] Information processing relates to how one retains and manipulates information—how information is acquired, stored, selected, and then recalled. Children with learning disabilities may have difficulty with their perception of space or they may have a visual or auditory processing disorder.[40]

Individuals with impaired depth perception misjudge where objects are in space. As a result, they descend stairs one at a time, are unable to catch and kick balls, and avoid climbing apparatus. Figure-ground perception involves the ability to distinguish an object from its background. It requires selecting and attending to the appropriate visual cue among a number of other cues that are irrelevant to that task at a particular moment. If the visual object to which the individual is to respond is not well-defined, chances are the motor task will be performed less proficiently than desired. Individuals with poor depth perception almost always demonstrate deficits in visual figure-ground perception.

Another visual characteristic that may be impaired in this population is ocular saccadic abilities, which permit the learner to refix the eye on differing targets accurately and quickly. The ocular saccadic ability is required in sports in which an individual must concentrate on a moving ball as well as a moving target (e.g., in football, when a quarterback throws a ball to a second receiver after seeing that the first potential receiver is covered, and in basketball, when focusing on a rebounding ball and then refocusing vision to find an outlet player to pass to). Any visual deficiency that interferes with visual discrimination needed for the proficient performance of a given sport will impair the performance of that sport.

The auditory mechanism may not be as critical in the performance of sport activity as is the eye; however, an impaired ability to use auditory information may result in performance that is below normative expectations. Some of the sport activities requiring auditory discrimination and perception are dancing and floor routines in gymnastics. Auditory figure-ground discrimination is important to skill proficiency. Anytime there are extraneous auditory sounds, auditory figure-ground perception is needed (e.g., when players participating in a noisy gym must attend closely to hear the coaches' instructions and officials' calls).

Ayres[2] suggests that individuals with learning disabilities may have deficits in motor planning. Eichstaedt and Kalakian[16] describe motor planning as the ability to execute behaviors in a proper sequential order. Sport skill tasks require the integration of discrete component parts in sequence for task success. When learning a motor task, each component part of the skill must be planned and carried out in sequence before the skill can be executed correctly. With practice, the skill becomes a subroutine, which is stored in long-term memory, and motor planning requirements are lessened. However, when learning new skills with component parts that must be sequenced, each component part must be present for the skill to be learned. Individuals with learning disabilities who demonstrate difficulty with motor planning may not have the necessary components (e.g., vestibular, kinesthetic, or visual information) available to them.

LANGUAGE DIFFERENCES

The physical education teacher should recognize individual language usage differences among students with learning disabilities.[15] Such knowledge can be used to modify teaching strategies that involve communication through language. There are at least three language categories: (1) receptive language, (2) expressive language, and (3) inner language.

Receptive language involves the ability to comprehend the meaning associated with language. Deficits in receptive language may be either visual or auditory. Visual deficits are reflected by the inability to organize and interpret visual information appropriately. For example, a child may be unable to interpret facial gestures appropriately. Auditory receptive language deficits may be reflected in a failure to follow directions or an inability to discriminate between sounds.

Expressive language involves the ability to communicate through either audition or the visual mechanism. Auditory deficits are expressed through impaired speech, whereas visual expressive language deficits are writing problems. Problems in visual expressive language are the inability to reproduce simple geometric forms, the persistent reversal of letters, the rotation or inversion of letters, and the reversed sequence of letters.

Inner language processes refers to the ability to transform experience into symbols. This, of course, is dependent on experiences. Inasmuch as young children gain much of their experience with the world through play and motor activity, environmental exploration with the body is an important aspect of the development of inner language.

MEMORY DEFICITS

Many individuals with learning disabilities also have deficits in long-term and short-term memory. Four steps are necessary for learning to occur: (1) a stimulus must be registered in the brain, (2) that stimulus must be maintained while its relevance is determined, (3) the stimulus must be processed in light of material present in long-term memory, and (4) the stimulus must be placed in long-term memory. Thus, deficits in either short-term or long-term memory limit the benefits of prior experiences and practice.

Memory is also a prerequisite for closure, the ability to recognize a visual or an auditory experience when only part is presented. The partial image is compared with complete images that are stored in memory for identification. Visual closure occurs when a baseball player is batting. The batter must make inferences as to where the ball will be when it crosses the plate. If a batter is not able to estimate where the ball will cross the plate, he or she cannot determine

where the bat should be swung. More experienced batters have more comparative images stored in their memory banks; thus, they are better able to estimate the flight of an incoming ball than are less experienced batters.

Individuals with learning disabilities also may be deficient in cue selection. Cue selection is the ability to attend to relevant cues and block out irrelevant stimuli. Individuals with memory, visual, or auditory deficits will not make efficient cue selections.

SHORT ATTENTION SPAN

Approximately 80% of all individuals with specific learning disabilities are estimated to also have some form of attention deficit disorder.[35]

Testing to Determine Motor Functioning Levels

Appropriate tests to use with this population include any instruments that will provide information about the functioning of neurological building blocks (vestibular, kinesthetic, visual efficiency, and reflex development), balance, fine motor control, and visual-motor control. An instrument that can provide several clues about the motor functioning level of this population is the Bruininks-Oseretsky Test of Motor Proficiency-2. Subtests that are helpful for pinpointing possible vestibular, kinesthetic, visual efficiency, bilateral coordination, and physical fitness delays are the gross motor, upper-limb coordination, and visual-motor control sections of the fine motor subtest. Rather than using the subtest scores to determine whether delays exist, it is recommended that the evaluator examine the performance of specific components of the subtests. When Shawn was tested using the Bruininks-Oseretsky test, his performance was as follows:

- He scored at the 6-year, 11-month level on the balance subtest. He balanced for 10 seconds with his eyes open and only 5 seconds with his eyes closed.
- He scored at the 7-year, 11-month level on the bilateral coordination subtest; however, he could not demonstrate any of the tasks requiring him to coordinate movements on the opposite side of the body.
- He scored at the 7-year, 8-month level on the strength subtest. He demonstrated 6 bent-knee push-ups and 6 sit-ups.
- His upper-limb coordination subtest score was at the 10-year, 5-month level, with no areas of concern.
- He scored at the 6-year, 11-month level on the visual-motor control subtest and at the 6-year, 8-month level on the upper-limb speed and dexterity subtest. He erred on all of the tracing mazes tasks and when trying to draw geometric figures.

Teaching Strategies

Regardless of the type of program a physical educator favors, tests should be administered to determine the motor functioning level of the child with a specific learning disability. After areas of deficiency have been identified, activities can be selected to promote development in these problem areas. If appropriate activities are selected and carefully taught, the prognosis for the motor development of these students is quite good.

General points to keep in mind when working with these students follow:

- Whenever possible, use a New Games approach that accommodates a wide range of motor competency, so that students' self-concepts are enhanced rather than demoralized by failure to contribute.
- Use a positive behavior management program to get students to finish tasks (e.g., use tokens or let them select their favorite activity once each day if they stay on task).

- Give brief instructions and ask the children to repeat those instructions before starting an activity. Doing this prevents problems that arise from the limited memory some of the children demonstrate.
- To enhance the children's opportunities for success and willingness to persist at tasks, break tasks into small learning steps and praise every legitimate effort they make.
- Help students define their learning goals and determine how to monitor their progress.[31]

See **Table 13-2.**

THE PHYSICAL EDUCATION PROGRAM

It is critical that learning disabled students' participation be limited in group activities that are beyond their capabilities. Such practices only reinforce their feelings of inferiority. When including these students with the regular physical education class, the more activities that use an individualized approach that enables each student to work at his or her level without being compared with peers, the better will be the students' opportunity to realize some success. At the elementary school level, activities should promote development of the neurological building blocks before concentrating on perceptual-motor integration or motor output behaviors. The greatest amount of carryover will occur if educators "fill in the blanks" of missing building blocks and perceptual components before teaching motor output behaviors. At the middle and high school levels, programs should encourage and reward individual effort. Examples are changing the way games are played to accommodate a variety of performance capabilities and having personal fitness programs that are specifically patterned to affect an individual's present level of performance.

TABLE 13-2 Teaching Strategies

Use a New Games approach.
Use positive behavior management.
Give brief instructions.
Break tasks into small steps.
Help students define learning goals.[31]
Teach students how to monitor their progress.[31]

When providing small-group or whole-class programs for students with specific learning disabilities, it is easier to focus on their particular needs. However, there is controversy among physical educators as to whether a bottom-up developmental approach or a task-specific, top-down approach should be used in the instruction of motor skills for students with learning disabilities. A bottom-up approach to facilitate movement efficiency would begin with sensory stimulation activities to provide prerequisite components for meaningful, culturally relevant skills. With such an approach, there would be extended periods during which students were engaging in specific activities to facilitate basic sensory and reflex systems. Once the basic sensory and reflex systems were functioning, and those stimuli were integrated, perceptual-motor development as well as learning of specific motor skills would occur. Admittedly, the number of components of sensory input systems as well as perceptual-motor functions is considerable. All of the senses, the integration of each of the senses, the perceptual-motor characteristics of the individual, the way in which information is processed, and associative and organizational structures of perceptual skills that can be linked with each of the sensory modes are taken into consideration. Effective use of this approach requires extensive knowledge on the part of the teacher and the willingness to delay instruction in what many consider culturally relevant skills.

The top-down approach to facilitating movement efficiency would start with the culturally relevant skills and work down toward prerequisite components when it became apparent a learner was not benefiting from direct instruction of a specific task. Which approach to use can be determined through thorough evaluation and interpretation of results. When evaluation results clearly indicate no sensory or reflex deficits, the most economical method would be the top-down approach. Also, the older the learner, the less appealing the bottom-up approach is.

MODIFICATIONS

Teaching and program modifications that are helpful for students with specific learning disabilities include the following:

- *Control attention.* One of the methods for controlling attention is to establish routines that are repeated day after day. This enables the child to develop a pattern of activities. The teaching techniques, behavior modification program, and organizational patterns should be kept as structured and consistent as possible.

- *Control extraneous stimuli in the environment.* In addition to stable routines, the environment should appear relatively the same from one day to the next. Positioning of equipment and systematic procedures to store equipment should be established and maintained.
- *Control of desired behaviors.* There should be instructionally relevant stimuli to focus students' attention (e.g., designate specific spots on the floor where students are to begin class each day). Visual cues can indicate where the hands are to be placed for a push-up or a forward roll. Specific visual or auditory information can be introduced that indicates to the individual specifically what to do with body parts to enhance motor control.

- *Control methodology.* If the learner has a tendency to disassociate visually or auditorily, use the whole-part-whole method of teaching. Later, attention to details of performance can be emphasized.
- *Use more than one sensory modality.* In addition to verbally describing the task to be performed, use visual stimuli (e.g., a picture, drawing, or demonstration). In this way, if the learning disabled student has either visual or verbal deficits, another sensory avenue can be used to comprehend the instruction. Kinesthetic aids, such as manually moving a child through sequences, can also be used.

SUMMARY

Specific learning disability is a condition that is manifested through disabilities in listening, thinking, writing, speaking, spelling, and mathematical calculations. The majority of children with this disability also demonstrate soft neurological signs early. Frequently, these soft neurological signs are later expressed in delayed motor development. In addition to addressing the specific types of academic subject delays these students demonstrate, physical educators must determine and correct physical and motor delays. To determine what types of delays these students are experiencing, testing must be done. Selected parts of the long form of the Bruininks-Oseretsky Test of Motor Proficiency-2 can be used to identify areas of concern. When including this type of student in the regular physical education class, either select activities that will be of benefit to them and to their classmates or allow for individualized programs for all students. When dealing with students with specific learning disabilities, there are two types of programs that will benefit them: (1) a bottom-up approach that focuses on facilitating deficit sensory input and reflex systems is appropriate for younger children, and (2) a top-down, skill-development approach that focuses on instruction in specific performance tasks that are available in the community is critical for middle and high school students. During the school years, every effort should be made to address the academic, motor, and life skills these individuals require to attain independence and cope in the community.

REVIEW QUESTIONS

1. What is meant by the term *specific learning disability?*
2. What are the cognitive, affective, and motor characteristics of individuals with specific learning disabilities?
3. What teaching strategies could a physical educator use to promote attending behavior of the student with specific learning disabilities?
4. What activities could a physical educator include in an elementary physical education class that would benefit both the students with learning disabilities and those without?
5. What types of information are helpful to the young adult with specific learning disabilities who is trying to cope in the community?

REFERENCES

1. American Academy of Child & Adolescent Psychiatry. (2013). *Children with learning disorders.* Retrieved from www.aacap.org
2. Ayres, A. J. (1980). *Sensory integration and the child.* Los Angeles: Western Psychological Services.
3. Ayres, A. J. (1972). *Sensory integration and learning disorders.* Los Angeles: Western Psychological Services.
4. Berman, S., Cicchino, N., Hajinazarian, A., Mescher, M., Holland, S., & Horowitz-Kraus, T. (2014, January). An fMRI study of a dyslexia biomarker. *Journal of Young Investigators,* www.jyi.org
5. Brain Gym International. *A chronology of annotated research study summaries in the field of educational kinesiology.* Ventura, CA: The Educational Kinesiology Foundation, www.braingym.org

6. Cavendish, W. (2013). Identification of learning disabilities: Implications of proposed DSM-5 criteria for school-based assessment. *Journal of Learning Disabilities, 46*(1), 52–57. DOI: 10.1177/0022219412464352.

7. Center for the Study of Learning, Georgetown Medical Center. *What is functional magnetic resonance imaging?* Retrieved from www.csl.georgetown.edu

8. Cermak, S., & Larkin, D. (2002). *Developmental coordination disorder.* Albany, NY: Thomson Delmar Learning, Inc.

9. Clay, R. (2007). *Functional magnetic resonance imaging: A new research tool.* Washington, DC: American Psychological Association.

10. Council for Exceptional Children. (2007). *A primer on the IDEA 2004 regulations.* Retrieved from http://www.cec.sped.org/AM

11. Dennison, P., & Hargrove, G. (1985). *Personalized whole brain integration.* Glendale, CA: Edu-Kinesthetics.

12. deQuiros, J. B., & Schrager, O. L. (1979). *Neuropsychological fundamentals in learning disabilities.* Novato, CA: Academic Therapy.

13. Devlin, H. (2013). *What is functional magnetic resonance imaging (fMRI).* FMRIB, Department of Clinical Neurology, University of Oxford, www.psychcentral.com

14. American Psychiatric Association (APA). (2013). Specific learning disabilities *Diagnostic and statistical manual of mental disorders,* 5th edition (*DSM-5*). Arlington, VA: American Psychiatric Publishing.

15. Dunn, J., & Leitschuh, C. (2014). *Special physical education.* Dubuque, IA: Kendall Hunt Publishing.

16. Eichstaedt, C. B., & Kalakian, L. H. (1987). *Developmental/adapted physical education.* New York: Macmillan.

17. Ellemberg, D., & St-Louis-Deschenes, M. (2010). The effect of acute physical exercise on cognitive function during development. *Psychology of Sport and Exercise, 11*(2), 122–126.

18. Federal Register. (2006, August). Individuals with Disabilities Education Improvement Act (IDEIA), 34 CFR 300.307.

19. Fletcher, J., Lyon, R., Fuchs, L., & Barnes, M. (2007). *Learning disabilities: From identification to intervention.* New York: Guilford Press.

20. Frostig, M., & Maslow, P. (1970). *Movement education: Theory and practice.* Chicago: Follett.

21. Haapala, E., Poikkeus, A., Tompuri, T., Kukkonen-Harjula, K., Leppänen, P., Lindi, V., & Lakka, V. (2013). Associations of motor and cardiovascular performance with academic skills in children. *Medicine & Science in Sports & Exercise, 1.* DOI: 10.1249/MSS.0000000000000186.

22. Idan, O., & Margalit, M. (2014). Socioemotional self-perceptions, family climate, and hopeful thinking among students with learning disabilities and typically achieving students from the same classes. *Journal of Learning Disabilities, 47*(2), 136–152. DOI: 10.1177/0022219412439608.

23. Iverson, S., Berg, K., Ellertsen, B., & Tonnessen, F. (2005). Motor coordination difficulties in a municipality group and in a clinical sample of poor readers. *Dyslexia, 11,* 217–231. DOI: 10.1002/dys.297.

24. Jongmans, M., Smits-Engelsman, B., & Schoemaker, M. (2003). Consequences of comorbidity of developmental coordination disorders and learning disabilities for severity and pattern of perceptual-motor dysfunction. *Journal of Learning Disabilities, 36*(6), 528–537. DOI: 10.1177/00222194030360060401.

25. Kephart, N. (1971). *The slow learner in the classroom.* Columbus, OH: Charles E. Merrill.

26. Kim, K., Redkin, N., Lee, K., & Hirsch, J. (1997). Distinct cortical areas associated with native and second languages. *Nature, 388*(6638), 171–174. DOI: 10.1038/40623.

27. Kirby, A., & Sugden, D. (2007). Children with developmental coordination disorder. *Journal of the Royal Society of Medicine, 100*(4), 182–186. DOI: 10.1258/jrsm.100.4.182.

28. Lavay, B. (2011). Specific learning disabilities. In Winnick, J. (Ed.), *Adapted physical education and sport* (5th ed.). Champaign, IL: Human Kinetics.

29. May-Benson, T. A., & Koomar, J. (2010). Systematic review of the research evidence examining the effectiveness of interventions using a sensory integrative approach for children. *American Journal of Occupational Therapy, 64*(3), 403–414. www.ajot.aota.org

30. National Center for Learning Disabilities. (2014). *The state of learning disabilities* (3rd ed.). www.ld.org

31. National Research Council. (2005). *How students learn.* Washington, DC: Academic Press.

32. O'Connor, R., Bocian, K., Sanchez, V., & Beach, K. (2014). Access to a responsiveness to intervention model: Does beginning intervention in kindergarten matter? *Journal of Learning Disabilities, 47*(4), 307–328. DOI: 10.1177/0022219412459354.

33. Price, G., Halloway, I., Rasanen, P., Vesterinen, M., & Ansari, D. (2007). Impaired parietal magnitude processing in developmental dyscalculia. *Current Biology, 17*(24), 1042–1043.

34. Rose, C., Espelage, D., Monda-Amaya, L., Shogren, K., & Aragon, S. (2015). Bullying and middle school students with and without specific learning disabilities: An examination of social-ecological predictors. *Journal of Learning Disabilities, 48*(3), 239–254. DOI: 10.1177/0022219413496279.

35. Silver, L. (2006). *The misunderstood child: Understanding and coping with your child's learning disabilities* (4th ed.). New York: Three Rivers Press.

36. Temple, E., Poldrack, R., Salidis, J., Deutsch, G., Tallal, P., Merzenich, M., & Gabrieli, E. (2000). Disrupted neural responses in phonological and orthographic processing in dyslexic children: An fMRI study. *NeuroReport, 12*(2), 299–307.

37. Tsai, C., Wu, S., & Huang, C. (2008). Static balance in children with developmental coordination disorder. *Human Movement Science, 27*(1), 142–153. DOI: 10.1016/j.humoov.2007.08.002.

38. United States Department of Education, Office of Special Education Programs. (2006). *Building the legacy: IDEIA 2004, Identification of specific learning disabilities.* www.ed.gov

39. United States Department of Education, Office of Special Education and Rehabilitative Services. (2014). *Thirty-sixth annual report to Congress on the implementation of the Individuals with Disabilities Education Act.* Washington, DC.

40. University of Michigan Health System. (2012). *Your child: Learning disabilities.* Retrieved from www.med.umich.edu

CHAPTER 14

Emotional Disturbance

OBJECTIVES

- Explain the mental health crisis in this country and the role of the schools in prevention and remediation.
- Describe the two major categories of mental health disorders.
- Briefly describe the effect of urbanization on mental health.
- Describe the behaviors of children with early onset depression.
- List the behaviors of a child/adolescent that are warning signals related to suicide.
- Briefly describe some of the indicators in the education setting that a child is struggling with a mental health disorder.
- Explain developmentally appropriate physical education programs for learners with mental health disorders.

Over one-third of all new teachers leave the profession in the first 3 years of their careers. Most of these teachers leave because of the frustrations of dealing with inappropriate student behavior. Clearly, the major issue facing educators is emotional disturbances.

Courtesy of Kristi Roth

This chapter will deal with the continuum of emotional disturbance. Least serious, a student may choose to ignore a teacher's directions the morning after her mother "grounded" her for being late for curfew. Most serious and socio-pathological, the student may commit suicide or shoot his classmates and teachers. The physical educator must be prepared to deal with such possibilities and everything in between.

A critical part of teaching all children in this society is the process of creating an emotionally safe physical education program. Lu and Bachanan wrote,

> Given the importance of emotional well-being in students' lives, physical education programs should promote emotional development as a major goal. Building a comprehensive educational plan that includes strategies to address students' emotional needs and that teaches them emotional-regulation skills is a valuable and necessary step in the physical education course-planning process.[21]

Definition of Emotional Disturbance

Emotional disturbance is a mental disorder describing a wide range of behavioral disorders or mental illness conditions. Each condition differs based on characteristics and treatments.[7] The New Freedom Commission on Mental Health, 2003, released a vision statement regarding mental health:

> We envision a future when everyone with a mental illness will recover, a future when mental illnesses can be prevented or cured, a future when mental illnesses are detected early, and a future when everyone with a mental illness at any stage of life has access to effective treatment and supports—essentials for living, working, learning, and participating fully in the community.[30]

The mental health crisis in this country is staggering in its broad and specific impact on individuals, their families, and the society. Many mental disorders begin in childhood or adolescence and many go undiagnosed for several years.[29] Millions of individuals in this society are impacted by mental health disturbances.[30]

New Freedom Commission reported that the social stigma associated with mental illness, a fragmented health care delivery system, significant financial requirements, and unfair private health insurance programs compromise the quality of life for individuals with mental illness.[30]

The goals for a transformed mental health system, outlined by the commission, include: (1) Americans understand that mental health is essential to overall health; (2) mental health care is consumer- and family-driven; (3) disparities in mental health services are eliminated; (4) early mental health screening, assessment, and referral to services are common practice; (5) excellent mental health care is delivered and research is accelerated; and (6) technology is used to access mental health care and information.[30]

Inappropriate social behaviors must be seen within a broad context. The three primary categories that must be considered are (1) behavior, (2) pathology, and (3) ecology.[40] The behavior must be considered in terms of its frequency, intensity, and variety. The pathology, or diagnostic labels (typically associated with educational assessment and special education labels), must be considered as well. As important, the behavior must be considered within the context of the family, community, and society in which the child lives.

Some of the elements defining a specific behavior disorder may be (1) a description of the problem behavior, (2) the setting in which the problem behavior occurs, and (3) the person who regards the behavior as a problem.

The physical educator and other school professionals are faced, increasingly, with a larger society in which the definition of appropriate behavior is not clear. For example, seemingly responsible adults engage in road-rage behaviors they would never demonstrate at work. The same, seemingly responsible adults use language in the locker room they would never use in front of a spouse or their own children. Television and radio programs, videos, and video games are increasingly violent and pornographic.

The school is, very simply, a microcosm of the larger society. Though expectations regarding student behavior were very clear for the teachers in *Little House on the Prairie*, and parents supported teacher decisions regarding behavior, that is simply no longer true within the contemporary public education system. The challenges are overwhelming but must be addressed.

Emotional disturbance is defined in IDEIA Sec 300.7 as follows:

(i) The term means a condition exhibiting one or more of the following characteristics over a long period of time and to a marked degree that adversely affects a child's educational performance:

  (A) An inability to learn that cannot be explained by intellectual, sensory, or health factors.

  (B) An inability to build or maintain satisfactory interpersonal relationships with peers and teachers.

  (C) Inappropriate types of behavior or feelings under normal circumstances.

  (D) A general pervasive mood of unhappiness or depression.

  (E) A tendency to develop physical symptoms or fears associated with personal or school problems.

(ii) The term includes schizophrenia. The term does not apply to children who are socially maladjusted, unless it is determined that they have an emotional disturbance.[7]

It must be understood that federally mandated special education services are available only to students who have been assessed and determined to have a serious emotional disturbance. Students with other disorders may be able to receive support as a result of other federal initiatives—for example, programs designed to prevent truancy—and/or support from school-based counseling, music therapy, and gang reduction programs.

Continuum of Emotional Disorders

Mental health behaviors must be considered on a continuum that ranges from those that are deemed "appropriate" to those that are deemed "inappropriate," or from those that are considered "socially acceptable" to those that are considered "socially unacceptable." Within the broad continuum of mental health disorders is a continuum for each type of disorder. For example, a student may experience significant anxiety (the specific type of disorder) when faced with state-mandated achievement tests; this anxiety is transient and usually ceases after the tests have been completed. On the other end of the continuum, within the category of "anxiety disorders," a student may have school phobia so traumatic that the student must be home-schooled.

Students who find themselves in situations in which there is a significant conflict between the expectations of the professionals in the school system and the expectations of the parents and immediate community struggle to make sense of their reality. One of the problems associated with the classification and identification of behaviors is that the determination of "appropriate" and "acceptable" behavior is situational. A student who is praised and honored in the home for being an active, inquisitive, curious learner who questions adults while seeking information may be perceived as "insolent" by an insecure teacher who expects students to accept the teacher's opinions without question.

Of significant concern is the fact that African American students are overrepresented in special education classes that serve students with emotional or behavioral issues.[9] This overrepresentation is caused by a significant failure to embrace active/interactive learning styles. Essentially, there appears to be a "mismatch" between the cognitive (learning) styles of children from minority cultural groups and the cognitive styles emphasized in the schools. As a result, children may be inappropriately identified as having a mental health issue and may be inappropriately taught, increasing the disorder.[25]

The *situation* is a significant component of the determination of an emotional disorder. The *severity* of the behavior is another important variable. Almost everyone occasionally reacts to stress, fatigue, grief, or uncertainty in ways that might be considered "abnormal" or "inappropriate." For example, a child may act out by destroying her toys after learning her parents are planning to divorce. If the violent, destructive behavior continues, the child may need significant intervention.

Although, typically, a mental health disorder is one in which a specific behavior, or a cluster of behaviors, persists over a period of time, one significant, atypical, antisocial behavior may be an indicator of a significant emotional disorder that may have been unnoticed or undiagnosed. For example, a second-grader who stabs a classmate with a knife in order to join his older brother's gang may never have exhibited this type of antisocial behavior before, yet the nature of the behavior makes it vital for serious consideration to be given to the child's emotional disorder.

Types of Mental Health Disorders

It is important for the physical educator to distinguish carefully between the student who may, occasionally, misbehave and the student who has been diagnosed as having an emotional disorder. As teachers struggle to teach more and more students who do not follow rules, who reject discipline, and who despise authority, the lines between students who exhibit problematic behavior and those who actually have a psychoeducational diagnosis become difficult to distinguish. It is also important for the physical educator to understand that a child with an emotional disorder may exhibit a variety of symptoms over a given period of time that make a specific diagnosis impossible.

During the last few years an attempt has been made to reclassify mental health disorders to enable mental health personnel to better determine appropriate intervention strategies. The two categories decided upon are *internalizing disorders* and *externalizing disorders.* Internalizing disorders are expressed within an individual, disorders that make the person feel bad.[41] Externalizing disorders are expressed overtly, disorders that make others feel bad.[6] The specific types of disorders in each of these categories follows.

Internalizing Disorders

Anxiety disorders
    Generalized anxiety disorder
    Obsessive-compulsive disorder
    Panic disorder
    Posttraumatic stress disorder
    Phobias
Eating disorders
Mood disorders
    Depression
    Bipolar disorder
    Seasonal affective disorder
    Manias

Externalizing Disorders

Attention deficit/hyperactivity disorder (ADHD)
Conduct disorders
    General conduct disorder
    Oppositional defiant disorder

Suicidal behavior
Drug and alcohol use and abuse

INTERNALIZING DISORDERS

Anxiety Disorders

Anxiety disorders cause intense feelings of anxiety and tension when there is no real danger. The symptoms cause significant distress and interfere with daily activities. Children with anxiety disorders usually do anything to avoid situations that provoke anxiety. The physical signs of anxiety are restlessness, irritability, disturbed sleep, muscle aches and pains, gastrointestinal distress, and difficulty concentrating. Anxiety disorders are often accompanied by the symptoms of depression and can lead to chronic anxiety, such as phobia, posttraumatic stress disorder, or panic disorder.

Generalized Anxiety Disorder   Generalized anxiety disorder (GAD) "is characterized by exaggerated worry and tension, often expecting the worst, even when there is no apparent reason for conern."[4] People with this condition tend to worry throughout their waking moments and are unable to turn off their fears. They usually expect the worst, even though there is no reason for concern. One-third of the adults afflicted with GAD had their first symptoms in childhood. Women are twice as likely as men to have the condition.[4]

Obsessive-Compulsive Disorder   Obsessive-compulsive disorder (OCD) is a condition that causes people "to have unwanted and intrusive thoughts (obsessions) they can't stop thinking about, and they feel compelled to repeatedly perform ritualistic behaviors and routines (compulsions) to try and ease their anxiety."[24] Some spend a great deal of time performing rituals, such as hand-washing or counting, in an attempt to rid themselves of unwanted thoughts and feelings. Others are constantly afraid they will do something wrong, such as bring harm to someone or make a foolish statement. Adults are usually aware of their condition; however, children who are obsessive-compulsive do not realize their actions are excessive.[33]

Panic Disorder   Many children experience occasional panic attacks. These are characterized by nausea, abdominal distress, sweating, trembling, shaking, shortness of breath, dizziness, and crying or chest pain/discomfort. Few suffer from panic disorder, which usually originates in childhood and adolescence and is more common among women than men.[5]

Phobias   A phobia is a significant, persistent, yet unrealistic and often debilitating fear of an event, a person, an activity, or an animal/insect. For example, school phobia is a significant, and often overwhelming, fear of going to school. Agoraphobia ("fear of the marketplace" in Greek) is an anxiety disorder characterized by an intense fear of being trapped in a situation in which no help is available, losing control, or doing something embarrassing in the presence of others. Agoraphobia can be brought on by repeated panic attacks and can, ultimately, cause a person to have a significant fear of leaving the home.

Posttraumatic Stress Disorder   Posttraumatic stress disorder is characterized by an overwhelming traumatic event that is re-experienced; this causes intense fear, helplessness, horror, and avoidance of stimuli associated with the trauma.[24] *Posttraumatic stress disorder* used to be a term associated with combat veterans, victims of criminal violence, and people whose lives were significantly affected by such events as September 11, 2001, or the Sandy Hook school shootings of 2012. Increasingly, children living in abusive homes and children who are living in homes within violent communities are demonstrating symptoms associated with posttraumatic stress disorder.

Eating Disorders

Eating disorders include anorexia nervosa, bulimia nervosa, and binge eating. Individuals with anorexia nervosa have an intense fear of gaining weight. As a result, they severely limit their caloric intake. About 95% of the people who have the condition are female, and onset is usually in adolescence.[24]

Individuals with bulimia nervosa have frequent episodes of uncontrolled overeating followed by inappropriate compensatory behavior to prevent weight gain, such as vomiting, purging, or excessive exercise. These individuals, unlike those with anorexia nervosa, usually have a normal weight. The incidence is 1% to 3% of adolescent girls.[24] Individuals with the condition are prone to impulsive behavior, as well as drug and alcohol abuse.

Binge eating is eating excessively and not attempting to rid oneself of the extra calories. It usually occurs after adolescence, and it commonly leads to obesity.[24]

Depression is characteristic of individuals with an eating disorder.[24]

Mood Disorders

Mood disorders are characterized by significant and prolonged moods over which the person has no control. Mood disorders include depression, bipolar disorder, seasonal affective disorder, and manias.

Courtesy of Kristi Roth

Childhood Depression Depression is among the most common of mental health disorders. The World Health Organization estimates that 350 million people worldwide suffer from depression.[22] Increasingly, the Americans who struggle with depression are children.

Childhood depression is a mood disorder that resembles depression in adults but shows up in very different ways in children. Children with depression may appear persistently sad, may no longer enjoy activities they normally enjoyed, or may be agitated or irritable. Depressed children may frequently complain of physical problems, such as headaches and stomachaches, and have frequent absences from school or poor performance in school. They may appear bored or low in energy and have problems concentrating. A major change in eating or sleeping patterns is frequently a sign of depression in children and adolescents.

It appears that child abuse is a causative factor in childhood depression. Prolonged sexual abuse and incest appear to be significant. See **Table 14-1** for symptoms of early onset of depression.

Childhood Bipolar Disorder Bipolar disorder is a serious, debilitating disorder that involves extreme mood swings or highs (mania) and lows (depression). During the manic phase, the individual may be elated, irritable, or hostile. The child may experience inflated self-esteem and may be boastful. The child may be overactive, may experience weight loss because of increased activity, and may not require sleep. In the depressive phase, the individual may be depressed, irritable, or anxious. The child may lack self-confidence and have low self-esteem. The child may focus on the negative and appear hopeless and helpless. The child will experience significant fatigue.[24]

TABLE 14-1 Symptoms of Depression in Children and Adolescents[11]

Loss of interest in activities that previously caused pleasure
Withdrawal from people who had been significant
Irritable mood
Significant weight loss
Sleep disturbance nearly every day
Significant fatigue
Physical symptoms, including headaches and stomachaches
Feelings of worthlessness
Poor self-esteem
Difficulty concentrating and paying attention
Poor school performance
Alcohol and other drug abuse
Thoughts of suicide or death

Seasonal Affective Disorder   Seasonal affective disorder (SAD) is a mood disorder characterized by depression, lack of energy, a tendency to over-sleep, and cravings for starchy or sweet foods during months of the year when there is prolonged limited sunshine. More than half a million people in the United States suffer from SAD, usually during the winter. The condition primarily affects adults over the age of 20 years; however, it has been diagnosed in some children and adolescents.[36]

Manias   *Mania is* a term used to describe an elevated, expansive, or irritable mood that lasts more than 1 week. Additional symptoms include inflated self-esteem, greater talkativeness than usual, racing of thoughts, distractibility, and decreased need for sleep. The condition frequently begins in the teenage years, and it puts these individuals at risk of using poor judgment about people and appropriate behaviors.[3]

EXTERNALIZING DISORDERS

Attention Deficit/Hyperactivity Disorder

Attention deficit/hyperactivity disorder (ADHD) has received increasing attention since being included in the 1999 revision of IDEA. The types of the conditions and suggestions for testing and teaching children with ADHD are fully covered in Chapter 18 of this text.

Conduct Disorders

It is estimated that 2% to 16% of children in the United States have conduct disorder. According to the *Diagnostic and Statistical Manual of Mental Disorders (DSM-5):*

> Conduct disorder is characterized by behavior that violates either the rights of others or major societal norms. To be diagnosed with conduct disorder, the symptoms must cause significant impairment in social, academic or occupational functioning.[2]

> Oppositional defiant disorder consists of a pattern of angry/irritable mood, argumentative/defiant behavior, or vindictiveness lasting at least six months.[2]

There are two basic subtypes of antisocial behavior that must be considered within the school setting. Covert antisocial behavior begins with "minor behaviors," such as lying and cheating. Later the behavior includes stealing, shoplifting, vandalism, fire-setting, and burglary. Overt antisocial behavior begins with early disobedience and defiance. Later the child begins to be involved in more serious aggression—bullying and intimidating.[46] Eventually, the individual is involved in rape, serious assault, or murder.[43] Consideration must be given when the child begins to demonstrate antisocial behaviors. "Early starters" begin demonstrating antisocial behaviors early in elementary school. "Late starters" begin to demonstrate the antisocial behaviors in middle school and high school. Clearly, students who begin demonstrating the behaviors earlier are at more serious risk for long-term participation in, and the escalation of, inappropriate behaviors.[35]

See **Table 14-2** for behaviors of children with conduct disorders and **Table 14-3** for the diagnostic criteria of conduct disorders.

Suicidal Behavior

The World Health Organization has reported that the link between suicide and mental health is well-established in high-income countries. Many happen impulsively due to personal crisis.[49] In the United States, more than 30,000 people commit suicide each year; approximately 1 million deaths by suicide occur worldwide.[31] Suicide is epidemic, particularly

TABLE 14-2   Behaviors of Children with Conduct Disorder[24, 48]

- Lack sensitivity to the feelings of other children
- Act aggressively with little remorse
- Tend to be suspicious
- Believe other children are threatening
- Have difficulty tolerating frustration
- Are impulsive
- Are reckless
- Bully and make threats
- Boys tend to
  - Fight
  - Steal
  - Vandalize
- Girls tend to
  - Lie
  - Engage in prostitution
  - Run away

TABLE 14-3   Diagnostic Criteria of Conduct Disorders[1]

A. A repetitive and persistent pattern of behavior in which the basic rights of others or major age-appropriate societal norms or rules are violated, as manifested by the presence of three (or more) of the following criteria in the past 12 months, with at least one criterion present in the past 6 months:

Aggression to People and Animals

1. Often bullies, threatens, or intimidates others
2. Often initiates physical fights
3. Has used a weapon that can cause serious physical harm to others
4. Has been physically cruel to people
5. Has been physically cruel to animals
6. Has stolen while confronting a victim (e.g., mugging)
7. Has forced someone into sexual activity

TABLE 14-3   Diagnostic Criteria of Conduct Disorders[1] (*Continued*)

Destruction of Property

  8. Has deliberately engaged in fire setting with the intention of causing serious damage

  9. Has deliberately destroyed others' property

Deceitfulness or Theft

10. Has broken into another's house, building, or car

11. Often lies to obtain goods or favors

12. Has stolen items without confronting a victim (e.g., shoplifting)

Serious Violations of Rules

13. Stays out at night despite parental rules, beginning before age 13 years

14. Has run away from home overnight at least twice while living in parent or surrogate home (or once for a lengthy stay)

15. Is often truant from school, beginning before age 13 years

B. The disturbance in behavior causes clinically significant impairment in social, academic, or occupational functioning.

C. If the individual is age 18 years or older, criteria are not met for antisocial personality disorder.

Modified from Phillip W. Long, M.D. *Conduct Disorder.* Internet Mental Health. http://www.mentalhealth.com/home/dx/conduct.html

among adolescents; it is the leading cause of injury and death worldwide.[31] Suicidal behavior includes suicide ideation (serious thoughts about suicide), attempted suicide, and completed suicide. Suicidal behavior also includes plans and actions that appear to be unlikely to be successful;[17] it is believed that these plans and actions are a plea for help. An attempted suicide is an act that is not fatal; this may also be a significant plea for help. See **Table 14-4** for the high-risk factors and behaviors associated with suicide.

Drug and Alcohol Use and Abuse

Illicit drugs for youth include marijuana, methamphetamines, hallucinogens, crack cocaine, heroin, Ecstasy, anabolic steroids, alcohol, and nicotine. Peak use of these drugs by teens in the United States occurred in the 1990s, but, thanks to preventive programs in our schools, use by teenagers is on the decrease. However, because of the negative impact drug usage has on mental health, any use should be of concern to educators.

TABLE 14-4   High-Risk Factors and Behaviors Associated with Suicide

- Talking about suicide
- Previous suicide attempt
- Making detailed suicide plans
- Family history of suicide or affective disorder
- Social isolation
- Depression
- Anxiety, restlessness, and motor agitation
- Significant feelings of guilt, inadequacy, and hopelessness
- Impulsive, hostile personality
- Alcohol or other drug abuse
- Preoccupation with death and dying
- Loss of interest in things in which the person was previously interested
- Calling relatives and friends with whom the person rarely has contact
- Giving away possessions
- Getting one's affairs in order

Alcohol abuse includes the use of any type of alcoholic beverage prior to the legal drinking age. Each year approximately 50,000 eighth-, tenth-, and twelfth-grade youth are surveyed to study drug and alcohol use. According to the 2014 survey, there is a continued decline in alcohol use by eighth, tenth, and twelfth graders since 2009. Nine percent of eighth graders, 23.5% of tenth graders, and 37.4% of twelfth graders reported use of alcohol within a month of the data collection. These percentages in 2009 were 14.9%, 30.4%, and 43.5%, respectively.[27, 28] According to the same survey, the percentage of youth smoking cigarettes has dropped but other forms of tobacco have become popular. Hookah use and e-cigarette use were measured for the first time in 2014. Approximately 8.7% of eighth graders, 16.2% of tenth graders, and 17.1% of twelfth graders reported use of e-cigarettes. Marijuana use remained stable in 2014 and continues to be used more than cigarettes in all three grade levels. The use of prescription drugs, such as Vicodin, has declined but the nonmedical use of stimulants (Adderall and Ritalin) has remained steady.

Each year approximately 5,000 youth under the age of 21 years die as a result of underage drinking. Those who begin drinking during their teen years are at the greatest risk (47%) of developing alcohol dependence at some point in their lives. Compared with other students, the approximately 1 million frequent heavy drinkers have mostly lower grades (D's and F's) and most often pose risks to themselves and others.[14]

According to the National Institute on Drug Abuse, "all drugs that are addicting can activate the brain's pleasure circuit," which is why people enjoy using drugs. Unfortunately, when a person continues to use drugs because he or she enjoys the pleasant feeling the drugs yield, fundamental, long-lasting changes occur in the brain. At some point in time (which varies from person to person), the brain "flips a switch," transforming the drug user into a drug addict who constantly craves more drugs. Obtaining the means to get more drugs becomes the focal point of the addict's life, and other things lose their importance.[45] Youth who use drugs often have co-existing disorders. Among the most common are conduct disorders and mood disorders, particularly depression.[23]

Living in a poor and hazardous environment, experiencing economic hardship, and dealing with parental depression are known to contribute negatively to the mental health of youth; thus, they are attracted to drugs that help them escape from reality.[50] However, it has been reported that youth are less likely to use illicit drugs if they are socially accepted at school and feel that their teachers treat them fairly. Teachers can and do make dramatic differences in students' lives.[34]

Incidence of Emotional Disorders

Because of the significant stigma attached to emotional disorders, the reported incidence is probably significantly lower than the actual number of affected individuals. It is also important to acknowledge the fact that special education services provided for students with mental health disorders are limited to those students who have been identified as having an emotional disturbance.

There has been an ever-increasing incidence of emotional disturbance in children from 3 to 21 years of age served in federally supported programs for individuals with disabilities. In fall 2012, 6.2% of children receiving special education services were those with emotional disturbance; this makes it the sixth most prevalent diagnosis under IDEIA (2004).[26]

The percentages of students with emotional disturbance who are served in particular education settings follow:

General classroom (80% or more):   44%
Separate school: 13%
Separate residential facility: 1.8%
Regular private school: 0.2%
Home/hospital: 1.1%
Correctional facility: 1.7%[26]

Causes of Emotional Disturbance

The causes of emotional disturbance can be understood only within the broad context of the total ecosystem of the individual. The disorders are a function of the interaction of a number of variables:[39]

- Heredity and genetic predisposition
- Biochemical and neurotransmitter imbalance, which may be congenital, appearing in utero and at birth; this may occur as a result of glandular dysfunction and may be adventitious, caused by the use or abuse or alcohol or other drugs
- Low birth weight and decreased head circumference
- Breakdown in the family unit
- Parental mood disorders, particularly in the mother, characterized by withdrawal, depression, or hostility
- Parental conflict
- Parenting difficulties; mental health disorders are particularly linked to abusive families
- Sexual and physical abuse and emotional neglect
- Lack of support by the extended family
- Poverty
- Peer pressure, particularly gang involvement
- Community expectations regarding behavior
- Inappropriate, inflexible teaching strategies

Teachers may contribute to emotional disturbance in the schools by discriminating against the students and criticizing them in a harsh manner.

Characteristics of Learners with Emotional Disturbance

Learners with emotional disturbance constitute a very heterogeneous group and struggle within the school setting. Disruptive and antisocial learners, in particular, are excluded from school groups and find it difficult to maintain friendships. The physical educator must work closely with the learners' parents, the school counselor, and the learners' primary educators within the school building. This is critical in order to learn each student's specific characteristics.

There is considerable evidence that children and youth with emotional disturbance have educational difficulties:[47, 10]

- Many children and youth with emotional disturbance receive inappropriate educational, social, and medical services; as a result, families make tremendous financial sacrifices to secure needed services for their children.
- Most students who have been diagnosed with an emotional disorder have lower grade point averages than their classmates.
- Many students have learning disabilities, not to be confused with problems with learning.
- Suspensions of students with emotional disturbance are high, even though children with emotional disturbance constitute less than 7% of all students receiving special education.
- These students have an increased likelihood to fail at least one high school course.
- Children and youth with mental health disorders are more likely to grow up to be underemployed, involved in criminal behavior, and to abuse substances.

When children and youth are struggling with emotional disturbance issues, the physical education teacher may be one of the first to notice the signs that a student is in trouble and needs help. The very nature of a physical education class—with a great deal of movement, excitement, and noise and the need to work as part of a team—makes some mental health disorders more evident than they would be if a learner were just sitting at a desk. The physical educator should be sensitive to the following indications that a student is having difficulty learning:

1. Poor work habits in practicing and developing motor skills
2. Lack of motivation in achieving goals not of an immediate nature

3. Disruptive class behavior
4. Lack of involvement in class activities
5. Inability to follow directions, daydreaming
6. Demands for constant attention of teacher and other students
7. Short attention span, distractibility
8. Poor coordination
9. Development of physical symptoms (stomachache, headache, etc.) when confronted with physical activities with which the person is not secure
10. Overactive, restlessness
11. Forgetfulness, memory impairment

Difficulty developing and maintaining quality personal relationships with the teacher or other students often makes the physical education experience a devastating one for learners with emotional disturbance. Indicators that a student is having difficulty with interpersonal relationships include the following:

1. Lack of conscience, hostile disobedience, resistance to authority
2. Loss of emotional control, temper tantrums
3. Formation of superficial relationships, if relationships are formed
4. Shyness, hypersensitivity, detachment, poor self-esteem, feelings of inadequacy
5. Aggressiveness, hostility, destructiveness, quarrelsomeness
6. Group values of delinquency
7. Fear, anxiety, apprehension of teachers and other students
8. Disrespect of others

The learner may demonstrate inappropriate behavior under "typical" conditions in the physical education class:

1. Unhappiness, depression
2. Inconsistencies in responses
3. Rigid expectations of everyday life
4. Carelessness, irresponsibility, apathy
5. Immaturity, impulsiveness
6. Tendency to seek retribution
7. Unreasonable expectations regarding own behavior

8. Incorrigibility
9. Tendency to attribute hostile intentions to the conduct of others

The learner with emotional disturbance may also demonstrate poor motor behavior in physical education:

1. Poor physical condition caused by withdrawal from activity
2. Retardation of motor skill development caused by withdrawal from activity
3. Disorientation in space and time
4. Poor body image

A Supportive Learning Environment for Children with Emotional Disturbance

School administrators and teachers must face the realities that exist in the public schools today. Clearly, the public schools mirror the increasing violence and unpredictability within the society. The "zero tolerance" response to violence in schools, while a good first step, is not adequate. Skiba and Peterson wrote that "a broader perspective, stressing early identification, comprehensive planning, prevention, and instruction in important social skills, is necessary if schools are to prevent the tragedies that happen too often in our schools."[37] School personnel must be involved in long-range planning and must emphasize partnerships among the school, family members, and the community.[37] Clearly, communities have a vested interest in schools' prevention and remediation programs because there is a relationship between a child's in-school disciplinary problems and juvenile offenses within the community.[40]

Special Considerations

The school should offer a variety of intervention strategies to address emotional disturbances, particularly antisocial behavior, in the school. The most basic of the interventions is "universal," a prevention-based approach. The interventions include a school-wide discipline program and a school curriculum that emphasizes the development of conflict resolution and anger management skills.[40] Individualized interventions designed for one learner or for a small group of learners in a self-contained classroom or small-group therapy setting are required for learners who already demonstrate inappropriate, asocial behavior.

One of the major problems associated with the education of students with an emotional disturbance is the stigma. Individuals who struggle with emotional disorders and their families may feel stigmatized and rejected and, in fact, may be stigmatized and rejected.[13] Unfortunately, this stigma often causes families to avoid seeking professional help, so identification of the problem is delayed.

The education of learners with disabilities cannot be seen in a framework outside the family unit. The parent/primary caregiver may be willing to share strategies that work with school administrators, teachers, coaches, and paraeducators. Family management practices are key to the collaboration between the school and the home:

- Many parents/primary caregivers learn how to identify problematic behavior and track occurrences of the behavior at home.
- To survive, parents/caregivers learn to use reinforcement techniques, such as praise, point systems, and rewards.
- Effective parents learn to use a "mild" consequence for inappropriate behavior, such as a 1-hour loss of screen time.
- Effective caregivers use strategies to communicate clearly with their child. They learn to use "alpha" commands or instructions instead of "beta" commands. An alpha command is clear, specific, and direct and allows the child a limited time to respond. A "beta" command or instruction is one that is vague and conveys only frustration and anger. For example, if a parent wants the child to put toys away, an alpha command is "William, put your toys in the closet." A beta command, however, is "William, I've had a really long day. And I need some cooperation around the house. I can't be expected to work all day and worry about dinner and then come home and find the house is a mess. The least you could do is put away your toys."

The physical educator should be aware that many children with an emotional disturbance take medication that affects their performance during the school day. It is critical that the physical educator know what medications a student is taking, particularly because some inhibit motor control and have a negative impact on balance, for example.

Most parents are thrilled if the physical educator takes enough interest in the student to ask for specific information about a medication. A physician will not release information about medication—or anything else, for that matter—to a teacher without signed parental permission. Most state education agencies have a standard form to request a release of information from a physician. The physical educator can ask the school nurse to complete such a request.

Psychological tests are required to establish the presence of an emotional disturbance. However, the psychological data and the labels associated with the data often do not provide specific information to assist the physical education teacher in planning instruction. The physical educator should work closely with the child's special education teachers, counselors, and family members to plan and modify instruction. If at all possible, the physical educator should adopt the instructional techniques and behavior management strategies used during the rest of the child's instructional day. This type of consistency is critical to the success of a student with an emotional disturbance. This will be considered more completely later in this chapter.

Specific ways the physical educator can collaborate with other professionals who work with the student as well as the student's individualized education program (IEP) team are as follows:

- Share information about the student's physical and motor needs.
- Listen to and act on relevant suggestions made by parents and other professionals.
- Share materials and ideas with individuals working with the student.
- Solicit support from parents and colleagues that contributes to the effectiveness of the physical education program.
- Use resource personnel effectively.[19]

Testing

The student with an emotional disturbance is typically able to participate in any state or local education agency-mandated physical fitness, motor, sport skill, or knowledge assessments regarding rules, techniques, and health and wellness concepts. Decisions regarding who will administer such tests are often left to the IEP or multidisciplinary team and may be a function of the placement of the student in general or adapted physical education.

FitnessGram and SHAPE America's Physical Best have been used to assess fitness skill with a wide variety of students and are typically appropriate for a child with an emotional disturbance. If the student has been identified as having a motor skill deficit, the choice of assessment instruments is determined primarily by the student's age. The Test of Gross Motor Development-2 may be very appropriate for an elementary-school-age student with an emotional disturbance. The Louisiana Competency Test for Adapted Physical Education may be very useful for a student in middle school or high school.

When testing students who have an emotional disturbance, the teacher must be sensitive to the fact that these students may feel extremely threatened by test situations. When placed in threatening situations, more acting-out behavior can be expected. Aggressive or withdrawal behavior can be avoided if the student does not have to perform in the presence of peers and if the teacher is supportive of the student's efforts. It is usually advisable, if testing a student with a serious disorder, to include the student's favorite teacher or a significant peer in the testing situation.

Teaching Strategies

The children who need great teachers the most may be the very children who are the most difficult to teach. The teacher of a child who has an emotional

disturbance must be grounded, self-assured, confident, patient, and competent. The teacher must be able to see the student's behavior within the broader context of an emotional disturbance and not respond to inappropriate behavior as if it were directed toward the teacher. The teacher's ability to separate self from inappropriate student behavior is critical. See **Table 14-5** for specific strategies of behavior management for the physical educator.

TABLE 14-5   Behavior Management: Learners with Emotional Disturbance[44]

- Effective intervention must duplicate the strategies used in other phases of the learner's life—school, home, recreation center, and/or work environment. This is crucial, so that the individual has consistent feedback and reinforcement.
- Teachers need to be well grounded and self-assured. Learners with mental health disorders often "push the buttons" of perceived authority figures. The teacher must be secure enough to understand that inappropriate emotions/behaviors are not directed at him or her. These behaviors include but are not limited to
  - Absolute rejection of the authority figure
  - Conflicting demands; one minute the learner may be clingy, demand constant attention, and seek affection and the next moment he or she may be shouting, "I hate you"
  - Temper tantrums, rages, and outbursts
  - Unpredictable changes in emotions and moods
  - Physical and/or verbal aggression
  - Significant withdrawal
  - Negativism, noncompliance, and refusal behaviors
  - Impulsiveness
  - Destruction of equipment and materials
- The limits and expectations regarding behavior must be clearly defined.
- Rules need to be posted in simple language or symbols or pictures. The learners need to be reminded daily of the rules and consequences if that behavior is not followed.
- Positive behavior and its positive consequences must be made clear; always "catch 'em being good" and reward the appropriate behavior.
- The minimum amount of reinforcement should be used to encourage appropriate behavior:
  - Smiles
  - Verbal praise
  - Verbal praise with a sign—"thumbs up"
  - Verbal praise paired with a physical reinforcer: high, medium, low, or behind the back "5"
  - Tangible reinforcers: stickers or praise notes for young learners
  - Primary reinforcers: goldfish or graham crackers
- With older learners, more appropriate reinforcers may be
  - Choice of activity
  - "Free time"
  - Choice of music to listen to in the background (careful screening is important)

(continues)

TABLE 14-5   Behavior Management: Learners with Emotional Disturbance[44] (*Continued*)

- Baseball or football cards
  - Sports posters
  - Slice of pizza
  - "Alone with me" time—teacher commits to time spent with the learner, shooting baskets or swimming laps together
- Inappropriate behavior and its negative consequences must be clear. The learner must be reminded that the behavior and consequence is a choice. The consequence must always occur and it must be explained to link cause-effect—for example, "I'm sorry, Timmy, but you chose to [cite misbehavior]. You know this is the consequence."

The teacher of a child with an emotional disturbance has a tremendous responsibility. The most critical responsibility is for consistent, effective classroom management designed to prevent problems and minimize behaviors that disrupt learning. In fact, many school-based discipline strategies, such as in-school and out-of-school suspensions, may actually be dumping grounds for students whose teachers are unprepared to manage their classroom. In fact, it appears that the practices of suspension and expulsion are associated with negative outcomes, which include poor student attitudes toward school, academic failure, retention in grades, and increased dropout rates.[18]

The principles that guide the teacher of children who have mental health disorders in physical education are, very simply, the *basic principles of good teaching*:

- Carefully model caring, sensitive, adult behavior.
- A gentle, calm, but structured teaching style will promote learning for all students, but particularly for students with mental health disorders.
- Teach so that children with all of Gardner's eight types of intelligence can learn.
- Establish and use a class routine.
- Set, define, and post positively worded rules and expectations that are age-appropriate. Make clear not only the behaviors that are appropriate but those that are inappropriate. (See **Table 14-6** for a brief example of positive gymnasium expectations.)
- Consistently acknowledge and reward appropriate behavior.

TABLE 14-6   Gymnasium Expectations Stated in a Positive Way

1. Raise your hand before speaking.
2. Remain on your spot until advised to leave it.
3. Keep your hands and feet to yourself.
4. Use school-appropriate language.
5. Use equipment as demonstrated.

- Consistently ensure fair and humane consequences for inappropriate behavior. Corporal punishment is not a fair and humane consequence in the public schools.[8]
- Remind the student of the consequences of inappropriate behavior.
- Emphasize cooperative activities.
- Ensure that each student has a designated spot with enough personal space to avoid physical contact with other students.
- Ensure there is a safe space to which a student can retreat for a self-imposed "time-out."
- Have enough equipment, so that young children, in particular, do not have to share equipment.
- Remove distracting objects. Bats, balls, and other play equipment should be kept out of sight until the time of use, if possible.
- Pair children carefully for learning tasks.
- Avoid activities that promote aggressive behavior—wrestling, for example.
- Ask for and use the behavior management plan developed by the student's IEP/multidisciplinary team.
- Select activities that allow all students to experience success.

The Physical Education Program

A developmentally appropriate, well-taught physical education program is critical for learners with emotional disturbance. The potential benefits of a quality physical education are, perhaps, even more important for learners with emotional disturbance than for other children.

It appears that a curriculum that is sensitive to students' interests and allows them to be involved in choices may help prevent acting-out and inappropriate behaviors, particularly in students with emotional disturbance.[16] Team teaching strategies that allow students to choose activities may be very helpful to the physical educator trying to create a good learning environment.

It appears particularly important to provide students the opportunity to participate, daily, in sustained, vigorous aerobic activities.[15] For preschoolers and young elementary school learners, the emphasis should be on simple dance activities, such as "Chug Along Choo Choo," "Bendable Stretchable," tricycling, bicycling, and vigorous, sustained playground activity. For older elementary-age learners, these activities should include walking, jogging, running, cross-country skiing, inline skating, and swimming. Middle and high school students can get the appropriate level of aerobic activity by walking, jogging, running, swimming, stationary cycling, stationary rowing, aerobic dancing, and aquarobics. (See **Table 14-7** for more information on aquatics.)

There is significant evidence that participation in aerobic activities may release endorphins, which improve mood and reduce stress. Exercise programs have been effective in reducing the stereotypical, self-injurious, and disruptive behavior of individuals with severe behavior disorders.[42] There

TABLE 14-7   Aquatics for Learners with Mental Health Disorders[44]

- The aquatics program must be such that the student's success is guaranteed. A careful initial assessment will ensure success. (Please refer to the Texas Woman's University Project INSPIRE Aquatics Web page: www.twu.edu/INSPIRE.)
- Start with "familiar" skills (e.g., walking, running, jumping in the water) and move slowly to unfamiliar skills.
- Create small learning stations or areas for students, so that there are "safe spaces." This can be done with lane lines, for example, or a tethered floating mat.
- From the time students enter the locker room, every minute must be planned and monitored carefully. The locker room is the most potentially volatile situation for these learners. Issues tied to abuse, in its many forms, are more evident in this vulnerable setting. Supervision is crucial.
- With a particularly confrontational student, the best environment may be one in which the learner is over his or her head. It may be easier for the teacher to control behavior if the learner is dependent on the teacher.
- Touch, even for spotting, needs to be explained carefully and done with care. A learner with a history of abuse may misinterpret well-intentioned touch.
- There must be a "fail safe" plan for an emergency—a student "out of control." The lifeguard on deck must be able to contact another teacher or an administrator instantly.

is also evidence that participation in systematic exercise may enhance self-esteem and body image.[12]

It appears there is some promise in the use of relaxation training for students with an emotional disturbance, particularly for students who are aggressive. Progressive muscle relaxation, meditation, yoga, guided imagery, and biofeedback have been found to reduce arousal.[38] Yoga and progressive muscle relaxation training hold particular promise for the physical educator who is teaching children and youth who demonstrate aggressive behavior. Preliminary research indicates that children with an emotional disturbance who exhibit aggressive behavior demonstrate less aggressive behavior after participating in a progressive muscle relaxation program based on Jacobson's work.[20] It also appears that there is significant promise in the use of challenge activities, cooperative, and team-building activities.[32]

Carefully designed instructional physical education programs can play a significant role in the lives of learners with an emotional disturbance. The curricular emphasis should be on aerobic activity, relaxation training, and cooperative, challenge-based activities that encourage effective communication with others. The program must support student efforts in and through consistency and positive behavior management strategies. Perhaps most important, the physical education classroom must be bully-free and safe (see behavior chapter for more specific information regarding creating a bully-free learning environment) and must encourage personal responsibility (see behavior chapter for information about Hellison's model).

Modifications/Adaptations/Inclusion Techniques

One of the major considerations for learners with mental health disorders is the least restrictive environment. For many learners with an emotional disturbance, the regular physical education program would be very restrictive and overwhelming. It is critical that the IEP/multidisciplinary team address the possibility of providing physical education within a self-contained program. There are some benefits to a self-contained placement: (1) a well-structured behavior management system (such as Boys Town); (2) teachers and aides specifically trained in the behavior management system; (3) a relatively small staff–student ratio; and (4) clearly defined physical boundaries, often behind closed, locked doors.[15] This consistency and safety may be extremely important to the education of learners with mental health disorders.

The only safe instructional strategy for including most students with an emotional disturbance in the general physical education program is to have the students work with a carefully trained paraeducator. The practice of assigning "peer tutors" is questionable, at best, for a number of reasons. Clearly, the most significant is that a learner with a mental health disorder is too unpredictable for another child to anticipate and address the learner's behaviors.

A physical educator serving a student with an emotional disturbance must adopt the behavior management plan developed by the IEP/multidisciplinary team. These students need *consistency*. A teacher who just "rolls out the ball" will not be able to serve these children—or others, for that matter.

It is also important that the same behavior management plan be used by all teachers and other school personnel working with the student. For example, the Boys Town curriculum has been adopted by many public schools that serve students with an emotional disturbance. Indeed, the best possible scenario is one in which school personnel and the family use the same strategies. This gives the student the best possible opportunity to succeed.

In many school-based programs for students with an emotional disturbance, the student literally "earns" the right, by demonstrating appropriate behavior, to participate in school programs, such as physical education. The unique characteristics of the physical education program must be discussed with the IEP/multidisciplinary team before any decision is made to include a student with a severe disorder in the physical education environment. Perhaps the major issue in many physical education programs, unfortunately, is large class size. Typically, the student with an emotional disturbance requires a great deal of attention. This is difficult, if not impossible, for the physical educator teaching three or more first-grade classes, for example, simultaneously.

SUMMARY

Increasingly, physical education teachers and other school professionals struggle to teach learners with mental health disorders. It is critical that the physical educator be able to identify the early signs of disorder. The physical education class may be the situation in which the signs are most easily identified. The physical educator must create a carefully designed classroom learning environment in which behavior management is used constructively to enhance learning and promote learners' self-esteem. The emphasis must be on vigorous, aerobic, developmentally appropriate, noncompetitive activity.

REVIEW QUESTIONS

1. What are some signs or symptoms of mental health disorders?
2. What is the impact of urbanization on mental health? What are other causes of mental health disorders?
3. What is a stigma?
4. What are some of the basic techniques the physical educator should use to teach learners with mental health disorders?
5. What should be the emphasis in the physical education curriculum for students with these disorders?
6. Describe the program implications—behavior management and safety—that are critical to learners with mental health disorders.

REFERENCES

1. American Academy of Child & Adolescent Psychiatry. (2013). Conduct disorder. Washington, DC. www.aacap.org
2. American Psychiatric Association. (2013). *Diagnostic and statistical manual of mental disorders* (5th ed.). Arlington, VA: American Psychiatric Publishing.
3. American Psychiatric Association. Mania. Retrieved from www.psch.org
4. Anxiety and Depression Association of America. (2015). Generalized anxiety disorder (GAD). Retrieved from www.adaa.org
5. Anxiety and Depression Association of America. (2015). Panic disorder and agoraphobia. Retrieved from www.adaa.org
6. Beers, M. H., Porter, R.S., Jones, T. V., Kaplan, J. L., & Berkwits, M. (2006). *The Merck manual of diagnosis and therapy*. Whitehouse Station, NJ: Merck Research Laboratories.
7. Center for Parent Information Resources. (2015). Emotional disturbance. Retrieved from www.parentcenterhub.org
8. Corrigan, D. Office of Special Education, Challenges for Personnel Preparation Conference, Washington, DC, September 8–10, 1999.
9. Codrington, J., & Fairchild, H. (2012). Special education and the miseducation of African American children: A call to action. A position paper of the Association of Black Psychologists.
10. Constantine, R. J., Andel, R., Robst, J., & Givens, E. M. (2013). The impact of emotional disturbances on the arrest trajectories of youth as they transition into young adulthood. *Journal of Youth and Adolescence, 42,* 1286–1298. DOI: 10.1007/s10964-013-9974-9.

11. *Early onset depression.* (2004). www.nami.org/helpline/depression-child.html

12. Ekeland, E., Heian, F., & Hagen, K. B. (2005). Can exercise improve self esteem in children and young people? A systematic review of randomized controlled trials. *Br Journal of Sports Medicine, 39,* 792–798. DOI: 10.1136/bjsm.2004.017707.

13. Farmer, E. M. Z., Mustillo, S., Burns, B. J., & Costello, E. J. The epidemiology of mental health programs and service use in youth: Results from the Great Smoky Mountains study. (2005). In Epstein, M. H., Kutash, K., & Duchnowsk, A. (Eds.). *Outcomes for children and youth with behavioral and emotional disorders and their families: Programs and evaluation best practices* (2nd ed.).

14. Hingson, R. W., Hereen, T., & Winter, M. R. (2006). Age at drinking onset and alcohol dependence. *Arch Peds Adol Med, 160*(7), 739–746.

15. Huettig, C., & Pyfer, J. (2002, September). *The role of the adapted physical educator in the mental health crisis.* Corvallis, OR: North American Federation of Adapted Physical Activity.

16. Kern, L., Bambara, L., & Fogt, J. (2002). Class-wide curricular modification to improve the behavior of students with emotional or behavioral disorders. *Behavioral Disorders, 27*(4), 317–326.

17. Lambert, M. T. (2003). Suicide risk assessment and management: Focus on personality disorders. *Current Opinion Psychiatry, 16*(l), 71–76, http://www.medscape.com/viewarticle/447415_print (pp. 1–7 online)

18. Lee, T., Cornell, D., Gregory, A., & Fan, X. (2011). High suspension schools and dropout rates for black and white students. *Education and Treatment of Children, 34,* 167–192.

19. Lieberman, L. (2007). *Paraeducators in physical education: A training guide to roles and responsibilities.* Champaign, IL: Human Kinetics.

20. Lopata, C. (2003). Progressive muscle relaxation and aggression among elementary students with emotional or behavioral disorders. *Behavioral Disorders, 28*(2), 162–172.

21. Lu, C., & Buchanan, A. (2014). Developing students' emotional well-being in physical education. *Journal of Physical Education, Recreation and Dance, 85,* 28–33.

22. Marcus, M., Yasamy, T, van Ommeren, T., Chisholm, D., & Saxena, S. (2012). Depression: A global public health concern. World Health Organization of Mental Health and Substance Abuse, www.who.int

23. Martin, K. (2007). *Substance-abusing adolescents show ethnic and gender differences in psychiatric disorders.* Bethesda, MD: National Institute on Drug Abuse, http://www.drugabuse.gov/NIDA_ notes/ NNVoll8Nl/Substance.html

24. Merck Manuals Professional Edition. *Posttraumatic stress disorder.* Retrieved from www.merckmanuals.com

25. Morgan, H. (2010). Improving schooling for cultural minorities: The right teaching styles can make a big difference. *Educational Horizons, 88,* 114–120.

26. National Center for Educational Statistics. (2014). Digest of education statistics. Retrieved from http://nces.ed.gov

27. National Institute on Drug Abuse. (2014). High school and youth trends. National Institutes of Health (NIH).

28. National Institute on Drug Abuse. (2014). Monitoring the future survey results. National Institutes of Health (NIH).

29. National Institute of Mental Health (NIMH). (2010). *Child and adolescent mental health.* Available online at http://www.nimh.nih/health/topics/child-and-adolescent-mental-health/index.shtml

30. New Freedom Commission on Mental Health. (2003). http://www.mentalhealth commission.gov/reports/FinalReport/FullReport.htm

31. Nock, M., Borges, G., Bromet, E., Cha, C., Kessler, R., & Lee, S. (2008). Suicide and suicidal behavior. *Epidemiologic Review, 30,* 133–154. DOI: 10.1093/epirev /mxn002.

32. Pierangelo, R., & Giuliani, G. (2008). *Classroom management for students with emotional and behavioral disorders: A step by step guide of educators.* Thousand Oaks, CA: Corwin Press.

33. Przeworski, A. (2012). Mothers critical of their kids with OCD. *Child Psychiatry & Human Development, 43,* 337–353.

34. Resnick, M. D., Bearman, P. S., & Blum, R. W. (1997). Protecting adolescents from harm. *J of American Medical Association, 278*(10), 823–832.

35. Schubert, C. A., & Mulvey, E. P. (2014). Behavioral and health problems, treatment, and outcomes in serious youthful offenders. *Juvenile Justice Bulletin,* U.S. Department of Justice, Office of Juvenile Justice and Delinquency Prevention.

36. *Seasonal affective disorder.* (2007). Retrieved from http://familydoctor.org /online/famdocen/home/common/mentalhealgth/depression

37. Skiba, R., & Peterson, R. (2000). School discipline at a crossroads: From zero tolerance to early response. *Exceptional Children, 66*(3), 335–347.

38. Smith, C., Hancock, H., Blake-Mortimer, J., & Eckert, K. (2007). A randomized comparative trial of yoga and relaxation to reduce stress and anxiety. *Complementary Therapies in Medicine, 15,* 77–83. DOI: 10.1016/j.ctim.2006.05.001.

39. Smith, D. D. (2007). Emotional and behavioral disorders. In *Introduction to Special Education.* New York: Pearson Education, Inc.

40. Sprague, J., & Walker, H. (2000). Early identification and intervention for youth with antisocial and violent behavior. *Except Child, 66*(3), 367–379.

41. Tandon, M., Cardeli, E., & Luby, J. (2009). Internalizing disorders in early childhood: A review of depressive and anxiety disorders. *Child and Adolescent Psychiatry Clinics of North America, 18,* 593–610. DOI: 10.1016/j.chc.2009.03.004.

42. Tartakovsky, M. (2015). Helping your child reduce self-harming behavior. *PsychCentral.* www.psychcentral.com

43. Tatem-Kelly, B., Loeber, R., Keenan, K., & DeLamatre, M. (1997). Developmental pathways in boys' disruptive and delinquent behavior. *Juvenile Justice Bulletin.*

44. Texas Woman's University Project INSPIRE Web page. (2003). www.twu .edu/inspire

45. *The science behind drug abuse.* (2007). Bethesda, MD: National Institute on Drug Abuse, http://teens.drugabuse.gov/mom/tg_effects.asp

46. Tompsett, C., & Toro, P. (2010). Predicting overt and covert antisocial behaviors: Parents, peers and homelessness. *Journal of Community Psychology, 38,* 469–485. DOI: 10.1002/jcop.20375.

47. Wagner, M., Friend, M., Bursuck, W., Kutash, K., Duchnowski, A., Sumi, C., & Epstein, M. (2006). Educating students with emotional disturbances: A national perspective on school programs and services. *Journal of Emotional and Behavioral Disorders, 14,* 12–30.

48. WebMed Mental Health Center. (2015). Mental health and conduct disorder. Retrieved from www.webmed.com

49. World Health Organization. (2014). *Suicide.* Retrieved from www.who.int

50. Zaff, J. F., & Calkins, J. (2007). Background for community-level work on mental health and externalizing disorders in adolescence. *Child Trends.* http://www.childtrends.org/what_works/youth_development

CHAPTER 15

Physically Disabling Conditions

OBJECTIVES

- Describe at least one physically disabling condition that is representative of each of the three categories in this chapter.
- Describe the types of spina bifida and the types of physical education program modifications required of each.
- Describe how to modify three physical education activities to include a student using a wheelchair.
- Give three examples of principles for adapting physical activity to accommodate persons with physical disabilities.

There are many different types of physically disabling conditions. Physical impairments can occur at more than 500 anatomical sites. Each person who has a disabling condition has different physical and motor capabilities. Thus, each person must be treated in such a manner that his or her unique educational needs are met.

In this chapter we suggest a procedure to accomplish this task. The processes involved in this procedure are to (1) identify the specific clinical condition, (2) identify which activities are contraindicated on the basis of medical recommendations, (3) determine needed functional physical fitness and motor skills, (4) determine the activities that will assist the development of the desired fitness and motor skills, and (5) determine aids and

491

devices that will enable the individual to function in the least restrictive environment.

More than 20 disabilities are discussed in this chapter. Many of these conditions, though differing in cause, result in similar movement limitations. To aid you in focusing on the commonalities across physically disabling conditions, the format of this chapter is slightly different from that of some of the other chapters dealing with specific populations. Under the headings of "Neurological Disorders," "Orthopedic Disabilities," and "Traumatic Injuries," specific conditions are identified and defined, the incidence and cause of each condition are given, the characteristics are delineated, special considerations are discussed, and suggestions for programming and teaching are presented. Following the unique aspects of all of the specific conditions are common testing suggestions, modifications, adaptations, and inclusion techniques.

Definition and Scope of Physically Disabling Conditions

Physical disabilities affect the use of the body as a result of deficiencies of the nerves, muscles, bones, and/or joints. The three main sources of disabilities are neurological impairments, orthopedic (musculoskeletal) disabilities, and traumatic injuries. Neurological disabilities are chronic, debilitating conditions that result from impairments of the central nervous system. The neurological conditions discussed in this chapter are amyotrophic lateral sclerosis, cerebral palsy, epilepsy, multiple sclerosis, muscular dystrophy, Parkinson's disease, poliomyelitis and post-polio syndrome, and spina bifida.

Orthopedic conditions are deformities, diseases, and injuries of the bones and joints. The orthopedic conditions discussed in this chapter are arthritis, arthrogryposis, congenital hip dislocation, coxa plana, Osgood-Schlatter condition, osteogenesis imperfecta, osteomyelitis, spondylolysis, and spondylolisthesis.

Traumatic conditions are the result of damage to muscles, ligaments, tendons, or the nervous system as a result of a blow to the body. Traumatic brain injuries, spinal cord injuries, and amputations are discussed in this chapter.

Because of the number of conditions included in this chapter, case studies have only been developed to be representative of each of the three groups of disabilities. Spina bifida represents the neurological disorder category; juvenile rheumatoid arthritis, the orthopedic disabilities category; and traumatic brain injury, the traumatic injuries section.

NEUROLOGICAL DISORDERS

Amyotrophic Lateral Sclerosis

Amyotrophic lateral sclerosis (ALS) is a progressive and fatal disease of the nerves from the spinal cord to the muscles. Although the number fluctuates, at any given time approximately 20,000 people in the United States can have the disease. The disease is infrequent in school-age populations and is more common for individuals 40–70 years of age, with the median age of onset being 55 years.[4] It affects men two to three times as often as women. Lou Gehrig, the hall-of-fame first baseman of the New York Yankees, who finally missed a game after more than 2,000 successive starts, was forced to retire as a result of the disease. It has since been named Lou Gehrig disease.

Characteristics and Testing   The central features of the disease are atrophy and muscle wasting, resulting in marked weakness in the hands, arms, shoulders, and legs and in generalized weakness. The site of onset is random, and it progresses asymmetrically. Cramps are common, and muscular weakness may cause problems with swallowing, talking, and respiration.[47] Concomitant spinal conditions include ruptured intervertebral disks, spinal cord tumors, and spinal malformations. Manual muscle testing is used to determine the amount of functional strength.

Special Considerations   The drug Rilutek has been shown to prolong survival.[36] The rate of decline of muscular strength varies, with some losing strength quickly, and others more slowly.[7] More than half of those diagnosed with ALS live more than 3 years after the diagnosis has been made.[47]

The Physical Maintenance Program The major goal of the ALS physical activity program is to maintain physical capability as long as possible. There is some anecdotal evidence that exercise that strengthens the healthy muscle fibers permits an individual with ALS to maintain strength and a higher level of function over time. Walking and recumbent cycling daily are recommended for maintaining endurance. Range-of-motion exercises with free weights and the use of weight machines are recommended for maintaining strength.[7] It might also be desirable to focus attention on activities that maintain efficient movement of the body for the activities of daily living. Leisure skills should be taught that have functional use at present or in the near future. The nature of the physical activities will depend on the physical capabilities of the individual at each point in time. The caregiver should be supportive and understanding. Consultation with an occupational therapist should be sought for advice about assistive devices to enable the activities of daily living.

Cerebral Palsy

Cerebral palsy is a condition, rather than a disease. The term *cerebral palsy* is defined as a nonprogressive lesion of the brain before, during, or soon after birth (before age 5 years). The condition is lifelong, impairing voluntary movement. It is one of the most common causes of childhood physical disability and the most frequent cause of severe disabilities in children.[32, 44]

The incidence of cerebral palsy is 1.5 to 4 per 1,000 live births.[11] Although earlier studies indicated that the vast majority of cerebral palsy cases were caused by perinatal factors, such as prolonged labor, instrumental deliveries, and breech births, it is now believed that only 15% of cases result from these causes.[32] Certain groups of infants, including those with prolonged birth anoxia, very low birth weight, and abnormal neurological symptoms, are candidates for cerebral palsy.[47] Children with cerebral palsy possess poor postural adjustment. As a result, simple gross motor movements (e.g., kicking, throwing, and jumping) are difficult to perform effectively.[48]

Characteristics and Types The degree of motor impairment of children with cerebral palsy ranges from serious physical disability to little physical disability. The limbs affected are identified with specific titles:

- Monoplegia involves a single limb.
- Hemiplegia indicates involvement of both limbs on one side, with the arm being more affected than the leg.

- Paraplegia indicates involvement of both legs with little or no involvement of the arms.
- Quadriplegia, or tetraplegia, denotes involvement of all the limbs to a similar degree.
- Diplegia is an intermediate form between paraplegia and quadriplegia, with most involvement being in the legs.

Because the extent of the brain damage that results in neuromotor dysfunction varies greatly, diagnosis is related to the amount of dysfunction and associated motor involvement. Severe brain injury may be evident shortly after birth. However, cases of children with cerebral palsy who have slight brain damage and little motor impairment may be difficult to diagnose. In the milder cases, developmental lag in the motor and intellectual tasks required to meet environmental demands may not be detected until the children are 3 or 4 years old. As a rule, the clinical signs and symptoms of cerebral palsy reach maximum severity when children reach the age of 2 to 4 years.

Individuals with cerebral palsy usually demonstrate persistence of primitive reflexes and frequently are slow to develop equilibrium (postural) reflexes. It is difficult for most performers to execute simple gross motor movements effectively unless appropriate postural adjustments occur to support such movements and individuals are given additional time to plan and execute the movements.

Some of the secondary impairments that accompany cerebral palsy are intellectual disabilities, hearing and vision loss, emotional disturbance, hyperactivity, learning disabilities, loss of perceptual ability, and inability to make psychological adjustments.[54] Laskin[56] reports that 60% of all children with cerebral palsy have seizures. Seizures are sudden involuntary changes in behavior that range from a short period of loss of consciousness to jerks of one or two limbs or the whole body.[32]

Various authors agree that more than 50% of children with cerebral palsy have oculomotor defects. In other words, many children with brain injury have difficulty coordinating their eye movements. For this reason, these children may lack depth perception and have difficulty accurately determining the path of moving objects.

The different clinical types of cerebral dysfunction involve various obvious motor patterns, commonly known as hard signs. There are four clinical classifications: spasticity, athetosis, ataxia, and mixed. Of persons with cerebral palsy, 70% are clinically classified as spastic, 20% as athetoid, and 5% as ataxic; the remaining are mixed conditions (usually spasticity and athetosis).[32]

Muscular spasticity is the most prevalent type of hard sign among persons with cerebral palsy. It results from damage to an area of the cortical brain.[11, 28] One characteristic of spasticity is that muscle contractures that restrict muscular movement and hypertonicity give the appearance of stiffness to affected limbs. This makes muscle movement jerky and uncertain. Children with spasticity have exaggerated stretch reflexes, which cause them to respond to rapid passive stimulation with vigorous muscle contractions. Tendon reflexes are also hyperactive in the involved part. When the upper extremities are involved, the characteristic forms of physical deviation in persons with spastic cerebral palsy include flexion at the elbows, forearm pronation, and wrist and finger flexion. When the spastic condition involves the lower extremities, the legs may be rotated inward and flexed at the hips, the knees may be flexed, and a contracted gastrocnemius muscle holds the heel off the ground. A scissors gait is common among persons with this type of cerebral palsy. Spasticity is most common in the antigravity muscles of the body. Contractures are more common in children with spastic cerebral palsy than in children with any of the other types of cerebral palsy. In the event that contractures are not remedied or addressed, permanent contractures may result. Consequently, good posture is extremely difficult to maintain. Individuals with spastic hemiplegia or paraplegia usually have normal intelligence; however, they may demonstrate some learning disabilities. Intellectual disability is more frequently seen in individuals with spastic quadriplegia and mixed forms of cerebral palsy.[47]

Athetosis, which results from basal ganglia involvement, is the second most prevalent clinical type of cerebral palsy. The distinguishing characteristic of the individual with athetosis is recognizable incoordinate movements of voluntary muscles. These movements take the form of wormlike motions that involve the trunk, arms, legs, and tongue or muscle twitches of the face. The unrhythmical, uncontrollable, involuntary movements increase with voluntary motion and emotional or environmental stimuli and disappear during sleep. Because of the presence of primitive reflexes and the inability to control muscles, the individual with athetosis has postural control difficulties that threaten balance. Impairment in the muscular control of hands, speech, and swallowing often accompanies athetosis.

Ataxia, a primary characteristic of the ataxic type of cerebral palsy, is a disturbance of equilibrium that results from involvement of the cerebellum or its pathways.[45] The resulting impairment in balance is evident in the walking gait. The gait of the person with ataxic cerebral palsy is wide and unstable, which causes weaving during locomotion. Standing is often a problem. Kinesthetic awareness seems to be lacking in the individual with ataxia. Weakness, incoordination, and intention tremor create difficulties with rapid or fine movements.[47]

Mixed forms are the least common of all types of cerebral palsy. Spasticity and athetosis are the most frequent characteristics.

Special Considerations   Increasingly, the medical community and society at large have come to understand that the focus of medical intervention should be on the prevention of disabilities through appropriate prenatal care and early intervention with children who may be at risk. Procedures most prevalent in the medical treatment of individuals with cerebral palsy are early intervention to promote a more normal neuromotor developmental sequence (physical therapy), casting, orthotics (bracing), medication, and neurosurgical management.[22] Physical therapy focuses on reducing the effect of persisting primitive reflexes and promoting range of motion at the joints. Casting involves placing a cast on an extremity to hold it in line with the limb to which it is attached. Orthotics help delay the development of contractures, limit the amount of spasticity that can occur, and decrease consumption of energy. Medication usually serves two functions: aiding in the relaxation of muscle groups when neuromuscular exercise therapy is attempted and controlling epileptic seizures through the use of anticonvulsant drugs. Neurosurgical management involves surgery to release tight muscles and tendons.

The Physical Education Program and Teaching Strategies   There is no treatment for the repair of a damaged brain. However, the portion of the nervous system that remains intact can be made functional through a well-managed training program. Intervention by the physical educator and other personnel is needed to build functional developmental motor patterns with the operative parts of the body. Each child should be evaluated closely, and programs that foster those functional abilities should be formulated. Developmental programs should be constructed to correct deficiencies that respond to treatment. The specific child should be considered when the exercise regimen is being determined. Because of their numerous involuntary muscular activities, children with athetosis are much more active than children with spasticity and ataxia.

There is growing evidence that some of the sensory and perceptual delays can be improved through training. Sensorimotor and perceptual-motor training programs are designed to reduce primitive reflex involvement and develop locomotor patterns, balance, rhythm, and ocular control. These areas are the focus of physical therapists early in the life of the child. All of these activities are inherent in most elementary physical education programs; however, the quality of physical education programs could be improved by consciously selecting activities of this nature for classes that include students with spastic cerebral palsy.

The individualized education program (IEP) of the student with cerebral palsy should include activities to address the individual's unique needs. Some therapeutic activities and techniques follow:

1. Muscle stretching to relieve muscle contractures, prevent deformities, and permit a fuller range of purposeful motion (consult with physical therapists about this procedure)
2. Gravity exercises that involve lifting the weight of the body or body part against gravity
3. Muscle awareness exercises to control specific muscles or muscle groups
4. Neuromuscular re-education exercises that are performed through the muscles' current range to stimulate the proprioceptors and return the muscles to greater functional use (consult with physical therapists about this procedure)
5. Reciprocal exercises to stimulate and strengthen the action of the protagonist
6. Tonic exercises to prevent atrophy or maintain organic efficiency
7. Relaxation training to assist in reducing muscle contractures, rigidity, and spasms
8. Postural alignments to maintain proper alignment of musculature
9. Gait training to teach or reteach walking patterns (consult with physical therapists about this procedure)
10. Body mechanics and lifting techniques to obtain maximum use of the large muscle groups of the body

11. Proprioceptive facilitation exercises to bring about maximum excitation of the motor units of a muscle with each voluntary effort to overcome motor-functioning paralysis (consult with physical therapists about this procedure)
12. Ramp climbing to improve ambulation and balance
13. Progressive, resistive exercise to develop muscle strength

Failure to provide children with cerebral palsy the opportunity to participate in progressive exercise may leave them short of their potential development. The opportunities for physical education to maximize the physical development of these children are great. Furthermore, children with cerebral palsy frequently do not develop adequate basic motor skills because of their limited play experiences.

When a child with cerebral palsy participates in a group activity, it may be necessary to adapt the activity to the child's abilities or to modify the rules or environment. A child with quadriplegic spastic cerebral palsy may be given the opportunity to play the bells during a rhythm activity, instead of being asked to dance with his or her feet. A child with rigid cerebral palsy who uses a wheelchair may "hold" one handle on a parachute with the edge of his or her chair. A child with ataxia may play a sitting circle game with classmates while propped in the teacher's lap or propped against a wall.

In addition to adaptation of activity, the capabilities of each individual must be considered. Children with spasticity, those with athetosis, and those with ataxia differ greatly in function. For instance, the child with spasticity finds it easier to engage in activities in which motion is continuous. However, for the child with athetosis, relaxation between movements is extremely important to prevent involuntary muscular contractions that may thwart the development of skills.[22]

Children with ataxia have different motor problems—they are usually severely limited in all activities that require balance. The motor characteristics of the basic types of cerebral palsy, as well as of each child, are important variables in the selection of activities. Rest periods should be frequent for children with cerebral palsy. The length and frequency of the rest periods should vary with the nature of the activity and the severity of the disability. The development of a sequence of activities varying in degree of difficulty is important. This sequencing provides an opportunity to place each child in an activity that is commensurate with his or her ability and proposes a subsequent goal to work toward.

Physical activities described under the definition of physical education in IDEIA (2004) are appropriate for children with cerebral palsy. At the early elementary level, the focus should be on the development of sensorimotor function, body image, and rhythmicity. Appropriate motor activities include fundamental motor patterns, such as walking, running, and jumping, and fundamental motor skills, such as throwing, kicking, and catching. Aquatics is a vital part of the curriculum for children with cerebral palsy. The buoyancy of the water frees the child from the pull of gravity, which activates many primitive reflexes and allows for greater range of motion. Rhythm activities are also a vital part of the quality physical education program for children with cerebral palsy; expressive dance may prove to be vital in the development of language and communication, as well as motor skills. If possible, the physical education program for children with cerebral palsy at the elementary school level should include age-appropriate, geographically-appropriate leisure and recreation skills. Horseback riding is a particularly effective intervention activity for children who are severely involved.[30] Other leisure and recreation skills are important parts of the total program. The child should be introduced, for example, to the skills needed to participate in bowling, including the use of automatic grip release balls and ramps, if necessary.

The middle school curriculum should focus on the development of physical fitness, body mechanics, and relaxation techniques. Once again, aquatics is a vital component of the curriculum. Increased focus should be placed on exposing the student to community-based leisure and recreation activities and, where appropriate, competitive sports programs.

In the high school program, it is important that students with cerebral palsy maintain adequate levels of physical fitness, practice body mechanics, and develop more sophisticated relaxation techniques. The secondary student's IEP must address techniques that will allow the student to make the transition from school-based to community-based leisure and recreation programs. For example, the IEP may address the skills necessary for the student to register for and participate in an adult bowling or archery league.

These skills may include independent management of a ramp, for example. In addition, these students should be made familiar with the activities and programs of the U.S. Cerebral Palsy Athletic Association.

Epilepsy

Epilepsy is a disturbance resulting from abnormal electrical activity of the brain. The condition is a chronic disorder that causes repeated seizures if not treated.[23] A seizure is a "sudden surge of electrical activity in the brain that can cause changes in behavior and/or unusual sensations, muscle spasms, loss of consciousness, and convulsions."[23] Epilepsy is not a specific disease but a group of symptoms that may be associated with several conditions. Almost 3 million Americans have epilepsy, and there are 125,000 new cases each year, with about 50% of those being children.[43] Many persons with epilepsy experience their first attack during childhood. Common causes are brain damage at birth, alcohol or other drug abuse, severe head injury, brain infection, and brain tumor.[41]

Characteristics and Types   There are several types of epilepsy, and each type has a particular set of characteristics. Although there are several methods of classifying various types of epilepsy, the one most commonly used includes four categories of seizure: tonic-clonic (formerly referred to as grand mal), absence (formerly referred to as petit mal), focal, and psychomotor.

Tonic-clonic is the most severe type of seizure. The individual often has an "aura" that immediately precedes the seizure, and the aura may give the individual some warning of the imminence of the seizure. The aura is usually a somatosensory flash—a particular smell, a blur of colors, or an itching sensation, for example. The seizure itself usually begins with bilateral jerks of the extremities, followed by convulsions and loss of consciousness. The person may be incontinent during the seizure, losing control of the bowels and bladder. After the seizure, the individual is usually confused, often embarrassed, and exhausted.[47]

The onset of the absence seizure is sudden and may last for only a few seconds or for several minutes. Usually, the individual simply appears to stare into space and have a lapse in attention. It is often characterized by twitching around the eyes or mouth. There is a loss of consciousness but no collapse. The individual remains sitting or standing. Seizures of this type usually affect children between the ages of 5 and 15 years. The student with absence seizures may experience serious learning difficulties. It is not uncommon for a child to have hundreds of absence seizures a day. If a child has 100 seizures and each lasts only 30 seconds, the child will have lost a full 50 minutes of learning time.[47]

The focal seizure is similar to the tonic-clonic seizure. It is characterized by a loss of body tone and collapse. The student usually remains conscious during the attack, but speech may be impaired. In Jacksonian focal seizures, there is a localized twitching of muscles in the extremities, which moves up the arm or leg. If the seizure spreads to other parts of the brain, generalized convulsions and loss of consciousness result.

A psychomotor seizure is characterized by atypical social-motor behavior for 1 or 2 minutes. The behaviors may include uncontrollable temper tantrums, hand clapping, spitting, swearing, or shouting. The individual is unaware of the activity during and after the seizure. Psychomotor seizures can occur at any age.

Many factors can cause seizures. Some of these factors are (1) emotional stress, such as fear, anger, or frustration; (2) excessive amounts of alcohol; and (3) menstruation.

Special Considerations   Teachers should be cognizant of which students have epilepsy and whether they are taking drugs to control their seizures. Anticonvulsant drugs are the preferred medical treatment for most individuals with epilepsy, and they can prevent convulsive seizures in more than half of the people who have them. However, these drugs are slightly less effective for absence seizures. The type of drug that should be given and the optimum dosage are difficult to determine and highly individualized. Teachers should be sensitive to the side effects of these drugs, which may impair motor performance. Dilantin, for example, can produce lethargy, dizziness, and mental confusion. Phenobarbital sometimes contributes to drowsiness and learning difficulties. Drugs taken to control absence seizures may lead to drowsiness and nausea.[47] These side effects may be detrimental to the student's performance and safety in certain activities. Information about the student's drug treatment program should be discussed during the IEP meeting.

Physical education teachers should be familiar with procedures for handling seizures. Perhaps the most significant procedure for handling a seizure is to educate the student's class members about epilepsy. If the child's classmates are knowledgeable about seizures, the child will not have to suffer from embarrassment after a seizure has taken place.

In the event a child has a tonic-clonic seizure, the physical educator should do the following:[29]

1. Help the student to the floor or ground and place the student in a back-lying position.
2. Clear the area of dangerous objects.
3. Loosen all restraining clothing, such as a belt or shirt collar.
4. If the student is experiencing breathing difficulty, tilt the student's head back to open the airway.
5. Do not try to insert an object into the person's mouth or attempt to restrain the individual who is having a seizure.
6. Once the convulsion has stopped, place a blanket or towel over the student to eliminate embarrassment if the student has lost bowel or bladder control.
7. Allow the student to rest.
8. Report the seizure to the appropriate school official.

A tonic-clonic seizure is not life-threatening and should be treated as a routine event. The seizure process is dangerous only if the student moves into status epilepticus—has a series of tonic-clonic seizures without a break. If this happens, emergency medical personnel must be contacted immediately.

If the student experiences a focal or psychomotor seizure, the child should be removed to an isolated part of the gymnasium, if possible. If the student experiences an absence seizure and the teacher is aware of it, the teacher should repeat any instructions given previously.

The Physical Education Program and Teaching Strategies   If medication is effective and the child's seizures are under control, the student should be able to participate in a physical education program. However, activities that involve direct blows to the head, including boxing, soccer, and full-contact karate, should be avoided. Performing activities while a considerable height from the floor, swimming in cold water, and scuba diving without supervision should also be avoided. Swimming should be carefully supervised. Individuals who have uncontrolled seizures should avoid gymnastics, ice hockey and ice skating, sailing and waterskiing, and horseback riding.[51]

Multiple Sclerosis

Multiple sclerosis is a chronic and degenerative neurological disease affecting primarily older adolescents and adults. It is a slowly progressive disease of the central nervous system, leading to the disintegration of the myelin coverings of nerve fibers in the brain and spinal cord, which results in hardening or scarring of the tissue that replaces the disintegrated protective myelin sheath.[47]

Characteristics   The symptoms of multiple sclerosis are sensory problems (such as visual disturbances), tremors, muscle weakness, spasticity, speech difficulties, dizziness, mild emotional disturbances, partial paralysis, fatigue, and motor difficulties.[56] Multiple sclerosis generally appears between the ages of 20 and 40 years and results in several periods of remission and recurring exacerbation. Some persons have frequent attacks, whereas others have remissions that last several years.[47]

The Physical Activity Program   There is no treatment that can repair the damage to the nervous system caused by degeneration. However, each person should be evaluated individually, and physical activity programs should be administered to maintain maximum functioning.[2] Regular physical activity can be used to alleviate symptoms associated with multiple sclerosis.[37] In addition, Jacobson relaxation techniques[19] and active and passive range-of-motion exercises should be used to counter contractures in the lower extremities. The goal of these programs is to maintain functional skills, muscle strength, and range of motion. It is particularly important to teach the skills necessary for the functional use of walkers, crutches, and wheelchairs. In addition, the individual should be given the opportunity to develop compensatory skills—skills needed because of changes in central nervous system function—for example, skills to compensate for disequilibrium. Braces may be introduced at the later stages of the disorder to assist with locomotion. Many individuals with this condition are heat sensitive, which means their condition worsens when their body temperature increases. Exercising in an air-conditioned setting during extreme outdoor temperatures is recommended.[29]

Inactivity and the use of prednisone, which is an anti-inflammatory drug, may contribute to the progressive weakening of the muscles needed for daily activity. Instructors should constantly encourage as active a lifestyle as possible. Individuals should be urged to participate in an exercise program that maintains cardiovascular-respiratory functioning and sufficient muscle strength to allow participation in the activities of daily living. Research on the step-rates of individuals with multiple sclerosis reports that persons with mild to moderate involvement can meet the recommended amount of daily activity; combining moderate and vigorous intensity in bouts of 10 minutes is recommended.[2] Because involvement of the lower extremities interferes with balance, stationary cycles using the arms or legs are recommended for physical activity programming. Begin with an unloaded warm-up and progress to exercising in 3- to 5-minute increments. Weight training is recommended 2 to 3 days a week, using 8 to 15 repetitions of submaximal weights. Swimming and aquatic aerobic exercises are recommended because they require less effort than activities on land.[25] Individuals who enjoy competition should be encouraged to participate in wheelchair sports when their condition is in remission.

Muscular Dystrophy

Muscular dystrophy is a group of inherited, progressive muscle disorders that differ according to which muscles are affected.[45] All types result in the deterioration of muscle strength, power, and endurance. The rate of progressive degeneration is different for each set of muscles.[52] Although the exact incidence of muscular dystrophy is unknown, estimates place the number of persons with the disorder in excess of 200,000 in the United States. It is estimated that in more than half of the known cases, the age of onset falls within the range of 3 to 13 years.

Characteristics and Types   The physical characteristics of persons with muscular dystrophy are relevant to the degenerative stage as well as to the type of muscular dystrophy. In the late stages of the disease, connective tissue replaces most of the muscle tissue. In some cases, deposits of fat give the appearance of well-developed muscles. Despite the muscle atrophy, there is no apparent central nervous system impairment.

The age of onset of muscular dystrophy is of importance to the total development of the child. Persons who contract the disease after having had an opportunity to secure an education, or part of an education, and develop social and psychological strengths are better able to cope with their environment than are those who acquire the disease before the acquisition of basic skills.

Although the characteristics of individuals with muscular dystrophy vary according to the stage of the disease, some general characteristics are as follows:

1. There is a tendency to tire quickly.
2. There may be a loss of fine manual dexterity.
3. There is sometimes a lack of motivation to learn because of isolation from social contacts and limited educational opportunities.
4. Progressive weakness tends to produce adverse postural changes.
5. Emotional disturbance may exist because of the progressive nature of the illness and the resulting restrictions placed on opportunities for socialization.

There are numerous classifications of muscular dystrophy based on the muscle groups affected and the age of onset. However, three main clinical types of muscular dystrophy have been identified: Duchenne (pseudohypertrophic), Becker, and facioscapulohumeral (Landouzy-Dejerine).[45]

The Duchenne (pseudohypertrophic) type is an X-linked recessive disorder that usually presents itself between ages 2 and 3 years. It occurs in 1 in every 4,700 live male births. It affects the pelvic girdle first, followed by the shoulder girdle.[47] Symptoms that give an indication of the disease are the following:

1. Waddling gait
2. Toe walking
3. Lordosis
4. Frequent falls
5. Difficulty getting up after falling
6. Difficulty climbing stairs[47]

Imbalance of muscle strength in various parts of the body occurs as the disease progresses. Deformities develop in flexion at the hips and knees. The spine, pelvis, and shoulder girdle also eventually become atrophied. Contractures and involvement of the heart may develop with the progressive degeneration of the disease. The motorized wheelchair has increased the independence of children in the advanced stages of muscular dystrophy. Though unable to perform activities of daily living, the child using a motorized wheelchair retains a measure of mobility that promotes independence and allows integration into many school-based and community-based programs.

Becker muscular dystrophy is also an X-linked disorder; however, it is less severe than the Duchenne type. The advancement of this type of dystrophy mimics the Duchenne type, but the Becker type progresses more slowly. As a result, few individuals are required to use wheelchairs until they approach adulthood, and most survive into their thirties or forties.[47]

The facioscapulohumeral (Landouzy-Dejerine) type of muscular dystrophy, which is the third most common type, is characterized by weakness of the facial muscles and shoulder girdles. The onset of symptoms or signs of the facioscapulohumeral type is usually recognized in early childhood and more noticeable in the teenage years. Both genders are equally subject to the condition. Persons with this form of muscular dystrophy have trouble raising their arms above their head, whistling, drinking through a straw, and closing their eyes. A child with this type of disease often appears to have a masklike face, which lacks expression. Later, involvement of the muscles that move the humerus and scapula will be noticed. Weakness usually appears later in the abdominal, pelvic, and hip musculature. The progressive weakness and muscle deterioration often lead to scoliosis and lordosis. This type of muscular dystrophy is often milder than the Duchenne type, and life expectancy is normal. Facioscapulohumeral muscular dystrophy usually progresses slowly, and ambulation is seldom lost.[47]

Special Considerations   Duchenne muscular dystrophy is one of the most serious disabling conditions that can occur in childhood. Although not fatal in itself, the disease contributes to premature death in most known cases because of its progressive nature. The progress of the condition is cruel and relentless as the child loses function and moves toward inevitable death. However, it is worth noting that scientific research may be close to solving unanswered questions regarding the disease, and eventually the progressive deterioration may be halted.

The Physical Education Program and Teaching Strategies   An individually designed activity program may significantly contribute to the quality of life of the individual affected by muscular dystrophy. Inactivity seems to contribute to the progressive weakening of the muscles of persons with muscular dystrophy. Exercise of muscles involved in the activities of daily living to increase strength may permit greater functional use of the body and slow the progression of the disease.[26] Furthermore, exercise may assist in reducing excessive weight, which is a burden to those who have muscular dystrophy. Movement in warm water—aquatic therapy—may be particularly beneficial for the child with muscular dystrophy. It aids in the maintenance of muscle tonus and flexibility, and it encourages circulation.

The child's diet should be closely monitored. Prevention of excess weight is essential to the success of the rehabilitation program of persons with progressive muscular dystrophy. For individuals whose strength is marginal, any extra weight is an added burden on ambulation and on activities of daily living.

A great deal can be done to prevent deformities and loss of muscle strength from inactivity. If a specific strengthening and stretching program is outlined during each stage of the disease, the child may extend the ability to care for most of his or her daily needs for many additional years. In addition to the administration of specific developmental exercises for the involved muscles, exercises should include the development of walking patterns, posture control, muscle coordination, and the stretching of contractures involved in disuse atrophy. Because little is known about the frequency, intensity, amount, and duration of exercise required to produce a beneficial effect, all exercises should be selected after the study of contraindications specified by a physician.[34] It is desirable to select activities that use the remaining strengths, so that enjoyment and success can be achieved.

All the types of muscular dystrophy cannot be considered to be the same; therefore, the physical and social benefits that children can derive from physical education and recreation programs are different. However, all children with muscular dystrophy can profit from a well-designed program to enhance quality of life. The focus of the program, particularly for children with Duchenne muscular dystrophy, is on the development of leisure and recreation skills that will be appropriate as the child progressively loses function. For example, a child with Duchenne muscular dystrophy should be taught to fish and to play bocce because those are skills that can be enjoyed throughout the life span. Also, the child should be given the opportunity to learn board and electronic games that will provide entertainment and joy.

One focus of the program should be the development of relaxation techniques. The progressive loss of functional skills causes a great deal of stress, as does facing the inevitability of an early death; the quality of the child's life can be enhanced if the child has learned conscious relaxation skills.

Perhaps more important, dance, music, and art therapy should be a part of the child's total program. Movement and dance, even dance done in a motorized wheelchair, can help the child or adolescent express emotions—grief, rage, frustration, love, or joy. Music and art therapy provide vital avenues of expression as the child loses motor capabilities. In addition, a trained therapist can be of value as the child moves through the stages of grief. The intent of the program is to enhance the quality of the child's life and, with professional support, allow the process of dying to be as humane, caring, and ennobling as possible. Specific programs are suggested in **Table 15-1**.

Parkinson's Disease

Parkinson's disease is a slow, progressive disorder that results in physical debilitation. The disease usually appears gradually and progresses slowly. It may progress to a stage where there is difficulty with the routine activities of daily living. There is no known cause; however, it is believed to result from a combination of genetics and environment (e.g., exposure to toxins). The signs and symptoms of Parkinson's are believed to happen because of a decrease in the neurotransmitter dopamine, produced in the basal ganglia.[46] The condition may be aggravated by emotional tension or fatigue. It affects about 1.5 adults in the United States over the age of 50 years. A juvenile form of Parkinsonism, which has its onset prior to age 40 years, has also been identified.

TABLE 15-1   Recommended Programming Ideas for Persons with Muscular Dystrophy[52]

Provide realistic short-term goals to the individuals and parents.
Use submaximal resistance exercises while focusing on maintaining muscle endurance, peak power, and strength.
When muscles are weaker the goal becomes range of motion exercises against gravity.
Include as many game-like, fun situations as possible.
Stretch to prevent contractures and maintain flexibility.
Exercise with a partner, drink fluids, and avoid strenuous exercise in high heat and humidity.

Characteristics   The observable characteristics of Parkinson's disease are infrequent blinking and lack of facial expression, tremor of the resting muscles, a slowing of voluntary movements, muscular weakness, abnormal gait, and postural instability.[47] These motor characteristics become more pronounced as the disease progresses. For instance, a minor feeling of sluggishness may progress until the individual is unable to get up from a chair. The walking gait becomes less efficient and can be characterized by shuffling of the feet for the purpose of postural stability. In addition, voluntary movements, particularly those performed by the small muscles, become slow, and spontaneous movements diminish.

In general, most persons require lifelong management consisting of physical therapy and drug therapy. Physical therapy consists of heat and massage to alleviate the muscle cramps and relieve the tension headaches that often accompany rigidity of the muscles of the neck.

The Physical Activity Program   Because of the degenerative nature of the disease, the goals of physical activity programs are to preserve muscular functioning for purposive movement involved in the activities of daily living and required for the performance of leisure and recreation skills. The types of physical activities that may be of value are general coordination exercises to retard the slow deterioration of movement and relaxation exercises that may reduce muscular incoordination and tremors. In addition, balance activities and those that teach compensation for lack of balance should be included. Exercises directed at maintaining postural strength and flexibility should be a part of the program plan. Care must be taken when the individual is on antiparkinsonian medications because of the varied side effects.[45] A physician's and/or a physical therapist's guidance should be sought as the disease progresses.

Poliomyelitis and Post-Polio Syndrome

Poliomyelitis (polio) is an acute viral infection with a wide range of manifestations.[47] In the serious cases (nonparalytic and paralytic), an inflammation affects the anterior motor cells in the spinal cord, which in turn affects the muscles. Extensive vaccination has virtually eradicated polio; however, an increasing number of individuals who had polio as children are developing a post-polio syndrome (PPS). Almost one-fourth of the individuals who contracted polio during peak epidemics are now developing symptoms similar to those they experienced during the initial onset of the disease.[9]

Characteristics and Types   There are two basic patterns—minor illness (abortive) and major illness (paralytic or nonparalytic). Minor poliomyelitis accounts for 80% to 90% of the clinical infections and occurs chiefly in children.[45] This form does not involve the central nervous system. The symptoms are headache, sore throat, mild fever, and nausea.

Major poliomyelitis involves the central nervous system. In addition to the symptoms of minor poliomyelitis, the individual may experience a fever, severe headache, stiff neck, and general and specific pain in and acute contractions of one or more muscle groups in the upper and lower extremities or the back. Individuals with the nonparalytic form recover completely. Individuals with the paralytic form develop paralysis of muscle groups throughout the body. Two-thirds of these individuals have residual, permanent weakness.[45]

Post-polio syndrome occurs many years after a paralytic poliomyelitis attack. The characteristics include muscle fatigue and decreased endurance, accompanied by weakness, and atrophy in selected muscles.[47]

The Physical Activity Program   Exercise programs should focus on motor tasks that develop strength, endurance, flexibility, and coordination. Orthopedic deformities resulting from the residual effects of polio do not totally restrict movement. Children quickly learn to compensate for the inconvenience of an impaired foot or arm. At the elementary school level, many children with polio can achieve considerable athletic success. However, as they progress through school life, accumulated developmental lags, as a rule, influence skill development. Wheelchair sports are popular for individuals with polio who cannot walk.

For adults who experience post-polio syndrome, it appears that the muscle units that were not originally impaired become fatigued from overwork. These individuals appear to benefit from moderate-intensity aerobic exercise and resistive training.[10]

Spina Bifida

Spina bifida is the most common congenital spinal defect. The condition is a result of defective closure of the vertebral column. The severity ranges from spina bifida occulta, with no findings, to a completely open spine (spina bifida cystica).[47] The incidence of spina bifida is estimated at 1 per 1,500 live births in the United States, making it one of the most common birth defects that can lead to physical disability.

Characteristics   In spina bifida occulta, the vertebral arches fail to fuse; however, there is no distension of the spinal cord lining or of the cord itself. In spina bifida cystica, the protruding sac can contain just the lining (meninges) of the spinal column (meningocele) or both the meninges and the spinal cord (myelomeningocele).[43] See **Figures 15-1** and **15-2**. Meningocele usually can be repaired with little or no damage to the neural pathways. Myelomeningocele, the more common of the two types, produces varying degrees of neurological impairment, ranging from mild muscle imbalance and sensory loss in the lower limbs to paralysis of one or both legs. The child's ability to walk depends on the level of the lesion. Persons with lesions at the low lumbar level can walk, and persons with high lumbar or thoracic levels can walk.[12] Paralysis usually affects bladder and bowel function,[47] and bladder and kidney infections are frequent. Nearly all children born with myelomeningocele have or soon develop hydrocephalus.[1] In these cases, usually a shunt is inserted to drain off cerebrospinal fluid that is not being reabsorbed properly. Removing the excess cerebrospinal fluid protects the child against brain damage resulting from pressure on the brain. Many children who are paraplegic from spina bifida are able to

Meningocele

Courtesy of Association for Spina Bifida and Hydrocephalus.

Figure 15-1   Meningocele
In this form of spina bifida, the sac contains tissues that cover the spinal cord (meninges) and cerebrospinal fluid. This fluid bathes and protects the brain and spinal cord. The nerves are not usually badly damaged and are able to function; therefore, there is often little disability present. This is the least common form.

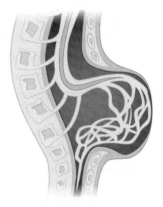

Myelomeningocele
Courtesy of Association for Spina Bifida and Hydrocephalus.

Figure 15-2   Myelomeningocele (Meningomyelocele)
This is the more common of the two meningoceles and the most serious.
Here the sac or cyst contains not only tissue and cerebrospinal fluid but also
nerves and part of the spinal cord. The spinal cord is damaged or not properly
developed. As a result, there is always some degree of paralysis and loss of
sensation below the damaged vertebrae. The amount of disability depends
very much on where the spina bifida is and the amount of nerve damage
involved. Many children and adults with this condition experience problems
with bowel and bladder control.

move about with the aid of braces and crutches. It is also interesting to note
that many children who have spina bifida are allergic to latex.

Even though children with spina bifida have normal intelligence, many
have some learning difficulties. The most common difficulties are poor
hand–eye coordination, distractibility, hyperactivity, and memory, sequencing, and reasoning problems.[12]

Special Considerations   Activities that could distress the placement of any
shunts or put pressure on sensitive areas of the spine must be avoided. Of
considerable concern is the prevention of contractures and associated foot
deformities (e.g., equinovarus) through daily passive flexibility exercises.

Many social problems result from spina bifida. In addition to the physical disability, there are often problems associated with bowel and bladder
control, which draw further attention to the children as they function in a

social environment. In many cases, this has a negative social impact on the children. Often, children with spina bifida need catheterization. If someone must do it for them, the attention of others is drawn to these circumstances. However, in many cases older children can be taught to catheterize themselves. The physical disability and the associated physiological problems result in stressful social situations because groups must adapt to the child with spina bifida's physical disabilities and associated physiological problems.

The Physical Education Program and Teaching Strategies   No particular program of physical education or therapy can be directly assigned to the student with spina bifida. Some students have no physical reaction and discover the condition only by chance through X-ray examination for another problem. On the other hand, a person may have extensive neuromuscular involvement requiring constant medical care. A program of physical education or therapeutic exercise based on the individual's needs should be planned.

The child with spina bifida myelomeningocele is often able to participate in a general physical education program more effectively using a wheelchair than using a walker or crutches and braces. While the child with spina bifida should be encouraged to walk whenever possible, it may be difficult for the child to participate in activities safely in a crowded gymnasium.

ORTHOPEDIC DISABILITIES

Arthritis

The term *arthritis* is derived from two Greek roots: *arthro-,* meaning joint, and *-itis,* meaning inflammation. Nearly 53 million adults and 300,000 children are being told by a physician that they have some form of arthritic disease.[5] Because arthritis inflicts a low mortality and high morbidity, the potential for increasing numbers of those impacted is great. It is assumed that many factors predispose one to arthritis: infection, hereditary factors, environmental stress, dietary deficiencies, trauma, and organic or emotional disturbances.

Types, Causes, Incidence, and Characteristics   In most cases, arthritis is progressive, gradually resulting in general fatigue, weight loss, and muscular stiffness. Joint impairment is symmetrical, and characteristically the small joints of the hands and feet are affected in the earliest stages. Tenderness and pain may occur in tendons and muscular tissue near inflamed joints. As the inflammation in the joints becomes progressively chronic, degenerative and proliferative changes occur to the synovial tendons, ligaments, and articular cartilages. If the inflammation is not arrested in its early stages, joints become ankylosed and muscles atrophy and contract, eventually causing a twisted and deformed limb. Three common forms of arthritis are rheumatoid arthritis, osteoarthritis, and ankylosing spondylitis.

Rheumatoid arthritis impacts more than 1.5 million people in the United States. It is a systemic disease of unknown cause. Seventy-five percent of the cases occur between the ages of 30 and 60 years and in a ratio of 3 to 1, women to men. A type of rheumatoid arthritis called Still's disease, or juvenile arthritis, attacks children before the age of 7 years. Approximately 300,000 children in the United States are diagnosed with rheumatoid arthritis, making it a major impairment among young children.[5] The most significant physical sign is the thickening of the synovial tissue in joints that are actively involved (inflamed). Inflamed joints are sensitive to the touch. Individuals with rheumatoid arthritis are stiff for an hour or so after rising in the morning or after a period of inactivity.

Osteoarthritis, the second most frequent type of arthritis, is a disorder of the hyaline cartilage, primarily in the weight-bearing joints. It is a result of mechanical destruction of the coverings of the bone at the joints because of trauma or repeated use. Although evidence of the breakdown can be documented during the twenties, discomfort usually does not occur until individuals are in their forties. Initially, the condition is not inflammatory, and it impacts only one or a few joints. Pain is the earliest symptom, and it increases initially with exercise. The condition affects men and women equally; however, recent studies demonstrate that athletes may be at the greatest risk for developing osteoarthritis. Athletes who participate in sports with a high percentage of high impact, plus fast acceleration and deceleration, put themselves at the greatest risk. These activities include soccer, long distance running, weight lifting, and wrestling.[15]

Osteopenia is low bone mineral content, a condition that frequently leads to osteoporosis, which results in fragile bones and a high risk of fractures. Youth who fail to attain peak bone mass during their adolescent years are at highest risk for developing osteoporosis in later life. Teenagers with juvenile rheumatoid arthritis who do not use corticosteroids demonstrate mild to moderate osteopenia, which puts them at high risk for developing osteoporosis later in life.[5]

Special Considerations   Interventions for arthritis include proper diet, rest, drug therapy, reduction of stress, and exercise. Because of its debilitating effect, prolonged bed rest is discouraged, although daily rest sessions are required to avoid undue fatigue. A number of drugs may be given to the patient, depending on individual needs; for example, salicylates, such as aspirin, relieve pain; gold compounds may be used for arresting the acute inflammatory stage; and adrenocortical steroids may be used to control the degenerative process. Drugless techniques for controlling arthritis pain, such as biofeedback, self-hypnosis, behavior modification, and transcutaneous nerve stimulation, are often used as adjuncts to more traditional types of treatment.

The Physical Activity Program and Teaching Strategies   Physical exercise is crucial to reduce pain and increase function. The exercises required by patients with arthritis fall into three major categories: exercises to improve and maintain range of motion, exercises that strengthen the muscles that surround and support affected joints, and aerobic exercises to improve cardiovascular endurance. The physical educator should encourage gradual or static stretching, isometric muscle contraction, and low-impact aerobic exercise daily. Exercising in a pool, biking, and rowing are highly recommended.

Maintenance of normal joint range of movement is of prime importance for establishing a functional joint. Stretching may first be passive; however, active stretching is of greater benefit because muscle tone is maintained in the process. Joints should be moved through pain-free range of motion several times daily.

Isometric exercises that strengthen the muscles that support affected joints should be practiced during the day when the pain and stiffness are at a minimum. Although weight-bearing isotonic exercises have long been advised against, in recent studies intensive weight-bearing exercises have been shown to be very beneficial. Because individuals with rheumatoid arthritis are at high risk for osteoporosis and cardiovascular problems, an ongoing program that includes both weight-bearing exercises and aerobic exercise is recommended.

Aerobic exercises that require a minimum of weight bearing should be used. Bicycling, swimming, and aquatic aerobics are recommended.[24] Whenever possible, water activities should take place in a heated pool because the warmth enhances circulation and reduces muscle tightness. The Arthritis Foundation recommends a water temperature between 83°F and 88°F.[53] One recreational activity that has been shown to improve cardiovascular endurance and to counteract depression, anxiety, and tension is dancing.[5]

An individual with arthritis may need rest periods during the day. These should be combined with a well-planned exercise program. Activity should never increase pain or so tire an individual that normal recovery is not obtained by the next day.

Arthrogryposis (Curved Joints)

Arthrogryposis is a condition of flexure or contracture of joints (joints of the lower limbs more often than joints of the upper limbs) that is present at birth. The incidence is estimated to be 1 in 3,000 births.[6]

Characteristics   The limbs may be fixed in any position. However, the usual forms are with the shoulders turned in, the elbows straightened and extended, the forearms turned with the palms outward (pronated), and the wrists flexed and deviated upward with the fingers curled into the palms. The hips may be bent in a flexed position and turned outward (externally rotated), and the feet are usually turned inward and downward. The spine often evidences scoliosis, the limbs are small in circumference, and the joints appear large and have lost their range of motion. Deformities are at their worst at birth, and a regular exercise program improves function; active physical therapy early in life can produce reduced contracture and improved range of motion.

Several physical conditions are associated with arthrogryposis, including congenital heart disease, urinary tract abnormalities, respiratory problems, abdominal hernias, and cleft palate. Intelligence is usually normal. Children with arthrogryposis may walk independently but with an abnormal gait, or they may depend on a wheelchair.

Special Considerations   Surgery is often used to correct hip conditions, as well as knee and foot deformities. Surgery is sometimes used to permit limited flexion of the elbow joint, as well as greater wrist mobility.

The Physical Education Program and Teaching Strategies   The awkwardness of joint positions and mechanics causes no pain; therefore, children with arthrogryposis are free to engage in most types of activity. Muscle strengthening and range-of-motion exercises are recommended.[6]

Congenital Hip Dislocation

Congenital hip dislocation, which is also known as developmental hip dislocation, is a disorder in which the head of the thigh bone (femur) doesn't fit properly into, or is outside of, the hip socket (acetabulum) (see **Figure 15-3**). It is estimated that it occurs more often in females than in males; it may be bilateral or unilateral, occurring most often in the left hip.

The cause of congenital hip dislocation is unknown, with various causes proposed. Heredity seems to be a primary causative factor in faulty hip development and subsequent dysplasia. Actually, only about 2% of developmental hip dislocations are congenital.

Characteristics   Generally, the acetabulum is shallower on the affected side than on the nonaffected side, and the femoral head is displaced upward and backward in relation to the ilium. Ligaments and muscles become deranged, resulting in a shortening of the rectus femoris, hamstring, and adductor thigh muscles and affecting the small intrinsic muscles of the hip. Prolonged malpositioning of the femoral head produces a chronic weakness of the gluteus medius and minimus muscles. A primary factor in

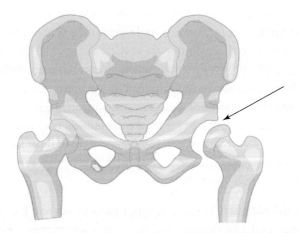

Figure 15-3   Developmental Hip Dislocation

stabilizing one hip in the upright posture is the iliopsoas muscle. In developmental hip dislocation, the iliopsoas muscle displaces the femoral head upward; this will eventually cause the lumbar vertebrae to become lordotic and scoliotic.

Detection of a hip dislocation may not occur until the child begins to bear weight or walk. Early recognition of this condition may be accomplished by observing asymmetrical fat folds on the infant's legs and restricted hip adduction on the affected side. The Trendelenburg test (see **Figure 15-4**)

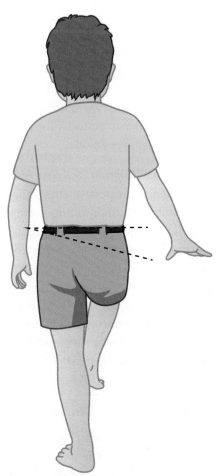

Figure 15-4   Trendelenburg Test

will reveal that the child is unable to maintain the pelvic level while standing on the affected leg. In such cases, weak abductor muscles of the affected leg allow the pelvis to tilt downward on the nonaffected side. The child walks with a decided limp in unilateral cases and with a waddle in bilateral cases. No discomfort or pain is normally experienced by the child, but fatigue tolerance to physical activity is very low. Pain and discomfort become more apparent as the individual becomes older and as postural deformities become more structural.

Special Considerations   Medical treatment depends on the age of the child and the extent of displacement. Young babies with a mild involvement may have the condition remedied through gradual adduction of the femur by a pillow splint, whereas more complicated cases may require traction, casting, or surgery to restore proper hip continuity. The thigh is slowly returned to a normal position.

The Physical Education Program and Teaching Strategies   Active exercise is suggested, along with passive stretching of contracted tissue. Primary concern is paid to reconditioning the movement of hip extension and abduction. When adequate muscle strength has been gained in the hip region, a program of ambulation is conducted, with particular attention paid to walking without a lateral pelvic tilt. Most children in the physical education or recreation program with a history of developmental hip dislocation will require specific postural training, conditioning of the hip region, continual gait training, and general body mechanics training. Swimming is an excellent activity for general conditioning of the hip, and it is highly recommended. Activities should not be engaged in to the point of discomfort or fatigue.

Coxa Plana (Legg-Calvé-Perthes Disease)

Coxa plana is the result of abnormal softening of the femoral head. It is a condition identified early in the twentieth century independently by Legg of Boston, Calvé of France, and Perthes of Germany. Its gross signs

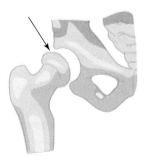

Figure 15-5   Coxa Plana

reflect a flattening of the head of the femur (see **Figure 15-5**), and it is found predominantly in boys between the ages of 5 and 10 years.[47] It has been variously termed osteochondritis deformans juvenilis, pseudocoxalgia, and Legg-Calvé-Perthes disease. The exact cause of coxa plana is not known; trauma, infection, and endocrine imbalance have been suggested as possible causes.

Characteristics   Coxa plana is characterized by degeneration of the capital epiphysis of the femoral head. Osteoporosis, or bone rarefaction, results in a flattened and deformed femoral head. Later developments may also include widening of the femoral head and thickening of the femoral neck. The last stage of coxa plana is characterized by a self-limiting course in which there is a regeneration and an almost complete return of the normal epiphysis within 2 to 3 years.[47] However, recovery is not always complete, and there is often some residual deformity. The younger child with coxa plana has the best prognosis for complete recovery.

The first outward sign of this condition is often a limp favoring the affected leg, with pain in the hip or referred to the knee region. The individual with coxa plana experiences progressive fatigue and pain on weight bearing, progressive stiffness, and a limited range of movement.

Treatment of coxa plana primarily entails the removal of stress placed on the femoral head by weight bearing. Bed rest is often used in the acute stages, with ambulation and non-weight-bearing devices used for the remaining period of incapacitation. The sling and crutch method for non-weight-bearing is widely used for this condition (see **Figure 15-6**). Weight-bearing exercise is contraindicated until the physician discounts the possibility of a pathological joint condition.

The Physical Education Program and Teaching Strategies The individual with an epiphyseal affection of the hip presents a problem of muscular and skeletal stability and joint range of movement. Stability of the hip region requires skeletal continuity and a balance of muscle strength, primarily in the muscles of hip extension and abduction. Prolonged limited motion and non-weight-bearing may result in contractures of the tissues surrounding the hip joint and an inability to walk or run with ease. Abnormal weakness of the hip extensors and abductors may cause shortening of the hip flexors and adductors and lead the individual to display the Trendelenburg sign (review Figure 15-4).

A program of exercise must be carried out to prevent muscle atrophy and general deconditioning. When movement is prohibited, muscle-tensing exercises for the muscles of the hip region are conducted, together with isotonic exercises for the upper extremities, trunk, ankles, and feet.

When the hip becomes free of symptoms, a progressive, isotonic, non-weight-bearing program is initiated for the hip region. Active movement

Figure 15-6 Sling and Crutch for Hip Conditions

emphasizing hip extension and abduction is recommended. Swimming is an excellent adjunct to the regular exercise program.

The program of exercise should never exceed the point of pain or fatigue until full recovery is accomplished. A general physical fitness program emphasizing weight control and body mechanics will help the student prepare to return to a full program of physical education and recreation activities.

Osgood-Schlatter Condition

Osgood-Schlatter condition is not considered a disease but, rather, the result of trauma to the patellar tendon where it inserts on the tibia. Major features are pain, swelling, and tenderness over the insertion point.[47]

Osgood-Schlatter condition usually occurs in active boys and girls when their bones are growing most rapidly (ages 8 to 15 years).[20] This is a very common cause of knee pain in adolescents, particularly those who participate in activities requiring jumping and cutting, such as volleyball and soccer.[31] The condition occurs twice as frequently in the left knee than in the right knee.

Characteristics   In the early stages, there is pain in front of the shin 2 to 3 inches below the kneecap. Swelling occurs a few months later. The symptoms range from mild knee pain during activity to constant pain.[19] The physical educator may detect this condition based on the student's complaints. When this happens, parents should be notified to contact their physician.

Special Considerations   If Osgood-Schlatter condition is not properly cared for, deformity and a defective extensor mechanism may result; however, it may not necessarily be associated with pain or discomfort. In most cases, Osgood-Schlatter condition is acute, is self-limiting, and does not exceed a few months' duration. However, even after the arrest of symptoms, Osgood-Schlatter condition tends to recur after irritation.

Local inflammation occurs when the legs are used, and it eases with rest. The individual may be unable to kneel or engage in flexion and extension movements without pain. The knee joint must be kept completely immobilized when the inflammatory state persists. Forced inactivity, provided by a plaster cast, may be the only answer to keeping an overactive adolescent from using the affected leg.

The Physical Education Program and Teaching Strategies   Early detection may reveal a slight condition in which the individual can continue a normal activity routine, excluding sport participation, excessive exercise, strenuous running, jumping, deep knee bending, and falling on the affected leg. All physical education activities must be modified to avoid quadriceps muscle strain while preparing for general physical fitness. Moderate stretching of the quadriceps and hamstrings done for 10 seconds may relieve some of the pain and allow for activity.

While the limb is immobilized in a cast, the individual is greatly restricted; weight bearing may be held to a minimum, with signs of pain at the affected part closely watched by the physician. Although Osgood-Schlatter condition is self-limiting and temporary, exercise is an important factor in full recovery. Physical education activities should emphasize the capabilities of the upper body and nonaffected leg to prevent their deconditioning.

After arrest of the condition and removal of the cast (or relief from immobilization), the patient is given a graduated reconditioning program. The major objectives at this time are re-education in proper walking patterns and the restoration of normal strength and flexibility of the knee joint. Strenuous knee movement is avoided for at least 5 weeks, and the demanding requirements of regular physical education classes may be postponed for extended periods, depending on the physician's recommendations. Although emphasis is placed on the affected leg during rehabilitation, a program must also be provided for the entire body.

The following are criteria for the individual to return to a regular physical education program:

1. Normal range of movement of the knee
2. Quadriceps muscle strength equal to that of the unaffected leg
3. Evidence that Osgood-Schlatter condition has become asymptomatic
4. Ability to move freely without favoring the affected part

After recovery, the student should avoid all activities that tend to contuse, or in any way irritate again, the tibial tuberosity.

Osteogenesis Imperfecta (Brittle Bone Disease)

Osteogenesis imperfecta is a condition marked by both weak bones and elasticity of the joints, ligaments, and skin. It occurs once in 20,000 births.[8]

Most cases are the result of a dominant genetic defect, although some cases result from a spontaneous mutation. There are four types, ranging from mild to severe involvement.

Characteristics   The bones of children with this condition are abnormally frail and may have multiple fractures at the time of birth. The underlying layer of the eyeball (choroid) shows through as a blue discoloration. Individuals who live are shorter than average and have a triangular-shaped face.

As growth occurs in individuals with the condition, the limbs tend to become bowed. The bones are not dense, and the spine is rounded and often evidences scoliosis. The teeth are in poor condition, easily broken, discolored, and prone to cavities. The joints are excessively mobile, and the positions that the children may take show great flexibility.

Special Considerations   No known chemical or nutrient has been shown to correct osteogenesis imperfecta, and the most satisfactory treatment is the surgical insertion of a steel rod between the ends of the long bones. This treatment, plus bracing, permits some youth to walk. Many persons with brittle bone disease need a wheelchair at least part of the time, and those with severe cases require a wheelchair exclusively.

The Physical Education Program and Teaching Strategies   Some authorities have suggested that physical activities are to be ruled out for this population, whereas others encourage exercise to promote muscle and bone strength. Swimming and water therapy are strongly recommended. These individuals are also encouraged to maintain a healthy weight and avoid activities that deplete bone (e.g., smoking, steroid use).[8]

Physical education teachers should be sensitive to the presence of children in their classes whose bones are highly susceptible to injury, trauma, or breakage because of this and related conditions. These children, who approach normalcy in other areas, continue to require a highly adapted physical education program that is limited to range-of-motion exercises. Although osteogenesis imperfecta is diagnosed only in severe cases, many children seem to have a propensity for broken bones. Physical educators should take softness of bones into consideration when developing physical education programs for children.

Osteomyelitis

Osteomyelitis is an inflammation of a bone and its medullary (marrow) cavity. Occasionally referred to as myelitis, this condition is caused by bacteria, mycobacteria, and fungi.[47] In its early stages, osteomyelitis is described as acute. If the infection persists or recurs periodically, it is called chronic. Because chronic osteomyelitis can linger on for years, the physical educator should confer with the physician about the nature of an adapted program.

Characteristics   In children, the long bones are affected. In adults, the condition settles in the vertebrae and the pelvis. Pain, tenderness, and soft-tissue swelling are present, and heat is felt through the overlying skin. There are limited effects on range of joint movement. The child may limp because of the acute pain.

Special Considerations   If medical treatment is delayed, abscesses work outward, causing a sinus (hole) in the skin over the affected bone, from which pus is discharged. This sinus is covered with a dressing that must be changed several times daily. The medical treatment is rest and intensive antibiotic therapy. Through surgery, the infected bone can be scraped to evacuate the pus.

The Physical Education Program and Teaching Strategies   Rehabilitation activity under the direction of a physician can restore motor functions, so that normal activity can be resumed. Exercise is always contraindicated when infection is active in the body.

Spondylolysis and Spondylolisthesis

Spondylolysis and spondylolisthesis result from a congenital malformation of one or both of the neural arches of the fifth lumbar vertebra or, less frequently, the fourth lumbar vertebra. Spondylolisthesis is distinguished from spondylolysis by anterior displacement of the fifth lumbar vertebra on the sacrum. Both conditions may be accompanied by pain in the lower back.

Forward displacement may occur as a result of sudden trauma to the lumbar region. The vertebrae are moved anteriorly because of an absence of bony continuity of the neural arch, and the main support is derived from ligaments that surround the area. In such cases, individuals often appear to have severe lordosis.

Spondylolysis occurs more frequently in teenagers who are involved in athletics than in the general population. The highest incidence in adolescents occurs in persons involved in activities requiring hyperextension and/or rotation of the lumbar spine, such as diving, weight lifting, wrestling, football, and gymnastics.[50] However, it is also a growing concern for competitive swimmers who use the butterfly stroke or the breaststroke.[21]

Characteristics   Many individuals have spondylolysis, or even spondylolisthesis, without symptoms of any kind, but a mild twist or blow may set off a whole series of low back complaints and localized discomfort or pain radiating down one or both sides.

Special Considerations   The pathological condition eventually may become so extensive as to require surgical intervention.

The Physical Education Program and Teaching Strategies   Proper programming may involve a graduated exercise program to help prevent further aggravation and, in some cases, remove many symptoms characteristic of the condition. A program should be initiated that includes stretching the lower back, strengthening abdominal muscles, walking to stimulate blood flow, and engaging in a general conditioning program. Games and sports that overextend, fatigue, or severely twist and bend the lower back should be avoided. In most cases, the physician will advise against contact sports and heavy weight lifting.

TRAUMATIC INJURIES

Traumatic Brain Injuries

Definition   A traumatic brain injury is an injury to the head that results in minor to serious brain damage; it is the major cause of injury, death, and long-term neurological impairment in children and adolescents.[49] It is the most common cause of acquired disability in childhood and adolescence.[17] The effects of head injuries on school behavior depend on the extent of the insult to the brain tissue.

Incidence   The Centers for Disease Control and Prevention report that in the decade 2001–2010 approximately 2.5 million traumatic brain injuries (TBIs) occurred in the United States that restricted activities, required medical attention, or caused death.[38] In 2009, an estimated 250,000 children under the age of 19 years were treated for sports and recreational injuries that include a diagnosis of TBI.[14]

Causes   Falls are the leading cause of TBI, accounting for 40% of all TBIs in the United States. Fifty-five percent of children 0 to 14 years of age and 81% of adults over the age of 65 years acquired a TBI from a fall. Being hit by an object (unintentional blunt trauma) is the second leading cause followed by motor vehicle accidents. Assaults account for 10% of all reported TBI.

Characteristics   The location and severity of brain damage greatly affect the characteristic behaviors of the child and the speed of recovery. Generally, attention/concentration, memory, executive functions, cognition, and motor and language functions are impaired to some extent. The more severe the injury, the more persistent the behavior, learning, and academic problems.[10] Although rapid recovery of most functions occurs during the first 2 or 3 years after injury, problems frequently persist for longer periods. When the frontal lobe is involved, cognitive impairments occur in attention, executive functioning, and problem solving.[38] Damage to the temporal regions of the brain results in problems with learning new information. Gross motor impairments including static and dynamic balance as well as activities requiring coordination of the two sides of the body are usually impacted the most.[55] Difficulty processing and integrating information, as well as abnormal brain activity, contributes to negative behaviors, including low tolerance for frustration, aggression, impulsiveness, and noncompliance. In addition, seizures are three times more likely among individuals with TBI, with the risk doubling as late as 5 years after the injury. The extent and frequency of these problems should be addressed in the student's IEP.[39]

Testing   The type of test administered will depend on the extent and severity of the student's brain damage. If an individual is having difficulty organizing sensory input, decision and movement time will be compromised, as well as movement efficiency. The type of teaching approach (bottom-up or top-down) a teacher uses will dictate the assessment instrument used. The teacher who wants to address functional performance will measure physical fitness and specific sporting skills. The teacher who uses the bottom-up approach will elect to sample sensory input function.

If the evaluator is more interested in simply pinpointing the areas of motor functioning that have been affected, a motor development or motor proficiency test, such as the Test of Gross Motor Development–2 or the Bruininks-Oseretsky Test of Motor Proficiency-2 (balance, strength, and bilateral coordination subtests) should be administered.

Special Considerations   The extent of the brain damage will determine the number of special considerations that must be made. The person who has acquired a TBI will have good days and bad days. On a good day, it is relatively easy to attend, follow directions, and tolerate minor frustrations. On a bad day, everything is blown out of proportion—it is hard to sit still, listen to instructions, overlook minor problems, and comply with rules. The sensitive teacher will attend carefully to clues that indicate the type of day the student with brain damage is experiencing and will adjust expectations for the student accordingly. Allowance must always be made for basic organizational problems and learning difficulties that have resulted from the insult to the brain tissue.

It is critical that students who have a TBI, no matter how mild, be carefully monitored before returning to participation in sports because TBIs that follow one another have a confounding effect.[33] The reason for this is that the effects of repeated concussions are cumulative. The Centers for Disease Control (CDC) provides five gradual steps in their *Return to Play Progression*, adapted from the International Concussion Consensus Guidelines.[39] The steps, presented in **Table 15-2** are for physical educators, athletic trainers, and coaches who monitor an athlete's return to play.[13]

TABLE 15-2   Return to Play Progression

Step	Goal	Activities
1: Light aerobic activity	Only to increase an athlete's heart rate. Duration: 5–10 minutes	Exercise bike, walking, or light jogging. NO weight lifting, jumping, or hard running.
2: Moderate activity	Limited body and head movement. Duration: reduced from typical routine	Moderate jogging, brief running, moderate-intensity stationary biking, and moderate-intensity weight lifting
3: Heavy, noncontact activity	More intense but noncontact. Duration: close to typical routine	Running, high-intensity stationary biking, weight lifting, noncontact sport skills.
4: Reintegrate in full-contact practice.		
5. Return to competition.		

Teaching Strategies   Physical education personnel should be particularly attentive to the post-trauma student's ongoing psychomotor, cognitive, and behavior problems. Care must be exercised in sequencing motor tasks, providing instructions, and simplifying motor demands. Tasks should be reduced to their simplest components without making the student feel babied; instructions should be brief and to the point; and game strategies should be simple rather than complex. The student should be given the option of taking himself or herself out when the demands of the class prove to be too frustrating to handle on a given day. Any adjustments that will reduce the student's frustration to a minimum and increase his or her ability to cooperate in a group setting will contribute to the student's success in physical education.

The Physical Education Program   Physical exercise has been shown to improve motor function, elevate mood, and contribute to perceptions of better health in individuals with TBIs.[16] The type of physical education provided for the student with a TBI will depend on the test results and the teacher's judgment of the student's capability. The more individualized the program, the less frustration the student will experience. If the student is given opportunities to pursue his or her own exercise program, a buddy system should be effective in keeping the student with a TBI on task and following appropriate safety procedures.

The physical education program should include aerobics and strength exercises, as well as stretching. Initially, the student should avoid high-intensity exercises, particularly those affecting blood pressure, such as resistance training. Instead, he or she should use low to moderate exercise intensities that do not evoke symptoms (e.g., headache, confusion, dizziness, nausea, numbness, fatigue). As strength and endurance improve, the exercise intensity can be increased.

Depending on the extent and severity of brain damage, the following are educational modifications that may need to be included in the IEP:[39]

- Reduce the number of classes
- Scheduling of the most demanding classes in the morning, when the student is fresh
- A resource room with the assistance of an aide
- Rest breaks as needed
- Adapted physical education or a modified regular physical education program

- Peer tutoring
- Counseling
- Provisions for taping lectures and extra time for completing written work and examinations

The individual with a strong support system of friends and family will have greater opportunities to be active in community settings than will the individual who has little or no outside support. Persons with TBIs who understand the components of a healthy lifestyle and who have been taught to select activities that will promote that lifestyle will seek out opportunities to stay active on their good days. On their bad days, their support group will provide them with the encouragement and motivation they need to expend the extra effort to stay active. Caution should be exercised when selecting activities. Highly competitive sports, particularly those that involve contact, can easily provoke a sensitive individual and result in undesirable impulsive, aggressive behaviors. Less competitive games and exercise routines will provide the same level of benefit without the potential negative emotional and physical outcomes.

Spinal Cord Injuries

Spinal cord injuries usually result in paralysis or partial paralysis of the arms, trunk, legs, or any combination thereof and loss of sensation, depending on the locus of the damage. The spinal cord is housed in the spinal, or vertebral, column. Nerves from the spinal cord pass down into the segments of the spinal column. Injury to the spinal cord affects the innervation of muscle. The higher up the vertebral column the level of injury, the greater the restriction of body movement. There are 12,000 new cases of spinal cord injury in the United States every year and 80% of those occur among young adult males (20–29 years of age).[42, 57]

Characteristics   Spinal cord injuries are classified according to the region of the vertebrae affected. The regions affected are cervical, thoracic, lumbar, and sacral. There are two broad types of spinal cord injury: tetraplegia and paraplegia. Tetraplegia (quadriplegia) means the injury is between the C1 vertebra and the T1. Affected body parts include head, neck, shoulders, arms, hands, upper chest, pelvic organs, and legs. A person with paraplegia has lost feeling in his or her lower body including the chest, stomach, hips, legs, and feet. The vertebrae affected are from T2 down to S5.[40]

A description of the movement capability at each level of the lesion follows:

- Fourth cervical level. There is use of only the neck muscles and the diaphragm. Upper limb function is possible only with electrically powered assistive devices. The individual needs complete assistance moving to and from the wheelchair.
- Fifth cervical level. There is use of the deltoid muscles of the shoulder and the biceps muscles of the arm. The arms can be raised; however, it is difficult to engage in manipulative tasks. Persons with this level of involvement can perform many activities with their arms. However, they need assistance with transfer to and from the wheelchair.
- Sixth cervical level. There is use of the wrist extensors, and the person can push the wheelchair and use an overhead trapeze (a bar hung overhead to be grasped). Some persons afflicted at this level can transfer the body to and from the wheelchair.
- Seventh cervical level. There is use of the elbow and wrist extensors. Movement of the hand is impaired. However, the person afflicted at this level may be able to perform pull-ups and push-ups and participate in activities that involve the grasp release mechanism.
- Upper thoracic levels. There is total movement capability in the arms but none in the legs. There is some control in the muscles of the upper back. The individual can control a wheelchair and may be able to stand with the use of long leg braces.
- Lower thoracic levels. There is control of the abdominal musculature that rights the trunk. Using the abdominal muscles makes it possible to walk with the support of long leg braces.
- Lumbar levels. There is control of the hip joint, and there is a good possibility of walking with controlled movement.
- Sacral level. There is muscular functioning for efficient ambulation. The functional level of the bladder, anal sphincters, and external genitals may be impaired.

Special Considerations   In general, spinal cord injury results in motor and sensory loss below the level of injury, autonomic nervous system dysfunction if the injury is at T3 or lower (e.g., bowel/bladder, cardiovascular, and temperature regulation), spasticity, and contractures.[40] Specific physical characteristics are as follows:

1. Inappropriate control of the bladder and digestive organs
2. Contractures (abnormal shortening of muscles)
3. Heterotopic bone formation, or the laying down of new bone in soft tissue around joints (during this process, the area may become inflamed and swollen)
4. Urinary infections
5. Difficulty in defecation
6. Decubitus ulcers on the back and buttocks (caused by pressure of the body weight on specific areas)
7. Spasms of the muscles
8. Spasticity of muscles that prevents effective movement
9. Overweight because of low energy expenditures
10. Scoliosis
11. Respiratory disorders

Persons with spinal cord injury have muscle atrophy and impaired aerobic work capacity because of fewer remaining functional muscles and impaired blood flow. If the injury is above T3, the heart rate may be affected (120 beats per minute is high). Athletes with spinal cord injuries between C6 and T7 have maximal heart rates of 110 to 130 beats per minute. Thermal regulation may also be impaired because of a loss of normal blood flow regulation and the inability to sweat below the level of injury.[35] For this reason, individuals with tetraplegia should not be left in the sun or cold for any length of time. Individuals with tetraplegia who exercise are encouraged to wear support hose and use abdominal strapping to promote venous blood flow to the heart.[35]

The Physical Education Program and Teaching Strategies   The physical education program for persons with spinal cord injury should be based on a well-rounded program of exercises for all the usable body parts, including activities to develop strength, flexibility, muscular endurance, cardiovascular endurance, and coordination. Physical activity is necessary because not only does a regular exercise regime strengthen the cardiovascular system but it also enhances a person's functional independence, overall sense of well-being, and quality of life.[18] Young children need to be taught ways to use their wheelchairs in a variety of environments and should be encouraged to interact with their ambulatory peers. Middle school and high school students should develop the physical fitness necessary to participate in the sports of their choice.

Movement and dance therapies have been used successfully in rehabilitation programs for persons who have spinal cord injuries. **Table 15-3** includes modifications that can be made in a typical warm-up session for a kindergarten or first-grade class.

The emphasis in the physical education program should be on functional movement skills. The child, if using a wheelchair, should be given every opportunity to move in the chair. Individuals with upper body function can perform most physical education activities from a wheelchair. In consultation with a physical therapist, the physical educator should integrate wheelchair mobility training into programming. The child should practice moving in the chair with activities that modify the movement variables of time, space, force, and flow. For example, the child should be able to do the following:

1. Time
   a. Wheel fast, then slow.
   b. Wheel to a 4/4 beat.
2. Space
   a. Wheel up and down inclines.
   b. Wheel on cement, linoleum, grass, a gymnasium floor, and so on.
   c. Wheel around obstacles.
   d. Wheel over sticks.
   e. Wheel, holding a glass of water.
   f. Wheel, holding a ball on lap.
3. Force
   a. Wheel with a buddy sitting on lap.
   b. Wheel while pulling a partner on a scooter board.
   c. Push hard and see how far the chair will roll.
4. Flow
   a. Roll forward, spin in a circle, roll forward.
   b. Roll forward, stop, roll backward, stop.

The same type of movement activities should be made available to the child using crutches and braces.

TABLE 15-3 Warm-up Session with Modifications for Children Using Wheelchairs

Class Activity (Song/Dance)	Modifications
"Warm-up Time"	
Clap hands	None
Swing arms	None
Bend knees	Child lifts knees with hands.
Stamp feet	Child slaps feet with hands.
"What a Miracle"	
Clap hands	None
Stamp feet	Child slaps feet with hands.
Swing arms	None
Bend and stretch legs	Child lifts knees with hands.
Twist and bend spine	None
One foot balance	Child pushes into push-up position.
"Swing. Shake, Twist, Stretch"	
Swing	Child swings arms or head.
Shake	Child shakes hands, elbows, or head.
Twist	Child twists trunk.
Stretch	Child stretches arms.
"Bendable, Stretchable"	
Stretch to sky; touch floor	Child stretches to sky, touches toes.
"Run, Run, Run in Place"	
Run in place	Child spins chair in circle.
"Simon Says Jog Along"	
Jog	Child rolls chair in time to music.
Walk	Child rolls chair in time to music.

In addition to wheelchair mobility, younger children should be taught fundamental motor skills, such as throwing, hitting, and catching. Once these skills are mastered, games that incorporate these skills can be played. Modifications of games that have been described previously are appropriate for children using wheelchairs. Children using wheelchairs can participate in parachute games and target games without accommodation. They can maintain fitness of the upper body through the same type of exercises as their nondisabled peers. Strengthening of the arms and shoulder girdle is important for propelling the wheelchair and for changing body positions when moving in and out of the wheelchair. Swimming is a particularly good activity for the development of total physical fitness. The emphasis should be on the development of functional movement skills.

It is possible to increase the heart rate response, blood pressure response, stroke volume and cardiac output, and respiration rate and depth through the use of arm exercises.[18] Stretching exercises should always be used to improve flexibility and enable an individual to achieve full joint range of motion. They are also critical for reducing the chance of stress injuries to muscles, tendons, and ligaments.

Routine exercise programs are critical for the individual who uses a wheelchair for ambulation, because the act of manually wheeling the chair produces imbalances in muscle strength. Imbalances in muscle strength lead to postural deviations that, if left unaddressed, will eventually become structural and further impair the individual's health. The physical educator who helps the individual using a wheelchair develop a realistic exercise program that can be continued throughout life will contribute to the quality of that person's life.

Amputations

A person with an amputation is missing part or all of a limb. Amputation is sometimes performed to arrest a malignant condition caused by trauma, tumors, infection, vascular impairment, diabetes, or arteriosclerosis.[58] The number of amputees in the United States is nearly 2 million.[3]

Characteristics and Types   Amputations can be classified into two categories: acquired amputation and congenital amputation. The amputation is acquired if one has a limb removed by operation; it is congenital if one is born without a limb. Congenital amputations are classified according to the site and level of limb absence. When an amputation is performed through a joint, it is referred to as a disarticulation.

Special Considerations   Many individuals with an amputation elect to use a prosthetic appliance to replace the missing limb. The purpose of the prosthetic device is to enable the individual to function as normally as possible. The application of a prosthetic device may be preceded by surgery to produce a stump. After the operation, the stump is dressed and bandaged to aid shrinkage of the stump. After the fitting of the prosthesis, the stump must be continually cared for. It should be checked periodically and cleaned to prevent infection, abrasion, and skin disorder. The attachment of a false limb early in a child's development will encourage the incorporation of the appendage into natural body activity more than if the prosthesis is introduced later in life. The type of prosthesis selected depends on whether it will be used for daily activities and recreational purposes or for a specific activity, such as distance running or sprinting.[27]

The Physical Education Program and Teaching Strategies   The ultimate goal of a person with an amputation is to perform physical activity safely. Amputees must develop skills to use prostheses. The remaining muscles needed for prosthetic use must be strengthened, and standing and walking must be practiced until they become automatic. To regain adequate postural equilibrium, individuals with lower limb amputation have to learn to link altered sensory input to movement patterns. Practice in walking, turning, sitting, and standing is needed.[3]

Amputees are often exposed to beneficial exercise through the use of the prosthesis. Exercises should be initiated to strengthen muscles after a stump heals. Training also enhances ambulation, inhibits atrophy and contractures, improves or maintains mechanical alignment of body parts, and develops general physical fitness.

Several adaptations of physical activity can be made for children with impaired ambulation. For these children, the major disadvantages are speed of locomotion and fatigue to sustained activity. Physical fitness of amputees should be an important part of a physical education program. Some accommodations that can be made are shortening the distance the child must travel and decreasing the speed needed to move from one place to another.

Persons with amputations below the knee can learn ambulation skills well with a prosthesis and training. Persons with amputations above the knee but below the hip may have difficulty developing efficient walking gaits. Amputations at this level require alteration of the gait pattern. Steps are usually shortened to circumvent lack of knee function.

Authorities agree that children with properly fitted prostheses should engage in regular physical education activities. Amputees have considerable potential for participation in adapted sports and games. The National Amputee Golf Association, for example, provides clinics nationwide to introduce children and adults with disabilities to the sport of golf and to train teachers and coaches to adapt methods and instruction to meet the needs of amputees. There are opportunities for persons with prostheses to participate in official sports competition. Persons with above-the-knee amputations can walk well and engage in swimming, skiing, and other activities with the proper aids. Persons with arm amputations who have use of their feet can participate in activities that require foot action, such as soccer and running events, as well as other activities that involve the feet exclusively.

Testing   Assessing the present level of performance of students who are amputees is important for structuring a quality physical education/activity program. The Brockport Physical Fitness Test, Project M.O.B.I.L.I.T.E.E., and the *Physical Best and Individuals with Disabilities Handbook* by SHAPE America all suggest accommodations for ambulatory and nonambulatory individuals. In addition to formal testing, it is frequently just as important to appraise individuals' functional movement capabilities. Movement programs can then be developed to meet the unique needs of students with differing limb involvement. The assessment should provide information about the potential for movement of each action of the body. This would involve knowledge of the strength, power, flexibility, and endurance of specific muscle groups. In addition, there should be information about which movement actions can be coordinated to attain specific fundamental movement and sport-specific outcomes.

SUMMARY

The three types of physical disabilities discussed in this chapter are neurological conditions, orthopedic disabilities, and conditions caused by trauma. Afflictions can occur at more than 500 anatomical sites. Each student with a disability has different physical and motor capabilities and is to be provided with accommodations that enable participation in modified games and sport activity. Contraindicated activity as identified by medical personnel must be avoided.

Physical educators should address two types of program considerations to meet the physical education needs of persons with physical disabilities. One is to implement developmental programs that enhance prerequisite motor patterns, sport skills, and physical and motor fitness. The other is to structure the environment so that students with disabilities can derive physical benefits through participation in competitive sporting activities (this may be facilitated by the use of aids for specific types of activities and disabilities).

The physical educator should be ready to accommodate the individual program needs of persons with a disability by identifying unique needs through formal and functional assessment, using adaptive devices to permit activity involvement, and modifying activities to enable the student to participate in a variety of settings.

REVIEW QUESTIONS

1. Identify some activities that will benefit a child with cerebral palsy.
2. Discuss the type of physical education program that would benefit a teenager who has returned to school after suffering a moderate traumatic brain injury.
3. Explain how the level of spinal cord injury affects the type of activity a person can participate in.
4. What are some specific examples of ways physical education activities can be modified to accommodate a student using a wheelchair?
5. What types of spina bifida are there and what accommodations must be made for each?

REFERENCES

1. Adzick, S., et al. (2011). A randomized trial of prenatal versus postnatal repair of myelomeningocele. *New England Journal of Medicine, 364*(11). DOI: 10.1056 /nejmoa1014379.
2. Agiovlasitis, S., & Motl, R. (2014). Step-rate thresholds for physical activity intensity in persons with multiple sclerosis. *Adapted Physical Activity Quarterly, 31*, 4-18. DOI: 10/1123/apaq.2003.0008.
3. Amputee Coalition. (2015). www.amputeecoalition.org
4. Amyotrophic Lateral Sclerosis Association. (2015). www.alsa.national.org
5. Arthritis Foundation. (2007). www.arthritis.org
6. Bamshad, M., Heest, A., & Pleasure, D. (2009). Arthrogryposis: A review and update. *Journal of Bone and Joint Surgery, 91*, 40–46. DOI: 10.2106/jbjs.i.00281.
7. Bello-Haas, V., & Krivickas, L. (2009). Amyotrophic lateral sclerosis. In Durstine, J. L., Moore, G., Painter, P., & Roberts, S. (Eds.). *ACSM's exercise management for persons with chronic diseases and disabilities* (3rd ed.). Champaign, IL: Human Kinetics.
8. Biggin, A., & Munns, C. (2014). Osteogenesis imperfect: Diagnosis and treatment. *Pediatrics, 12*, 279–288. DOI: 10.1007/s11914-014-0225-0.

9. Birk, T. J. (2003). Polio and post-polio syndrome. In Durstine, J. L., & Moore, G. (Eds.). *ACSM's exercise management for persons with chronic diseases and disabilities* (2nd ed.). Champaign, IL: Human Kinetics.

10. Brain Injury Association of America. (2015). *Brain injury in children.* Retrieved from www.biausa.org

11. Centers for Disease Control. (2015). http://www.cdc.gov/ncbddd/cp/facts.html

12. Centers for Disease Control and Prevention. (2015). http://www.cdc.gov/ncbddd/spinabifida/infant.html

13. Centers for Disease Control and Prevention. (2015). *Managing return to activities.* Retrieved from www.cdc.gov

14. Centers for Disease Control and Prevention. (2014). *Traumatic brain injury in the United States: Fact sheet.* Retrieved from www.cdc.gov

15. Driban, J., Hootman, J., Sitler, M., Harris, K., & Cattano, N. (2015). Is participation in certain sports associated with knee osteoarthritis? A systematic review. *Journal of Athletic Training.* DOI: 10.4085/1062-6050-50.2.08.

16. Driver, S. (2008). Development of a conceptual model to predict physical activity participation in adults with brain injuries. *Adapted Physical Activity Quarterly, 25,* 289–307.

17. Driver, S., Harmon, M., & Block, M. (2003). Devising a safe and successful physical education program for children with brain injury. *JOPERD, 74*(7), 41–49.

18. Figoni, S. F. (2009). Spinal cord injury. In Durstine, J. L., Moore, G., Painter, P., & Roberts, S. (Eds.). *ACSM's exercise management for persons with chronic diseases and disabilities* (3rd ed.). Champaign, IL: Human Kinetics.

19. Goldman, R. (2014). *Healthline.* Retrieved from http://www.healthline.com/health/what-is-jacobson-relaxation-technique

20. Golijan, E. (2014). *Rapid Review Pathology* (4th ed.). Philadelphia, PA: Elsevier Health Sciences.

21. Grierson, M., Speckman, R., Harrast, M., & Herring, S. (2015). Stress fractures of the lumbar spine. In Miller, T., & Kaeding, C. (Eds.). *Stress fractures in athletes.* Springer.

22. Günel, M. K., Türker, D., Ozal, C., & Kara, O. K. (2014). *Physical Management of Children with Cerebral Palsy.* Cdn. Intechopen.com.

23. Healthology. (2007). www.healthology.com

24. Hurkmans, E., van der Giesen, F., Vlieland, T., Schoones, J., & Van den, E. (2009). Dynamic exercise programs (aerobic capacity and/or muscle strength training) in patients with rheumatoid arthritis. Cochrane Database Syst Rev. DOI: 10.1002/14651858.

25. Jackson, K., & Mulcare, J. (2009). Multiple sclerosis. In Durstine J. L., Moore, G., Painter, P., & Roberts, S. (Eds.). *ACSM's exercise management for persons with chronic diseases and disabilities* (3rd ed.). Champaign, IL: Human Kinetics.

26. Kilmer, D. D. (2002). Response to resistive strengthening exercise training in humans with neuromuscular disease. *Am J Phys Med Rehabil, 81* (Suppl), S121–S126.

27. Kistenberg, R. (2014, February). Prosthetic choices for people with leg and arm amputation. *Physical Medicine and Rehab Clinics of NA, 25*(1).

28. Laskin, J. (2003). *Cerebral palsy.* In Durstine, J. L., Moore, G. (Eds.). *ACSM's exercise management for persons with chronic diseases and disabilities* (2nd ed.). Champaign, IL: Human Kinetics.

29. Lava, M. (2015). Epilepsy seizure types and symptoms. *WebMD.* http://www .webmd.com/epilepsy/guide/types-of-seizures-their-symptoms

30. Long, S. (2013). Hippotherapy as a tool for improving motor skills, postural stability, and self confidence in cerebral palsy and multiple sclerosis. *Sound Neuroscience: An Undergraduate Neuroscience Journal, 1*(2). http:/soundideas .pudgetsound.edu/soundneuroscience/vol1/iss2/3

31. Mayo Clinic. (2015). http://www.mayoclinic.org/diseases-conditions /osgood-schlatter

32. McBride, M. (2013). Cerebral palsy syndromes. *Merck Manuals Professional Edition.*

33. McCrory, P., Meeuwisse, W., Johnson, K., Dvorak, J., Aubry, M., Molloy, M., & Cantu, R. (2009). Consensus statement on concussion in sport. *Journal of Sports Medicine, 43* (suppl), i76-i84. DOI: 10.1136/bjsm.2009.058248.

34. McDonald, C. M. (2002). Physical activity, health impairments, and disability in neuromuscular disease. *Am J Phys Rehabil, 81*(Suppl), S108–S120.

35. McKinley, W. (2014). Cardiovascular concerns in spinal cord injury. *Medscape,* www.emedicine.medscape.com

36. Medline Plus. (2003). www.nlm.nih.gov/medlineplus/ency

37. Molt, R., Arnett, P., Smith, M., Barwick, F., Ahlstrom, B., & Stover, E. (2008). Worsening of symptoms is associated with lower physical activity levels in individuals with multiple sclerosis. *Multiple Sclerosis, 14*(1), 140–142. PMID: 18089672.

38. National Center for Injury Prevention and Control. (2014). *Report to Congress: Traumatic brain injury in the United States: Epidemiology and rehabilitation.* Atlanta, GA: Centers for Disease Control and Prevention.

39. National Information Center for Children and Youth with Disabilities. (2015). *Traumatic brain injury.* Retrieved from www.nichcy.org

40. National Institute of Child Health and Development. (2013). *Spinal cord injury: Condition information.* National Institute of Health, www.nichd.nih.gov

41. National Institute of Neurological Disorders and Stroke. (2015). *NIH.* http:// www.ninds.nih.gov/disorders/epilepsy/detail_epilepsy.htm

42. National Spinal Cord Injury Statistical Center. (2012). *Spinal cord injury facts and figures at a glance.* Retrieved from www.nscisc.uab.edu

43. Neurology Channel. (2007). www.neurologychannel.com/cerebralpalsy

44. Oskoui, M., Coutinho, F., Dykeman, J., Jetté, N., & Pringsheim, T. (2013). An update on the prevalence of cerebral palsy: A systematic review and meta-analysis. *Developmental Medicine and Child Neurology, 55*(6), 509–519. DOI: 10.1111/dmcn.12080.

45. Protas, E. J., Stanley, R. K., & Jankovic, J. (2003). Parkinson's disease. In Durstine, J. L., Moore, G., Painter, P., & Roberts, S. (Eds.). *ACSM's exercise management for persons with chronic diseases and disabilities* (2nd ed.). Champaign, IL: Human Kinetics.

46. Rajab, A., Yoo, S. Y., Abdulgalil, A., Kathiri, S., Ahmed, R., Mochida, G. H., Bodell, A., Barkovich, A. J., & Walsh, C. A. (2006). An autosomal recessive form of spastic cerebral palsy (CP) with microcephaly and mental retardation. *Am J Med Genet Part A, 140A*, 1504–1510.

47. Rubin, M. (2014). Amyotrophic lateral sclerosis and other motor neuron diseases. *Merck Manuals Professional Edition.*

48. McBride, M. (2013). Cerebral palsy syndromes. *Merck Manuals Professional Edition.*

49. Salavati, M., Rameckers, E., Steenbergen, B., & van der Schans, C. (2014). Gross motor function, functional skills and caregiver assistance in children with spastic cerebral palsy (CP) with and without cerebral visual impairment (CVI). *European Journal of Physiotherapy, 16*(3), 159–167. DOI: 10.3109/21679169.2014.899392.

50. Su, F. (2013). *Traumatic brain injury in children.* Medscape. www.emedicine.medscape.com

51. Tallarico, R., Madom, A., & Palumbo, M. (2008). Spondylosis and spondylolisthesis in the athlete. *Sports Medicine Arthrosc, 16*(1), 32–38. DOI: 10.1097/jsa.0b013e318163be50.

52. Thiele, E. (2006). *Activities, safety and first.* Massachusetts General Hospital. http://www2.massgeneral.org/childhoodepilepsy/child/activities.htm

53. United Cerebral Palsy of Central California. (2003). www.ccucp.org/prg

54. University of Washington Medicine: Orthopaedics and Sports Medicine. (2015). *Water exercises: Pool and arthritis.* Retrieved from www.orthop.washington.edu

55. Unnithan, V. B., Clifford, C., & Bar-Or, O. (1998). Evaluation by exercise testing of the child with cerebral palsy. *Sports Medicine, 26*, 239–251.

56. Walker, W., & Pickett, T. (2007). Motor impairment after severe traumatic brain injury: A longitudinal multicenter study. *Journal of Rehabilitation Research & Development, 44*, 975–982. DOI: 10.1682/JRRD.2006.12.0158.

57. White, L. J., & Castellano, V. (2006). Exercise and brain health—implications for multiple sclerosis: Part 1—neural growth factors. *Sports Medicine, 38*(2), 91–100. PMID: 18201113.

58. World Health Organization. (2013). *Spinal cord injury.* Retrieved from www.who.int

59. Ziegler-Graham, K., MacKenzie, E. J., Ephraim, P. L., Travison, T. G., & Brookmeyer, R. (2008). Estimating the prevalence of limb loss in the United States: 2005 to 2050. *Archives of Physical Medicine and Rehabilitation, 89*(3), 422–429.

CHAPTER 16

Communicative Disorders

- List three motor characteristics of elementary and high school children who are deaf.
- Describe the culture of the Deaf community.
- Demonstrate five specific signs that can be used in physical education to communicate with students who are deaf or hard of hearing.
- List five techniques a teacher can use for enhancing communication with students who are deaf or hard of hearing.
- Differentiate between the three major instructional approaches used with deaf learners: bilingual/bicultural, total communication, and auditory-verbal (oral) therapy.
- List the strategies a physical education teacher can use when working with a professional interpreter.
- Explain effective teaching strategies for working with a learner who is deaf-blind.
- Describe strategies for teaching students with receptive and expressive language disorders.

Fundamental to the human experience is communication with other human beings. Children who have difficulty expressing their thoughts, feelings, ideas, and dreams or understanding struggle to make sense of their surroundings.

© Lopolo/Shutterstock

It is difficult to make sense of their world and all the stimuli and experiences to which they are exposed without the capacity to describe, evaluate, and share these experiences.

Without supports and accommodations, children with communicative delays and disorders may have a difficult time being successful in the educational environment. While they may have good physical and motor skills, they may struggle with the social experiences in the physical education program.

Deafness and Hearing Impairments

© spass/Shutterstock

Significant challenges face the physical educator seeking to provide a *quality* educational experience for deaf learners. Part of the challenge is associated with the growing educational trend to consider students who are deaf or hearing impaired as bilingual members of a bicultural minority,[49] rather than children with a disability. This trend is emerging, in part, to honor the unique culture, language, history, and legacy of the Deaf community. Deafness, with a capital "D," espouses more than just limited hearing. The Deaf community identify with Deaf culture. People who are Deaf communicate with each other and with hearing people using American Sign Language (ASL) or the visual language of their country of origin. In addition to supporting the education of children in both ASL and English, Deaf culture involves traditions and social conventions and methods of interaction.[16] When interacting with individuals with hearing impairments, it is important to ask their preferred mode of communication and honor the culture they identify with.

In addition to broader cultural issues, children who have permanent hearing loss usually have delays in expressive and receptive language, play and other social skills, and motor development. The purpose of this chapter is to provide the physical educator with information necessary to teach learners who are deaf or hearing impaired, deaf-blind, and speech and language delayed.

Definition of Deaf or Hearing Impaired

Deafness and hearing impairment are disabilities defined by the Individuals with Disabilities Education Act. Deafness means a hearing impairment so severe that the child is impaired in processing linguistic information through hearing, with or without amplification. Hearing impairment, whether permanent or fluctuating, adversely affects a child's educational performance.

The continuum of hearing loss and the ability to understand speech ranges from that of little significance to that of extreme disability (see **Table 16-1**). The degree of an individual's deafness is determined by the level of decibel loss and the individual's ability to perceive conversation.[55]

TABLE 16-1   Characteristics of Children with Hearing Loss[13, 26]

Mild Hearing Loss (15–30 Decibel Hearing Loss)

- Children develop speech and language spontaneously.
- They may have difficulty hearing faint speech.

Moderate Hearing Loss (31–60 Decibel Hearing Loss)

- Children will benefit from hearing aids as soon as possible after diagnosis.
- Children will rely on visual information to supplement auditory information.
- They may have difficulty with delayed language and speech skills, particularly in the pronunciation of consonants.
- They will do better in a classroom setting with preferential seating.

Severe Hearing Loss (61–90 Decibel Hearing Loss)

- Children will have difficulty hearing conversational speech.
- They will be able to respond to sounds that are high in intensity, at close range, with amplification.
- They will require amplification and significant speech and language therapy to function in the educational setting.

(continues)

TABLE 16-1   Characteristics of Children with Hearing Loss[13, 26] (*Continued*)

Profound Hearing Loss (91–120 Decibel Hearing Loss)

- Children with a profound hearing loss are unlikely to benefit from auditory input and will rely on tactile and visual cues.
- They will usually need to use total communication or manual communication.
- With little residual hearing, they may still have intelligible speech.

Total Hearing Loss (121+ Decibel Hearing Loss)

- Children with total hearing loss do not hear even with an auditory amplification device.
- They will depend on vision as their primary modality.

Incidence of Hearing Impairments in Children

Approximately 77,000 students, between the ages of 3 to 21 years, received educational services in 2012–2013 because of an educational diagnosis of deafness or hearing impairment.[46] These students received their education in the following settings:

- <40% of instruction inside regular classroom: 13%
- 40%–79% of instruction inside regular classroom: 16.8%
- >80% of instruction inside regular classroom: 56.7%
- Separate public school facility: 8.6%
- Separate private school facility: 1.3%
- Residential facility: 3.4%
- Home/hospital: 0.20%
- Correctional facility: 0.10%[64]

Causes of Hearing Impairments

The time of onset of deafness is a critical factor in its impact on the child's learning. The acquisition of speech and language skills, like the acquisition of motor skills, is basic to the subsequent development of the individual. Essentially, individuals are divided into two basic categories, those who are prelingually deaf and those who are postlingually deaf. Prior to the invention of the cochlear implant device, if a child became deaf before the acquisition of any linguistic or speech skills, prelingually, the child had little, if any, chance of acquiring typical speech and language skills. If an individual experiences a hearing loss after having acquired speech and language skills, postlingually, the individual may have already acquired and be able to retain typical speech and language skills.

All 50 states have laws requiring early hearing detection and intervention in newborns, and the majority of states provide hearing screening in school-age children. Early detection allows for early intervention. Early intervention is critical for infants and young children with hearing loss. The earlier the diagnosis can be made, the earlier the infant or child and the family can receive the health and educational services vital to the development of the infant or child.

There are three major types of hearing impairments: (1) conductive, (2) sensorineural, and (3) mixed.

CONDUCTIVE HEARING IMPAIRMENTS

A conductive hearing loss causes fluctuating hearing levels. A conductive hearing impairment is, typically, a condition in which the intensity of sound is reduced before reaching the inner ear, where the auditory nerve begins. A conductive hearing loss can also result when the membranes in the inner ear undergo physical changes that reduce the transfer of energy to the hair cells.

The most prevalent cause of conductive hearing loss is otitis media, an infection of the middle ear. Hearing impairments and deafness from otitis media are particularly critical if a young child has suffered a series of infections at a young age. Intermittent or persistent conductive hearing loss as a result of otitis media may have a significant impact on the subsequent learning and behavior of school-age children. It may interfere with a child's detection and recognition of speech.

Another infection that can cause conductive hearing loss is mastoiditis. Mastoiditis occurs when there is chronic inflammation of the middle ear that spreads into the cells of the mastoid process within the temporal bone. Other causes of conductive hearing loss include perforation of the eardrum from a blow to the head, allergies that make the eustachian tube swell, tumors of the external auditory canal, the presence of foreign objects in the external ear, insect bites, and an excessive buildup of ear wax.

SENSORINEURAL HEARING IMPAIRMENTS

A sensorineural hearing loss (SNHL) may also filter and distort sound. It also may interfere with a child's detection and recognition of speech. A sensorineural hearing loss is caused by an absence or a malfunction of the sensory unit. The damage may be present in the cochlea (sensory) or the eighth cranial nerve (neural). If the dysfunction is in the inner ear, the individual has difficulty discriminating among speech sounds. The individual can hear sound but has difficulty making sense of high-frequency sounds. Causes of SNHL include maternal rubella (German measles); venereal disease during pregnancy; lesions or tumors in the inner ear or on the eighth cranial nerve; infections of childhood, including mumps, meningitis, and encephalitis; head trauma; aging; or hereditary hearing loss. One of the major causes of significant hearing loss is noise. Noise-induced hearing loss results from exposure to any source of intense and/or constant noise, an environmental toxin, over an extended period of time.

MIXED HEARING LOSS

Mixed hearing loss is a combination of conductive and sensorineural hearing loss. Subsequently there is damage in both the outer or middle ear and in the inner ear or auditory nerve. In this type of hearing loss, the conductive cause of the hearing loss has the potential to respond to treatment; however, the sensorineural cause is often permanent.

Characteristics of Students with Hearing Impairments

UNILATERAL HEARING LOSS

A child with a unilateral hearing loss (normal hearing in one ear but not the other) may struggle in the school environment. He or she is frequently misunderstood as being able to hear "what he or she wants to hear." In fact, the child with a unilateral hearing loss has difficulty hearing the teacher, especially if the acoustics are bad (e.g., in the gymnasium), and the teacher is at any distance from the child. In order to track sound, the child may move his or her head and body toward the sound; unfortunately, a teacher without specific training may assume the child is simply fidgeting and not attending.[12]

CLUES THAT INDICATE HEARING LOSS

Early identification of deafness and hearing loss is critical.[14] Parents and teachers should be alert to signs of hearing loss:[1, 14]

1. Hearing and comprehension of speech
   a. General indifference to sound
   b. Lack of response to the spoken word
   c. Response to noise, not words
   d. Head and body leaning toward the source of sound
   e. Requests that statements be repeated
   f. Tinnitus—buzzing, ringing, roaring, whistling, or hissing sounds
2. Vocalization and sound production
   a. Monotonal quality
   b. Indistinct speech
   c. Lessened laughter
   d. Vocal play for vibratory sensation
   e. Head banging, foot stamping for vibratory sensation
   f. Yelling, screeching to express pleasure or need
3. Visual attention
   a. Augmented visual vigilance and attentiveness
   b. Alertness to gesture and movement
4. Social rapport and adaptation
   a. Intensified preoccupation with things rather than persons
   b. Puzzling and unhappy episodes in social situations
   c. Suspiciousness and alertness, alternating with cooperation
   d. Marked reaction to praise and affection
5. Emotional behavior
   a. Tantrums to call attention to self or need
   b. Frequent stubborn behavior
   c. Frustration and anger when not understood
6. Motor behavior
   a. Vertigo, an abnormal sensation of rotary movement associated with difficulty in balance, gait, and navigation of the environment[1]
7. Physical development and health
   a. Earaches, particularly chronic
   b. Jaw pain
   c. Chronic sinus infections[1]

Courtesy of Kristi Roth

Hearing loss can have a profound effect on behavior, language and speech development, learning and cognitive function, play, and social adjustment. Comprehension and language production are significantly affected by hearing loss. In both conductive and sensorineural hearing losses, the development of auditory skills that are critical prerequisites to the development of receptive and expressive language skills, as well as speech intelligibility, is delayed. The auditory skills that are compromised include detection, discrimination, recognition, comprehension, and attention. If an infant or a developing child is unable to hear the oral language produced in his or her environment, it is impossible for the child to reproduce the language. If the child is unable to hear the rhythm and rhyme, the form (syntax), the use of language (pragmatics), the tone, the timbre and flow of the language, and the content (semantics), the child will be unable to produce sounds that replicate what was heard. It is generally understood that the more severe the hearing loss, the less intelligible a child's speech will be.[57]

The young child with deafness or a hearing impairment is particularly apt to struggle within the traditional school setting. Until the child is able to read, the child relies heavily on hearing to learn.[39] Even the child with a minimal hearing loss struggles in school learning environments and may become fatigued because of the extra effort necessary to hear and follow directions.[20, 47] This struggle is even worse in the gymnasium. This places the child with deafness or a hearing impairment at a significant disadvantage. However, if these children are given the opportunity to develop all of his or her intelligences (Gardner's eight intelligences)—the musical, logical-mathematical, or bodily-kinesthetic, for example—there is no reason they cannot succeed in school.

Technological Hearing Assistance

The child's ability to function will also be impacted by the type of hearing assistance he or she has and the length of time he or she has had corrected hearing. The National Institute on Deafness and Other Communication Disorders describes hearing aids:

> A hearing aid is an electronic, battery-operated device that amplifies and changes sound to allow for improved communication. Hearing aids receive sound through a microphone, which then converts the sound waves to electrical signals. The amplifier increases the loudness of the signals and then sends the sound to the ear through a speaker.[61]

Hearing aids come in five models: in-the-ear aids, behind-the-ear aids, canal aids, body aids, and implantable aids. An audiologist decides which type of hearing aid will be beneficial for the individual who is deaf or hearing impaired. Bluetooth-enabled hearing aids can be purchased to enable a listener to hear content coming directly from a Bluetooth-enabled device, such as an app on a mobile device, a speaker system in a gym, or even a small microphone clipped onto the teacher. Implantable aids increase the transmission of sounds entering the ear.

Cochlear implants are available for surgical implantation in children with bilateral severe-to-profound hearing loss and who have made little progress in the development of auditory skills.[8] (See **Figure 16-1.**) An implant has four basic parts: "a microphone that picks up sound from the environment; a speech processor, which selects and arranges sounds picked up by

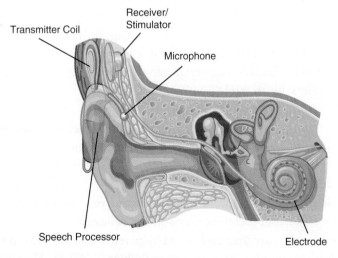

Figure 16-1   Ear with Cochlear Implant
Courtesy of National Institutes of Health

the microphone; a transmitter and receiver/stimulator, which receive signals from the speech processor and convert them into electric impulses; and electrodes, which collect the impulses from the stimulator and send them to the brain."[44] Essentially, the implant finds and transmits usable sounds to existing auditory nerves. The use of a cochlear implant by children who are prelingually profoundly hearing impaired presents a tremendous advantage for these children over children who use a hearing aid, particularly if they are educated in an oral setting (without the use of sign language). Studies have shown that these children understand and produce language at a level comparable to that of hearing children of the same age.[18, 62]

At the time most students who are deaf or have a hearing impairment leave school at age 20 years, their average reading skills are at grade 4.5, and their overall academic skills are behind those of their hearing peers.[59] It must be remembered, however, that most students who graduate from public high schools in the United States have functional reading skills typical of a fourth- or fifth-grader. That is, of course, a major concern.

The most significant problem tied to deafness/hearing impairment in young children is their difficulty with play. Play is the foundation of the development of young children. Difficulty with communication makes it difficult for a young child who is deaf or hearing impaired to play with other children.

Children who have a hearing impairment may, indeed, develop symbolic play even in the absence of spoken language. However, language does not develop in the absence of play.[35] It appears that young children who have a hearing impairment develop the skills to engage in "pretend play" without oral/verbal communication. Apparently, it is much like the play typical of young children who have not yet developed spoken language—the play of young toddlers, for example.

Each child's psychosocial development is based on how well or how poorly others in the environment accept him or her (see **Table 16-2**). Unfortunately, the psychosocial development of some children who have a hearing impairment is delayed because of the negative stereotypes attributed to them.[38] Stereotypes associated with individuals who have a hearing impairment include nonsocial behavior, reservedness, lack of communicativeness, and preference for solitary behavior.[7]

Children who are deaf and raised by parents who are deaf, about 10% of the children who are deaf, are generally better adjusted than deaf children reared by hearing parents. This should be no surprise. If the child's

TABLE 16-2   Holcomb's Categories of Identity of Individuals Who Are Deaf[22]

Balanced Bicultural

The person who is deaf feels equally comfortable in deaf and hearing cultures.

Deaf-Dominant Bicultural

The person is primarily involved in the Deaf community but can relate well to hearing people.

Hearing-Dominant Bicultural

The person feels comfortable in the hearing community and has limited involvement in the Deaf community, perhaps because of lack of access.

Culturally Separate

The person identifies with and prefers to associate exclusively with others who are deaf.

Culturally Isolated

The person rejects involvement with other individuals who are deaf. The person is comfortable in and prefers the hearing community and perceives sign language to be a "crutch" for those unable to learn oral skills.

Culturally Marginal

The person is uncomfortable in the Deaf community and the hearing community.

Culturally Captive

The person is deaf and has had no opportunity to meet others who are deaf and learn about deaf culture.

parent has experienced the confusion, frustration, and pain associated with difficulty communicating with others and has experienced discrimination within the community and larger society, the parent will be much more likely to understand the feelings of his or her child. In addition, the infant born to deaf parents has a definite advantage in communication skills because the child is exposed to sign language from infancy, in the same way that a hearing child of hearing parents is exposed to the parents' oral language from infancy.

In addition, if the parent's natural language is sign, the child and parent will find it much easier to communicate than will a child and parent learning the language together. It is easy to compare this to the process a child goes through learning a verbal-based language. If the parent's native language, for example, is Spanish, it will be easy for the child to learn Spanish; the language is used in the home, and the inferences, nuances, and intricacies of the language are shared daily. If both the parents and the child are struggling to learn English as a second language, the process is much more difficult.

MOTOR CHARACTERISTICS OF INDIVIDUALS WITH HEARING IMPAIRMENT

Impairment of the semicircular canals, vestibule of the inner ear, and/or vestibular portion of the eighth cranial nerve has a negative effect on balance. Siegel, Marchetti, and Tecclin[56] reported significantly depressed balance performance by children with sensorineural hearing loss of below 65 decibels. Another study that did not examine etiological factors evaluated motor performance and vestibular function of a group of children with hearing impairments. The vast majority (65%) of the studied group demonstrated abnormal vestibular function but normal motor proficiency except for balance, whereas 24% had normal vestibular function and motor proficiency, including balance. Eleven percent had normal vestibular function but poor motor proficiency and balance.[19]

Butterfield et al.[6] found that 9 of 18 deaf boys and girls attending a residential school for the deaf had significant balance deficits, as evidenced by extraneous movement on Subtest 2, Item 8 of the Bruininks-Oseretsky Test of Motor Proficiency. Each child was asked to walk on a balance beam and step over a stick, held at knee level, without falling off the balance beam. The students who fell appeared dependent on the visual system for their information about their performance; they watched their feet while walking on the beam. Each student who fell appeared dependent on the visual mechanism for information about his or her balance. This is typical of children with a vestibular deficit, though no specific test was used to determine if such a deficit was present.

Butterfield and Ersing[5] found the time the deafness/hearing impairment is acquired may have an impact on balance. Congenitally deaf/hearing impaired individuals have poorer balance than those with acquired deafness. Children with sensorineural hearing loss demonstrate reduced dynamic visual acuity (the ability to see clearly while the head is moving), which directly impacts motor performance.[37] This has significant implications for the physical education instruction and safety of students with this type of hearing loss. Soto-Rey et al. found that when tested in a controlled environment, athletes with hearing impairments have a significantly shorter reaction time to visual stimuli when compared to athletes without disabilities.[58] However, the educator must be careful not to generalize about the motor performance of children, but customize instruction based on their individual ability.

The Physical Education Program

Hearing loss interferes with the child's ability to function within the physical education environment. The hearing loss may affect the child's ability to (1) comprehend class material, (2) follow directions, (3) follow class rules, (4) exhibit age-appropriate classroom behaviors, (5) follow and participate in class discussions, (6) interact well with peers, (7) attend to important stimuli in the learning environment, (8) express and understand emotions, and (9) avoid inappropriate acting-out behaviors.[47, 53, 55]

There are considerable differences in the ways individuals with hearing impairments respond to stimuli. Programming, accommodations, instruction, and supports should be carefully planned and detailed in the child's individualized education program (IEP). The basis for this IEP is the assessment.

Testing

Any evaluation instrument that allows the evaluator, or a peer, to demonstrate the skills involved can be used with students with a hearing impairment. Most elementary and middle school students with a hearing impairment can participate in the physical fitness and motor competency tests that are part of the general physical education program.

The Test of Gross Motor Development-II (TGMD-II) is very appropriate for the elementary- and middle-school-age child who is deaf or hearing impaired to determine if the child has a motor delay. In addition, the balance subtest from the Bruininks-Oseretsky Test of Motor Proficiency-2 (BOT-2) can be used to determine whether there is a possibility of vestibular delay. Comparison of static balance ability with eyes open and eyes closed will provide clues to vestibular delay or damage. Note that, if the child has balance problems caused by sensorineural damage to the eighth cranial nerve, which carries the vestibular impulse, activities to stimulate the vestibular system will not help the balance problem. In these cases, it is best simply to teach the child compensatory skills to execute the balance moves needed to be successful in motor activities.

Almost all elementary, middle school, and high school children are capable of participating in school, school district, or state-mandated physical fitness tests without major accommodation. Certainly, every effort should be made to meet the individual needs of all students being assessed.

When assessing students with hearing impairments, evaluators should ensure the student's primary method of communication is utilized. Utilization of an interpreter, amplification, reduced background noise, demonstrations, video clips, and photos are common strategies used to ensure the student understands the directions and expectations of the assessment.

Curriculum Design

The objectives of a physical education program for children with a hearing impairment are the same as those for children without a hearing impairment. An important area of concern is balance. If vestibular functioning appears to be delayed and damage to the eighth cranial nerve can be ruled out, activities that encourage spinning, rolling, rocking, rapid changes in direction, and rapid start/stops should be emphasized. Rajendran et al. found that a 6-week vestibular-specific neuromuscular training program improved the postural control and motor skills of children with hearing impairments.[51] Examples of activities that stimulate the vestibular system are dances such as "Freeze" or games such as "Red Light/Green Light." Should eighth cranial nerve damage be suspected, balance should be taught directly. Balance activities that can be included in a program are (1) standing on one foot, so that the other foot can be used for kicking and trapping; (2) walking a balance beam to develop leg, hip, and trunk strength; and (3) performing drills that build balance skills for chasing, stopping, starting, and dodging.

INTEGRATING STUDENTS WITH A HEARING IMPAIRMENT

It should no longer be assumed that all persons who are deaf or have a hearing impairment should fit or want to fit into and function in the hearing world. In some large cities, there are whole communities of individuals who are deaf who choose to live together to share their unique culture, lifestyle, and language.

Requiring individuals who are deaf or hard of hearing to meet the demands of the hearing population's culture may not always be in their best interest. The issue of the placement of children who are deaf in an inclusive environment is a highly emotional and controversial issue within the Deaf community. Parents of some students prefer to enroll them in residential or day schools that have segregated programs. Many parents prefer these schools because they have a higher percentage of teachers who are deaf educators, and the students have the opportunity to participate in an extensive array of academic and vocational courses, as well as a wide range of athletic and social programs.[60] Physical educators can make a major contribution to the education of a child who is deaf by being sensitive to his or her individual needs and providing an appropriate and acceptable physical education program. It is important to note that simply "sharing" a physical space does not mean that students with and without hearing impairments will automatically develop empathy and mutual understanding.[42] The physical educator must help create an environment that allows quality interaction and quality time; the students must participate in educational experiences designed to foster empathy and understanding.

The most inviting school for students who are deaf or hearing impaired is one in which the administration, faculty, staff, and students are prepared to welcome the students within the community. A model strategy would be that beginning in kindergarten, all students receive instruction in ASL, so that they can communicate with their peers who have a hearing impairment. The principal and all members of the faculty, and most staff members, should be able to communicate in sign as well. Physical educators can regularly incorporate simple signs into daily instruction, such as stop, listen, look, walk, play, help, ball, and run. They can also teach the class a Sign of the Week and keep a bulletin board with all of the signs. There are several mobile applications that will show the signs for words. Having an iPad or mobile device available for peers to look up signs can increase communication.

Physical educators can be challenged to assist all students to develop effective social skills through participation in integrated settings. Certain physical education activities enable the integration process to be accomplished with minimum support systems. Activities that require less social interaction and communication skills are movement exploration programs in the elementary school and individual sports, such as bowling, archery, and weight lifting, at the advanced levels. More complex team sports, such as basketball, which requires frequent response to whistles and verbal communication involved in strategic situations among teammates, require more modifications.

Organized football is perhaps the most difficult because of the need for ongoing information exchange between coaches and players while the game is in progress. The task is not impossible, however. Derrick Coleman was the first deaf offensive player in the NFL and the first deaf player to compete in the Super Bowl with his winning team, the Seattle Seahawks. He relies on hearing aids, lip reading, and visual cues to overcome his communication barriers.

Teaching Strategies

COMMUNICATION

For optimum learning to occur, a teacher must be able to communicate effectively with his or her students (see **Table 16-3).** Students with hearing losses have the greatest opportunity to learn when they have maximum hearing correction and a teacher who has mastery of the communication system the student has elected to use. Technological advances continue to improve methodology for maximizing hearing capability. And computer-mediated instruction has opened up a world of communication and information exchange for individuals who are deaf or hearing impaired. Speech-to-text features on mobiles devices, amplification apps on mobile phones, and Bluetooth-enabled hearing aids are a few of the technological advances that assist individuals with hearing impairments.

In some school districts, interpreters are hired to assist children to succeed in school. If the physical educator has a child who is receiving assistance from an interpreter, the physical educator and interpreter need to remember the following:

- The interpreter is *not* in the gymnasium or on the playground as a co-teacher or paraeducator. The interpreter is a highly skilled professional with a specific responsibility to the student he or she is serving. "Educational interpreters are responsible for receiving the spoken word and translating it into sign language and translating it into the spoken word."[2]
- Even if an interpreter is present, the physical educator is still ultimately responsible for effective communication with the student who is deaf or hearing impaired.

The physical educator must be aware of the fact that each cochlear implant is "mapped" at the time it is fitted. Typically, this is done by an audiologist, who calibrates the device. Static electricity may "demap" the cochlear implant. The physical educator must help the child avoid activities that may "demap" the implant—for example, running on carpeting, sliding

TABLE 16-3   Communication Strategies for Teachers Working with Students Who Are Deaf or Hearing Impaired[2]

- If a student is using an interpreter, the students in the class must be taught to communicate directly with the student who is deaf or hearing impaired, not the interpreter.
- If the student is working with a sign interpreter, the interpreter should be positioned, at the request of the student, directly in front of the student, near the teacher on the platform or in front of the gymnasium, or following the teacher about the room.
- If the student is working with an oral interpreter, the interpreter should be posted close to the student for presenting information via mouth movement, facial expression, gestures, and appropriate rephrasing.
- If the student is using an assistive learning device, the teacher can wear a lapel microphone attached to an amplifier in his or her pocket.
- Group discussions that include students who are deaf or hearing impaired must be carefully controlled.
  - Only one student can speak at a time.
  - A student who relies on speech reading should be given the time to refocus on the new speaker.
- The teacher should use the following strategies to enhance oral communication:
  - The teacher should enunciate clearly and speak at a moderate pace.
  - The teacher should face the class.
  - During question-and-answer periods, the teacher should repeat the questions carefully.
  - If the teacher needs to write on the board, he or she should write, then stop, and give the students time to process what has been written before going on. The use of overhead projectors allows the teacher to continue to face the class.
  - The teacher should not wear facial hair and should not chew gum.
  - Visual materials and handouts are particularly helpful.
- The teacher should use the following strategies to enhance the student's written communication:
  - The teacher should meet with the student regularly to review and correct written work.
  - The teacher should help the student learn to use spelling/grammar checks available as part of most computer software and to understand the changes the software makes.
- The teacher may encourage best performance on a test by allowing the student to take a written exam and then giving the student the opportunity to explain answers orally.

down slides, and rolling inside carpeted barrels.[21] The physical educator can rub gym mats or other equipment that often generates static electricity with fabric softener sheets to prevent this issue.

Educators, particularly physical educators teaching in gymnasiums or outside on playgrounds and play areas, should be aware of the availability of frequency modulated (FM) systems. The FM system is worn by the teacher and the student who is deaf or hearing impaired. It picks up the teacher's voice and transmits the speech signals directly to the student's ear.[11] Although expensive, the systems are often available to students and their families for use in the school setting as rentals.

Communication Systems

The three prevalent philosophies in the education of persons who are deaf or hard of hearing are the bilingual-bicultural method, auditory-verbal therapy (oral) method, and the total communication method. Each emphasizes the need for early identification, early intervention, and timely medical and audiological management.

The bilingual-bicultural philosophy considers ASL (or the native sign language) to be the child's native language. Spoken and written language is taught as a second language. Both languages are taught and developed as distinct languages. Research shows that if deaf children know both English as well as sign language, they are more successful academically, socially, and with language development.[54]

The oral approach emphasizes communication through oral language in and through (1) required amplification, (2) significant language and communication stimulation, and (3) maximized opportunities to use residual hearing.[12] There is a significant emphasis on the role of the parents and family members as communication models.[12] ASL is not typically taught or encouraged.

The total communication method combines the auditory-verbal therapy method with the use of signs and fingerspelling. Children are provided amplification of sound and are taught through speech reading, fingerspelling, and signs. They express themselves through speech, fingerspelling, and signs.

The term *total communication* refers to both a method of instruction and a philosophy of education. As a philosophy, it refers to the right of every person who is deaf or hard of hearing to select whatever form of communication is preferred. That is, depending on the circumstances, the person should have the right to choose to communicate through speech, signs, gesture, or writing. If taught through a total communication system, a person has the option to communicate in a way that best suits his or her need. A barrier to the total communication system is the lack of universality and consistency of the selected modes of communication. With a wide variety of methods of communication, it decreases the chances of a peer, teacher, coworker, or community member of fluency in the deaf individual's chosen modes of communication. A variety of forms of manual communication systems may be incorporated into the total communication method.

The manual communication systems range from simple homemade gestures to fingerspelling. Signing systems between these two extremes include Pidgin Sign Language, ASL, Manually Coded English, and fingerspelling. A description of each follows:

- *Homemade gestures.* A primitive gestural system is developed to communicate between individuals or among small groups.
- *Pidgin Sign Language.* This is a mixture of English and ASL. Key words and phrases are signed in correct order; prepositions and articles are usually omitted.[47]
- *American Sign Language.* ASL is a visual-gestural language that is governed by rules. The visual-gestural language involves executing systematic manual and nonmanual body movements simultaneously. Manual movements involve shapes, positions, and movements of the hands; nonmanual gestures involve the shoulders, cheeks, lips, tongue, eyes, and eyebrows. The rules that govern this language relate to how the language works (e.g., functions of the language, meaning, structure, and organization of sentences and the sound, or phonetic, system).[9, 46]
- *Manually Coded English.* Signs are produced in English order, and fingerspelling is used for words and concepts that do not have a sign equivalent. Forms of Manually Coded English include Seeing Essential English, Signing Exact English, and Signed English. All are variations of ASL that attempt to model the vocabulary and syntax of the English language.[50]
- *Fingerspelling.* Each word is spelled letter by letter using a manual alphabet that consists of 26 letters. The hand is held in front of the chest, and letters are formed by using different single-hand configurations. Fingerspelling is also known as the Rochester method because it originated at the Rochester School for the Deaf in the late nineteenth century.[50]

Effective communication with students with a hearing impairment is a challenge to physical educators. Teachers can improve their instructional ability by learning to communicate in a variety of ways to meet student needs, and by working with the student, school personnel, parents, and speech-language pathologists to provide consistency in communication and educational strategies. Examples of hand signals and/or basic survival signs are shared in **Figures 16-2** and **16-3**.

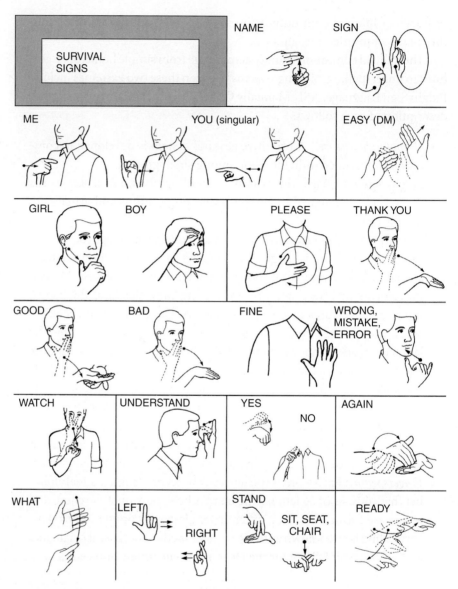

Figure 16-2   Survival Signs

Reprinted with permission from the *Journal of Physical Education, Recreation and Dance*.

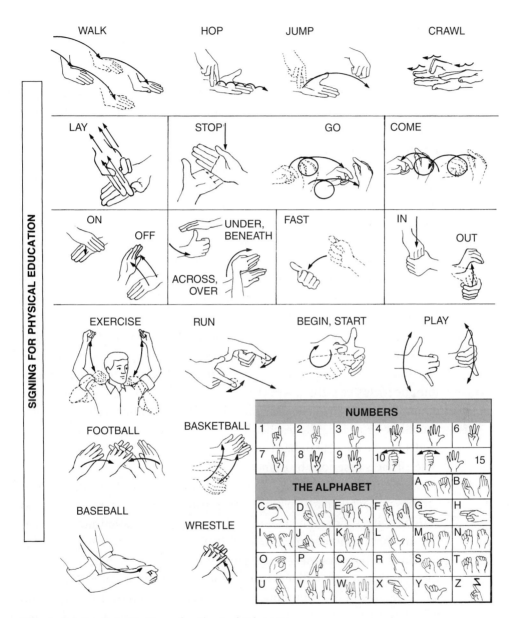

Figure 16-3   Specific Signs for Physical Education

Reprinted with permission from the *Journal of Physical Education, Recreation and Dance*.

TEACHING STRATEGIES

In the past several decades, the emphasis in most special education programs has been on the process of teaching—teaching strategies and techniques—rather than the content of what is taught. This appears to be particularly true within deaf education,[3] and the adapted physical educator and general physical educator who seek to communicate with students who are deaf or hearing impaired have focused on the process of teaching rather than the nature of the curriculum.[36] There must be a greater emphasis on the physical education curriculum, and decisions regarding that curriculum must be outcome-based and focused on the functional ability of the student.[45] An emphasis on hands-on demonstration, technological support, peer-to-peer instruction, self-paced learning, high expectations, independent learning opportunities, and exposure to a great deal of communication and interaction heightens the effectiveness of the learning environment.[4] Carefully trained peer tutors increase the physical activity levels of deaf students in inclusive elementary physical education programs.[29]

The introduction of a child who is deaf or hearing impaired into a general physical education class without prearranged support systems may be devastating. A peer support system is an excellent way to ease a student into the inclusive setting. As is the case with all support systems, only the amount of assistance necessary for the individual to experience success should be provided. The teacher has the major responsibility for assisting students who are deaf or hard of hearing to adjust to the learning environment. That is best done by example.

The ability to communicate effectively is important in instructional settings and while participating in play, games, leisure, recreation, fitness activities, and sports. When there is effective communication and the learning environment is properly managed, there may be little need to modify the demands of the physical activity.[5] However, when communication impairments are present, the student may perform motor and social skills less well, solely because of the communication problem. The physical educator who works with students who are deaf or hearing impaired must do everything possible to ensure effective communication (see **Table 16-4**) and to provide effective physical education experiences (see **Tables 16-5** and **16-6**)

According to Ling,[32] no single method can meet the individual needs of all children with hearing disorders, and multiple modes of communication

TABLE 16-4 Techniques for the Physical Educator to Enhance Communication

1. Position yourself where the child who is deaf can see your lips and maintain eye contact; do not turn your back on the child and talk (e.g., writing on the board).

2. When out of doors, position yourself so that you, rather than the child who is deaf, face the sun.

3. Use only essential words or actions to transmit messages.

4. Use visual attention-getters. These include large pictures and a variety of visual materials: written words, line drawings, cutouts from magazines, labels and wrappers, signs and logos, and graphic organizers.[34]

5. Make sure that the teaching environment has adequate lighting.

6. Allow the child to move freely in the gymnasium in order to be within hearing and sight range.

7. Encourage the use of residual hearing.

8. Use the communication method (oral, total communication) that the child uses.

9. Present games with straightforward rules and strategies.

10. Familiarize the student with the rules and strategies of a game before introducing the activity.

11. Learn some basic signs and use them during instruction (e.g., good, bad, okay, better, worse, line up, start, go, finish, stop, help, thank you, please, stand, sit, walk, run).

12. Use visual materials to communicate body movements (e.g., lay out footprints to indicate the foot placements required in a skill).

13. Refrain from having long lines and circle formations when presenting information to the class.

14. Keep objects out of your mouth when speaking.[40]

15. Use body language, facial expression, and gestures to get an idea across.[40]

16. Avoid verbal cues during the game or activity. It is important that the student who is deaf fully understands his or her role before the game or activity and that the role does not change.[40]

17. Inside facilities should be equipped with special lighting systems easily turned on and off by the instructor to get the students' attention.[40]

18. Use flags or bright objects to get the attention of students out of doors. However, make it clear to students that it is their responsibility to be aware of your presence throughout the lesson. Under no circumstance should you allow students to manipulate you by ignoring attempts to get their attention.

19. Captioned videotapes and other visual aids can be helpful in explaining strategies.

20. Demonstrate or have another student demonstrate often. It may help the student form a mental picture of how to perform a particular skill correctly.

21. Keep instructions simple and direct.

22. Emphasize action rather than verbal instruction.

23. Stand still while giving directions.

24. Correct motor errors immediately.[40]

(continues)

TABLE 16-4 Techniques for the Physical Educator to Enhance Communication (*Continued*)

25. Select activities that allow all the children to be actively involved throughout; avoid activities that require children to spend a great deal of time sitting and waiting to participate.

26. Make use of the "buddy system" to help the student understand instructions and know when a phase of the activity is completed.

27. Assign a home base to every student in the class. The home base of the student who is deaf/hearing impaired should be close to the space from which you usually communicate.

28. Delimit the area in which members of the class may move.

29. Provide a structured environment.

30. Use the same sequence of activities for each class—for example, warm-up, dance, calisthenics, jogging/running, and so on.

31. Supply a visual schedule to the student who is deaf; it will help the student predict what is coming and to prepare for it. Be sure to refer consistently to the name of each segment of the day using the same name.[34]

TABLE 16-5 Aquatics for Individuals Who Are Deaf or Hearing Impaired

• Hearing aids will need to be removed before individuals who are deaf or hearing impaired enter the pool area. In fact, they should probably be removed in the locker room and stored carefully in a locked locker.

• The individual who is deaf or hearing impaired should wear earplugs and waterproof headbands to prevent water from entering the ear canal.

• A visual emergency signal must be in place.
  • Flicking on and off the lights, above and below water level
  • Warning flags waved by the lifeguard or teacher

• In an open-water swimming area, the designated safe swimming area must be carefully delineated and marked by colorful buoys. The individual who is deaf or hearing impaired must always swim with a buddy; in fact, it is the best practice in aquatics for all individuals always to swim with a buddy.

• In a pool, the deep-water areas must be carefully identified and separated from the shallow end.

• Demonstrations, particularly by classmates, are effective in presenting information.

• The individual who is deaf or hearing impaired should not dive to enter the pool area and certainly should not snorkel or scuba dive without his or her physician's permission because of the risk associated with increased hydrostatic pressure.

• The individual who is deaf or hearing impaired may experience difficulty with the maintenance of equilibrium. The individual must be given the opportunity to explore the aquatic environment and a variety of positions within that environment and to practice vital safety skills, such as recovering to a stand from a float or glide.

TABLE 16-6   Teaching Strategies for Including the Student Who Is Deaf or Hearing Impaired[4, 13, 17, 52]

- Group discussions must be carefully controlled for students who rely on speech reading (lip reading).
  - The speech reader must be given enough time to refocus on the next speaker.
  - Only one student may speak at a time.
- The teacher of a student who relies on speech reading should not wear facial hair, particularly mustaches and beards, which obstruct sight of the lips and mouth.
- The classroom or gymnasium must be well-lighted; the speakers must avoid being in shadows.
- Group discussions must be carefully controlled for students who rely on an interpreter.
  - The interpreter must be seated within easy view of the student yet in a position that does not interfere with contact with other students.
  - Participants in the group discussion (and any discussion) must be taught to talk directly to the student and not the interpreter.
- The teacher may wear a lapel microphone, attached to an amplifier, for the student who is wearing an assistive listening device.

should be used. Verbal instructions that describe movements are ineffective for deaf individuals who cannot read lips. It is critical that precise visual models be presented individuals who are deaf. To promote kinesthetic feedback, it is also helpful to move a child through the desired movement pattern. This helps the student feel the temporal-spatial relationship of movements associated with a skill. Using both visual and kinesthetic instruction provides opportunities for two avenues of sensory information. A quick visual model followed by physical prompting of the behavior may facilitate learning.

Some older children who are deaf can read lips and thus receive directions through verbal means. If the child has residual hearing or is skilled at lip reading, the physical educator should make the environment conducive to reception of the spoken word. Instruction must be given close enough to the child that precise movement of the lips and tongue can be deciphered. The instructor should be in front and in clear view of the deaf student. When movement in a game requires the child to perform an activity at a distance at which lips cannot be read, it is then necessary to use a combination of signing to communicate. Eichstaedt and Seiler[14] have suggested 45 signs specific to physical education to communicate with the deaf. Another source of communication with these students is trained hearing paraprofessionals (teacher aides) or peers who can facilitate instruction by gaining the attention of the

Courtesy of Kristi Roth

child who has a hearing impairment and then relaying instructions through visual models, signs, or tactile inputs that guide the child into class activities.

One of the major problems associated with physical education programs for learners who are deaf have a hearing impairment is the poor acoustical conditions that exist in many classrooms.[33, 48] The poor acoustics and reverberation effects in the typical classroom are nothing like those that exist in the gymnasium. Most gymnasiums are essentially large, empty rooms with wood floors, high ceilings, and few materials or surfaces to absorb sound. As a result, any child is bombarded by the noise and may find it difficult to listen to and hear directions. Adding sound-absorbing materials, such as carpet, acoustic ceiling tiles, curtains, and corkboard, may help reduce the reverberations.[4]

DEAF-BLIND

Definition

Deaf-blind means concomitant hearing and visual impairments, the combination of which causes such severe communication and other developmental and educational needs that they cannot be accommodated in special education programs solely for children with deafness or children with blindness.[24]

Incidence

In the 2012–2013 academic year, approximately 1,000 deaf-blind school-age children were provided educational services in the United States.[46] Approximately one-third of those children received their education in public separate facilities or residential schools. The percentage of children receiving services in diverse educational settings are

- <2l% of instruction outside regular classroom: 27%
- 21%–60% of instruction outside regular classroom: 10.5%

- >60% of instruction outside regular classroom: 32.5%
- Separate school facility: 18%
- Residential facility: 8.4%
- Home or hospital: 2.8%[47]

CHARACTERISTICS

Children who are deaf-blind have a significant loss of both vision and hearing. They have less than 20/20 vision in a visual field of 20 degrees or less. In addition, they have a loss of hearing of 25 decibels or more. Children who are deaf-blind have problems that are similar to those of blind children and deaf children. This makes it very difficult for them to acquire basic communication skills. Residual sight, hearing, or both are the basis of communication. If there is no residual sight or hearing, communication is primarily tactile and kinesthetic, through touch and movement. Individuals with congenital deaf-blindness, when compared to those with acquired deaf-blindness, more commonly exhibit impairments in social interaction, independent living skills, and cognition.[10]

Wheeler and Griffin[65] have suggested a motor-based approach to teaching communication and language skills to young children who are deaf-blind. The critical role of the physical educator, as the motor expert, in each of the following phases must be emphasized:

- *Resonance.* In this phase, the physical educator mirrors and expands on movements the student initiates. For example, if the student is holding a ball, the teacher may grasp the ball as well and begin to move it in a circular path.
- *Coactive movement.* In this phase, the emphasis is on the physical relationship between the teacher and the student, including frequent touch and physical contact between the two. It also includes movements done together—for example, sitting, singing, rocking, and playing "row, row, row your boat."
- *Nonrepresentation reference.* In this phase, the teacher helps the student develop the basis of body image by encouraging the student to replicate the position of a three-dimensional object—for example, the teacher, a doll, a teddy bear, or a "gumby."

- *Deferred imitation.* The teacher, in this phase, asks the student to imitate a series of body positions, which become increasingly complex. An example of this activity is playing "angels in the snow."

Children and adolescents who are deaf-blind find it difficult to communicate with others. Their educators may fail to understand or may miss their interactive signals because the signals are often subtle and may be difficult to interpret.[25] It is clear that those who wish to communicate with children who are deaf-blind, notably their educators, must be given the opportunity to learn observation skills to identify communicative intents and to analyze those intentions in different interactional situations.[25] For example, the physical educator must be trained to notice the signals a deaf-blind child gives to communicate, particularly in the gymnasium or on the playground. Additionally, the development of trust between the physical educator and the student who is deaf-blind is imperative. The gym can be a large and intimidating space, as the environment is constantly changing. The student-teacher bond will promote exploration and engagement in new experiences in the student who is deaf-blind.[15]

Lieberman[28] recommended that the physical educator use significant tactile and physical communication strategies to teach children who are deaf-blind. One strategy is moving a child's body, using physical guidance, through a skill. Another is providing a demonstration while the child feels the teacher's body.

Typically, the deaf-blind child in the educational environment is helped by a professional known as an "intervenor." This professional helps the deaf-blind child gain access to the information in the environment.[41] As with the interpreter for the deaf, this professional is there solely to serve the student. Additional communication strategies for individuals who are deaf-blind can be found in **Table 16-7**.

THE PHYSICAL EDUCATION PROGRAM

The significant efforts of adapted physical education professionals, notably Dr. Lauren Lieberman, Dr. James Cowart, and Dr. Steven Butterfield, have increased the physical education opportunities for students who are deaf-blind. The opportunities for students who are deaf-blind to master and enjoy leisure, recreation, fitness, and sport activities to enhance their physical fitness are vast.

TABLE 16-7   Communication Modes for Students Who Are Deaf-Blind

Nonlinguistic Communication Modes

Touch Cues: The teacher prompts the student with touch to cue him or her about what is expected (e.g., stand up, sit down, stop an activity).

Objects: An actual object or small model of the object is given to the child to represent the activity to be completed. For example, the student may be handed a jump rope when it is time to go to physical education.

Calendars/Communication Shelves: Objects can be placed on a shelf in the order they will happen. This will allow the student to understand sequencing, time, and order. For example, the student may have a toy bike, a baseball, and a CD in order on a shelf to represent the daily lesson of stationary biking, baseball, and dance.

Signals and Gestures: Students who are deaf-blind may use signals or gestures to indicate their wants or needs. For example, letting go of a guide's arm could indicate a desire to stop activity.

Co-active Movement: Students may determine the skill to perform by watching the teacher through their remaining visual field or physical contact, and imitate what they "see."

Linguistic Communication Modes

Voice: Used when students who are deaf-blind have some residual hearing.

Sign Language: If the students has some residual vision, perform the signs in close proximity, in their functional field of vision, slowly, with short phrases, and repeat signs.

Tactile Sign Language: In tactile sign language the person who is deaf-blind communicates by placing his or her hands over the signs being expressed.

Tangible Symbols and Alphabet Systems: Braille, foam letters, or pictures are all forms of tangible symbols.

Tadoma: The listener places his or her hands over the face and neck of the speaker while he or she is speaking.

Adapted from Engelmann et al., 1999.

Lieberman[28] has suggested that students who are deaf-blind can use the same types of techniques to run as individuals with visual impairments. These include using a guide wire, a sighted guide, or a tethered partner, and running toward a voice. Tandem bicycling and duo cycling are also recommended.

Another excellent strategy for enjoying physical activity and developing cardiovascular respiratory fitness is the use of fitness equipment typically found in YMCA/YWCAs, city recreation centers, and/or health clubs: treadmill walking, treadmill running, stationary bicycling, and tethered swimming.

Lieberman and Stuart[31] identified the recreation preferences of deaf-blind adults. A large percentage (65%) identified fitness activities as a preferred activity. The physical educator can play a vital role in preparing deaf-blind students for other preferred recreation activities, including dancing, outdoor recreation activities, and water activities.

The quality of life of an individual who is deaf, hearing impaired, or deaf-blind can be enhanced in and through quality physical education programs that prepare students for a life of leisure, recreation, fitness, and sport activities. The creative and resourceful teacher can make a huge difference in the lives of these students.

Students with visual impairments and who are deaf-blind face many barriers to successful inclusion in general physical education. These barriers include a lack of training for physical educators; the inherent pace and nature of the physical education curriculum and lessons; fear on the part of teachers, the student, and parents; low expectations for the student; student lack of confidence; and lack of appropriate equipment.[30] Ultimately, a dedicated IEP team who communicates openly about struggles and advocates for solutions can help overcome most of these issues. There are excellent videos and webinars online for physical educators to use as training resources. A creative approach to the physical education curriculum can promote inclusion. For example, include students who are deaf-blind in units or electives in which they can thrive, such as adventure and cooperative education, fitness, yoga, dance, golf, swimming, and track and field. The careful collaboration of the IEP team, including the student, parents, therapists, and teachers, can help everyone gain confidence and find solutions to overcome barriers to participation in physical education.

Speech and Language Disorders

The global term *speech disorders* refers to difficulties in producing speech sounds or problems with voice quality that interfere with an individual's ability to communicate effectively. A speech disorder may be characterized by an interruption in the flow or rhythm of speech—called fluency disorder or dysfluency (e.g., stuttering). Speech disorders may also be problems with the way sounds are formed, called articulation, or phonological, disorders, or they may be difficulties with the pitch, volume, or quality of the voice.[43] The most common speech disorder that requires careful consideration by the physical educator is stuttering. The National Dissemination Center for Children with Disabilities (NICHCY) defines a language disorder as "an impairment in the ability to understand and/or use words in context."[43]

Some individuals with language disorders have difficulty using appropriate words and confuse their meanings, some struggle to express their ideas, some use inappropriate grammatical patterns, some have a small vocabulary, and some have difficulty following directions. One or a combination of these characteristics may occur in children who are affected by language-learning disabilities or a developmental language delay.[43] It is common for students with autism, specific learning disabilities, or intellectual disabilities to have a receptive or expressive language disorder. Though most children with speech and language-learning disorders as their only disability do not have any gross motor delays, the physical educator teaches children with speech and language-learning disorders in every class.

A brief introduction to select speech and language-learning disorders is included in this chapter. Most students with speech and hearing disorders have typical gross motor skills, and physical education can provide a quality educational experience with simple modifications to honor the students' individual needs.

DEFINITION

Speech and language impairment is a communication disorder, such as stuttering, impaired articulation, or a voice impairment, that adversely affects a child's educational performance.[24]

INCIDENCE

In 2012–2013 more than 1,356,000 children between ages 6 and 21 years received instruction to address speech and language disorders.[63] The vast majority of those children spent most of their time in the general education program. A large number of children with a different primary disability—for example, intellectual disability, autism, or deafness/hearing impairment—also have speech and language disorders.[19]

CAUSES

One of the major causes of speech and language-learning disorders is hearing loss. Even a minor or fluctuating hearing loss (e.g., as a result of otitis media), particularly during the early developmental period, may have a significant negative impact on the development of speech and language skills.

In addition, neurological disorders, traumatic brain injury, alcohol or other drug abuse, physical impairments (e.g., cleft lip or cleft palate), and vocal abuse (e.g., use of cigarettes or caffeine) can cause speech and language-learning disorders.[43]

FLUENCY DISORDERS: STUTTERING AND CLUTTERING

Individuals who stutter experience disruptions in the smooth flow of their speech more often than the average speaker of their age. Interruptions in the flow of speech, called dysfluencies, are the most obvious feature of stuttering. The interruptions differ from person to person. Common dysfluencies include part- or whole-word repetitions, phrase repetitions ("m-m-m-mummy"), prolonged sounds at the beginning of words ("C-a-a-an I h-h-h-have that?"), hesitations, and silent blocks when the person silently struggles to begin a word. Although virtually ALL young children exhibit some dysfluencies, very early stuttering is distinct from normal dysfluency. See **Table 16-8** for specific tips for the physical educator who is teaching a child who stutters.

TABLE 16-8 Tips for the Physical Educator Teaching a Child Who Stutters[61]

- Listen to and answer the child in a patient, calm, and unemotional way.
- Talk privately with the child who stutters. Explain to the child that when we learn to talk—just like learning new things in physical education—we make mistakes. We bobble sounds, just as we bobble a ball, or we repeat or get tangled up on words, just as our feet get tangled in a jump rope.
- Assure the child that stuttering does not bother you. You want him or her to talk, so that you can learn the way he or she feels, what he or she thinks about, and what he or she has learned and wants to learn.
- Initially, until he or she adjusts to the physical education class, ask the child questions that can be answered with one or two words.
- If every child is going to be asked a question, call fairly early on the child who stutters. The stuttering will be worse if the child has to wait and worry.
- Listen to what the child is saying. Respond to that, rather than the stuttering.
- Give appropriate responses to what the child is saying, such as head nods and smiles. Don't interrupt the child with "uh-huh" or "yes." The verbalization will cause the child to hesitate.
- Maintain natural eye contact when the child is talking.
- Don't rush the child by interrupting or finishing words for him or her.
- With the child and his or her parents' permission, spend a brief period of time early in the semester sharing specific information about stuttering or do "empathy" experiences to help the child's classmates understand the problem.

Cluttering is often characterized by rapid, slurred, or imprecise speech, in which the child seems to get "stuck," as if the child's mind is going faster than his or her mouth.

RECEPTIVE LANGUAGE DISORDER

A receptive language dysfunction is a central auditory processing deficit. A receptive language dysfunction is a difficulty in the decoding and storing of auditory information, typically incoming verbal messages (see **Table 16-9**). A child with a receptive language disorder may have difficulty understanding directions given in class, so using visuals (demonstrations, pictures, and videos) can be beneficial. It is also helpful to give the student a visual cue and make eye contact when it is time for him or her to listen. Slowing instruction and inserting pauses can also allow the student time for processing.

EXPRESSIVE LANGUAGE DISORDER

An expressive language dysfunction is one in which the individual has difficulty with verbal expression. The individual struggles to put words together to formulate thoughts and to share those thoughts with others. Strategies for assisting students with expressive language disorder include allowing them time to think about a response, repeating back the correct form of mispronounced words or sentence structures (without requiring them to repeat it again), providing the student with choices of the correct word form, and allowing them to restate the word or sentence selecting the correct choice.

TABLE 16-9   Signs and Symptoms of Receptive Language Dysfunction[27]

- The child demonstrates echolalia. He or she repeats back words or phrases either immediately or at a later time without understanding the meaning.
- The child is unable to follow directions, though he or she may follow routine, repetitive directions.
- The child shows inappropriate, off-target responses to "wh" questions—"who," "what," "when," "where," and "why."
- The child demonstrates re-auditorization; he or she repeats back a question first and then responds to it.
- The child has difficulty responding appropriately to "yes/no" and "either/or" questions.
- The child does not attend to spoken language.
- The child uses a lot of jargon.

SUMMARY

Children with communicative delays and disorders require careful planning and modifications for success in the educational environment. Though they may have excellent physical and motor skills, they may struggle with the psychosocial component of the physical education experience.

When working with students who are deaf or hard of hearing, physical educators are concerned primarily with the extent to which the hearing loss affects ability to participate in play, leisure, recreation, and sport activity. The classification of hearing loss is often based on the location of the problem within the hearing mechanism. Conductive losses interfere with the transfer of sound. Sensorineural problems result from damage to the inner ear and/or the eighth cranial nerve. Central hearing impairments occur at the brain stem or the auditory cortex. Hearing aids and cochlear implants are used to amplify sound and enhance the communication capability of individuals who are deaf or hard of hearing. Types of communication systems used to communicate with individuals who are deaf or hard of hearing are the bilingual/bicultural method, auditory-verbal (oral) method, and the total communication method. Considerations for effective communication by teachers of the individuals who are deaf or hearing impaired during instruction are teacher-learner position, visual feedback, intensity of the commands, and special attention to the environment. Few changes are required in the physical education program. Athletic opportunities should be provided for students who are deaf or hard of hearing, so that they have the opportunity to participate in activities that will provide enjoyment and help maintain a healthy lifestyle after their school years.

Teaching the learner who is deaf-blind is challenging for the physical educator, but a good teacher can open up a world of leisure, recreation, sport, and fitness activities the learner who is deaf-blind can enjoy throughout a lifetime.

The physical educator, teaching children with speech and language-learning disorders, should use strategies to ease the communication barriers and promote social interaction.

REVIEW QUESTIONS

1. What are the differences between prelingual and postlingual deafness?
2. What strategies can the physical educator use to communicate with and teach the deaf and hearing impaired?
3. What are some teaching strategies that can be used with students who are deaf-blind?

REFERENCES

1. Beers, M. H., Porter, R. S., Jones, T. V., Kaplan, J. L., & Berkwits, M. (Eds.). (2006). *The Merck manual of diagnosis and therapy.* Whitehouse Station, NJ: Merck Research Laboratories.

2. Best, C., Lieberman, L., & Amdt, K. (2002). Effective use of interpreters in general physical education. *JOPERD, 73*(8), 45–50.

3. Bowe, F. (1991). *Approaching equality: Education of the deaf.* Silver Springs, MD: TJ Publishers.

4. Brackett, D. (1997). Intervention for children with hearing impairment in general education settings. *Lang Speech Hear Serv Schools, 28*, 355–361.

5. Butterfield, S. A., & Ersing, W. F. (1986). Influence of age, sex, etiology and hearing loss on balance performance by deaf children. *Percept Mot Skills, 62*, 659–663.

6. Butterfield, S. A., et al. (1998). Kinematic analysis of a dynamic balance task by children who are deaf. *Clin Kines, 52*(4), 72–78.

7. Cambra, C. (1996). A comparative study of personality descriptors attributed to the deaf, the blind, and individuals with no sensory disability. *Am Ann Deaf, 141*(l), 24–28.

8. Cochlear Corporation. (2000). Package insert for Nucleus 24 Contour (brochure). Sydney, Australia.

9. Crowe, T., & Horak, F. (1988). Motor proficiency associated with vestibular deficits in children with hearing impairments. *Phys Ther, 68*, 1493–1499.

10. Dalby, D. M., Hirdes, J. P., Stolee, P., Strong, J. G., Poss, J., Tjam, E. Y., Bowman, L., & Ashworth, M. (2009). Characteristics of individuals with congenital and acquired deaf-blindness. *Journal of Visual Impairment & Blindness, 103*(2), 93–102.

11. DiPietro, M. A., Williams, P., & Kaplan, H. (2007). *Alerting and communicating devices for deaf and hard of hearing people—what's new.* Laurent Clerc National Deaf Education Center, Gallaudet University. http://clerccenter.gallaudet.edu/InfoToGo/418.html

12. Duquette, C., Durieux-Smith, A., Olds, J., Fitzpatrick, E., Eriks-Brophy, A., & Whittingham, J. (2002). Parents' perspectives on their roles in facilitating the inclusion of their children with hearing impairment. *Exceptionality Education Canada, 12*(l), 19–36.

13. Easterbrooks, S. (1999). Improving practices for students with hearing impairments. *Except Child, 65*(4), 537–554.

14. Eichstaedt, C. B., & Seiler, P. (1978, May). Communicating with hearing impaired individuals in a physical education setting. *JOPERD,* 19–21.

15. Engleman, M. D., Griffin, H. C., Griffin, L. W., & Maddox, J. I. (1999). A teacher's guide to communicating with students with deaf-blindness. *TEACHING Exceptional Children, 31*(5), 64–70.

16. Gallaudet website. https://www.gallaudet.edu/clerc-center/information-and
-resources/info-to-go/educate-children-(3-to-21)/resources-for-mainstream
-programs/effective-inclusion/including-deaf-culture/about-american-deaf-culture
.html

17. Garay, S. (2002). Listening to the voices of deaf students. *Teaching Except Child, 35*(4), 44–48.

18. Geers, A. E., Nicholas, J. G., & Sedey, A. L. (2003). Language skills of children with early cochlear implantation. *Ear and Hearing, 24*(1) (Supp.), 46S–58S.

19. Hall, B., Oyer, H., & Haas, W. (2001). *Speech, language, and hearing disorders: A guide for teachers.* Boston: Allyn & Bacon.

20. Hicks, C., & Tharpe, A. (2002). Listening effort and fatigue in school-age children with and without hearing loss. *J Speech, Lang & Hearing Research, 45*(3), 573–585.

21. Hilgenbrinck, L. (2003). *Disability fact sheet on cochlear implants.* Project INSPIRE. www.twu.edu/INSPIRE

22. Holcomb, T. K. (1997). Development of deaf bicultural identity. *Am Ann Deaf, 142*(2), 89–93.

23. *IDEA part B trend data.* http://www.ideadata.org/PartBTrendDataFiles.asp

24. Individuals with Disabilities Education Act Amendments of 1997 [P.L. 105–17].

25. Janssen, M. J., Riksen-Walraven, M., & Van Dijk, J. (2003, April). Contact: Effects of an intervention program to foster harmonious interactions between deaf-blind children and their educators. *J Vis Impair & Blindness,* 215–229.

26. Karchmer, M. A., & Allen, T. A. (1999). The functional assessment of deaf and hard of hearing students. *Am Ann Deaf, 144*(2), 68–71.

27. *Kid speech.* (2003). http://www.kidspeech.com/signs.html

28. Lieberman, L. (2002). Fitness for individuals who are visually impaired or deaf-blind. *RE:view, 34*(1), 13–23.

29. Lieberman, L., Dunn, J., van der Mars, H., & McCubbin, J. (2000). Peer tutors' effects on activity levels of deaf students in inclusive elementary physical education. *APAQ, 17*(l), 20–39.

30. Lieberman, L. J., & Houston-Wilson, C. (1999). Overcoming the barriers to including students with visual impairments and deaf-blindness in physical education. *RE:view, 31*(3), 129–138.

31. Lieberman, L., & Stuart, M. (2002). Self-determined recreation and leisure choices of individuals with deaf-blindness. *J Visual Impairment & Blindness, 96*(10), 724–736.

32. Ling, D. (1984). *Early total communication intervention: An introduction in early intervention for hearing-impaired children: Total communication options.* San Diego, CA: College Hill Press.

33. Loizou, P. (1998, September). Introduction to cochlear implants. *IEEE Signal Processing Magazine,* 101–130.

34. Luckner, J., Bowen, S., & Carter, K. (2001). Visual teaching strategies for students who are deaf or hard of hearing. *Teaching Except Child, 33*(3), 38–44.

35. Lyon, M. E. (1997). Symbolic play and language development in young deaf children. *Deafness and Ed, 21*(2), 10–20.

36. Lytle, R. R., & Rovins, M. R. (1997). Reforming deaf education: A paradigm shift from how to teach to what to teach. *Am Ann Deaf, 142*(1), 7–15.

37. Martin, W., Jelsma, J., & Rogers, C. (2012). Motor proficiency and dynamic visual acuity in children with bilateral sensorineural hearing loss. *International Journal of Pediatric Otorhinolaryngology, 76*(10), 1520–1525.

38. Martinez, C., & Silvestre, N. (1995). Self-concept in profoundly deaf adolescent pupils. *Inter J Psychol, 30*(3), 309–316.

39. Matkin, N. D., & Wilcox, A. M. (1999). Considerations in the education of children with hearing loss. *Ped Clin North Am, 46*(1), 143–152.

40. Minter, M. G. (1989). Factors which may prevent full self-expression of deaf athletes in sports. *Palaestra, 5*, 36–38.

41. Morgan, S. (2001). "What is my role?" A comparison of the responsibilities of interpreters, intervenors, and support service providers. *Deaf-Blind Perspectives, 9*(1), 1–3.

42. Most, T., Weisel, A., & Tur-Kaspa, H. (1999). Contact with students with hearing impairments and the evaluation of speech intelligibility and personal qualities. *J Spec Ed, 33*(2), 103–111.

43. NICHCY. (2003). http://www.kidsource.com/NICHCY/speech.htm

44. National Institute on Deafness and Other Communication Disorders. (2003). *Cochlear implants.* Retrieved from http://www.nidcd.nih.gov/health/hearing/coch.asp

45. Nowell, R., & Marshak, L. (1994). An orientation for professionals working with deaf clients. In Nowell, R., & Marshak, L. (Eds.). *Understanding deafness and the rehabilitation process.* Boston: Allyn & Bacon.

46. O'Rourke, I. J. (1987). *ABC's of signing.* Silver Springs, MD: National Association of the Deaf.

47. Pakulski, L., & Kaderavek, J. (2002). Children with minimal hearing loss: Interventions in the classroom. *Interventions in School & Clinic, 38*(2), 96–104.

48. Palmer, C. V. (1997). Hearing and listening in a typical classroom. *Lang Speech Hear Serv Schools, 28*, 213–217.

49. Parasnis, I. (1997). Cultural identity and diversity in deaf education. *Am Ann Deaf, 142*(2), 72–79.

50. Paul, P., & Quigley, S. (1990). *Education and deafness.* New York: Longman.

51. Rajendran, V., Roy, F. G., & Jeevanantham, D. (2013). A preliminary randomized controlled study on the effectiveness of vestibular-specific neuromuscular training in children with hearing impairment. *Clinical Rehabilitation, 27*(5), 459–467.

52. Reich, L. M., & Lavay, B. (2009). Physical education and sport adaptations for students who are hard of hearing. *Journal of Physical Education, Recreation & Dance (JOPERD), 80*(3), 38–42.

53. Rieffe, C., Terwogt, M., & Smit, C.(2003). Deaf children on the causes of emotions. *Educational Psychology, 23*(2), 159–168.

54. Rochester Institute of Technology. *Deaf education: A new philosophy.* Retrieved from http://www.rit.edu/showcase/index.php?id=86

55. Ross, M., Brackett, D., & Maxon, A. B. (Eds.). (1991). *Assessment and management of mainstreamed hearing-impaired children.* Austin, TX: PRO-ED.

56. Siegel, J., Marchetti, M., & Tecclin, J. (1991). Age-related balance changes in hearing-impaired children. *Phys Ther, 71,* 183–189.

57. Singer, B. D., & Bashir, A. S. (1999). What are executive functions and self-regulation and what do they have to do with language-learning disorders? *Lang Speech Hear Serv Schools, 30,* 265–273.

58. Soto-Rey, J., Pérez-Tejero, J., Rojo-González, J. J., & Reina, R. (2014). Study of reaction time to visual stimuli in athletes with and without a hearing impairment. *Perceptual & Motor Skills, 119*(1), 123–132.

59. Stewart, D. A. (1991). *Deaf sport: The impact of sports within the deaf community.* Washington, DC: Gallaudet University Press.

60. Stinson, M. (1994). Affective and social development. In Nowell, R., & Marshak, L. (Eds.). (1994). *Understanding deafness and the rehabilitation process.* Boston: Allyn & Bacon.

61. *Stuttering.* (2003). Retrieved from http://www.mankato.msus.edu/dept/comdis/kuster/stutter.html

62. Uchanski, R. M., & Geer, A. E. (2003). Acoustic characteristics of the speech of young cochlear implant users: A comparison with normal-hearing age-mates. *Ear and Hearing, 24*(l) (Supp.), 90S–105S.

63. U.S. Department of Education. National Center for Education Statistics. https://nces.ed.gov/fastfacts/display.asp?id=64

64. U.S. Department of Education. National Center for Education Statistics. https://nces.ed.gov/programs/digest/d13/tables/dt13_204.60.asp

65. Wheeler, L., & Griffin, H. C. (1997). A movement-based approach to language development in children who are deaf-blind. *Am Ann Deaf, 142*(5), 387–390.

CHAPTER 17

Visual Impairments

OBJECTIVES

- Identify and describe three types of visual impairments.
- List the general characteristics of students with visual impairments.
- List five ways to modify the play environment to make it safe for students who are blind.
- List eight ways to modify activities to accommodate a student with a visual impairment.
- Describe equipment specially designed to enable sport participation by individuals with limited or no sight.

Visual impairments include both permanent and functional conditions. Children with visual disorders represent a unique challenge to the physical educator, because in addition to their visual impairments they usually demonstrate developmental lags. Many of these children have not had opportunities to physically explore the environment during their early years. As a result, intact sensorimotor systems are not stimulated adequately, and motor development suffers.

United States Association of Blind Athletes

Low vitality and perceptual-motor development lags can prevent children from participating in activities not contraindicated by the primary visual disorder.

Definition of Visual Impairments

There are varying degrees of visual impairment. Individuals at one end of the continuum have little residual vision and are unable to perceive motion and discriminate light. If a person is not totally blind, it is still possible to make functional use of whatever vision remains. Some persons who are considered blind are capable of perceiving distance and motion but do not have enough residual vision to travel; others, although classified as legally blind, can perceive distance and motion and have enough usable residual vision to move about with a minimal amount of assistance.

Children with loss of vision are, for educational purposes, classified as partially sighted, low vision, legally blind, and totally blind. The term "partially sighted" indicates some type of visual problem that requires a need for special education. These persons have less than 20/70 visual acuity in the better eye after correction, have a progressive eye disorder that will probably reduce vision below 20/70, or have a very limited field of vision (20 degrees at its widest point). The term "low vision" refers to a severe visual impairment, not necessarily limited to distance vision. Individuals with low vision are unable to read a newspaper at the normal viewing distance, even with the aid of glasses or contact lenses. Persons who are "legally blind" are those who have visual acuity of 20/200 or less in the better eye after maximum correction or a very limited field of vision (20 degrees at its widest point). Totally blind persons must use braille or other nonvisual media to learn.[24]

For a child to qualify under the law for special services in physical education, the visual disability must adversely affect the child's physical education performance or safety. Children with a visual impairment, including blindness, qualify for adapted/developmental physical education programs by demonstrating one or both of the following:

1. A visual impairment that, even with correction, adversely affects a child's educational performance; the term "visual impairment" includes partial sight and blindness.
2. Hearing and visual impairments that occur together, also called deafblindness, the combination of which causes such severe communication and other developmental and educational needs that the child cannot be accommodated in special education programs solely for children with deafness or blindness.

Functional conditions not covered under the law that have an impact on motor performance efficiency are depth perception, eye–hand coordination, visual form perception, visual memory, visual-spatial development, and visual-spatial integration. Children who have any of these conditions may experience movement problems, even though they are not classified as having a visual impairment as identified in the Individuals with Disabilities Education Improvement Act (IDEIA, 2004).

Incidence of Visual Impairments

Approximately 28,000 students, between the ages of 3 to 21 years, received educational services in 2012–2013 who had an educational diagnosis of visual impairment and 1,000 who had an educational diagnosis of deafblindness.[27] These students received their education in the following settings:

Deaf-blindness

- <40% of instruction inside regular classroom: 32.5%
- 40%–79% of instruction inside regular classroom: 10.5%
- >80% of instruction inside regular classroom: 27%
- Separate public school facility: 18.1%
- Separate private school facility: 8.4%
- Residential facility: 0.7%

- Home/hospital: 2.8%
- Correctional facility: 0%[64]

Visual Impairment

- <40% of instruction inside regular classroom: 11.3%
- 40%–79% of instruction inside regular classroom: 13.1%
- >80% of instruction inside regular classroom: 64.3%
- Separate public school facility: 5.9%
- Separate private school facility: 3.8%
- Residential facility: 1.1%
- Home/hospital: 0.06%
- Correctional facility: 0%[27]

In 2013 there were 7.3 million blind and visually impaired persons aged 16–75 years or older in the United States.[17]

Causes of Visual Impairments

The underlying causes of visual loss are existing visual conditions, structural anomalies, and inefficient extraocular muscle control. Existing conditions impact the integrity of the visual impulse in the eye, on the optic nerve, or in the visual cortex. These conditions include diabetes, accidents and injuries, poisoning, tumors, excessive oxygen at birth, and prenatal influences, such as rubella and syphilis. Structural anomalies include deviations of the eye structure. Functional causes that compromise visual efficiency are extraocular muscle imbalances caused by postural deviations, poor reading habits, and visual acuity problems. Risk factors for pediatric visual impairment include:

- Prematurity, low birth weight, with a need for oxygen treatment at birth or bleeding in the brain.
- Family history of retinoblastoma, congenital cataracts, or metabolic or genetic disease.
- Infection of the mother during pregnancy such as rubella, toxoplasmosis, cytomegalovirus, HIV, herpes, gonorrhea, or chlamydia.
- Central nervous system disorders including cerebral palsy, seizures, or hydrocephalus.[16]

VISUAL CONDITIONS

Visual conditions that cause blindness or visual impairments in children include congenital causes, diseases, insult or injury to the eye, and aging. In the United States, cortical visual impairment, retinopathy of prematurity, and optic nerve hypoplasia are the three leading causes of pediatric blindness.[25] Additional congenital causes more commonly seen in children are albinism and retinitis pigmentosa. Cortical visual impairment is a condition in which the visual input received is not processed accurately in the brain, which causes visual messages to be distorted. Retinopathy of prematurity occurs when the growth of the blood vessels in the retina is disturbed during fetal development and is often linked with premature birth. Children with retinopathy of prematurity have an increased risk of retinal detachment. Optic nerve hypoplasia occurs when the number of nerves within the optic nerve bundle is reduced.[2] With albinism, there is a lack of pigment in the eyes. Extreme light sensitivity may require the use of dark glasses. Retinitis pigmentosa is a hereditary condition in which the retinal rods become defective, which initially reduces night vision.

Common visual conditions seen in older adults include cataracts and glaucoma. Cataracts can be caused by aging, exposure to X-rays, disease, smoking, or exposure to heat from infrared or ultraviolet light.[15] Cataracts cause an opacity of the normally transparent lens. Glaucoma is generally considered a disorder resulting from aging; however, it can occur in any age group.[15] Glaucoma creates increased pressure inside the eye, which results in visual loss and decreased peripheral vision. As deterioration continues, central vision is reduced.

IMPAIRMENTS TO THE EXTRAOCULAR MUSCLE SYSTEM

Singular binocular vision involves coordinating the separate images that enter each eye into a single image in the visual cortex of the brain. When the two eyes function in unison and are coordinated, the images entering the eyes are matched in the visual cortex, and binocular fusion results. If, however, one or more of the six extraocular muscles attached to the outside of each eyeball is out of balance, the eyes do not function in unison. When this occurs, the images from one eye deviate from those of the other eye, and the images do not match in the visual cortex. The amount of visual distress experienced because of mismatched images depends on the degree of

United States Association of Blind Athletes

deviation of the eyes and the ability of the central nervous system to correct the imbalance.

There can be several conditions as a result of impairment to the extraocular muscle system. Strabismus is a condition where one eye moves normally while the other eye turns out or in. Nystagmus involves pendular, horizontal swinging of the eyes which can impact the ability to direct the eyes in the desired location and to accommodate for near and far vision. Amblyopia or "lazy eye" results when the image from an eye has been suppressed by the brain for a long time because a conflict exists between the two eyes. The eye with amblyopia does not function because the brain will not accept the deviant image. Individuals who use each eye independently from the other, suppressing first one eye and then the other, are known as alternators. When a person has visual suppression problems with one or both eyes, depth perception is always compromised. See **Table 17-1** for descriptions of visual impairment conditions and specialists.

TABLE 17-1 Visual Impairment Conditions and Specialists

Term	Description
Alternator	Uses each eye independently of the other (e.g., one eye may be used for near-point activities and the other for distance activities)
Amblyopia	A type of strabismus that causes the affected eye to be nonfunctional
Astigmatism	A refractive error caused by an irregularity in the curvature of the cornea of the lens; vision may be blurred
Esophoria	A tendency for an eye to deviate medially toward the nose
Esotropia	A condition in which the eye(s) turn(s) inward (cross-eyed)
Exophoria	A tendency for an eye to deviate laterally away from the nose
Exotropia	A condition in which the eye(s) turn(s) outward

TABLE 17-1   Visual Impairment Conditions and Specialists (*Continued*)

Term	Description
Hyperopia	A condition in which the light rays focus behind the retina, causing an unclear image of objects closer than 20 feet from the eye (far-sighted)
Hyperphoria	A tendency for an eye to deviate in an upward direction
Hypertropia	A condition in which one or both eyes swing upward
Hypophoria	A tendency for an eye to deviate in a downward direction
Hypotropia	A condition in which one or both eyes swing downward
Myopia	A condition in which the light rays focus in front of the retina when a person views an object 20 feet or more away from the eye (near-sighted)
Nystagmus	Rapid movement of the eyes from side to side, up and down, in a rotatory motion, or in a combination of these motions
Ophthalmologist	A licensed physician specializing in the treatment of eye diseases and optical defects
Optician	A technician who grinds lenses and makes glasses
Optometrist	A specialist in examining the eyes for optical defects and fitting glasses to correct those defects
Orthoptic vision	The ability to use the extraocular muscles of the eyes in unison
Orthoptician	A person who provides eye exercises to refine control of the eye (e.g., visual developmental specialist)
Refractive vision	The process by which light rays bend as they enter or pass through the eyes
Tunnel vision	A loss of side vision (also called peripheral vision) while retaining clear central vision
Visual developmental specialist	An optometrist or ophthalmologist with specialized training in evaluating and correcting orthoptic visual problems

Characteristics of Visual Impairments

Vision loss requires exposure, intervention, and therapy to promote general development of motor, academic, intellectual, psychological, and social characteristics. There are widespread individual differences among persons with limited vision. The onset of blindness has an impact on the development of the child. The child with congenital blindness lacks visual information on which motor responses may be built. Also, overprotection may hamper the development of the individual who is congenitally blind. Frequently, parents and teachers tend to restrict the activity of children who are blind.[12] The over-protection complicates development because the child is not permitted to explore the environments necessary for the development of motor responses. It is obvious that, depending on when blindness occurred, the child who is blinded after birth will have some opportunities to explore environments and receive environmental information through the visual senses for development. However, certain characteristics appear more often in children with visual impairments than in sighted persons. Some of the characteristics that have implications for physical education are motor development, physical fitness, and psychological and social adjustment.

MOTOR DEVELOPMENT

Limited vision restricts physical motor activity, which limits the range and variety of experiences children may encounter. Infants who are blind exhibit inhibited development of self-initiated postures and locomotion.[26] When compared to typically developing infants, infants born with visual impairments do not exhibit differences in motor patterns until around 3 months of age. Reduction of head control, particularly in head lift can be seen around 3 months and continues until 6–7 months. The vestibular system experiences abnormal development due to a lack of visual stimuli and subsequent vestibular development, until at least 1 year of age in children with visual impairments. However auditory stimuli (interesting and different sounds) resulted in a correction of the head position, particularly when the trunk was supported. Infants with visual impairments also exhibit a delay in gaining postural control and in postural stability (balance).[22] Because postural control precedes gross and fine motor development, these children are slow to walk, run, skip, reach, grasp, and develop other gross and fine motor skills.

The child with normal sight makes judgments as to where objects are in space by pairing sensory information from vision with movement information received when moving to and from objects. Because persons with severe visual impairments cannot visually compare objects at varying distances in the environment, they are unable to formulate visual judgments. Many subsequently rely on auditory information to determine depth and distance from objects.

Studies have confirmed these delays. Ribadi, Rider, and Toole[23] indicate that congenitally blind individuals are less capable on static and dynamic balance tasks than are their sighted peers. The ways that delayed balance impacts movement patterns were described by Gordon and Gavron.[4] They studied 28 running parameters of sighted and blind runners and found that, as a group, the blind runners did not have sufficient forward lean while running. They demonstrated insufficient hip, knee, and ankle extension at takeoff, which limited their power, and their range of motion of the hip and the ankle was limited.

Visual information that assists with performing specific motor skills is integrated with information from the vestibular apparatus and kinesthetic signals resulting from reflex and voluntary movements. Organization of these sensory inputs plays a central role in successfully maintaining posture and executing movement. Sensory organization is responsible for determining the timing, direction, and amplitude of movement based on information from vision, kinesthesis, and the vestibular sense. The execution of static and dynamic balance requires a combination of several senses, one of which is vision. When vision is compromised, other senses must be used more fully.

PERCEPTUAL DEVELOPMENT

Children with limited vision use other sensory abilities better as a result of increased attention to them in attempts to learn about and cope with the environment. A sighted person might be unaware of particular auditory stimuli, whereas a person who is blind might attach great significance to them.

These children need to use full kinesthetic, auditory, tactile, and space perception. Each form of perception contributes to the blind child's ability to adapt to the environment. The kinesthetic and vestibular systems can enable a person with limited vision to maintain balance. Balance experience is acquired through participation in activities that require quick changes of direction. The kinesthetic receptors are stimulated if the tasks, such as weight lifting or pushing and pulling movements, increase the amount of pressure applied to the joints.

PHYSICAL FITNESS

Individuals with visual impairments demonstrate a wide range of physical fitness. Individuals who adopt a passive lifestyle can be expected to demonstrate poor physical fitness; however, when appropriate activity programs are available, individuals who are blind can develop excellent levels of physical fitness. Children with visual impairments have less muscular and cardiovascular endurance, less muscular strength, and more body fat than children who are sighted.[12] Lieberman et al. found that children and adolescents aged 10–17 years have low passing rates in the areas of upper-body strength, cardiovascular endurance, and body composition when assessed with the Brockport Test of Physical Fitness.[8] Loss of vision, by itself, is not a limiting condition for physical exercise. A considerable amount of developmental exercises to promote muscular strength, power, and endurance can be administered to such children.[5] Exposure, accommodation, and opportunities can address the fitness discrepancies.

PSYCHOLOGICAL AND SOCIAL ADJUSTMENT

The emotional and social characteristics of persons with visual impairments vary. Research regarding the social maturity of children who are blind reveals that, in general, they receive significantly lower social maturity scores than do sighted children.[6]

The psychological and social adjustment of individuals with severe visual impairments depends a great deal on the extent and success of their interactions with others. Sighted persons acquire social habits by observing and imitating people they esteem. Individuals with severe visual impairments do not have the same opportunity to develop those skills because they are unable to observe social interactions. Any limitation in observing and interpreting the gestures of individuals as they talk limits the information about what a person is attempting to communicate. Lack of opportunity to read body language and assess the social surroundings in terms of what is appropriate may limit the social development of individuals who are blind.

Some individuals who are blind may exhibit self-stimulatory behavior, such as rocking the body or head, placing fingers or fists into the eyes, flicking the fingers in front of the face, and spinning the body around repetitiously. The cause of these self-stimulatory behaviors is unknown; however, it is suspected that the individuals are attempting to access vestibular, kinesthetic, and tactile stimuli to substitute for loss of visual stimulation. The lack of opportunity and experience in social interaction, as well as external behaviors that are not understood by peers can inhibit the social integration of children with visual impairments. Symptoms that might indicate eye disorders and might be observed by educators appear in **Table 17-2.**

TABLE 17-2 Symptoms Indicative of Common Disorders of the Eye

1. Confuses right/left directions
2. Complaints of dizziness or frequent headaches
3. Poor balance
4. Frequent rubbing of the eyes
5. Difficulty concentrating, short attention span; easily distracted
6. Difficulty following a moving target
7. Squinting
8. Eyes turn in or out
9. Walking overcautiously
10. Faltering or stumbling
11. Running into objects not directly in the line of vision
12. Failure to see objects readily visible to others
13. Sensitivity to normal light levels
14. Difficulty in estimating distances
15. Complaints of double vision
16. Going down steps one at a time
17. Poor hand–eye and/or foot–eye coordination
18. Avoidance of climbing apparatus
19. Holding the head close to the desk during paper-and-pencil tasks
20. Turning the head and using only one eye while moving

Modified from The Visual Fitness Institute Symptoms of Visual Skill Disorders website (http://visualfitness.com/symptoms.html).[28]

Functional visual problems related to misalignment of the eyes are frequently treated using vision training, or vision therapy, defined as the teaching and training process for the improvement of visual perception and/or the coordination of the two eyes for efficient and comfortable binocular vision. The purpose of vision therapy is to treat functional deficiencies in order for the person to achieve optimum efficiency and comfort.[3] Although the value of this type of therapy has long been debated, when carried out by well-trained visual behavioral specialists, there is strong scientific support for its efficacy in modifying and improving oculomotor, accommodative, and binocular system disorders.[1]

The Physical Education Program

TESTING

Students with visual impairments must be approached in accordance with their unique educational needs. Physical fitness and motor proficiency and skill tests should be administered to all students, regardless of visual status. Physical fitness tests that might be used with students with visual impairments include the Brockport Physical Fitness Test, Test of Gross Motor Development-2, Project M.O.B.I.L.I.T.E.E., and the balance and bilateral coordination portions of the Bruininks-Oseretsky Motor Proficiency Test-2. Regardless of what tests are used, modifications must be made to accommodate the lack of vision. Utilization of audible equipment, manual guidance, and tactile modeling may be necessary when administering motor assessments to students with visual impairments. Recommendations for exercise testing are presented in **Table 17-3**.

Two excellent instruments to use to document how youth participate in everyday activities outside of mandated school activities is the Children's Assessment of Participation and Enjoyment (CAPE) and Preference for Activities of Children (PAC). It can be used to measure formal and informal physical-based activity and self-improvement activities. It is designed for use with youth between the ages of 6 and 21 years.[7]

Curriculum Design

Effective physical educators respect all students, regardless of their ability level; are skilled observers of motor performance; recognize and accommodate individual differences; and use teaching methods and curricula appropriate for the students. Such professionals establish educational environments conducive to optimum growth. They assess the needs, abilities, and limitations of all of their students and design a program to meet those

TABLE 17-3   Recommendations for Exercise Testing for Students with Visual Impairments

Have all instructions described verbally or on audiotape.
Allow the person to describe or demonstrate the test protocol before the test begins.
Give tactile and verbal reinforcement to motivate the participant.
Allow the person to lightly touch the tester when necessary.

needs. The least restrictive environment should be carefully determined by the individualized education program (IEP) team and based on a comprehensive evaluation. The inclusion of students with visual impairments in the general physical education class requires careful planning, but often reduces self-limiting behaviors and increases confidence. A study by Lieberman, Houston-Wilson, and Kozub identified reasons general physical educators were hesitant to include children with visual impairments in their classes. The physical educators studied reported a lack of (1) professional preparation, (2) appropriate equipment, (3) adequate programming, and (4) time in their schedule.[11] Teachers who have had some experience with students who have low vision or are blind are more positive about including this population in the general physical educational environment. To enhance attitudes about including individuals with visual impairments in the general physical educational environment, it has been suggested that physical educators be given the opportunity to observe their students in the classroom setting and be provided workshops on ways to teach these students effectively.[29]

The mission of physical education programs for all students is to develop independent recreational sport and physical activity in the community and habits of healthful living. Promotion of independent participation without restrictions is imperative for the development of self-efficacy in physically active environments. Students with visual impairment who participate in physical activities with their sighted peers are less likely to engage in vigorous physical activities.[14] However, when students with visual impairments are provided with appropriate physical education experiences that accommodate their individual needs, they are more likely to engage in sports outside of school.[21]

The ultimate goal of the class atmosphere for children with vision losses is to provide experiences that will help them be successful in all activities they desire to engage in. The selection and method of experiences in the physical education program are critical. These experiences should not be overprotective to the extent that growth is inhibited; rather, the experiences should provide challenges yet remain within the range of the children's capabilities for achieving skill objectives.

PEER ASSISTANCE

Peers without disabilities can assist children with disabilities in inclusive settings. Peer tutors are more effective when they have been trained to assist their partner with a visual impairment. Training should include information on the residual vision of their partner, type of visual impairment, communication, guiding, modification, modeling, physical assistance, cuing, and instructional techniques.[10] The nature of the assistance depends on the nature of the task. Guiding is one method of assistance commonly utilized in physical education. Students with low vision may choose to have peers who serve as sighted guides. When children without disabilities serve as peer tutors, it is necessary to manage their time so as not to impede their own education. Often training a team of peer tutors who rotate is the most effective strategy for equal inclusion.

ORIENTATION AND MOBILITY TRAINING

Mobility is the ability to move from one point to a second point. Orientation is the ability to relate body position to other objects in space. Obviously, these abilities are related and required for efficient movement in a variety of environments.

Orientation and mobility training is an adaptive technique that helps students with visual impairments learn about their physical space. This training increases their confidence in moving with greater authority and provides greater safety while they are participating. It is a valuable way to enhance participation in the physical education program.

Although professionals use specific techniques in orientation and mobility training, physical educators can reinforce many of the concepts that are a part of sophisticated training programs. Practicing and establishing routes in physical education can increase confidence and independence. Some example routes are traveling from the locker room to a home spot or home spot to an activity start location. Activities in the physical education class that would reinforce professional orientation and mobility training programs are (1) practice walking straight lines while maintaining good posture, (2) locate sounds in the environment, (3) follow instructions where movements have to be made that conform to the instructions (memory), (4) practice the reproduction of specific walking distances with respect to time, (5) find one's way back to starting points on different surfaces, and (6) practice changing body positions.

Orientation and mobility training programs help individuals with visual impairments cope effectively with physical surroundings. Working closely with the student's orientation and mobility specialists in the physical education environment is highly beneficial for both the students and physical educators. Understanding how to effectively facilitate independent ambulation can promote student confidence. Physical educators need to know what mobility devices are acceptable for their students and how to help them learn to use them effectively. Orientation and mobility programs should also help students with visual impairments interact with their peers, as well as with the physical facilities and equipment.

SAFETY

The instructional environment for individuals with visual impairments should be safe and familiar and have distinguishing landmarks. As a safety precaution, play areas should be uncluttered and free from unnecessary obstructions. Children with visual impairments should be thoroughly introduced to unfamiliar areas by walking them around the play environment before they are allowed to play or introduced to game boundaries with a tactile board.

The characteristics of the instructional environment can be amplified. For instance, gymnasiums can be well-lighted to assist those who have residual vision. Boundaries for games can have various compositions, such as a base or path of dirt and concrete or grass for other areas. Brightly colored objects are easier to identify. Also, equipment can be designed and appropriately placed to prevent injuries. For instance, volleyball standards are best if stored out of the gym area.

There are two parts to the management of safe environments. One is the structure of the environment, and the other is the teacher's guidance of the children as they participate in the environment. Suggestions to ensure safe play are presented in **Table 17-4**.

The following are applications of safety principles:

Principle	Safety Measure
Protection of aids	Protect all body parts; use spotting in gymnastics.
Protection of eyeglasses	Use a restraining strap to hold glasses in place.
Safe equipment	Use sponge ball for softball, volleyball, or any other projectile activities.
Safe environment	Check play areas for obstacles and holes in the ground.
Activity according to ability	Avoid activities that require children to pass each other at high speeds
Close supervision of all potentially dangerous activity	The teacher positions self close to the student with a visual impairment during activity, anticipates dangerous situations, and helps the student avoid them.

TABLE 17-4 Safety Measures to Prevent Injury

1. Alter the playing surface texture (sand, dirt, asphalt); increase or decrease the grade to indicate play area boundaries.
2. Use padded walls, bushes, or other soft, safe restrainers around play areas.
3. Use brightly colored objects as boundaries to assist those with residual vision.
4. Limit the play area.
5. Limit the number of participants in the play area.
6. Play in slow motion when introducing a new game.
7. Protect the eyes.
8. Structure activities commensurate with the ability of the student with a visual impairment.
9. Protect visual aids, such as eyeglasses.
10. Select safe equipment.
11. Structure a safe environment.
12. Instruct children to use the environment safely.
13. Do not allow students with aphakia (absence of the natural lens of the eye, as when a cataract has been surgically removed), a detached retina, or severe myopia to engage in high-impact activities, such as jumping.

Teaching Strategies

Physical educators who instruct students with visual impairments have an added dimension to their work. Rather than using the old standby, demonstration, as their main form of communicating a desired movement, they must be prepared to substitute a variety of other forms of sensory experiences that are meaningful to the student with a visual impairment.

Some excellent ideas teachers can use to enhance the perceived competence of children with visual impairments are presented in **Table 17-5**.

TABLE 17-5 Strategies to Improve Perceived Competence in Children with Visual Impairments[24]

- Introduce role models.
- Use motor behavior assessments.
- Use guided discovery as a teaching method.
- Use peer tutors.
- Increase opportunities for independent mobility.
- Facilitate social interaction.
- Teach students to take the initiative to get involved in activities.

TEACHING MODIFICATIONS

One of the factors parents of children with visual impairments identify as barriers to physical activity is a lack of opportunities that accommodate their child's needs.[20] Physical educators need training in conditions causing visual impairments and in how to accommodate and provide opportunities for students with visual impairments. Because of the great visual content included in the components

United States Association of Blind Athletes

of certain games, some skill activities are more difficult than others to adapt for persons with visual impairments. In the case of total blindness, participation in the more complex activities may be extremely difficult to modify. However, the skills constituting a game can be taught, and lead-up games with appropriate modifications are usually within the student's grasp. The adaptation of the physical education program for individuals with visual impairments should promote their confidence to cope with their environment by increasing their physical and motor abilities. It should also produce in them a feeling of acceptance as individuals in their own right. To achieve these goals, the program should include the adaptation of the general program of activities, when needed; additional or specialized activities, depending on the needs of the child; and special equipment, if needed. Additionally, there should be an emphasis on development of skills beneficial to sports and activities designed for athletes with visual impairments, such as goalball, beep baseball, One-Touch, tandem biking,

United States Association of Blind Athletes

and Showdown. Campabilities.org provides descriptions of these activities and more, along with modifications and assessment materials. Additional modifications that can be made to enable the participation of persons with visual limitations are detailed in **Table 17-6**. Modifications for students in an aquatic environment are described in **Table 17-7**.

The level of residual vision among individuals with visual impairments will vary. Questioning students about their vision is an appropriate practice. Individuals can see different colors, at different angles (peripheral, central), in different lighting, and even in different times of the day. Individuals with visual impairments must depend on receiving information through sensory media other than vision. Audition is a very important sensory medium of instruction. Another sensory medium that can be used

TABLE 17-6   Activity Modifications for Students with Visual Impairments

Activity	Modification
Aerobic dance	Include verbal description of movement with demonstration.
Archery	Beeper is affixed to center of target.
Bicycling	Child assumes rear seat position on tandem bicycle with sighted partner in front seat.
Bowling	Beeper is attached above pins at end of lane.
Canoeing	Child assumes bow position, with sighted partner in stem.
Frisbee	Frisbee has a beeper attached.
Horseshoes	Beeper is affixed to stake. Path to horseshoe pit is made of wood chips or sand.
Running	Guide wires or a sighted guide.[18]
Swimming	Lane lines designate swimming lanes. Pool has constant sound source for orientation. Small bells are suspended near gutters and are activated by waves as a person approaches the end of the pool. Sprinkler spray water at the end of a lane to cue the lane is ending.
Softball	Sand or wood chips are used for base paths. T-stand is used for batting, instead of batting from pitcher. Different texture of ground or floor is used when near a surface that could result in serious collision. Beeping ball is used with tee or without. Bases have beeping modules affixed.
Weight training	Equipment and weights are put in the same place. Weights have braille indicators.
Class management	Environment is ordered and consistent. Reference points indicate location of the child in the play area. Auditory cues identify obstacles in the environment Tactile markings are on the floor. Boundaries of different textures are used.

TABLE 17-7   Aquatics for Learners with Visual Impairments

- The swimmer should wear goggles to prevent any possible damage from chlorine and other chemicals in the water.
- Bright, colorful toys should be used, such as beach balls, kickboards, pails and shovels, water-use stuffed animals, and water squirters (not squirt guns).
- The swimmer must be given the opportunity to explore the learning environment to orient himself or herself. This careful exploration can be enhanced if there is a constant sound source: a soft radio or the like for the swimmer to use for orientation.
- The swimmer must be given a chance to learn self-protective skills that include sensing the end of the lane because of the reaction of the waves in response to the incoming body, sensing the presence of another swimmer because of splashing and waves, and announcing intentions if planning to jump into the water.
- A swimmer who is totally blind may learn best if given the opportunity to "feel" the movement of another; this is particularly effective if paired with patterning the movement of the swimmer.
- When lap swimming, open turns, rather than flip turns, give the swimmer a little leeway to find the wall, rather than being surprised by it.
- Lane lines help the swimmer stay oriented in the pool. The swimmer may want to wear tight-fitting gloves to avoid being cut by the lane lines if off course.

For more information refer to Project INSPIRE Aquatics pages: www.twu.edu/INSPIRE.

is kinesthesis. Tactile modeling (inspection of the demonstrator or object through touch) and physical guidance (performing a skill with the student) are two instructional strategies that can allow students to understand how to perform movements.[19] Often children with visual impairments have little or no understanding of spatial concepts, such as location, position, direction, and distance. Skin and muscular sensations that arise when the student is moved through movement skills provide the information he or she needs to participate. Manual and tactile guidance methods accompanied by verbal corrections are often effective in the development of motor skills.

Providing information, rules, and tests in braille can facilitate acquisition of knowledge for students with visual impairments. Other low-vision aids include magnifying lenses, field enlargement lens systems, telescopic lenses mounted on eyewear frames, nonoptical aids, such as special illumination, filters, large-print materials, and even mobile devices.

Students with visual impairments need to know the effects of their performance on physical tasks because they receive little or no visual feedback. Effective feedback is an important reinforcing property to be incorporated into physical activity for persons with visual impairments.[13] Persons with visual limitations need concrete experiences with objects and events for learning to occur. To assist learners with visual impairments in understanding positioning of themselves or objects around them, the clock method can be used. For example, if a student is attempting to find a hold on a climbing wall, the belayer can encourage the climber to sweep at 2 o'clock, or a student can tap the edge of a basketball hoop with their cane to determine the height of the goal.

To promote participation with sighted players and develop the ability to refine auditory tracking skills, audible balls should be introduced early and utilized frequently. With the audible ball, blind players can know where the ball is most of the time. Audible balls emit beeping sounds for easy location. They may be the size of a softball, soccer ball, or playground ball. The beep baseball is a regular softball with a battery-operated electronic beeping sound device. Through continuous sound, this special equipment tells the blind person where the ball is at all times. A goal ball is constructed with bells inside it. When the ball moves, the bells help the players locate it. One of the skills of the game is to roll the ball smoothly to reduce auditory information (less sound from the bells) to make it more difficult for blind players to locate it. Audible goal locators are motor-driven noisemakers. They indicate the position of backboards in basketball, targets in archery, pins in bowling, and stakes in horseshoes. Audible bases, which are plastic cones 60 inches tall with a noisemaker inside, are used in the game of beep baseball. Audible locators can also be used as boundaries or to identify dangerous objects in the environment.

Other auditory feedback strategies include buzzers or bells inserted inside a basketball hoop to inform the person when a basket has been made. Gravel can be placed around the stake in horseshoes to indicate the accuracy of the toss.

Both guide wires and guide runners have been shown to be effective for runners. Sighted guides can facilitate safe walking and running by providing their upper arm and allowing the student with a visual impairment to grasp above the elbow, with their thumb on the outside and the fingers on the inside of the guide's arm. They also can guide using a tether, which both partners grasp. Tethers can be headbands, string, or rope. Once trust is established, verbal guiding is another possibility. A guide runner is a person who runs alongside the visually impaired runner and verbally describes the distance to the finish. In competition, the guide runner is also permitted to touch the elbow of a runner who has a visual impairment to indicate any lateral off-step. Individuals with visual impairments can participate in alpine skiing with the help of a guide who stays within 5 to 8 feet of the skier with low vision. The guide and the skier ski independently; however, the guide keeps an eye on both the course and the skier who is visually impaired. A guide wire or rope can also provide a safe and independent accommodation for running and walking. Guide wires are ropes or heavy string stretched 36 inches above the lane markers; they help runners feel the perimeters of the lane. Even elementary-age children can learn to run using some form of guidance.[9]

There are several considerations that physical educators must make to effectively accommodate children with low vision in the diverse activities and environments where instruction takes place. The application of principles

TABLE 17-8   Physical Education Principles for Working with the Visually Impaired

1. Use large-print letters and numbers (which can be perceived by many persons who are partially sighted) or braille on posters and task cards.
2. Position students with visual impairments where they can best hear instructional information. This may be directly in front of the instructor.
3. Encourage the use of residual vision.
4. Design appropriate light contrasts between figure and ground when presenting instructional materials.
5. Utilize equipment that features colors students with residual vision can see well.
6. Utilize tactile modeling and physical guidance along with precise verbal cues.
7. Use sighted peers to provide individual attention and maximize participation.
8. Allow students to orient themselves to the environment prior to the start of activity. Develop toothpick models of game and court set-up and boundaries.
9. Allow the person with the visual impairment to decide if assistance is needed or wanted.[12]
10. Keep equipment and objects in the same place. Moving objects without telling the person with a visual impairment can be frustrating to that person.
11. Assist with the initiation of social interactions with peers.
12. Give clear auditory signals with a whistle or megaphone.
13. Instruct through manual guidance.
14. Use braille to teach cognitive materials before class.
15. Encourage tactual exploration of objects to determine texture, size, and shape.
16. Address the child by name.
17. Individualize instruction and build on existing capabilities. Do not let the child exploit visual limitations to the extent of withdrawing from activity or underachieving in motor performance.
18. Use the sensory mode that is most effective for specific learners (tactile, kinesthetic, haptic, auditory).
19. Manage the instructional environment to minimize the need for vision. Use chains where children touch one another. Participate from stationary positions. Establish reference points to which all persons return for instruction.

of accommodation may help the physical educator teach a wide variety of activities. A number of practical guidelines are presented in **Table 17-8.**

SUMMARY

United States Association of Blind Athletes

Children with visual impairments vary in functional ability to participate in physical activity. Persons classified as partially sighted have less than 20/70 acuity, and individuals are classified as blind if their acuity is 20/200 or less. *Low vision* is a term that is used when referring to individuals with a severe visual impairment. There are two basic categories of blindness: congenital blindness means that the person was born blind; adventitious blindness means the person was blinded after birth.

The underlying causes of visual loss are existing visual conditions, structural anomalies or injuries, and inefficient extraocular muscle control. Those associated with curvature of the light rays as they enter or pass through the eye are myopia, hyperopia, and astigmatism. Visual conditions include albinism, cataracts, glaucoma, retinitis pigmentosa, and retinopathy of prematurity. Nystagmus, suppression, and tropias are associated with difficulties in depth perception. Phorias are tendencies for the eyes to misalign.

Functional visual impairments may be identified by the Snellen test. They also may be identified by observing abnormal eye conditions, movement patterns and preferences, and visual discrimination. Low-vision clinics offer comprehensive evaluations and assistance to individuals with visual disorders.

Vision loss has serious implications for motor, intellectual, psychological, and social development. Vision loss early in life may delay the mastery of motor responses, which can affect other areas of development. Planned physical experiences will enhance physical and motor fitness and may counter maldevelopment in other areas.

Training programs in mobility increase the degree of independence of persons who are blind. Accompanying direct instruction to develop travel vision and motor skills is a technique for adaptation. This can be accomplished by modifying activity and instructional environments and introducing special aids, devices, or equipment.

Persons with visual disorders should be trained with self-help or recreational skills that can be used in the community. This may enable participation in some of the community sports programs for the blind and visually limited.

A process that will integrate players who are blind into inclusive physical activities involves the assessment of the social and physical skill level of the individual to ensure success in the activity, appropriate placement in a continuum of environments with the appropriate sighted support systems and sequential withdrawal of support systems and movement to less restrictive participation environments that are commensurate with improved motor and social skills.

REVIEW QUESTIONS

1. How do the movement capabilities of a child with slight loss of vision differ from those of a child who is totally blind?
2. What are the general characteristics of persons with limited vision that impair physical performance of skills?
3. What social adjustment problems do students who are blind face when being included in the general physical education program?
4. What are five ways the physical education environment can be modified to include a student who is visually impaired?
5. What are the essential components for integrating players who are blind with sighted players in physical activity?

REFERENCES

1. American Academy of Optometry and American Optometric Association. (2003). *Vision, learning and dyslexia: A joint organizational policy statement.* Retrieved from http://www.aaopt.org/JointStatement.html
2. American Association for Pediatric Opthalmology and Strabismus: Optic Nerve Hypoplasia. http://aapos.org/terms/conditions/83. 2016.
3. Ciuffreda, K. J. (2002). The scientific basis and efficacy of optometric vision therapy in nonstrabismic, accommodative, and vergence disorders. *Optometry, 73,* 735–762.
4. Gordon, B., & Gavron, S. J. (1987). A biomechanical analysis of the running pattern of blind athletes in the 100 meter dash. *APAQ, 4,* 192–203.
5. Horvat, M., Ray, C., Croce, R., & Blasch, B. (2004). A comparison of isokinetic muscle strength and power in visually impaired and sighted individuals. *Isokinetics and Exercise Science, 12*(3), 179–183.
6. Jindal-Snape, D. (2004). Generalization and maintenance of social skills of children with visual impairment: Self-evaluation and role of feedback. *Journal of Visual Impairment and Blindness, 98*(8), 470–483.

7. King, G., Law, M., King, S., Hurley, P., Rosenbaum, P., Hanna, S., Kertoy, M., & Young, N. (2004). *Children's Assessment of Participation and Enjoyment (CAPE) and Preference for Activities of Children (PAC)*. San Antonio, TX: Harcourt Assessment.

8. Lieberman, L., Byrne, H., Mattern, C., Watt, C., & Fernández-Vivó, M. (2010). Health-related fitness of youths with visual impairments. *Journal of Visual Impairment & Blindness, 104*(6), 349–359.

9. Lieberman, L. J., Butcher, M., & Moak, S. (2001). A study of guide-running techniques for children who are blind. *Palaestra, 17*(3), 20–26.

10. Lieberman, L. J., & Houston-Wilson, C. (2002). *Strategies for inclusion: A handbook for physical educators*. Champaign, IL: Human Kinetics.

11. Lieberman, L. J., Houston-Wilson, C., & Kozub, F. M. (2002). Perceived barriers to including students with visual impairments in general physical education. *APAQ, 19*, 364–377.

12. Lieberman, L., & Lepore, M. (1998, Winter). Camp abilities: Developmental sports camp for youths who are visually impaired. *Palaestra, 28–31*, 46.

13. Lieberman, L. J., Ponchillia, P. E., & Ponchillia, S. K. V. (2012). Physical education and sports for people with visual impairments and deafblindness: Foundations of instruction. *American Foundation for the Blind.*

14. Longmuir, P. E., & Bar-Or, O. (2000). Factors influencing the physical activity levels of youths with physical and sensory disabilities. *Adapted Physical Activity Quarterly, 17*, 40–53.

15. Merck Manuals Consumer Version. (2015). http://www.merckmanuals.com/home

16. My Child Without Limits. http://www.mychildwithoutlimits.org/understand/vision-loss/what-are-the-causes-of-vision-loss/

17. National Federation for the Blind. https://nfb.org/blindness-statistics

18. National Information Center for Children and Youth with Disabilities. (2003). http://www.nichcy.org/pubs/factshe/fsl3text.htm

19. O'Connell, M., Lieberman, L., & Petersen, S. (2006). The use of tactile modeling and physical guidance as instructional strategies in physical activity for children who are blind. *Journal of Visual Impairment & Blindness, 100*(8), 471–477.

20. Perkins, K., Columna, L., Lieberman, L., & Bailey, J. (2013). Parents' perceptions of physical activity for their children with visual impairments. *Journal of Visual Impairment & Blindness, 107*(2), 131–142.

21. Ponchillia, P., Strause, B., & Ponchillia, S. (2002). Athletes with visual impairments: Attributes and sports participation. *Journal of Visual Impairment & Blindness, 96*, 267–272.

22. Prechtl, H., Cioni, G., Einspieler, C., Bos, A., & Ferrari, F. (2001). Role of vision on early motor development: Lessons from the blind. *Developmental Medicine & Child Neurology, 43*(3), 198–201.

23. Ribadi, H., Rider, R. A., & Toole, T. (1987). A comparison of static and dynamic balance and congenitally blind and sighted blindfolded adolescents. *APAQ, 4,* 220–225.
24. Shapiro, R., Leberman, L. J., & Moffett, A. (2003). Strategies to improve perceived competence in children with visual impairments. *RE:view, 35*(2), 69–80.
25. Steinkuller, P. G., Du, L., Gilbert, C., Foster, A., Collins, M. L., & Coats, D. K. (1999, February). Childhood blindness. *J AAPOS, 3*(1), 26–32.
26. Tobin, M. J., Bozic, N., Douglas, G., Greaney, J., & Ross, S. (1997). Visually impaired children: Development and implications for education. *European Journal of Psychological Education, 12,* 431–447.
27. U.S. Department of Education, National Center for Education Statistics. https://nces.ed.gov/fastfacts/display.asp?id=64
28. Visual Fitness Institute. (2003). *Symptoms of visual skill disorders.* Retrieved from http://visualfitness.com/symptoms.html
29. Wall, R. (2002). Teachers' exposure to people with visual impairments and the effect on attitudes toward inclusion. *RE:view, 34*(3), 111–119.

CHAPTER 18

Other Health Impairments

OBJECTIVES

- Identify teaching techniques that can be used to keep youth with attention deficit disorders on task.
- Describe the precautions that should be taken when a child with AIDS is included in the general physical education program.
- Describe the characteristics of a person with anemia.
- Describe the role of exercise in asthma.
- Describe the role of exercise in a child with cystic fibrosis.
- Explain the value of exercise for individuals with diabetes.
- List emergency procedures for treating a diabetic attack brought on by hyperglycemia or hypoglycemia.

The federal laws that have been passed in the United States during the past 40 years virtually ensure a free and appropriate public education to every individual who has a real or perceived impairment that limits major life activities. Other health impairment, by federal definition, means that a child has limited strength and vitality or alertness with respect to the environment due to chronic or acute health problems, such as asthma, attention deficit/hyperactivity disorder, diabetes, leukemia, and sickle cell anemia, that adversely affect a child's educational performance.

In addition to the major health impairments identified in the federal definition of the Individuals with Disabilities Education Improvement Act (IDEIA, 2004), acquired immune deficiency syndrome (AIDS), anemia, childhood cancer, and cystic fibrosis will also be addressed in this chapter.

When children with health impairments improve their motor performance, they also benefit socially and psychologically. Physical education programs that increase exercise tolerance and improve recreational sport skills may also enhance self-care and social competence. Improved physical performance capability usually gives the student a great psychological boost. Involving students in skill and physical development activity programs often helps break a cycle of passive, debilitating physical and social lifestyles.

Most of the conditions discussed in this chapter require medical attention. When this is the case, it is advisable to request permission of the parents to consult with the student's physician to ensure that the type of exercises and activities selected for the student will not aggravate the condition. When the physical educator notices the symptoms that are described in this chapter being demonstrated by a student who is not diagnosed as having a health impairment, the child should be referred to the school nurse for additional evaluation.

Attention Deficit/Hyperactivity Disorder

Individuals with attention deficit/hyperactivity disorder (ADHD) have difficulty attending in school, work, and social situations. They are easily distracted and frequently make careless mistakes because they rush through tasks without thinking. They have difficulty organizing their schoolwork and other responsibilities. They often appear to be daydreaming or not listening. When they do attempt tasks, their work is usually very messy and only partially completed. These individuals typically make every effort to avoid activities that demand sustained self-application, mental effort, and close concentration. They also have difficulty "reading" social situations and, as a result, make comments out of turn, initiate conversations at inappropriate times, and intrude on others. They are often judged to be lazy, uncaring, and unreliable, when in reality they simply cannot focus their attention for any length of time.

Many children with ADHD:

- Fail to give close attention to detail
- Have difficulty sustaining attention during play activity
- Fail to listen carefully when spoken to
- Fail to follow through on directions
- Have difficulty organizing tasks and activities
- Are reluctant to engage in tasks that require sustained effort
- Lose things necessary for activities
- Become distracted by extraneous stimuli
- Are forgetful of daily activities[55]

Persons with ADHD may have problems with social relationships, which include less positive social behavior, fewer positive peer interactions, lower rates of peer reinforcement, lower self-esteem, and fewer cooperative social behaviors.[23]

DEFINITION

ADHD is a neurodevelopmental disorder characterized by inattentiveness, impulsiveness, and hyperactivity. The IDEIA (2004) includes attention deficit disorder and attention deficit/hyperactivity disorder in the list of conditions that could render a child eligible for special services under the category of "other health impaired."[26] Three distinct forms of ADHD have been identified: (1) attention deficit/hyperactivity disorder predominantly inattentive, (2) attention deficit/hyperactivity disorder predominantly hyperactive-impulsive, and (3) attention deficit/hyperactivity disorder combined.

INCIDENCE

The Centers for Disease Control and Prevention (CDC) estimates that approximately 11% of children ages 4–17 years (6.4 million) have been diagnosed with ADHD as of 2011. Males are diagnosed twice as frequently as females and the average age of diagnosis is approximately 7 years of age.[18]

CAUSES

The cause of ADHD is unknown. However, the difficulties with self-inhibition that persons with ADHD have strongly suggest involvement of the prefrontal cortex, basal ganglia, and cerebellum.[57] When higher control centers such as these are involved, inhibition and executive functions are compromised.[48] The disorder is believed to be genetic; however, negative responses to food additives; sensitivity to chemicals, fungi, and molds; and exposure to toxins are believed to contribute to ADHD.[18]

CHARACTERISTICS

Many children and youth with ADHD are more impulsive than their peers in making choices. This can significantly interfere with their ability to regulate physical activity, inhibit behavior, and attend to physical education tasks in developmentally appropriate ways. Impulsivity can cause devastating consequences, including failure in school, antisocial behavior, and interpersonal difficulties. Other adverse consequences associated with impulsivity are difficulties attending to instruction, following instructions, completing instructional activities, and complying with class rules.[52] Three-quarters of hyperactive-inattentive children have coexisting conditions, including oppositional defiance disorder (50%), depression (38%), and anxiety (25%).[55]

The characteristics associated with each type of ADHD appear in **Table 18-1**.

TABLE 18-1   Characteristics of the Types of Attention Deficit/Hyperactive Disorders

ADHD predominantly inattentive—makes careless mistakes, inattentive, doesn't seem to listen, doesn't follow through on instructions, difficulty organizing tasks, avoids/dislikes tasks requiring sustained mental effort, loses things necessary for tasks, easily distracted, forgetful in daily activities
ADHD predominantly hyperactive-impulsive—fidgets and/or squirms in seat, leaves seat often, runs about or climbs excessively, difficulty playing or engaging in leisure activities quietly, often on the go, talks excessively, blurts out answers before question is complete, has difficulty waiting turn, interrupts or intrudes on others
ADHD combined—the most common type in children and adolescents, a combination of characteristics demonstrated in the other two types

American Psychiatric Association. (2013). *DSM-V-TR Diagnostic and Statistical Manual of Mental Disorders* (5th ed.). Washington, DC: American Psychiatric Association.

SPECIAL CONSIDERATIONS

The management of ADHD has received considerable study. A combination of drug therapy and psychological therapy shows the greatest promise for improving behavior and academic performance. Drug therapy most frequently is used with individuals who demonstrate ADHD. The three most common drugs prescribed are methylphenidate (Ritalin), dextroamphetamine (Dexedrine), and pemoline (Cylert),[23] all of which are central nervous system stimulants.[29] Improvements in attentiveness, information processing, and short-term memory result in academic performance gains.

THE PHYSICAL EDUCATION PROGRAM AND TEACHING STRATEGIES

The decision about which teaching strategy to use depends on the age and needs of the student. The bottom-up teaching approach using group games for elementary-age children and stations for middle school students can be used to address underlying neurological building block deficits. After age 12 years, a top-down, task-specific approach is best. Social development skills should be emphasized in the physical education program. Direct instruction, positive reinforcement of appropriate behavior, and peer coaching should be used whenever possible.[23] In addition to the many opportunities team play offers to aid in teaching socially appropriate responses, interactive computer-facilitated social interventions that address social problem solving can be helpful. Computer-facilitated scenarios that represent social environments and the range of choices within those environments can be used with youngsters with ADHD to help them understand how to select appropriate social responses.[27] The use of punitive measures with these youngsters should be avoided.[52] General points to keep in mind when working with these students are presented in **Table 18-2**.

TABLE 18-2   Tips for Teaching Students with ADHD

- Change activities frequently to accommodate the short attention span.
- Use a positive behavior modification program to keep the student on task.
- Incorporate 3 to 5 minutes of conscious relaxation at the end of the physical education period.
- Give brief instructions.
- Use activities that promote cooperation among all students (e.g., New Games).

Because of the physical and motor deficits many of these students demonstrate, whenever possible games and activities that limit competition should be stressed. Students with ADHD do not need to participate in activities they have little hope of succeeding in. To require them to do so sets them up for failure and contributes to poor self-esteem. The more activities that use an individualized approach and allow the students to work at their own level, the better the chance the students have at succeeding.

AIDS

Acquired immune deficiency syndrome (AIDS) has swept a deadly path throughout the world. Although AIDS was not recognized as a disease entity until 1981, the CDC estimates more than 1.2 million people in the United States are living with human immunodeficiency virus (HIV).[19]

DEFINITION

AIDS is the development of opportunistic infections and/or certain secondary cancers known to be associated with HIV infection. HIV disease (all stages of infection before the development of AIDS) is a progressive disease that is a result of the virus's infecting the CD_4 cells of the immune system. As HIV disease progresses, all of the CD_4 cells in the body are depleted, which results in the suppression of the immune system.[31] AIDS is the final stage of a series of diseases caused by HIV infection.

INCIDENCE

The World Health Organization reports that in 2013 nearly 35 million people worldwide are living with HIV/AIDS. In 2013, an estimated 47,352 people were diagnosed with HIV infection in the United States. In that same year, an estimated 26,688 people were diagnosed with AIDS.[17, 30] Nearly 30% of those infected with HIV are women.[4] In 2010, youth aged 13–24 years in the United States accounted for approximately 265 of HIV infections.

CAUSES

The HIV virus is spread from one person to another via body fluids. The primary transmission fluids are blood and blood products, semen, vaginal secretion, breast milk, and amniotic fluid. In the United States, the high-risk categories for receiving and transmitting the virus are homosexual or bisexual males (57% of cases), intravenous drug abusers, prostitutes and those who frequent them, transfusion recipients and hemophiliacs (particularly those who received transfusions before 1985), and those who have sexual contact with any of these groups. A child can get the HIV virus from the mother during pregnancy, childbirth, and breastfeeding.[20]

CHARACTERISTICS

HIV infection causes a wide range of symptoms ranging from flulike symptoms to full-blown AIDS. There are three recognized stages of development. During stage 1, the person tests positive for HIV, but no symptoms are present. This stage can last as long as 10 years. During stage 2, there are severe weight loss and wasting, chronic diarrhea, nonproductive cough with shortness of breath, dementia, fevers of unknown origin, chronic fatigue, swollen lymph glands, and decreased food consumption. With appropriate drug intervention, this stage can last several years. In stage 3, fully developed AIDS is apparent, which puts the individual at risk for infection and malignancy. Children born to HIV-positive mothers demonstrate significant mental and motor delays.[12]

SPECIAL CONSIDERATIONS

Because of the manner in which the virus is spread, caution should be exercised if the child with HIV/AIDS becomes injured and there is blood loss. Although the risk of contracting HIV/AIDS through providing first-aid assistance is minimal, the precautions to protect against all infectious diseases should be followed. Those precautions state that staff must routinely use appropriate barrier precautions to prevent skin and mucous membrane exposure to blood and body fluids containing visible blood in the following ways:

1. Whenever possible, wear disposable plastic or latex gloves. Use towels or cloth between yourself and blood or body fluids when gloves are not available.
2. Always wear gloves whenever you are in contact with blood, body fluids, diapering, or invasive procedures if you have an open wound or a lesion.

3. Toys should be cleansed by immersing them in a germicidal solution and rinsed thoroughly after use each day.
4. Cleaning up spills of body fluids requires the use of gloves. All surfaces should be cleansed with a germicide solution and rinsed, then air dried.
5. Soiled clothes and diapers should be placed in a plastic bag and given to the parent to clean at home.
6. Trash should be placed in a plastic bag and tied securely for removal.
7. All staff must use hand-washing techniques between handling each child during feedings, diapering, and nose cleaning.[46]

THE PHYSICAL EDUCATION PROGRAM AND TEACHING STRATEGIES

All schools should require that HIV infection, HIV disease, and AIDS information be included in the school curriculum; however, increasingly in the United States sex-related topics are being removed from health education content. To deny a teacher the right to share information critical to a student's health and welfare seems shortsighted and contrary to good educational practice; however, teachers must follow administration policies or risk dismissal. In schools where these topics cannot be included in the curriculum, the school administration should be encouraged to allow medical resources in the community to provide this vital information and to solicit parental support for accessing those professionals.

A student who is HIV-positive can be included in the physical education program without the teacher's being aware of the condition. A physician may not disclose the status of a child's health to a third party without parental consent.[40] This information may, or may not, be shared with the school. If the teacher is aware of a student with an HIV condition, precaution should be taken to avoid an injury that leads to bleeding. Most schools have developed policies to follow, should such injuries occur. Ways to prevent the possibility of contamination through contact with blood should be part of those policies, and they should be followed to the letter.

The physical education teacher should consult with each student's physician to determine activity levels. Because of the progressive nature of HIV diseases, students' levels of physical and motor performance should be assessed frequently and their program modified to accommodate their levels of function. However, for children who are rapidly deteriorating physically, it may be realistic to develop a program that will promote the maintenance of existing skills and capabilities. Each child with HIV/AIDS is different because of the many forms of the illness; however, the ultimate goal should always be to include the student in as many activities as possible. For individuals who are medically stable, evidence suggests that exercise is safe for those with HIV/AIDS.[31]

Anemia

DEFINITION

Anemia is a condition of the blood in which there is a deficiency of red cells or hemoglobin (a molecule in red blood cells that carries oxygen) in circulation.[10] There are several forms of anemia, which are classified as either acquired or congenital.[7] Examples of each are presented in **Table 18-3**.

Anemia requires medical intervention for management. The usual treatment includes nutritional supplements and transfusion. Anemia caused by disease is addressed by treating the disease.

Iron deficiency is commonly seen in teenage girls and especially in those who are active in sports. Care must be taken that nonanemic iron deficiency does not lead to anemic iron deficiency.

Sickle cell anemia, one of the most well-known forms of anemia, is an inherited disorder. In this form of anemia, not all of the person's hemoglobin works correctly. Some of the hemoglobin forms rodlike structures, which cause the blood cells to be sickle-shaped and stiff. These cells clog small blood vessels and prevent some tissues and organs from receiving adequate

TABLE 18-3   Types of Anemia

Acquired
- Nutritional, such as iron, B_{12}, or folic acid deficiency
- Acute or chronic blood loss, as from a peptic ulcer or hemorrhoids
- A result of disease, such as leukemia, juvenile rheumatoid arthritis, destruction of red blood cells by abnormal antibodies formed in a disease state

Congenital
- Sickle cell
- Spherocytosis (abnormal red blood cell membranes)

amounts of oxygen. When this occurs, severe pain results, and damage to organs and tissues frequently occurs.[6] The sites of the body most commonly affected by sickle cell anemia are the bones (usually the hands and feet in young children), intestines, spleen, gallbladder, brain, and lungs. Chronic ankle ulcers are a recurrent problem. Episodes of severe abdominal pain with vomiting may stimulate severe abdominal disorders. Such painful crises usually are associated with back and joint pain. Sickle cell anemia affects African Americans and Hispanics from the Caribbean, South or Central America, and parts of South Africa.[7] Individuals of Mediterranean, Middle Eastern, and Indian ancestry have a similar form of anemia, which results from unbalanced hemoglobin synthesis.[10]

Sports anemia affects athletes with low values of red blood cells or hemoglobin. These athletes range from fit individuals performing daily submaximum exercise to individuals participating in prolonged severe exercise and strenuous endurance training.

INCIDENCE

The prevalence of iron deficiency anemia for adolescent girls and adult women in the United States is 2% and 5%, respectively; the reported incidence in high school and college female athletes ranges as high as 19%. In the United States, estimates of nonanemic iron deficiency, which can, if uncorrected, lead to iron deficiency anemia, are 11% for adult women and 9% for adolescent girls. The sickle cell anemia trait is carried by about 8% of African Americans and 6% of Hispanics.[5]

CAUSES

There are many causes of anemia, which can be categorized as either congenital or acquired. The congenital form is present at birth. An example of this form is sickle cell anemia. The acquired form may occur at any time during one's life and persist or move into remission. Some of the specific causes of anemia are as follows:

- Iron deficiencies in the diet
- Inadequate or abnormal utilization of iron in the blood
- Menstrual loss (a primary source of iron loss in females)

- Chronic posthemorrhaging when there is prolonged moderate blood loss, such as that caused by a peptic ulcer
- Acute posthemorrhaging caused by a massive hemorrhage, such as a ruptured artery
- Decreased production of bone marrow
- Vitamin B_{12} deficiency
- Deficiency in folic acid, which is destroyed in long-term cooking
- Mechanical injury or trauma that impacts blood circulation
- Gastrointestinal loss, common in runners
- Urinary loss in the presence of urinary tract trauma
- Sweat loss when exercise is prolonged
- Disorders of red blood cell metabolism
- Defective hemoglobin synthesis[10, 32]

Primary diseases that give rise to anemia as a secondary condition include malaria, septic infections, and cirrhosis. In addition, poisons, such as lead, insecticides, and arsenobenzene, may contribute to anemia. Diseases associated with endocrine and vitamin deficiencies, such as chronic dysentery and intestinal parasites, can also cause anemia.

CHARACTERISTICS

The physical education teacher should be aware of the characteristics that anemic persons display. Some of the symptoms that signify anemia are an increased rate of breathing, a bluish tinge of the lips and nails (because the blood is not as red), headache, nausea, faintness, weakness, and fatigue. Severe anemia results in vertigo (dizziness), tinnitus (ringing in the ears), spots before the eyes, drowsiness, irritability, and bizarre behavior.[10] Children found to be iron deficient in early childhood, if treated only short-term (2 weeks), demonstrate poor cognitive and motor development, as well as poor school achievement into middle childhood. Young children treated for longer periods of time overcome their performance deficiencies. Iron-deficient school-age children who are treated usually overcome their cognition deficits but do not catch up in school achievement.[28] The performance effects of iron deficiency anemia are presented in **Table 18-4**.

TABLE 18-4   Performance Effects of Iron Deficiency Anemia

Diminished VO$_2$ max

Decreased physical work capacity

Lowered endurance

Increased lactic acidosis

Increased fatigue

SPECIAL CONSIDERATIONS

Anemia is symptomatic of a disturbance that, in many cases, can be remedied. Persons who have anemia because of a disease process have different medical needs than athletes with sports anemia who are apparently healthy. The school nurse should be alerted if a student is suspected of being anemic. The nurse will be able to recommend specific medical intervention to enable treatment to be determined and initiated. Inasmuch as there are several varieties of anemia, the method of treatment depends on the type of anemia present. Treatment of iron deficiency anemia usually involves physician-directed iron supplementation. Physicians usually prescribe several months of iron therapy coupled with supplements of vitamin C for individuals who are nonanemic iron deficient.[32] Aplastic anemia may be corrected by bone marrow transplantation and by use of the male hormone testosterone, which is known to stimulate the production of cells by the bone marrow if enough red marrow is present for the hormone to act on. Vitamin B$_{12}$ is stored in the liver and is released as required for the formation of red blood cells in the bone marrow.[45]

There is no drug therapy for sickle cell anemia. The symptoms are treated as they appear. During painful episodes, pain-killing drugs and oral and intravenous fluids reduce pain and prevent complications.[6] The initial symptoms of overexertion are headache or dizziness, leg cramps, chest pain, and left upper quadrant pain. Continuing exercise under those conditions can lead to coma and death. Children with sickle cell anemia must rest when feeling tired, drink extra fluids when active, and dress appropriately for the weather. Also, activities that expose persons to cold weather or high altitudes, such as backpacking and skiing, should be avoided. Coaches are advised that during preseason conditioning all athletes should train wisely, stay hydrated, heed environmental stress, and be alert to their reactions to heat.

THE PHYSICAL EDUCATION PROGRAM AND TEACHING STRATEGIES

The alert physical educator should be able to assist in the identification of anemia and thus refer the student to medical authorities. Undiagnosed anemia may curtail motor skill and physical development and thus may set the child apart from peers in social experiences. The student who has been identified as having anemia should be evaluated to determine physical fitness and motor skill development levels, so that an appropriate intervention program can be started.

The primary difficulty the student will experience is lowered stamina. Both the teacher and the student must be sensitive to the need to curtail activity levels, so that the student does not overexert during the physical education class period. Indications that the student is reaching a point of fatigue include loss of body control (e.g., running into other players, stumbling or falling frequently), irritability, loss of temper, breathlessness, and an unwillingness to continue to participate. Should any of these behaviors appear, if the student does not ask to sit out, the teacher should insist on an immediate rest period. The student will be the best judge of when to return to activity. In the meantime, the teacher should offer encouragement and be supportive.

The final decision regarding the nature of physical education activities for a student with anemia should be made by medical personnel. A well-conceived and supervised physical education program can be of great value because exercise stimulates the production of red blood cells through the increased demand for oxygen. However, to be beneficial, an activity must be planned qualitatively with regard to the specific anemic condition. It is not uncommon for children who have anemia to be delayed in the development of physical strength and endurance.

Asthma

DEFINITION

Asthma is a pulmonary disease characterized by reversible airway obstruction, airway inflammation, and increased airway responsiveness to a variety of stimuli.[10]

INCIDENCE

Asthma is the single most chronic disease in childhood, affecting 5 million children in the United States. The number of individuals with asthma has increased in the last few decades.[39] The condition is disproportionately high among inner-city children.[34] Asthma-related illness accounts for 15 million school days missed annually.[39]

CAUSES

The disease is a result of the body's reaction to an allergen, such as animal dander, mold spores, pollens, or house dust mites; to a nonallergenic stimulus, such as cold air or exercise; or to chemical substances, such as tobacco smoke, fungi, mold, and polluted indoor air.[9] The airways become obstructed because of a combination of factors, including a spasm of smooth muscle in the airways, edema of the mucosa in the airways, increased mucus secretion, infiltration of the cells in the airway walls, and eventual permanent damage to the lining of the airways.[10]

CHARACTERISTICS

The symptoms of asthma vary widely. Some asthmatics just wheeze and have a dry cough. Others have a tight chest, wheeze and cough frequently, and have increased difficulty breathing following exposure to allergens, viral infections, and exercise.[10] An attack usually begins with an irritating cough, and the student complains of a tightness in the chest and difficulty breathing, especially during inspiration. The severity of the attack can be measured by the symptoms (see **Table 18-5**). The early warning signs of

TABLE 18-5   Levels of Severity of an Asthma Attack[10]

Stage	Symptoms and Signs
I: Mild	Adequate air exchange, mild shortness of breath, diffuse wheezing
II: Moderate	Respiratory distress at rest, marked wheezing, use of accessory muscles to breathe, difficulty breathing
III: Severe	Marked respiratory distress, cyanosis, inability to speak more than a few words, marked wheezing, and use of accessory muscles to breathe
IV: Respiratory failure	Severe respiratory distress, lethargy, confusion, marked use of accessory muscles to breathe

an asthmatic attack are (1) a feeling of pressure on the chest, (2) chronic, persistent cough, (3) shortness of breath, (4) exercise intolerance, (5) sore throat, (6) restlessness, (7) headache, (8) runny nose, (9) clipped speech, (10) changes in breathing patterns, and (11) change in face color.[2]

Exercise-induced asthma (EIA) is acute airway narrowing after strenuous exertion. The symptoms include chest tightness, shortness of breath, coughing, wheezing, fatigue, and prolonged recovery time. The reaction starts 5 to 20 minutes after beginning to exercise. The symptoms peak about 5 to 10 minutes after stopping exercise.[25] A second reaction 3 to 9 hours after exercising can occur. About 50% of asthmatics have a refractory period of 2 to 4 hours after ceasing to exercise. During the refractory period, their airways respond to a second bout of exercise 50% better than during the initial exercise period.[56]

SPECIAL CONSIDERATIONS

Most individuals with asthma who are under a physician's care take either oral or inhaled medication to control their condition. The use of medication before exercise will allow most individuals with asthma to perform to the level of their nonasthmatic peers.[14] Two categories of medication are used to reverse or prevent airflow obstruction for both acute and chronic asthma: anti-inflammatory agents and bronchodilators. Corticosteroids (taken orally intravenously, or as an inhalant) and nonsteroidal inhalants, such as cromolyn sodium, are used to control inflammation. Bronchodilators include beta 2-agonists and methylxanthines, such as theophylline. Beta 2-agonists are the most effective bronchodilators to prevent and reverse EIA. One or two doses just before exercise will greatly enhance the student's ability to persist with an exercise bout. Those who do not benefit from beta 2-agonist inhalants frequently use the nonsteroidal inhalant cromolyn sodium because it blocks the postexercise bronchoconstriction that occurs several hours after exercise.[2, 22]

An indoor environment that contains mold, dust, or insects can trigger and exacerbate respiratory symptoms.[34] Recently, it has been reported that chlorinated byproducts that contaminate the air in indoor pools can promote the development of asthma in some children. As a result, chlorinated pool use prior to ages 6 to 7 years is discouraged.[11]

THE PHYSICAL EDUCATION PROGRAM AND TEACHING STRATEGIES

It is important for individuals with asthma to participate in the regular physical education class because of the physical and psychological benefits of exercise and the opportunities to socialize with classmates. The teacher must be aware of the student's condition, limitations, and anxieties in order to adjust the activity demands on the student and to foster understanding among other students in the class. A moderate or severe asthma attack can be very frightening to the child who is having the attack, as well as to the classmates who observe it. The teacher should request permission from the parents and the child who has asthma to provide information about asthma to the entire class.

Inasmuch as children with asthma vary in their capabilities to participate in intense activity, each student's physical education program should be individualized as much as possible. This is not to say the program should be watered down for these students. Clearly, many persons with asthma are world-class athletes and experience EIA. Thus, assumptions should not be made about the physical capabilities of students with asthma. For the most part, students with asthma can participate in the regular program without modification; however, environmental controls, special instruction in breathing and conscious relaxation, and a carefully controlled progressive exercise program are critical for these students.

All students should be taught to breathe through the nose and trained in abdominal breathing. Breathing through the nose allows the air to warm as it enters the body and controls the rate of expiration. Conscious relaxation and abdominal breathing are recommended as part of the cool-down to reduce post-exercise reactions.[3] Abdominal (deep) breathing can be accomplished by having the students lie on their backs on the floor and place one or both hands on their abdomens as they proceed with the following instructions:

1. Inhale slowly and naturally through the nose deep enough to push the diaphragm down (which will cause the hands on the abdomen to rise).
2. Exhale slowly against pursed lips to keep the small airways open.
3. Pause without holding the breath and count to self 1,001, 1,002. During this pause, allow the exhalation to come to a natural, unforced conclusion.
4. Repeat the first three steps for several minutes.

Abdominal breathing exercises will increase the strength and endurance of the respiratory muscles and will allow greater amounts of air to be inhaled and to be made available for exercise. Students with asthma should be cautioned that breathing in this manner may initially increase their phlegm and cause them to cough and wheeze. After extended training, those reactions will be greatly reduced.

At the elementary school level, every class should end with 3 to 4 minutes of relaxation techniques. At the middle and high school levels, relaxation sessions should be included at the end of any class using high-cardiovascular endurance activities. Training in relaxation is particularly critical for the individual with asthma because the practice can be used to lower the impact of anxiety on the body. When an individual's anxiety level is lowered, the tendency to cough and wheeze is also reduced.

Progressive exercise programs are a must for the individual with compromised endurance, whether it is a result of asthma, a sedentary lifestyle, or some other reason. Regular exercise that is gradually increased in frequency and intensity will improve respiration, circulation, physical functioning, and muscle strength.[22] Specific exercise guidelines are presented in **Table 18-6.**

Unless a physician indicates otherwise, no special modifications other than allowing the student to reduce his or her activity level and rest when needed are required for the student with asthma. However, until the student has developed skills and fitness levels commensurate with his or her peers, the student's progress should be carefully monitored to ensure ease of participation and continual improvement. The student should be given

TABLE 18-6   Exercise Guidelines for Individuals with Asthma[2]

1. Choose exercises that can be performed in a warm, humid environment, such as a pool.
2. If exercising outside in cold weather, wear a scarf or mask over the mouth to limit exposure to cold and pollutants.
3. Breathe through the nose whenever possible to warm and humidify inspired air.
4. Work out inside when pollutant or allergen levels are high outside.
5. Do 5 to 10 minutes of stretching and breathing exercises before a high-intensity workout.
6. Work out slowly for the first few minutes after warm-up.
7. Do a 10- to 20-minute cool-down after a workout.

American College of Allergy, Asthma & Immunology. *Asthma attack.* Retrieved from http//acaai.org

TABLE 18-7   Intervention for an Asthma Attack

1. Remove the student from the group to reduce anxiety.
2. Encourage the student to relax and breathe deeply and slowly.
3. If an inhaler is typically used it should be readily available.
4. Have the student get into a comfortable position.
5. Encourage the student to spit if needed to get rid of any mucous plugs.

Modified from Rimmer, J. H. (1994). *Fitness and rehabilitation programs for special populations.* Madison, WI: Brown & Benchmark.

responsibility for taking the appropriate dosage of medication before exercise and regulating his or her exercise pace. To keep the student's anxiety about the possibility of an asthma attack to a minimum, the teacher should ensure that the appropriate program is followed, should be attentive to the status of the student, and should provide needed encouragement. If a student experiences an asthma attack, the procedure presented in **Table 18-7** is recommended.

Childhood Cancer

DEFINITION

Cancer is a cellular malignancy whose unique characteristic is a loss of normal cell control. The body loses control of its cells' growth and the distribution of cells by function. There is a lack of differentiation of cells; the cells tend not to assume a particular function in the body. In addition, these unique, apparently random cells have the ability to invade local, healthy tissues and to metastasize (spread), destroying the healthy cells.[10]

INCIDENCE

Childhood cancer, a devastating disease, is the major cause of death by disease in children. The National Cancer Institute estimates 10,380 new cases of cancer diagnosed in children ages 0 to 14 years in 2015. Acute lymphocytic leukemia (ALL), brain and other central nervous system tumors, and neuroblastoma are predicted to account for more than half of the new cases in 2015.[44] Cancer is the second leading cause of death in childhood.[37]

CAUSES

The onset of childhood cancer appears to be related to the relationship between the child's genetic/familial endowment and the child's environment. If the child has a chromosomal aberration, as is seen in Down syndrome, trisomy G, and Klinefelter's syndrome, the child is more likely than another to develop childhood cancer.[13] Chromosomal instability also is related to the development of childhood cancers, as are inherited traits for immunodeficiency. The best example of this is the child born with AIDS; that child is highly likely to develop AIDS-related cancers.

The transformation of a cell from normalcy to malignancy is thought to occur in one cell through a series of two or more steps. The development of cancer cells, or malignancies, is initiated by a cell that is affected by an event. This cell then becomes an "initiated" cell. If this cell is further stimulated by an event, the cell may become precancerous. Any subsequent conversion or modification of this cell causes it to become malignant. Then the malignant cell "clones" itself. It appears that most tumors are clonal expansions of cells that grow unchecked because of acquired changes in the genes that regularly control the growth and development of cells.[43]

Common cancer-causing environmental substances include soot and mineral oil, arsenic, asbestos, hair dyes, painting materials, and lead.[14] If an infant is exposed to a large dose of lead, one of the child's cells may become an initiated cell. If that cell is subsequently exposed to additional large doses of lead, precancerous cell growth may be promoted. Any further modification of the cell may cause it to become malignant and then clone itself, metastasizing into other, healthy tissues.[43]

CHARACTERISTICS

The general symptoms of childhood cancer include the following:

- Fatigue
- Weight loss
- Cough
- Changes in blood composition
- Changes in bowel activity
- Persistent pain
- Skeletal pain

- Fever
- Sweating[10]

TYPES OF CHILDHOOD CANCERS

Leukemias

Leukemias are cancers of the white blood cells, involving bone marrow, circulating white blood cells, and organs such as the spleen and lymph nodes.[10] The factors that predispose a child to the development of leukemia are the same as those that predispose a child to the development of other forms of childhood cancer. These include the Epstein-Barr virus, the human T-cell lymphotropic virus, ionizing radiation, and chromosomal disorders (such as Down syndrome and Fanconi's anemia).[10] Acute leukemia is the most common form of malignancy in childhood,[44] representing 33% of childhood cancers.[37] There are two major forms: acute lymphoblastic leukemia (ALL) and acute nonlymphoblastic leukemia (ANLL).

Central Nervous System Tumors

The most common primary childhood brain tumors are astrocytomas, medulloblastomas, and ependymomas.[38] These primary childhood tumors tend to remain confined to tissues within the central nervous system but are devastating in their impact on the total human being. Most of the general signs and symptoms of brain tumors are significantly related to elevated levels of intracranial pressure caused by the presence of abnormal tissue growth.[10]

Hodgkin's Disease

Hodgkin's disease in childhood is similar to the Hodgkin's disease that affects adults. About 15% of those affected by Hodgkin's disease are younger than 15 years of age. It is a chronic condition in which large, multinucleated reticulum cells (Reed-Sternberg cells) are present in lymph node tissue or in other nonreticular formation sites. The presence of these cells causes lesions. The primary lesions are located in the lymph nodes, spleen, and bone marrow.

Neuroblastoma

A neuroblastoma is the most common cancer in infants accounting for 6% of all childhood cancers.[1] It is a solid tumor arising in the adrenal gland or from the adrenal sympathetic chain.[10] Approximately 700 new cases are diagnosed each year with 90% of children diagnosed by age 5 years.[1]

Wilms' Tumor

Wilms' tumor is a malignant embryonal tumor of the kidney. It usually occurs in children under the age of 5 years, but occasionally in older children. A genetic effect has been identified in some cases.[10]

Soft-Tissue Tumors

One of the more common forms of soft-tissue tumors in children is rhabdomyosarcoma, representing approximately 3%–4% of all childhood cancers.[36] This malignancy affects the muscle tissue and can arise from any type of muscle tissue.[10]

Bone Tumors

The two best-known childhood bone malignancies are Ewing's sarcoma and osteosarcoma. Ewing's sarcoma is the second most common form of malignant primary bone tumor of childhood.[10] It is a round cell bone tumor of childhood. The primary bone tumor usually appears in the extremities and most commonly metastasizes to the lungs and bone marrow. Osteosarcoma appears between the ages of 10 and 20 years. Pain and a noticeable mass are the usual symptoms. It is most common in the knee joint and is highly malignant.

Retinoblastoma

A retinoblastoma is a malignant tumor that arises from the immature retina. The disease may be inherited and has been traced to an autosomal dominant trait.[10] It has a significant negative impact on the child's vision.

SPECIAL CONSIDERATIONS

New and innovative treatments of childhood cancer have increased the likelihood that children who are diagnosed early will have a chance of survival. More than 73% of children with cancer are cured by surgery, chemotherapy, radiation, or a combination of these treatments.[44] Many of these survivors return to school and attempt to restore relative normalcy to their lives. The teacher must be aware of the side effects of the cancer and its treatment and be sensitive to the psychosocial needs of the student.

The side effects of the childhood cancers and their treatments have a negative impact on the following:

- General intelligence
- Age-appropriate developmental progress
- Academic achievement
- Visual and perceptual motor skills
- Memory
- Receptive and expressive language and attention/concentration[15]

THE PHYSICAL EDUCATION PROGRAM AND TEACHING STRATEGIES

The teacher needs to be sensitive to the physical deficits and needs of the child survivor of cancer and work in close cooperation with the child's physician, rehabilitation therapist, and parents to develop a program that addresses the student's unique health needs. In addition, the teacher must be aware of the significant psychosocial effects that a life-threatening illness has on the child, the parents and siblings, members of the extended family, and friends. The child who is able to return to school, to move from the more restricted hospital/homebound education program to the less restricted public school program, will face peers with a history of markedly different experiences. It is frequently difficult for the child to make the transition from a life-and-death situation to a life of play, games, and sports. However, play, games, and sports often are a vital link to normalcy for the child.

The physical education program for students recovering from cancer should be designed to meet demonstrated specific needs. If the child's physical development lags behind his or her peers, opportunities should be provided to promote development in the needed area. In elementary schools where a movement education program is in place, it is relatively easy to provide for individual differences. In more structured educational settings, care must be taken not to place the child in a game or play situation beyond his or her capabilities. These children should be assigned less active roles that will enable them to participate as they gain the needed skills and performance levels of their classmates. Highly competitive activities should be avoided, so that these students are not placed in a situation where the level of play creates a potential for injury, or where their need to restrict their all-out efforts results in negative reactions from teammates.

Physical fitness regimens should begin at the student's present level of performance and slowly build toward higher levels of fitness.

Cystic Fibrosis

DEFINITION

Cystic fibrosis is a disease of the exocrine glands primarily affecting the gastrointestinal and respiratory systems.[10] A defect in a gene prevents chloride from entering or leaving cells, which results in production of a thick, sticky mucus that clogs ducts or tubes in some organs. The primary organs affected are the lungs, pancreas, small intestine, and sweat glands.[24]

INCIDENCE

The disease affects 1 in every 3,300 Caucasian births, 1 in every 15,300 African American births, and 1 in every 32,000 Asian American births. Treatments have improved in the last several years and it is now estimated that approximately 50% of those with cystic fibrosis are adults.[50]

CAUSES

Cystic fibrosis is an inherited disorder that is generally fatal. It is the most common life-shortening genetic disease in the Caucasian population.

CHARACTERISTICS

The disease is characterized by the production of abnormally thick mucus, impaired absorption of fat and protein, a high concentration of sodium and chloride in the sweat, and progressive lung damage. As the disease progresses, pulmonary function deteriorates and exercise tolerance diminishes.[47]

The symptoms and severity of cystic fibrosis vary from apparently normal to markedly impaired health. Nearly all of the exocrine glands are affected to some degree. The lungs appear normal at birth, but thick mucous secretions eventually clog the bronchial tubes and impair breathing.[10] There is usually continuing destruction of pancreatic tissue. Older children may also have diabetes. There is considerable variance in the physical capabilities among children with cystic fibrosis.

SPECIAL CONSIDERATIONS

Increased understanding about cystic fibrosis and the value of aggressive intervention programs has resulted in improved prognosis over the past 50 years. Successful intervention includes a special diet, control of infection, and pulmonary therapy.

Diet

To offset the undernourishment that results from the under absorption of fat and protein, additions to the diet and supplements are used. The recommended special diet includes an intake of calories and protein that exceeds the Recommended Dietary Allowance (RDA) by 30% to 50% and a normal-to-high total fat intake. Twice the recommended daily allowance of multivitamins and supplemental vitamin E in water-miscible form are used to strengthen the immune system. Salt supplements during periods of exposure to high temperature and sweating reduce the risk for heat-associated illnesses.[50]

Control of Infection

A high incidence of pulmonary infections requires intermediate- to long-term use of antibiotics, depending on the individual. The use of ibuprofen has been shown to slow the rate of pulmonary function decline in children 5 to 13 years of age. Vitamin K supplements are recommended for individuals receiving long-term antibiotic therapy and individuals with liver involvement.[10] Immunizations against whooping cough, measles, and flu are routine.

Pulmonary Therapy

Progressive bronchiolar and bronchial obstruction leads to infection of the bronchi and breakdown of lung tissue. Every effort is made to clear the bronchi of the thick mucus that accumulates continually. Pulmonary involvement leads to death in over 90% of individuals with cystic fibrosis.

Pulmonary therapy to lessen the accumulation of mucus consists of postural drainage, percussion, vibration, and assistance with coughing on indication of pulmonary involvement. Oral and aerosol bronchodilators are also used to reverse airway obstruction.[10] In severe cases, the constant use of supplemental oxygen is necessary.

THE PHYSICAL EDUCATION PROGRAM AND TEACHING STRATEGIES

It may be helpful for physical education teachers to understand the behavior and medical treatments of individuals with cystic fibrosis. The following are some common behaviors and needs they demonstrate:

- They need to cough out the mucus in their lungs. Therefore, they should be encouraged to do so. Other students in the class need to understand that cystic fibrosis is not a communicable disease.
- The student's diet may be different from the norm; as such, the child may need to make frequent trips to the restroom.
- Although individuals with cystic fibrosis may have less stamina than others, it is important that they participate in modified physical activity commensurate with their abilities.
- Some may be on medication for both pancreatic and lung involvement and may subsequently need to take medication during physical education class.
- Some individuals may also demonstrate asthma or exercise-induced asthma and will require the use of bronchodilator therapy prior to physical activities.[47] Aerosol bronchodilator drugs are helpful in some cases and may need to be administered in class.
- Precautions should be taken to minimize the probability of respiratory infections.
- Teenagers frequently demonstrate a declining tolerance for exercise. Their physical education activity should be modified accordingly.

The physical education program for young children with cystic fibrosis should not differ from that of their classmates. Students at the middle and high school levels should be encouraged to participate within their own limitations. They should be discouraged from engaging in highly competitive sports in which there are pressures to exercise beyond what is a safe level for the individual. Individual physical fitness programs should begin with low-intensity exercise and gradually increase to comfort levels. Building in physical activity three to five times weekly is recommended. If an individual has severe dysfunction, days of rest must be interspersed with exercise days. The types of exercise programs that have been shown to benefit the individual with cystic fibrosis include running, swimming, bicycling, and active play.

Diabetes

DEFINITION

Diabetes is a general term referring to a variety of disorders that are primarily divided into two groups: diabetes mellitus and diabetes insipidus.[21] Diabetes mellitus is a group of diseases characterized by hyperglycemia resulting from defects in insulin secretion, insulin action, or both.[35] Diabetes insipidus results from an inability to concentrate urine in the kidneys. There are two types of diabetes insipidus: pituitary and nephrogenic.

At the recommendation of a committee sponsored by the American Diabetes Association, diabetes mellitus, which is the most common form of diabetes, has been divided into the following four classifications:

- Type 1—diabetes mellitus, formerly called insulin-dependent diabetes—IDD or juvenile
- Type 2—diabetes mellitus, formerly called non-insulin-dependent diabetes—NIDD
- Type 3—other specific types of diabetes mellitus
- Type 4—gestational diabetes mellitus[54]

INCIDENCE

Diabetes was the seventh leading cause of death in the United States in 2010. Approximately 29.1 million Americans have diabetes mellitus equaling 9.3% of the population, and 8.1 million of them do not know they have the disease.[4] It is estimated that 1.25 million American adults and children have Type 1 diabetes. The incidence of diabetes insipidus is much lower.

CAUSES

Diabetes mellitus has diverse genetic, environmental, and pathogenic origins.[10] Type 1 results in beta cell destruction, which usually leads to absolute insulin deficiency. Type 2 is characterized by insulin resistance in peripheral tissue and/or insulin secretory defects in a beta cell. Because 30% of adults and 25% of children in the United States are obese, they are considered pre-diabetic, meaning they are at high risk of developing Type 2 diabetes.[33] Type 3 causes include genetic defects of beta cell function, diseases of the exocrine pancreas, genetic defects in insulin action, endocrinopathies, and drug- or chemical-induced diabetes. Type 4, gestational diabetes, is brought on by the metabolic stress of pregnancy; a genetic basis has not been confirmed.[54]

Both pituitary and nephrogenic diabetes insipidus have genetic bases. Pituitary diabetes insipidus results from damage to the pituitary gland and/or hypothalamus, which leads to a deficiency of antidiuretic hormone (ADH); it can be inherited or acquired. Nephrogenic diabetes insipidus is a genetic disorder that is caused by a lack of response of resorption of the renal tubules. Because fluids are not resorbed in the kidneys, urine is excreted frequently in a nonconcentrated form. The recommended treatment is adequate and ongoing water intake.[10]

CHARACTERISTICS

In diabetes mellitus, the body is unable to burn up its intake of carbohydrates because of a lack of insulin production by the pancreas. The lack of insulin in the blood prevents the storage of glucose in the cells of the liver. Consequently, blood sugar accumulates in the bloodstream in greater than usual amounts (hyperglycemia). The chronic hyperglycemia of diabetes mellitus results in long-term damage to, dysfunction of, and failure of various organs, especially the eyes, kidneys, nerves, heart, and blood vessels.

Type 1 diabetes mellitus accounts for 10% to 15% of all diabetes mellitus. It must be controlled with insulin. An equal number of males and females are afflicted with the condition. The amount of insulin needed by these individuals varies widely. The biggest risk with this group is to take in more insulin than can be utilized, which will result in a hypoglycemic coma. Although Type 1 diabetes mellitus can occur at any age, it is usually acquired before age 30 years. It is the form that is most prevalent in school-age children. The onset is acute (sudden), and early symptoms include weight loss despite normal or increased dietary intake, frequent urination, and fatigue.[10] Persons with Type 1 diabetes may lower their need for insulin by exercising;

however, they must monitor their carbohydrate intake before exercise and their blood sugar before, during, and after exercise, modifying their short-acting insulin injections accordingly.[35]

Type 2 diabetes mellitus is also characterized by hyperglycemia but, because individuals with this disease usually retain some insulin secretion capability, ongoing insulin therapy is usually not necessary. A far greater number of females than males are afflicted with this form of diabetes. Obesity, a sedentary lifestyle, and a family history of diabetes characterize Type 2 diabetes mellitus. Like Type 1, common symptoms include fatigue; weakness; thirst; frequent urination; lethargy; dry, hot skin; lack of hunger; a fruity or winelike odor; heavy, labored breathing; and eventual stupor or unconsciousness.[51] Children with Type 1 or 2 well-controlled diabetes who were raised in nonstimulating environments demonstrate significantly delayed gross and fine motor development as late as 12 years of age.[49]

Type 3, other, specific types of diabetes mellitus, results from conditions and syndromes that impact glucose tolerance, such as cystic fibrosis, organ transplants, acromegaly, renal dialysis, and drugs and chemical agents.[10] Care of the person with Type 3 diabetes is tied directly to the primary condition or syndrome.

Type 4, gestational diabetes mellitus, is usually not identified until a woman becomes pregnant. All pregnant women should be screened for this type of diabetes because untreated gestational carbohydrate intolerance results in increased fetal and neonatal loss. The problem occurs in about 4% of all pregnancies; however, the incidence is higher in Mexican Americans, Indians, Asians, and Pacific Islanders.[10] Many pregnant women with Type 4 diabetes must take insulin during their pregnancy; however, diet modification, moderate exercise, maintenance of normal body weight, and weekly monitoring of glucose levels also aid in controlling the condition.

SPECIAL CONSIDERATIONS

Individuals with diabetes mellitus should be encouraged to exercise because regular, long-term exercise provides many benefits that contribute to control of the disease. However, unless strict food and insulin guidelines are followed, a single exercise bout can lead to negative reactions. Three negative exercise reactions that can occur but are avoidable are hypoglycemia (abnormally low blood sugar level), hyperglycemia (an excess amount of blood sugar), and ketoacidosis.

Hypoglycemia

Hypoglycemia is the greatest concern of the individual who has Type 1 diabetes mellitus. Signs of hypoglycemia include double vision, fatigue, excessive hunger, increased heart rate, nervousness, headache, numbness, palpitations, slurred speech, excessive sweating, and tremor.[3, 54]

Because school-age children who are diabetic most frequently have Type 1 diabetes, if they have a negative reaction to exercise, it will probably be in the form of hypoglycemia. Hypoglycemic reactions can occur because of an error in insulin dosage, a missed meal, unplanned exercise, or no apparent cause.[10] A hypoglycemic reaction should be suspected when a student who has Type 1 diabetes mellitus demonstrates any or all of the following symptoms:

- Confusion
- Inappropriate behavior
- Visual disturbance
- Stupor
- Seizures

Should a student have a hypoglycemic reaction in class, the intervention presented in **Table 18-8** should be performed.

Hypoglycemic reactions can be prevented by decreasing insulin or increasing carbohydrate consumption before, during, and after exercise. There are formulas for determining how much short-acting insulin can be reduced (never change the dosage of long-acting insulin); also, alternate injection sites should be selected (e.g., inject into the abdomen or a limb not used during exercise).

TABLE 18-8   Intervention to Counter a Hypoglycemic Reaction

1. Give some form of sugar immediately (improvement should be evident within a few minutes). Use fast-acting sugar in the form of a small box of raisins, 4 ounces of regular (not diet) cola or fruit juice, five small sugar cubes, six or seven Life Savers, or 1–2 teaspoons of honey.[54]
2. When improvement occurs, give additional food and then have the child resume normal activities.
3. If the child does not improve after sugar intake, call parents, the physician, and emergency medical assistance.
4. If the child becomes unconscious or is unable to take the sugar, immediately call for medical assistance.

Hyperglycemia

Hyperglycemia is also a problem for the active individual with either Type 1 or Type 2 diabetes mellitus. Hyperglycemia results when daily exercise volume is suddenly reduced without increasing insulin or any oral agents being used to control glucose levels. The symptoms of hyperglycemia are increased thirst and increased urination.

Ketoacidosis

Ketoacidosis is a violent reaction to a lack of circulating insulin. It is caused by the failure to take an appropriate dose of insulin or by an acute infection or trauma that requires additional insulin.[8] Students who forget to take their insulin or experience an acute infection or trauma may have a ketoacidotic reaction, with the following symptoms:

- Abdominal pain
- Dehydration caused by excessive urination
- Drowsiness
- Fruity-smelling breath
- Nausea
- Glucose and ketones in the urine

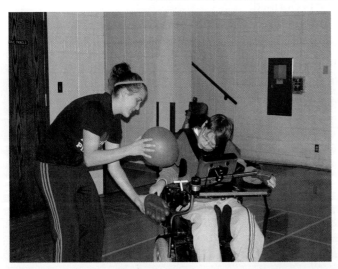

This condition requires immediate treatment with insulin, fluids, and electrolytes. Delayed intervention can cause lethargy, which may lead to a coma.[10]

THE PHYSICAL EDUCATION PROGRAM AND TEACHING STRATEGIES

The physical educator should be aware of students' individual needs. The school nurse can be very helpful in providing information about students who have existing medical conditions. After students with medical conditions are identified, programs of exercise should be established (with medical counsel) according to the needs of each student. The limits on the activity each child with diabetes can perform vary; therefore, it is important that the physical educator be clear about the status of each child.

Information should be gathered from the primary physician, the student, and the student's caregivers. Awareness of the knowledge and attitudes of the student and his or her parents concerning the benefits of physical activity, the extent to which the student is able to monitor his or her own blood sugar levels, and the student's understanding of the condition all impact the type of physical education program the teacher recommends for the student. In addition, once a program of activity is initiated, the teacher is responsible for carefully monitoring the student's progress.

Every year more studies validate the roles of exercise and proper diet in the management of diabetes. As this knowledge reaches primary care physicians, they are better able to counsel individuals with diabetes and their caregivers about the importance of maintaining ongoing regimens of appropriate exercise and diet. The knowledgeable physician is the conscientious physical educator's best ally. The physical educator should seek both cooperation and advice from the physician. Information gathered should include the type of diabetes, the type of diet and therapeutic intervention, the knowledge level of the student and the student's parents or caregivers, recommendations of desirable activity levels, and contraindications.[42]

Successful management of diabetes requires that the student participate in a regimen of care. Noncompliance with health practices related to diabetes can have serious short- and long-term effects. In general, a student with Type 1 or Type 2 diabetes mellitus should have the information presented in **Table 18-9**.

Regular exercise programs are of value to all individuals with diabetes, and it is particularly important that the child with diabetes be provided proper instruction that can be used throughout life. Exercise is an essential component of an effective treatment program for many diabetics. In developing an exercise program, it is desirable to provide activity that meets the student's interests and needs and still uses the large muscles of the body. Sport activity and aerobic exercise, such as walking, jogging, cycling, swimming, and cross-country skiing, are particularly desirable. Gary Hall, a world-class swimmer who was diagnosed with Type 1 diabetes at age 24 years, went on to win a gold medal in the 50-meter freestyle race during the 2000 Olympiad.

TABLE 18-9   Required Practices of Students with Type 1 or Type 2 Diabetes Mellitus[53]

1. Blood sugar levels should be monitored before, during, and after workouts, and the diet should be adjusted to make up for energy lost during exercise. If the blood sugar is less than 100 mg/dl, a snack should be eaten that contains at least 15 to 30 grams of carbohydrate (e.g., a slice of bread or 60 to 120 calories of fruit or crackers).

2. Always eat something 2 to 3 hours before and after exercise.

3. Prevent dehydration by drinking 2 cups of water 2 hours before exercise, 1 to 2 cups 30 minutes before, 1/2 cup every 15 minutes during exercise, and enough afterward to regain any weight lost during the workout.

4. Spend 5 to 10 minutes warming up before exercising and cooling down after exercising with stretching and slow, large-muscle activity (e.g., walking, jogging).

5. Exercise with a buddy who knows the signs of hypoglycemia, hyperglycemia, and ketoacidosis.

6. Wear appropriate, well-fitting shoes for the activity (soft leather with few seams are best), and check feet regularly for infected blisters, scratches, or open wounds. Don't ever burst a blister.

7. Carry insulin, oral drugs, or hard candy with you.

8. Wear identification that gives your name, address, parents' home and work phone numbers, physician's name and phone number, and type of diabetes.

9. In addition, a student with Type 1 diabetes should:

   a. Keep a logbook to record levels of blood sugar, dosage of insulin, amount and type of food eaten, and type and intensity of exercise. That information will help the student establish the relationship among those factors and be better able to adjust for low and high levels of blood sugar.

   b. Review the effect the frequent use of short-acting insulin has on blood sugar levels before, during, and after.

   c. Not exercise if the blood sugar reading is less than 60 mg/dl.

   d. Time exercise to miss the peak period of administered insulin. Begin exercising no earlier than 1 hour after taking the insulin.

   e. Choose insulin administration sites away from actively exercising muscle groups.

   f. Take a high-carbohydrate snack, such as fruit juice, bread, or plain cookies, before exercise. Eat about 15 grams of carbohydrate or more if needed.

   g. For moderate bouts of exercise, reduce the dose of short-acting insulin by 10%. For vigorous bouts of exercise, reduce the dose of short-acting insulin by up to 50%.

   h. If using only intermediate-acting insulin, reduce the morning dose by 30% to 40% for moderate to vigorous exercise in the morning, midday, or early afternoon.

   i. Prevent nighttime hypoglycemia by exercising earlier in the day and by reducing insulin dosages in the evening after exercising. If hypoglycemia persists, monitor blood sugar levels at night and take additional carbohydrates before sleep.

10. The teacher may want to develop a checklist with all of this information for the student. Until the routine becomes habitual, the student can refer to the checklist daily and occasionally share the results with the teacher.

Data from Taunton, J. E., & McCargar, L. (1995). Staying active with diabetes: Quick and helpful exercise tips. *Physician Sportsmed, 23*(3), 55–56.

He was able to maintain his 8-hour-daily, 6-days-a-week practice regime by working closely with a physician who specialized in diabetes.[41]

The child with diabetes can and should participate, in general, in the activities of the unrestricted class. However, many people with diabetes are more susceptible to fatigue than are their nondiabetic peers. Therefore, the physical educator should be understanding in the event that the student with diabetes cannot withstand prolonged bouts of more strenuous exercise. The intensity of aerobic activities will be determined by the present levels of performance assessed through testing. Individuals who have been sedentary and have not been able to develop adequate physical fitness levels should begin slowly and progress at a rate commensurate with their capability. The student's reactions during and after exercise will dictate the intensity, duration, and frequency levels. To aid the teacher in monitoring student status, a buddy who has been trained to recognize the previously described adverse reactions to exercise should be assigned to exercise with the student with diabetes.

SUMMARY

Other health impairment, by federal definition, means that a child has limited strength, vitality, attentiveness, or alertness due to chronic or acute health problems. In addition to health impairments listed in the federal definition of the IDEIA, other impairments that might limit a student's participation in physical education are ADHD, AIDS, anemia, asthma, childhood cancer, cystic fibrosis, or diabetes. The physical educator should understand the nature of each of these conditions, how the conditions can affect a student's performance capabilities, and the types of program modifications that best meet the needs of each student.

Most of the conditions discussed in this chapter require medical attention. When this is the case, it is advisable to request permission from the parents to consult with the student's physician to ensure that the type of exercises and activities selected for the student will not aggravate the condition. In most situations, mild exercise will benefit the student. However, in the case of the diabetic student, the type of diabetes must be known before specific exercise programs can be developed.

REVIEW QUESTIONS

1. What techniques can a physical education teacher use to keep a student with an attention deficit/hyperactive disorder on task?
2. How should persons with Type 1 diabetes adjust their insulin levels to accommodate increased exercise?

3. How should the physical education program be modified for students with asthma?
4. Summarize the Universal Precautions to protect against all infectious disease. Which are most pertinent to physical education?
5. What are the characteristics of a person with anemia?
6. What precautions must be used in developing an individual exercise program for a child with cystic fibrosis?
7. How do the emergency treatment procedures for hypoglycemia and hyperglycemia differ?

REFERENCES

1. American Cancer Society. (2014). *Neuroblastoma.* Retrieved from www.cancer.org
2. American College of Allergy, Asthma, & Immunology. (2012). *Asthma attack.* Retrieved from http://acaai.org
3. American Diabetes Association. (2015). *Hypoglycemia.* Alexandria, VA: American Diabetes Association, www.diabetes.org
4. American Diabetes Association. (2014). *Statistics about diabetes.* Alexandria, VA: American Diabetes Association, www.diabetes.org
5. American Sickle Cell Anemia Association. (2007). *How common is sickle cell anemia?* Retrieved from http://www.ascaa.org/FAQS
6. American Sickle Cell Anemia Association. (2007). *How is sickle cell anemia treated?* Retrieved from http://www.ascaa.org/FAQS
7. *Anemia.* (2003). http://www.sleeptight.com/EncyMaster/A/anemia
8. Ayala, G. M., Guadalupe, X., Miller, E. Z., Riddle, C., Willis, S., & King, D. (2006). Asthma in middle schools: What students have to say about their asthma. *J of School Health, 76*(6), 208–214.
9. Bardana, E. J. (2001). Indoor pollution and its impact on respiratory health. *Annals of Allergy, Asthma & Immun, 87*, 33–40.
10. Beers, M. H., Porter, R. S., Jones, T. V., Kaplan, J. L., & Berkwits, M. (Eds.). (2006). *The Merck manual of diagnosis and therapy* (18th ed.). Whitehouse Station, NJ: Merck Research Laboratories.
11. Bernard, A., Carbonnelle, S., de Burbure, C., Michel, O., & Nickmilder, M. (2006). Chlorinated pool attendance, atopy, and the risk of asthma in childhood. *Environmental Health Perspectives, 114*(10), 1567–1573.
12. Blanchette, N. (2001). Cognitive and motor development in children with vertically transmitted HIV infection. *Brain Cogn, 46*, 50–53.
13. Bocskay, K., Orjuela, M., Warburton, D., & Perera, F. (2005). Chromosomal aberrations in cord blood are associated with prenatal exposure to carcinogenic polycyclic aromatic hydrocarbons. *Cancer Epidemiologic Biomarkers Prevention, 14*, 506–511.
14. Boulet, L., & O'Byrme, P. (2015). Asthma and exercise-induced bronchoconstriction in athletes. *New England Journal of Medicine, 372*, 641–648.

15. Butler, R. W., & Haser, J. K. (2006). Neurological effects of treatment for childhood cancer. *Mental Health and Developmental Disabilities Research Reviews, 12*(3), 184–191.

16. Centers for Disease Control and Prevention. (2007). *HIV.* Retrieved from http://www.cdc.gov/hiv/resources/factsheets/at-a-glance.htm

17. Centers for Disease Control and Prevention. (2015). *HIV among youth.* Retrieved from http://www.cdc.gov/hiv/group/age/youth/

18. Centers for Disease Control and Prevention. (2015). *Attention-Deficit/ Hyperactivity Disorder: Data and statistics.* Retrieved from www.cdc.gov

19. Centers for Disease Control and Prevention. (2007). *HIV in the United States.* Retrieved from www.cdc.gov

20. Centers for Disease Control and Prevention. (2015). *HIV transmission.* Retrieved from www.cdc.gov

21. Chapman, I. (2015). Central diabetes insipidus. Retrieved from www.merckmanuals.com

22. Clark, C., & Cochran, L. (2009). Asthma. In Durstine, J. L., Moore, G., Painter, P., & Roberts, S. (Eds.). *Exercise management for persons with chronic diseases and disabilities* (3rd ed.). Champaign, IL: Human Kinetics.

23. DuPaul, G., & Stoner, G. (2014). *ADHD in the schools: Assessment and intervention* (3rd ed.). New York, NY: Guilford Press.

24. Microsoft® Encarta® online encyclopedia. (2003). *Cystic fibrosis.* Retrieved from www.encarta.msm.com/encnet

25. eMedicineHealth. (2007). *Exercise-induced asthma.* Retrieved from http://www.emedicinehealth.com/exercise-induced_asthma/article_em.htm

26. Federal Register. (2006, August). Individuals with Disabilities Education Improvement Act (IDEIA), 34 CFR 300.307.

27. Fensternmacher, K., Olympica, D., & Sheridan, S. M. (2006). Effectiveness of a computer-facilitated, interactive social skills training program for boys with attention deficit hyperactivity disorder. *School Psychology Quar, 21*(2), 197–224.

28. Grantham-McGregor, S., & Cornelius, A. (2001). A review of studies on the effect of iron deficiencies on cognitive development in children. *Anemia Suppl, 131,* 649s–668s.

29. Greenhill, L. L. (2002). Stimulant medication treatment of children with attention deficit hyperactive disorder. In Jensen, P., & Cooper, J. (Eds.). *Attention deficit hyperactivity disorder.* Kingston, NJ: Civic Research Institute.

30. Global Statistics. (2014). *HIV/AIDS epidemic.* Retrieved from www.aids.gov

31. Hand, G., Lyerlly, G., & Dudgeon, W. (2009). Acquired immune deficiency syndrome. In Durstine, J. L., Moore, G., Painter, P., & Roberts, S. (Eds.). *Exercise management for persons with chronic diseases and disabilities* (3rd ed.). Champaign, IL: Human Kinetics.

32. Harris, S. S., & Tanner, S. (1995). Helping active women avoid anemia. *Physician Sportsmed, 23,* 35–47.

33. Healthlink Medical College of Wisconsin. (2007). *Childhood obesity causes diabetes and other health problems.* Retrieved from http://healthlink.mcw.edu /article/941223597.html

34. Kercmer, C. M., Dearborn, D. G., & Schluchter, M. (2006). Reduction in asthma morbidity in children as a result of home remediation aimed at moisture sources. *Environmental Health Perspectives, 114*(8), 1574–1580.

35. Kishore, P. (2015). *Diabetes mellitus.* Retrieved from www.merckmanuals.com

36. Korones, D. (2007). *Rhabdomyosarcoma.* Merck Manuals, http://www .merckmanuals.com/professional/pediatric-cancers/rhabdomyosarcoma

37. Korones, D. (2015). *Overview of pediatric cancer.* Merck Manuals, www .merckmanuals.com

38. Korones, D. (2015). *Brain tumors in children.* Merck Manuals, www .merckmanuals.com

39. Kiley, J. P., Collins, J. L., Frumkin, H., & Price D. A. (2006). Managing asthma in schools. *J of School Health, 76*(6), 2001, 59.

40. Lin, L., & Liang, B. (2005). HIV and health law: Striking the balance between legal mandates and medical ethics. *AMA Journal of Ethics, 7*, 1–6.

41. Mazur, M. L., & Hall Jr., G. (2001). Best swimmer in the world. *Diabetes Forecast, 54*(7), 58–62.

42. Morrato, E., Hill, J., Wyatt, H., Ghushchyan, M., & Sullivan, P. (2006). Are health care professionals advising patients with diabetes or at risk for developing diabetes to exercise more? *Diabetes Care, 29*, 543–548. DOI: 10.2337 /diacare.29.03.06.dc05-2165.

43. National Cancer Institute. (2015). *What is cancer?* Retrieved from http://www .cancer.gov/about-cancer

44. National Cancer Institute. (2015). *A snapshot of pediatric cancer.* Retrieved from www.cancer.gov/research/progress/snapshots/pediatric

45. National Heart, Lung, and Blood Institute. (2012). *How is anemia treated?* Retrieved from www.nhlbi.nih.gov

46. New York City Department of Education. (2012). *HIV/AIDS curriculum.* New York, NY: Board of Education of the City of New York.

47. Nixon, P. (2009). Cystic fibrosis. In Durstine, J. L., Moore, G., Painter, P., & Roberts, S. (Eds.). *Exercise management for persons with chronic diseases and disabilities* (3rd ed.). Champaign, IL: Human Kinetics.

48. Pelsser, L. M., Frankena, K., Toorman, J., Savelkoul, H. F., Pereira, R. R., & Buitelaar, J. K. (2009). A randomised controlled trial into the effects of food on ADHD. *European Child & Adolescent Psychiatry, 18*, 12–19.

49. Ratzon, N., Greenbaum, C., Dulitzy, M., & Ornoy, A. (2000). Comparison of the motor development of school-age children born to mothers with and without diabetes mellitus. *Phys & Occup Therapy in Pediatrics, 20*(l), 43–57.

50. Rosenstein, B. J. (2014). *Cystic fibrosis.* Merck Manuals Professional Edition. www.merckmanuals.com

51. Rosenthal-Malek, A., & Greenspan, W. (1999, January/February). The student with diabetes in my class. *Teaching Excep Child*, 38–43.
52. Stahr, B., Cushing, D., Lane, K., & Fox, J. (2006). Efficacy of a function-based intervention in decreasing off-task behavior exhibited by a student with ADHD. *J of Positive Behavior Interventions*, 8(4), 201–211.
53. Taunton, J. E., & McCargar, L. (1995). Staying active with diabetes: Quick and helpful exercise tips. *Physician Sportsmed*, 23(3), 55–56.
54. The Expert Committee on the Diagnosis and Classification of Diabetes Mellitus. (2003). Report of the expert committee on the diagnosis and classification of diabetes mellitus. *Diabetes Care*, 26, S5–S16.
55. Woodward, R. (2006). The diagnosis and medical treatment of ADHD in children and adolescents in primary care: A practical guide. *Pediatric Nursing*, 32(4), 363–369.
56. Worrell, K., Shaw, M. R., Postma, J., & Katz, J. R. (2015). A systematic review of the literature on screening for exercise-induced asthma considerations for school nurses. *The Journal of School Nursing*, 31(1), 70–76.
57. Yu-Feng, Z., et al. (2007). Altered baseline brain activity in children with ADHD revealed by resting-state functional MRI. *Brain and Development*, 29, 83–91.

abdominal strength Muscular strength of the abdominal muscles.

abduction Away from the midline of the body.

accessibility The extent to which an environment can be used by all persons.

accommodation Tailoring of an educational program to a student's abilities and severity of disability.

accountability Evidence that students with disabilities have received appropriate education services.

acquired immune deficiency syndrome (AIDS) The development of opportunistic infections and/or certain secondary cancers known to be associated with HIV infection.

adapted physical education The art and science of developing, implementing, and monitoring a carefully designed physical education instructional program for a learner with a disability, based on a comprehensive assessment, to give the individual the skills necessary for a lifetime of rich leisure, recreation, and sport experiences to enhance physical fitness and wellness.

adapted physical education national standards (APENS) Comprehensive national criteria detailing the professional preparation standards expected of adapted physical educators who seek accreditation.

adapted physical educator A physical educator with highly specialized training in the assessment and evaluation of motor competency; physical fitness; play; and leisure, recreation, and sport skills.

adaptive skill areas Communication, home living, community use, health and safety, leisure, self-care, social skills, self-direction, functional academics, and work.

adduction Toward the midline of the body.

administrative feasibility The extent to which it is practical to use a given test.

admission An indicator that a student qualifies for special services because of an identifiable disability that interferes with educational progress.

adventitious Acquired after birth.

affective function Emotions resulting from experiences, beliefs, values, and predispositions.

agility The ability to change direction while moving.

air conduction hearing aid A hearing aid that is hooked to receivers located in the outer ear canal.

albinism Lack of pigment in the eyes.

alternate-form reliability The degree to which scores from two different tests purported to measure the same things agree when administered to the same group.

alternator A person who visually suppresses images received by one eye and then the other eye.

amblyopia Cortical suppression of visual images received by one or both eyes.

ambulatory Able to walk.

Americans with Disabilities Act of 1990 (ADA) Public Law 101–336, which widened civil rights protections for persons with disabilities to all public accommodations and addressed private discrimination.

amputation Missing part or all of a limb.

annual goals Statements that describe in measurable terms what a specific learner with a disability should be able to accomplish in a given year.

anxiety disorder Intense feeling of anxiety and tension when there is no real danger.

aphasia An impairment of language that affects the production or comprehension of speech and the ability to read or write.

Applied Behavioral Analysis A style of teaching, used with learners who have autism, that involves a series of trials to shape a desired behavior or response; also known as the Lovaas approach.

arthritis Inflammation of a joint.

arthrogryposis A congenital condition that results in flexure or contracture of joints.

assessment A problem-solving process that involves gathering information from a variety of sources.

assistive technology A piece of equipment or product system that increases, maintains, or improves the functional capabilities of persons with disabilities.

assistive technology service Any service that directly assists an individual with a disability in the selection, acquisition, or use of an assistive technology device.

asthma A pulmonary disease characterized by reversible airway obstruction, airway inflammation, and increased airway responsiveness to a variety of stimuli.

astigmatism A refractive error caused by an irregularity in the curvature of the cornea of the lens; vision may become blurred.

asymmetrical tonic neck reflex A reflex that causes extension of the arm on the face side and flexion of the arm on the posterior skull side when the head is turned.

at risk Refers to individuals whose development is jeopardized by factors that include poverty, homelessness, prenatal and postnatal maternal neglect, environmental deprivation, child abuse, violence, drug abuse, and racism.

ataxia A disturbance of equilibrium that results from the involvement of the cerebellum or its pathways.

athetosis A clinical type of cerebral palsy characterized by uncoordinated movements of the voluntary muscles, often accompanied by impaired muscle control of the hands and impaired speech and swallowing.

atlantoaxial instability Greater than normal mobility of the two upper cervical vertebrae.

atrophy Wasting away of muscular tissue.

audible ball A ball that emits a beeping sound for easy location by a person with limited vision.

audible goal locator A motor-driven noisemaker that enables a person with limited vision to identify the placement of a base or boundary.

audiologist A specially trained professional who can provide comprehensive evaluations of individuals' hearing capabilities.

autism spectrum disorder A complex developmental disability that affects a person's ability to communicate and interact with others. ASD is defined by a certain set of behaviors and is a "spectrum condition" that affects individuals differently and to varying degrees.

backward chaining The last of a series of steps is taught first.

balance The ability to maintain equilibrium in a held (static) or moving (dynamic) position.

basic neurological building blocks Sensory input systems, including primitive reflexes, the vestibular system, refractive and orthoptic vision, audition, the tactile and kinesthetic systems, and equilibrium reflexes.

Becker muscular dystrophy A disease of the muscular system very similar to Duchenne muscular dystrophy except that it progresses more slowly.

behavior disorder A condition in which the behavioral response of a student is so different from generally accepted, age-appropriate, ethnic, or cultural norms as to result in significant impairment in self-care, social relationships, educational progress, classroom behavior, work adjustment, or personal happiness.

behavior intervention plan A program designed to teach acceptable alternatives to behaviors addressed during a functional behavior assessment.

behavior management plan Specific intervention strategies, included in the IEP, that address how to deal with a student's behavior that interferes with his or her learning or disrupts the learning of others.

behavior management strategies Techniques for structuring the environment to produce changes in behavior.

behavior modification (behavior therapy) The changing of behavioral characteristics through the application of learning principles.

benchmarks Standards of performance for each grade level set at the local, district, or state level.

body awareness The way in which people picture their bodies and their attitude toward and knowledge of their bodily capabilities and limitations.

body composition The percentage of body fat in relation to lean tissue in the body.

body image The system of ideas and feelings a person has about his or her structure.

body righting reflex The reflex that enables segmental rotation of the trunk and hips when the head is turned.

bone conduction hearing aid A hearing aid that is placed in contact with the mastoid bone.

bottom-up strategy The process whereby the sensory input system is evaluated and then ability tests are used to determine which deficits are in evidence.

cardiovascular/cardiorespiratory endurance The ability of the heart, lungs, and blood vessels to direct needed oxygen to the muscles.

cataract A condition in which the normally transparent lens of the eye becomes opaque.

center of gravity A point in the human body where the pull of gravity on one side is equal to the pull of gravity on the other side.

central auditory processing problems Deafness resulting from damage to the brain stem or the cortex.

cerebral palsy A lifelong condition resulting from a nonprogressive lesion of the brain before, during, or soon after birth (before age 5 years) that impairs voluntary movement.

certified adapted physical educator (CAPE) An indicator that an individual has demonstrated knowledge of adapted physical education by passing the Adapted Physical Education National Standards test.

chaining Leading a person through a series of teachable components of a motor task.

checklist A screening instrument used to delineate critical aspects of movements.

Child Find A national effort to identify children who have developmental disabilities or are at risk for developmental delays.

childhood disintegrative disorder (CDD) A condition, which presents itself between the ages of 2 and 10 years, that results in a regression in many areas, including movement, social and language skills, and bladder and bowel control; also known as Heller's syndrome.

choice making A teaching strategy that provides persons with autism opportunities to make choices.

chromosomal abnormalities Deviations in the structure of the chromosome.

circuit training Exercising at a series of stations, with different types of activities at each station.

cochlear implant An electronic device, which is surgically implanted into a bone in the skull, that stimulates the remaining fibers of the auditory division of the 8th cranial nerve and enables persons who are profoundly deaf to hear and distinguish among environmental sounds and warning signals.

cognitive behavioral methods Intervention strategies designed to teach learners with autism to monitor their own behavior and provide self-reinforcement.

cognitive function The ability to organize, reorganize, and contemplate information in the brain.

collaboration A process in which two or more professionals share ideas and responsibilities.

communicative disorders Conditions that interfere with one's ability to understand or be understood.

community-based assessment Assessment that focuses on the skills needed to live independently in the community.

concussion Impaired functioning of an organ, especially the brain, as a result of a violent blow or impact.

condition shifting A program in which several conditions of behavioral objectives are altered to produce activities that are sequenced from less to greater difficulty.

conditions A description of how the learner is to perform an objective.

conduct disorder Specific actions, or failures to act, that cause a student to be in trouble within the home, school, or community.

conductive hearing impairment A condition in which the intensity of sound is reduced before reaching the inner ear, where the auditory nerve begins.

congenital Present at birth.

construct validity The degree to which a test measures what its author claims it measures.

content analysis Breaking down discrete or continuous tasks into parts, or components.

content-referenced Components of a task or steps in a sequence of tasks.

content-related validity The degree to which the contents of a test represent an identified body of knowledge.

contingency contracting An agreement between the student and the teacher that indicates what the student must do to earn a specific reward.

continuous reinforcement schedule Reinforcing a behavior every time it is demonstrated.

contraindicated exercise Activities that are to be avoided because of their potential for harm.

convergence The ability to turn the eyes inward (medially) while visually tracking an object moving toward the body.

criteria for eligibility Requirements for being qualified to receive special education services mandated by law.

criterion for mastery A stated level of performance indicating the attainment of an objective.

criterion-referenced Measurement against a predetermined level of mastery.

criterion-related validity The degree to which a test compares with another acceptable standard of the same performance.

criterion shifting Programs in which the level of mastery (number of repetitions, distance traveled, speed, or range of motion) is modified to make the task easier or more difficult.

cross-lateral Coordination of both sides of the body.

cross-pattern creep Coordinating movements of legs and arms on opposite sides of the body while supporting the body on hands and knees.

cystic fibrosis An inherited disease of the exocrine glands primarily affecting the gastrointestinal and respiratory systems.

deaf A hearing impairment so severe that the person is impaired in processing linguistic information through hearing, with or without amplification, which adversely affects educational performance.

deaf-blind The loss of both hearing and vision.

deaf community Individuals who are deaf or have a hearing impairment who share a common language, values, culture, and experiences.

depth perception The ability to visually determine the position of objects in space by comparing the images entering each eye with each other.

developmental approach A bottom-up teaching strategy that addresses the lowest levels of motor development found to be deficient.

developmental delay When a child is less developed, physically or mentally, than is expected for his or her age.

developmentally appropriate learning environment A learning situation that is sensitive and responsive to the unique needs of children.

developmentally appropriate movement experience Play and movement opportunities, based on individual need, that allow a child to choose to participate in play and movement activities with success.

developmentally appropriate movement/play assessment Observing and recording children's cognitive, social-emotional, communication and language, and sensorimotor development as they interact with their environment.

diabetes A chronic metabolic disorder in which the cells cannot use glucose.

diabetes insipidus A condition that results from an inability to concentrate urine in the kidneys.

diabetes mellitus A group of diseases characterized by hyperglycemia resulting from defects in insulin secretion, insulin action, or both.

diplegia A neurological condition involving both the arms and the legs, with the most involvement in the legs.

direct services The professions identified by law with responsibility for providing educational services to students with disabilities (e.g., classroom teachers and physical educators).

directionality The perception of direction in space.

disabled Having physical, social, or psychological variations that significantly interfere with normal growth and development.

disorder An abnormal mental, physical, or psychological condition.

dissociative disorder A condition characterized by an inability to integrate memories, perceptions, identity, or consciousness normally.

divergence The ability to turn the eyes outward (laterally) while visually tracking an object moving away from the body.

dorsiflexion Bending the foot upward (flexion).

dorsiflexion of the head Extending the head toward the back of the body.

Duchenne muscular dystrophy (pseudohypertrophic) A disease of the muscular system characterized by progressive weakness and atrophy of the pelvic girdle followed by the shoulder girdle muscles.

due process The procedure to be followed to determine the extent to which an individual's constitutional rights have been made available.

duration recording Noting the length of time a behavior occurs.

dysplasia Separation of the hip joint.

early childhood intervention (ECI) Providing developmentally appropriate programs for infants and toddlers ages birth to 3 years.

early childhood intervention (ECI) natural settings initiative Educating infants and toddlers ages birth to 3 years in their most natural environments.

echolalia Echoing the language of another.

ecological inventory A checklist of behaviors needed to function in a given environment.

educational accountability A particular educational program, method, or intervention can be demonstrated to cause a significant positive change in one or more behaviors.

educational services The curricula, programs, accommodations, placements, behavior management plans, and personnel available to students.

emotional disturbance A condition resulting in exhibiting, over a long period of time or to a marked degree, behaviors that adversely affect a student's educational performance that cannot be explained by intellectual, sensory, or health factors.

empathy experiences Attempts to get the "feel" of having a disability by participating in activities while having a sensory or motor limitation placed on oneself (e.g., being blindfolded, ambulating in a wheelchair, wearing ear covers).

epilepsy A disturbance, resulting from abnormal electrical activity of the brain, that briefly alters consciousness, motor activity, sensory phenomena, or behavior.

equilibrium dysfunction An inability to maintain static and/or dynamic balance.

equilibrium reflexes Reflexes that help a person maintain an upright position when the center of gravity is suddenly moved beyond the base of support.

esotropia A condition in which the eyes turn inward, such as cross-eyes.

event recording Noting the number of times a specifically defined behavior occurs within a time interval.

Every Student Succeeds Act (ESSA) Public Law 114-95, 2015; replaces the No Child Left Behind Act to provide children with significant opportunity to receive a fair, equitable, and high-quality education.

evidence-based practice Utilizing instructional procedures and curricula that have been validated as effective by scientific research and/or the best available evidence.

exclusionary time-out Removing a student from the immediate environment to eliminate the possibility of the student's disrupting the class through inappropriate behavior.

exercise-induced asthma (EIA) An acute airway narrowing after strenuous exertion.

exertion level The amount of effort required for a task.

exotropia A condition wherein an eye deviates laterally away from the nose.

expressive language The ability to communicate feeling, emotions, needs, and thoughts through speaking and gesturing (facial or manual).

extensive support Regular and ongoing supports with some ability to complete self-care tasks independently.

externalized mental disorders Disorders expressed overtly that make others feel bad.

extinction The removal of reinforcers that previously followed a behavior.

extraocular muscles of the eyes The six pairs of muscles attached to the eye that permit movement of the eyes.

facilitated communication The practice of using a helper to support the hand, wrist, or shoulder of a person with autism to enable that learner to make selections on a communication device, such as a keyboard.

facioscapulohumeral muscular dystrophy (Landouzy-Dejerine) A disease of the muscular system characterized by weakness of the facial muscles and shoulder girdles.

fading Gradually withdrawing help from a task.

fatigability Easily tired.

fetal alcohol spectrum disorders (FASD) A range of physical, mental, behavioral, and learning disabilities that can occur in an individual whose mother drank alcohol during pregnancy.

fixed-interval ratio reinforcement schedule Reinforcing the occurrence of a desirable behavior demonstrated a set number of times according to a predetermined schedule (e.g., one reinforcer for every three instances of desired behavior).

flexibility Range of motion available at any one or a combination of joints.

focal seizure A seizure that involves a loss of body tone and collapse while remaining conscious.

formal tests Tests that have been developed for a specific purpose and have been standardized.

forward chaining The first step of a series of tasks is taught first.

fragile X syndrome An abnormality of the X chromosome, which results in a folic acid deficiency and leads to learning disabilities or mild to severe intellectual disability.

free appropriate public education (FAPE) The entitlement of all children to an education, without charge, that meets their specific needs.

full inclusion Educating all children in supported, heterogeneous, age-appropriate, natural, child-focused classroom, school, and community environments.

functional behavioral assessment (FBA) The process of identifying the important controllable and causal functions related to a student's undesirable behavior.

functional skills Movements that can be used for a variety of tasks.

gait training Teaching or reteaching an individual to ambulate by walking.

general curriculum The educational offerings that are available to children without disabilities.

general physical education Physical and motor instruction available to students from kindergarten through high school.

generalization The transfer of abilities and skills from the training environment to nontraining environments.

glaucoma A condition in which the pressure of the fluid inside the eye is too high, causing loss of vision.

Gowers' sign Moving from a hands and knees kneeling position to an upright position by pushing the hands against the legs in a climbing pattern.

guide runner A person with vision who runs alongside a runner who is visually impaired and verbally describes the distance to the finish or touches the runner's elbow to indicate any lateral off-step.

guide wire Rope or heavy string stretched 36 inches above lane makers that helps runners with limited vision feel the perimeters of the lanes.

hard-of-hearing A hearing impairment, whether permanent or fluctuating, that adversely affects a person's educational performance but is not included under the category of deaf.

health-related fitness Components of physiological functioning that are believed to offer protection against degenerative diseases.

health-related tests Assessment instruments that include measures of cardiovascular endurance, muscular strength, percentage of body fat, and flexibility.

hemiplegia A neurological condition involving both limbs on one side, with the arm being more affected than the leg.

heterogeneous groupings Amassing students with different levels of abilities together.

heterophoria A tendency toward visual malalignment.

heterotropia Malalignments of the eyes in which one or both eyes consistently deviate from the central axis.

hierarchical order A continuum of ordered activities in which a task of lower order and less difficulty is prerequisite to a related task of greater difficulty.

homogeneous grouping Amassing students with similar levels of abilities together.

human immunodeficiency virus (HIV) infection Infection caused by a retrovirus, resulting in a wide range of clinical manifestations, varying from asymptomatic carrier states (HIV-positive) to severely debilitating and fatal disorders related to defective cell-mediated immunity.

hydrocephalic Refers to an abnormal condition that results when cerebral spinal fluid is not reabsorbed properly, thus collecting around the brain.

hyperopia A condition in which light rays focus behind the retina, causing an unclear image of objects closer than 20 feet from the eye.

hyperreflexiveness Overactive or overresponsive reflexes.

hypertropia A condition in which one or both eyes swing upward.

hypotonia Low muscle tone that often results in reduced muscle strength.

hypotropia A condition in which one or both eyes turn downward.

IDEA Individuals with Disabilities Education Act of 1990; P.L. 101–476. Legislation that ensures individualized Free Appropriate Public Education for qualifying students with disabilities.

IDEIA Individuals with Disabilities Education Improvement Act of 2004. The reauthorization of IDEA.

impulse control The ability to resist an impulse, a drive, or a temptation to perform a harmful, disruptive, or inappropriate behavior.

inappropriate reflex behavior Persistence of primitive reflexes beyond age 1 year and/or failure to demonstrate all of the equilibrium reflexes after the first year of life.

incidental learning Learning that is unplanned.

inclusion Serving all students in the general education program.

inclusive environment An environment designed to accommodate a variety of learners regardless of functional abilities.

indirect services Services provided by related service personnel to enable a student with a disability to function more fully.

individualized education program (IEP) Specially designed instruction to meet the unique needs of a person for self-sufficient living.

individualized education program (IEP) document An individual student's formal IEP report, which must be approved by parents/guardians and educational professionals.

individualized education program (IEP) meeting A formally scheduled gathering of parents and educational professionals to discuss a student's present level of educational performance, goals, and educational alternatives.

individualized education program (IEP) process The procedure followed to develop an appropriate educational experience.

individualized family service plan (IFSP) A family-centered plan for assessing and prioritizing needs and programming and for providing services for at-risk children under the age of 3 years.

individualized physical education program An activity program developed from assessment information to meet the unique needs of an individual with a disability.

individualized transition plan (ITP) The specific strategies needed to move a child with a disability smoothly from home to preschool, preschool to school, or school to community.

Individuals with Disabilities Education Act Amendment of 1997 Federal legislation that reaffirmed IDEA, emphasized education for all students in the general education program, and increased parental participation in the assessment and IEP processes.

Individuals with Disabilities Education Act of 1990 (IDEA) Federal legislation that replaced the term *handicapped* with *disability* and expanded on the types of services offered to persons with disabilities and types of conditions covered in the law.

informal tests Tests that have been developed for a general purpose and have not been standardized.

inner language process The ability to transform experience into symbols.

instructional environment A setting designed for the education of students.

intellectual disabilities Significant limitations in intellectual and adaptive behavior originating before age 18 years.

interest boosting Involving a child in an activity to engage his or her interest in positive behaviors.

intermittent support Supports on an as-needed basis at high or low intensity.

interval recording Counting the occurrence or nonoccurrence of a behavior within a specified time interval.

intervention strategies Techniques for weakening or eliminating disruptive behaviors or reinforcing desirable behaviors or practices.

IQ-discrepancy model A difference between a student's cognitive and achievement test scores.

isokinetic exercises Exercises that provide resistance through the entire range of movement, either by pushing one limb against the other or by using an exercise machine that provides resistance equal to the amount of pull throughout the range of motion.

isometric (static) muscular contraction The amount of tension in the muscle equals the amount of applied resistance, so that no movement occurs.

isotonic exercises Exercises using progressive resistance with free weights or a machine with stacked weights.

joint laxity Loose ligaments.

juvenile arthritis (Still's disease) A form of rheumatoid arthritis that afflicts children before the age of 7 years.

ketoacidosis The body's violent reaction to a lack of insulin circulating in the blood.

kinesthetic guidance Manually moving a student through the correct movement pattern, so that the student can get the "feel" of the motion.

kinesthetic system Muscles, tendons, joints, and other body parts that help control and coordinate activities such as walking and talking.

labyrinthine portion of inner ear The part of the inner ear, located in the vestibule, that responds to movements of the head against gravity.

labyrinthine righting reaction An equilibrium reflex that causes the head to move to an upright position when the head is suddenly tipped while the eyes are closed.

language disorder An impairment in the ability to understand and/or use words in context, both verbally and nonverbally.

laterality An awareness of the difference between both sides of the body.

least restrictive environment (LRE) The setting that enables an individual with disabilities to function to the fullest of his or her capability.

legally blind Visual acuity of 20/200 or less in the better eye after maximum correction or having a visual field that subtends an angle of 20 degrees or less.

levels of motor function Basic neurological building blocks, integration processes, functional motor skills, and sport and recreational skills.

limited support Mild supports to assist with navigating everyday situations.

local education agency (LEA) The school district or education cooperative responsible for implementing state policy and interpreting that policy to meet the needs of learners within the district or cooperative.

locus of control The extent to which behavior is determined from within oneself or is dependent on others.

low vision A severe visual impairment, not necessarily limited to distance vision.

maintenance The perpetuation of a trained behavior after all formal intervention has ceased.

malnutrition Faulty or inadequate nourishment resulting from an improper diet.

manual communication system Techniques for communicating, including Pidgin Sign Language, American Sign Language, Manually Coded English, and fingerspelling.

manual guidance Physically moving a person through a movement.

manual muscle testing Evaluating the strength of a muscle by having an individual attempt to move a limb while the evaluator physically resists the movement.

mastoiditis Infection of the air cells of the mastoid process.

mediation A primary process used to resolve conflicts.

medical diagnostic service personnel Medical personnel who provide diagnostic services to children with disabilities and verify the disability status of individuals.

medically fragile Children with special health management needs who require technology, special services, or some form of ongoing medical support for survival.

meditation The art and technique of blocking out thoughts that create tension and refocusing attention and energy on soothing, quieting mental activity.

meningocele A protruding sac containing the lining of the spinal column.

midline problem An inability to coordinate limbs on opposite sides of the body.

mobility training An adaptive technique that is applied to the blind and enhances the ability to travel.

modeling Demonstration of a task by the teacher or reinforcement by another student who performs a desirable behavior in the presence of the targeted student.

momentary time sampling Noting whether a behavior is occurring at the end of specified time intervals.

monoplegia A neurological condition involving a single limb.

mood disorders A group of heterogeneous, typically recurrent illnesses that are characterized by pervasive mood disturbances, psychomotor dysfunction, and vegetative symptoms.

motor coordination The ability to use the muscles of the body to efficiently produce complex movement.

motor fitness Agility, power, speed, and coordination.

motor milestones Significant movement patterns and skills that emerge at predictable times during the life of a typically developing child.

motor-planning deficit An inability to determine and execute a sequence of tasks needed to achieve a goal.

motor stereotypies Rhythmic, repetitive, fixed, predictable movements such as handflapping, pacing, spinning, twirling a string, or drumming.

motor tics Sudden twitches of the entire body, shoulders, and/or head; eyeblinks or rolling of the head; repetitive tapping, drumming, or touching behaviors; and grimacing.

multidisciplinary motor team A group of direct service and related service providers who cooperate to determine and provide for students' physical and movement needs.

multiple sclerosis A chronic degenerative neurological disease primarily affecting older adolescents and adults.

muscle tension recognition and release Tensing and relaxing muscle groups at will; also known as differential relaxation.

muscular dystrophy A group of inherited, progressive muscle disorders that differ according to which muscles are affected and that result in deterioration of muscle strength, power, and endurance.

muscular endurance The ability of a muscle to contract repetitively.

myelomeningocele A protruding sac that contains the spinal cord and the lining of the spinal column.

myopia A refractive condition in which rays of light focus in front of the retina when a person views an object 20 feet away or more.

National Center on Health, Physical Activity and Disability (NCHPAD) A project funded by the Centers for Disease Control and Prevention to provide a clearinghouse for research and practice information to promote healthy lifestyles for persons with disabilities.

National Consortium for Physical Education for Individuals with Disabilities (NCPEID) An organization formed in 1973 to promote, stimulate, and encourage significant service delivery, quality professional preparation, and meaningful research in physical education and recreation for individuals with disabilities.

natural environment A community setting where individuals function.

negative support reflex A reflex in which there is flexion of the knees when pressure is removed from the feet.

neurological components Sensory input systems and perceptual processes that underlie movement patterns and skills and affective and cognitive functioning.

neurological disability A chronic, debilitating condition resulting from impairments of the central nervous system.

No Child Left Behind Act of 2001 National legislation that requires statewide accountability for all students' achievement in reading or language, mathematics, and science.

nonexclusionary time-out Removing the student from an activity but allowing the student to remain in the vicinity of the class.

normalization Making available to individuals with disabilities patterns and conditions of everyday life that are as close as possible to the norms and patterns of the mainstream of society.

normative-referenced test A test that measures an individual in comparison with others of the same age. Comparison standards are reported in percentiles, age equivalencies, and/or stanines.

nystagmus Rapid movement of the eyes from side to side, up and down, in a rotatory motion, or in a combination of these movements.

obesity Pathological overweight in which a person is 20% or more above the normal weight (compare with *overweight*).

occupational therapist A professional who improves functional living and employment skills.

ocular saccadic ability The ability to refix the eye on differing targets accurately and quickly.

ocular-motor control The ability to fixate visually on objects and track their movement.

oculomotor defects Difficulties coordinating the movement of both eyes, resulting in depth perception deficits.

Office of Special Education and Rehabilitative Services (OSERS) The unit within the Department of Education that is responsible for setting the agenda and providing direction regarding the delivery of educational services for students with disabilities.

oppositional-defiant disorder An antisocial behavior characterized by extreme disobedience, aggression, loss of temper, and arguments with adults and others in authority.

optical righting reaction An equilibrium reflex that causes the head to move to the upright position when the body is suddenly tipped and the eyes are open.

oral communication method Hearing-impaired persons are provided amplification of sound and are taught through speech reading (lip reading).

orientation and mobility Services provided to students who are blind or visually impaired to enable them to systematically use skills to orient them within their environments in schools, at home, and in the community.

orientation training A program that helps persons with visual impairments cope effectively with their physical surroundings.

orthopedic conditions Deformities, diseases, and injuries of the bones and joints.

orthoptic vision The ability to use the extraocular muscles of the eyes in unison.

orthoptics The science of correcting deviations of the visual axis of the eye.

Osgood-Schlatter condition Epiphysitis of the tibial tubercle.

osteoarthritis A disorder of the hyaline cartilage, primarily in the weight-bearing joints, resulting from trauma or repeated use.

osteogenesis imperfecta (brittle bone disease) A condition marked by both weak bones and elasticity of the joints, ligaments, and skin.

osteomyelitis Inflammation of a bone and its medullary cavity; sometimes referred to as myelitis.

other health impairment Limitations in strength and vitality or alertness with respect to the environment that are a result of chronic or acute health problems, such as asthma, attention deficit disorders, diabetes, epilepsy, a heart condition, hemophilia, lead poisoning, leukemias, nephritis, rheumatic fever, and sickle cell anemia, that adversely affect a child's educational performance.

otitis media Infection of the middle ear.

overcorrection Repeated practice of an appropriate behavior whenever an inappropriate behavior is demonstrated.

overload principle Improving muscular strength by gradually increasing the resistance used over time (days or months).

overweight Any deviation of 10% or more above the ideal weight for a person (compare with *obesity).*

paraeducator Education support professionals who assist with routine duties required of teachers. Also referred to as teacher assistant or instructional assistant.

paraplegia A neurological condition involving both legs with little or no involvement of the arms.

partial-interval time sampling Noting whether a behavior was demonstrated anytime during given periods of time.

partially sighted Having less than 20/70 visual acuity in the better eye after correction, having a progressive eye disorder that will probably reduce vision below 20/70, or having peripheral vision that subtends an angle less than 20 degrees.

peer tutor A same-age or cross-age (older) student who assists other students.

percentage of body fat The amount of body fat in relation to muscle, bone, and other elements in the body.

perceptual function The ability to integrate sensory input information into constructs in the central nervous system.

perceptual-motor abilities Balance, cross-lateral integration, body image, spatial awareness, laterality, and directionality.

perinatal During the birth process.

pervasive support Constant, high-intensity supports across multiple environments.

phobia A significant, persistent, yet unrealistic and often debilitating fear of an event, a person, an activity, or an animal or insect.

physical fitness A physical state of well-being that allows people to perform daily activities with vigor, reduces their risk of health problems related to lack of exercise, and establishes a fitness base for participation in a variety of activities; also physical properties of muscular activity, such as strength, flexibility, endurance, and cardiovascular endurance.

physical lag A deficit in physical fitness components or function of a specific body part.

physical restraint Holding students to prevent them from physically harming themselves or someone else.

physical therapist A professional who evaluates and treats physical impairments through the use of various physical modalities.

Picture Exchange Communication System Exchange of a picture of an item or activity to obtain or participate in that item or activity.

placement Alternative educational environments available to students with disabilities.

planned ignoring Choosing not to react to a behavior to avoid reinforcing the behavior.

play therapy A type of intervention, used with emotionally disturbed children, that involves using play to provide insight into emotional problems.

plumb line (posture) test Comparing body landmarks with a gravity line to assess posture.

portfolio assessment process Using a variety of techniques to gather ongoing information about a child's developmental progress.

positive learning environment A learning environment in which all students feel valued, safe, and successful.

positive reinforcement A pleasing consequence that follows an action.

positive support reflex A reflex that causes the legs to extend and the feet to plantar flex when one is standing.

postnatal After birth.

posttraumatic stress disorder A recurring intense fear, helplessness, or horror as a result of direct or indirect personal experience of an event that involves actual or threatened death, serious injury, or threat to personal integrity.

posture screen Comparing body landmarks with a grid of vertical and horizontal lines to evaluate all segments of the body in relationship to each other.

Prader-Willi syndrome A condition characterized by neonatal hypotonia and feeding difficulty followed by excessive appetite, pica behavior, and obesity starting in early childhood.

Premack principle Student will be allowed to participate in a preferred activity after completion of the nonpreferred activity.

prenatal During pregnancy.

present level of educational performance The skills, behaviors, and patterns an individual can demonstrate at any given time.

primitive reflexes Automatic reactions that should appear in an infant's movement repertoire during the first 6 months of life.

principle of normalization Routines of life that are typical for individuals without disabilities.

problem-oriented exercise management Developing a therapeutic exercise plan based on the assessment of subjective and objective data.

programmed instruction An instructional strategy to promote students' abilities to direct their own learning.

progressive relaxation Consciously releasing tension in specific muscle groups.

progressive resistive exercise Systematically adding resistance to an exercise to place additional demand on a muscle for the purpose of increasing strength.

prompting Physically holding and moving the body parts of a learner through an activity properly.

proprioceptive facilitation Exercises designed to excite motor units of a muscle to overcome paralysis.

proprioceptors Sensory receptors, located in the muscles, joints, tendons, deep tissues, and vestibular portion of the inner ear, that respond to movement.

protective extensor thrust reflex A reflex that causes immediate extension of the arms when the head and upper body are suddenly tipped forward.

proximity control Positioning oneself close to a child to encourage on-task behavior.

psychomotor seizure Uncontrollable atypical social-motor behavior, including temper tantrums, hand clapping, spitting, swearing, and shouting for one or two minutes.

psychosocial competence A sense of self-confidence necessary to participate in successful interpersonal relationships.

psychosocial development The level of one's psychosocial competence.

quadriplegia (tetraplegia) A neurological condition involving all of the limbs to a similar degree.

reasonable accommodation Modification of policies, practices, and procedures, including the provision of auxiliary aids and services, to enable a person with disabilities to use a facility.

receptive language An ability to comprehend meaning associated with language.

reciprocal exercises Exercises to stimulate and strengthen a muscle's agonist (protagonist).

recreation therapist A professional who works with physical and adapted physical educators and who provides information for individuals with disabilities to help them make wise decisions in the use of leisure time.

refractive vision The process by which light rays are bent as they enter the eyes.

regular education program Routine educational services available to students without disabilities.

rehabilitation counselor A specially trained person who provides services that focus on career development, employment preparation, and the achievement of independence and integration in the workplace and community.

reinforcement of appropriate target behavior Rewarding a student for demonstrating a prespecified target behavior.

reinforcement of behavior other than target behavior Rewarding a student for not demonstrating a prespecified misbehavior during a predetermined time limit.

reinforcement of incompatible behavior Rewarding a student for demonstrating a behavior that is incompatible with the target misbehavior (e.g., rewarding a student for assisting rather than fighting with a peer).

reinforcement schedule The frequency with which reinforcers are given.

related services Services that help a person with disabilities benefit from direct services.

relaxation therapy Teaching a person to achieve a state of both muscular and mental tension reduction by the systematic use of environmental cues.

reliability Consistency.

removal of seductive objects Controlling behavior by eliminating from view equipment children are attracted to.

repetition The number of times a work interval is repeated under identical conditions.

reprimand A form of punishment that involves verbally chastising a student for inappropriately exhibiting a target behavior.

resistance training The use of isotonic or isokinetic exercise to improve musculoskeletal strength.

response generalization Changes in behavior that were not specifically targeted for change.

response maintenance generalization Changes in behavior that continue to be demonstrated after reinforcement has stopped.

response to intervention A multi-tier approach to the early identification and support of students with learning and behavior needs.

restructure of classroom program Modifying a class routine to control student behavior.

retinitis pigmentosa Degeneration of the retina, producing gradual loss of peripheral vision.

retinoblastoma A malignant tumor that arises from the immature retina.

retinopathy A complication, resulting from long-standing diabetes, that is characterized by blurred vision, sudden loss of vision in one or both eyes, and black spots or flashing lights in the field of vision.

retinopathy of prematurity A visual impairment caused by excess oxygen during incubation of premature infants.

reverse mainstreaming The infusion of individuals without disabilities into educational and recreational settings to interact with persons with disabilities.

rheumatoid arthritis A systemic disease that causes inflammation, and eventual thickening, of the synovial tissue that surrounds joints.

scaffolding Providing an educational environment and a support system that allow a child to move forward and continue to build new competencies.

school health service personnel School staff, usually registered nurses, who monitor student health records, administer medicine, and provide other prescribed medical services.

school reform initiatives Alterations in the structure, curriculum, and management of schools to improve the effectiveness of the learning environment.

schoolwide behavior management system A systematic, collaborative strategy to prevent and manage students' behavior in a positive fashion that involves teachers, staff, parents, and students.

scoliosis Lateral and rotational deviation of the vertebral column.

scripting A description of an event that a student reads through prior to participation in that event.

self-correct To think about and modify one's own behavior.

self-management Shifting responsibility for behavior from the teacher or parent to the student.

self-management practice The ability to control one's own behavior.

sensorineural hearing impairment A loss of hearing caused by the absence or malfunction of the cochlea or 8th cranial nerve.

sensory input system dysfunction The failure of a sensory system to function because of a delay in development or neurological impairment.

sensory integration deficit The failure to process sensory information at the central nervous system level.

serious emotional disturbance A condition exhibiting one or more of the following characteristics over a long period of time and to a marked degree that adversely affects educational performance: (1) inability to learn that cannot be explained in other ways, (2) inability to maintain or build satisfactory interpersonal relationships, (3) inappropriate types of behavior or feelings, (4) general pervasive mood of unhappiness or depression, and (5) tendency to develop physical symptoms or fears associated with personal or school problems.

shaping Reinforcement of small, progressive steps that lead toward a desired behavior.

short-term instructional objectives Measurable intermediate steps that lead from the present level of performance to an annual goal.

shortened gestation An in utero life of less than 36 weeks. Gestations of less than 27 weeks result in at-risk infants.

shunt A drainage tube that is inserted to drain cerebral spinal fluid that is not being reabsorbed.

sickle cell anemia An inherited form of anemia that affects the bones, spleen, gallbladder, brain, and lungs.

signal interference Providing the student with a visible sign that a behavior is undesirable.

simulated training environment A teaching situation with task demands similar to those in the natural environment.

situation or setting generalization Changes in behavior that occur from one environment to another and from one person to another.

skill problems Behaviors that interfere with a student's motor performance learning or efficiency.

skills Abilities to perform complex tasks competently as a result of reinforced practice.

social stories Brief, individual stories that describe social situations and provide specific behavioral cues.

social toxins Factors, such as violence, poverty, hunger, homelessness, inadequate parenting, abuse and neglect, racism, and classism, that seriously compromise the quality of life of children.

social worker A professional who provides individual and group counseling/assistance to children and their families.

somatosensory strip in cerebral cortex The section of the cortex, just posterior to the central sulcus, that serves as a repository for incoming sensory information.

spasticity A clinical type of cerebral palsy characterized by muscle contractures and jerky, uncertain movements of the muscles.

spatial awareness The ability to replicate space in the "mind's eye" without visual input.

spatial relations The position of objects in space, particularly as the objects relate to the position of the body.

special physical education Adapted physical education.

specific learning disability A disorder in one or more of the basic psychological processes involved in understanding or using language, spoken or written, which may manifest itself in the imperfect ability to listen, speak, read, write, spell, or do mathematical calculations.

speech disorder Difficulties producing speech sounds and problems with voice quality that interfere with an individual's ability to communicate effectively.

speech therapist A professional who evaluates children with speech and language deficits and provides intervention programs.

spina bifida A congenital separation or lack of union of the vertebral arches.

spina bifida cystica A congenital separation of the vertebral arches, resulting in a completely open spine with a protruding sac.

spina bifida occulta A congenital separation of the vertebral arches with no distension of the spinal cord lining or of the cord itself.

splinter skill A particular perceptual or motor act that is performed in isolation and that does not generalize to other areas of performance.

sport-specific skills Movements that are used to perform sport activities.

standardized test A test that has been administered to a large group of persons under the same conditions to determine whether the test discriminates among ages and populations.

static stretching Maintaining a muscle stretch for 30 to 60 seconds.

status epilepticus A continual series of tonic-clonic seizures with no letup.

stimulus change Modifying the environment to discourage the expression of an undesirable behavior.

strabismus Crossed eyes resulting from the inability of the eye muscles to coordinate.

strength The ability of a muscle to contract against resistance.

stress-coping training Teaching a person to identify tension-producing situations and practice relaxation before or when confronted with those situations.

structural postural deficiencies Postural imbalances that involve abnormalities in the bones and joints.

supination Rotation of the palm of the hand upward, or abduction and inversion of the foot.

support personnel Individuals who assist the direct service provider in enabling students with disabilities to function in the least restrictive environment.

symmetrical tonic neck reflex A reflex in which the upper limbs tend to flex and the lower limbs extend when ventroflexing the head. If the head is dorsiflexed, the upper limbs extend and the lower limbs flex.

tactile defensive Having an aversion to touch and other tactile stimulation.

tactile system Knowledge of where the body ends and space begins and the ability to discriminate among pressure, texture, and size.

task analysis Breaking a task into parts to determine which motor components are present.

task signals Indicators that provide structure to the instructional environment.

task-specific approach Teaching a skill directly and generalizing it to a variety of environments. If the skill cannot be learned, the prerequisites are taught.

teaching style The instructional approach used by the teacher.

test objectivity A test's freedom from bias and subjectivity.

test reliability A measure of a test instrument's consistency.

test standardization Administering an evaluation instrument to a large group of persons under the same conditions to determine whether the instrument discriminates among the group members.

test validity How truthful a test is.

test-retest reliability The degree to which scores agree when the same test is administered twice to the same persons.

tetraplegia (quadriplegia) Involvement of all of the limbs to a similar degree.

three-year comprehensive re-evaluation Laws require that every student with a disability who qualifies for special education services receive a full re-evaluation at least every 3 years.

tic A sudden, rapid, recurrent, nonrhythmic, stereotyped movement or vocalization.

tinnitus Ringing in one or both ears in the absence of external stimuli.

token economy A form of contingency management in which tokens are earned for desirable behavior.

tonic exercises Passive movements of a muscle group to reduce the possibility of atrophy and to maintain organic efficiency.

tonic labyrinthine reflexes Reflexes that are present when one maintains trunk extension when supine and trunk flexion when prone.

tonic-clonic seizure A seizure that involves severe convulsions accompanied by stiffening, twisting, alternating contractions and relaxations, and unconsciousness; formerly referred to as a grand mal seizure.

torticollis Involuntary muscle contraction in the neck, causing the head to be twisted; wryneck.

total communication method The hearing-impaired person elects to communicate through speech, signs, gesture, or writing.

Tourette syndrome A genetic disorder that results in multiple motor tics and one or more vocal tics.

transdisciplinary Representing different professions or disciplines.

transdisciplinary, play-based assessment (TPBA) Two or more professionals sharing information about children they have observed in structured and unstructured play situations for the purpose of determining levels of functioning.

transition Change from one situation to another (e.g., from home to a school setting or from the school setting to a community environment).

transition service personnel Specially trained professionals who provide the expertise to ensure that individuals with disabilities have the skills needed to work and function in the community.

transition services Services available to facilitate the process of a child with a disability first entering public school, moving from a preschool to a school program, or moving from the school setting to a community setting.

traumatic brain injury (TBI) Blows to the head that result in minor to serious brain damage.

traumatic conditions Conditions resulting in damage to muscles, ligaments, tendons, or the nervous system as a result of a blow to the body.

travel vision Residual vision in blind persons that enables travel.

Trendelenburg test A test for hip dislocation that is performed by standing on one leg.

Type 1 diabetes mellitus A form of diabetes that is characterized by hyperglycemia and must be controlled with insulin therapy.

Type 2 diabetes mellitus A form of diabetes that is characterized by hyperglycemia but for which ongoing insulin therapy is usually not necessary.

Type 3, other specific types, diabetes mellitus Forms of diabetes that result from conditions and syndromes that impact glucose tolerance.

Type 4, gestational, diabetes mellitus A form of diabetes that occurs in some pregnant women.

undernutrition Insufficient nourishment, resulting in detriments to health and growth.

validity Truthfulness.

values clarification The process of identifying and clarifying prejudices, attitudes, and notions.

variable-interval ratio reinforcement schedule Modifying the number of behaviors reinforced according to a predetermined schedule (e.g., one reinforcer for every three instances followed by one reinforcer for every five instances of desirable behavior).

ventroflexion of the head Flexing the head toward the front of the body.

vestibular sense Response to balance.

vestibular system The inner ear structures that are associated with balance and position in space.

video modeling Videotapes that show a person engaging in a desirable target behavior.

vision specialist A specially trained professional who evaluates the extent of visual disabilities and designs intervention programs that make possible a successful educational experience.

visual behavioral specialist (visual developmental specialist) An optometrist or ophthalmologist who has specialized training in assessing and remediating misalignments of the eyes.

visual disability Having a classification as partially sighted or blind.

vocal tics Involuntary utterings of noises, words, or phrases, including sniffing, throat clearing, repeated coughing, coprolalia, involuntary laughing, a variety of sounds or yells, barking, grunting, and echolalia.

whole-interval time sampling Noting whether a behavior occurred throughout an entire interval.

zero tolerance A school policy to expel students from school or to place them in an alternative educational environment if they engage in specified disruptive behaviors.

Page numbers followed by *f* indicate figure; and those followed by *t* indicate table.